STANDARD LESSON COMMENTARY

King James Version

1998 ~ 1999

International Sunday School Lessons

edited by

DOUGLAS REDFORD AND JONATHAN UNDERWOOD

published by

STANDARD PUBLISHING

Eugene H. Wigginton, *President*

Mark A. Taylor, *Publisher*

Richard C. McKinley, *Director of Curriculum Development*

Carla Crane, *Assistant Director of Curriculum Development*

Hela M. Campbell, *Office Editor*

Forty-sixth Annual Volume

©1998

The STANDARD PUBLISHING Company

division of STANDEX INTERNATIONAL Corporation

8121 Hamilton Avenue, Cincinnati, Ohio 45231

Printed in U. S. A.

In This Volume

Fall Quarter, 1998 (page 1)
God Calls a People to Faithful Living

Writers

LESSON DEVELOPMENT: Orrin Root
VERBAL ILLUSTRATIONS: Charles R. Boatman

LEARNING BY DOING: Richard A. Lint
LET'S TALK IT OVER: Kenton K. Smith

Winter Quarter, 1998-99 (page 113)
God Calls Anew in Jesus Christ

Writers

LESSON DEVELOPMENT: J. Michael Shannon (1-4),
Johnny Pressley (5-13)
LEARNING BY DOING: Alan Weber

VERBAL ILLUSTRATIONS: Gene Appel (1-4),
Robert C. Shannon (5-13)
LET'S TALK IT OVER: David A. Baynes

Spring Quarter, 1999 (page 225)
That You May Believe

Writers

LESSON DEVELOPMENT: Edwin V. Hayden (1-9),
Robert C. Shannon (10-13)
VERBAL ILLUSTRATIONS: James G. VanBuren

LEARNING BY DOING: Howard Wakefield
LET'S TALK IT OVER: Kenton K. Smith

Summer Quarter, 1999 (page 337)
Genesis: Beginnings

Writers

LESSON DEVELOPMENT: Larry Pechawer (1-4),
John W. Wade (5-13)
VERBAL ILLUSTRATIONS: Richard W. Baynes

LEARNING BY DOING: Mark Plunkett (1-8),
Richard A. Lint (9-13)
LET'S TALK IT OVER: David Morley

Artists

TITLE PAGES: James E. Seward

Cover design by DesignTeam

Lessons based on International Sunday School Lessons © 1995 by the Lesson Committee.

II

Index of Printed Texts, 1998-99

The printed texts for 1998-99 are arranged here in the order in which they appear in the Bible. Opposite each reference is the number of the page on which it appears in this volume.

The *Standard Lesson Commentary:*
Your Tool for Better Teaching

For almost fifty years, the *Standard Lesson Commentary* has provided a valuable resource for adult Sunday school teachers. Many churches, desiring lessons that focus on what the Bible says and how it applies to our times, have found that the *Commentary* helps them achieve these important goals.

The strength of the *Standard Lesson Commentary* has always been its thorough treatment of the lesson Scripture. Five of the eight pages in each lesson are devoted to this. Printed texts are taken from the International Sunday School Lessons. These lessons are arranged in a six-year program that allows the teacher and student, by the completion of the series, to participate in a comprehensive survey of the entire Bible. The lessons to be covered in a given year are highlighted at the beginning of every fall quarter. See page 2 of this *Commentary*, and you will note that the 1998-99 lessons begin a new six-year program with an Old Testament survey ("God Calls a People to Faithful Living").

With this year's *Commentary*, we have included some new features that we hope will make it an even more beneficial resource for you to use. Most of these are found within the eight introductory pages that appear at the beginning of every quarter. For example, each set of introductory material now includes **two pages of Bible helps** relevant to the upcoming quarter. On one page is an appropriate **map** for the quarter, while on the other (on the reverse side of the same sheet) you will find a **time line, chart, or other feature** that will call attention to something noteworthy about that quarter's lessons. (For the fall quarter's helps, see pages 5 and 6 of this *Commentary*.) Note that these pages are **perforated** so that you can tear them out if you wish and save them. By the end of the six-year program of study, you will have collected what we hope will be a very useful set of Bible study helps!

Another special feature in the introductory pages begins with the winter quarter. There you will find a two-page article referred to as **"Teacher Tips."** These articles are written to provide you as a teacher with some practical suggestions as to how to communicate God's Word more effectively to your students. Specific illustrations of the general principles stated in these articles are taken from the upcoming quarter's lessons, making these "tips" of immediate value.

Within the introductory pages, we have kept what we hope will be features that will continue to be an asset to your teaching. There is always a two-page essay **previewing the lessons** that will be studied during the new quarter. Read it carefully before the quarter begins so that you can get a good summary of "coming attractions." You will also find the **quarterly quiz** at the beginning of each quarter. As the instructions at the top of the quiz explain, there are a number of ways in which you can use this quiz in your teaching. You may photocopy the quiz if you like (or feel free to add any other questions that you wish).

We'd like to call your attention to a couple of items within these pages at the beginning of this year's *Commentary*. On the next two pages (5 and 6) you will find a **questionnaire** that we would like for you to fill out and return to us at Standard Publishing. The questionnaire will give us an idea of how you like some of the regular features in the *Commentary* and also whether there are any new features that we need to consider adding. Please take a few moments to fill it out and send it to us (the page is perforated and no postage is required). If you happen to be a first-time user of the *Commentary*, you may want to use the book for a couple of quarters or perhaps the entire year before sending in your questionnaire. At any rate—don't forget! We are always glad to receive input from the people who are using our materials.

One final word to those of you who have used the *Standard Lesson Commentary* for some time. The *Commentary* has also been available for a number of years in a quarterly format known as *Bible Teacher and Leader*. With this fall quarter, the *Bible Teacher and Leader* will be available in a new **large print** edition! Standard Publishing has received a number of requests for such a product, and we are happy to be able to offer it. If you are interested, call Standard Publishing at 1-800-543-1353, talk to the individual in your church who orders your Sunday school materials, or call your local Christian bookstore.

We're hoping that what we've done this year with the *Standard Lesson Commentary* will help to keep it a valuable tool—only sharper than ever!

We Need Your Help

We at Standard Publishing continually strive to improve our adult Sunday school materials to make them more helpful to you. You can help us serve you better by completing this questionnaire. When you have done so, fold as indicated on the back. Glue or tape the flap down and mail the questionnaire to us. We will pay the postage. Thank you!   —The Editors

Teacher, please tell us a little about yourself:
In what age bracket are you?
❑ 20-30   ❑ 41-50   ❑ 61-70
❑ 31-40   ❑ 51-60   ❑ over 71
Check the highest level of formal education you have completed.
❑ 8th grade   ❑ high school ❑ college
(If college, how many years? _____)
For how many years have you taught Sunday school? _____

Please tell us a little about your students:
Check the age range of your students.
❑ 20-30   ❑ 41-50   ❑ 61-70
❑ 31-40   ❑ 51-60   ❑ over 70
Check the category that best describes the area from which your students come.
❑ city   ❑ suburban
❑ rural   ❑ small town
Check which best describes your class.
❑ men   ❑ women   ❑ both

Please tell us a little about your teaching:
What teaching method do you use most often?
❑ lecture   ❑ discussion   ❑ activities
Please list the versions of the Bible you prefer to use in your class.
First choice: _____
Second choice: _____
Third choice: _____

Please tell us what you think about the *Standard Lesson Commentary*:
Do you think each lesson in the *Commentary* presents an important Bible truth?
❑ always   ❑ usually
❑ sometimes   ❑ seldom
Do you find the Lesson Aims helpful?
❑ always   ❑ usually
❑ sometimes   ❑ seldom
Do you use the Lesson Outline in preparing and presenting the lesson?
❑ always   ❑ usually
❑ sometimes   ❑ seldom
Do you find the Lesson Introduction helpful?
❑ always   ❑ usually
❑ sometimes   ❑ seldom

Is the explanation of the Scripture adequate and appropriate for the age group you teach?
❑ always   ❑ usually
❑ sometimes   ❑ seldom
Do you find the Verbal Illustrations accompanying the explanation of the Scripture helpful?
❑ always   ❑ usually
❑ sometimes   ❑ seldom
Does the application presented in the lesson enable you to apply the Bible truths to your students' everyday lives?
❑ always   ❑ usually
❑ sometimes   ❑ seldom
Please give us your evaluation of the "Learning by Doing" section.
❑ very useful   ❑ somewhat useful
❑ not useful
Please evaluate the "Let's Talk It Over" page.
❑ very useful   ❑ somewhat useful
❑ not useful
Do you use the *Adult Visuals?*
❑ always   ❑ usually
❑ sometimes   ❑ seldom
What teaching aids do you find most helpful?
❑ maps   ❑ charts   ❑ posters
❑ Bible art   ❑ time lines   ❑ filmstrips
❑ quarterly quizzes ❑ role-play scripts
❑ teaching games   ❑ overhead transparencies
❑ other _____

What features do you like best about the *Standard Lesson Commentary?*

What changes would you suggest to improve the *Standard Lesson Commentary?*

Would you be interested in seeing the *Standard Lesson Commentary* become available on CD-ROM for computer users?
❑ yes   ❑ no   ❑ I'm not sure
How many in your class might find a CD-ROM *Commentary* useful?
❑ several   ❑ a few   ❑ none

BUSINESS REPLY MAIL
FIRST–CLASS MAIL   PERMIT NO. 760   CINCINNATI OH

POSTAGE WILL BE PAID BY ADDRESSEE

ADULT CURRICULUM DEPT.
STANDARD PUBLISHING
8121 HAMILTON AVE
CINCINNATI OH 45231-9943

⊦⊦⊦⊦⊦⊦⊦⊦⊦⊦⊦⊦⊦⊦⊦⊦⊦⊦⊦⊦⊦⊦⊦⊦⊦⊦⊦⊦⊦⊦⊦⊦

- FOLD HERE -

Additional Comments:

PLEASE TAPE OR GLUE ENDS TOGETHER BEFORE MAILING.

How to Say It

Listed below are some of the names and other hard to pronounce words that you will encounter in the lessons covered in this book. (Because of space limitations, not every word that appears in the "How to Say It" boxes in each lesson has been included, but these will be the ones most often needed for general Bible study.) Notice that the page is perforated so that you can tear it out and keep it for later use in teaching or personal Bible study.

ABANA. *Ab*-uh-nuh.
ABIAH. Uh-*bye*-uh.
ABIMELECH. Uh-*bim*-eh-lek.
ABRAM. *Ay*-brum.
AHAB. *Ay*-hab.
AHAZ. *Ay*-haz.
AHIJAH. Uh-*high*-juh.
AI. *Ay*-eye.
AMAZIAH. Am-uh-*zye*-uh.
ANAK. *Ay*-nak.
ANTIPAS. *An*-tih-pus.
ARAM. *Air*-um.
AREOPAGUS. Air-ee-*op*-uh-gus.
ARIMATHEA. *Air*-uh-muh-*thee*-uh (*th* as in *thin*; strong accent on *thee*).
ASAPH. *Ay*-saff.
ASHTAROTH. *Ash*-tah-rawth.
ASHTORETH. *Ash*-toe-reth.
ASSYRIA. Uh-*sear*-ee-uh.
ATHENS. *Ath*-unz.

BAAL. *Bay*-ul.
BAALIM. Bay-uh-*leem*.
BABEL. *Bay*-bul.
BABYLON. *Bab*-uh-lun.
BABYLONIANS. Bab-uh-*low*-nee-unz.
BARABBAS. Buh-*rab*-us.
BARJONAH. Bar-*jo*-nuh.
BATHSHEBA. Bath-*she*-buh.
BEERSHEBA. Beer-*she*-buh.
BELSHAZZAR. Bel-*shazz*-er.
BETHABARA. Beth-*ab*-uh-ruh.
BETHSAIDA. Beth-*say*-uh-duh.
BILHAH. *Bill*-ha.
BOANERGES. Boe-uh-*nur*-geez.

CAESAR AUGUSTUS. *See*-zer Aw-*gus*-tus.
CAESAREA PHILIPPI. Sess-uh-*ree*-uh Fuh-*lip*-pie or *Fill*-uh-pie.
CANAANITE. *Kay*-nuh-nite.
CAPERNAUM. Kuh-*per*-nay-um.
CHALDEES. Kal-*deez*.
CLEOPAS. *Klee*-uh-pass.
CORINTH. *Kor*-inth.
CORINTHIANS. Kor-*in*-thee-unz.
CORNELIUS. Kor-*neel*-yus.
CYRENIUS. Sye-*ree*-nee-us.
CYRUS. *Sye*-russ.

DAMARIS. *Dam*-uh-ris.
DAMASCUS. Duh-*mass*-kus.
DARIUS. Duh-*rye*-us.
DIDYMUS. *Did*-uh-mus.
DIONYSIUS. Die-oh-*nish*-ih-us.
DOTHAN. *Doe*-thun (*th* as in *thin*).

EBAL. *Ee*-bull.
EDOMITES. *Ee*-dum-ites.
ELIEZER. El-ih-*ee*-zer.
ELIJAH. Ee-*lye*-juh.
ELISHA. Ee-*lye*-shuh.
EMMAUS. Em-*may*-us.
ENOCH. *Ee*-nock.
ENOS. *Ee*-nuss.
EPHESUS. *Ef*-uh-sus.
EPHRAIM. *Ee*-fray-im.
EPHRATH. *Ef*-rath.
EZEKIEL. Ee-*zeek*-yul or Ee-*zeek*-ee-ul.

GALILEAN. Gal-uh-*lee*-un.
GAMALIEL. Guh-*may*-lee-ul.
GEHENNA. Geh-*hen*-uh.
GERAR. *Gear*-ar.
GERIZIM. *Gair*-ih-zim or Guh-*rye*-zim.
GETHSEMANE. Geth-*sem*-uh-nee.
GIDEON. *Gid*-ee-un.
GILEAD. *Gil*-ee-ud.
GILGAL. *Gil*-gal.
GOLGOTHA. *Gahl*-guh-thuh.
GOMORRAH. Guh-*more*-uh.

HADES. *Hay*-deez.
HAGAR. *Hay*-gar.
HAGGAI. *Hag*-eye or *Hag*-a-eye.
HAI. *Hay*-eye.
HARAN. *Hair*-un.
HEBRON. *Hee*-brun or *Heb*-run.
HERODIANS. Heh-*roe*-dee-unz.
HINNOM. *Hin*-um.

IMMANUEL. Ih-*man*-you-el.
ISCARIOT. Iss-*care*-ee-ut.
ISHMAEL. *Ish*-may-el.
ISHMAELITES. *Ish*-may-el-ites.

JABBOK. *Jab*-ock.
JAIRUS. *Jye*-rus or *Jay*-ih-rus.

JAPHETH. *Jay*-feth.
JEBUSITES. *Jeb*-yuh-sites.
JEHOIACHIN. Jeh-*hoy*-uh-kin.
JEHOIAKIM. Jeh-*hoy*-uh-kim.
JEHORAM. Jeh-*ho*-rum.
JEHOVAH-JIREH. Jeh-*ho*-vuh-*jye*-ruh.
JEHU. *Jay*-hew.
JERICHO. *Jair*-ih-ko.
JEROBOAM. Jair-uh-*boe*-um.
JESHUA. *Jesh*-you-uh.
JEZEBEL. *Jez*-uh-bel.
JOSES. *Joe*-sez.

KETURAH. Keh-*too*-ruh.
KIDRON. *Kid*-ron.

LABAN. *Lay*-bun.
LAMECH. *Lay*-mek.
LEVITES. *Lee*-vites.
LUZ. Luzz.

MAASEIAH. May-uh-*see*-yuh.
MACEDONIA. Mass-uh-*doe*-nee-uh.
MACHPELAH. Mack-*pea*-luh.
MAGDALA. *Mag*-duh-luh.
MAGDALENE. *Mag*-duh-leen or
        Mag-duh-*lee*-nee.
MANASSEH. Muh-*nass*-uh.
MEDES. Meeds.
MELCHIAH. Mel-*kye*-uh.
MELCHIZEDEK. Mel-*kizz*-ih-dek.
METHUSELAH. Muh-*thoo*-suh-luh.
MIDIANITES. *Mid*-ee-un-ites.
MIZPEH. *Miz*-peh.
MOLECH. *Mo*-lek.
MOREH. *Moe*-reh.
MORIAH. Mo-*rye*-uh.

NAAMAN. *Nay*-uh-mun.
NAHOR. *Nay*-hor.
NATHANAEL. Nuh-*than*-yull (*th* as in *thin*).
NAZARENE. *Naz*-uh-reen.
NAZARETH. *Naz*-uh-reth.
NEBUCHADNEZZAR. *Neb*-uh-kad-*nezz*-er
        (strong accent on *nezz*).
NEGEB. *Neg*-eb.
NEHEMIAH. Nee-huh-*my*-uh.
NICODEMUS. Nick-uh-*dee*-mus.
NINEVEH. *Nin*-uh-vuh.

OMRI. *Ahm*-rye.

PARACLETE. *pair*-uh-kleet.
PARAN. *Pair*-un.
PASHUR. *Pash*-er.
PATMOS. *Pat*-mus.
PENIEL. Peh-*nye*-el.
PENUEL. Pih-*nu*-el.
PHARAOH. *Fair*-o or *Fay*-roe.
PHARISEES. *Fair*-ih-seez.
PHARPAR. *Far*-par.
PHILISTINES. Fuh-*liss*-teens or *Fill*-us-teens.
POTIPHAR. *Pot*-ih-far.
PTOLEMY. *Tahl*-uh-me.

RABBI. *Rab*-eye.
RABBONI. Rab-*o*-nye.
RAMAH. *Ray*-muh.
REHOBOAM. Ree-huh-*boe*-um.
REUBEN. *Roo*-ben.

SADDUCEES. *Sad*-you-sees.
SALOME. Suh-*lo*-me.
SAMARITANS. Suh-*mare*-uh-tunz.
SANHEDRIN. San-*heed*-run or *San*-huh-drin.
SARAI. *Seh*-rye.
SEIR. *See*-ir.
SEPTUAGINT. Sep-*too*-ih-jent.
SEPULCHRE. *sep*-ull-kur.
SHALEM. *Shay*-lem.
SHECHEM. *Sheck*-em or *Shee*-kem.
SICHEM. *Sye*-kem.
SIMEON. *Sim*-ee-un.
SINAI. *Sye*-nye or *Sye*-nay-eye.
SODOM. *Sod*-um.
SUCCOTH. *Soo*-kawth.
SYCHAR. *Sigh*-kar.
SYNAGOGUE. *sin*-uh-gog.

TARSUS. *Tar*-sus.
TEKOA. Tih-*koe*-uh.
TERAH. *Tair*-uh.
THEOPHILUS. Thee-*ahf*-ih-luss.
TIBERIAS. Tie-*beer*-ee-us.
TOPHET. *Toe*-fet.

UZZIAH. Uh-*zye*-uh.

ZACCHEUS. Zack-*kee*-us.
ZEBEDEE. *Zeb*-uh-dee.
ZECHARIAH. Zek-uh-*rye*-uh.
ZEDEKIAH. Zed-uh-*kye*-uh.
ZEPHANIAH. Zef-uh-*nye*-uh.
ZERUBBABEL. Zeh-*rub*-uh-bull.

Fall Quarter, 1998

God Calls a People to Faithful Living
(Old Testament Survey)

Special Features

Lessons

Unit 1: God Fashions a People

Unit 2: God's People Reject His Laws

Unit 3: God Works Through People

Unit 4: God Judges and Renews

About These Lessons

The lessons of the current quarter launch us on a new six-year study of the Bible. These lessons give an overview, or survey, of the Old Testament. It is hoped that this survey will help the student put into context the lessons learned from Old Testament Scriptures throughout the six-year period.

Sep
6

Sep
13

Sep
20

Sep
27

Oct
4

Oct
11

Oct
18

Oct
25

Nov
1

Nov
8

Nov
15

Nov
22

Nov
29

The Journey Begins

As you can see from the chart below, this year's studies begin a new six-year cycle of Sunday school lessons. By the end of the six years, you will have been guided on a journey through the Book of books—the Bible.

Since this is the first year of the cycle, the first two studies for the year are primarily foundational and introductory. The fall quarter begins with an Old Testament survey, followed by a New Testament survey in the winter.

After these surveys, we begin a more detailed look at specific portions of Scripture. The first is the Gospel of John, which is our focus for the spring quarter. (Each year will see most or all of one quarter devoted to the life of Christ.) The summer quarter closes the year with a focus on the book of Genesis. With that we begin a six-year chronological study of the Old Testament.

By the time we finish the cycle, which will occur with the summer quarter of 2004, we will have entered a new decade, a new century, a new millennium! What will our world be like by then? Will Jesus have returned? Regardless of what changes take place in the years ahead, God's Word will remain our unchanging source of truth. To make learning it and living it our aim and our passion is the best way to prepare for what the future holds.

May God bless you as you begin this fascinating journey!

International Sunday School Lesson Cycle
September, 1998—August, 2004

YEAR	FALL QUARTER (Sept., Oct., Nov.)	WINTER QUARTER (Dec., Jan., Feb.)	SPRING QUARTER (Mar., Apr., May)	SUMMER QUARTER (June, July, Aug.)
1998-1999	God Calls a People to Faithful Living (Old Testament Survey)	God Calls Anew in Jesus Christ (New Testament Survey)	That You May Believe (John)	Genesis: Beginnings (Genesis)
1999-2000	From Slavery to Conquest (Exodus, Leviticus, Numbers, Deuteronomy, Joshua)	Emmanuel: God With Us (Matthew)	Helping a Church Confront Crisis (1 and 2 Corinthians)	New Life in Christ (Ephesians, Philippians, Colossians, Philemon)
2000-2001	The Emerging Nation (Judges, 1 and 2 Samuel, 1 Kings 1-11, 1 Chronicles, 2 Chronicles 1-9)	Good News of Jesus (Luke)	Continuing Jesus' Work (Acts)	Division and Decline (1 Kings 12-22, 2 Kings 1-17, 2 Chronicles 10-28, Isaiah 1-39, Amos, Hosea, Micah)
2001-2002	Jesus' Ministry (Parables, Miracles, Sermon on the Mount)	Light for All People (Isaiah 9:1-7; 11:1-9; 40-66; Ruth, Jonah, Nahum)	The Power of the Gospel (Romans, Galatians)	Worship and Wisdom for Living (Psalms, Proverbs)
2002-2003	Judgment and Exile (2 Kings 18-25, 2 Chronicles 29-36, Jeremiah, Lamentations, Ezekiel, Habakkuk, Zephaniah)	Portraits of Faith (Personalities in the New Testament)	Jesus: God's Power in Action (Mark)	God Restores a Remnant (Ezra, Nehemiah, Daniel, Joel, Obadiah, Haggai, Zechariah, Malachi)
2003-2004	Faith Faces the World (James, 1 and 2 Peter, 1, 2, 3 John, Jude)	A Child Is Given (Samuel, John the Baptist, Jesus) Lessons From Life (Esther, Job, Ecclesiastes, Song of Solomon)	Jesus Fulfills His Mission (Death, Burial, and Resurrection Texts) Living Expectantly (1, 2 Thessalonians, Revelation)	Hold Fast to the Faith (Hebrews) Guidelines for the Church's Ministry (1, 2 Timothy, Titus)

Here We Go Again

by Orrin Root

SIX YEARS AGO, we began a cycle of lessons designed to lead us through the Bible in a span of six years. The cycle began with a survey of the Old Testament in thirteen lessons. That cycle was completed with the summer 1998 lessons, and now, with the fall 1998 quarter, we are ready to begin another six-year cycle. It should come as no surprise that we begin with a survey of the Old Testament in thirteen lessons.

This does not mean that we are repeating the lessons we used six years ago. When we plan to cover the Old Testament in thirteen lessons, obviously we have to leave some huge gaps between lessons. Six years ago we skipped the first eleven chapters of Genesis to begin with Abraham, the father of God's chosen people. This time we skip only two chapters at the beginning. We start with Genesis 3, which records the entrance of sin into the world.

After this first lesson from Genesis, we bypass the rest of the book and leap forward to consider the Hebrews' deliverance from slavery in Egypt. It looks as if we are ignoring a lot of important material. But don't be alarmed. Next summer's studies will feature thirteen lessons drawn entirely from Genesis. (See the shaded portion of the cycle on the opposite page.) As we proceed through the thirteen lessons of this fall, we will find other large gaps in our study; but we can expect each gap to be partially filled through later studies.

Think of this fall's study as providing a framework that will aid us in putting future Old Testament studies in their proper context. (The time line found on page 6 will help you place the lessons in their proper historical context.) We need to be diligent in learning and remembering the framework. Then we will see how future lessons fit into the overall plan of the Old Testament. Notice how other lessons later in the cycle—often in the fall or summer quarters—continue our study of the Old Testament.

NEW FEATURE!

Notice the map and chronological chart on pages 5 and 6. Similar pull-out features will appear in each quarter through the current cycle. By the end of the cycle, you will have a good set of maps and charts for a variety of teaching situations.

Unit One: God Fashions a People

This unit of lessons reminds us of how God worked in a mighty way to establish a nation that would be His own special people—His "peculiar treasure" (Exodus 19:5). **Lesson 1**, however ("God's Creation Marred by Sin"), focuses on the tragic entry of sin into the world through the disobedience of Adam and Eve in the Garden of Eden (Genesis 3). How grateful we should be that the second Adam, Jesus Christ, came to undo the work of the devil (1 Corinthians 15:45; Hebrews 2:14, 15)!

Lesson 2 ("God's People Delivered From Slavery") highlights God's deliverance of Israel, using Moses to lead them out of bitter bondage in Egypt. The events recorded in **Lesson 3** ("God's Expectations Made Plain") occurred forty years later. As the people of Israel stood on the verge of entering the promised land, Moses repeated the law that had been given nearly forty years earlier, not long after the Israelites had left Egypt (Deuteronomy 5:1-21). **Lesson 4** ("God's Actions Remembered") tells how God stopped the flow of the Jordan River while His people crossed on dry land to the other side. They erected two monuments in memory of this miracle (Joshua 4).

Unit Two: God's People Reject His Laws

Lesson 5 ("Cycle of Sin and Judgment") calls attention to one of the most dismal periods of Israel's history—the period of the judges (about 1350-1050 B.C.). The Israelites became attracted to the gods of the people around them, whom they had failed to drive out of the land as God commanded. God's punishment (by means of oppression from pagan tribes) brought the nation back to obedience; but before long the people fell prey once again to idolatry. This happened many times in the span of about three centuries (Judges 2:11-23; 11:26). **Lesson 6** ("Demand for a King") notes how the people of Israel asked Samuel for a king. God granted this request, but He warned the people of what lay ahead for them (1 Samuel 8).

Our survey then moves past the reigns of Israel's first three kings (Saul, David, and Solomon) to the time when the kingdom was divided (931 B.C.). **Lesson 7** ("Jeroboam's Sin") tells how Jeroboam, the first king of the northern kingdom (Israel), set up two golden calves for the people in the north to worship. He also instituted other practices that were counter to what God had established in His law.

Unit Three: God Works Through People

The lessons in the previous unit show how God worked directly to deliver His people from bondage, to give them His laws, and to lead them into the land He had promised to give them. This next unit reminds us of the important truth that God also works through people to accomplish His purposes. **Lesson 8** ("God Works Through Prophets") tells how Naaman, a leader of the Syrian army, came to Israel in search of healing from his leprosy. God healed him when he humbly followed the instructions of God's messenger Elisha (2 Kings 5:1-14).

Lesson 9 ("God Gives His Spokesman Courage") focuses on the ministry of the prophet Amos. God sent this shepherd/farmer to denounce the sins of the northern kingdom. The religious hierarchy, represented by Amaziah the priest, opposed the prophet; but God gave him courage to deliver His message of judgment upon a sinful, complacent people (Amos 7).

Lesson 10 ("God Works Through Song Writers") is taken from Psalm 73. Asaph's song describes his own intense spiritual struggle and how he regained a proper perspective on his surroundings. Through this inspired songwriter, God works to help us through similar crises of faith.

Unit Four: God Judges and Renews

In 722 B.C., the northern kingdom of Israel was conquered by the Assyrians. Its people were scattered among various foreign countries (2 Kings 17:1-6). The southern kingdom of Judah exhibited far greater faithfulness toward God; and because of the godly leadership of King Hezekiah, God rescued Judah from the Assyrians (2 Kings 18:13–19:36). Eventually, however, evil kings guided the nation into wrongdoing. With the concluding unit of this quarter, we move forward to the time when the southern kingdom of Judah was under siege from the Babylonians. God's judgment was in the process of falling upon His stubborn, unrepentant people. **Lesson 11** ("False Hopes and Judgment") records the prophet Jeremiah's warnings to the nation. His words included a promise of God's judgment, "the which whosoever heareth, his ears shall tingle" (Jeremiah 19:3). But Jeremiah also extended God's gracious invitation to choose "the way of life" (Jeremiah 21:8).

Ezekiel, who was taken to Babylon in 597 B.C., served God as a prophet among the captives there. He gave the disheartened exiles God's promise that His people would be set free one day to return to their homeland (Ezekiel 37). This is the theme of **Lesson 12** ("Hope From God's Promise").

The final lesson of the quarter ("Renewal and Worship") brings us to the year 445 B.C., when Nehemiah came to Jerusalem as governor of Judah. His first aim was to rebuild the city wall that had been destroyed more than a century earlier. The people worked enthusiastically, and the wall was completed in only fifty-two days (Nehemiah 6:15). Nehemiah, with the assistance of Ezra, then began to give attention to teaching the law of Moses to the people. By this time, the observance of the Feast of Tabernacles was at hand; and that festival was observed in the ancient way and with the joy that God intended for His people to experience (Nehemiah 8).

In approximately 430 B.C., the prophet Malachi wrote the final book of the Old Testament. It shows that the people of God were once again becoming negligent in their obedience, as their ancestors had done so many times before. This series of studies surveying the Old Testament demonstrates the need for a new covenant offering the forgiveness of sins and the power to conquer the power of sin in one's life. Such a covenant was foretold by the prophet Jeremiah (Jeremiah 31:31-34), and it was established by Jesus approximately four hundred years after the completion of the Old Testament Scriptures.

Today the church—those who have accepted God's gracious offer of forgiveness in Jesus—has much to learn from these studies surveying the Old Testament. We are now the people whom God calls to "faithful living." Are we living up to such a high and holy calling?

Answers to Quarterly Quiz
on page 8

Lesson 1—1. the serpent. 2. Adam blamed the woman (Eve); Eve blamed the serpent. **Lesson 2**—1. Abraham, Isaac, Jacob. 2. Pharaoh. 3. midnight. **Lesson 3**—1. "Thou shalt have none other gods before me." 2. Sabbath. 3. false. **Lesson 4**—1. tribe, Jordan. 2. Gilgal. **Lesson 5**—1. Baal, Ashtaroth. 2. hot. **Lesson 6**—1. Bethel, Gilgal, Mizpeh. 2. Joel and Abiah. 3. nations. **Lesson 7**—1. David. 2. Bethel and Dan. 3. feast. **Lesson 8**—1. Syria. 2. Elisha. 3. Jordan, seven. **Lesson 9**—1. Amos. 2. Amaziah. **Lesson 10**—1. the prosperity of the wicked. 2. sanctuary. **Lesson 11**—1. break. 2. Zedekiah. **Lesson 12**—1. valley, bones. 2. true. **Lesson 13**—1. scribe. 2. law. 3. booths, seventh.

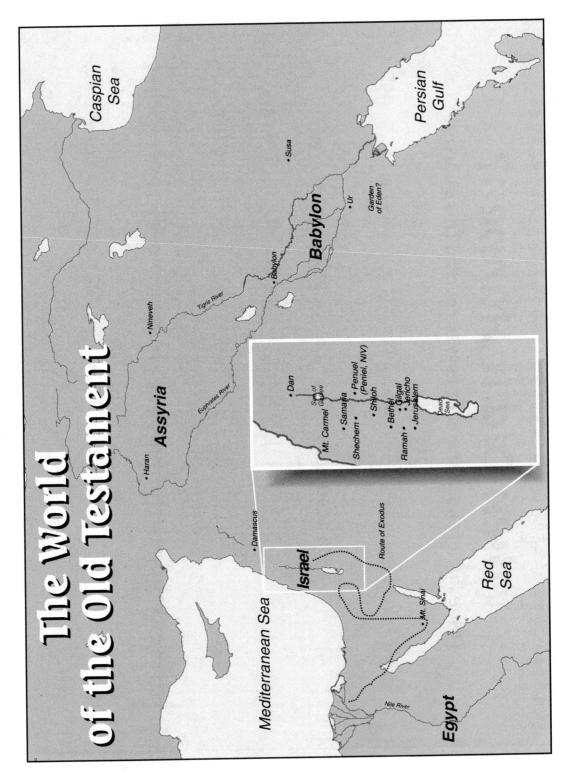

The World of the Old Testament

When Did It Happen?

(Time line of Old Testament events covered this quarter)

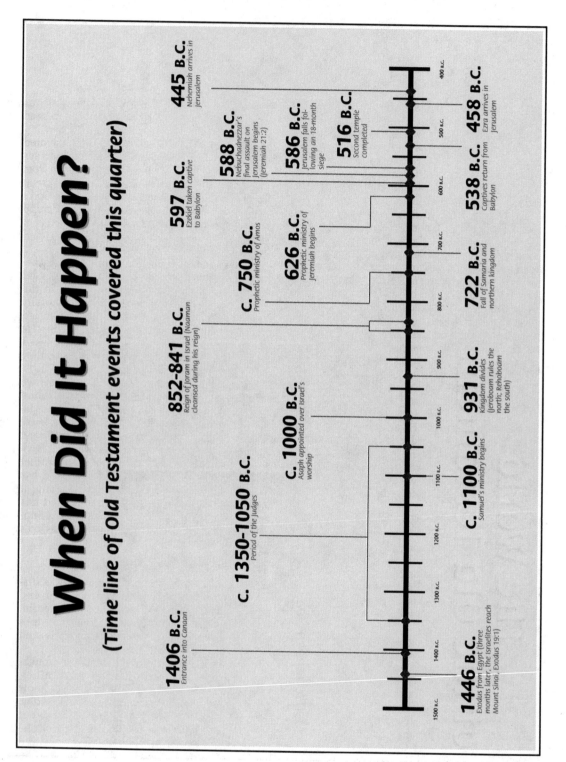

1446 B.C.
Exodus from Egypt (three months later, the Israelites reach Mount Sinai, Exodus 19:1)

1406 B.C.
Entrance into Canaan

c. 1350–1050 B.C.
Period of the Judges

c. 1100 B.C.
Samuel's ministry begins

c. 1000 B.C.
Asaph appointed over Israel's worship

931 B.C.
Kingdom divides (Jeroboam rules the north; Rehoboam the south)

852–841 B.C.
Reign of Joram in Israel (Naaman cleansed during his reign)

c. 750 B.C.
Prophetic ministry of Amos

722 B.C.
Fall of Samaria and northern kingdom

626 B.C.
Prophetic ministry of Jeremiah begins

597 B.C.
Ezekiel taken captive to Babylon

588 B.C.
Nebuchadnezzar's final assault on Jerusalem begins (Jeremiah 21:2)

586 B.C.
Jerusalem falls following an 18-month siege

538 B.C.
Captives return from Babylon

516 B.C.
Second temple completed

458 B.C.
Ezra arrives in Jerusalem

445 B.C.
Nehemiah arrives in Jerusalem

1500 B.C. 1400 B.C. 1300 B.C. 1200 B.C. 1100 B.C. 1000 B.C. 900 B.C. 800 B.C. 700 B.C. 600 B.C. 500 B.C. 400 B.C.

Yielding to the Hand of God

by Mark B. Reed

ALMOST TOTAL DEVASTATION lay in every direction, and who was responsible? The causal observer would say the Babylonians had come and destroyed everything in Jerusalem. But what really happened? The whirlwind that leveled God's people was actually the downward spiritual cycle that Israel had been on for several centuries.

The history of Israel may be likened to a series of circles that moved downward, forming the shape of a funnel. Each generation repeated the history of its predecessor, except on a lower level, spiraling downward faster and faster. At the top the pace moved in a slow, wide circle. It was easy to step out of, but too tempting just to enjoy the ride. Those who chose to stay on found themselves sinking into a slightly tighter spin. The deeper they sank, the faster they spun and the harder it became to get off. In the end, the swirling wind sucked in the nation, and Israel plunged to its destruction. However, the destruction was not total. God left a remnant intact as the twister vanished into history.

Where was God while Israel whirled in repeated unfaithfulness? He was pursuing them. He taught them His Word, and they chose to disobey it. He punished them, and they cried out in repentance. He delivered them and patiently taught them again; and when they chose to disobey, the cycle began once more.

Listening to God

Throughout the Old Testament we see the hand of God working among His people—touching them, speaking to them, delivering them, and warning them. Blessed with such tender care, why did Israel fail so miserably to achieve the "holy nation" status to which God called them (Exodus 19:6)? How did Israel get into this cycle in the first place?

Consider Adam and Eve's decision to listen to the serpent instead of to God. God had made His expectations clear; Adam and Eve ignored them. Today we live in a noisy world. With so many voices and so many distractions, listening to God requires discipline. Almost every generation of Israel struggled with listening. In the wilderness, their growling stomachs and grumbling complaints drowned out God's voice. Under the pressures of everyday life and toiling just to make ends meet, Israelites in the days of the judges were too busy and too burdened to attend to spiritual matters. Distracted by idolatrous pleasures, the northern kingdom refused to heed God's prophets.

Whenever Israel listened to God, He favored them just as He promised. The faithful always digest, decide, and act on what they hear from God. When doubts from their reasoning creep in, they expel them and say, "I will trust God's wisdom, even though my emotions or my mind tells me something different."

Remembering God's Touch

The Israelites also failed to remain faithful because they forgot who they were, who their God was, and what He had done for them. In the days of the judges, the people became morally lax and spiritually malnourished. They cried when God disciplined them, forgetting how He had delivered their forefathers during the desert wandering. Overwhelmed by their defeats, they lost sight of the victories of their past.

What is it that causes us forget? Like Israel we sometimes worry that God may not come through on His promise. Like the children of Israel at the foot of Sinai, waiting on Moses to return, we think God has abandoned us. We get wrapped up in our own circumstances that have us spinning. We get so busy with the "now" that we fail to take time to reflect on what God has done in the past for others and for us. Faithful Christians hang on to the reminders God has given, such as His written Word, the Lord's Supper, and their own personal testimonies to God's hand at work.

Faithful to the Faithful One

God proved faithful throughout Israel's history. He promised He would provide for and protect Israel if they honored Him, and He did. He promised He would punish them and take away His blessing if they acted unfaithfully, and He did. God proved faithful. Israel did not.

God's hand sweeps through our lives—touching our days, our circumstances, our families, and our friends. We don't have to see it to know it's there. We don't even have to see its results. We only have to trust God's promise, reach out for His hand, and lean on it. Learning from Israel's mistakes can save us much misery and self-destruction. To be faithful in listening, remembering, and obeying will deliver us from the whirlwind that engulfed Israel.

Quarterly Quiz

The questions on this page may be used in several ways: as a pretest at the beginning of the quarter; as a review at the end of the quarter; or as a review after each lesson. The questions are based on the Scripture text of each lesson (King James Version). **The answers are on page 4.**

Lesson 1

1. Who is described as "more subtile than any beast of the field"? *Genesis 3:1*
2. When confronted by God with their disobedience, whom did Adam blame? Whom did Eve blame? *Genesis 3:12, 13*

Lesson 2

1. God heard the groaning of the Israelites and remembered His covenant with _____, _____, and _____. *Exodus 2:24*
2. Who said, "I know not the Lord, neither will I let Israel go"? *Exodus 5:2*
3. At what hour did the Lord smite all the firstborn in Egypt? *Exodus 12:29*

Lesson 3

1. What is the first of the Ten Commandments? *Deuteronomy 5:7*
2. The _____ was to be observed on the seventh day. *Deuteronomy 5:14*
3. The command to keep the Sabbath Day did not apply to the Israelites' servants. T/F *Deuteronomy 5:14*

Lesson 4

1. One man out of every _____ of Israel was to take a stone from the _____ River. *Joshua 4:1, 2*
2. In what town did Joshua set the twelve stones taken from the river? *Joshua 4:20*

Lesson 5

1. Give the names of the pagan deities that the Israelites served during the days of the judges. *Judges 2:13*
2. The anger of the Lord is described as _____ against Israel. *Judges 2:14, 20*

Lesson 6

1. Name the three towns where Samuel traveled in a circuit to serve as judge. *1 Samuel 7:16*
2. Give the names of Samuel's two sons whom he appointed as judges. *1 Samuel 8:2*
3. The people desired a king in order to be like the _____. *1 Samuel 8:5, 20*

Lesson 7

1. Jeroboam feared that his kingdom might return to the house of _____. *1 Kings 12:26*

2. In what two locations did Jeroboam set up his golden calves? *1 Kings 12:29*
3. Jeroboam established a _____ to be observed in the eighth month. *1 Kings 12:32*

Lesson 8

1. Naaman was the "captain of the host" of the army of (the Philistines, Syria, Edom). *2 Kings 5:1*
2. Who said, "Let him come now to me, and he shall know that there is a prophet in Israel"? *2 Kings 5:8*
3. Naaman was told to wash in the _____ River _____ times. *2 Kings 5:10*

Lesson 9

1. Who said, "I was no prophet, neither was I a prophet's son"? *Amos 7:14*
2. Name the priest of Bethel who told Amos to go back to the land of Judah. *Amos 7:12*

Lesson 10

1. Psalm 73 is the testimony of a man who envied (the power of rulers, the prosperity of the wicked, the innocence of children). *Psalm 73:3*
2. Asaph, the writer of Psalm 73, found understanding when he entered the _____ of God. *Psalm 73:17*

Lesson 11

1. Jeremiah was told to take a potter's "earthen bottle," then to _____ it before the men who were with him. *Jeremiah 19:1, 10*
2. What king desired Jeremiah to inquire of the Lord regarding Jerusalem? *Jeremiah 21:1, 2*

Lesson 12

1. The hand of the Lord carried Ezekiel to a _____ full of _____. *Ezekiel 37:1*
2. God told Ezekiel that the bones represented the whole house of Israel. T/F *Ezekiel 37:11*

Lesson 13

1. Which word is used to describe Ezra (governor, prophet, scribe)? *Nehemiah 8:13*
2. The people gathered before Ezra to understand the words of the _____. *Nehemiah 8:13*
3. The people learned that the Israelites were to live in _____ during the feast of the _____ month. *Nehemiah 8:14*

God's Creation Marred by Sin

DEVOTIONAL READING: **Romans 7:15-25a.**

LESSON SCRIPTURE: **Genesis 3.**

PRINTED TEXT: **Genesis 3:1-13.**

Genesis 3:1-13

1 Now the serpent was more subtile than any beast of the field which the LORD God had made. And he said unto the woman, Yea, hath God said, Ye shall not eat of every tree of the garden?

2 And the woman said unto the serpent, We may eat of the fruit of the trees of the garden:

3 But of the fruit of the tree which is in the midst of the garden, God hath said, Ye shall not eat of it, neither shall ye touch it, lest ye die.

4 And the serpent said unto the woman, Ye shall not surely die:

5 For God doth know that in the day ye eat thereof, then your eyes shall be opened, and ye shall be as gods, knowing good and evil.

6 And when the woman saw that the tree was good for food, and that it was pleasant to the eyes, and a tree to be desired to make one wise, she took of the fruit thereof, and did eat, and gave also unto her husband with her; and he did eat.

7 And the eyes of them both were opened, and they knew that they were naked; and they sewed fig leaves together, and made themselves aprons.

8 And they heard the voice of the LORD God walking in the garden in the cool of the day: and Adam and his wife hid themselves from the presence of the LORD God amongst the trees of the garden.

9 And the LORD God called unto Adam, and said unto him, Where art thou?

10 And he said, I heard thy voice in the garden, and I was afraid, because I was naked; and I hid myself.

11 And he said, Who told thee that thou wast naked? Hast thou eaten of the tree, whereof I commanded thee that thou shouldest not eat?

12 And the man said, The woman whom thou gavest to be with me, she gave me of the tree, and I did eat.

13 And the LORD God said unto the woman, What is this that thou hast done? And the woman said, The serpent beguiled me, and I did eat.

GOLDEN TEXT: Adam and his wife hid themselves from the presence of the LORD God amongst the trees of the garden.—Genesis 3:8.

Lesson Aims

After this lesson a student should be able to:
1. Describe Adam and Eve's sin and its result.
2. Explain the nature and consequences of sin as they relate to God, man, and Satan.
3. Determine to obey God and resist Satan in one specific area of his or her life.

Lesson Outline

Introduction

Steve was caught in the act. There were witnesses. His guilt could not be denied. At the advice of his attorney, he pleaded no contest. As a result, Steve was convicted of stealing a six-pack of beer.

When asked about the incident, Steve said that it was a joke—a part of the initiation into his college fraternity. But the storekeeper was not amused; the police were not amused; and the judge was not amused. Perhaps the older fraternity members were more guilty than Steve, but Steve was the one who had to spend time in jail instead of in class.

You can think of similar cases. Consider the boy who spends his after-school hours on the streets and gets involved with drugs. We can blame the pusher who entices him, the parents who abandon him to the streets, or the system that compels both parents to work in order to earn a living; but the boy is the one who suffers the addiction and has to endure detention in a juvenile facility.

A. An Ancient Rule

The excuses may seem plausible, but they cannot overturn a fundamental principle: a person has to endure the consequences of what he does. This principle has been in operation for a long time, and it applies in matters much more serious than fraternity nonsense. Ultimately it is a matter of life and death. "The wages of sin is death," proclaimed Paul. But there was more to his message. Thanks to divine grace he could add, "The gift of God is eternal life through Jesus Christ our Lord" (Romans 6:23).

B. Lesson Background

Today's lesson begins a survey of the Old Testament, entitled "God Calls a People to Faithful Living." Obviously, to conduct such a survey in only thirteen lessons is not an easy task. It requires being quite selective as to what Scriptures will be covered.

The book of Genesis itself is filled with several "high points." Within the space of just the first two chapters, the following events are described:

God created the heaven and the earth.

God shaped the earth in wonderful ways, creating mountains and valleys, rivers, seas, and oceans, plains and rolling hills.

God made fish to swim in the sea, birds to fly in the air, and animals to walk on the ground.

God made man in His own image and gave him dominion over the other creatures.

God appointed the man He created to be the caretaker of a lovely garden that provided food for both man and beast.

Realizing that it was not good for that man to be alone, God provided a wonderful "help meet for him" (Genesis 2:18)—a woman.

In the middle of this garden, God designated one tree from which the man and the woman were not permitted to eat. Disobedience to this command would bring death.

Within this year (during the summer quarter of 1999, to be exact) three entire months will be given to studies from Genesis. There we will be able to go into greater detail concerning some of the themes mentioned above and others that are found within this important book.

For now, however, we begin our Old Testament survey with one of the "low points" found in Genesis: "God's Creation Marred by Sin."

I. Temptation
(Genesis 3:1-5)

Supposed wise men of today look at the deteriorating slums of our great cities and say that poverty is the cause of crime. The first three chapters of Genesis, however, are enough to tell us to look elsewhere for the cause. There was no poverty in Eden, yet that was where sin burst into bloom and brought forth its deadly fruit. Abundance is no shield against temptation.

A. The Tempter (v. 1a)

1a. Now the serpent was more subtile than any beast of the field which the LORD God had made.

Subtile is a word that reminds us of human nature. Like each of us, it has a good side and a bad side. In a good sense, it means wise, sagacious, or perceptive. In a bad sense, it means cunning, sly, or tricky. Here it is used in its bad sense, as we see from the verses that follow. The *serpent* was the trickiest creature in Eden.

B. The Question (v. 1b)

1b. And he said unto the woman, Yea, hath God said, Ye shall not eat of every tree of the garden?

The *woman* was Eve, wife of the first man Adam (Genesis 3:20). The serpent approached her with a question. Here *yea* has a meaning similar to "indeed." The *New International Version* reads, "Did God really say . . . ?" By expressing surprise that God would say, *Ye shall not eat of every tree of the garden*, the serpent implied that He was unreasonable to say it. We might paraphrase the serpent's words as follows: "Is it possible that God said this? It sounds so silly."

Have you ever heard a snake talking? None of us has ever heard a snake use human language. While the Bible does not specifically say so, it is generally supposed that Satan took possession of this serpent and miraculously enabled it to speak the devil's own thoughts. Here, close to the beginning of the Bible, we see Satan in the guise of a serpent, and near the end of the Bible we see him described as "that old serpent" (Revelation 20:2). He is the same deceitful character throughout Scripture! [See question #1, page 16.]

C. The Law (vv. 2, 3)

2, 3. And the woman said unto the serpent, We may eat of the fruit of the trees of the garden: but of the fruit of the tree which is in the midst of the garden, God hath said, Ye shall not eat of it, neither shall ye touch it, lest ye die.

The woman was fully aware of the order given by God, recorded in Genesis 2:16, 17. *Neither shall ye touch it* is not included there, and so we wonder why Eve mentioned it here. Perhaps God had said more than is recorded in that verse, or perhaps the man and woman had made the addition in their own thinking. In any case, the woman fully understood that God wanted her and her husband to leave *the fruit of the tree . . . in the midst of the garden* alone.

D. The Lie (vv. 4, 5)

4. And the serpent said unto the woman, Ye shall not surely die.

Now the *serpent* spoke more boldly. Flatly he accused God of lying. Why didn't the woman stop listening at that point? God's Word is true; He "cannot lie" (Titus 1:2). Satan, on the other hand, "is a liar, and the father of it" (John 8:44). He seeks to contradict whatever God has said. But Eve kept on listening; and to this very day liars are denying the Word of God, and uncounted thousands of unwary people are listening to and liking what the liars have to say. All the attacks directed toward the Bible come down to the issue of truth: can we trust what God has said? Is He telling the truth, or is He lying? Satan will cast any amount of doubt he can on this matter, just as he did with Eve. [See question #2, page 16.]

5. For God doth know that in the day ye eat thereof, then your eyes shall be opened, and ye shall be as gods, knowing good and evil.

Having accused God of lying, the serpent proceeded to give the devil's twisted explanation of why God had lied. God wanted to keep something from His creatures, the devil claimed. The forbidden fruit would make Adam and Eve *as gods*—or as God Himself, actually. The Hebrew word for *gods* (plural) is *elohim*, which is also the form normally used to represent God, as at the beginning of this verse. God was afraid of competition, said the devil. God did not want the man and the woman to be all they could be. Today this argument is often stated as follows: "God doesn't want you to have any fun. His rules will only limit your freedom. Ignore them, and you'll really begin to live."

VISUALS FOR THESE LESSONS

The *Adult Visuals* packet contains classroom-size visuals designed for use with the lessons in the Fall Quarter. The packet is available from your supplier. Order No. 192.

II. Sin
(Genesis 3:6)

With the benefit of hindsight, we easily see what the woman should have done. She should have said, "Get out of here! God said to leave this fruit alone, and that settles it!"

But Eve kept on listening and kept on thinking. She allowed the devil's lie to guide her thoughts. Too many people spend time thinking about the devil's offer when they should simply follow Jesus' example and say, "Get thee behind me, Satan!"

A. Unwary Thinking (v. 6a)

6a. And when the woman saw that the tree was good for food, and that it was pleasant to the eyes, and a tree to be desired to make one wise.

The seed of doubt planted in Eve's mind grew and blossomed. She kept looking at the forbidden *tree*, and what she saw seemed to confirm the devil's lie. She *saw that the tree was good for food*. Obviously that fruit was edible, and *it was pleasant to the eyes*. How could it be bad when it looked so good? Besides all that, it was *a tree to be desired to make one wise*. That was evident in its name: "the tree of the knowledge of good and evil" (Genesis 2:17). Shouldn't one use every opportunity to learn more and to become wiser?

Not necessarily! Adam and Eve already knew right from wrong. They knew it was right to obey God and wrong to disobey Him. So they already knew good and evil in a proper sense. What eating the fruit would obtain for them was experiential knowledge of evil. They had never experienced the evil of disobedience before, and Satan made them feel that was a deprivation.

No doubt the fruit really was edible. No doubt it actually was pleasant to the eyes. But God's Word is truth! If we do not keep that assurance firmly in mind, Satan is always ready to twist the truth to support his position, thus leading us to a false conclusion. It is helpful to compare the

Visual for lesson 1

This visual is a map of the Old Testament world. You will find this map useful throughout the fall quarter.

qualities Eve found attractive in the tree with those that John says are part of "the world" that Christians are not to love: "the lust of the flesh, and the lust of the eyes, and the pride of life" (1 John 2:16).

B. Unwary Action (v. 6b)

6b. She took of the fruit thereof, and did eat.

This seemed to be the only thing to do, given all the apparently positive qualities of the tree. If the *fruit* was pretty and tasty and promised good results, how could anyone refuse it?

There was another way, and that was to trust the Lord. He said to leave that fruit alone. He said it would do more harm than good. If we really put our trust in God and His Word, no lie is plausible enough, no argument is strong enough, and no facts are persuasive enough to make us disobey His plain command.

C. Unwary Sharing (v. 6c)

6c. And gave also unto her husband with her; and he did eat.

Was there any discussion between the two, any objection from Adam, or any persuasion by Eve? If so, it is not recorded. The Scripture simply records the awful fact. Husband and wife shared their guilt just as they had earlier shared their innocence. [See question #3, page 16.]

How often have you compounded your sin by involving another unwary person in it with you?

EATING THE WRONG FOOD

During the Christmas shopping season in 1996, one of the most popular toys was a battery-powered Cabbage Patch "Snack Time Kid" doll. Unlike the ordinary Cabbage Patch doll that had been sold for years, this new version was able to "eat" a variety of fake food that came with it.

However, the Snack Time Kid turned out to have an appetite for food that it wasn't supposed to eat, sometimes with unfortunate results. After the gifts were unwrapped on Christmas morning, several children across America found that a stray lock of their hair "tasted" just as good to the Kid as the fake food it was supposed to "eat." One Kid even chewed the hair out of the scalp of a little girl, and because there was no "ON-OFF" switch, the doll had to be dismantled to free the child.

Our first parents, Adam and Eve, ate some food that brought even more disastrous results. Their simple act of taking a bite of the forbidden fruit had a calamitous effect on them and all who have followed them. With their sin came a dismantling of their paradise. Toil and suffering became a part of the human condition, not to mention the loss of intimate fellowship with God.

Human experience ever since that day so long ago confirms the truth that our Designer knew what He was doing when He warned Adam and Eve against eating the "forbidden fruit."

—C. R. B.

III. Consequences
(Genesis 3:7-13)

A. Shame (v. 7)

7. And the eyes of them both were opened, and they knew that they were naked; and they sewed fig leaves together, and made themselves aprons.

Adam and Eve had been *naked* before, and in their innocence such a state had seemed normal and proper (Genesis 2:25). But now they were ashamed. Something was abnormal and improper about their nakedness, for sin had entered their lives.

B. Fear (v. 8)

8. And they heard the voice of the LORD God walking in the garden in the cool of the day: and Adam and his wife hid themselves from the presence of the LORD God amongst the trees of the garden.

There are different kinds of fear. Fear of God, also referred to as reverence, awe, or submission, is wholesome and proper. Unless this fear underlies our learning, our knowledge becomes flawed and twisted (Proverbs 1:7). At this point, however, Adam and Eve felt another kind of fear, a cringing fear that moved them to cover their nakedness (v. 7) and to hide from God. The *garden*, which had been a place of fellowship with God, was now a place to hide from Him. Such fear results from the guilt produced by sin.

C. Exposure (vv. 9-11)

9. And the LORD God called unto Adam, and said unto him, Where art thou?

Guilty *Adam* longed to be hidden. But God would not have it so. He was like the shepherd in search of His lost sheep (Luke 15:4). He asked the question *Where art thou?* not for His sake (as though God did not know where Adam was), but to evoke Adam's confession.

10. And he said, I heard thy voice in the garden, and I was afraid, because I was naked; and I hid myself.

No one can hide from God (Psalm 139:7-12). Adam quickly realized that, and told God where he was and why he had hidden himself. Some who are not so wise spend years trying to "hide" themselves in work or fun or riotous living, but

God is not deceived. How much better it is to hear His *voice* and answer! [See question #4, page 16.]

11. And he said, Who told thee that thou wast naked? Hast thou eaten of the tree, whereof I commanded thee that thou shouldest not eat?

Adam could not be hidden, and neither could his sin. God knows our sins as well. When will we stop our futile efforts to hide from Him? When will we acknowledge our sin and seek His gracious forgiveness (1 John 1:9)?

D. Excuses (vv. 12, 13)

12. And the man said, The woman whom thou gavest to be with me, she gave me of the tree, and I did eat.

"It's not my fault." How often have you heard that excuse, or how often have you offered it yourself? Adam said, "It's Eve's fault. She gave me the fruit." Adam's excuse also included an element of blaming God as well, as he referred to *the woman whom thou gavest to be with me.* "You gave me that woman to be my helper. If You had given me one who was more obedient to You, I would have obeyed too. It's not my fault!"

But the Word of God firmly rejects any and all excuses—whether Adam's, yours, or mine. You are responsible for your misdeeds; I am responsible for mine. [See question #5, page 16.]

13. And the LORD God said unto the woman, What is this that thou hast done? And the woman said, The serpent beguiled me, and I did eat.

Eve echoed her husband's excuse: "It's not my fault." *"The serpent beguiled me.* It's his fault." She, like Adam, was trying to blame another party for what had happened. And like Adam's excuse, hers was to no avail.

Other consequences of this sinful act are described in the rest of the chapter. God's final word to Adam was a reminder of the sentence of death that he now faced, just as God had promised (v. 19). Satan's earlier claim, "Ye shall not surely die," was a lie.

Some critics of the Bible take delight in pointing out that Adam did not die that very day, as God had said he would (Genesis 2:17). In fact, he lived more than eight hundred years after his sin (Genesis 5:4, 5). So God was wrong, the critics say, or else the Bible does not truthfully report what He said. Bible students have pointed out at least three ways of reconciling God's promise with what happened to Adam:

How to Say It

ELOHIM (Hebrew). El-oh-*heem.*

1. In a spiritual sense, Adam did die on the day of his sin. Spiritual death means alienation or separation from God. Such alienation is seen first in Adam's attempt to hide from God (v. 8), and then in the separation of being expelled from the garden (Genesis 3:23, 24).

2. The word *day* can designate a period of time, not necessarily a twenty-four hour period. For example, "Now is the day of salvation" (2 Corinthians 6:2). Paul wrote that centuries ago, and the day of salvation has not ended yet. Adam's sin ended his era of innocence and began his era of punishment; and within that era he died.

3. Literal, physical death is not instant. It is a long process, as we know when we see vitality dwindling in a man of eighty or ninety. Adam not only was sentenced to death on the very day he sinned; before the sun went down, he actually began dying. From that time forward, the process of death went on unchecked until it was complete.

Perhaps all of these ingredients were involved in the sentence of death pronounced upon man. What is most important to acknowledge is that God kept His promise. Neither He nor His Word can be charged with error.

MAKING EXCUSES

The rookie pitcher's fast ball was *fast,* and his curve had some "stuff" on it. Some people thought he had a good career ahead of him. By August of his first year in the minor leagues, he was enjoying an 18-5 win-loss record. Then, diving after a ball in the outfield, he fell and cracked his shoulder. He would never pitch again.

The young pitcher could have made excuses for his bad luck and wandered off into some other career. Few people would have blamed him. But instead of making excuses, he focused on his other talents. By the time he set aside his spikes, bat, and glove for the last time, he had earned a record of 3,630 hits, 475 home runs, 1,949 runs scored, and 1,951 runs batted in. That player was Stan "the Man" Musial, one of the greatest baseball players of all time.

How we handle "bad luck" or foolish mistakes or terrible sins tells a lot about our character. Unfortunately, Adam and Eve did not fare well on this score. As soon as God approached them with the fact of their disobedience, they began to make excuses. We too sometimes find it easier to make excuses than to acknowledge responsibility for our failure, but God sees through our masks and calls our action *sin.* How much better it is to take responsibility for our actions, learn from our failures, and turn our lives in a new direction.   —C. R. B.

Conclusion

Adam sinned, and Adam died according to God's promise. So did Adam's children and grandchildren. So did our grandparents, and so shall you and I. "By one man sin entered into the world, and death by sin; and so death passed upon all men, for that all have sinned" (Romans 5:12). No one is exempt. From Adam to my ancestors and on to my grandchildren, the long funeral procession winds its way toward multiplied millions of tombs. Is there no way of escape?

A. The Way of Life

Of course, there is a way of escape. "For God so loved the world, that he gave his only begotten Son, that whosoever believeth in him should not perish, but have everlasting life" (John 3:16). Jesus said, "I am the resurrection, and the life: he that believeth in me, though he were dead, yet shall he live: and whosoever liveth and believeth in me shall never die" (John 11:25, 26). What Adam did through his sin, Jesus undid by giving His life as a sinless sacrifice for us!

B. Prayer

How gracious You are, our Father and Creator! And how unworthy we are! With sorrow we confess that we too have disobeyed You. We beg You to forgive us through Jesus Christ our Lord, and we give ourselves to your service in grateful trust. Amen.

C. Thought to Remember

Christ undid what Adam did.

Home Daily Bible Readings

Monday, Aug. 31—The Serpent as Tempter (Genesis 3:1-7)

Tuesday, Sept. 1—Disobedience Brings Fear (Genesis 3:8-13)

Wednesday, Sept. 2—Disobedience Has Consequences (Genesis 3:14-19)

Thursday, Sept. 3—Expulsion From the Garden (Genesis 3:20-24)

Friday, Sept. 4—Who Will Rescue Me? (Romans 7:15-25a)

Saturday, Sept. 5—No Condemnation (Romans 8:1-11)

Sunday, Sept. 6—Alive in Christ (1 Corinthians 15:12-22)

Learning by Doing

This page contains an alternate lesson plan emphasizing learning activities.
Classes desiring such student involvement will find these suggestions helpful.

Learning Goals

After this lesson each student will be able to:

1. Describe Adam and Eve's sin and its result.
2. Explain the nature and consequences of sin as they relate to God, man, and Satan.
3. Determine to obey God and resist Satan in one specific area of his or her life.

Into the Lesson

As you begin the lesson, write the word *freedom* on the chalkboard or a sheet of newsprint. Emphasize that God has given us the freedom to make choices. Ask the students to suggest some of the choices they made during the past week.

Most of the choices we make are routine and superficial. What will we wear? What will we have for breakfast? However, some choices are life-changing. Ask the students to suggest some of life's more important decisions. (Examples: what career to pursue, whom to marry, and how we will respond to Jesus' call to discipleship.)

Observe that, when temptation confronts us, we must choose to resist or to give in. In today's lesson, Adam and Eve chose to give in.

Into the Word

Ask a volunteer to read Genesis 3:1-6. Class members should listen for factors that influenced Eve to choose to disobey God—like these:

1. She entered into a dialogue with the tempter (vv. 1-3). What should she have done?

2. She allowed the tempter to plant a seed of doubt in her mind about the goodness of God (vv. 4, 5). How should she have responded to the tempter's accusation that God was acting selfishly by forbidding access to the tree?

3. She looked with lustful longing at something that was forbidden (v. 6). How can we overcome the temptation to look with longing at something (or someone) God has forbidden?

4. She involved someone else in her sin (v. 6). What responsibility did Adam have to make a personal choice to resist temptation?

The sins of Adam and Eve resulted in some grave consequences. Direct your students to Genesis 3:7-13, asking them to identify the consequences of sin that appear in that passage.

First, Adam and Eve received firsthand experience of what sin is and how it feels to sin.

Second, they became aware of their nakedness (v. 7). In their pristine state, nakedness was no problem. Now that their minds had been corrupted by sin, it caused shame.

Third, sin broke their fellowship with God (v. 8). It made them afraid to face God.

Fourth, their sin put a strain on the relationship between Adam and Eve. When confronted by God over his sin, Adam put the blame on his wife (v. 12).

Divide the class into four groups to consider the consequences of sin spelled out in Genesis 3:14-19, often called "the curse." Ask the members of Group 1 to find aspects of the curse that relate to the serpent—Satan (vv. 14, 15); Group 2, aspects that relate to Eve (v. 16); Group 3, aspects that relate to Adam (vv. 17-19); Group 4, aspects that relate to the earth (vv. 17b, 18).

After about five minutes, call for reports from the groups.

Into Life

Begin the application part of the lesson by writing the word *responsibility* on the chalkboard or on a sheet of newsprint. The flip side of freedom is responsibility. We are free to make choices, but we must bear the responsibility for the choices we make.

Ask the students to cite some of the excuses people use to escape responsibility for the bad choices they make. Here are a few suggestions:

- "Everybody does it."
- "I had an unhappy childhood."
- "I was just doing what I was told."
- "If it feels good, why not do it?"
- "Life is too short to worry about what other people think."

Challenge your students to make wise choices—and then to take personal responsibility for the choices they make. If a bad choice resulted in a spiritual failure, they need to confess their sin and repent.

We all have areas where we are spiritually vulnerable—areas where Satan attacks repeatedly. In closing, ask your students to think about the area where they are most vulnerable. Then pose this question: "What will you do during this coming week to obey God and resist Satan in the specific area of your life where you are most vulnerable?"

Challenge your students to make a commitment to stand firm and resist temptation. Then close with a prayer of commitment.

Let's Talk It Over

The questions on this page are designed to encourage review of the lesson Scriptures and to promote discussion of the lesson by the class. The answers provided are only discussion starters. Let your class talk it over from there.

1. Satan spoke through a snake in the garden. In what outwardly innocent forms does he appear to us? What are some ways we can resist such tactics?

Today Satan spreads lies through a variety of impressive outlets: glossy magazines, books written in scholarly language, expertly crafted plays and films, and the like. We must recognize that however attractively they are packaged, lies are still lies. Satan also uses glamorous people to propagate his false doctrines. Movie and television performers, professional athletes, successful businessmen, and smooth-talking politicians have all been recruited by the evil one to propagate moral and spiritual falsehoods. They can make sin seem righteous and respectable. Paul's reminder in 2 Corinthians 11:14 and 15 is important to keep in mind: "Satan himself masquerades as an angel of light. It is not surprising, then, if his servants masquerade as servants of righteousness" (*New International Version*).

2. To contradict the clear teaching of the Word of God is to lie. How much do you think we need to emphasize this fact? Why?

The Bible is under a relentless assault by unbelievers. Shortsighted scholars claim to find inaccuracies within its pages. Entertainers mock its teachings. Many religious leaders substitute human philosophies for its eternal truths. Under such circumstances, believers cannot afford to be halfhearted in their defense of God's Word. If we believe the Bible is divine truth, unchanging and unchangeable, we must say so. If we are convinced that human beings have no right to deny what God has affirmed, we must say so. If we realize that anti-Scriptural doctrines endanger the immortal souls of men, women, and children, we must label such doctrines as lies. Let us imitate the apostle Paul, who declared, "Let God be true, but every man a liar" (Romans 3:4).

3. What are some ways in which husbands and wives tempt one another to sin?

They may tempt one another in regard to the love of money and possessions. A wife may pressure her husband into striving for promotions and wage increases, and thereby cause him to ignore moral principles for the sake of such advancement. A husband may insist on his wife's working outside the home, and thereby cause her to neglect her responsibilities to her children. Certainly there have been instances of marriage partners encouraging one another in the use of recreational drugs, the drinking of alcoholic beverages, and other practices that can damage health. Too often the "for better or for worse" of the traditional wedding ceremony has been the prelude to a mutual plunge into the "for worse" of moral corruption.

4. What are some ways people today attempt to hide themselves and their sins from God?

It is likely that some of the busyness in which people are caught up today represents an unconscious effort to avoid thinking about God, sin, and eternity. We tend to hide from God in our hectic schedules, our unending activities, and our frantic rushing from one appointment to another. People also hide in their pleasures. By keeping their minds occupied with food and drink, sex, recreation, and the like, they are able to keep God at a distance. Also, the epidemic abuse of drugs and alcohol is surely a means of hiding from God. People try to quiet their consciences by means of these substances so as to avoid facing their guilt and the God whose laws they have violated. We need to ponder Psalm 139:1-12 and its declaration that there is no way we can hide from our Creator.

5. Whom or what do people sometimes blame for their sins? Why is it pointless to divert guilt from oneself to someone or something else?

It is easy to blame much of our misbehavior on the influence of our parents or the general environment in which we grew up. We can say that our parents were too strict or too lenient. We can complain that we had too few or too many possessions. But has any person living experienced an ideal upbringing? If we can excuse our sins on the basis of childhood influences, no one in the final analysis can be guilty. Many people point to their experiences of prejudice or oppression as a justification for their sins. It is a sad fact that racial minorities, people with physical or mental handicaps, and others have been subjected to unjust treatment in our society. However, this injustice simply does not provide a license for sinful, rebellious behavior.

God's People Delivered From Slavery

DEVOTIONAL READING: Psalm 105:37-45.

LESSON SCRIPTURE: Exodus 2:23-25; 5:1, 2; 11:1-8; 12:29-32; 15:1, 2, 19-21.

PRINTED TEXT: Exodus 2:23-25; 5:1, 2; 12:29-32; 15:1, 2.

Exodus 2:23-25

23 And it came to pass in process of time, that the king of Egypt died: and the children of Israel sighed by reason of the bondage, and they cried, and their cry came up unto God by reason of the bondage.

24 And God heard their groaning, and God remembered his covenant with Abraham, with Isaac, and with Jacob.

25 And God looked upon the children of Israel, and God had respect unto them.

Exodus 5:1, 2

1 And afterward Moses and Aaron went in, and told Pharaoh, Thus saith the LORD God of Israel, Let my people go, that they may hold a feast unto me in the wilderness.

2 And Pharaoh said, Who is the LORD, that I should obey his voice to let Israel go? I know not the LORD, neither will I let Israel go.

Exodus 12:29-32

29 And it came to pass, that at midnight the LORD smote all the firstborn in the land of Egypt, from the firstborn of Pharaoh that sat on his throne unto the firstborn of the captive that was in the dungeon; and all the firstborn of cattle.

30 And Pharaoh rose up in the night, he, and all his servants, and all the Egyptians; and there was a great cry in Egypt: for there was not a house where there was not one dead.

31 And he called for Moses and Aaron by night, and said, Rise up, and get you forth from among my people, both ye and the children of Israel; and go, serve the LORD, as ye have said.

32 Also take your flocks and your herds, as ye have said, and be gone; and bless me also.

Exodus 15:1, 2

1 Then sang Moses and the children of Israel this song unto the LORD, and spake, saying, I will sing unto the LORD, for he hath triumphed gloriously: the horse and his rider hath he thrown into the sea.

2 The LORD is my strength and song, and he is become my salvation: he is my God, and I will prepare him a habitation; my father's God, and I will exalt him.

GOLDEN TEXT: The children of Israel sighed by reason of the bondage, and they cried, and their cry came up unto God by reason of the bondage. And God heard their groaning, and God remembered his covenant with Abraham, with Isaac, and with Jacob.—Exodus 2:23, 24.

God Calls a People to Faithful Living
Unit 1: God Fashions a People
(Lessons 1-4)

Lesson Aims

After this lesson a student should be able to:
1. Relate the details of Israel's exodus from Egypt.
2. Describe how God in His providence continues to grant victory and release to His people.
3. Pinpoint an area of life where he or she needs God's deliverance from the power of sin and death.

Lesson Outline

INTRODUCTION
  A. Learning From Disaster
  B. A New Beginning
  C. Lesson Background
 I. THE BURDEN OF BONDAGE (Exodus 2:23-25)
  A. Israel's Cry Heard (v. 23)
  B. God's Covenant Remembered (v. 24)
  C. God's Loving Concern (v. 25)
 II. REQUEST REJECTED (Exodus 5:1, 2)
  A. Moses' Request (v. 1)
  B. Pharaoh's Denial (v. 2)
    Call Waiting
III. REQUEST GRANTED (Exodus 12:29-32)
  A. Disaster (vv. 29, 30)
  B. Permission (vv. 31, 32)
    A Great Price
IV. PRAISE THE LORD! (Exodus 15:1, 2)
  A. The Lord's Triumph (v. 1a)
  B. Egypt's Defeat (v. 1b)
  C. Help for God's People (v. 2a)
  D. Grateful Promise (v. 2b)
CONCLUSION
  A. Today's Tyranny
  B. Prayer
  C. Thought to Remember

Introduction

A. Learning From Disaster

Last week we read how disaster came to Adam and Eve. They disobeyed God and lost their home in Eden. Later, their son Cain was born. We do not know if he was told about what had happened in Eden. If so, he did not learn from his parents' disaster. Cain murdered his brother, and in so doing brought a new disaster upon himself (Genesis 4:1-16).

Did the next generation of Adam's family learn from his disaster? No, in fact it seems that each generation grew more wicked than the one before it. There were exceptions, of course. Enoch walked with God so well that God took him home, bypassing death (Genesis 5:21-24; Hebrews 11:5). For the most part, however, man's condition continued to deteriorate until "God saw that the wickedness of man was great in the earth, and that every imagination of the thoughts of his heart was only evil continually" (Genesis 6:5).

Such a state was intolerable. God destroyed most of mankind with a great flood, but saved one righteous family (Noah's) so that He could begin again (Genesis 6:9—8:22; 1 Peter 3:20).

B. A New Beginning

Did Noah's family all learn from the disastrous flood and walk faithfully with God? They did not. The new beginning proved to be merely the beginning of another slide toward increasing wickedness. The attempt to construct the tower of Babel, whose builders declared, "Let us make us a name" (Genesis 11:4), gave evidence that man was still seeking to live in defiance of his Creator.

However, God did not destroy most of humanity again, as He had through the flood. Instead, He chose one man of faith to be the father of a nation that would have God's special guidance and blessing—a nation designed to show the rest of the world how good and how profitable it is to obey God.

To begin this favored nation, God brought Abraham from Mesopotamia (Ur of the Chaldees) to the fruitful land east of the Mediterranean Sea. He promised that this land would belong to Abraham and his descendants (Genesis 13:14-17; 15:18-20; 17:8). They were required, however, to live in obedience to the Lord and His covenant (17:9).

C. Lesson Background

After approximately two centuries in the land of promise, Abraham's descendants, seventy of them (Genesis 46:27), journeyed to Egypt to escape a great famine. These migrants were welcomed cordially and given a place in the most productive section of the land; for Abraham's great-grandson, Joseph, was a ruler in Egypt at this point and second in command only to the king. Within a few centuries, this family of seventy became a throng of, according to some estimates, two to three million.

The centuries following Joseph brought new leaders to the throne of Egypt and new policies for dealing with the increasing population of

Hebrews. (It is possible that the various policies described in Exodus 1 reflect attempts by different Egyptian rulers to control the Hebrews.) The policies included reducing the Hebrews to slavery and working them to death (v. 11), ordering each Hebrew baby boy to be killed upon delivery (vv. 15-19), and commanding that every Hebrew baby boy be thrown into the river (v. 22).

One boy escaped this last murderous edict and was brought up as a son of the king's daughter. However, at the age of forty he murdered an Egyptian and, to escape the wrath of the king, fled eastward across the desert to Midian (Exodus 2:11-15). There, while tending sheep, this man Moses was prepared by God to shepherd His people. In the meantime, the oppression of the Hebrews worsened.

I. The Burden of Bondage (Exodus 2:23-25)

A. Israel's Cry Heard (v. 23)

23. And it came to pass in process of time, that the king of Egypt died: and the children of Israel sighed by reason of the bondage, and they cried, and their cry came up unto God by reason of the bondage.

The king of Egypt died, but the new king brought no relief to the oppressed *children of Israel*. Terribly overworked and driven by the whips of brutal taskmasters, they *sighed*, or "groaned," as the *New International Version* renders it. Apparently the practice of killing the baby boys had been discontinued. The Egyptians realized that the Hebrew males served a more useful purpose if allowed to grow and become numbered among the slaves.

At this point, the people's condition appeared hopeless. In their misery they *cried* to the Lord. The Hebrew words rendered *cried* and *cry* in this verse suggest a loud cry, reflecting a desperate appeal for help from someone deeply troubled. Reading the record now, we see a bright glimmer of hope, for *their cry came up unto God*. However, they did not yet know that God had heard and was already planning an end to their misery. [See questions #1 and 2, page 24.]

B. God's Covenant Remembered (v. 24)

24. And God heard their groaning, and God remembered his covenant with Abraham, with Isaac, and with Jacob.

All told, the people of Israel had been enslaved more than four hundred years in Egypt (Genesis 15:13; Exodus 12:40). By now they must have been wondering whether God knew or cared about their suffering. But He knew, and He cared deeply. He *heard their groaning*. He

How to Say It

BABEL. *Bay*-bul.
CHALDEES. Kal-*deez*.
ENOCH. *E*-nock.
MEDITERRANEAN. *Med*-uh-tuh-*ray*-nee-un (strong accent on *ray*).
MESOPOTAMIA. *Mes*-uh-puh-*tay*-mee-uh (strong accent on *tay*).
MIDIAN. *Mid*-e-un.
PHARAOH. *Fair*-o or *Fay*-roe.

knew all about their distress. He *remembered his covenant*—the promise He had made to their ancestors. *Abraham* was the man whom God had called from Mesopotamia to begin a new nation. *Isaac* was Abraham's son; *Jacob* was Isaac's son. To each of these, God had given the promise that their descendants would live in the land of promise (Genesis 15:18-21; 26:1-3; 35:9-12). [See question #3, page 24.]

When we say someone *remembered* something, we generally imply that the person had forgotten and then was bringing the matter to mind once again. This is not the way we should understand the word here. God had not forgotten His promise and only now remembered. He had been aware of His people's plight all along, and now the time for action had come. That God *remembered* His promise means that He would now take action according to that promise.

C. God's Loving Concern (v. 25)

25. And God looked upon the children of Israel, and God had respect unto them.

God not only heard the groaning of the *children of Israel*; He also *looked* and saw all their suffering. For the phrase *had respect unto them*, the Hebrew text literally reads, God "knew." Thus by the use of two simple words ("looked" and "knew"), the stage is set for God's calling of Moses (Exodus 3, 4) to be the instrument through whom His people would be set free.

II. Request Rejected (Exodus 5:1, 2)

For forty years Moses lived as a fugitive and a shepherd in Midian. Then God sent him back to Egypt to lead the Hebrew slaves to freedom (Exodus 3:9, 10).

A. Moses' Request (v. 1)

1. And afterward Moses and Aaron went in, and told Pharaoh, Thus saith the LORD God of Israel, Let my people go, that they may hold a feast unto me in the wilderness.

When Did It Happen?
(Time line of Old Testament events covered this quarter)

Visual for
lesson 2

This visual is a time line that you will find useful throughout the quarter. Locate the events of today's lesson on it.

Aaron was Moses' older brother (Exodus 7:7). God had appointed him to help Moses in rescuing the enslaved children of Israel (Exodus 4:10-16). *Pharaoh* is another title for the king of Egypt (the two terms are used interchangeably in Exodus). This was most likely the successor of the pharaoh from whom Moses had fled forty years earlier (Exodus 2:11-15, 23).

The brothers first told the elders of the Israelites that God was about to set them free (Exodus 4:29-31), as Moses had been commanded (3:16, 17). *Afterward* they went to the king. Boldly they told him that God was saying, *Let my people go.* They did not yet tell him that the departure would be permanent; they asked only for permission to go into the *wilderness* for a religious holiday—a *feast* to the Lord. He later explained this as a "three days' journey into the desert" to hold a sacrifice to the Lord (v. 3). Apparently Moses was testing what Pharaoh's reaction to a very minor request would be.

B. Pharaoh's Denial (v. 2)

2. And Pharaoh said, Who is the LORD, that I should obey his voice to let Israel go? I know not the LORD, neither will I let Israel go.

We wonder if the king was angry, or only amused at this point. King though he was, it might be politically expedient for him to listen to Egyptian priests and defer in small ways to Egyptian gods. These Hebrews, however, were saying that the ruler of mighty Egypt was to take orders from the God of slaves. To the king, this must have seemed ridiculous. His reply was unequivocal: he was not going to *let Israel go.* [See question #4, page 24.]

CALL WAITING

The "call waiting" service offered by the telephone companies is either a blessing or a curse, depending on one's point of view. If the party we are talking to has "call waiting," it can seem like an impertinent imposition on our time. How could an unknown caller possibly be more important to the person we are conversing with than we are?

On the other hand, most of us have been on the phone at times when we wished we had an easy way to bring the call to a close. Now, science has come to our aid! Someone has invented an inexpensive gadget that enables a person to duplicate the "call waiting" sound with the mere touch of a button. Appropriately enough, its trade name is "Gotta Go." When your patience with a long-winded caller or telemarketing agent wears thin, just push the button, click the phone off for a few seconds, and then tell your caller, "Sorry, but this is an important call; I've gotta go." However, like so many deceptive "solutions" to modern problems, this one works best if you can silence your conscience.

Pharaoh acted as if he had "call waiting" when Moses asked for permission for the Israelites to go into the wilderness to worship. He asked, "Who is the Lord? He's not important enough for me to talk to Him." But Pharaoh eventually learned a lesson we all need to heed: it's very dangerous to "hang up" on God!   —C. R. B.

III. Request Granted
(Exodus 12:29-32)

"Who is the Lord, that I should obey his voice to let Israel go?" Pharaoh asked. He received a clear and powerful answer to this question in the days that followed. The Lord is God! He controls things animate and inanimate, and uses them against people who defy Him. The Egyptians saw this demonstrated in a powerful way through the plagues that befell Egypt (Exodus 7:14—10:23). After the first nine, despite the devastation that Egypt had experienced, Pharaoh remained defiant. He told Moses to get out of his sight: "Get thee from me, take heed to thyself, see my face no more; for in that day thou seest my face thou shalt die" (Exodus 10:28). Thus the power of God was poised for the tenth and most fearsome plague.

A. Disaster (vv. 29, 30)

29. And it came to pass, that at midnight the Lord smote all the firstborn in the land of Egypt, from the firstborn of Pharaoh that sat on his throne unto the firstborn of the captive that was in the dungeon; and all the firstborn of cattle.

What a *midnight* that was! *The firstborn of Pharaoh* was dead, and in every home *in the land of Egypt* a similar disaster took place. Only Hebrew homes were spared. And in the stalls and pastures throughout Egypt, *all the firstborn of cattle* were dead as well.

30. And Pharaoh rose up in the night, he, and all his servants, and all the Egyptians; and there was a great cry in Egypt: for there was not a house where there was not one dead.

Apparently the dead did not die quietly in their sleep. Whole families were awakened during the midnight tragedy. *Pharaoh* in his royal palace was stricken with grief, and *all his servants* with him. Beyond the palace walls, *all the Egyptians* were grief-stricken as well. *There was a great cry in Egypt:* a wail rose from every home. Only in Hebrew houses was there no such mourning.

B. Permission (vv. 31, 32)

31, 32. And he called for Moses and Aaron by night, and said, Rise up, and get you forth from among my people, both ye and the children of Israel; and go, serve the Lord, as ye have said. Also take your flocks and your herds, as ye have said, and be gone; and bless me also.

By this time, the king's haughty defiance had been replaced by humble deference. Filled with grief and terror, he could not wait for daylight. While it was still *night*, he sent messengers to bring *Moses and Aaron*. Hastily he granted all they had asked, urgently telling them to leave his country. Pharaoh was a beaten and broken man; his surrender was complete. The God of the Hebrews had carried out a tenfold curse, and had driven him to his knees. In his humiliation, Pharaoh begged Moses for a parting blessing instead of another curse: *bless me also.*

When the people of Israel received word of their release from slavery, they were ready! They had not gone to bed that night. They had packed their goods. They had earlier celebrated their first Passover (Exodus 12:1-28), for death had passed over them and fallen on the Egyptians. [See question #5, page 24.]

A GREAT PRICE

In 1967, a violinist at the University of California at Los Angeles (UCLA) borrowed a school violin for an off-campus practice session. After practice, the musician put the violin and its case on the roof of his car and drove off without thinking. That was the last he saw of the violin, which had been crafted in 1732 by the famed Antonio Stradivari.

In 1995, UCLA recovered this $800,000 violin, but not before a lawsuit and a payment of $11,500 to a descendant of the woman who found the instrument alongside a freeway on-ramp. Not knowing the violin's rightful owner, the woman's family had "held it captive" for twenty-eight years. The university concluded that $11,500 was a small price for the redemption of its prized violin.

The people of Israel had been "lost" for over four hundred years before God redeemed them from their captivity to the Egyptians. But when the time came for redemption, it was the Egyptians who paid a great price. During one terrible night, the firstborn in all the land—from Pharaoh's household to the firstborn cattle in the stable—had to give their lives as the price for Israel's freedom.

Whenever valuable property changes hands, whether it is human slaves or a precious musical instrument, there is a cost involved. As Christians we may be thankful that when our freedom from sin was purchased, God Himself is the one who paid the price, giving His only Son.
—C. R. B.

IV. Praise the Lord! (Exodus 15:1, 2)

Most know what happened after the Israelites left Egypt. Pharaoh had second thoughts about his decision to free the Hebrews. How could he have allowed such an enormous work force to escape? So Pharaoh summoned his army to seize Moses and Aaron, and to bring the runaway slaves back to their toil.

As the Egyptian troops approached the Hebrews' camp, they found the Hebrews apparently "entangled in the land" (Exodus 14:3). They seemed to be "hemmed in" against the Red Sea, trapped in a virtual "no man's land." Then Pharaoh received another extraordinary answer to his earlier query, "Who is the Lord?" The Lord was the one who could push back the sea, leaving a wide stretch of dry land across it, with water standing like a wall on either side. Between those walls the fleeing Hebrews walked—millions of them, with their backpacks, loaded wagons, and animals. Pharaoh's troops hurried after them, but the walls of water collapsed, drowning the entire army.

Now the triumph over Pharaoh and his army was complete. The people of God were safely beyond the waters, and Pharaoh no longer possessed an army to go after them. It was time to celebrate!

A. The Lord's Triumph (v. 1a)

1a. Then sang Moses and the children of Israel this song unto the Lord, and spake, saying, I will sing unto the Lord, for he hath triumphed gloriously.

Moses took no credit for the Hebrews' deliverance. The triumph belonged to *the Lord*, and all His people knew it. The Lord had disciplined Egypt by means of the ten plagues, forcing Pharaoh to release the slaves; and when Pharaoh had changed his mind and sought to reverse his decision, the Lord had won a final victory. [See question #6, page 24.]

B. Egypt's Defeat (v. 1b)

1b. The horse and his rider hath he thrown into the sea.

The Egyptian army had looked invincible with its thundering chariots and well-trained cavalry. The people of Israel had cried out in terror at the sight of them (Exodus 14:10). But with a single stroke, the Lord had ended their threat.

C. Help for God's People (v. 2a)

2a. The LORD is my strength and song, and he is become my salvation.

Earlier that day, the Hebrews had felt themselves without *strength*, ready to go back to their life of slavery in Egypt (Exodus 14:11, 12). But they were never without strength when the Lord was with them. His strength was their strength, and before it Egypt was as feeble as the Hebrews felt before Egypt. The Lord was their *salvation*, their deliverance, their preservation, their safety. For these reasons, He was their *song*—their hymn of praise and thanksgiving. Note the use of the personal pronoun *my*; these were to be words of praise for each Israelite to offer.

D. Grateful Promise (v. 2b)

2b. He is my God, and I will prepare him a habitation; my father's God, and I will exalt him.

This was now Israel's "pledge of allegiance." The Lord, Jehovah, *is my God*—the one I will worship, the one on whom I can depend, the one I will obey.

I will prepare him a habitation. This may be a prophecy of the magnificent tabernacle soon to be built in the desert under Moses' leadership (Exodus 25-27). Even so, the Lord who lives in the infinite Heaven above us also lives on earth with each of His obedient people (John 14:23). Such a devoted follower of the Lord prepares for Him a habitation or sanctuary in his heart.

Many scholars prefer a different understanding of this phrase, however. The *New International Version* has, "I will praise him." This translation has parallelism to its credit, a frequent device of Hebrew poetry. Thus translated, the verse reads: "He is my God, and I will praise Him; my father's God, and I will exalt Him." Either way, the dominant theme is worship, whether in the sanctuary or *habitation* of the *King James* translation or in the praises promised in the *New International Version* and other modern translations.

I will exalt him. Glory, honor, and highest praise to the Lord! This was the song of Moses and the grateful Hebrews. Is it not the song of every grateful Christian today?

Conclusion

A. Today's Tyranny

The slavery in which Egypt held Israel for so many long years was cruel and oppressive. However, it is only one illustration of the slavery in which Satan has held mankind ever since the entrance of sin into the world (see last week's lesson from Genesis 3). In today's world, examples of such bondage are abundant. The sad irony is that so many believe that they are on the road to freedom. They, like Eve, have been duped by the father of lies (John 8:44).

This slavery has only one solution. It is found in the One who declared, "If the Son therefore shall make you free, ye shall be free indeed" (John 8:36). Hebrews 2:14 and 15 tells us that Jesus came "that through death he might destroy him that had the power of death, that is, the devil; and deliver them, who through fear of death were all their lifetime subject to bondage."

Thank God that through Jesus the chains of mankind's worst bondage can be broken.

B. Prayer

We trust You, Father. Yours is the wisdom and Yours is the power. Thank You for delivering us from the horrible slavery of sin through the gospel of our Lord Jesus. Help us to live daily by Your power, so that sin will not have dominion over us. Use us to guide others to the freedom that we have found. In Jesus' name. Amen.

C. Thought to Remember

Freedom from the bondage of sin is the greatest freedom of all.

Home Daily Bible Readings

Monday, Sept. 7—Israelites Enslaved (Exodus 2:11-25)

Tuesday, Sept. 8—Moses Called (Exodus 3:1-12)

Wednesday, Sept. 9—"I Am That I Am" (Exodus 3:13-22)

Thursday, Sept. 10—Pharaoh Resists God (Exodus 4:27—5:9)

Friday, Sept. 11—God Repeats the Promise (Exodus 6:1-9)

Saturday, Sept. 12—Free at Last! (Exodus 14:19-25)

Sunday, Sept. 13—God Remembered the Holy Promise (Psalm 105:23-26)

Learning by Doing

This page contains an alternate lesson plan emphasizing learning activities.
Classes desiring such student involvement will find these suggestions helpful.

Learning Goals

As a result of this lesson, each student in your class should be able to:

1. Relate the details of Israel's exodus from Egypt.

2. Describe how God in His providence continues to grant victory and release to His people.

3. Pinpoint an area of life where he or she needs God's deliverance from the power of sin and death.

Into the Lesson

Briefly summarize the historical background to build a bridge between last week's lesson and this lesson. (See sections B and C on page 18.) Explain why the Hebrews were in Egypt and why they were slaves.

Introduce the lesson by asking your students if they ever have felt powerless. At one time or another we all feel as if we are being victimized by "the system" or an unfair law or a tyrannical boss or someone else. Ask your students to share some of their experiences with powerlessness. How did their powerlessness cause them to feel? How did they deal with their powerlessness?

The Hebrew slaves in Egypt knew all about powerlessness. They were oppressed and depressed, and no one came to deliver them. In today's lesson we look at what God did to get His people out of their predicament.

Into the Word

God knows our situation. That comes through strongly in today's lesson. To demonstrate that, ask your students to look for the action verbs in Exodus 2:24 and 25, and then to explain how each action verb shows not only God's knowledge of our situation but also His concern.

1. God "heard" (v. 24). God hears everything that is said. But here the implication is that He heard with compassion, as a father listens to his children.

2. God "remembered" (v. 24). He remembered the covenant He had made with Abraham and his descendants. While the people had forgotten (violated) the covenant, God honored it.

3. God "looked" (v. 25). God's look implies action. When God looks, things happen.

4. God "had respect" (v. 25). This means God was concerned about His people. He was moved to action by their plight.

Write the word *providence* on the chalkboard. Ask a volunteer to define or describe providence. (Providence is God's provision for His people through miraculous or natural means, often unnoticed until later, when one can look back and see that God was at work through one's circumstances.) Ask, "How can God's providence be seen in the situation of the Israelites in bondage in Egypt?" Draw special attention to Exodus 5:1, 2 and 12:29-32 of today's text. List the class's ideas on the chalkboard. Here are some suggestions:

1. By God's providence Moses was adopted by Pharaoh's daughter and reared with both the best Hebrew instruction and the best Egypt had to offer.

2. Moses spent forty years in the desert being prepared by God to lead His people.

3. Pharaoh's resistance (Exodus 5:1, 2) provided an opportunity for God to demonstrate His power over the Egyptian gods.

4. In the tenth plague (Exodus 12:29-32) Pharaoh was humbled before God, and the Israelites were delivered with Pharaoh's blessing.

5. Even when Pharaoh changed his mind and sent his army after the Israelites, God's providence delivered His people through the Red Sea, and the Egyptians were drowned.

When you have a good list of ideas, ask, "How does God in His providence continue to grant victory and release to His people?" Discuss how you and your students have seen God's providence at work.

Into Life

It is proper to celebrate spiritual victories. Moses and the Israelites celebrated their victory over the Egyptians by singing a song of praise to God. (Read Exodus 15:1, 2.)

Provide hymnals and ask the students to look for hymns that offer praise and thanksgiving to God. Compile a list of these hymns on the chalkboard. Your class might want to sing or recite in unison one of the hymns of praise.

God can deliver your students from the forces and the powers of evil just as surely as He delivered the ancient Hebrews. Hand out index cards, and ask each student to write down a specific area of life in which he or she needs God's deliverance. Then close with prayer, asking God to give your students the strength to trust Him to provide the deliverance they need.

Let's Talk It Over

The questions on this page are designed to encourage review of the lesson Scriptures and to promote discussion of the lesson by the class. The answers provided are only discussion starters. Let your class talk it over from there.

1. The Hebrew people groaned under the weight of literal slavery. What kinds of slavery make people groan in our time?

Jesus once said, "Whosoever committeth sin is the servant of sin" (John 8:34). It is obvious that many human beings today are servants, or slaves, of sin. Some people are trapped in the tangled web of lying. They have practiced deception so long that they have forfeited the trust of other human beings. Some people are snared in illicit sexual relationships. They have lost any sense of genuine love and commitment toward a member of the opposite sex. Some people are enslaved to alcohol or drugs. As a result they have jeopardized their physical health, hindered their ability to do productive work, and damaged social relationships. Some people are held fast by their excessive pride. They are unable to humble themselves before God or accept constructive criticism from other human beings.

2. Of course, some people so enslaved seem not to realize they are in bondage. They do not groan; they celebrate. How can we take God's message of freedom to people who do not realize they are enslaved?

We need to help people see the consequences of their behavior. Some are objective and easily documented, like the health problems associated with promiscuity, drunkenness, or drug abuse. Others are spiritual and hard to see unless one has a spiritual perspective. To help a person see either kind of consequence, however, requires us to get near the person, spend time with him or her, and establish a relationship of trust from which we can share our concerns. Each of us needs to be, like Jesus, "a friend of publicans and sinners" (Matthew 11:19).

3. God was concerned about the sufferings of His people. How can we gain a stronger sense of God's concern for all who suffer today?

John 3:16 sums up God's attitude perfectly: "God so loved the world. . . ." If we would gain a sense of God's concern, we must first develop His kind of love. On one occasion, when Jesus was trying to move to a place of solitude and quiet, crowds followed Him and the apostles to that place. His reaction is described in Mark 6:34: "And Jesus, when he came out, saw much

people, and was moved with compassion toward them, because they were as sheep not having a shepherd: and he began to teach them many things." Jesus' focus was always outward. If the church is going to share God's concern for the lost, its members must focus outward—on the lost—and spend less time seeking personal comfort and convenience.

4. Pharaoh's stubborn resistance to the Lord is one of the striking details in the story of the ten plagues. What are some examples of similar stubbornness in our time?

The worst kind of stubbornness is that displayed by people who refuse to accept Jesus Christ as Savior. In spite of believers' appeals to trust in Christ and follow Him, they stubbornly cling to their own way of life.

Unfortunately, even Christians can exhibit a Pharaoh-like stubbornness. They resist God's call to sacrificial giving of their financial resources or God's challenge to undertake a position of spiritual leadership.

5. When all the firstborn in Egypt died, Pharaoh got a dramatic answer to his question, "Who is the Lord?" Is it proper to use disasters in our own time to help people realize who the Lord is? Why or why not?

We cannot draw a close parallel between the disaster that rocked Egypt and natural disasters today. The death of the firstborn in Egypt was specifically prophesied for a specific purpose. It was a judgment on Egypt and its king. Still, natural disasters remind us that there is much that we cannot control. If our hope is anchored in this life only, we are at risk. Let us use such occasions to remind people that the One who created the earth can give hope beyond this life in eternity.

6. The Israelites sang a hymn to glorify God for the victory He gave. Why do we sing hymns?

If our hymns merely fill in time in our services, or if we sing mainly because it is a part of our worship that makes us feel good, then we have missed the point. Every hymn we sing should address God with praise or tell of His greatness to others. If they make us feel good, that is a by-product. They first and foremost give glory to God.

God's Expectations Made Plain

DEVOTIONAL READING: Isaiah 49:1-6.

LESSON SCRIPTURE: Deuteronomy 5:1-21.

PRINTED TEXT: Deuteronomy 5:6-21.

Deuteronomy 5:6-21

6 I am the LORD thy God, which brought thee out of the land of Egypt, from the house of bondage.

7 Thou shalt have none other gods before me.

8 Thou shalt not make thee any graven image, or any likeness of any thing that is in heaven above, or that is in the earth beneath, or that is in the waters beneath the earth:

9 Thou shalt not bow down thyself unto them, nor serve them: for I the LORD thy God am a jealous God, visiting the iniquity of the fathers upon the children unto the third and fourth generation of them that hate me,

10 And showing mercy unto thousands of them that love me and keep my commandments.

11 Thou shalt not take the name of the LORD thy God in vain: for the LORD will not hold him guiltless that taketh his name in vain.

12 Keep the sabbath day to sanctify it, as the LORD thy God hath commanded thee.

13 Six days thou shalt labor, and do all thy work:

14 But the seventh day is the sabbath of the LORD thy God: in it thou shalt not do any work, thou, nor thy son, nor thy daughter, nor thy manservant, nor thy maidservant, nor thine ox, nor thine ass, nor any of thy cattle, nor thy stranger that is within thy gates; that thy manservant and thy maidservant may rest as well as thou.

15 And remember that thou wast a servant in the land of Egypt, and that the LORD thy God brought thee out thence through a mighty hand and by a stretched out arm: therefore the LORD thy God commanded thee to keep the sabbath day.

16 Honor thy father and thy mother, as the LORD thy God hath commanded thee; that thy days may be prolonged, and that it may go well with thee, in the land which the LORD thy God giveth thee.

17 Thou shalt not kill.

18 Neither shalt thou commit adultery.

19 Neither shalt thou steal.

20 Neither shalt thou bear false witness against thy neighbor.

21 Neither shalt thou desire thy neighbor's wife, neither shalt thou covet thy neighbor's house, his field, or his manservant, or his maidservant, his ox, or his ass, or any thing that is thy neighbor's.

GOLDEN TEXT: I am the LORD thy God, which brought thee out of the land of Egypt, from the house of bondage. Thou shalt have none other gods before me.—Deuteronomy 5:6, 7.

God Calls a People to Faithful Living
Unit 1: God Fashions a People
(Lessons 1-4)

Lesson Aims

After this lesson a student should be able to:
1. Recite the Ten Commandments.
2. Explain the relevance of these Commandments today.
3. Suggest a means by which obedience to one specific Commandment can be improved in one's personal life or in his or her community.

Lesson Outline

INTRODUCTION
  A. A Great Advantage
  B. Lesson Background
 I. THE LORD AND YOU (Deuteronomy 5:6-11)
  A. The Liberator (v. 6)
  B. The One and Only (vv. 7-10)
  C. The Reverend One (v. 11)
II. THE SABBATH AND YOU (Deuteronomy 5:12-15)
  A. A Holy Day (v. 12)
  B. Work and Rest (vv. 13, 14)
  C. Memorial of Deliverance (v. 15)
    It's About Time!
III. OTHER PEOPLE AND YOU (Deuteronomy 5:16-21)
  A. Honor to Parents (v. 16)
  B. No Murder (v. 17)
  C. No Adultery (v. 18)
  D. No Stealing (v. 19)
  E. No False Testimony (v. 20)
  F. No Coveting (v. 21)
    Concerned for Others
CONCLUSION
  A. The Nation God Made
  B. Man-made Nations
  C. Prayer
  D. Thought to Remember

Introduction

A. A Great Advantage

The people of Israel had been slaves in Egypt for generations. They had no experience with government and no understanding of how to form a nation. Then, suddenly, they were free. Their bondage was behind them, but so were their homes and their means of making a living. Imagine how hard it would be to mold some two to three million such people into a nation.

But the people of Israel had one great advantage: they were *God's* people. He was in charge. He showed them which way to travel; He fed them with manna; He brought water from the rock to quench their thirst. Most significant of all, He gave them laws to govern their emerging nation. Was ever another infant nation so well cared for? If Israel's obedience had been as reliable as the Lord's provisions, the results would have been remarkable.

B. Lesson Background

By crossing the Red Sea, the people of Israel escaped from Egypt and entered the wilderness of the Sinai Peninsula. After two months of travel, they camped in a broad plain beside towering Mount Sinai. There they stayed for nearly a year, receiving God's laws and building the tabernacle as God had planned and instructed. God's laws covered many important areas of life, but the core of these laws was the Ten Commandments, which were written on two tablets of stone "with the finger of God" (Exodus 31:18).

In the second year of their journey, the people came to the southern border of the land God had promised them for their permanent home. There the people's faith fell prey to fear. Frightened by the big men and the fortified cities of Canaan, they refused to enter the promised land.

Because of their faithless spirit, the Israelites were sentenced to live in the desert for thirty-eight more years. The total number of years of wandering (forty) was based on one year for each day of the forty-day mission to explore the land of Canaan (Numbers 14:34). Those adults who had balked at the border of Canaan died during those years of wandering, to be replaced by a new generation.

In the fortieth year of their wandering, Israel approached the promised land once more, this time from the east. There Moses reviewed events from the past forty years. In it he repeated the Ten Commandments that had been given thirty-eight years earlier. Those Ten Commandments are the focus of our study this week.

I. The Lord and You
(Deuteronomy 5:6-11)

A. The Liberator (v. 6)

6. I am the LORD thy God, which brought thee out of the land of Egypt, from the house of bondage.

Before revealing the contents of His law, God revealed Himself and reminded the Israelites who He was. He was *the Lord* their *God*. Here *the Lord* represents the Hebrew name that has come into our language as *Jehovah.* That name describes the I AM (Exodus 3:14): He is the only God who really exists. Next, God reminded the people that He had freed them from their *bondage* in *Egypt.* That reminder served two purposes.

First, the people were reminded of God's power. Their release from Egypt had been accomplished by a series of mighty miracles: the ten plagues on Egypt and the marvelous opening of the Red Sea. The God who was powerful enough to bring His people out of Egypt would be powerful enough to bring them into the land of promise. They needed not to be afraid, as their fathers had been years before.

Second, the people were reminded of God's goodness to them. He had liberated them from generations of cruel slavery. Simple gratitude should have moved them to receive God's law and to obey it gladly, and to move boldly into the promised land in spite of the dangers.

B. The One and Only (vv. 7-10)

7. Thou shalt have none other gods before me.

To many of us, this command against the worship of other gods may seem irrelevant, since there may be no pagan shrines or temples where we live. However, let us never forget our Master's warning: "Ye cannot serve God and mammon" (Matthew 6:24). Paul adds that covetousness is idolatry (Colossians 3:5). Not all the world's idols are carved statues made of gold, silver, or bronze. We are to "flee from idolatry" in any form (1 Corinthians 10:14). [See question #1, page 32.]

8. Thou shalt not make thee any graven image, or any likeness of any thing that is in heaven above, or that is in the earth beneath, or that is in the waters beneath the earth.

This verse is not meant to forbid any artistic painting or sculpture. In Exodus we read that God ordered His people to make representations of various items as furnishings for the tabernacle: cherubim (25:18), almonds and their flowers (25:33), and pomegranates and bells (28:33, 34). On one occasion He even commanded Moses to fashion a snake (Numbers 21:8). To be understood, this verse must be read with the following one.

9. Thou shalt not bow down thyself unto them, nor serve them: for I the LORD thy God am a jealous God, visiting the iniquity of the fathers upon the children unto the third and fourth generation of them that hate me.

Now we see what verse 8 is saying: We must not make graven images and *bow down unto,* or worship, them. God is not *jealous* just because a

This visual beautifully illustrates today's Golden Text. Display it as you begin to discuss verses 5 and 6.

Visual for lesson 3

sculptor prepares a beautiful statue; He is jealous when the sculptor or anyone else worships that statue. Consider once again the snake that Moses was commanded to construct. When it was used for God's stated purpose, it was a blessing; but in later years, when people began to treat it as an object of worship, it became an abomination worthy of destruction (2 Kings 18:4).

God's jealousy is not an evil thing, as human jealousy usually is. He does not demand all our worship just for His own gratification; He demands it because it is bad for us to worship anyone or anything else. It is *iniquity,* and it will bring bad results to our *children* and grandchildren as well as to us.

While children do not share the guilt of their father unless they also do wrong, they may share some of the results of his wrongdoing. For example, a man engages in illicit behavior and contracts AIDS. He transmits it to his wife, and she passes it on to the unborn children in her womb. Or a man is greedy and resorts to fraud for the sake of gain. He is caught and forced to pay a heavy fine in order to reimburse those he has defrauded. His children are reduced to poverty along with him. In addition, they are likely to lose the trust and respect of neighbors because of their father's wrongdoing.

10. And showing mercy unto thousands of them that love me and keep my commandments.

Here is the brighter side of the picture. When a man gives the Lord all his worship, all his allegiance, and all his obedience, he brings the Lord's *mercy* and blessing not only to himself, but also to his children and grandchildren who follow his example. Is there any doubt which way is the right one to choose?

C. The Reverend One (v. 11)

11. Thou shalt not take the name of the LORD thy God in vain: for the LORD will not hold him guiltless that taketh his name in vain.

"Holy and reverend is his name" (Psalm 111:9). God's name is to be held in reverence, as God Himself is. *In vain* represents a Hebrew expression that has varied meanings and can apply to much more than just swearing. This Commandment is violated when God's name is used for any evil purpose; it is violated when His name is used lightly, frivolously, and with no meaning or purpose at all; it is violated when one swears falsely by God; it is violated when one swears profanely by God; and it is violated when one uses God's name as a mere expression of surprise, alarm, or indignation. "I don't mean anything by it," a man says to excuse such frivolous use of God's name. But "without meaning" is one of the meanings of *in vain*. The name of the Lord ought never to be spoken or written without reverence. [See question #2, page 32.]

II. The Sabbath and You
(Deuteronomy 5:12-15)

A. A Holy Day (v. 12)

12. Keep the sabbath day to sanctify it, as the LORD thy God hath commanded thee.

The words are slightly different in Exodus 20:8: "Remember the sabbath day, to keep it holy." But the meaning is the same. *To sanctify* is to make holy, to set apart, and to dedicate to some special use or purpose. The seventh day was to be set apart from the others and to be dedicated to rest from labor, as we see in the following verse. God had prepared the people for this Commandment when He began providing manna for them (Exodus 16:22-30).

B. Work and Rest (vv. 13, 14)

13. Six days thou shalt labor, and do all thy work.

As a rule, a man ought to *work* and earn his living. This is not only permitted, but commanded (1 Thessalonians 4:11, 12; 2 Thessalonians 3:10-12). But he ought to work no more than *six days* a week.

14. But the seventh day is the sabbath of the LORD thy God: in it thou shalt not do any work, thou, nor thy son, nor thy daughter, nor thy manservant, nor thy maidservant, nor thine ox, nor thine ass, nor any of thy cattle, nor thy stranger that is within thy gates; that thy

---

How to Say It

CANAAN. *Kay*-nun.
DEUTERONOMY. Due-ter-*ahn*-uh-me.
SINAI. *Sye*-nye or *Sye*-nay-eye.

---

manservant and thy maidservant may rest as well as thou.

Ordinary daily *work* was to stop on the *sabbath*. All the people were to rest: children as well as parents, slaves as well as masters, foreigners as well as Israelites. Even the domestic animals were to have a day of rest.

C. Memorial of Deliverance (v. 15)

15. And remember that thou wast a servant in the land of Egypt, and that the LORD thy God brought thee out thence through a mighty hand and by a stretched out arm: therefore the LORD thy God commanded thee to keep the sabbath day.

According to Exodus 20:11 the Sabbath law was based on God's rest after creation, but in our text another thought is added. Verse 14 ends with the command that a Hebrew must give his slave a day of rest; verse 15 adds a reminder that the Hebrew himself had been a slave *in the land of Egypt* until God had manifested His *mighty* power to set him free. The *sabbath day* was to be a weekly reminder of God's rescue of the Hebrews and of His special covenant with them. [See question #3, page 32.]

IT'S ABOUT TIME!

For some people in the United States, time stood still for a few minutes on November 18, 1883. For other people that day, time jumped forward. It all depended on which of the country's fifty-six time zones one lived in.

In earlier times, the shadow on a local sundial had been sufficiently accurate for most communities. As the modern era dawned, life became more complicated and timekeeping became more sophisticated: clocks were set according to a telegraph signal from an observatory that performed star sightings on clear nights.

The increasing popularity of railroad travel precipitated the change to four "standard" time zones on that Sunday in 1883. Without a time standard, no one knew when a train was on time.

God established the Sabbath as a standard by which the people of Israel could measure their use of time. It was to be a holy day, set aside for the worship of God. It was a day of rest, dedicated to remembering that God had delivered them from bondage—especially significant for a nation of freed slaves who had never known a day off.

The New Testament does not include commands regarding a "Sabbath" day, but it does indicate the significance of the first day of the week for Christians (Acts 20:7; 1 Corinthians 16:2). We do well to make this day one in which we rest from our labors and remember the One who delivered us from our bondage to sin. —C. R. B.

III. Other People and You (Deuteronomy 5:16-21)

The first four Commandments deal with the duties of God's people toward Him. The other six deal with one's duties toward others.

A. Honor to Parents (v. 16)

16. Honor thy father and thy mother, as the LORD thy God hath commanded thee; that thy days may be prolonged, and that it may go well with thee, in the land which the LORD thy God giveth thee.

This is named first among one's duties to others, perhaps because its results are so widespread and so far reaching. God calls parents to teach His law to their children (Deuteronomy 6:6, 7) and children to honor their parents as well as God by learning and obeying that teaching. When these Commandments are obeyed, generation after generation does right. The result is healthful, helpful, and peaceful living. Such living generally results in longer life, for obedient children do not destroy their lives by participating in self-destructive acts such as taking drugs, drinking alcohol, or provoking fights.

B. No Murder (v. 17)

17. Thou shalt not kill.

Several of our English translations read "murder" instead of *kill*, both here and in Exodus 20:13. This seems to be a more accurate reading, for the Hebrew word used here is never used of justifiable killing.

The sixth Commandment was never intended to forbid capital punishment. We know this because God Himself commanded capital punishment for a variety of acts. These acts include murder, striking or cursing a parent, kidnapping (Exodus 21:12-17); adultery, fornication, or rape (Deuteronomy 22:22-25); cursing God (Leviticus 24:15, 16); breaking the Sabbath (Exodus 31:14); witchcraft (Exodus 22:18); and idolatry (Exodus 22:20). Neither was the Commandment meant to prohibit killing during a just and honorable war. God sent His people into the promised land with orders to "utterly destroy" the evil people living there (Deuteronomy 7:1, 2). This Commandment forbids the willful taking of an innocent human life.

C. No Adultery (v. 18)

18. Neither shalt thou commit adultery.

Promiscuous sex was popular among ancient pagans, as it is among unbelievers today. But God's law permitted sexual relations only between a man and a woman married to each other. As noted under the previous verse, not only was *adultery* (when a married person has sexual relations with someone other than his or her spouse) forbidden, but also rape and fornication of any kind (Deuteronomy 22:22-25).

D. No Stealing (v. 19)

19. Neither shalt thou steal.

The right to ownership of private property is crucial for the security and stability of any society. Stealing is wrong, whether done by force, by stealth, or by deceit.

E. No False Testimony (v. 20)

20. Neither shalt thou bear false witness against thy neighbor.

Like our English translation, the Hebrew term for *false witness* suggests false testimony given in a court of law. Such a "false report" in a judicial setting was forbidden (Exodus 23:1). When applied to our conduct toward a *neighbor*, this command prohibits any attempt to twist the truth in our speech, whether by lying or gossip.

F. No Coveting (v. 21)

21. Neither shalt thou desire thy neighbor's wife, neither shalt thou covet thy neighbor's house, his field, or his manservant, or his maidservant, his ox, or his ass, or any thing that is thy neighbor's.

Desire and *covet* may be regarded as synonyms; in fact, the Hebrew word here translated *desire* is translated *covet* in Exodus 20:17. It is not wrong to want a wife or a house or a field; but it is wrong for anyone to have an envious wish for *any thing that is* his or her *neighbor's.* Such envious wishing makes one unhappy, and may turn such a one into a thief.

All these Commandments concerning relations with others are summed up in Leviticus 19:18: "Thou shalt love thy neighbor as thyself." If I really do that, I will not feel bad because my neighbor has a better house than I have. I will rejoice in his blessing as much as I would if the house were mine. [See question #4, page 32.]

CONCERNED FOR OTHERS

Malden Mills is one of the last large textile mills remaining in New England. It is the largest employer in the village of Methuen, Massachusetts. But one night just before Christmas of 1995, the mill burned to the ground. Immediately fourteen hundred people were out of a job. They expected the fire to close the mill forever.

But the citizens of Methuen were not counting on the moral character of Aaron Feuerstein, the seventy-year-old owner of the mill. The morning after the fire, he said, "With God's help, we will overcome what has happened." Then he gave every worker a paycheck and a $275 Christmas bonus. Two days later, Feuerstein announced that everyone would be paid for at least thirty days, and promised that the mill would be back in operation within ninety days. He later extended the pay for another thirty days. The mill was rebuilt on the promised schedule, and the grateful town now views Feuerstein as a hero.

The latter part of the Ten Commandments may be summarized as a demand that we be concerned about the welfare of others rather than our own desires. There are few better modern examples of this principle than Aaron Feuerstein. At a time in his life when he could have "picked up his marbles and gone home" (with few people blaming him for doing so), he demonstrated a godly concern for others that is worthy of emulation.

—C. R. B.

Conclusion

A. The Nation God Made

The nation God made possessed several advantages over others. First, its leader was faultless, all-wise, and all-powerful. He was the Lord, Jehovah, maker of Heaven and earth, the one and only God. Second, this faultless God let His people know exactly what He expected of them. The laws he gave were as faultless as Himself. We have just surveyed the Ten Commandments. God also revealed additional laws to His people to govern the details of their daily living. These were exactly the laws needed in the nation God established. They stood for centuries, needing no additions or amendments.

The success of this nation depended not only on the excellence of the leader and His laws, but also on the response of the people. The faultless laws would not accomplish their purpose unless they were obeyed.

B. Man-made Nations

No other nation can claim what ancient Israel could—that it is a nation God made. All other nations, both past and present, are man-made nations. This is not to belittle the influence of God in their making—at least some of them. Many Americans see God's hand at work in the founding of their nation. The collapse of the Soviet Union and the emergence of free nations that resulted may well be another example of God's providence. But God did not provide these nations with their constitutions or any of their laws. Congresses and parliaments meet almost continuously to make new laws and revise old ones.

Still, the success of any nation depends on its people more than on its leaders and its laws. Why haven't laws put a stop to murder? Because people are killers. Why does stealing continue in spite of laws? Because sneak thieves pilfer in darkness, armed robbers operate in daylight, and officials high in industry and government embezzle millions of dollars. Why does the tragic toll of death on the highways continue? Because people ignore the laws made for their safety.

The need is not for new laws as much as for new hearts. Any nation can rise to heights unexpected and marvelous if its people will go beyond the Ten Commandments and keep the commandments directed at the heart: "Thou shalt love the Lord thy God with all thine heart, and with all thy soul, and with all thy might" (Deuteronomy 6:5) and "Thou shalt love thy neighbor as thyself" (Leviticus 19:18).

The faultless covenant God made at Sinai included those commandments. However, that covenant was inadequate because people did not keep the commandments. So God offered a New Covenant, whose crowning feature is forgiveness of sins (Jeremiah 31:31-34). Jesus Christ is the mediator of that better covenant (Hebrews 8:6). The hope of the world lies in turning to Him and in leading others to open their hearts to His rule.

C. Prayer

How gracious You are, our Father! How grateful we are for Your forgiveness! Continue to bless us, we pray, and grant us wisdom, strength, and courage to do Your will day by day. In Jesus' name. Amen.

D. Thought to Remember

God's commandments are designed to add to, not take away, our enjoyment of life.

Home Daily Bible Readings

Monday, Sept. 14—No Other Gods (Deuteronomy 5:1-10)

Tuesday, Sept. 15—Observe the Sabbath Day and Keep It Holy (Deuteronomy 5:11-15)

Wednesday, Sept. 16—Honor Your Father and Mother (Deuteronomy 5:16-21)

Thursday, Sept. 17—Recite Them to Your Children (Deuteronomy 6:1-9)

Friday, Sept. 18—When Your Children Ask (Deuteronomy 6:20-25)

Saturday, Sept. 19—The Greatest Commandment (Matthew 22:34-40)

Sunday, Sept. 20—A Light to the Nations (Isaiah 49:1-6)

Learning by Doing

This page contains an alternate lesson plan emphasizing learning activities.
Classes desiring such student involvement will find these suggestions helpful.

Learning Goals

As a result of this lesson, each of your students should be able to:

1. Recite the Ten Commandments.

2. Explain the relevance of these Commandments today.

3. Suggest a means by which obedience to one specific Commandment can be improved in his or her personal life or in the community.

Into the Lesson

Make several large "road signs" (Speed limit, Stop, etc.) and post them around the room. Begin the lesson by asking the students to imagine that there are no traffic laws: no speed limits, no stop signs, no yield signs, no one-way signs, no do-not-enter signs. Each person is free to drive in any way he or she desires. What would it be like to drive in such a "lawless" environment?

Ask, "What does this tell us about human nature? What does it tell us about the need for laws and the enforcement of those laws? What kind of society would we have if there were no laws?"

In today's lesson we look at the laws God gave His people after they were released from slavery and able to establish their own nation. Through these laws God told the people what He required of them and established a system of national order.

Into the Word

The Ten Commandments are familiar to us all, but can any of your students recite the Commandments in order? Have them listed them on the chalkboard or on a large poster, and have the class read through the list in unison. Then cover all or part of one of them and have the class read through the list again—including the one that is covered. Keep covering more of the list and reading through the list together until the class can recite the entire list without seeing any of the words.

God's ten laws fall naturally into two categories: laws that govern our relationship with God, and laws that govern our relationships with other people. Divide the class into two groups. Group 1 will examine Deuteronomy 5:6-11 to see what the first four Commandments tell us about our relationship with God. Group 2 will examine Deuteronomy 5:12-21 to see what

Commandments 5-10 tell us about our relationships with others.

Give Group 1 some magazines and ask them to create a montage of pictures, logos, and other symbols of items that can become "gods" to people today. The purpose here is to emphasize that whatever comes between us and God is an idolatrous item of worship.

Ask Group 2 to write some headlines typical of the daily newspaper. Then ask them to review the list and note which Commandment(s) was (were) likely broken to result in each action that made the news. The idea here is to see how disregard for God's law contributes to today's social ills.

After a few minutes have each group report. As Group 1 concludes its report, note that the collage deals with the first two Commandments, but there are two more that concern our relationship with God. Discuss the third and fourth Commandments with the class, using questions 2 and 3 on page 32.

As Group 2 concludes its report, note that the tenth Commandment sums up many of the others. Use question 4 on page 32 to discuss this issue.

Into Life

Ask, "How important are these commands for us today? Why?" Your students' first reaction will be to affirm that the Ten Commandments are very important. Challenge them on this. Note that even very few Christians keep the fourth Commandment. Even if they do no work on Sunday, the Commandment says "the sabbath," which means "seventh," or Saturday. If we don't have to keep Saturday holy, why do we have to observe the other nine Commandments? This should lead to a probing of the principles behind each command. Observing the Lord's Day (Sunday) keeps the spirit of the fourth Commandment, just as watching our tempers is important to keeping the spirit of the sixth (Matthew 5:21, 22).

Remind your students that God has told us what He requires. Our task is to translate those requirements into standards for everyday living. In closing, tell your students to select one of the Ten Commandments that they have not been following as carefully as they should. Challenge them to make a conscious effort to improve its observance during the coming week.

Let's Talk It Over

The questions on this page are designed to encourage review of the lesson Scriptures and to promote discussion of the lesson by the class. The answers provided are only discussion starters. Let your class talk it over from there.

1. What are some examples of "other gods" people today place before God?

People may not bow before them in classic "pagan worship," but homes, automobiles, recreational vehicles, and similar possessions certainly appear to be idols to many human beings. In this age of humanistic influence man himself is an idol to great numbers of people. Modern-day humanists insist that man has no need for God, the Bible, salvation, prayer, Heaven, and other such religious beliefs or practices. Others claim to worship God, but their concept of God has no basis in the truth revealed in Scripture. They have fashioned their own god as surely as did those who cast golden idols!

2. What are some ways in which people misuse the name of God and the name of Jesus Christ?

The lesson writer notes several examples that your class can discuss. But what about the individual who begins a statement, "As God is my witness," or concludes with, "So help me, God"? Another example is afforded by those who speak glowingly of God, Christ, and the Bible merely to convey the impression of piety. These hypocrites do this for the purpose of political influence or financial gain or self-glorification.

One writer mentions a friend who bought a used car because "the Lord led" him to that specific car. But the car turned out to be a lemon! The writer questioned whether the Lord had really led his friend to make the purchase and wondered whether we take God's name in vain when we carelessly claim God's leading for our own decisions.

3. The command to refrain from work on the Sabbath is not given to Christians in the New Testament. But should we set aside one day of each week for rest? If so, why?

We must avoid any legalistic approach to Sabbath-keeping. God's original intent in giving the Sabbath Commandment was to benefit man—see Mark 2:27. Unfortunately the Jewish rabbis through their traditions made it more of a burden than a source of relief from labor. It is equally unfortunate that some Christian teachers have attempted to make Sunday into a legalistic and burdensome "Christian Sabbath." Of course, our bodies require rest just as much as the bodies of Old Testament believers did. And we are responsible for caring for our bodies as temples of the Holy Spirit—see 1 Corinthians 6:19. Setting aside one day each week for rest, whether it be Sunday or some other day, is a sensible method for giving our body proper care. (See "It's About Time" on page 28 for another writer's view on this issue.)

4. It is interesting to note that obeying the command to refrain from coveting helps one in obeying some of the commands that precede it. How is this so?

The command to refrain from coveting someone else's wife could make the prohibition against adultery unnecessary. While some acts of adultery may occur spontaneously and unexpectedly, it is likely that most of them result from a period of illicit desire. The command to refrain from coveting someone else's property could make the prohibition against stealing unnecessary. Sometimes stealing results from the desperation felt by poor, hungry individuals. But it is often the outcome of a longtime attraction toward another person's possessions. We may also wonder how often dishonoring of parents, murder, and the bearing of false witness are the fruit of a heart set on covetousness.

5. Some observers have pointed out that many people treat the Ten Commandments as though they were the "ten suggestions." How can we change that?

In today's permissive moral climate people work out their own systems of right and wrong on the basis of personal taste and convenience, treating this passage and all the rest of the Bible as merely one option among many. Christians must by word and by example uphold the standard that God has set down in His Word. But when Christian divorce rates approach the secular, we are not upholding the standard of the seventh Commandment. When we take advantage of an opportunity for financial gain that we have not honestly earned, we are not upholding the standard of the eighth. We need to realize that the blame for treating the Commandments as suggestions lies partly with the church, and we must work to correct that.

God's Actions Remembered

DEVOTIONAL READING: Psalm 78:1-8.

LESSON SCRIPTURE: Joshua 3:7—4:24.

PRINTED TEXT: Joshua 4:1-3, 8-11, 20-24.

Joshua 4:1-3, 8-11, 20-24

1 And it came to pass, when all the people were clean passed over Jordan, that the LORD spake unto Joshua, saying,

2 Take you twelve men out of the people, out of every tribe a man,

3 And command ye them, saying, Take you hence out of the midst of Jordan, out of the place where the priests' feet stood firm, twelve stones, and ye shall carry them over with you, and leave them in the lodging place, where ye shall lodge this night.

. . . .

8 And the children of Israel did so as Joshua commanded, and took up twelve stones out of the midst of Jordan, as the LORD spake unto Joshua, according to the number of the tribes of the children of Israel, and carried them over with them unto the place where they lodged, and laid them down there.

9 And Joshua set up twelve stones in the midst of Jordan, in the place where the feet of the priests which bare the ark of the covenant stood: and they are there unto this day.

10 For the priests which bare the ark stood in the midst of Jordan, until every thing was finished that the LORD commanded Joshua to speak unto the people, according to all that Moses commanded Joshua. And the people hasted and passed over.

11 And it came to pass, when all the people were clean passed over, that the ark of the LORD passed over, and the priests, in the presence of the people.

. . . .

20 And those twelve stones, which they took out of Jordan, did Joshua pitch in Gilgal.

21 And he spake unto the children of Israel, saying, When your children shall ask their fathers in time to come, saying, What mean these stones?

22 Then ye shall let your children know, saying, Israel came over this Jordan on dry land.

23 For the LORD your God dried up the waters of Jordan from before you, until ye were passed over, as the LORD your God did to the Red sea, which he dried up from before us, until we were gone over:

24 That all the people of the earth might know the hand of the LORD, that it is mighty: that ye might fear the LORD your God for ever.

GOLDEN TEXT: When your children shall ask their fathers in time to come, saying, What mean these stones? then ye shall let your children know, saying, Israel came over this Jordan on dry land.—Joshua 4:21, 22.

God Calls a People to Faithful Living
Unit 1: God Fashions a People
(Lessons 1-4)

Lesson Aims

After this lesson students should be able to:
1. Tell how Israel crossed the Jordan River and why they set up memorial stones.
2. Recall spiritual milestones in their lives or in the lives of their families and church.
3. Praise and thank God for what He has done, as represented in these milestones.

Lesson Outline

INTRODUCTION
   A. Memories
   B. Lesson Background
I. MEMORIAL STONES (Joshua 4:1-3)
   A. Significant Committee (vv. 1, 2)
   B. Significant Stones (v. 3)
II. MONUMENT IN THE RIVER (Joshua 4:8-11)
   A. Mission Accomplished (v. 8)
   B. Lasting Monument (v. 9)
     Did It Happen or Not?
   C. Significant Spot (vv. 10, 11)
III. MONUMENT ON THE BANK (Joshua 4:20-24)
   A. The Monument (v. 20)
   B. The Meaning (vv. 21-23)
     Looking Backward
   C. The Message (v. 24)
CONCLUSION
   A. Disappointment
   B. Blessing
   C. Prayer
   D. Thought to Remember

Introduction

A. Memories

How we love our memories! When I moved to Cincinnati, I found in a little downtown park a statue of William Henry Harrison. He served as the ninth President of the United States, but the statue shows him as a soldier, sitting tall on his handsome horse. Harrison's tenure as President lasted only thirty-one days, so his battlefield heroics outshine his White House career.

At the other end of the park is a statue of James A. Garfield. He, too, was a notable soldier, but the statue represents him in civilian clothes; for he is better remembered as the twentieth President of the United States.

Perhaps your town has a relic, statue, or monument dedicated to the memory of some person or event. This week we focus attention on a pair of monuments erected more than three thousand years ago. They served to commemorate an event that will not be forgotten while the world stands.

B. Lesson Background

Last week we saw Israel encamped on the east bank of the Jordan River. There Moses recounted the laws that God had given the people to follow, including the Ten Commandments (Exodus 20:1-17; Deuteronomy 5:6-21).

Moses died soon after this (Deuteronomy 34:1-8). After a month of mourning for him, it was time for the people to cross the Jordan and continue their conquests on the west side of the river. Joshua had already been appointed as Moses' successor to provide leadership for the people (Numbers 27:15-23).

The Bible records how the Jordan was flooded at the time the people prepared to cross (Joshua 3:15; 4:18). However, when the priests who were carrying the ark of the covenant placed their feet in the river, the waters miraculously separated. The waters from the north "rose up upon a heap" (3:16), leaving an area of dry ground over which the people could cross. Priests carrying the ark of the covenant stopped in the middle of the dry riverbed. The waters did not come near them, but remained motionless until all the Israelites crossed to the other side (v. 17).

I. Memorial Stones
(Joshua 4:1-3)

Even after the all people had reached Jordan's west bank, the priests who carried the ark remained in the riverbed. Another important matter needed to be taken care of.

A. Significant Committee (vv. 1, 2)

1, 2. And it came to pass, when all the people were clean passed over Jordan, that the LORD spake unto Joshua, saying, Take you twelve men out of the people, out of every tribe a man.

The business at hand involved *all the people*, so the committee included *twelve men*—one taken *out of every tribe*.

B. Significant Stones (v. 3)

3. And command ye them, saying, Take you hence out of the midst of Jordan, out of the place where the priests' feet stood firm, twelve stones, and ye shall carry them over with you, and leave them in the lodging place, where ye shall lodge this night.

Like the men who carried them, the *stones* represented the twelve tribes of Israel. The monument formed from these stones would become a monument for the entire nation, commemorating the crossing of the river by all twelve tribes. Nothing is said about the size of the stones, but it seems reasonable to suppose that each man chose a stone as big as he could easily carry to the bank. [See question #1, page 40.]

II. Monument in the River (Joshua 4:8-11)

Verses 4-7 record how Joshua explained the purpose of the stones to the men who would carry them. The stones constituted a memorial of the miraculous crossing of the Jordan. We omit this explanation at this point, because it is repeated in the last part of our printed text.

A. Mission Accomplished (v. 8)

8. And the children of Israel did so as Joshua commanded, and took up twelve stones out of the midst of Jordan, as the LORD spake unto Joshua, according to the number of the tribes of the children of Israel, and carried them over with them unto the place where they lodged, and laid them down there.

The *twelve stones* from the *midst of Jordan* were carried to the bank as *the Lord* had instructed Joshua. This verse repeats the fact that the stones represented the entire nation, all *twelve* tribes. However, before we read more about the significance of those stones, we are told how twelve other stones were selected and used.

B. Lasting Monument (v. 9)

9. And Joshua set up twelve stones in the midst of Jordan, in the place where the feet of the priests which bare the ark of the covenant stood: and they are there unto this day.

In the middle of the river, Joshua built a second monument to mark the place where *the priests* had stood with *the ark of the covenant.* That monument was still there when this record was written, but we do not know how much later this was.

Some students believe that a monument in the river would be useless because it would be hidden by the water or because the flowing stream would soon demolish it. Perhaps moved by such thinking, the translators of the *New International Version* indicate that Joshua built only one monument, the one on the bank. A footnote in the *NIV* text allows the possibility of a second monument, one in the river where the priests had stood.

The original text seems to support the dual-monument understanding, and nothing about the practicality of the idea seriously challenges this understanding. The Jordan flows slowly— one writer calls it "sluggish"—and would not quickly dislodge a monument. Large, heavy stones could have been used in the riverbed, since they did not have to be carried far. Probably the place chosen was a ford, where the river was shallow and fairly calm except in time of flood. The top of the monument may have been seen above the water during the dry season. If any stones were displaced, travelers could replace them as they went by. The monument in the middle of the river would serve as a useful visual aid when parents explained to their children the meaning of the monument on the bank.

DID IT HAPPEN OR NOT?

Admiral Richard E. Byrd was long thought to have been the first person to fly over the North Pole. However, just a few years ago Byrd's long-lost diary was found in some archives at Ohio State University's Byrd Polar Research Institute; and the diary indicates that he may never have reached his goal. Experts at the Institute have determined that Byrd's navigational notes testify that he turned back two hours and one hundred sixty-five miles short of his goal.

A similar fate has dampened the assertions of Robert E. Peary, who claimed to have reached the North Pole by dogsled in 1909. Peary's claim had been controversial for many years, and has also been set aside recently by experts in the field of navigation.

When we hear that "heroes" have been either mistaken or willfully deceitful about what they have accomplished, we are disappointed. We like to trust in the authenticity of great events as they have been reported to us.

Israel's crossing the Jordan River on dry land was an event of great significance. It was important that future generations have no doubt about what had happened. The building of a monument at the place of the event so soon after it had occurred served as a testimony to what God had done. As Christians we also would do well to remind ourselves of the memorials that testify to God's great works on our behalf.   —C. R. B.

How to Say It

BABYLON. *Bab*-uh-lun.
CANAAN. *Kay*-nun.
GILGAL. *Gil*-gal.
JERICHO. *Jair*-ih-co.
SHILOH. *Shy*-low.

C. Significant Spot (vv. 10, 11)

10. For the priests which bare the ark stood in the midst of Jordan, until every thing was finished that the LORD commanded Joshua to speak unto the people, according to all that Moses commanded Joshua. And the people hasted and passed over.

The *ark* was supported on long poles that extended in front of the ark and behind it. The two or more priests who carried the ark probably kept these poles on their shoulders. They stood still in the middle of the riverbed until all the people reached the other side, until the twelve stones had been carried out of the riverbed, and until the second group of twelve stones had been formed into a monument near where they stood. As long as the ark remained in that spot, the riverbed was dry. [See question #2, page 40.]

The ark of the covenant was the visible symbol of God's presence and power. Its position at that spot in midstream indicated the power of God holding back the flow of the waters and piling them into a mountain upstream. The monument placed in that specific location would serve as a lasting memorial of such a wonderful event.

11. And it came to pass, when all the people were clean passed over, that the ark of the LORD passed over, and the priests, in the presence of the people.

When *all the people* were safe on the west bank of the river and the two memorials had been completed, *the priests* left their post in the middle of the river and carried *the ark* to the bank where *the people* were standing.

III. Monument on the Bank (Joshua 4:20-24)

When the priests had carried the ark to the other side of the Jordan, the river returned to flood stage where it had been previously (vv. 15-18). The people then made camp at a place called Gilgal, which was beyond the reach of the flooded river. It was also situated near the east side of Jericho (v. 19), to which Joshua had already sent spies in preparation for the conquest of the city.

A. The Monument (v. 20)

20. And those twelve stones, which they took out of Jordan, did Joshua pitch in Gilgal.

To *pitch* means to set up, or erect, as one pitches a tent. Literally the Hebrew word means "caused to rise." Joshua made the *twelve stones* rise in a heap. These were not squarely hewn blocks such as we might use for a monument. They were stones taken from the bed of the

Jordan—water-worn and probably not uniform in shape or size. The monument may have appeared to be nothing more than a pile of large stones. But it was meant to serve a high and holy purpose. Passersby would notice the heap of stones and wonder how it came to be there. God intended for them to be told, as the following verses show.

B. The Meaning (vv. 21-23)

21. And he spake unto the children of Israel, saying, When your children shall ask their fathers in time to come, saying, What mean these stones?

The people of Israel were to gather three times a year for the feasts of Passover, Pentecost, and Tabernacles (Leviticus 23). Travelers coming to Shiloh (Joshua 18:1), and later Jerusalem, from east of the Jordan would likely ford the river at the place where the Israelites had crossed. Even if it were somewhat out of their way, they might deliberately choose to cross near the monument in order to see it. *Children* would see the odd pile of stones and *ask* about it. That would give *fathers* a wonderful opportunity to tell how the power and goodness of God had been displayed at that very place.

22. Then ye shall let your children know, saying, Israel came over this Jordan on dry land.

Travelers going to the Feast of Tabernacles in the autumn would probably find the river low enough to cross. Small *children* could be carried across, while adults probably would be wet to the knees or the waist. Children would be surprised to hear that anyone ever *came over this Jordan on dry land*. If the people were going to the Feast of Passover in the spring, the water would be higher and the children's amazement greater. "How did they do that?" they would ask. [See question #3, page 40.]

23. For the LORD your God dried up the waters of Jordan from before you, until ye were passed over, as the LORD your God did to the Red sea, which he dried up from before us, until we were gone over.

Through generations to come, the same explanation would be passed on from parents to children. If this trip took place in the autumn, children might see the pile of rocks in the river as they were crossing. Parents could then begin their teaching in midstream, promising to show the children the other monument at Gilgal.

This story of God's power and goodness would open the door for parents to tell of another miracle—the crossing of the *Red sea* years earlier. Children would learn not only of wondrous events in the distant past, but also of God's continuing care for them as they walked

Visual for
lesson 4

Today's visual reminds us of some of the memorable things God did for Israel. Discuss, "What memorable things has God done for you?"

over the ancient trail and crossed the same river that their ancestors had crossed. [See question #4, page 40.]

LOOKING BACKWARD

Marathon running has become a very popular sport, with many large cities holding their own annual event. One of the strangest entries among the 22,000 who ran the 1987 New York City Marathon was Yves Pol. He ran the entire 26.2 miles *backward*!

The thirty-four-year-old Pol had two friends who ran alongside to warn him of any obstacles along the way. In spite of their help, he fell several times. Nevertheless, he finished in four hours and forty minutes, two and one-half hours behind the winner, but ahead of about half of his competitors.

Joshua's memorial of stones from the Jordan River was set up to cause Israel to look backward. He told the Israelites that in times to come, they should tell their children the meaning of those stones. In this way, the nation was never to forget what God had done for them. By looking backward into the past, they would maintain a proper appreciation of their present circumstances and could gain a perspective with which to face the future courageously. Unfortunately in the years to come, Israel would often forget to look back and, as a result, would lose its spiritual bearings.

Facing forward as we run the race of life is better than facing backward, but an occasional backward glance will help us to remember how God has upheld us along the way.   —C. R. B.

C. The Message (v. 24)

24. That all the people of the earth might know the hand of the LORD, that it is mighty: that ye might fear the LORD your God for ever.

The miraculous stopping of the Jordan had a number of purposes. Obviously it was intended to get the people of Israel to the other side of the river. Another purpose is stated in the last part of this verse: *that ye might fear the Lord your God for ever.* There were hard battles to be fought on the west side of the river. The people would have to face the fierce people and fortified cities that had frightened Israel some forty years earlier (Numbers 13:25—14:4). The present generation of Israel needed this assurance of God's power, an assurance that would make them *fear* Him— that is, regard the Lord with such reverence and awe that they would be more afraid to disobey Him than to go into battle against intimidating peoples and strong city walls.

An additional purpose reached beyond Israel. This miracle was performed so *that all the people of the earth might know the hand of the Lord, that it is mighty.* First of all, some of the residents of Jericho likely witnessed the crossing, and would realize that the Israelites were equipped with something much greater than any human power. That news would spread quickly to other cities in Canaan. As it was, the people of Jericho were already frightened because they knew how Israel had crossed the Red Sea forty years earlier and conquered territories east of the Jordan (Joshua 2:8-11). Now they would recognize that the power that had opened the sea was still with Israel, and they would face these invaders with terror instead of confidence.

In addition, the people of that area were not isolated. Traders from distant places were constantly passing through. Soon the news of the stopped river and the mountain of water would be told in places as far away as Egypt and Babylon. More than three thousand years later, you and I are reading again this record, and we too are reminded that the hand of the Lord is mighty.

Conclusion

A. Disappointment

The Israelites experienced a devastating setback when they moved on to attack another town and suffered a humiliating defeat. The people had to stop and take inventory, get rid of sin in the camp, and muster their courage and try again in spite of the disappointment (Joshua 7:1—8:29).

In our town, Harvey was a disappointed man. As a new employee in the supermarket he did his work well, but without a smile. "I'm not much for church," he grumbled in response to my invitation.

He had been "much for church" in another town, I knew. He had been a leading elder and a popular teacher of the young adult class. There he owned a store and prospered. But he had overextended himself in the roaring twenties, and in the crash of 1929 he lost his store. Now in 1930 he was working for low wages, with never a smile. And he never went to church.

The people of Israel experienced many disappointments. Expecting an uneventful trip to a land flowing with milk and honey, they found themselves sentenced to forty years of hard living in the desert. More than once they thought of giving up their dream and going back to slavery in Egypt (Exodus 14:10-12; 16:1-3; 17:3; Numbers 14:1-4).

B. Blessing

There was disappointment in the desert, but there was blessing, too. There was manna every morning, and in times of need God provided an abundance of water. God gave the people victory over hostile desert tribes and other enemies east of the Jordan. He provided a dry path over which to cross the Jordan. He guided the people to a convincing triumph over Jericho. Then why did anyone ever think of going back to Egypt?

First, blessings that come continually are apt to be undervalued. The manna was there every day. Picking it up was part of the daily routine week after week and year after year. Soon people forgot that it was a special gift from God. Gathering it every morning, they may have come to think that they were earning their daily bread. When they forgot that God was with them continually and was the source of their blessings, they were ready to be discouraged by any disappointment or setback. [See question #5, page 40.]

Second, even the greatest of our blessings tend to grow dim in our memories and lose their power to move us. That is the reason God desired that memorials be built to commemorate the crossing of the Jordan. That is the reason

Home Daily Bible Readings

Monday, Sept. 21—Hear the Words of the Lord (Joshua 3:7-13)
Tuesday, Sept. 22—A Memorial Forever (Joshua 3:14—4:9)
Wednesday, Sept. 23—The Lord Exalted Joshua (Joshua 4:10-24)
Thursday, Sept. 24—The Conquest of Jericho Begins (Joshua 6:1-7)
Friday, Sept. 25—The Walls Came Tumbling Down (Joshua 6:12-25)
Saturday, Sept. 26—God's Covenant Transgressed (Joshua 7:1-9)
Sunday, Sept. 27—That the Next Generation May Know (Psalm 78:1-8)

Jesus ordained the Lord's Supper—to remind us that He died that we might live. "This do in remembrance of me," He said (1 Corinthians 11:24). We need to count our blessings, both the tremendous and the tiny, and live to bless the Lord who blesses us.

So I tried to turn Harvey's thoughts to his blessings. He had a good job at a time when thirty percent of the men in town were unemployed. His wife had been faithful in bad times as well as in good, and her salary as a schoolteacher enabled the couple to save for retirement as well as live comfortably. His sons both had good jobs in other towns.

Harvey remained stubborn. He felt that God had let him down and no longer was worthy of his worship. So I tried another tack.

"Do you know what hard times are for?"

"Sure!" he said savagely. "They're to break a man down and trample him in the dirt and take all the joy out of life."

"No," I told him, "they're to build a man up and give him new joy." The reply was a disgusted grunt.

Harvey had been a Sunday school teacher, so I started to quote James 1:2-4: "Count it all joy when ye fall into divers temptations. . . ."

"I know," Harvey broke in impatiently. ". . . knowing this, that the trying of your faith worketh patience. But let patience have her perfect work. . . ." He stopped short for two seconds, and then his voice lost its angry edge and became slower, more thoughtful: ". . . that ye may be perfect and entire, wanting nothing."

We were silent for a long moment. Then Harvey said in a hushed voice, "It's talking about *me*. I never knew that."

After another period of silence he went on. "I need to be alone, preacher. I've got some thinking to do."

So one glad day Harvey came to himself, came to the Lord, and came to the church. There was joy among the angels in Heaven and among God's people on earth. If anyone was happier than Harvey's loyal wife, it was Harvey himself.

C. Prayer

Thank You, Father, for the countless blessings that have made our lives happy, and thank You for the trials and disappointments that have made our spirits strong. Open our eyes to see the opportunities that lie ahead—opportunities for new conquests and new triumphs in Your work. May we accept Your leading and profit by both our triumphs and our troubles. Amen.

D. Thought to Remember

God is with us when we are with Him.

Learning by Doing

This page contains an alternate lesson plan emphasizing learning activities.
Classes desiring such student involvement will find these suggestions helpful.

Learning Goals

After this lesson your students should be able to:

1. Tell how Israel crossed the Jordan River and why they set up memorial stones.
2. Recall spiritual milestones in their lives or in the lives of their families and church.
3. Praise and thank God for what He has done, as represented in those milestones.

Into the Lesson

Before class, write these two open-ended sentences on the chalkboard or on a large poster:

The most significant experience of my life was when. . . .

To help me remember that experience, I. . . .

As the students arrive, direct them to the statements and tell them to think about how they would complete each statement. Then introduce the lesson by asking for personal responses. Encourage your students to talk about their significant experiences and what they do to remind themselves of good times.

We all use memorial devices to help us remember significant events and experiences: a first date, baby's first steps, a spiritual victory, a first car or house, a great battle. Mementos and memorials remind us of what happened and help us feel the way we felt in those times.

In today's lesson we learn about the value of spiritual memorials.

Into the Word

Lay the historical groundwork for this lesson by telling the story of the miraculous crossing of the Jordan River (see the Lesson Background, page 34). You may want to ask a student to do this for you.

An alternative method of presenting the story of the Jordan crossing is to divide the class into three-person groups and have the students pretend they are reporters covering the event for a newspaper. Give each group a different assignment, based on Joshua 3, for stories and sidebars related to the event. After about ten minutes, call for reports from each group.

Memorial stones play a significant role in this lesson. Ask the students to talk about some of the memorials and monuments they have seen. You can start the ball rolling by telling about a monument you have seen.

Tell your students to read Joshua 4:1-3, 8, 20-24, and then ask these questions:

• Why did the Hebrews set up memorial stones at the place where they crossed the Jordan? (To remind themselves of what God had done and to spark questions from those who did not know what had happened.)

• Who were to be told the story of what God had done for His people at the Jordan? (Future generations of Hebrews [vv. 22-23] and anyone else who might ask [v. 24].)

Read Joshua 4:9-11, and ask these questions:

• What did Joshua do—perhaps while the twelve men were gathering the stones for the monument at Gilgal? (He set up another monument of twelve stones in the riverbed.)

• Why do you think he did this? (Marking the precise spot in the river where the priests stood would be a dramatic symbol and would serve as evidence that the event really did happen.)

• What might be the effect on future generations to see the pile of stones rising out of the water in the middle of the Jordan? (Their faith would be strengthened and God would be praised when they saw the clear evidence to support the story of God's stopping the Jordan.)

Into Life

We do not need to see the same miraculous signs to believe in the God who has done these mighty deeds. We don't need for God to dry up a river or part a sea. We believe they happened just as we believe God raised Jesus from the dead. Discuss some of the reasons we can have faith even if we have not seen these events with our own eyes. (See John 20:24-31.)

Providentially, however, God does work even in our own lives in wonderful and faith-building ways. Hand out index cards, and tell each student to think of a time when God has done something wonderful or providential in his or her life. Then say, "Write a word or phrase on your card that reminds you of what God has done for you in the past. Then write 'Thank You, God,' on your card."

Next, give each person in the class a small stone. Tell your students to take these stones home and put them—together with the index cards—in a place where they will be seen every day to serve as reminders of what God has done in their lives.

Let's Talk It Over

The questions on this page are designed to encourage review of the lesson Scriptures and to promote discussion of the lesson by the class. The answers provided are only discussion starters. Let your class talk it over from there.

1. God called for the use of stones in building a memorial to the Jordan River crossing. Jesus instituted the Lord's Supper by employing bread and grape juice in a memorial meal. Why did God chose such common materials for memorials? Do you think this is a precedent we ought always to follow? Why or why not?

Perhaps God meant in this way to illustrate how His truth and salvation have been given not only to the elite, but especially to common people (1 Corinthians 1:26-31). Certainly one reason God appointed such items as memorials was their availability. Stones were no doubt abundant in the Jordan, but a memorial made of marble or ivory would have been very difficult to construct! Today it is a simple matter for us to obtain the elements for the Lord's Supper.

Still, there is a place for extravagance. The ark of the covenant that the priests carried was overlaid with gold inside and out. Solomon's temple had gold and silver and bronze in abundance. Let us not be legalistic in the way we apply Biblical precedents.

2. The priests stood in the middle of the Jordan riverbed while the people crossed, the stones were gathered, and the monument was built. All this time the water must have been piling up higher and higher. What kind of test do you think that would have been on the priests' faith? What tests your faith today? How do you stand firm when your faith is tested?

We might recall Peter's walking on water. At first he was successful, but then he let the storm around him shake his faith, and he sank (Matthew 14:28-33). We can only imagine how the priests must have felt, but if the piling waters were in view, there was potential for doubt. (The location of the city of Adam, Joshua 3:16, is unknown, so we do not know whether the heap of waters was visible to the people.)

Today we are tested by a variety of things, maybe more by what we do not see than by what we do. Sometimes it's hard to see God at work, or to imagine the good He is going to work out of our situation (Romans 8:28). Reminders like this passage of Scripture help us remain faithful.

3. God made special mention of using the memorial to the Jordan River crossing as a means of instructing children. How are memorials especially useful for this purpose?

Educational experts emphasize the importance of using visual aids in teaching. God recognized this need long ago. The tabernacle and its furnishing served this purpose. The manna did also, at the same time it provided food for the Israelites. In the New Testament Jesus employed all kinds of visual aids in His teaching: birds of the air, a sower with his seed, the elements of the Lord's Supper, etc. Children learn from memorials, sacred and secular. These visual aids stimulate them to ask questions and aid them in remembering the lessons taught.

4. Apparently the memorial on the bank at Gilgal and the memorial in the river have both perished. What relevance do you see in this passage, then, since we cannot point to the stones and tell the story?

The fact that they were there is still important. They were still present when this account was written (Joshua 4:4). If they had not been, this account would have been rejected as false. So it reaffirms our trust in the Bible as an accurate historical record. The Bible itself becomes our memorial marker, telling us of this and many other mighty works of God. Its reliability has been tested and proven, and its record is "written for our admonition" (1 Corinthians 10:11).

5. The lesson writer points out how we tend to take many of God's blessings for granted, because they come to us continually. How can we overcome this tendency?

It is a helpful exercise for us to ponder occasionally how easily such blessings could be taken away. For example, Jesus taught us to pray, "Give us this day our daily bread" (Matthew 6:11). Contemplating our well-stocked pantry and refrigerator, not to mention the proximity of our local grocery store, we may regard this prayer as unnecessary. But how easily could all that food disappear! A fire or flood or destructive storm could ruin it. A swift reversal of our economic status could rapidly deplete it. Some "positive thinkers" would declare that we ought not to engage in this kind of contemplation. But it can be a healthy antidote to smugness, complacency, and ingratitude.

Cycle of Sin and Judgment

DEVOTIONAL READING: Psalm 78:17-32.

LESSON SCRIPTURE: Judges 2.

PRINTED TEXT: Judges 2:11-20a.

Judges 2:11-20a

11 And the children of Israel did evil in the sight of the LORD, and served Baalim:

12 And they forsook the LORD God of their fathers, which brought them out of the land of Egypt, and followed other gods, of the gods of the people that were round about them, and bowed themselves unto them, and provoked the LORD to anger.

13 And they forsook the LORD, and served Baal and Ashtaroth.

14 And the anger of the LORD was hot against Israel, and he delivered them into the hands of spoilers that spoiled them, and he sold them into the hands of their enemies round about, so that they could not any longer stand before their enemies.

15 Whithersoever they went out, the hand of the LORD was against them for evil, as the LORD had said, and as the LORD had sworn unto them: and they were greatly distressed.

16 Nevertheless the LORD raised up judges, which delivered them out of the hand of those that spoiled them.

17 And yet they would not hearken unto their judges, but they went a whoring after other gods, and bowed themselves unto them: they turned quickly out of the way which their fathers walked in, obeying the commandments of the LORD; but they did not so.

18 And when the LORD raised them up judges, then the LORD was with the judge, and delivered them out of the hand of their enemies all the days of the judge: for it repented the LORD because of their groanings by reason of them that oppressed them and vexed them.

19 And it came to pass, when the judge was dead, that they returned, and corrupted themselves more than their fathers, in following other gods to serve them, and to bow down unto them; they ceased not from their own doings, nor from their stubborn way.

20a And the anger of the LORD was hot against Israel.

GOLDEN TEXT: The LORD raised up judges, which delivered them out of the hand of those that spoiled them. And yet they would not hearken unto their judges.—Judges 2:16, 17.

God Calls a People to Faithful Living
Unit 2: God's People Reject His Laws
(Lessons 5-7)

Lesson Aims

After this lesson a student should be able to:

1. Describe Israel's repeated cycle in the time of the judges: peace and prosperity; growing disobedience to God; punishment; repentance; and the return of peace and prosperity.

2. Give examples of how a similar cycle has plagued the life of an individual, a family, or a nation.

3. Commit themselves, as followers of Jesus, to breaking this cycle in their lives or to helping another in doing so.

Lesson Outline

INTRODUCTION
  A. This Worsening World
  B. Lesson Background
I. ISRAEL'S WORSENING CONDITION (Judges 2:11-13)
  A. Evil (v. 11)
  B. Ingratitude (v. 12)
  C. Worship of Other Gods (v. 13)
II. PUNISHMENT (Judges 2:14, 15)
  A. Defeat (v. 14)
  B. God's Hand Against Them (v. 15a)
  C. Fair Warning (v. 15b)
    A Paradise That Wasn't
III. RESCUE AND RENEWED EVIL (Judges 2:16, 17)
  A. Deliverance From Enemies (v. 16)
  B. Departure From God (v. 17)
    Defrauding God
IV. REPEATED CYCLE (Judges 2:18-20a)
  A. God's Compassion (v. 18)
  B. Growing Disobedience (v. 19)
  C. God's Anger (v. 20a)
CONCLUSION
  A. Slow Learners
  B. Quick Forgetters
  C. Enrolling Learners
  D. Prayer
  E. Thought to Remember

Introduction

When World War I was heating up in Europe, Grandma observed that wars always brought lower moral standards and wild, reckless living. She had seen it during the Civil War, and now she could see it again. A prominent couple in

our town was getting a divorce. The crime rate was increasing. Grandma thought a lady's bathing costume was indecent because the skirt barely covered the knee, and the calf of the leg was clad only in a stocking. Gloomily Grandma predicted a time when one marriage in ten would end in divorce, when we would not dare to leave home without locking the door, and when women would swim without stockings.

Sadly, Grandma's "prophecies" have come true—and to a degree that even she would not have dreamed possible.

A. This Worsening World

Becoming worse is not confined to the twentieth century. The Bible tells how a spotless world became so corrupt that God destroyed it and started again with Noah and his family. Again, idolatry and sin became rampant; then God called Abraham to start a new nation that would be blessed by having His laws to know and obey. In spite of having such knowledge and in spite of having numerous opportunities to see God's mighty power at work, this nation repeatedly forsook the Lord and fell prey to idolatry and to all the vices that normally accompany idol worship.

B. Lesson Background

When the Jordan River stopped to let the children of Israel cross, and when the walls of Jericho fell flat, God's people saw ample evidence of His power and had ample reason to trust and obey Him. Similar evidence continued to mount as the people proceeded to take the promised land. On the positive side, God gave victory after victory to His people, even causing the sun to stand still on one occasion so they could successfully complete a battle (Joshua 10:12-14). On the negative side, a single act of disobedience resulted in an embarrassing defeat. Only when the sin was discovered and punished did God's blessing return (Joshua 7, 8).

In approximately seven years, God's people conquered as much land as they needed. They divided it among their tribes and settled down to peaceful living, though minor hostilities continued (Judges 1). Joshua and other godly leaders were a powerful influence for righteousness as long as they lived (Joshua 24:1-31; Judges 2:7). But in time that generation passed away, and there arose a generation that did not remember how greatly the Lord had helped His people (Judges 2:10).

How could this have happened? How could the knowledge of the Lord have disappeared so quickly from the people's thinking? God had told the people to teach His words diligently to their children (Deuteronomy 6:6, 7). Obviously this had not taken place; and because it had not, within one generation the law of God had faded from the people's memory. Any nation that fails to remember its history and respect its heritage is traveling a perilous path.

I. Israel's Worsening Condition (Judges 2:11-13)

A. Evil (v. 11)

11. And the children of Israel did evil in the sight of the LORD, and served Baalim.

Baalim is the plural of *Baal*, a Hebrew word meaning "master" or "lord." The word *Baalim* describes the various representations of the god Baal; for each town could have a Baal of its own, probably represented by a crude image in a shrine of some sort.

While different towns may have held different myths about their Baals, it was generally believed that the god Baal controlled the fertility of people, animals, and crops. His followers attempted to gain his favor by offering sacrifices to him. In addition, they often engaged in "religious" prostitution to induce Baal to grant fertility to themselves or their farms.

Of course, the Baalim had no Ten Commandments by which their followers should live. They did not teach people to be unselfish, helpful, kind, or forgiving. People who *served Baalim* naturally *did evil* more and more as they became more oblivious toward the Lord and His ways. Such is the consequence of making God in man's image.

B. Ingratitude (v. 12)

12. And they forsook the LORD God of their fathers, which brought them out of the land of Egypt, and followed other gods, of the gods of the people that were round about them, and bowed themselves unto them, and provoked the LORD to anger.

Judges 1 tells how, in many cases, certain tribes of Israel failed to destroy the Canaanite inhabitants of the territories that had been allotted to them under Joshua. (God had clearly told them to do this, as Deuteronomy 7:1-5 states.) In the course of time, Israelites of the generation following Joshua's became acquainted with some of the pagans living near them. Perhaps those pagans did not seem to be as terrible as they were reported to be. After all, they were farmers and shepherds just as the Israelites were. Wouldn't it be better for all concerned to try to work together?

The problem was that the Israelites began to turn from the true God to the *other gods* of the

pagans. As noted earlier, these gods had no moral standards. As the worship of them increased among the Israelites, so did all kinds of wrongdoing; and so did the *anger* of the Lord. He had warned the people of this very danger (Deuteronomy 7:4, 5). Now His words were proving true. [See question #1, page 48.]

C. Worship of Other Gods (v. 13)

13. And they forsook the LORD, and served Baal and Ashtaroth.

Ashtaroth is the plural form of *Ashtoreth*, just as *Baalim* is the plural of *Baal*. The Ashtaroth included imaginary goddesses that were associated with the various Baalim (usually as their lovers). By serving such gods, the Israelites were violating the First Commandment: "Thou shalt have no other gods before me" (Exodus 20:3). They needed a drastic wake-up call.

II. Punishment (Judges 2:14, 15)

A. Defeat (v. 14)

14. And the anger of the LORD was hot against Israel, and he delivered them into the hands of spoilers that spoiled them, and he sold them into the hands of their enemies round about, so that they could not any longer stand before their enemies.

God's wake-up call came in the form of *spoilers*, a term describing raiding parties from the pagan peoples nearby. They came to steal cattle, sheep, or grain—and they did not hesitate to kill anyone who was in their way.

In Joshua's time the army of Israel, with the help of God, had swept across the land, capturing cities and villages as it did so. But now the people of Israel had no such army. The men of the various tribes had settled in their towns and villages. They were not organized, trained, or equipped to resist the spoilers. Most significant, God no longer helped them; and for that reason, *they could not any longer stand before their enemies.* That God *sold them* does not mean that God received any payment from the raiders; it means that He handed the Israelites over to their oppressors as if they had been bought.

B. God's Hand Against Them (v. 15a)

15a. Whithersoever they went out, the hand of the LORD was against them for evil.

The hand of the Lord signifies His power at work. We saw in last week's lesson how that power had allowed the Israelites to cross the Jordan River (Joshua 4:23, 24). Now it *was against them for evil.* The spoilers were the weapon in

The Judges of Israel

Today's visual is a chart of the judges of Israel. Point out the periods of oppression that preceded the call of several of the judges and the periods of rest that followed.

Visual for lesson 5

God's hand to punish His people, though they did not worship or even acknowledge Him. The phrase *for evil* does not mean that the punishment was wrong. The word for *evil* does not necessarily imply a moral evil; it is a general term for something bad or harmful or unpleasant. It means that the punishment was harmful; it hurt the people, just as a spanking hurts an unruly child. It—like the spanking—was designed to prevent a far greater harm: the people's continued descent into paganism and wickedness. [See question #2, page 48.]

C. Fair Warning (v. 15b)

15b. As the LORD had said, and as the LORD had sworn unto them: and they were greatly distressed.

The Israelites could not claim that the punishment came without warning. Plainly and in clearest detail the Lord had promised this very punishment (and many others) if the people disobeyed Him (Deuteronomy 28:15-68; see especially v. 25). That promise was as certain as the promise of blessing for obedience (Deuteronomy 28:1-14).

A PARADISE THAT WASN'T

In 1905, the Colorado River overflowed its banks and broke through irrigation heads near the California-Mexico border. The floodwaters poured into the Salton Basin, a saline depression some thirty miles northeast of San Diego, California. The water created what is now called the Salton Sea, a huge lake more than two hundred feet below sea level. The lake has no outlet, but evaporation has reduced its size by about a third from its original surface area. Runoff into the lake has stabilized it at its current size, and the water is now more salty than that of the ocean.

About forty years ago, developers decided to turn the Salton Sea into a paradise of resorts, yacht clubs, golf courses, and seaside residential communities. However, their plans have been stymied by some unanticipated problems. Because the water that now flows into the Salton Sea contains the runoff from agricultural irrigation and from untreated sewage and refuse from the large city of Mexicali, Mexico, the Salton Sea is not only getting more salty; it is also becoming increasingly polluted. The result is that the developers' dreams of a desert paradise have not come true. Their punishment for not doing sufficient research into their project was the loss of several million dollars' investment.

The Israelites thought they had moved to a paradise when they reached the promised land. They thought they could live without regard to the laws of the God who gave them the land, but they were terribly mistaken. For their disobedience to His commands, God allowed their enemies to overpower them.

Whatever "paradise" we seek to build on earth, this principle remains true: No place can be a paradise if we ignore or violate the laws of our Creator.　　　　　　　　　　　　—C. R. B.

III. Rescue and Renewed Evil (Judges 2:16, 17)

God's punishment accomplished its intended purpose: the distressed Israelites realized that they had turned away from God. In their misery they turned back to Him and begged Him for help. As we progress through the book of Judges, we see this same plea to the Lord recorded again and again (Judges 3:9, 15; 4:3; 6:6; 10:10, 15). The Lord's wondrous patience is seen in His response to these cries, for each time He provided the deliverance that His people sought.

A. Deliverance From Enemies (v. 16)

16. Nevertheless the LORD raised up judges, which delivered them out of the hand of those that spoiled them.

How did God rescue His people from oppression when they turned to Him with cries for help? He provided *judges*. A judge was a leader—one from among the people—who rallied them to take a brave stand against the enemies who were plundering them. Since the judge represented God's presence with the people, their resistance was successful; and their oppression ended. This happened again and again over approximately three hundred years (Judges 11:26).

The judges differed widely in their abilities and their actions. Deborah is described as someone who actually "judged" cases that were brought before her (Judges 4:5). Gideon is noted for his military leadership rather than for settling disputes. Samson was a one-man army. God used him to wreak havoc among the Philistines, but we are not given any detailed information about his teaching or judging. [See question #3, page 48.]

B. Departure From God (v. 17)

17. And yet they would not hearken unto their judges, but they went a whoring after other gods, and bowed themselves unto them: they turned quickly out of the way which their fathers walked in, obeying the commandments of the LORD; but they did not so.

When an enemy had been defeated and robbery and oppression were ended, the judge who had led the people to victory would urge them to keep living in obedience to God so that peace and prosperity would continue. But the people *would not hearken*. All too soon they lapsed again into idolatry and sin. As an unfaithful wife turns away from a good husband to play the harlot with other men, unfaithful Israel turned away from the true God to go *a whoring after* the *gods* of the pagans. In so doing, they violated their covenant as God's people just as an unfaithful spouse violates the sacred covenant of marriage. *Their fathers* (including Joshua and Caleb) had gone in the way of righteousness, *obeying the commandments of the Lord*. In contrast, *they did not so*.

DEFRAUDING GOD

Weddings are usually a time of hope and joy, with family and friends gathered to share with the happy couple as they start a new life together. However, a bizarre twist was given to the concept of marriage in Florida just a couple of years ago. The bride was hospitalized and lying in a deep coma, just hours from death. Before she died, her boyfriend forged a marriage license, and "married" her with the help of an unscrupulous notary public. Using the credit cards belonging to his dead "wife," the man then spent $20,000 fraudulently before he was arrested for the crime.

The Bible often compares the relationship between God and Israel with a marriage. But Israel seemed more like the faithless and fraudulent groom in the incident we have just related than a loving mate whose joy is found in being faithful. Israel's lack of faith and gratitude for her deliverance from slavery showed itself in her slide toward idolatry after God brought her safely to the promised land.

It is easy enough for us to look back at the Israelites and condemn their idolatry. We must not forget, however, that the church is the "bride of Christ." Dare we examine our lives to see if we have defrauded our Lord, who died to deliver us from slavery to sin?　　—C. R. B.

IV. Repeated Cycle
(Judges 2:18-20a)

What is told briefly in verses 16 and 17 is now repeated in more detail. It is something that happened repeatedly in the approximately three centuries that we call the time of the judges.

A. God's Compassion (v. 18)

18. And when the LORD raised them up judges, then the LORD was with the judge, and delivered them out of the hand of their enemies all the days of the judge: for it repented the LORD because of their groanings by reason of them that oppressed them and vexed them.

Whenever the Lord provided a leader for the Israelites, their *enemies* were defeated. The result was that the land had "rest" (Judges 3:11; 3:30; 5:31) until the people strayed from God once again. *The Lord was with the judge* as long as that judge lived. The influence of the judge kept the people obedient. Sometimes the "rest" He provided lasted for forty years (Judges 3:11; 5:31; 8:28). In one case it lasted eighty (Judges 3:30). The phrase *it repented the Lord* should not cause us to think the Lord had to repent from evil. The basic meaning of *repentance* is change, so this verse affirms that the people's response to their situation changed the way the Lord dealt with them. (See Jeremiah 18:7-10.)

B. Growing Disobedience (v. 19)

19. And it came to pass, when the judge was dead, that they returned, and corrupted themselves more than their fathers, in following other gods to serve them, and to bow down unto them; they ceased not from their own doings, nor from their stubborn way.

Peace, prosperity, and happiness might last forty years or eighty; however, *when the judge was dead* and when his impact no longer was present in the land, gradually the people began again to join in pagan worship. They began again to lie, cheat, steal, and kill. These were *their own doings*; and stubbornly they continued

---

How to Say It

ASHTAROTH. *Ash*-tah-rawth.
ASHTORETH. *Ash*-toe-reth.
BAAL. *Bay*-ul.
BAALIM. Bay-uh-*leem*.
CALEB. *Kay*-leb.
CANAANITE. *Kay*-nuh-nite.
JERICHO. *Jair*-ih-co.

in them until God withdrew His protection and allowed an enemy to conquer them. [See question #4, page 48.]

C. God's Anger (v. 20a)

20a. And the anger of the LORD was hot against Israel.

It was not just the greed of the desert tribes that brought them in to devastate Israel; it was the *anger of the Lord*, which *was hot against Israel*. "The Lord is merciful and gracious, slow to anger, and plenteous in mercy" (Psalm 103:8). But it would not be kind or merciful for Him to let people go on forever destroying themselves. When the sin of Israel became intolerable, God's anger was hot, swift, and terrible. The kindest thing He could do for His people was to plunge them into suffering, for in their suffering they realized what they were doing and stopped it. In suffering they turned to God and begged for help; and when they did so, His help was as swift and powerful as His anger. What then became of those innumerable desert dwellers who invaded and terrorized Israel? "All the host ran, and cried, and fled" (Judges 7:21). The Lord's power was more than adequate when His people were ready to trust and obey Him.

Conclusion

A. Slow Learners

In previous lessons we have seen that certain people were slow in learning to obey God. Let's suppose they were in "obedience school" and give them grades.

Lesson 1. Adam and Eve may have learned to obey, but their descendants became so disobedient that God drowned most of them. Give those people an F.

Lesson 2. The plagues taught Pharaoh to obey God; but then he had to have another lesson, and it cost him his army. Give Pharaoh an F.

Lesson 3. The people of Israel were privileged to receive the Ten Commandments from God, but they started breaking them before they saw them carved in stone. Give them an F for that session.

Lesson 4. Give an A to Joshua and his comrades. They led an obedient nation as long as they lived. But when they died, the people quickly forgot the Lord and all He had done.

How would you grade your church in its obedience to God? How would you grade yourself? Is your grade better or worse than it would have been a year ago? [See question #5, page 48.]

B. Quick Forgetters

In this lesson we have seen that God used oppression by foreign powers to teach Israel to obey Him. Once they learned in only seven years (Judges 6:1). Another time it took them forty years (Judges 13:1). Yet regardless of the time, their "learning" was short-lived. In one instance it was eighty years before they had to have another lesson (Judges 3:30). More often it was only forty years (Judges 3:11; 5:31; 8:28).

Today some of us who are older may think that people do not obey God as well as we did when we were young. What do you think? Are we going to need a lesson as severe as the kind that Israel received in the days of the judges?

C. Enrolling Learners

How can we bring more people to church and Sunday school so they will learn to obey God better? Give each of these plans a grade to indicate how effective you think it would be in your particular situation.

1. Advertise by newspaper, radio, or TV.
2. Have a revival meeting.
3. Have some sermons on obeying God.
4. Mail written invitations.
5. Invite people by telephone.
6. Send callers in person to invite people.
7. Plan a "Friend Day" and encourage each member to bring a neighbor.
8. Have a special class to teach Christians how to win others to Christ.

D. Prayer

Merciful Father, we confess that our own obedience has not been perfect. Please forgive us. Today we promise both to obey You better and to try to lead others to obey You. Amen.

E. Thought to Remember

You can obey God better.

Learning by Doing

This page contains an alternate lesson plan emphasizing learning activities.
Classes desiring such student involvement will find these suggestions helpful.

Learning Goals

As a result of this lesson, your students should be able to:

1. Describe Israel's repeated cycle in the time of the judges: peace and prosperity; growing disobedience to God; punishment; repentance; and the return of peace and prosperity.

2. Give examples of how a similar cycle has plagued the life of an individual, a family, or a nation.

3. Commit themselves, as followers of Jesus, to breaking this cycle in their lives or to helping another do so.

Into the Lesson

Begin the lesson by presenting the students with this challenge:

If you were devising the ideal strategy for being a victorious Christian in a basically non-Christian society and culture, which of the following elements would you include in your strategy?

• **Avoid** everyone who is hostile to the Christian faith.

• **Destroy** everyone who is hostile to the Christian faith.

• **Have only limited contact with** those who are hostile to the Christian faith.

• **Embrace with open arms** those who are hostile to the Christian faith for the purpose of winning them to Christ.

Encourage your students to explain their reasons for choosing the responses they choose.

When the Hebrews occupied the land of Canaan, God told them to exterminate all the Canaanites. But they failed to do that. In today's lesson we see what happened as a result of their being exposed to idolatrous religions and pagan practices.

Into the Word

Fill in the historical bridge between last week's lesson and this lesson. (Use information from the Lesson Background on page 42.) The time of the judges was one of the darkest periods in Israel's history. The period was characterized by a repeating cycle of peace and prosperity; growing disobedience to God; punishment; repentance; deliverance and the return of peace and prosperity.

Divide the class into four groups to explore the text and describe each step in the cycle. Ask

each group to read the printed text, Judges 2:11-20a, and then focus on a particular portion of the text to identify and describe one part of the cycle. Group 1 should focus on verses 11-13, 17, 19 (disobedience); group 2: verses 14, 15a, 20a (punishment); group 3: verses 15b, 18b (repentance); group 4: verses 16, 18a (deliverance and return to peace).

Allow ten minutes for study in the groups; then write "Peace and Prosperity" on the chalkboard. Draw a "cycle" like the one below, but without the labels. Have each group supply the proper labels as it gives its report.

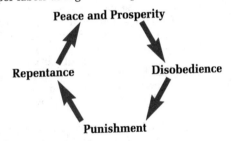

Into Life

God always expects His people to exert a positive influence on the people they live with and around. Unfortunately, after the death of Joshua the Hebrews forgot God and began to worship and serve the false gods of the Canaanites. Ask:

• Why did this happen?

• Why is it that a righteous person seems more likely to be influenced to go astray by a wicked environment than a sinful person is to be influenced to give up his sins and reform his life by a godly environment?

Ask your class members to suggest some of the dangers and hazards of living in a society that is basically non-Christian and hostile to Christ and the gospel. Discuss, "How can we safeguard ourselves from the influence of evil around us and strengthen our witness to the culture to lead people to Christ?"

In closing, emphasize that God is still in the business of delivering those who are bound by the consequences of their own self-destructive behaviors. Ask each adult to think about this question: "What do you want deliverance from today?" Offer a closing prayer, asking God to deliver your students from the things that bind them today.

Let's Talk It Over

The questions on this page are designed to encourage review of the lesson Scriptures and to promote discussion of the lesson by the class. The answers provided are only discussion starters. Let your class talk it over from there.

1. The influence of the pagan peoples around them was one factor in the Israelites' tendency to forsake God. How can we combat the influence of ungodly neighbors and acquaintances?

The Israelites had ceased to engage in actual warfare against their pagan neighbors. But they needed to recognize that there was still a spiritual war going on—a war for their minds and hearts. We Christians must keep in mind that we are also at war (Ephesians 6:10-18). We must be alert to where the battles of this war are fought: our schools; the offices of elected and appointed government officials; the media—television, movies, books and magazines; and the like. We must filter everything we see and hear through the filter of the gospel—and much of it won't pass at all! We need to be especially careful about what influences our children, and see to it that they have wholesome information and good role models from which to develop their worldview.

2. God inflicted punishment on the Israelites when they sinned. This was done to lead them to repentance. Do you think God still does this? If not, why not? If so, can you cite examples?

In Hebrews 12:4-13 is an extended discussion of God's loving discipline. There we are reminded that God is a wise and loving Father who disciplines us for our own good. We who are human parents should give a great deal of thought to our own administering of punishment and use that as a stepping-stone to understanding better how and why God disciplines.

Without the divine inspiration that guided the prophets like those who wrote the Scriptures, it would be difficult or impossible to cite specific cases of God's intervention to bring discipline. But whether God *causes* certain unpleasant events or just *allows* them, it is clear He expects us to learn from them and to adjust our lifestyles when they are out of harmony with His will.

3. Should we pray for God to raise up leaders like the judges today? Why or why not?

Not all the judges lived exemplary lives. Samson, for one, had many faults. We certainly don't want to encourage behavior like his promiscuity or short-sightedness. But the most important aspect of the judges' work was calling the people back to God. We can certainly pray for God to raise up leaders who will boldly call people to faith in God, righteousness, and repudiation of the devil. We can pray that they will be leaders who will be living examples of the message they proclaim. And we can pray that their leadership will be so powerful as to make a deep and lasting impression on the church and on society.

4. The judges' influence lasted only as long as they lived. How can modern Christian leaders extend their influence beyond their lifetimes?

Paul told Timothy: "And the things that thou hast heard of me among many witnesses, the same commit thou to faithful men, who shall be able to teach others also" (2 Timothy 2:2). Note that this describes a chain of Christian influence. Ministers, elders, teachers, and godly parents must all be concerned with teaching God's Word, and they must aim at enabling their students to teach. Ultimately, however, it is each believer's own responsibility to accept and apply the teaching. In the case of the Israelites, "they would not hearken unto their judges" (Judges 2:17).

5. The lesson writer notes that many people in Bible history failed to learn the lessons of obedience that God intended to teach them. What lessons do we need to learn from this text about the consequences of sin?

First, we need to know that sin has consequences. We cannot expect to go on sinning without adversely affecting our relationship with God.

Second, we need to know God wants the best for us. Even when He allowed spoilers to ravage Israel, His intent was for Israel's repentance and renewed relationship with Him. God wants that for us, too (1 Corinthians 10:6-13; Romans 8:28).

Third, we need to know that, when God forgives us our sins, He does not intend for us to erase our sins and their consequences from our memories. If we forget them, we may repeat them. Then we will have to endure the consequences again. In our forgetfulness we may plunge ourselves into the same sad cycle Israel experienced. If we sin, suffer, repent, and then stumble back into the same sin again, we will miss the joy and victory that should be part of the Christian life. We will be, as Peter notes, like "the sow that was washed [turning again] to her wallowing in the mire" (2 Peter 2:22).

Demand for a King

DEVOTIONAL READING: Psalm 24:7-10.

LESSON SCRIPTURE: 1 Samuel 7:15—8:22.

PRINTED TEXT: 1 Samuel 7:15—8:9, 19-22.

1 Samuel 7:15-17

15 And Samuel judged Israel all the days of his life.

16 And he went from year to year in circuit to Bethel, and Gilgal, and Mizpeh, and judged Israel in all those places.

17 And his return was to Ramah, for there was his house; and there he judged Israel; and there he built an altar unto the LORD.

1 Samuel 8:1-9, 19-22

1 And it came to pass, when Samuel was old, that he made his sons judges over Israel.

2 Now the name of his firstborn was Joel; and the name of his second, Abiah: they were judges in Beersheba.

3 And his sons walked not in his ways, but turned aside after lucre, and took bribes, and perverted judgment.

4 Then all the elders of Israel gathered themselves together, and came to Samuel unto Ramah,

5 And said unto him, Behold, thou art old, and thy sons walk not in thy ways: now make us a king to judge us like all the nations.

6 But the thing displeased Samuel, when they said, Give us a king to judge us. And Samuel prayed unto the LORD.

7 And the LORD said unto Samuel, Hearken unto the voice of the people in all that they say unto thee: for they have not rejected thee, but they have rejected me, that I should not reign over them.

8 According to all the works which they have done since the day that I brought them up out of Egypt even unto this day, wherewith they have forsaken me, and served other gods, so do they also unto thee.

9 Now therefore hearken unto their voice: howbeit yet protest solemnly unto them, and show them the manner of the king that shall reign over them.

19 Nevertheless the people refused to obey the voice of Samuel; and they said, Nay; but we will have a king over us;

20 That we also may be like all the nations; and that our king may judge us, and go out before us, and fight our battles.

21 And Samuel heard all the words of the people, and he rehearsed them in the ears of the LORD.

22 And the LORD said to Samuel, Hearken unto their voice, and make them a king. And Samuel said unto the men of Israel, Go ye every man unto his city.

GOLDEN TEXT: The LORD said to Samuel, Hearken unto their voice, and make them a king.—1 Samuel 8:22.

<table>
<tr><td>

God Calls a People to Faithful Living
Unit 2: God's People Reject His Laws
(Lessons 5-7)

</td></tr>
</table>

Lesson Aims

After this lesson students should be able to:
1. Give the details of how Israel asked for, and was given, its first king.
2. Give examples of occasions when individuals have chosen a secular solution to a spiritual problem.
3. Suggest steps they can take to effect a spiritual solution to a current problem.

Lesson Outline

INTRODUCTION
  A. God's Dilemma
  B. Lesson Background
I. A CHANGE REQUESTED (1 Samuel 7:15—8:5)
  A. Circuit Judge (vv. 15-17)
  B. Disappointing Sons (8:1-3)
  C. Call for a King (vv. 4, 5)
    Being Like Everyone Else
II. A CHANGE CONSIDERED (1 Samuel 8:6-9)
  A. Samuel's First Reaction (v. 6)
  B. God's Perspective (vv. 7-9)
III. A CHANGE ALLOWED (1 Samuel 8:19-22)
  A. Repeated Request (vv. 19, 20)
    Spiritual Middle Age
  B. Divine Permission (vv. 21, 22)
CONCLUSION
  A. Who Wants Responsibility?
  B. Prayer
  C. Thought to Remember

Introduction

"I guess I'll hold my nose, vote for Smith, and hope he doesn't make too many mistakes." Thus a businessman regretfully announced his decision as an election drew near. The thought of voting for Candidate Smith was as repulsive to him as a foul odor; but the thought of voting for Smith's opponent was even worse. So he decided to do his civic duty and ended up voting for a candidate with whom he was not really satisfied.

Have you ever chosen between two candidates when you would have liked to vote against both of them? Or perhaps you chose one of two courses of action when you were against both of them. We usually refer to this as "choosing the lesser of two evils." Such dilemmas are not un-common. They start early, like when Mom asks, "Do you want spinach or brussels sprouts?" Sometimes they take on moral value, as when we have to choose between keeping something in confidence and telling the secret to help a friend.

A. God's Dilemma

Even the Lord sometimes chooses the lesser of two evils. For example, He hates divorce (Malachi 2:16). Yet, when He gave laws to His people, He allowed for divorce in certain instances (Deuteronomy 24:1). Why? Because the alternative would have been worse. If a cruel, abusive man hated his wife and could not legally divorce her, he might treat her horribly. Therefore, "because of the hardness of [men's] hearts," as Jesus put it (Matthew 19:8), divorce was allowed. This week's lesson tells of another time when God permitted something of which He did not approve.

B. Lesson Background

Samuel was the last of the many judges who led Israel during the few troubled centuries after Joshua died and before there was a king. Samuel grew up in the tabernacle "before the Lord" (1 Samuel 1:22) and was reared by Eli, a priest who also judged Israel. Samuel was still young when the people of Israel realized that God had chosen him as a prophet (1 Samuel 3:19-21).

Eli died when he heard that the ark of the covenant had been captured by the Philistines (1 Samuel 4:15-18). Even after the ark's return to Israel (1 Samuel 6), the Philistines continued to harass Israel. Then Samuel challenged the people to put away their false gods and rededicate themselves to serve the Lord alone (1 Samuel 7:3, 4). Later, while Samuel was leading a time of confession and fasting, the Philistines prepared to attack Israel. The Lord came to His people's aid through a thunderstorm, and the Philistines were routed (vv. 5-14). They were kept under control "all the days of Samuel" (v. 13).

The first portion of our printed text summarizes Samuel's ministry in Israel.

I. A Change Requested (1 Samuel 7:15—8:5)

A. Circuit Judge (7:15-17)

15. And Samuel judged Israel all the days of his life.

The people of Israel gave their complete support to Samuel as their leader. Three reasons for this are easily seen.

1. Because Samuel's words had proved to be true, the people understood that he was a prophet of God (1 Samuel 3:19, 20).

2. Samuel had led the Israelites to a decisive victory over the oppressive Philistines (1 Samuel 7:3-11). The people accepted him as their leader as naturally as the United States accepted Washington's leadership after the American Revolution and Eisenhower's after World War II.

3. Experience showed that Samuel's judgments were just and that he was a man of integrity. Later the people would tell him, "Thou hast not defrauded us, nor oppressed us, neither hast thou taken aught of any man's hand" (1 Samuel 12:4).

16. And he went from year to year in circuit to Bethel, and Gilgal, and Mizpeh, and judged Israel in all those places.

Samuel held court in three towns: *Bethel, Gilgal,* and *Mizpeh.* These towns were fairly close to each other, and all were located in the territory of the tribe of Benjamin. Judges and preachers followed the same circuit strategy on the American frontier, where the population was sparse and travel was not easy.

Samuel probably was not the only person who functioned in this capacity, especially since the territory described here was rather limited. Perhaps some of the cases were handled by Levites in the various Levitical cities (Numbers 35:1-8). In addition, Samuel apparently organized a group that came to be known as the "company of the prophets" (1 Samuel 10:5-10; 19:20). These apprentices may have assisted Samuel in carrying out his responsibilities, particularly as he grew older. [See question 1, page 56.]

17. And his return was to Ramah, for there was his house; and there he judged Israel; and there he built an altar unto the LORD.

After holding court in the three places named in the preceding verse, Samuel would go back home to *Ramah.* That had been his parents' home (1 Samuel 1:19). Likely Samuel had inherited their property, or part of it. He *judged,* or held court, at Ramah also, thus making four stops in his circuit. He also *built an altar* in Ramah on which to offer sacrifices to *the Lord.*

B. Disappointing Sons (8:1-3)

1. And it came to pass, when Samuel was old, that he made his sons judges over Israel.

Perhaps Samuel's already heavy caseload was growing heavier, while he himself was losing energy as he grew *old.* It seemed reasonable to get some help, which Samuel found by appointing his *sons* as *judges.*

2. Now the name of his firstborn was Joel; and the name of his second, Abiah: they were judges in Beersheba.

Samuel's four stopping points were close together in central Israel. *Beersheba,* on the other hand, was approximately fifty miles away in the southern part of the country. It was more convenient for people that far away to have a court closer to where they lived.

3. And his sons walked not in his ways, but turned aside after lucre, and took bribes, and perverted judgment.

Samuel had managed the nation admirably, but he had not done so well with his own household. *His sons* had become selfish and greedy for *lucre,* or "dishonest gain" (*New International Version*). They cared nothing for law or justice; they saw their judgeship only as an opportunity to enrich themselves. They sold each decision to the highest bidder.

C. Call for a King (8:4, 5)

4. Then all the elders of Israel gathered themselves together, and came to Samuel unto Ramah.

The corruption of Samuel's sons was known all over the country. *Elders* in the towns *of Israel* had supported Samuel and his exemplary leadership, but now they were justly alarmed at the prospect of Samuel's sons in leadership roles.

5. And said unto him, Behold, thou art old, and thy sons walk not in thy ways: now make us a king to judge us like all the nations.

Samuel had been known as a just judge for a long time, but he had been known even longer as a prophet of God (1 Samuel 3:20). With the help of the Lord, perhaps he would provide Israel with a *king* who would be as capable a leader as Samuel himself. With such a man in charge, peace and prosperity would continue. Besides, *all the nations* around Israel had kings, and they seemed to be getting along quite well. If Israel were given a king who was better than any other, would it not become a nation more prosperous and respected than any other? [See question 2, page 56.]

BEING LIKE EVERYONE ELSE

There is something to be said for being like everyone else—speaking the same language, for instance. Numerous regional dialects have added color to American speech, but they have

---

How to Say It

ABIAH. Uh-*bye*-uh.
BEERSHEBA. Beer-*she*-buh.
GILGAL. *Gil*-gal.
LEVITES. *Lee*-vites.
LEVITICAL. Leh-*vit*-ih-kul.
MIZPEH. *Miz*-peh.
PHILISTINES. Fuh-*liss*-teens or *Fill*-us-teens.
RAMAH. *Ray*-muh.

also made it difficult at times for people from different regions to communicate.

Boontling is one such regional dialect. It developed in Boonville, a once remote village in northern California. Boontling has some two thousand words and phrases that differ from standard English. Several local men who were called into the army during World War I had to learn standard English before they could serve. Now cars, telephones, and television have erased Boonville's cultural distance from the outside world, just as these advances are blurring regional distinctions everywhere. Only a few old-timers still speak Boontling. As one of them said, "We've all piked for dusties now; our harpin' days are gone." ("We've all died now; our speaking days are over.")

Israel's problem was not that they wanted to communicate with their neighbors; it was that they wished to be governed like them. What they refused to hear from God was that having a king as their neighbors did would have dire results: they would experience the same moral and spiritual problems as their neighbors. Wanting to be like the world is *still* a problem for the people of God, isn't it?   —C. R. B.

II. A Change Considered (1 Samuel 8:6-9)

Samuel had some thinking to do. Probably the request for a king surprised him. He knew he had been judging justly and that his judgment was acceptable to most. Perhaps he did not realize how bad his sons were. So he was surprised when so many leaders came asking for a change.

A. Samuel's First Reaction (v. 6)

6. But the thing displeased Samuel, when they said, Give us a king to judge us. And Samuel prayed unto the LORD.

The elders' request *displeased Samuel*. At this point we are not told why, but at least two reasons are quite possible.

First, Samuel probably took such a request personally. He felt that he was being rejected. This is indicated by God's words to him in verse 7. After all Samuel had done for his country, it seemed to him most ungrateful for the people to disregard the plan for leadership that he had proposed. (Perhaps, deep-down, he was also displeased with himself and with his failure to do a better job with his sons.)

Second, Samuel knew enough about national affairs to know that a king would not solve Israel's problem. Having a king would be no better than having a judge, unless the king was a better man. The elders likely recognized that they would not find a king who was a better man

than Samuel—but they hoped to find one better than his sons.

Despite the hurt he felt, Samuel reacted to the request in the right way. Instead of criticizing or denouncing the elders' appeal, he *prayed unto the Lord*. Samuel preferred to give the elders no answer until he could give them God's answer. [See question 3, page 56.]

B. God's Perspective (vv. 7-9)

7. And the LORD said unto Samuel, Hearken unto the voice of the people in all that they say unto thee: for they have not rejected thee, but they have rejected me, that I should not reign over them.

Now we see the real problem with the elders' request. It was a rejection of God and His rule over Israel. We should note that God had provided in the law for a time when the people would desire a king (Deuteronomy 17:14-20). The problem was not so much the request for a king as the reason for the request. God had called Israel to be His own "peculiar treasure" (Exodus 19:5), distinct from all other nations. Now the elders were asking to be "like all the nations." In effect, the people were abandoning the covenant that God had made with them. They had forgotten that God was their real King.

Some students feel that, since God had made provision for a king in the law, then He must have expected Israel to have a king at some time. They suggest, then, that God intended for David to be the first king of Israel, and this request represents a case of the people running ahead of God and His timing.

However we analyze the details of the case, we come to the same conclusion: the people rejected God's plan and came up with their own.

8. According to all the works which they have done since the day that I brought them up out of Egypt even unto this day, wherewith they have forsaken me, and served other gods, so do they also unto thee.

Rejecting God was just what the people had been doing ever since leaving Egypt—not all the time, but again and again. This was evident in our lesson last week.

9. Now therefore hearken unto their voice: howbeit yet protest solemnly unto them, and show them the manner of the king that shall reign over them.

Both in verse 7 and here in verse 9, we see that God told Samuel to *hearken* to the elders and do as they asked. Why? As your own child grew toward manhood, didn't you sometimes decide that it was best to let him go his own mistaken way and learn from his error? So God let the people have their way, and later generations

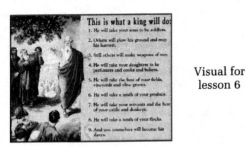

This is what a king will do:
1. He will take your sons to be soldiers.
2. Others will plow his ground and reap his harvest.
3. Sell others will make weapons of war.
4. He will take your daughters to be perfumers and cooks and bakers.
5. He will take the best of your fields, vineyards and olive groves.
6. He will take a tenth of your produce.
7. He will take your servants and the best of your cattle and donkeys.
8. He will take a tenth of your flocks.
9. And you yourselves will become his slaves.

Visual for
lesson 6

This visual illustrates the prophet Samuel's warning the people of the consequences of having a king (1 Samuel 8:11-18).

learned the disadvantages of having another *king* besides the Lord.

If you have ever decided to let your child go his own mistaken way, perhaps you also explained why you thought that way was mistaken. Likewise the Lord told Samuel to *protest solemnly* and to explain why having a king was not best for them. (See verses 10-18.) A king, said Samuel, would become an expensive commodity for his people. He would draft their sons into military service and put their daughters to work in the royal kitchen. He would confiscate the farmers' best fields and vineyards for his servants. He would levy a heavy tax on crops and livestock. The people would then cry to the Lord because of oppression by their king, as they had cried because of oppression by enemies; but this time the Lord would not be as quick to respond. [See question 4, page 56.]

III. A Change Allowed
(1 Samuel 8:19-22)

No doubt the elders had discussed their concerns at length before they approached Samuel. They thought the solution they proposed was the best possible one. Even with Samuel's warning about what a king would cost the nation, they could not be swayed from their choice. They repeated their request more emphatically, this time with additional support from the people.

A. Repeated Request (vv. 19, 20)

19. Nevertheless the people refused to obey the voice of Samuel; and they said, Nay; but we will have a king over us.

Usually these elders had gratefully accepted Samuel's leadership, but this time they resisted. Again they stated their request, this time more as a demand: *We will have a king over us.*

20. That we also may be like all the nations; and that our king may judge us, and go out before us, and fight our battles.

The elders repeated their wish to *be like all the nations.* But Israel had been set apart to be different from all the nations, to be the one nation in all the world that was governed by God's law, and to be a living demonstration that the way of obedience to God is the best way there is. To be like all the nations would be to forsake the very purpose for which the nation of Israel had been created.

Another reason for the elders' request was *that our king may judge us.* They wanted the king to be responsible for enforcing the law and administering justice. We wonder if the elders hoped that a king would relieve them of their own leadership responsibilities. Obviously he would not. Even if Israel had a king, each of the elders would still be responsible for obeying the law and guiding the younger generation to obey it.

Finally, the elders desired that the king *go out before us, and fight our battles.* They wanted the king to be responsible for Israel's national defense. But had they forgotten that there was a better protection already available—the protection of the Lord God Almighty? He would keep them safe if they would obey His law. He had proved that again and again. Was the desire for a king an attempt by the people to bypass their responsibility to obey God? If so, they were badly mistaken. No king (no matter how capable he might be) could take the responsibility of obedience from God's people.

SPIRITUAL MIDDLE AGE

People who have just entered the decade of their forties like to comfort themselves (and annoy younger people) with the boast that "life begins at forty." However, they often fail to complete the sentence: "Life begins (to become more troublesome) at forty." Forgetfulness, aches and pains where there used to be none, concerns for aged parents (not to mention "grown-up" but not yet mature children), wrinkles, thinning hair, and expanding waistlines all seem to be part of the life that "begins at forty."

Now to the aid of such individuals comes a "middle-aged baby book" to help middle-agers remember all those bits of information that no longer come readily to mind: birth dates, anniversaries, waist size (as if they wanted to think about that!), Social Security number, E-mail address, and other facts and figures.

Israel seems to have been suffering from that middle-age scourge of forgetfulness. Things the people should have remembered seem to have been beyond their ability to recall when they most needed to do so. Among those items were God's dealings with Israel. He had been their king and provider from the time of Moses. They forgot what God had done; they followed other gods; now they wanted another king.

Let us pray that we might be less forgetful of God's goodness than Israel was!   —C. R. B.

B. Divine Permission (vv. 21, 22)

21. And Samuel heard all the words of the people, and he rehearsed them in the ears of the LORD.

When the discussion was over, Samuel again went to *the Lord* in prayer. The decision in this matter would affect the nation for centuries to come. Samuel wanted it to be the Lord's decision, not his.

22. And the LORD said to Samuel, Hearken unto their voice, and make them a king. And Samuel said unto the men of Israel, Go ye every man unto his city.

Again the Lord told Samuel to let the people have their way, make their mistake, and thus learn their lesson. Samuel then told the assembled elders to go home and wait for God to make known His choice of a man to be king. Chapters 9 and 10 tell how this was done, resulting in the selection of Saul as Israel's first king.

Conclusion

Why didn't the elders of Israel come to Samuel and say, "Let us share the responsibility"? They could have said, "With your help we can do the judging in our towns. Our fellow citizens know us and respect us. We're not inspired prophets, but we can study the law together and know how to apply it. We can appeal to you for help when we have difficult problems."

Why didn't the elders say something like that? You know the answer. Seldom does anyone ask for added responsibility unless a salary

Home Daily Bible Readings

Monday, Oct. 5—Hannah Prays for a Male Child (1 Samuel 1:3-11)

Tuesday, Oct. 6—Hannah Does As She Promised (1 Samuel 1:21-28)

Wednesday, Oct. 7—"Speak, Lord; for Thy Servant Heareth" (1 Samuel 3:1-10)

Thursday, Oct. 8—Samuel Administers Justice (1 Samuel 7:15—8:9)

Friday, Oct. 9—Samuel Listens to the People and God (1 Samuel 8:10-22)

Saturday, Oct. 10—Pray for All in Authority (1 Timothy 2:1-7)

Sunday, Oct. 11—Saul Becomes Israel's First King (1 Samuel 11:5-15)

goes with it. The elders wanted a king, not themselves, to be responsible for the national behavior and the national welfare.

A. Who Wants Responsibility?

The United States elected a President in 1996. Shortly before the election, there was a so-called debate between the two leading candidates. Ordinary citizens were allowed to question the candidates.

The questions were not surprising. A teacher asked a candidate if he would provide more funds for public education. A working mother inquired what help would be available for day care for her children. A small business owner wanted to know how a candidate would encourage small businesses. A naval man asked if there would be more pay for people in the armed services. No one asked what a President would expect of ordinary citizens or what a citizen could contribute to the general welfare. The universal question seemed to be, "What's in it for me?"

In essence, this was the primary concern of Samuel's two sons, who had become selfish and dishonest judges. It was also the issue being raised by the elders of Israel when they requested a king of Samuel. The king was to fight their battles, although God had been doing so all along! God, however, required obedience to His law. Perhaps with a king would come less responsibility on their part. This is often the thinking of those who seek to address spiritual problems by non-spiritual means.

The question, "What's in it for me?" may not necessarily be associated with greed or corruption. "We have forsaken all, and followed thee; what shall we have therefore?" Simon Peter once asked of Jesus, and Jesus answered plainly. If we sacrifice much in serving Him, even in this world we will get far more than we give; and in the world to come, we will have eternal life (Matthew 19:27-29). But God's people must also ask, "What can I give?" "How can I contribute?" "Where can I help?"

Look around your church. What needs to be done? What can *you* be responsible for doing? [See question 5, page 56.]

B. Prayer

What a wealth of opportunities You have placed before us, our Father! There are so many things that need to be done! Open our eyes to see them, we pray, and strengthen our wills to do them. In Jesus' name. Amen.

C. Thought to Remember

Meet your responsibilities. Don't try to pass them off to someone else.

Learning by Doing

This page contains an alternate lesson plan emphasizing learning activities.
Classes desiring such student involvement will find these suggestions helpful.

Learning Goals

Following this lesson, your students should be able to:

1. Give the details of how the Israelites asked for and were given their first king.

2. Give examples of occasions when individuals have chosen a secular solution to a spiritual problem.

3. Suggest steps they can take to effect a spiritual solution to a current problem.

Into the Lesson

Ask your students to imagine what would happen if they suddenly were transported to a land where everyone wore white. No colors, no creativity, no originality. Only white. Ask, "How long do you think it would take before you stopped wearing colorful clothes and began wearing only white?"

"Everybody does it. Why can't we be like everyone else?" How often have the parents in your class heard that refrain from their teenagers! Actually, we all want to fit in—parents and teens alike. Even those in our society who adopt bizarre and outlandish styles are trying to please others who dress and act the same way.

In today's lesson we hear the lament, "We want to be like everyone else."

Into the Word

Samuel bridged the period of the judges and the prophetic age. He was the last of the judges and the first prophet.

For all his good qualities, Samuel shows that even a wise and godly leader does not always leave a great legacy.

Read 1 Samuel 7:15-17. Ask, "What good qualities do we see here in Samuel's life?" (He was faithful: he judged "all his life"; he was accessible: traveling in a circuit; he was spiritual: he "built an altar unto the Lord.")

Now read 1 Samuel 8:1-9, 19-22. Observe that there was a real problem in Israel, and the elders were attempting to solve it with their proposal to Samuel. Divide the class into three groups to work on the following assignments.

1. The problem. What was the problem the people identified? How serious a problem was it? (Samuel was old, so his influence would soon be gone, but his sons were corrupt; they would not lead as faithfully as Samuel had [v. 5].)

2. A secular solution. Israel's problem was spiritual, but the people chose a secular solution. What was it? Why was that attractive to them? (To have a king. This would make them more like other nations [v. 5] and give them a special leader to lead them into battle [v. 20].)

3. A spiritual solution. What spiritual solutions might they have come up with to solve their problem? What would you have suggested if you had been one of the Israelites? (They could have asked Samuel to appoint godly men to serve with him as judges and learn to serve in the same faithful way he had. They could have demanded that Samuel's sons be held accountable for their actions and reform or give up their positions. Your students will have many good ideas.)

Observe that Samuel at first refused but later gave in. In between, he prayed. Discuss the importance of prayer when making a significant decision.

Note also that God gave in to the people's request even though it was not in their best interest. Discuss why He would do that. Does God sometimes let us have our own way even though He knows it is not best for us? Can you think of some examples of this? (See "God's Dilemma" on page 50.)

Into Life

Israel's desire to conform and be like everyone else led them to accept a secular solution to their problem (a change in government) rather than a spiritual solution (a change of heart).

Ask, "What are some spiritual problems facing our church and/or community today?" Make a list on the chalkboard as your students suggest items. These may include pornography, abortion, declining academic standards, crime, loss of faith in absolute truth, divorce, and others.

Ask the class to choose three or four of the problems and then assign a task force to consider each one. Each task force will answer two questions regarding the problem: (1) What are some secular solutions that have been implemented to deal with this problem? (2) What would be a spiritual solution to the problem, and how could we implement this solution?

Give the groups ten minutes to work; then ask for reports. Choose one of the spiritual solutions and take it on as a class project. Pray about it in your closing prayer.

Let's Talk It Over

The questions on this page are designed to encourage review of the lesson Scriptures and to promote discussion of the lesson by the class. The answers provided are only discussion starters. Let your class talk it over from there.

1. Samuel's practice of traveling in a circuit made him more accessible to the people. How important do you think it is for a leader to be accessible? Why? Do you think a leader can be too accessible? Why or why not?

Jesus warned about leaders who "exercise dominion" over others and told His disciples that they were not to lead in that way, but by being servants (Matthew 20:25-28). A servant must be accessible. One cannot meet people's needs without meeting people!

At the same time, Moses was too accessible to the people, as his father-in-law pointed out (Exodus 18:13-23). One carefully must balance accessibility with his own needs for refreshment and devotion, as well as the needs of his own family.

2. Israel wanted to "be like all the nations." What are some ways a similar desire to be like others creates problems for Christians?

We may want to be like others in terms of money and possessions. The quest for material wealth can tempt us to employ ungodly methods to obtain it, such as lying, cheating, or taking advantage of others' trust. Young people often attempt to gain acceptance by adopting the use of the same kind of language, hair styles, and fashion as their friends. The erosion of moral standards is, at heart, an attempt to be like others. When enough people view a behavior as acceptable, many others go along because they don't want to be "different." It takes courage and faith to stand against such a tide, but Christians must take that stand.

3. It is interesting to note how Samuel more than once responded to the elders' demands by praying to God, and how we sometimes wish that God would speak to us as He did to Samuel, making His answer clear! How can we understand God's answer to our prayers? How can we be sure we are acting according to His answer and not just as we think He should answer?

Important decisions need much prayer, not just a quick "God bless the decisions we make." Some suggest "putting out a fleece," as Gideon did (Judges 6:36-40). Too often, however, the "fleece" we choose is too much of a natural event to be very indicative. Besides, Jesus often reproved those who asked for a miraculous sign, so many students believe putting out a fleece to be improper.

Jesus did encourage persistent prayer (Luke 18:1) and praying with others (Matthew 18:19, 20). We need to pray humbly and honestly, seeking the Lord's will and not just an endorsement of our own plans.

4. Apparently, the Israelite elders did not want to think through the consequences of asking for a king, so God told Samuel to "show them the manner of the king" they were wanting to have over them. What are some present-day examples of human beings acting without pondering the consequences of their actions?

It is clear that many people enter into marriage without giving adequate consideration to the consequences. They need to ponder the sacrifices they will have to make and the crises they will face. Another example is afforded by those who choose to smoke, drink alcoholic beverages, gamble, or dabble in the occult. The consequences may be addiction, damage to their health, financial ruin, or spiritual bondage. Still another example involves people who resort to lying, deception, and cheating. They may face such consequences as a ruined reputation, the loss of friends, and the inability to find and hold employment.

5. The lesson writer suggests that some people never seem to get past the question, "What's in it for me?" How does the preoccupation with this question harm the church? How can we help people to think first of what's good for the Lord's kingdom instead of what's good for themselves?

This attitude stands in contrast to New Testament teaching. Paul wrote in Philippians 2:4: "Look not every man on his own things, but every man also on the things of others." We are to give high priority to ministering to one another and to meeting one another's needs. This truth must be emphasized at all levels of our church teaching, for young people learn early to "look out for Number One." This servant's attitude must be modeled as well. If we teach one thing but practice another, our teaching will have been in vain!

Jeroboam's Sin

October 18
Lesson 7

Devotional Reading: Psalm 48:9-14.

Lesson Scripture: 1 Kings 12.

Printed Text: 1 Kings 12:20, 25-33.

1 Kings 12:20, 25-33

20 And it came to pass, when all Israel heard that Jeroboam was come again, that they sent and called him unto the congregation, and made him king over all Israel: there was none that followed the house of David, but the tribe of Judah only.

. . . .

25 Then Jeroboam built Shechem in mount Ephraim, and dwelt therein; and went out from thence, and built Penuel.

26 And Jeroboam said in his heart, Now shall the kingdom return to the house of David:

27 If this people go up to do sacrifice in the house of the LORD at Jerusalem, then shall the heart of this people turn again unto their lord, even unto Rehoboam king of Judah, and they shall kill me, and go again to Rehoboam king of Judah.

28 Whereupon the king took counsel, and made two calves of gold, and said unto them, It is too much for you to go up to Jerusalem: behold thy gods, O Israel, which brought thee up out of the land of Egypt.

29 And he set the one in Bethel, and the other put he in Dan.

30 And this thing became a sin: for the people went to worship before the one, even unto Dan.

31 And he made a house of high places, and made priests of the lowest of the people, which were not of the sons of Levi.

32 And Jeroboam ordained a feast in the eighth month, on the fifteenth day of the month, like unto the feast that is in Judah, and he offered upon the altar. So did he in Bethel, sacrificing unto the calves that he had made: and he placed in Bethel the priests of the high places which he had made.

33 So he offered upon the altar which he had made in Bethel the fifteenth day of the eighth month, even in the month which he had devised of his own heart; and ordained a feast unto the children of Israel: and he offered upon the altar, and burnt incense.

**Oct
18**

Golden Text: The king took counsel, and made two calves of gold, and said unto them,
It is too much for you to go up to Jerusalem: behold thy gods, O Israel,
which brought thee up out of the land of Egypt.—1 Kings 12:28.

God Calls a People to Faithful Living
Unit 2: God's People Reject His Laws
(Lessons 5-7)

Lesson Aims

After this lesson your students should be able to:

1. Describe the counterfeit religion Jeroboam established to consolidate his kingdom.

2. Contrast the counterfeit religion of Jeroboam with the true religion God had ordained.

3. Identify some counterfeit religious ideas that challenge the "faith . . . once delivered," and suggest ways to keep one's religion free of counterfeits.

Lesson Outline

Introduction

"Like father, like son." So says an oft-quoted proverb, and in a multitude of cases we see that it is true. However, there are many cases in which it has been proved inaccurate. Last week we saw Israel's era of the judges end with the admirable work of Samuel, who was a prophet of God as well as a judge of Israel. In his old age he shared the work of judging with his sons, who, unlike their father, were greedy and corrupt. Unhappy at the prospect of having the peo-

ple governed by such men, the elders of Israel asked Samuel to provide a king to rule the nation. The Lord told Samuel to grant this request, and Israel became a monarchy. Three kings ruled in succession before the time when the events recorded in this week's lesson occurred.

A. Saul

The first king of Israel was Saul. He began his reign with an impressive victory over Israel's enemies; but later he became arrogant, foolishly going his own way instead of obeying the Lord. An example of his folly is seen in his treatment of David. Saul made David the head of his army, then jealously tried to have him killed because he was so successful. Eventually Saul's disobedience resulted in God's rejection of him and the choice of "a man after [God's] own heart" (1 Samuel 13:14). The record of Saul's reign is found in 1 Samuel 9—31.

B. David

After Saul's death David became king, first of his own tribe of Judah and then of all Israel. He built the nation of Israel into a great empire, subduing the surrounding pagan peoples. His later years were marred by his own scandalous conduct, and by two rebellions led by two of his sons. Still, David preserved a strong and stable empire, and turned it over to his son Solomon. Events of David's reign are found in 2 Samuel 5:1—1 Kings 2:12.

C. Solomon

Gifted with special wisdom from the Lord, Solomon brought his country to the peak of its power and glory. The ancient empires of Egypt and Mesopotamia were both in periods of decline at that time, allowing Israel to reign supreme as the greatest empire of all. Yet with all his wisdom, Solomon ruined the latter part of his reign with foolish choices. He married several pagan wives and allowed them to desecrate Jerusalem with their pagan gods. Through excessive taxation and forced labor, he burdened his own people so heavily that they were on the verge of rebellion when his kingship ended. The record of Solomon's reign is found in 1 Kings 2:13—11:43.

D. Lesson Background

While Saul, David, and Solomon all showed arrogance and folly in the latter part of their reigns, Solomon's son Rehoboam *began* his reign with a very foolish decision. When the people gathered to crown him king, they asked him to reduce the heavy burdens that Solomon had placed upon them. Recklessly the young king vowed to increase their burdens instead. The greater part of the nation rebelled at this news. Judah, Rehoboam's own tribe, remained loyal to him, and the small tribe of Benjamin joined it; however, the northern tribes vowed to serve Rehoboam no more. They formed an independent nation and designated Jeroboam as their king.

Jeroboam had been an able administrator under Solomon; but when the king learned of a promise made by Ahijah the prophet to Jeroboam that he would one day become king of Israel, Solomon sought to kill him. Jeroboam then fled to Egypt (1 Kings 11:28, 37-40). Now he came back to govern the rebel nation in the north (thus fulfilling the prophet's words). That nation kept the name of "Israel," while the portion loyal to Rehoboam was called "Judah" (1 Kings 12:1-24).

I. New Nation
(1 Kings 12:20, 25)
A. Completing the Division (v. 20)

20. And it came to pass, when all Israel heard that Jeroboam was come again, that they sent and called him unto the congregation, and made him king over all Israel: there was none that followed the house of David, but the tribe of Judah only.

Here *all Israel* refers to the people of the rebellious tribes. They were to be called "Israel" from that time forth. Many people of the northern kingdom knew Jeroboam, for he had served quite capably among them during Solomon's administration (1 Kings 11:28). He was also among the leaders who took their request to Rehoboam and heard his refusal to address their concerns (1 Kings 12:12, 13). Apparently the rebels trusted Jeroboam and were unanimous in choosing him to be their king.

The house of David describes the royal family. Rehoboam was its member on the throne, though no longer recognized by the northern tribes. At this point only *the tribe of Judah* was loyal to Rehoboam; but when he prepared to go to war to

---

How to Say It

AHIJAH. Uh-*high*-juh.
ELOHIM (Hebrew). El-oh-*heem*.
EPHRAIM. *Ee*-fray-im.
JEROBOAM. Jair-uh-*boe*-um.
MESOPOTAMIA. *Mes*-uh-puh-*tay*-me-uh (strong accent on tay).
PENUEL. Pih-*nu*-el.
REHOBOAM. Ree-huh-*boe*-um.
SHECHEM. *Sheck*-em or *Sheek*-em.

---

force the rebellious tribes to remain in his kingdom, the tribe of Benjamin joined Judah instead of siding with the rebels (v. 21). [See question #1, page 64.]

B. Constructing New Cities (v. 25)

25. Then Jeroboam built Shechem in mount Ephraim, and dwelt therein; and went out from thence, and built Penuel.

Mount Ephraim does not refer to a single mountain crowned by a city. Rather, it designates the highlands belonging to the tribe of Ephraim.

In this case the word *built* does not mean that Jeroboam established a new city, for *Shechem* had a long history before this. It had been particularly significant in the time of Joshua as a place where Israel gathered to renew its commitment to God (Joshua 24:1, 25). Most likely Jeroboam built fortifications there, making it a stronger, better defended city. Perhaps he also built a royal palace, for he *dwelt therein*, making Shechem both his residence and his capital city for a time. Likewise Jeroboam fortified *Penuel*, establishing a strong point east of the Jordan River. From there his troops could control the main route of travel and trade on that side of the river.

II. New Places for Worship
(1 Kings 12:26-29)

According to the law of Moses, the men of Israel were required to assemble three times each year for the religious festivals of Passover, Pentecost, and Tabernacles (Exodus 23:14-17; Leviticus 23). Though given before Israel reached the promised land, these requirements looked forward to a special central place of worship in that land (Deuteronomy 12:5-7). For years that place had been the temple in Jerusalem; but now, out of fear of losing his newly gained power, Jeroboam began to think about instituting worship in other places besides Jerusalem.

A. Jeroboam's Dilemma (vv. 26, 27)

26. And Jeroboam said in his heart, Now shall the kingdom return to the house of David.

Despite his efforts to establish his authority and fortify his defenses, *Jeroboam* was still unsure of how firmly he was in control. He began to think of a very unpleasant scenario. The people in the north might *return* to Jerusalem to be ruled by Rehoboam, the king who belonged to *the house of David*. David was still recognized as a great national hero—the builder of Israel's empire. The people had rebelled without hesitation against his grandson when he had refused to lighten their financial burdens. Would they go back just as quickly if Rehoboam promised to do what they asked? If they did, Jeroboam would likely have to flee to Egypt again—assuming he could get away before being arrested and executed for treason.

27. If this people go up to do sacrifice in the house of the LORD at Jerusalem, then shall the heart of this people turn again unto their lord, even unto Rehoboam king of Judah, and they shall kill me, and go again to Rehoboam king of Judah.

Jeroboam knew that he needed the religious as well as the political support of the people if he were to reign successfully as their king. If they continued to view *Jerusalem* and Solomon's temple as their place of worship, Jeroboam's control in the north could be severely damaged. The three annual festivals in Jerusalem drew thousands of people, and included glorious ceremonies of worship in the stately temple. They were also festive occasions with joyful feasting, family reunions, and meetings of old friends. Would attending these gatherings cause them to regret their decision to sever ties with the house of David?

Jeroboam thought so, especially if Rehoboam reversed his earlier statement and promised lower taxes and less forced labor. Zealous men of Israel might then *kill* Jeroboam and *go again to Rehoboam*—back to the fold of David their hero. Jeroboam made plans to prevent this from happening.

B. Jeroboam's Solution (vv. 28, 29)

28. Whereupon the king took counsel, and made two calves of gold, and said unto them, It is too much for you to go up to Jerusalem: behold thy gods, O Israel, which brought thee up out of the land of Egypt.

The king took counsel, that is, he consulted his advisers. Together they made a plan to keep the people of the north from going to Jerusalem. Jeroboam *made two calves of gold.* He then told the Israelites, *It is too much for you to go up to Jerusalem.* They had asked for lighter burdens (v. 4); now Jeroboam was offering to remove the burden of a long trip to Jerusalem three times a year. That trip was *too much;* they could worship much closer to home.

Jeroboam's new religion consisted of a dangerous blend of truth and falsehood. He linked his religion with the act that led to Israel's establishment as a nation: their deliverance from slavery in *the land of Egypt.* However, he credited this deliverance to the *gods* who were represented by the golden calves. It is true that the word for *gods* here, *elohim,* is the same word used for the true God in the Old Testament, so

some students believe the calves were intended in some way to portray Him. When *Elohim* means God, however, whatever verb, adjective, or pronoun is used with it is singular, even though *Elohim* is a plural noun. But here the verb (*brought*) is plural, indicating that Jeroboam was not thinking of one God. Whether he saw the calves as gods or, as many pagans of the time, imagined the gods as riding the backs of the calves, is not clear. What is clear is the blatant violation of the first and second of the Ten Commandments. Jeroboam's act thus opened the door for the entry of idolatry into the northern kingdom. As verse 30 notes, "This thing became a sin." [See question #2, page 64.]

29. And he set the one in Bethel, and the other put he in Dan.

Bethel was located at the southern end of Jeroboam's kingdom, just ten miles north of Jerusalem; *Dan* was situated at the northern end, north of the Sea of Galilee. A family could travel to the place that was more convenient.

EXOTIC RELIGIONS

"Exotic Plants, Animals Imperil U. S. Ecosystem" read the newspaper headline. The article beneath it described a number of "exotic" invaders: non-native (foreign) species that threaten the well-being of native species. Among those mentioned were the South Pacific brown tree snake (up to eight feet long) that is entering Hawaiian homes through the plumbing, the kudzu vine that is choking southern waterways, and the zebra mussel that is clogging parts of the Great Lakes and the Saint Lawrence Seaway. These are but a few of the 4,500 species of exotic plants and animals that have taken up residence in places where they often have no natural enemies.

Jeroboam should have known that there is no room in the human heart for two gods if one of them is the God of the Bible. Nevertheless, he attempted to import other "exotic" gods into Israel's worship. The result of this was disastrous for God's people; for in time, their idolatry destroyed them.

Each of us needs to ask himself, "Have *I* placed any other gods before my Father in Heaven?"

—C. R. B.

III. New Sins
(1 Kings 12:30-33)

Jeroboam tried to pretend that he was continuing the proper worship of Jehovah. In fact he proceeded to institute a new system of worship. Verses 30-33 point out, one by one, the system's features that were established by the king, not by the Lord.

Visual for
lesson 1

You may find it helpful to display again the visual for lesson 1 and use it to locate some of the places mentioned in today's lesson.

A. Idols (v. 30)

30. And this thing became a sin: for the people went to worship before the one, even unto Dan.

This thing (Jeroboam's counterfeit religion) *became a sin.* Jeroboam's actions came to receive their own stigma in the Biblical record, as wayward kings as well as the people of Israel in general were frequently said to continue in "the sins of Jeroboam" (1 Kings 14:16; 15:30; 16:31; 2 Kings 3:3; 10:29, 31; 13:6; 14:24; 17:22). Because of these sins, God determined to destroy the house of Jeroboam "from off the face of the earth" (1 Kings 13:34).

The people went to worship before the one, even unto Dan. Obviously this does not mean that the people worshiped only at Dan and not at Bethel, for the following verses repeatedly mention worship at Bethel. Perhaps we should understand the statement to indicate the zeal with which the people accepted the new religion. Observe the irony: it was "too much" for the people to go to Jerusalem, yet they were willing to journey to distant Dan in the north to participate in the sinful practices encouraged by Jeroboam. [See question #3, page 64.]

B. Places and Priests (v. 31)

31. And he made a house of high places, and made priests of the lowest of the people, which were not of the sons of Levi.

The statement that Jeroboam *made a house of high places* is another one of uncertain meaning. Pagan places of worship were placed on hilltops so often that *high places* may refer to places of worship, whether located on hills or not. It appears that Jeroboam made a *house*, a temple or sanctuary of some sort, for each of his golden calves. Such an act represented still another attempt by Jeroboam to draw people in the northern kingdom away from worship in the temple in Jerusalem by providing them a convenient substitute.

Others believe that Jeroboam also built shrines on hills in other places throughout the northern kingdom, or attempted to use shrines that were already present as places to worship the gods represented by the calves at Dan and Bethel. First Kings 13:32, 33 indicates that there were other high places in the land. Bethel, however, remained the most prominent place of worship, and the one at which the king himself offered incense (1 Kings 13:1).

In addition, Jeroboam *made priests of the lowest of the people, which were not of the sons of Levi.* First Kings 13:33 offers a helpful commentary on the meaning of this verse: "Whosoever would, he consecrated him, and he became one of the priests of the high places." The Lord had appointed Aaron and his descendants to be priests, and they were members of the tribe of Levi (Hebrews 7:5). Now, however, Jeroboam chose priests from other tribes; essentially, anyone who wanted to could become a priest! Second Chronicles 11:13, 14 tells us that legitimate priests and Levites from "all Israel" came to Judah, for Jeroboam did not allow them to carry out their appointed tasks. Perhaps he did this because the priests and Levites in his kingdom refused to take part in his idolatry, but this is not stated in the Bible.

C. Festival (v. 32)

32. And Jeroboam ordained a feast in the eighth month, on the fifteenth day of the month, like unto the feast that is in Judah, and he offered upon the altar. So did he in Bethel, sacrificing unto the calves that he had made: and he placed in Bethel the priests of the high places which he had made.

In Judah the Feast of Tabernacles began on the fifteenth day of the seventh month (Leviticus 23:33-36). In yet another effort to lure people away from the worship in Jerusalem, Jeroboam instituted a similar feast in his domain and set its observance a month later than the Feast of Tabernacles. It has been noted that the change to the *eighth month* made this feast more convenient for farmers in the northern kingdom, where the harvest was approximately one month later than in Judah. He also *offered upon the altar,* probably making sacrifices similar to those prescribed for the Feast of Tabernacles (Numbers 29:12-39). Perhaps the *priests'* duties *in Bethel* resembled those of the priests in Jerusalem.

Thus Bethel housed a center of worship similar to the one in Jerusalem. No doubt it was smaller and less ornate than the one that Solomon had taken seven years to build in Jerusalem (1 Kings 6:37, 38), but it had all the proper religious ingredients, including priests, an altar, and sacrifices.

The differences, however, were critical. The temple was not in the place God had chosen. The feast was not in the month God had appointed. The priests did not belong to the priestly tribe. The sacrifices were offered *unto the calves that* Jeroboam *had made*. The entire system was counterfeit!

D. Ceremonies (v. 33)

33. So he offered upon the altar which he had made in Bethel the fifteenth day of the eighth month, even in the month which he had devised of his own heart; and ordained a feast unto the children of Israel: and he offered upon the altar, and burnt incense.

Here the counterfeit ceremonies are summarized. Sacrifices were offered, *incense* was *burnt*, and a *feast* was established in imitation of the ceremonies at Jerusalem. Yet none of it was commanded by the Lord; it was *devised* in Jeroboam's *own heart*. It was *ordained* by his own mouth, not by the mouth of the Lord. Thus it was doomed to fail. [See question #4, page 64.]

Conclusion

A. A Nation Divided

Among the nations of the world, Solomon's Israel was mightiest and most glorious. It is tragic that Israel became divided, and that it lost its power and glory, finally being dominated by other nations whose god was not Jehovah. Yet we must remember that the division of the nation was from the Lord (1 Kings 12:24).

Why did the Lord end the glory of His people? Because they no longer were behaving as His people should. Wise old Solomon acted foolishly. He overburdened his people to enhance the glory of his kingdom (1 Kings 12:4). Worse

Home Daily Bible Readings

Monday, Oct. 12—A Prophet's Message to Jeroboam (1 Kings 11:26-35)
Tuesday, Oct. 13— Jeroboam Flees to Egypt (1 Kings 11:36-43)
Wednesday, Oct. 14—Rehoboam Rejects the Advice of the Elders (1 Kings 12:1-19)
Thursday, Oct. 15—Rehoboam's Downfall; Jeroboam's Sin (1 Kings 12:20-33)
Friday, Oct. 16—Jeroboam's Sin and Its Consequences (1 Kings 13:1-10)
Saturday, Oct. 17—More Consequences of Jeroboam's Sin (1 Kings 13:33—14:10a)
Sunday, Oct. 18—Jeroboam's Son Dies (1 Kings 14:10b-20)

than that, he married pagan wives and brought their idolatry to Jerusalem with them (1 Kings 11:1-13). The nation was no longer blessed, for Jehovah no longer was its one and only God.

Solomon's son Rehoboam might have been able to prevent the division of the nation, had he listened to the right counsel. But Rehoboam ignored the advice of the older and wiser men, who counseled him to "be a servant" by lessening the burden on the people (1 Kings 12:7). Instead, he followed the suggestion of those who were younger and who wanted Rehoboam to establish himself as an aggressive, no-nonsense ruler. The result was full-scale revolt, and the division of God's people.

B. A Nation Deceived

Observe closely the subtle process by which Jeroboam drew the northern kingdom away from the true worship ordained by God in the law of Moses. He established a feast "like unto the feast that is in Judah" (1 Kings 12:32), only his fell on the fifteenth day of the eighth month rather than the fifteenth day of the seventh month, as the law directed. Jeroboam ordained priests, but they were not taken from the tribe designated by God to be the source of priests. He encouraged worship, but it was the worship of false gods, in violation of the First and Second Commandments. And all of this was done, claimed Jeroboam, to keep the people from having to go all the way to Jerusalem to worship.

Jeroboam's "conveniences" are a classic example of counterfeit religion at work. Most of us associate the term "counterfeit" with money. A counterfeit bill resembles the genuine brand so closely that it is usually hard for anyone except an expert to recognize the difference. The expert's job is to become so familiar with the genuine item that he can spot the counterfeit item with little trouble.

The application of this to God's people today should be clear. We need to become so familiar with God's Word that we cannot be led astray by "experts" or "scholars" who think they can improve on it. [See question #5, page 64.]

C. Prayer

King of kings and Lord of lords! Rule in our hearts; rule in our minds; rule in our lives. Help us to pattern our will after Your will, our thoughts after Your thoughts, our acts after Your desires. May we move closer to one another; but above all, may we stay close to You. Amen.

D. Thought to Remember

Learn to want what God wants. Never settle for an inferior substitute.

Learning by Doing

This page contains an alternate lesson plan emphasizing learning activities.
Classes desiring such student involvement will find these suggestions helpful.

Learning Goals

Following this lesson, your students should be able to:

1. Describe the counterfeit religion Jeroboam established to consolidate his kingdom.

2. Contrast the counterfeit religion of Jeroboam with the true religion God had ordained.

3. Identify some counterfeit religious ideas that challenge the "faith . . . once delivered," and suggest ways to keep one's religion free of counterfeits.

Into the Lesson

The history of the church is filled with stories of people who have used religion to further their own political or financial ends. Ask your students to suggest some recent examples of false leaders in the church who have misled their people for personal profit.

The self-centered misdeeds of some former high-profile televangelists may still be fresh in your students' minds. Another example is Jim Jones, who in the name of religion led nearly a thousand people in an act of ritual suicide. A more recent example of a misleading leader is David Koresh, whose egocentric theology turned *Waco* into a word that inspires horror and grief.

Jeroboam was a leader in the tragic tradition of Jim Jones and David Koresh. He corrupted and perverted religion for his own selfish purposes. In today's lesson we will see what he did and why he did it.

Into the Word

Fill in the events that happened in Israel's history since last week's lesson. (Refer to the Lesson Background on pages 58 and 59.) The crisis that divided the kingdom is described in 1 Kings 12:1-17. Tell your students to read that passage and then discuss, "What role did Solomon's policies and practices play in the breakup of the united kingdom? What role did Rehoboam play in the breakup? What role did Jeroboam play?"

Display a map of the divided kingdom. Ask the students to locate the northern kingdom of Israel, and then ask them to find Judah, the southern kingdom. Then have your students find the following towns on the map and describe why each is significant to this lesson:

- Shechem (v. 25).
- Penuel (v. 25).
- Jerusalem (v. 28).
- Bethel (v. 29).
- Dan (v. 29).

Lead your students in contrasting Jeroboam's counterfeit religion with the true religion that God had ordained and established. Write the following headings on the chalkboard: "Israel's True Religion" and "Jeroboam's Counterfeit Religion." Under the true religion heading write the following items:

1. The place of sacrifice was to be the temple at Jerusalem.

2. Priests were to come from the tribe of Levi only.

3. Images of God and idols were forbidden.

4. Three national feasts, or festivals, were to be observed at specified times each year: Passover, Pentecost, and Tabernacles.

5. Sacrifices were to be made to God alone.

6. Special incense was to be burnt to represent prayers offered to God.

Then ask the students to look for contrasting counterfeit elements in today's Bible passage (1 Kings 12:20, 25-33). Students may work individually or in groups. The following verses should reveal the necessary information to complete the chart: 1. v. 29; 2. v. 31; 3. v. 28; 4. v. 32; 5. v. 32; 6. v. 33.

Into Life

Like the united kingdom, churches have been divided and congregations have been split apart when counterfeit ideas have been introduced to replace the genuine. Sometimes these are presented to make worship more "convenient." At other times they are introduced by leaders eager to make a name (and a profit) for themselves.

Ask your students to name some counterfeit religious ideas or practices. Make a list on the chalkboard as these are mentioned. Let the class brainstorm for a while, naming as many ideas as they can in a short period of time. Then review the list. Are any of these counterfeits being practiced in your church? If so, what can be done about it?

In closing, issue a call to integrity and genuineness. Challenge each student to do something specific during the coming week that would tend to focus attention on the true gospel in your church.

Let's Talk It Over

The questions on this page are designed to encourage review of the lesson Scriptures and to promote discussion of the lesson by the class. The answers provided are only discussion starters. Let your class talk it over from there.

1. Rehoboam failed to address the grievances of the people. As a result, the nation was split and most of it formed a new nation, one that turned quickly to idolatry. Similarly, churches are split when certain members feel their needs or wishes are not being addressed. Is it ever right to split or leave a church? Why or why not?

Paul taught that it is a serious matter to sow division in the church. The first four chapters of 1 Corinthians deal with this issue, and he warns that a divisive person (*KJV:* heretic) must not be tolerated within the body (Titus 3:10, 11). Submission to the church leadership should typify the church (Hebrews 13:17). A Christian should never sow discord in the church simply to satisfy his or her own whims and preferences.

Occasionally, however, the leadership may abandon the truth. In such a rare case, true believers must take a stand for the Word of God. If that means leaving the fellowship, either individually or as a group, then such a drastic step may be necessary. It should be only as a last resort, however, and on clearly Biblical grounds.

2. Jeroboam instituted the new religious practices in his kingdom out of an effort at self-preservation. What are some evil practices that continue in our society because of the practitioners' concern for self-preservation?

The abortion industry may offer one example. It is not mere cynicism to suggest that some doctors and nurses advocate abortion because it is a source of tremendous income. Another example is the tobacco industry. Its leaders ignore extensive evidence in insisting that tobacco usage is harmless. The alcoholic beverage industry, similarly, promotes the concept of safe, responsible drinking and overlooks the terrible damage done by alcohol. Television and movie producers believe that by continuing to display sex, profanity, and violence, they are "just giving people what they want"—and will pay for.

3. Sometimes professing Christians will reject certain truths taught in the Bible. "My God is a loving God," they may say. "He could never send anyone to an eternal Hell." How would you answer, based on today's lesson text?

Some people today seem to think they can approach the Bible the way they do the salad bar: choose a little of this, a little of that, and leave whatever they don't like. Convenience is preferred over commitment. The counterfeit religion of the north was similarly formed by taking some aspects of true religion, combining them with falsehood, and coming up with a new religion that was more convenient.

But the God revealed in the Bible is a God of truth. He combines holiness and love, judgment and grace, and discipline and gentleness in His dealings with people. The violence typical of the northern kingdom of Israel, and its tragic end in 722 B.C., should be a lesson to each of us who wants to create his or her own God according to personal preference, convenience, or taste.

4. The text tells us that Jeroboam set up a feast at a time "which he had devised of his own heart." How does this human tendency to devise religious doctrines and practices out of our own heart affect the church today?

We have surely heard someone preface a statement with the words, "I know that the Bible teaches . . . but. . . ." They either explain away the significance of Biblical doctrines, or they substitute doctrines of their own. They proclaim a plan of salvation that is foreign to the New Testament and exchange the truth of the Bible for popular writings of human authors. Never has the plea for evangelism, doctrine, worship, and fellowship based on the New Testament been more urgent than today.

5. The lesson writer points out that it is a "subtle process" by which people are drawn away from the true worship ordained by God to a counterfeit. How can we tell whether a change is simply meeting the needs of contemporary people or is a compromise that may be the first step toward apostasy?

Paul said he was "all things to all men" (1 Corinthians 9:22), which suggests we need to use a variety of methods and means to accommodate people. But we must keep clearly in mind the end of that verse as well: "that I might by all means save some." We must be sure we maintain a faithfulness to our primary task as outlined in the Great Commission (Matthew 28:18-20). Philippians 4:8, 9 will also help us avoid a deadly compromise.

God Works Through Prophets

DEVOTIONAL READING: 2 Samuel 12:1-15.

LESSON SCRIPTURE: 2 Kings 5:1-19.

PRINTED TEXT: 2 Kings 5:1-14.

2 Kings 5:1-14

1 Now Naaman, captain of the host of the king of Syria, was a great man with his master, and honorable, because by him the LORD had given deliverance unto Syria: he was also a mighty man in valor, but he was a leper.

2 And the Syrians had gone out by companies, and had brought away captive out of the land of Israel a little maid; and she waited on Naaman's wife.

3 And she said unto her mistress, Would God my lord were with the prophet that is in Samaria! for he would recover him of his leprosy.

4 And one went in, and told his lord, saying, Thus and thus said the maid that is of the land of Israel.

5 And the king of Syria said, Go to, go, and I will send a letter unto the king of Israel. And he departed, and took with him ten talents of silver, and six thousand pieces of gold, and ten changes of raiment.

6 And he brought the letter to the king of Israel, saying, Now when this letter is come unto thee, behold, I have therewith sent Naaman my servant to thee, that thou mayest recover him of his leprosy.

7 And it came to pass, when the king of Israel had read the letter, that he rent his clothes, and said, Am I God, to kill and to make alive, that this man doth send unto me to recover a man of his leprosy? Wherefore consider, I pray you, and see how he seeketh a quarrel against me.

8 And it was so, when Elisha the man of God had heard that the king of Israel had rent his clothes, that he sent to the king, saying, Wherefore hast thou rent thy clothes? let him come now to me, and he shall know that there is a prophet in Israel.

9 So Naaman came with his horses and with his chariot, and stood at the door of the house of Elisha.

10 And Elisha sent a messenger unto him, saying, Go and wash in Jordan seven times, and thy flesh shall come again to thee, and thou shalt be clean.

11 But Naaman was wroth, and went away, and said, Behold, I thought, He will surely come out to me, and stand, and call on the name of the LORD his God, and strike his hand over the place, and recover the leper.

12 Are not Abana and Pharpar, rivers of Damascus, better than all the waters of Israel? may I not wash in them, and be clean? So he turned and went away in a rage.

13 And his servants came near, and spake unto him, and said, My father, if the prophet had bid thee do some great thing, wouldest thou not have done it? how much rather then, when he saith to thee, Wash, and be clean?

14 Then went he down, and dipped himself seven times in Jordan, according to the saying of the man of God: and his flesh came again like unto the flesh of a little child, and he was clean.

GOLDEN TEXT: Let him come now to me, and he shall know that there is a prophet in Israel.—2 Kings 5:8b.

God Calls a People to Faithful Living
Unit 3: God Works Through People
(Lessons 8-10)

Lesson Aims

As a result of studying this lesson, each student will be able to:

1. Retell the story of Naaman's healing.

2. Explain why Naaman found it difficult to obey God's prophet and what was the result when he did.

3. List some situations in which people find it difficult to obey God today, and suggest some ways to encourage them to do so.

Lesson Outline

INTRODUCTION
    A. Divided Israel
    B. Preserving the Truth
    C. Lesson Background
I. A SLAVE'S SUGGESTION (2 Kings 5:1-3)
    A. A Hapless Hero (v. 1)
    B. A Captive Slave (v. 2)
    C. A Word of Hope (v. 3)
      Prisoners of War
II. A KING'S PLEA (2 Kings 5:4-7)
    A. A Word to the King (v. 4)
    B. A Quick Response (v. 5a)
    C. From King to King (vv. 5b-7)
      Buying God's Favor
III. A PROPHET'S SOLUTION (2 Kings 5:8-14)
    A. The Prophet's Invitation (v. 8)
    B. The Prophet's Promise (vv. 9, 10)
    C. The Hero's Fury (vv. 11, 12)
    D. The Servants' Suggestion (v. 13)
    E. Obedience and Healing (v. 14)
CONCLUSION
    A. A Good Enemy
    B. The Temporary and the Permanent
    C. Prayer
    D. Thought to Remember

Introduction

A. Divided Israel

The nation of Israel was divided after King Solomon's death, as we saw in last week's lesson. In the northern kingdom, known as Israel, King Jeroboam promptly instituted new religious practices that were continued by later kings. The Bible calls them "the sins of Jeroboam" (1 Kings 14:16). The presence of evil in the north sunk to new depths when King Ahab married a pagan princess (Jezebel), who seemed determined to make Baal worship the state religion of Israel (1 Kings 16:29-33).

B. Preserving the Truth

In the troubled century following the division of the nation, God kept His truth alive and well in Israel by means of His prophets. Chief of these were Elijah and Elisha. In various places they gathered groups of faithful men, whom they trained to assist them in their prophetic tasks. The Bible calls them "sons of the prophets" (2 Kings 2:3, 5, 15). We have no idea how many of them there were; but when wicked Queen Jezebel set out to destroy the prophets, a hundred of them were saved by one man alone (1 Kings 18:13). The masses of people wavered in their allegiance between Jehovah and Baal (1 Kings 18:21) until Elijah's heroic action on Mount Carmel brought them to declare their loyalty to Jehovah alone (vv. 20-40). When Elijah complained to God that he alone was faithful, the Lord replied that there were seven thousand others who had not fallen prey to idolatry (1 Kings 19:13-18).

C. Lesson Background

During this same period there was intermittent war between Israel and Syria (also referred to as Aram)—the country to the north and east of the territory of Galilee. The Bible records a series of skirmishes that occurred during the reign of Ahab (1 Kings 20; 22:1-40). This tension provided the background for an incident that involved both these countries in a most unusual set of circumstances.

I. A Slave's Suggestion (2 Kings 5:1-3)

Our lesson story begins, not in Israel, but in Syria, the enemy country. However, a girl from Israel was living there.

A. A Hapless Hero (v. 1)

1. Now Naaman, captain of the host of the king of Syria, was a great man with his master, and honorable, because by him the LORD had given deliverance unto Syria: he was also a mighty man in valor, but he was a leper.

We would probably use a term such as "general of the army" where our text says *captain of the host*. In this case the army was that of Syria, not Israel. The general's *master* was *the king of Syria*. The king considered Naaman *a great man . . . and honorable*, because he was a proven champion in battle. He had delivered Syria from a particular danger: perhaps an attack by Israel, or perhaps an attack by Assyria, which was gaining in strength as the ninth century B.C. progressed. The writer of this history knew that the victory was really the Lord's; Naaman was only His tool. Nevertheless, the writer notes that the general was truly *a mighty man in valor,* or a genuine hero.

There was, however, a tragic side to Naaman's otherwise exemplary record: *he was a leper.* Apparently lepers were not isolated in Syria as they were in Israel (Leviticus 13:45, 46). It seems that Naaman was still able to command the Syrian army.

B. A Captive Slave (v. 2)

2. And the Syrians had gone out by companies, and had brought away captive out of the land of Israel a little maid; and she waited on Naaman's wife.

As part of the ongoing warfare between Syria and Israel, raiding parties (*companies*) sometimes invaded Israel to steal what they could: stores of grain, sheep and cattle, and, in some cases, human captives to be used as slaves. Among the captives was a girl who was now a servant of *Naaman's wife.* We can only guess how *little* or how young she was, but apparently she was old enough to help with some of the details of running a household.

C. A Word of Hope (v. 3)

3. And she said unto her mistress, Would God my lord were with the prophet that is in Samaria! for he would recover him of his leprosy.

From this verse we can tell that the girl was old enough to realize that Naaman had an incurable disease and to be concerned about his health. Before leaving Israel, she had been old enough to know that marvelous miracles were done through Elisha, *the prophet that is in Samaria.* At this point, she had been in Syria long enough to become attached to her captors and to be concerned about their well-being. It appears that she had been kindly treated, for she spoke freely, and apparently was sincere in her desire to see Naaman healed of his *leprosy.* Knowing the Syrians were enemies of her native country, she probably assumed that there was no way that Naaman could ever be *with* Elisha, but she wished he could.

We noted that in last week's lesson, Jeroboam established Shechem as the capital of the northern kingdom (1 Kings 12:25). Omri, a later king, established Samaria as the capital (1 Kings 16:24). This is the city where Elisha was residing. [See question #1, page 72.]

How to Say It

ABANA. *Ab*-uh-nuh or Uh-*ban*-uh.
AHAB. *Ay*-hab.
ARAM. *Air*-um.
ASSYRIA. Uh-*sear*-ee-uh.
BAAL. *Bay*-ul.
DAMASCUS. Duh-*mass*-kus.
ELIJAH. Ee-*lye*-juh.
ELISHA. Ee-*lye*-shuh.
JEHORAM. Jeh-*ho*-ram.
JEROBOAM. Jair-uh-*boe*-um.
JEZEBEL. *Jez*-uh-bel.
JORAM. *Jo*-ram.
MOAB. *Mo*-ab.
NAAMAN. *Nay*-uh-mun.
OMRI. *Ahm*-rye.
PHARPAR. *Far*-par.
SAMARIA. Suh-*meh*-ri-uh.
SHECHEM. *Sheck*-em or *Sheek*-em.
SYRIA. *Sear*-ee-uh.

PRISONERS OF WAR

War brings tragedies of many kinds, including some that affect innocent civilians. Early in World War II, Americans feared a Japanese invasion of the West Coast, so the United States military gathered 110,000 residents with Japanese ancestry into internment camps surrounded by barbed wire and guard towers. This was done in spite of the fact that more than two-thirds of these prisoners were loyal American citizens. After the war these internees were able to return to freedom, but four years of their lives had been lost, and many of them had lost all their property. Amazingly, and to their credit, the vast majority of them returned to freedom with little hostility toward the United States.

The girl who served Naaman's wife was also a prisoner of war. We would understand completely if she had rejoiced in her master's poor health. Instead, she told Naaman's wife how he could be healed. As Jesus would say centuries later, doing good to those who do evil to us identifies us as children of the heavenly Father (Matthew 5:44, 45).   —C. R. B.

II. A King's Plea
(2 Kings 5:4-7)

No doubt Naaman's wife lost little time to tell her husband what her servant girl had told her. The Hebrew servant's suggestion was taken seriously. Perhaps we should not be surprised at this, for there was no other hope for Naaman. He would die unless a miracle occurred.

A. A Word to the King (v. 4)

4. And one went in, and told his lord, saying, Thus and thus said the maid that is of the land of Israel.

Probably the *one* who *went in* to the king was Naaman himself. The Hebrew text can be translated "he went in" instead of "one went in." No one would be more interested in the Hebrew maiden's suggestion than Naaman, and no one could more easily have had access to the king.

B. A Quick Response (v. 5a)

5a. And the king of Syria said, Go to, go, and I will send a letter unto the king of Israel.

Enthusiastically *the king of Syria* told his general to go to Israel, and quickly. *Go to* is an old English expression of urgency, similar to our "Get going!" Furthermore, the king of Syria volunteered to write *a letter unto the king of Israel.* Apparently diplomatic channels were open between the two nations, in spite of the on-and-off war between them. Most likely this king of Israel was Jehoram (2 Kings 3:1), usually called Joram (2 Kings 8:16, 25, 29) to distinguish him from King Jehoram who ruled Judah at the same time. (The two names appear together in the three verses just cited.)

C. From King to King (vv. 5b-7)

5b. And he departed, and took with him ten talents of silver, and six thousand pieces of gold, and ten changes of raiment.

The general expected to pay handsomely for his healing. Footnotes in the *New International Version* estimate that he took about 750 pounds *of silver* and 150 pounds *of gold.* Using those figures and the current prices of gold and silver, we can estimate that Naaman carried nearly a million United States dollars. Fine clothing also was highly valued in those days, and *ten* good suits would last the prophet a long time.

BUYING GOD'S FAVOR

In the spring of 1996, a new series of hundred-dollar bills went into circulation throughout the United States. Supposedly the redesigned currency is more difficult to counterfeit. It features a larger picture of Ben Franklin and other harder-to-duplicate features.

However, just one week after the bill went into circulation came the first known attempt to pass a fake copy of the new bill. The counterfeiter was a West Virginia teenager with a computer and a laser printer. The bills weren't very good counterfeits, but that didn't stop the boy's uncle from trying to buy lunch with one of them at the local McDonald's! The boy was not arrested, apparently because he did not plan to circulate the bills (he even printed his own picture on some of them in place of Franklin's). His uncle, however, *was* arrested.

When Naaman went to Israel to seek a cure for his leprosy, he thought he could buy good health—a priceless commodity in anyone's estimation. Unlike the uncle in the West Virginia restaurant, Naaman offered something of real worth for his healing. Gold, silver, and beautiful garments were the tokens with which he tried to buy the favor of God's prophet.

However, Naaman learned a lesson that is timeless: God's favor cannot be purchased. His grace is offered to those who have humble and contrite hearts and are willing to do what He says. This principle still holds true. We must come to God on His terms, not ours.　—C. R. B.

6. And he brought the letter to the king of Israel, saying, Now when this letter is come unto thee, behold, I have therewith sent Naaman my servant to thee, that thou mayest recover him of his leprosy.

The Hebrew maiden had not claimed that *the king of Israel* could heal *leprosy;* she had said that the prophet could (v. 3). However, she had also said that the prophet was in Samaria; and Samaria was the capital city, where the king of Israel lived. Apparently the king of Syria reasoned that King Joram would know it if a prophet in his city could heal someone of his leprosy.

7. And it came to pass, when the king of Israel had read the letter, that he rent his clothes, and said, Am I God, to kill and to make alive, that this man doth send unto me to recover a man of his leprosy? Wherefore consider, I pray you, and see how he seeketh a quarrel against me.

Tearing one's own *clothes* was a way of expressing shock, dismay, or grief. *The king of Israel* felt all of these. An enemy king was demanding that he do something he could not possibly do. Then, because he could not fulfill those demands, the enemy king would respond by sending troops to punish him. This outlandish demand was simply a way of picking a fight, Joram thought; and he wanted no fight with Syria.

It should be noted that Joram's father (Ahab) had been defeated and killed when he had fought to recover some territory that Syria had taken from Israel (1 Kings 22:29-37). Now it seemed to Joram that Syria was looking for an excuse to start the war again, with the intention of seizing more of Israel's territory. [See question #2, page 72.]

III. A Prophet's Solution
(2 Kings 5:8-14)

Verse 7 probably records what Joram said to his advisers, while Naaman remained in a separate room and did not hear it. Perhaps Naaman was kept waiting for some time while the king and his counselors discussed how they could answer him. Meanwhile, word of the impossible demand leaked out, along with word of the king's fear. Swiftly the news spread throughout the city. There must have been a feeling of alarm everywhere, for no one wanted to resume the war with Syria. But Elisha was not alarmed. He knew that he could address Joram's concerns and grant the king of Syria's request.

A. The Prophet's Invitation (v. 8)

8. And it was so, when Elisha the man of God had heard that the king of Israel had rent his clothes, that he sent to the king, saying, Wherefore hast thou rent thy clothes? let him come now to me, and he shall know that there is a prophet in Israel.

Wherefore in King James English means "why." "Why have you torn your clothes?" the prophet wanted to know. "What are you worried about?" All Joram had to do was to send his visitor to Elisha's house. There the visitor would learn that *there is a prophet in Israel.* Joram himself knew how Elisha had helped him during a battle with Moab (2 Kings 3:4-27), and was probably aware of several of Elisha's miracles (2 Kings 4). No doubt it was with great relief that the king sent Naaman to see the prophet.

B. The Prophet's Promise (vv. 9, 10)

9. So Naaman came with his horses and with his chariot, and stood at the door of the house of Elisha.

Can you imagine this demonstration of pomp and pride? Naaman's *chariot* was likely the finest in all Syria except for the king's. He must have been accompanied by a formidable array of cavalry to protect the gold and silver that he carried. The entire entourage gathered at Elisha's door. The stage was set for a dramatic miracle. The general and his men were waiting with expectation.

10. And Elisha sent a messenger unto him, saying, Go and wash in Jordan seven times, and thy flesh shall come again to thee, and thou shalt be clean.

What a letdown! There was no dramatic miracle, no eloquent gesture, no loud cry to the Almighty, no striking ceremony whatsoever. The prophet himself did not even come out. He simply sent an unnamed *messenger* to tell his distinguished visitor to *go* and *wash* himself *seven times* in the *Jordan*, a little more than twenty miles away.

C. The Hero's Fury (vv. 11, 12)

11. But Naaman was wroth, and went away, and said, Behold, I thought, He will surely come out to me, and stand, and call on the name of the LORD his God, and strike his hand over the place, and recover the leper.

Naaman was wroth, or furious. He had expected an impressive ceremony that would enhance his honor before his men and produce instant healing. His pride was deeply hurt.

12. Are not Abana and Pharpar, rivers of Damascus, better than all the waters of Israel? may I not wash in them, and be clean? So he turned and went away in a rage.

Syria had *rivers,* too—*better than all the waters of Israel* in Naaman's estimation. If bathing in a river would heal leprosy, what was the matter with those rivers?

In a rage the general wheeled his chariot about and started back to Damascus. In his anger, disappointment, and wounded pride, Naaman was returning home without the one thing he had come all those weary miles to get. [See question #3, page 72.]

D. The Servants' Suggestion (v. 13)

13. And his servants came near, and spake unto him, and said, My father, if the prophet had bid thee do some great thing, wouldest thou not have done it? how much rather then, when he sayeth to thee, Wash, and be clean?

For how many miles did Naaman and his men race down the road before his rage began to cool? We do not know. Perhaps, as reason began to return, he became ashamed of his childish tantrum. At some point, Naaman's *servants* ventured to approach him: *My father*—the term was respectful, but it also spoke of closeness and affection. *If the prophet had bid thee do some great thing, wouldest thou not have done it?* Then why balk at a trivial request such as a sevenfold bath in the Jordan River? To Naaman's credit, he was able to recognize the common sense in his servants' advice. He turned his chariot toward the Jordan.

E. Obedience and Healing (v. 14)

14. Then went he down, and dipped himself seven times in Jordan, according to the saying of the man of God: and his flesh came again like unto the flesh of a little child, and he was clean.

Naaman's chariot stopped at the edge of the *Jordan.* The general waded into the "waters of Israel" that he had despised not long before (v. 12). He had been told to wash (v. 10), but apparently he did not take that to mean a thorough scrubbing. The record says that he *dipped himself* according to his instructions. Was he cleansed a little with each dipping so that after seven times he was clean, or did he come up diseased as ever for six times and then clean after the seventh? We are not told. All we know is that, after the seventh time, true to the prophet's word, *he was clean.* [See question #4, page 72.]

We can be certain that a feeling of joy accompanied Naaman and his troops all the way back to Damascus. There they shared their joy with the king who had sent them on their journey. And surely joy filled the heart of one little Hebrew maiden.

Conclusion

What was the prophet thinking? Syria was the enemy. Syria had stolen some of Israel's territory, and had killed King Joram's father when he tried to reclaim it. Syria was a constant threat to Israel, and Naaman was the general of Syria's army.

This visual shows Naaman coming up from the water the seventh time, clean and whole. The caption reminds us of the prophet's promise in verse 8.

Visual for lesson 8

Wouldn't it be better to let him die from his illness than to show him the way back to health?

A. A Good Enemy

Naaman was a soldier of Syria, Israel's enemy; but we see several indications that he was a man of fine character. In his military duties he appears to have been recognized as a genuine hero. In his home he seems to have been so kind to a slave girl that she was concerned about his welfare. When disappointment and wounded pride caused him at first to reject Elisha's advice, he listened to the wise counsel of his servants and accept what Elisha said. After Naaman was healed, he went back to the prophet with deep gratitude, an offer of payment, and an earnest vow to worship Jehovah (2 Kings 5:15-19).

We know that no one on earth really deserves God's mercy, but this man, numbered among Israel's enemies, seems to have been more worthy than many men of Israel. Would he also be more worthy than some in the church today?

B. The Temporary and the Permanent

The nations of the world are temporary. Only one kingdom will last forever. Hear Daniel the prophet: "In the days of these kings shall the God of heaven set up a kingdom, which shall never be destroyed: and the kingdom shall not be left to other people, but it shall break in pieces and consume all these kingdoms, and it shall stand for ever" (Daniel 2:44). To the apostle John, God gave this vision of the consummation of Daniel's prophecy: "The kingdoms of this world are become the kingdoms of our Lord, and of his Christ; and he shall reign for ever and ever" (Revelation 11:15). The greatest nation on earth will be pulled down, and so will the tiniest nation; but the kingdom of God and Christ will stand forever. [See question #5, page 72.]

Should not every citizen of Christ's kingdom give attention to the King's commands? Should not His desires become ours? He said, "Go ye into all the world, and preach the gospel to every creature" (Mark 16:15). Should not every citizen of the world make haste to find his way into the kingdom of God? This is something permanent!

C. Prayer

How wonderful are Your works, our Father and our King! Thank You for the prophets, through whom we know about the marvels You have done and the marvels You will do. By Your grace may we be good citizens of Your kingdom, now and forever. In Jesus' name. Amen.

D. Thought to Remember

God's kingdom is forever, and so are you!

Learning by Doing

This page contains an alternate lesson plan emphasizing learning activities.
Classes desiring such student involvement will find these suggestions helpful.

Learning Goals

Following this lesson, your students should be able to:

1. Retell the story of Naaman's healing.
2. Explain why Naaman found it difficult to obey God's prophet and what was the result when he did.
3. List some situations in which people find it difficult to obey God today, and suggest some ways to encourage them to do so.

Into the Lesson

Write the following scrambled sentence on the chalkboard or on a sheet of newsprint:

know shall there in that prophet is Israel he a

Have the students work in pairs or small groups to decipher the message. Award a token prize to the group who first comes up with, "He shall know that there is a prophet in Israel."

Then ask your students, "What is a prophet?" Many will probably say a prophet predicts the future, but that was a minor role of the Biblical prophet. Predicting the future served to validate the prophet's message. His first task was to speak for God to his generation.

Ask, "What, then, would be the value of knowing 'that there is a prophet in Israel'?" (Knowing there is a prophet presupposes there is a God for whom the prophet speaks.) In today's lesson we see one example of how God used the prophet Elisha to demonstrate His power.

Into the Word

Make copies of the following statements, arranged in random order. Have the students work in small groups to arrange the statements in chronological order after you have a volunteer read the printed text, 2 Kings 5:1-14. (The statements are printed here in order; you will want to scramble them on your handout.)

1. Naaman becomes a leper.
2. A servant girl mentions there is a prophet in Samaria who can heal Naaman.
3. The king of Syria sends Naaman to the king of Israel to have him cured of leprosy.
4. The king of Israel thinks the Syrian king is trying to pick a fight with him, and he tears his clothing in grief.
5. Elisha sends a message to the king of Israel to have Naaman come to him, and "he shall know that there is a prophet in Israel."
6. Through a servant Elisha orders Naaman to wash seven times in the Jordan River.
7. Naaman is angered, and he refuses to comply with the prophet's order.
8. Naaman goes to the Jordan and dips himself seven times.
9. Naaman is cured of leprosy.

Give the groups a few minutes to work; then ask someone which statement comes first. Work through the list so everyone has the correct order. Make comments as needed so everyone understands the significance of the events. For example, you'll want to point out Naaman's pride in initially refusing the prophet's order.

Into Life

Naaman found it difficult to obey God because of pride. Probably all of your students have wrestled with that same problem. Ask, "What other factors sometimes make it difficult for us to obey God?" As the class suggests ideas, discuss how one might overcome the problem. Here are some possibilities to help you get started if the class is slow to respond:

Ignorance. Sometimes we just don't know what God has commanded. How can we help people know God's will so they can obey it?

Laziness. Sometimes God's commands require diligence and effort. Not everyone has the discipline to give that. How can we help people to develop self-discipline?

Lust. Any evil desire can be called lust, not just wrong sexual desires. Face it, sin can be fun, and many in our culture live to have fun. How can we help people see that there are some things—many things—more important than having fun?

Science. The prophet's command seemed contrary to natural law and did not make sense to Naaman, so he rejected it. But God doesn't always explain Himself; He just asks for obedience. How can we learn to accept God's will even when it "doesn't make sense" to us?

For some people, salvation by grace doesn't make sense—they want to try to earn it. Close with a discussion of the importance of accepting God's grace by faith, including the importance of repentance and baptism. Design the discussion to help the students witness to others or to make their own confession of faith if they have not done so.

Let's Talk It Over

The questions on this page are designed to encourage review of the lesson Scriptures and to promote discussion of the lesson by the class. The answers provided are only discussion starters. Let your class talk it over from there.

1. The servant girl who waited on Naaman's wife could easily have been bitter about her captivity. In such a case she might have delighted to see her captor suffer. Instead, she seems to have been compassionate toward her enemy. How can we develop such a kindly spirit toward those who do us harm?

Joseph is another good example of someone who was mistreated but bore no ill will toward his brothers or his Egyptian masters. When he and his brothers were reconciled, he said, "Be not grieved, nor angry with yourselves, that ye sold me hither: for God did send me before you to preserve life" (Genesis 45:5). Joseph could see God's providence at work in the situation, and he became God's instrument of working good. We, too, need to remember God is capable of working all things together for the good of His people (Romans 8:28), and we can choose whether He will work through us or in spite of us!

2. How ironic that Naaman and the king of Syria seemed to have more faith in the God of Israel than Israel's own king! Why is it that we who know so well the Lord's mercies can sometimes forget them or fail to rely on His power? How can we maintain the childlike faith of the Israelite maid who initiated Naaman's journey of faith?

Perhaps the Israelite maid in captivity spent more time thinking about the Lord, possibly praying for her homeland and her family daily, than did the king, safe and secure in his palace. We need to remember that the Lord's blessings are "new every morning" (Lamentations 3:23). Perhaps if we started each day consciously looking for the Lord's blessings, we would not forget to think of Him when times of testing come.

3. Naaman's pride got in the way of his accepting the prophet's solution. What are some ways pride hinders people from making the decision to accept Jesus Christ as Savior? How can we help them overcome this barrier?

Pride keeps us from believing we need a Savior. We want to justify or excuse our sins rather than admit to them. Or we think we can make up for them by doing good deeds. But Jesus came to save sinners, and we must admit that we are sinners and that we cannot save ourselves.

Pride makes it difficult for us to respond to the gospel invitation. Some people feel it unnecessary to stand before an assembly just to express a simple faith in Jesus Christ as Son of God and Savior. Pride hinders a person from submitting to baptism. Immersion into Christ can be seen as an inconvenient, embarrassing act, and it requires an appropriate measure of humility to submit to it.

Love and patience are required to help such a person. We need to help him or her accept the truth of God's Word by modeling our own faith and obedience. When we admit our own failings and need for a Savior, we are more likely to be able to communicate with another person about his or her need for salvation.

4. Naaman was healed only when he followed the Lord's instructions to the letter. Yet today many people seem to be looking for spiritual shortcuts rather than explicitly obeying God's instructions regarding salvation, holiness, worship, service, or any number of issues. What is the danger of such a practice?

It is vital to follow instructions carefully when performing dozens of tasks, like preparing a tax return, assembling an item of furniture, baking a cake, changing a headlight in our automobile, or marking our ballots during an election. Why should we think that obeying God would require any less care? It is true that God looks at the heart (cf. 1 Samuel 16:7), but what kind of heart consciously resists the Word of God? True obedience is a matter of the heart!

5. Naaman was from Syria, a political enemy of Israel. Still, God healed him. What does this suggest to you about the mission of the church and God's interest in people outside our own geographical or political borders?

"God is no respecter of persons: but in every nation he that feareth him, and worketh righteousness, is accepted with him" (Acts 10:34, 35). It is easy for modern believers to focus too narrowly on God's work within their own race or nation. They may be slow to support missionary work, arguing that the money would be better spent at home. We must develop a vision for the gospel as wide as that of Jesus. He urged His disciples to go to "all nations" (Matthew 28:19).

God Gives His Spokesman Courage

DEVOTIONAL READING: Acts 4:13-22.

LESSON SCRIPTURE: Amos 6, 7.

PRINTED TEXT: Amos 6:1; 7:7-15.

Amos 6:1

1 Woe to them that are at ease in Zion, and trust in the mountain of Samaria, which are named chief of the nations, to whom the house of Israel came!

Amos 7:7-15

7 Thus he showed me: and, behold, the LORD stood upon a wall made by a plumbline, with a plumbline in his hand.

8 And the LORD said unto me, Amos, what seest thou? And I said, A plumbline. Then said the Lord, Behold, I will set a plumbline in the midst of my people Israel: I will not again pass by them any more:

9 And the high places of Isaac shall be desolate, and the sanctuaries of Israel shall be laid waste; and I will rise against the house of Jeroboam with the sword.

10 Then Amaziah the priest of Bethel sent to Jeroboam king of Israel, saying, Amos hath conspired against thee in the midst of the house of Israel: the land is not able to bear all his words.

11 For thus Amos saith, Jeroboam shall die by the sword, and Israel shall surely be led away captive out of their own land.

12 Also Amaziah said unto Amos, O thou seer, go, flee thee away into the land of Judah, and there eat bread, and prophesy there:

13 But prophesy not again any more at Bethel: for it is the king's chapel, and it is the king's court.

14 Then answered Amos, and said to Amaziah, I was no prophet, neither was I a prophet's son; but I was a herdman, and a gatherer of sycamore fruit:

15 And the LORD took me as I followed the flock, and the LORD said unto me, Go, prophesy unto my people Israel.

Nov
1

GOLDEN TEXT: Amos . . . said to Amaziah, I was no prophet, neither was I a prophet's son; but I was a herdman, and a gatherer of sycamore fruit: and the LORD took me as I followed the flock, and the LORD said unto me, Go, prophesy unto my people Israel.—Amos 7:14, 15.

God Calls a People to Faithful Living
Unit 3: God Works Through People
(Lessons 8-10)

Lesson Aims

As a result of studying this lesson, your students will be able to:

1. Describe the call and courageous ministry of Amos.

2. Suggest some reasons a man like Amos was called instead of a "professional" prophet.

3. List some situations in which a "nonprofessional" minister might serve the Lord more fruitfully than a "professional."

Lesson Outline

Introduction

The north side of Hickory Hill was not for sledding. Everyone knew that. It looked good from the top, but the lower part of the slope was steeper; and it ended with a vertical drop of six feet into Stony Creek. The south side was not so steep, but it was safer.

Four boys brought their sleds to the hilltop after school. To their disappointment, the south slope was not in good condition for sledding. The sunshine had melted most of the snow, and what was left was too soft to bear a sled.

"Let's go that way," Bert challenged, pointing to the north. There was a short argument; but it ended when Bert sneered, "You're all chicken," and flung himself and his sled on the north slope.

"Who's chicken?" yelled Chuck, following only six feet behind. The other two launched themselves side by side, their elbows almost touching. It was wonderful, like riding on the wind!

Then they came to the steeper slope of the lower hill. Bert thrust his foot into the snow to stop his sled. Chuck crashed into him, followed by two more sleds and boys. The tangled mass plunged over the steep bank and broke through thin ice into freezing water.

A. Israel's Slippery Slope

The history of the northern kingdom of Israel resembled the plunge of those boys into the icy water. Unable to resist the slippery slope of idolatrous pleasure, the nation plunged to disaster. King Ahab (encouraged by his wife Jezebel) led the nation on to the "steeper slope" by promoting the worship of Baal (1 Kings 16:29-33).

For several years after Ahab's death, wicked Jezebel continued to promote the worship of Baal. God then commanded the prophet Elisha to anoint Jehu as king. Jehu was commissioned to destroy the house of Ahab (2 Kings 10:11). He proceeded to demonstrate his zeal for Jehovah by rounding up and killing the worshipers of Baal (vv. 18-25). The Lord then promised that four generations of Jehu's family would rule in Israel (v. 30).

Despite his zeal for the Lord's cause, Jehu did not put a stop to "the sins of Jeroboam"—the worship of the golden calves at Dan and Bethel (2 Kings 10:29). Other sins continued along with this idolatry, to the point that God used Syria as His instrument to punish Israel (vv. 32, 33). However, the Lord was not yet ready to let Israel be destroyed (2 Kings 13:22, 23). He gave the northern kingdom one more chance.

B. One More Chance

Nearly a century and a half after Jeroboam led Israel into idolatry through his counterfeit religious practices, another Jeroboam (generally referred to as Jeroboam II) came to the throne of Israel. He belonged to the fourth generation of Jehu's family. Like the kings before him, he continued in the sins of the first Jeroboam. Nevertheless, the Lord gave him victory over Syria, and he regained much of the territory that had been taken earlier from the northern part of the kingdom of Israel (2 Kings 14:23-27). Apparently the Lord was giving His people one more opportunity to respond to His goodness with faithful obedience. To reinforce His appeal, the Lord sent the prophet Amos to denounce the sins of Israel and to call the people to repent and put an end to their sinful practices.

C. Lesson Background

From Amos 7:15 we see that Amos was one who "followed the flock," indicating that he likely took care of sheep or goats. Amos also referred to himself as a "herdman" (Amos 7:14). Since this Hebrew term is related to a word for cattle, Amos's responsibilities may have involved cattle as well. We cannot be certain just what Amos did with sycamore trees (v. 14). The *New International Version* indicates that he "took care of sycamore-fig trees"; the *King James Version* indicates that he "was a gatherer of sycamore fruit." Probably he did both.

Amos's home was in Tekoa (Amos 1:1), a town located in the southern kingdom of Judah, about twelve miles south of Jerusalem. However, God sent him to minister in the northern kingdom of Israel. Amos spoke at Bethel (Amos 7:13), the place where Jeroboam had set up one of his golden calves (1 Kings 12:28, 29).

As he began his message to Israel, Amos mentioned the pagan nations nearby. He named each one, spoke of its multiple transgressions, and foretold disaster to each one (Amos 1:3—2:3). No doubt the people of Israel applauded all of that. He even pointed out the sins of Judah to the south (2:4, 5), which must have made the northerners feel rather smug.

But then Amos turned his attention to Israel (which probably brought the applause abruptly to an end!). He spoke openly of Israel's sins and its coming punishment: "Therefore will I cause you to go into captivity beyond Damascus, saith the Lord" (Amos 5:27). Chapter 6 of Amos continues the prophet's denunciation of both Judah and Israel's sinfulness and complacency.

I. Discomfort for the Comfortable (Amos 6:1)

A. Woe to Judah (v. 1a)

1a. Woe to them that are at ease in Zion.

In English versions of the Old Testament, the word *woe* often represents a Hebrew expression of grief. The word itself is pronounced with a wailing sound, similar to the cry of one who is grieving. In our text, the word expresses the sorrows that would come to sinners who had closed their ears to the Lord's appeal through His prophets. Amos's words were directed to those who were *at ease*—complacent and unconcerned about the sins they and their countrymen had committed. Complacent now, they will soon moan in grief.

Originally *Zion* designated one of the hills on which Jerusalem stood. David captured this stronghold from the Jebusites (2 Samuel 5:6-9). Eventually the name Zion came to designate the entire city of Jerusalem (2 Kings 19:21; Psalm 48:2; Isaiah 1:8), as it does here.

B. Woe to Israel (v. 1b)

1b. And trust in the mountain of Samaria.

The mountain of Samaria was a hill, some three hundred feet high, on which the city of Samaria was built. Samaria was the capital of the northern kingdom. Its elevation made it easy to defend against attack, and for that reason its leaders felt secure from any outside threat. Like those in Jerusalem, they were apathetic about the sins of their people, and oblivious to the punishment that loomed before them. [See question #1, page 80.]

C. Woe to the Leaders (v. 1c)

1c. Which are named chief of the nations, to whom the house of Israel came!

The first part of this appears to be directed specifically at the leaders of the nation. The *New American Standard Bible* reads, "The distinguished men of the foremost of nations, to whom the house of Israel comes." Thus the initial *woe* of this verse was targeted toward the leaders—both religious and political—*to whom the house of Israel came* for guidance and direction. These men should have been encouraging the nation to know and obey God's law, but they were leading the people away from it. For that reason, "woe" was coming both to the leaders and to the nation that they led. Chapter 6 goes on to describe the luxurious living of these self-satisfied leaders (vv. 3-6), and the disaster that was coming to them and to their cities (vv. 7, 8). Because they were first in rank and responsibility, they would be the first to be taken captive (v. 7).

II. The Plumbline
(Amos 7:7-9)

Chapter 7 begins with two visions describing the possible punishments that awaited sinful Israel. In the first vision, grasshoppers "made an end of eating the grass of the land" (v. 2). In the second, a great fire dried up the ocean and destroyed part of the land. In each case, Amos pleaded with the Lord not to punish Israel in such a brutal manner. The Lord relented and withdrew the threat. Then came a vision of a plumbline.

A. Israel Tested (vv. 7, 8)

7. Thus he showed me: and, behold, the Lord stood upon a wall made by a plumbline, with a plumbline in his hand.

A *plumbline* is a string that has a weight attached to the end so it will hang straight down. Masons and bricklayers use such a line to be sure that the wall they are building is perfectly vertical, or "plumb." Building inspectors use one to see how well the masons and bricklayers did. In this vision, *the Lord* stood ready to test a *wall* that was already built.

8. And the LORD said unto me, Amos, what seest thou? And I said, A plumbline. Then said the Lord, Behold, I will set a plumbline in the midst of my people Israel: I will not again pass by them any more.

The wall to be tested was *Israel.* The nation was "out of plumb," but God had not taken action. Now, however, He said He would *not again pass by them any more.* His plumbline would show that the nation was not straight, and a wall that was not straight had to be torn down. Punishment for Israel was imminent.

B. Israel Condemned (v. 9)

9. And the high places of Isaac shall be desolate, and the sanctuaries of Israel shall be laid waste; and I will rise against the house of Jeroboam with the sword.

Isaac was the father of Jacob; Jacob was given the new name of Israel; and *Israel* became the name of the nation descended from Jacob. In this poetic verse, both *Isaac* and *Israel* refer to the northern kingdom known as Israel. Tested by God's plumbline, that nation was not upright. Corrective action would need to be taken, either to straighten the "wall" or to tear it down.

High places and *sanctuaries* are places of worship. Israel's places of worship included the two where golden calves were worshiped (at Bethel and Dan), and other idolatrous sites as well. All those places of false worship were going to be *laid waste.* They were out of line with God's law; they could not be permitted to stand.

The Lord had promised that King Jehu's family would rule Israel for four generations (2 Kings 10:30). Jeroboam II was the fourth generation of that family. The Lord had blessed him and the nation with victory in battle and with prosperity (2 Kings 14:23-29), but they had not responded with grateful obedience (v. 24). Now it was time to end the rule of Jehu's family, and it would end violently. *With the sword* the Lord would *rise,* not against Jeroboam himself, but *against the house of Jeroboam.*

Second Kings records how this prophecy was fulfilled. Jeroboam's death ended the presence of stable government in the northern kingdom. Over the next thirty years there were six kings in the north. All of them did what was evil in the sight of the Lord. Four of them were killed by assassins who then seized the throne. The last four had to pay tribute to Assyria. The last one refused tribute and was taken captive. Samaria was then captured by the Assyrians, the people of Israel were deported to foreign lands, and the nation of Israel was no more. (The record of the reigns of these last six kings is found in 2 Kings 15:8-31; 17:1-6.)

III. The Priest's Complaint
(Amos 7:10-13)

Having concluded our brief look at events after the time of Amos, we now go back to the time when Amos was preaching at Bethel. As might be expected, there was quite a protest when he denounced the sins of Israel and predicted its severe punishment.

A. Amaziah's Protest (vv. 10, 11)

10. Then Amaziah the priest of Bethel sent to Jeroboam king of Israel, saying, Amos hath conspired against thee in the midst of the house of Israel: the land is not able to bear all his words.

This *Amaziah* was a *priest* who likely led in the worship of the golden calf at *Bethel.* Naturally he was not pleased to have a prophet from Judah proclaiming the destruction of the sanctuary in Israel and the demise of the king who had given Amaziah his job. Amaziah's first reaction was to complain to *Jeroboam king of Israel.* He claimed that Amos was spearheading a conspiracy against the king. Such preaching could not be tolerated.

11. For thus Amos saith, Jeroboam shall die by the sword, and Israel shall surely be led away captive out of their own land.

It was true that Amos had predicted captivity for Israel (5:27; 6:7), but he had not said, *Jeroboam shall die by the sword.* He had predicted violence only against Jeroboam's *house*, or family (7:9). Probably Amaziah thought a bit of exaggeration would be more likely to stir the king to action, so he reported that the prophet had predicted a violent death for the king himself. How could any king let a preacher go on predicting his death? [See question #2, page 80.]

B. Amaziah's Threat (vv. 12, 13)

12. Also Amaziah said unto Amos, O thou seer, go, flee thee away into the land of Judah, and there eat bread, and prophesy there.

If King Jeroboam issued any reply, it is not recorded. Perhaps he was wise enough to know that Amos was not a violent revolutionary. Perhaps he did send men to investigate Amaziah's claim. Perhaps Amaziah proceeded with his next threat without waiting for an answer. This was to advise Amos to go back to *the land of Judah*, from which he had come.

The term *seer*, generally used respectfully of a prophet (1 Samuel 9:11; 2 Samuel 24:11), was used by Amaziah as a term of derision. Perhaps he was alluding to the various visions that Amos claimed to "see." The phrase *flee thee away* implied that he had better leave the country before the king's men came to arrest him. *There eat bread* suggested that he might be able to earn a living by preaching against Israel in Judah; but he could never expect people of Israel to pay him for denouncing their conduct and predicting their doom. [See question #3, page 80.]

13. But prophesy not again any more at Bethel: for it is the king's chapel, and it is the king's court.

Amaziah's veiled threat, "flee thee away," was suddenly much more direct. The sanctuary at *Bethel* was *the king's chapel*. Originally King Jeroboam I had it built; he put the calf there to be worshiped; he told the people to worship there; and he even burned incense on the altar (1 Kings 13:1). Who did this so-called prophet think he was—denouncing such a sacred place?

IGNORING BAD NEWS

Most of us prefer not to hear bad news. In fact, we practice hard at ignoring it. For example, scientists have been issuing warnings for years that the Pacific Northwest is ripe for an earthquake of epic proportions. About eleven hundred years ago, an area near Seattle rose twenty-three feet as a result of such a quake. In addition, there is evidence that Mount Rainier, just sixty miles from Seattle, could explode and send massive mud flows into the city. There is also the possibility of a *tsunami* (soo-*nah*-me)— a tidal wave—inundating Puget Sound as a result of an earthquake or volcanic explosion.

Home Daily Bible Readings

Monday, Oct. 26—Amos Speaks for God (Amos 1:1-8)
Tuesday, Oct. 27—Both Judah and Israel Have Transgressed God's Laws (Amos 2:4-8)
Wednesday, Oct. 28—Amos Condemns Those at Ease in Zion (Amos 6:1-7)
Thursday, Oct. 29—You Have Turned Justice Into Poison (Amos 6:8-14)
Friday, Oct. 30—I Am Setting a Plumbline in Israel (Amos 7:1-9)
Saturday, Oct. 31—Flee Away to the Land of Judah (Amos 7:10-17)
Sunday, Nov. 1—From Abundance to Agony (Luke 16:19-31)

Traditionally—and very much in keeping with human nature—Washingtonians have given little heed to warnings of such disasters. They are no different from people elsewhere. Californians have long denied the possibility of being personally harmed by their frequent earthquakes. Midwesterners tend to "stay put" in spite of killer tornadoes, life-threatening blizzards, and devastating floods year after year.

So it is not surprising that Israel's reaction to the divine judgment predicted by Amos was, in effect: "Go somewhere else with your prophecies of doom. If you can't say anything to make us feel good about ourselves, get lost!" The world still takes this approach to God's warnings about moral failure. Seems we haven't learned very much in the last 2,700 years!   —C. R. B.

IV. The Prophet's Answer (Amos 7:14, 15)

The priest of Bethel was a "professional." He was appointed by the king; he took his orders from the king; he was handsomely paid out of the offerings of worshipers. He could not understand a man like Amos, who was not concerned about his salary, the king's order, or his own safety. So Amos proceeded to explain how he had been called by Israel's real King.

A. Not a Professional (v. 14)

14. Then answered Amos, and said to Amaziah, I was no prophet, neither was I a prophet's son; but I was a herdman, and a gatherer of sycamore fruit.

Before God called him, Amos was *no prophet*. Neither was he *a prophet's son*. This latter term may mean a "student" rather than a literal son.

Visual for
lesson 9

This visual, showing Christians from many backgrounds teaching God's Word, challenges students to a ministry like Amos's.

In Elisha's time there were groups of such students in several locations (2 Kings 2:3, 5, 7). Apparently such a group was like a boarding school. Sons of the prophets lived together (2 Kings 6:1-7) and ate their meals together (2 Kings 4:38-44). Amos was not such a student. He was not trained to be a prophet; he did not choose to be a prophet; and he was certainly not one of the "professionals" who always gave the king the answer he wanted to hear (1 Kings 22:13). His life's work had been entirely different; he had been *a herdman, and a gatherer of sycamore fruit*. [See question #4, page 80.]

B. Appointed by the Lord (v. 15)

15. And the LORD took me as I followed the flock, and the LORD said unto me, Go, prophesy unto my people Israel.

This was how the shepherd/fig gatherer became a prophet. He had received his orders directly from *the Lord* Himself. This was why he was unconcerned about his pay or his safety, or about offending the king. He was obeying the King of kings, and trusting Him for whatever help or protection he needed.

Conclusion

There were numerous "sons of the prophets," whom God could have called to carry out His task; but He bypassed all of them and sent a shepherd to give His warning in Bethel, site of the king's idolatrous chapel. There were hundreds of shepherds in Israel, yet the Lord sent one from Judah to travel northward and confront His people with their sins.

God knows the hearts of His people, and He knows their abilities as well. But God's call is not so obvious to us as it was to Amos, and it often seems that inspiration must be replaced by diligent study. How can a farmer know if he ought to be a preacher, and how can a preacher know if he ought to be a farmer?

"There's a place for every worker in the vineyard of the Lord." So begins an old song, but it ends with this plea: "Help me, Lord, from this time onward, find and occupy my place."

A. Help Me Find My Place

Without such an unmistakable call as Amos received, how can I be sure what God wants me to do? Some simple questions may help.

1. What can I do? This is not as easy a question as it seems. Some of us have inflated opinions of our abilities. We handicap ourselves by being conceited and arrogant. Some of us are too modest. We handicap ourselves by underestimating our abilities. Paul advises each one of us "not to think of himself more highly than he ought to think." On the other hand, one should not think of himself less highly than he ought to think. Each one needs to see himself clearly and objectively: he needs "to think soberly, according as God hath dealt to every man the measure of faith" (Romans 12:3).

2. What do I like to do? A happy worker is a better worker. I am not likely to be a great success in any work I dislike. On the other hand, work may be both pleasant and profitable to me, and still be unworthy of my time and effort. So, "What do I like?" is not the only question I must consider.

3. How can I best help other people? Most honest workers are helpful: the doctor, the lawyer, the farmer, the mail carrier, the grocery seller, and a multitude of others.

4. How can I best glorify God? Some glorify God by preaching the gospel. Others glorify Him with honest and capable management in both the secular workplace and the church. Paul wrote, "Whatsoever ye do, do all to the glory of God" (1 Corinthians 10:31). Jesus said, "Let your light so shine before men, that they may see your good works, and glorify your Father which is in heaven" (Matthew 5:16). [See question #5, page 80.]

B. Prayer

Our Father, sometimes we feel confused by the many opportunities that lie before us—opportunities for service in the world and in the church. Yet in our confusion we are thrilled and thankful because You have supplied us and our brothers and sisters with abilities as numerous as the opportunities. By Your grace may we find the places of service for which You have designed us, and may each one fill his place as You would have it filled. Amen.

C. Thought to Remember

Do all that you do to the glory of God.

Learning by Doing

This page contains an alternate lesson plan emphasizing learning activities.
Classes desiring such student involvement will find these suggestions helpful.

Learning Goals

After this lesson your students will be able to:

1. Describe the call and courageous ministry of Amos.

2. Suggest some reasons why Amos was called instead of a "professional" prophet.

3. List some situations in which a "nonprofessional" minister might serve the Lord more fruitfully than a "professional."

Into the Lesson

Before class, write COURAGE on the chalkboard or on a sheet of newsprint. Then introduce the lesson by asking, "What was the most courageous thing you ever did?"

From this discussion develop a list of some of the things that require courage. Likely most items on your list will involve courage in the face of physical danger. Encourage the students to think also about issues of moral courage—like the determination to do what is right but unpopular or to speak the truth when no one wants to hear the truth.

In today's lesson we look at a man who had the courage to speak the truth even though that truth was unpopular. His courage came, not from an inner reservoir of human strength or willpower, but from God.

Into the Word

Direct your students to Amos 7:7-15 and ask them to look for evidences of who Amos was and what he did for a living.

• Amos was not a professional prophet. In other words, he was what many people today call "a layman" (v. 14).

• Amos was a "herdman" (v. 14). We usually think of a "herd" of cattle and a "flock" of sheep or goats, so the word *herdman* might suggest Amos either owned or cared for cattle. However, the term is generic enough that it could include caring for any kind of animal. Verse 15 implies that Amos was a shepherd—he was called as he "followed the flock."

• Amos was a "gatherer of . . . fruit" (v. 14), which may mean either that he owned the fruit orchard or tended it for another.

Observe that Amos was a resident of Tekoa in the southern kingdom, but he went to Bethel to deliver his prophetic message. (Show Tekoa and Bethel on a map.) Ask the students what they know of Bethel. (Some should remember that Jeroboam I put one of his idols there [lesson 7]). Amos's preaching inspired anger on the part of Israel's religious establishment (vv. 12, 13). Suppose a layman came to your church from a church in a neighboring county to criticize and condemn the way your students are living. How would they feel about that?

Ask the students to suggest reasons Amos needed courage to perform his role. (This could be done in small groups or by the class as a whole.) Some ideas include the following:

• Amos was an "outsider." He left his own home in Tekoa of Judah to prophesy against Israel at Bethel.

• Amos declared an unpopular truth in the face of powerful opposition (v. 10).

• Amos was not a professional prophet (v. 14). Some might question his authority for his ministry.

Call attention to Amos's use of the image of a plumbline (vv. 1-8). Bring a plumbline to class to show those who may not be familiar with this device.

Ask, "What is the purpose of a plumbline?" (To show if a brick wall is "true"—is being built straight without leaning.) "What if the wall is not 'plumb'?" (It will be in danger of falling; the builder will tear it down to build a straight one.)

Then discuss, "What function might a plumbline serve in evaluating our spiritual lives?"

Into Life

Since Amos was a layman instead of a "professional" prophet, your students can identify with him and his mission. Ask your students to think about some situations in which a layman might be more effective than a professional minister:

• Being an influence for Christ on the job.

• Being a witness in the neighborhood.

• Being salt and light for friends and family.

As "nonprofessionals," your students have a unique opportunity to be witnesses for Christ on the job, in the community, and in the home. In closing, challenge each student to complete this open-ended sentence:

"During the coming week, I will have the courage to be a witness for Christ to . . ."

Close with a prayer of commitment, asking God to help your students to be bold and courageous witnesses during the coming week.

Let's Talk It Over

The questions on this page are designed to encourage review of the lesson Scriptures and to promote discussion of the lesson by the class. The answers provided are only discussion starters. Let your class talk it over from there.

1. Amos attempted to awaken his hearers from their ease and complacency. How important is it for someone to do that today? Why? Who should take on the job? How?

As Edmund Burke has said—and as history has demonstrated again and again—"All that is necessary for the triumph of evil is that good men do nothing." Thus, there is a great need to be vigilant against complacency. We live in an affluent, comfortable society—the perfect breeding ground for complacency.

Christian leaders must make it a point to warn against complacency, but they cannot do it alone. Amos was neither a "prophet" nor "a prophet's son," but he took on the task. So must every concerned Christian today!

2. Amaziah twisted Amos's words; he did not give a true report about Amos to the king. How should we respond when we or our church is misrepresented in the media or some other public forum?

More and more the popular culture tries to put a bad "spin" on anything religious. Christian homeschoolers are portrayed as radical, antisocial revolutionaries. Conservative politicians are portrayed as heartless villains victimizing the poor. Any public official who acts on Biblical principles is accused of violating "the separation of church and state."

"Speaking the truth in love" (Ephesians 4:15) is the only response. We cannot control what other people say or do, but we can control ourselves. We have to make the truth known as much as we are able, and then love our neighbors enough to prove wrong those who slander us (1 Peter 3:16; see also 2:12).

3. Amaziah told Amos that he should go to his own land of Judah to do his prophesying. Today the pluralistic world seems to be telling the church to keep its preaching to itself—"Don't force your views on me." How should we respond to that?

Amos replied by telling Amaziah he had a mandate from God to preach in Israel. We, too, have a mandate from God. Perhaps we should answer in the words of Peter and John: "We cannot but speak the things which we have seen and heard" (Acts 4:20).

We also need to be sure that we do not come across as pushy, actually trying to "force" the gospel on people. We "persuade" people (2 Corinthians 5:11) and "implore" them, (2 Corinthians 5:20, *New International Version*), but we cannot force it on anyone.

4. Throughout history God has called people like Amos, out of common backgrounds, to be proclaimers of His truth. What is He calling you to do? How do you know? What will you do about it?

In general, God calls each of us to live for Him, to "let [our] light so shine before men, that they may see [our] good works, and glorify [our] Father which is in heaven" (Matthew 5:16). How each of us does that, however, may differ. To the Twelve Jesus said, "Follow me," but to the former demoniac in Gadara he said, "Go home to thy friends, and tell them how great things the Lord hath done for thee" (Mark 5:19). Perhaps God is calling some of your students to leave secular employment to be involved in vocational ministry. Perhaps there is someone who works with one of your students whom the Lord wants that person to reach through an effective witness on the job. Challenge all your students to be open to whatever challenges and opportunities the Lord lays before them.

5. The lesson writer points out that one question we must ask when seeking our proper place of service in the church is, "How can I best glorify God?" Why is it important for us to emphasize this question?

In our human weakness we may be tempted to ask, "How can I best glorify *me?*" Certain places of service can provide us the opportunity to nourish our pride or to strengthen our personal influence or to give us a heady sense of power. We must beware of seeking a place of service out of such unworthy motives. On the other hand, we may be tempted to avoid certain offices or responsibilities because they require sacrifice and could be difficult to fulfill. In this case we are asking, "How can I glorify God *on my own terms?*" But God gains glory when men and women of faith meet difficult challenges head-on, knowingly undertaking tasks that entail physical strain and emotional anguish.

God Works Through Song Writers

DEVOTIONAL READING: Psalm 27.

LESSON SCRIPTURE: Psalm 73.

PRINTED TEXT: Psalm 73:1-3, 12, 13, 16-18, 21-26.

Psalm 73:1-3, 12, 13, 16-18, 21-26

1 Truly God is good to Israel, even to such as are of a clean heart.

2 But as for me, my feet were almost gone; my steps had well-nigh slipped.

3 For I was envious at the foolish, when I saw the prosperity of the wicked.

. . . .

12 Behold, these are the ungodly, who prosper in the world; they increase in riches.

13 Verily I have cleansed my heart in vain, and washed my hands in innocency.

. . . .

16 When I thought to know this, it was too painful for me;

17 Until I went into the sanctuary of God; then understood I their end.

18 Surely thou didst set them in slippery places: thou castedst them down into destruction.

. . . .

21 Thus my heart was grieved, and I was pricked in my reins.

22 So foolish was I, and ignorant: I was as a beast before thee.

23 Nevertheless I am continually with thee: thou hast holden me by my right hand.

24 Thou shalt guide me with thy counsel, and afterward receive me to glory.

25 Whom have I in heaven but thee? And there is none upon earth that I desire besides thee.

26 My flesh and my heart faileth: but God is the strength of my heart, and my portion for ever.

Nov
8

GOLDEN TEXT: It is good for me to draw near to God: I have put my trust in the Lord GOD, that I may declare all thy works.—Psalm 73:28.

God Calls a People to Faithful Living
Unit 3: God Works Through People
(Lessons 8-10)

Lesson Aims

Having participated in this lesson, students will be able to:

1. Explain Asaph's envy and how he overcame it.

2. List several reasons believers sometimes envy unbelievers.

3. Suggest some ways Christians can encourage one another to keep an eternal, unenvious perspective.

Lesson Outline

INTRODUCTION
  A. Asaph's Struggle
  B. Lesson Background
 I. A SHAKEN FAITH (Psalm 73:1-3, 12, 13)
  A. Basic Belief (v. 1)
  B. Near Disaster (vv. 2, 3)
   Envy
  C. Summary (vv. 12, 13)
 II. A SURE FAITH (Psalm 73:16-18, 21, 22)
  A. Inspired by the Sanctuary (vv. 16, 17)
  B. Thinking Clearly (vv. 18, 21, 22)
III. SECURITY WITH GOD (Psalm 73:23-26)
  A. Companionship (v. 23)
  B. Guidance and Glory (v. 24)
  C. The One and Only (v. 25)
  D. Source of Strength (v. 26)
   "Amazing Grace"
CONCLUSION
  A. Watch Your Wanting
  B. Afterward
  C. Prayer
  D. Thought to Remember

Introduction

"I was so tired of being poor!" That was Bob's excuse. He and Betty had agreed that she should leave her job to become a housewife and mother, but getting by on one salary was harder than they expected. And then there was Jerry, Bob's college chum. He was making money "hand over fist." His salary was no more than Bob's, but he seemed to have a golden touch with investments.

One day Jerry volunteered to let Bob in on a "sweet deal." It would make forty percent in a

year, Jerry said, but he needed a few thousand dollars more to swing it. So Bob borrowed the money, using the equity in his home as security. He gave the money to Jerry, signed the papers Jerry put before him, and waited for his investment to turn a profit.

Unfortunately, the "sweet deal" turned out to be illegal. Because Bob's signature was on the papers, Bob is spending a year in prison. Betty is a single parent, and poorer than ever.

A. Asaph's Struggle

Asaph could have sympathized with Bob. He felt frustrated because of his own meager circumstances when compared with those who were making money "hand over fist." Furthermore, those making the money were clearly people of ungodly character. Asaph was on the verge of a spiritual tragedy (rather than a financial one), but by the grace of God he found an answer. He wrote a song about his experience, and from that song we take today's text.

Asaph's song is one of a hundred and fifty collected over the centuries of Old Testament history into the book we call the book of Psalms. One of them is called "A Prayer of Moses the man of God" (Psalm 90), so it must have been written approximately four hundred years before the time of Asaph. Others, such as Psalm 85, seem to have been written after Israel was released from captivity in Babylon, close to five hundred years after Asaph.

B. Lesson Background

Thus far in our survey of the Old Testament, we have had nine lessons in chronological order, though sometimes with wide gaps of time between lessons.

1. Adam and Eve bring sin into the world.
2. God's people escape from Egypt.
3. God's people receive His law.
4. God's people enter the promised land.
5. God's people are helped by judges.
6. Israel becomes a monarchy.
7. Israel is divided into two countries.
8. A Syrian general is healed in Israel.
9. Amos the prophet boldly confronts Israel with its sins.

Today's lesson does not follow lesson 9 in chronological order. We go back to the time between when the events in lessons 6 and 7 took place. David was king of Israel. Asaph was the chief of his musicians, whose duty was to help with the worship of the Lord in Jerusalem (1 Chronicles 16:4, 5; 2 Chronicles 5:12). Asaph is credited with writing twelve Psalms (50, 73-83), although some of these reflect the time after Jerusalem had been destroyed (74, 79, 83).

These may have been composed by a member of "the children of Asaph," who comprised a group of singers during the period after the exile (Nehemiah 7:44).

I. A Shaken Faith
(Psalm 73:1-3, 12, 13)

Psalm 73 is a very personal Psalm. Asaph writes from his own experience: his feelings and thoughts, his errors in judgment, and the firm conclusion that he eventually reached. His song is designed to help us reach the same firm conclusion when confronted with a similar spiritual crisis.

A. Basic Belief (v. 1)

1. Truly God is good to Israel, even to such as are of a clean heart.

Asaph begins this Psalm with a personal statement of faith. The rest of the song goes on to tell how he wavered in his belief, yet received an assurance that renewed his trust in God. At this point, however, the first line states Asaph's conviction that *God is good* to His people.

After the fashion of Hebrew poetry, the second part of this verse repeats the first part, but with some modification. God is good *to such as are of a clean heart,* or "to those who are pure in heart," as the *New International Version* renders it. This principle holds true for both Israel and the church: One will encounter God's wrath instead of His goodness if one's heart is contaminated by evil motives, selfish desires, and malicious thoughts. Such a condition will manifest itself in evil words and deeds. [See question #1, page 88.]

B. Near Disaster (vv. 2, 3)

2. But as for me, my feet were almost gone; my steps had well-nigh slipped.

In some of the earlier lessons in this series, we noted the slippery slope by which the people of Israel sank to the depths of idolatry and sin. Asaph himself had been on a similar slope, on the verge of losing his spiritual footing. The next verse tells how this happened.

3. For I was envious at the foolish, when I saw the prosperity of the wicked.

As he writes this song, Asaph is reflecting on the time when he *was envious at the foolish.* At the time when he was struggling with his faith,

How to Say It

ASAPH. *Ay*-saff.
GIBEON. *Gib*-e-un.

they did not seem so foolish. Their lifestyle appeared quite desirable, for it was a lifestyle of *prosperity. Wicked* people were getting rich, and Asaph was jealous. One who feels such jealousy is tempted to link wealth with wickedness, and to join in wickedness for the sake of getting rich. Verses 4-11 elaborate on the pride, prosperity, and corruption of foolish, wicked people who were doing remarkably well financially while appearing to thumb their noses at God. [See question #2, page 88.]

ENVY

"I'm just a valet, but I play God for a second and take charge of their cars," was the smug claim of a valet parking attendant at a Los Angeles restaurant. He then explained how he treats people who do not meet his standards. Local celebrities who have expensive cars and are good tippers will be called by name. Their cars will be parked near the entrance to the restaurant. At the very least, if their cars are parked farther away, they will be given preferential treatment over "lesser" people.

But too bad for you if you own an older or inexpensive car. And if the valet remembers you as a poor tipper, you may wait "forever" for him to bring your car to you. And then he just may leave a big, smudgy handprint on your window as he slams your door shut on you.

This may not be much of a problem to those of us who live in the suburbs or small towns, but in big cities where parking is at a premium, parking valets may well seem like gods. And then we may *really* be tempted to envy people who are more "blessed" with fame and wealth and convenience than we are. But while we are envying them, we should not forget the evil manner by which many of them obtained their wealth. We must remember that there are greater blessings than a fancy car, a convenient parking place, or any of a vast number of other things that our culture tempts us to view as "essentials." —C. R. B.

C. Summary (vv. 12, 13)

12. Behold, these are the ungodly, who prosper in the world; they increase in riches.

Here Asaph describes what each of us has observed going on *in the world:* ungodly people— people who care nothing about what God says or thinks—*prosper.*

13. Verily I have cleansed my heart in vain, and washed my hands in innocency.

While the wicked were getting rich, Asaph was trying diligently to keep his *heart* pure and his *hands* clean: he was thinking right and doing right. But what did he get for his efforts? Nothing but trouble and pain: "For all the day long have I been plagued, and chastened every morning" (v. 14). All his righteous living was *in vain*—useless and unprofitable. It wasn't fair! [See question #3, page 88.]

II. A Sure Faith
(Psalm 73:16-18, 21, 22)

The wealthy wicked were not thinking straight. They believed that evil was good for them because it paid off financially. In his envy, Asaph had begun to entertain this same twisted outlook. His thinking needed to be straightened out!

A. Inspired by the Sanctuary (vv. 16, 17)

16. When I thought to know this, it was too painful for me.

The *New International Version* reads, "When I tried to understand all this, it was oppressive to me." The facts could not be denied: the wicked seemed to be blessed in spite of their wickedness; Asaph and other honest men were struggling in spite of their righteousness. The more Asaph thought about this injustice and tried to understand it, the more he felt oppressed, burdened, weighed down, and pained by what appeared to be the facts of the matter.

17. Until I went into the sanctuary of God; then understood I their end.

A *sanctuary* is a holy place—a place set apart, or dedicated, to some sacred use or purpose. In Asaph's day, before Solomon built the magnificent temple in Jerusalem, two humbler places might have been called *the sanctuary of God*. One was the ancient tabernacle at Gibeon (1 Chronicles 21:29); the other was the tent in Jerusalem where David had placed the ark of the covenant (1 Chronicles 16:1). Asaph was chief of the musicians who was appointed at that time to "minister before the ark of the Lord" (1 Chronicles 16:4, 5). There in the sanctuary Asaph probably heard the teaching of the law, with its clear promise of blessing for obedience and cursing for disobedience (Deuteronomy 28). [See question #4, page 88.]

In the light of God's Word, it was evident that any advantage gained by the wicked was only temporary. In the light of God's Word, Asaph confessed, *Then understood I their end*. The final destiny of the wicked became apparent to him. He elaborates on this in the next verse.

B. Thinking Clearly (vv. 18, 21, 22)

18. Surely thou didst set them in slippery places: thou castedst them down into destruction.

Asaph himself had been close to *slippery places*—close to the point at which men coast

swiftly to sure *destruction*. But then he came to realize that the wealthy wicked whom he had envied were already there. Their final destiny would not change unless they changed their perspective as Asaph was now doing.

21. Thus my heart was grieved, and I was pricked in my reins.

As a result of his renewed perspective, Asaph became deeply and sincerely *grieved*. He was ashamed of what he had been thinking when he had envied the wealthy wicked; he was appalled by the thought of the destruction he had escaped. Perhaps he was also grieved for the sake of the wicked, who would meet such a horrible end.

The last part of this verse simply repeats the first part using other words (as is common in Hebrew poetry). The Hebrew word translated *reins* literally refers to the kidneys. The ancients thought of them (along with the heart) as the seat of one's inner feelings and emotions. (Note that the reins are said to "rejoice" in a wise son in Proverbs 23:16.)

22. So foolish was I, and ignorant: I was as a beast before thee.

Here the Hebrew word for *foolish* is not the one used earlier in verse 3. The word before us now describes the brutish behavior of an animal. This is consistent with the phrase *as a beast* in the latter part of the verse. The term *ignorant* literally says, "I did not know." Asaph's envy of the wicked had arisen from ignorance and lack of clear thinking. The perspective based on God's truth led him to the assurance that we see expressed in the rest of our printed text.

III. Security With God
(Psalm 73:23-26)

We who are reading this Psalm can have the same assurance as Asaph that our senseless blunders need not condemn us forever. God is merciful and gracious. He would rather forgive than destroy, rather reclaim than abandon. He is willing to be with us if we are willing to be with Him. But He will not be with us in the pursuit of any selfish, greedy, or wicked way. Only by choosing to walk in godly ways can we be assured of His company.

A. Companionship (v. 23)

23. Nevertheless I am continually with thee: thou hast holden me by my right hand.

Nevertheless, said Asaph—even though I was ignorant (v. 22) and "almost gone" (v. 2)—*I am continually with thee*. God's care for me is not one degree less than what it was before I embarked on my path of erroneous thinking. The

Home Daily Bible Readings

Monday, Nov. 2—My Feet Had Almost Stumbled (Psalm 73:1-14)

Tuesday, Nov. 3—I Went Into the Sanctuary of God (Psalm 73:15-20)

Wednesday, Nov. 4—I Was Foolish and Ignorant (Psalm 73:21-28)

Thursday, Nov. 5—Reassurance Is Found in Worship (Psalm 27:1-14)

Friday, Nov. 6—The Fate of the Wicked (Psalm 37:1-13)

Saturday, Nov. 7—Integrity Is Affirmed (Psalm 26:1-12)

Sunday, Nov. 8—The Lord Is Our Protector (Psalm 121:1-8)

second part of the verse adds another precious thought. Though I have learned to think straight, it is not by my wisdom that I am able to escape the destruction facing the wicked. Though I am willing to exert all my strength to stay close to God, it is not by my strength alone that I am able to prevail: *Thou hast holden me by my right hand.*

B. Guidance and Glory (v. 24)

24. Thou shalt guide me with thy counsel, and afterward receive me to glory.

The privilege of being with God includes the privilege of being guided by Him: by His *counsel*, which includes the wisdom of His Word. That leading is available to all of us if we make the effort both to know and to do what His Word teaches. *And afterward*, when I have followed God's leading faithfully, God will *receive me to glory*. Even in this world there is a glory that comes to one who walks with God over many years; but for the faithful follower of the Lord, there is more to come *afterward*. If this truth encouraged Asaph, how much more should it encourage us who live in the light of the empty tomb of Jesus?

C. The One and Only (v. 25)

25. Whom have I in heaven but thee? And there is none upon earth that I desire besides thee.

Heaven may have its angels—ten thousand times ten thousand, and more; but God is all I need. *On earth* I have family and friends and teachers and companions whose company I treasure; but all of them fade in comparison with God, whom I love with all my heart and with all my soul and with all my might (Deuteronomy 6:5). I'll walk with Him whether anyone else does or not. [See question #5, page 88.]

D. Source of Strength (v. 26)

26. My flesh and my heart faileth: but God is the strength of my heart, and my portion for ever.

My flesh and my heart faileth. My muscles, my mind, my motives, and my will are not enough to keep me walking faithfully with God in His way. *God is the strength of my heart.* My power fails, but His prevails. If my will is in accord with His will, and my mind agrees with His mind, and my motives are His motives, and my strength works with His strength, then with Asaph I can say, *God is . . . my portion for ever.*

"AMAZING GRACE"

"Amazing Grace," perhaps more than any other Christian hymn, has at times found a place even in the world of "secular" music. There is an amazing story behind this well-loved song.

During that tragic period of modern history when the African slave trade enriched Western profiteers, many people with Christian backgrounds rationalized their participation in this "business." One such man was an eighteenth-century Englishman, John Newton, who had grown up in a Christian home. However, when Newton went to sea as a young man, he left his faith behind.

Newton became captain of a slave ship and for years plied his gruesome trade, apparently without any influence from the faith he had once known. But the power of the gospel eventually overcame Newton, and he saw his trafficking in slaves for the awful sin that it was. Although he had amassed an ill-gained wealth that many would envy, through his conversion he came to realize that the grace of God and the gift of Heaven constituted a treasure worth far more:

> The Lord has promised good to me,
>   His word my hope secures;
> He will my shield and portion be
>   As long as life endures.

Newton's words echo those of Asaph in Psalm 73:25, 26: "There is none upon earth that I desire besides thee. . . . God is the strength of my heart, and my portion for ever."   —C. R. B.

Conclusion

Asaph was an extremely blessed man. As chief musician he was often in the Lord's sanctuary. He became acquainted with God's law; he led the sacred songs that praised it and reinforced its teaching.

As Christians, we are far more blessed than Asaph. Not only do we learn of God's Word in the sanctuary; we have it in our homes for daily study. We also have the books of the prophets who wrote after Asaph's time. Better still, we have the teaching of Christ and His apostles in the New Testament to add clarity and reinforcement to the lessons Asaph learned.

A. Watch Your Wanting

"Thou shalt not covet . . . any thing that is thy neighbor's" (Exodus 20:17). So said the law. Asaph violated that law when he envied the rich, even though they were wicked. Then in the sanctuary, he was reminded that he was envying people who were doomed to destruction. That was absurd.

It would be doubly absurd for us to fall into Asaph's error, especially when we have what Asaph never did—the teachings of Jesus and His apostles. Jesus said, "Take heed, and beware of covetousness: for a man's life consisteth not in the abundance of the things which he possesseth" (Luke 12:15). Paul wrote, "They that will be rich fall into temptation and a snare, and into many foolish and hurtful lusts, which drown men in destruction and perdition" (1 Timothy 6:9). We need to learn not to "trust in uncertain riches, but in the living God, who giveth us richly all things to enjoy" (v. 17).

What do you want most: to be rich, or to be with the Lord?

B. Afterward

I know that my Redeemer liveth,
  And on the earth again shall stand.

This joyous, triumphant hymn of Christian assurance is based on a similar statement of faith by Job (Job 19:25-27). Asaph may have been acquainted with the book of Job. As a musician, he probably knew the song of David that joyfully ends, "I will dwell in the house of the Lord for ever" (Psalm 23:6). From such sources, as well as from the direct inspiration of the Holy Spirit, Asaph seems to have expected not only God's guidance as long as he lived on earth, but also a glory that he would attain "afterward." Confidently he sang to the Lord, "Thou shalt guide me with thy counsel, and afterward receive me to glory."

The New Testament casts a flood of light on what earlier saints could view only dimly. It tells us, "Jesus Christ . . . hath abolished death, and hath brought life and immortality to light through the gospel" (2 Timothy 1:10). "The gift of God is eternal life through Jesus Christ our Lord" (Romans 6:23).

Is that fair? It is much better than fair! It is *grace*. The gift of eternal life is available because God loved the world (John 3:16). Even when we

This visual illustrates the golden text, which provides a good point on which to close today's lesson.

Visual for lesson 10

were sinners, He loved us—loved us so dearly that He gave His Son to die for us (Romans 5:8).

Yet even this matchless love is not irresistible. We can choose. We can accept the gift of eternal life, or we can receive the death that we have earned. Grievous sinners shall not inherit the kingdom of God (1 Corinthians 6:9, 10), but neither shall nice people who do not believe the good news of God's love (Mark 16:15, 16). Even church members who prefer to live like sinners can expect "judgment and fiery indignation" (Hebrews 10:26, 27).

Asaph nearly slipped, lured by the prospect of riches; and today we see many attracted by that same temptation. Others are seduced by pleasures incompatible with godliness. Then there are multitudes who just do not care. Sin has no overpowering attraction for them, but they make no effort to live for God. They are just coasting—but they are coasting downhill.

Asaph found straight thinking in the sanctuary. Here is a good example for all who are running away from God, or being lured away, or just drifting away. Go to church, and take Christian teaching to heart. Have a sanctuary at home where the family searches the Scriptures together. Let your thinking be shaped by God's Word. Then God will guide you by His counsel, and afterward receive you to glory.

C. Prayer

Almighty and everlasting Father, how richly You have blessed us with Your counsel! The call of riches is loud, and the call of pleasure is insistent; but above them all Your Word calls us day by day to the road that leads us afterward to glory. May Your power keep us on that road, we pray, and may Your grace forgive us when we foolishly turn aside. Amen.

D. Thought to Remember

Learn to view every circumstance from God's perspective.

Learning by Doing

This page contains an alternate lesson plan emphasizing learning activities.
Classes desiring such student involvement will find these suggestions helpful.

Learning Goals

After this lesson your students will be able to:

1. Explain Asaph's envy and how he overcame it.

2. List several reasons why believers sometimes envy unbelievers.

3. Suggest some ways Christians can encourage one another to keep an eternal, unenvious perspective.

Into the Lesson

Begin by asking your students to name their favorite Psalms. Likely several will say Psalm 23. Others may say Psalm 1. Ask if some would like to quote their favorite Psalms.

Psalms is a book of poetry. The writers—including David and Asaph—expressed their deepest feelings and thoughts in the poems that make up the book of Psalms. Point out that many of the hymns and gospel songs we sing as a part of worship are Psalms set to music.

Into the Word

Psalm 73 begins by stating a basic belief that Asaph had arrived at as the result of a significant crisis in his life (v. 1). The rest of the Psalm shows how he arrived at this basic belief. Begin this part of the lesson by writing GOD IS GOOD on the chalkboard. Then ask students to answer the question, "How has God been good to you in the past week?"

Asaph began to describe the crisis in his life in verse 2. Suggest that most of the significant insights in our lives develop out of crises. Maybe some of your students can tell about a time when a crisis gave them a new spiritual insight or a clearer view of God and His goodness.

Get at the heart of the lesson by writing the following open-ended sentence on newsprint and asking students to suggest completions:

"When I see a wicked person who
is successful and prosperous, I feel . . ."

Urge students to be honest, and to express how they really feel. Their responses probably will fall into two categories:

• "It isn't fair!" This questions the goodness and fairness of God. But did God ever promise that life would be fair?

• "If the wicked prosper, what's the use of trying to be righteous and trying to do the right

thing?" (see v. 13). This questions the value of right living—as if success and prosperity in this life is the only reason for right living.

Does anyone feel sorry for them? The apparent prosperity of the wicked is often what keeps such people from seeing their need for a Savior. We should pity them rather than envy them.

Asaph was not thinking clearly. He was looking at life from the wrong perspective. Direct your students to Psalm 73:16-18. In that passage, what did Asaph say he did to correct his faulty perspective? (He went to the sanctuary, probably the tent where the ark of God was kept. For us, this could mean a place of worship or any place where we can talk with God and meditate on His will.)

Asaph felt he had a legitimate gripe, and he took his complaint to God. Ask:

• What do you do when you feel that God is being unfair?

• How do you express your complaints to God?

• How does God respond to your complaints?

Into Life

Since we are human, and since we are surrounded by wicked people who prosper and good people who flounder physically, emotionally, and financially, we are susceptible to the faulty thinking that afflicted Asaph. However, we have some advantages that the psalmist did not have. Ask your students to suggest what some of these advantages are. For example:

1. We have the completed Scriptures, which show the ultimate end of both the wicked and the righteous.

2. We have Jesus, who loved us and died for us.

3. We have the indwelling of the Holy Spirit.

4. We have the support and encouragement of fellow Christians, many of whom have already struggled with this issue.

In closing, tell your students we need to make two responses to today's lesson: First, we need to encourage each other and remind each other of our blessings in Christ. Then we will not envy those who have earthly riches only. Second, we need to feel compassion for wicked and prosperous sinners. Encourage your students to make a commitment to do one thing during the coming week to encourage a fellow believer or reach out to a successful sinner. Close with prayer.

Let's Talk It Over

The questions on this page are designed to encourage review of the lesson Scriptures and to promote discussion of the lesson by the class. The answers provided are only discussion starters. Let your class talk it over from there.

1. "Truly God is good to Israel," Asaph said, and Christians also like to give God credit for the good things in their lives. The wicked are also "blessed" at times, but they do not give God credit. How would you answer a skeptic who said his—and your—blessings have nothing to do with God but are simply the result of hard work and personal effort?

The Christian believes James, that "every good gift and every perfect gift is from above, and cometh down from the Father of lights" (James 1:17). Often these are a matter of God's grace, given without regard for whether a person "deserves" such favor. Some are providential. As Creator, God is the source of such blessings as sunshine and rain, which He gives to the righteous and unrighteous alike (Matthew 5:45).

However, spiritual blessings (Ephesians 1:3) are the special inheritance of believers. The unbeliever can neither receive nor appreciate such blessings, which are superior to material blessings and enhance one's enjoyment of those blessings. The skeptic may be more impressed by the believer's contentment with lesser material blessings (1 Timothy 6:6, 7) than by an affluent Christian who gives God credit.

2. Asaph was troubled by the economic prosperity the wicked in his day were enjoying. We also may be tempted to envy the wicked for the same reason. How can we keep from envying such people?

Asaph came to his senses when he looked beyond the immediate situation and saw the results of the wicked's behavior (vv. 17, 18). There is nothing to envy in that! We, too, need to look more to the goal of our faith, to the eternal, and not get stuck in the temporal. Paul said whatever troubles we endure in this life "are not worthy to be compared with the glory" we will receive (Romans 8:18). If we focus on eternal matters, we will be touched with compassion for those who, though they may have much physical wealth now, are spiritually impoverished and without a Savior. We will want to share Jesus with them.

3. The psalmist was almost to the point of giving up. He felt he had "cleansed [his] heart in vain." Suppose a friend said, "I'm dropping out of church. It's just no use. I can't live the
Christian life, and it hasn't done me any good to try. I still have a huge credit card bill, I can't afford the mortgage, and my husband's job just got cut out with downsizing." How would you answer her?

Your friend will need compassion and encouragement. Perhaps you could share today's lesson text with her, or tell her of a time in your own life when you endured some lean times with the Lord's help.

4. Asaph gained victory over his temptation to envy the wicked when he "went into the sanctuary of God." How can our Christian worship help us to deal with envy and other temptations?

True worship should help us to focus on God instead of ourselves or others. This will help to realign our thinking. Recall that Peter was able to walk on the water as long as he kept his eyes on Jesus (Matthew 14:30). The writer of Hebrews tells us we need to be "looking unto Jesus" (Hebrews 12:2). True worship helps us do that.

In addition, worship that is centered in Biblical truth will provide us with many reminders of man's eternal destiny. We will find our attention drawn to the heavenly blessings awaiting the righteous and to the terrible fate in store for the wicked. Then, rather than giving ourselves to envying the wicked, we will be inspired to dedicating ourselves to evangelizing them.

5. Asaph finally came to realize that, if he had God, he had enough (v. 25). How can we help one another come to, and live with, the same realization?

What do we cherish most on earth? Do our family, our possessions, and our friends occupy a more important place in our heart than God does? Asaph's prayer is beneficial in causing us to take a fresh look at our priorities. We should be able to make that prayer our own. If not, then we are guilty of a form of idolatry, putting things or other persons ahead of God in our affections.

We need to demonstrate with our lifestyle that God comes first. When for the sake of the gospel we can sacrifice material wealth, either by giving it away or refusing to amass it, we will help others to appreciate the truth of Asaph's prayer.

False Hopes and Judgment

DEVOTIONAL READING: Joshua 24:14-28.

LESSON SCRIPTURE: Jeremiah 19; 21:1-10.

PRINTED TEXT: Jeremiah 19:1-4, 10, 11; 21:1, 2, 8-10.

Jeremiah 19:1-4, 10, 11

1 Thus saith the LORD, Go and get a potter's earthen bottle, and take of the ancients of the people, and of the ancients of the priests;

2 And go forth unto the valley of the son of Hinnom, which is by the entry of the east gate, and proclaim there the words that I shall tell thee:

3 And say, Hear ye the word of the LORD, O kings of Judah, and inhabitants of Jerusalem; Thus saith the LORD of hosts, the God of Israel; Behold, I will bring evil upon this place, the which whosoever heareth, his ears shall tingle.

4 Because they have forsaken me, and have estranged this place, and have burned incense in it unto other gods, whom neither they nor their fathers have known, nor the kings of Judah, and have filled this place with the blood of innocents.

. . . .

10 Then shalt thou break the bottle in the sight of the men that go with thee,

11 And shalt say unto them, Thus saith the LORD of hosts; Even so will I break this people and this city, as one breaketh a potter's vessel, that cannot be made whole again: and they shall bury them in Tophet, till there be no place to bury.

Jeremiah 21:1, 2, 8-10

1 The word which came unto Jeremiah from the LORD, when king Zedekiah sent unto him Pashur the son of Melchiah, and Zephaniah the son of Maaseiah the priest, saying,

2 Inquire, I pray thee, of the LORD for us; for Nebuchadrezzar king of Babylon maketh war against us; if so be that the LORD will deal with us according to all his wondrous works, that he may go up from us.

. . . .

8 And unto this people thou shalt say, Thus saith the LORD; Behold, I set before you the way of life, and the way of death.

9 He that abideth in this city shall die by the sword, and by the famine, and by the pestilence: but he that goeth out, and falleth to the Chaldeans that besiege you, he shall live, and his life shall be unto him for a prey.

10 For I have set my face against this city for evil, and not for good, saith the LORD: it shall be given into the hand of the king of Babylon, and he shall burn it with fire.

GOLDEN TEXT: Thus saith the LORD; Behold, I set before you the way of life, and the way of death.—Jeremiah 21:8.

God Calls a People to Faithful Living
Unit 4: God Judges and Renews
(Lessons 11-13)

Lesson Aims

After participating in this lesson, the students should be able to:

1. Summarize the warnings Jeremiah gave to Jerusalem in today's text.

2. List some of the false hopes that cause people to ignore God's warnings today.

3. Give thanks to God for Jesus, who gives us living hope in place of judgment.

Lesson Outline

INTRODUCTION
    A. Smashing Microscopes and Destroying
      Viruses
    B. Lesson Background
  I. WARNING (Jeremiah 19:1-4, 10, 11)
    A. The Audience (v. 1)
    B. The Place (v. 2)
    C. The Message (v. 3)
    D. The Reason (v. 4)
      Taking Risks
    E. The Illustration (vv. 10, 11)
      Getting Our Attention
  II. ANOTHER WARNING (Jeremiah 21:1, 2, 8-10)
    A. The King's Question (vv. 1, 2)
    B. The Lord's Advice (vv. 8, 9)
    C. The Prophet's Explanation (v. 10)
CONCLUSION
    A. God's Patience
    B. God's Punishment
    C. Prayer
    D. Thought to Remember

Introduction

More than a hundred years ago, according to an oft-repeated story, a missionary doctor had a microscope delivered to his outpost in central Africa. He wanted to examine the water supply of a tribe that was plagued by sickness and early death.

As the doctor expected, he found the water contaminated with deadly bacteria. In that isolated place he could think of but one remedy. The natives would have to learn to boil their drinking water. To begin a campaign of education, the doctor asked the chief to come and look through the microscope.

The chief was horrified when he saw the fearsome creatures wriggling in the water, but he had a ready solution. He picked up a heavy stone and smashed the microscope.

A. Smashing Microscopes and Destroying Viruses

Two weeks ago we read how Amos exposed the deadly virus of idolatry in Bethel. But instead of working to destroy the virus, Amaziah, the priest of Bethel, told Amos to take his message of doom back to Judah (Amos 7:7-13).

Last week we turned back to a time approximately two centuries before the time of Amos. Asaph was infected with the viruses of greed and envy. When he "went into the sanctuary of God" (Psalm 73:17), he saw those deadly monsters exposed by the microscope of God's truth. His response was better than that of the African chief or of Amaziah. Instead of smashing the microscope, he destroyed the viruses and gained renewed confidence in the Lord's promises.

This week we move forward to a time more than a century after Amos. The prophet Jeremiah was by this time exposing the viruses of idolatry and sin in Judah, as Amos had done in Israel. The people of Judah had already seen their sister nation to the north deported by the Assyrians, so they should have known how deadly was the virus with which they had been infected. But instead of taking action against the viruses, many people of Judah wanted to take action against Jeremiah (Jeremiah 26:8-11).

Jeremiah, however, remained undaunted; he continued to expose the sins that were destroying Judah. Though the people did not silence him, neither did they heed him. In time, the nation fell to Babylon.

An epidemic is never stopped by smashing a microscope, and a nation is never preserved by ignoring the truth.

B. Lesson Background

The book of Jeremiah is a collection of the messages that Jeremiah delivered during the approximately forty years of his ministry. In addition, the book includes important historical material. Many of Jeremiah's prophecies are not dated, including the one with which today's printed text begins. (The second portion, from chapter 21, names Zedekiah as king, so we are able to establish the time of that writing with more precision. Zedekiah was Judah's last king, so the events of chapter 21 come near the end of the nation, not long before the Babylonian captivity began.) Some students believe that the first section belongs to the time when King Josiah was leading Judah in obedience to God's law (2 Chronicles 34:29-33). Others link it to the time of Jehoiakim's reign, when Judah's subjection to Babylon had begun (see Daniel 1:1, 2). Jeremiah 19:3-5 seems to describe a time when the kings of Judah needed to be warned about their evil actions. Jehoiakim certainly merited such a warning (2 Kings 23:36, 37).

I. Warning
(Jeremiah 19:1-4, 10, 11)
A. The Audience (v. 1)

1. Thus saith the LORD, Go and get a potter's earthen bottle, and take of the ancients of the people, and of the ancients of the priests.

Thus saith the Lord. This lets us know that our text begins with instructions given by the Lord to Jeremiah. *A potter's earthen bottle* would be a jar of some sort made of clay and baked in an oven. This one was to serve as a visual aid for Jeremiah's message, much as another clay pot did earlier (18:1-10).

The term *ancients* translates the Hebrew word that is usually rendered as "elders." Jeremiah was told to gather an audience consisting of Judah's respected leaders. Perhaps these men would be more apt to listen to what the prophet had to say.

B. The Place (v. 2)

2. And go forth unto the valley of the son of Hinnom, which is by the entry of the east gate, and proclaim there the words that I shall tell thee.

The valley of the son of Hinnom is sometimes called the valley of Hinnom (Joshua 15:8; 18:16; Nehemiah 11:30). It lay outside the south wall of Jerusalem. Here what we might call the "city dump" was located. The Hebrew term for "valley of Hinnom" became, in Greek, *Gehenna,* which is the New Testament word translated "Hell."

Other versions refer to *the east gate* as "the potsherd gate." A gate leading to the dump might easily get such a name because the ground around it would be littered with fragments of broken clay pots discarded there.

C. The Message (v. 3)

3. And say, Hear ye the word of the LORD, O kings of Judah, and inhabitants of Jerusalem; Thus saith the LORD of hosts, the God of Israel; Behold, I will bring evil upon this place, the which whosoever heareth, his ears shall tingle.

The phrase *kings of Judah* probably refers to the entire royal family. Only one of them was actually king, but the Lord wanted all of them (including those who would one day be king) to know about the message. Jeremiah's words

applied to the powerful and mighty as well as to the common *inhabitants of Jerusalem.*

I will bring evil upon this place. This was the heart of Jeremiah's message. The word *evil* does not mean that the punishment of Jerusalem was wrong; it means that the punishment was harmful. It was to be so disastrous that anyone hearing about it would find *his ears* tingling with the shock of the news. Similar language is found in 1 Samuel 3:11 and 2 Kings 21:12. [See question #1, page 96.]

D. The Reason (v. 4)

4. Because they have forsaken me, and have estranged this place, and have burned incense in it unto other gods, whom neither they nor their fathers have known, nor the kings of Judah, and have filled this place with the blood of innocents.

Because they have forsaken me summarizes the basic sin committed by the people of Judah. We should recall God's words concerning Israel when the elders requested that Samuel give them a king: "They have rejected me" (1 Samuel 8:7). This is what Jeremiah's countrymen had done. The rest of this verse lists some of the evils that had accompanied forsaking God.

First, the people had *estranged this place.* Jerusalem was the place God had chosen, in order to put His name there (1 Kings 11:36). In a special sense, it was the city of God. But the people of Jerusalem had made the city a stranger to Him. He did not want His name associated with such a sinful place.

Second, they had *burned incense in it unto other gods.* The use of incense was permitted in the law of Moses (Exodus 30:1). But now, incense was being used in the worship of other gods—gods unknown to the people, *their fathers,* and their *kings.*

Third, they had *filled this place with the blood of innocents.* Taking *this place* to mean the valley of Hinnom, some students think this refers

This visual illustrates Jeremiah's dramatic demonstration of the destruction coming on Jerusalem.

(On the visual for lesson 13 is a map you may find useful for this lesson. See page 109.)

Visual for lesson 11

to the burning of innocent children in sacrifice to Molech, the bloodthirsty god of the Ammonites. This sometimes took place in the valley of Hinnom (Jeremiah 32:35). Among those who participated in this were King Ahaz and King Manasseh (2 Kings 16:2, 3; 21:1, 6).

However, in the verse before us it seems better to take *this place* to mean Jerusalem, where the acts by which innocent blood was shed were many. King Manasseh is said to have "shed innocent blood very much, till he had filled Jerusalem from one end to another" (2 Kings 21:16).

Verses 5-9 continue the description of the sins of Jerusalem and the punishment that was imminent.

TAKING RISKS

So you think you're safe in your own home? Think again! While at home, during a typical year:

• One of every 400 Americans will be injured in bed by the headboard falling on them or the bed frame collapsing.

• One in 13 will suffer an injury requiring medical attention.

• One in 350,000 will be electrocuted.

Things get worse, or at least more tragic, when we step outside our front door:

• One in 40,000 will die as pedestrians in urban traffic accidents.

• One in 11,000 will die *inside* an automobile.

These dangers and a multitude of others are discussed in *The Book of Risks* (1994), written by a University of Hawaii professor named Larry Laudan. Read it only if you're feeling especially brave! It is apparent that many risks must be accepted as the natural consequences of living in our complex, modern society.

But some risks we don't have to take. The punishment of ancient Judah reminds us that godlessness will bring certain retribution from the Lord. God's judgment came upon those people because of their wicked behavior. If we are wise, we will learn from them and take the necessary steps to avoid such risks.   —C. R. B.

E. The Illustration (vv. 10, 11)

10, 11. Then shalt thou break the bottle in the sight of the men that go with thee, and shalt say unto them, Thus saith the LORD of hosts; Even so will I break this people and this city, as one breaketh a potter's vessel, that cannot be made whole again: and they shall bury them in Tophet, till there be no place to bury.

As the climax to his brief message, Jeremiah was to *break* the clay jar, probably by hurling it to the ground so that it would shatter into pieces and be lost among the other fragments of pottery

---

How to Say It

AHAZ. *Ay*-haz.
AMAZIAH. Am-uh-*zye*-uh.
ASAPH. *Ay*-saff.
ASSYRIANS. Uh-*sear*-ee-unz.
BABYLON. *Bab*-uh-lun.
BABYLONIANS. Bab-uh-*low*-nee-unz.
CHALDEANS. Kal-*dee*-unz.
GEHENNA. Geh-*hen*-uh.
HINNOM. *Hin*-um.
JEHOIACHIN. Jeh-*hoy*-uh-kin.
JEHOIAKIM. Jeh-*hoy*-uh-kim.
JEREMIAH. Jair-uh-*my*-uh.
MAASEIAH. May-uh-*see*-yuh.
MANASSEH. Muh-*nass*-uh.
MELCHIAH. Mel-*kye*-uh.
MOLECH. *Mo*-lek.
NEBUCHADNEZZAR. *Neb*-uh-kad-*nezz*-er (strong accent on *nezz*).
NEBUCHADREZZAR. *Neb*-uh-kad-*rezz*-er (strong accent on *rezz*).
PASHUR. *Pash*-er.
TOPHET. *Toe*-fet.
ZEDEKIAH. Zed-uh-*kye*-uh.
ZEPHANIAH. Zef-uh-*nye*-uh.

---

that lay near the potsherd gate. The jar would be beyond repair—a fitting description of how Jerusalem and its people would be crushed because of their disobedience.

Tophet was a place in the valley of Hinnom where children were burned in pagan sacrifice, probably to the idol Molech (Jeremiah 7:31). It was to become the burial place of those sinners who would die during the siege and the destruction of Jerusalem, and it would be filled to overflowing with their corpses. [See question #2, page 96.]

GETTING OUR ATTENTION

"His employee's driving his car. So how come he's not worried?" The "he" in this case is a relaxed and smiling executive pictured in a magazine advertisement for a product called *DriveRight*. This "responsible driving monitor" is a computerized device that allows the boss to set the limits of speed and acceleration that he will allow while one of his employees drives his car.

When an employee/driver exceeds those limits, an alarm sounds a warning, indicating to the employee that the boss will have a record of the infraction. The boss will know how many times the limits have been violated as well as whether the errant employee has tried to tamper with the device. Presumably, the employee would receive appropriate discipline for violating the boss's driving standards.

Jeremiah's act of breaking the potter's vessel was God's way of getting Judah's attention and letting the people know that He was aware that they had violated His standards. God knew their long history of disregard for His will, both as individuals and as a nation.

God also knows when *our* behavior violates His standards. Jeremiah's words and actions are a warning to us as well: God is still serious about sin and its consequences. —C. R. B.

II. Another Warning
(Jeremiah 21:1, 2, 8-10)

Now we leap forward in time, perhaps about fifteen years. During this time, some important changes in Judah took place.

First, King Jehoiakim stopped paying the required tribute to Babylon. The consequences of such an act were predictable: Nebuchadnezzar returned to Judah with his army. During this time, Jehoiakim died and was replaced on the throne by Jehoiachin. After a reign of only three months, Jehoiachin was forced to surrender to Nebuchadnezzar. He was taken to Babylon, along with the leading men of his government and the craftsmen and smiths (who were capable of making weapons). In all, ten thousand captives were transported to Babylon. Zedekiah was left to be king in Jerusalem and to pay tribute to Babylon. The record of these events is found in 2 Kings 24.

Second, after ruling approximately eight years, Zedekiah stopped paying tribute. Nebuchadnezzar's troops returned and laid siege to Jerusalem for approximately a year and a half (2 Kings 25:1-3). With food supplies running dangerously low and despair running high, King Zedekiah sent a question to Jeremiah, with which the next part of our printed text begins.

A. The King's Question (vv. 1, 2)

1. The word which came unto Jeremiah from the LORD, when king Zedekiah sent unto him Pashur the son of Melchiah, and Zephaniah the son of Maaseiah the priest, saying.

Before relating *the word which came unto Jeremiah from the Lord*, we are given the explanation of what called for it. Jerusalem was surrounded by overwhelming numbers of Babylonian troops, and *King Zedekiah* sent two of his advisers to the prophet Jeremiah with the question that follows. [See question #3, page 96.]

2. Inquire, I pray thee, of the LORD for us; for Nebuchadrezzar king of Babylon maketh war against us; if so be that the LORD will deal with us according to all his wondrous works, that he may go up from us.

King Zedekiah understood that Jeremiah was a prophet *of the Lord*, so he asked Jeremiah to take his question to the Lord for an answer. Throughout Israel's history, the Lord had done many *wondrous works* on behalf of His people. At this point, Zedekiah may have been thinking especially of the Assyrian invasion a little more than a century earlier. The Assyrians had brought a massive army to capture Jerusalem, but the Lord had inflicted huge losses upon them (2 Kings 19:35, 36). Would the Lord now perform yet another miracle and do away with the Babylonians? This was likely what the king wanted to know.

We may wonder why the king of Babylon's name is spelled *Nebuchadrezzar* (with an *r* in the middle) rather than the more common *Nebuchadnezzar* (with an *n*). The spelling with the *r* is actually closer to the spelling of this name in the language of the Babylonians. The slight difference may simply have arisen out of the attempt to bring a foreign name into the Hebrew language. [See question #4, page 96.]

In verses 3-7 Zedekiah's question was answered in the plainest of terms. This time the Lord was going to fight against Jerusalem and Judah. He would not rescue them; He would turn them over to the Babylonians. The next verses of our printed text record the Lord's counsel to the people under siege in Jerusalem.

B. The Lord's Advice (vv. 8, 9)

8. And unto this people thou shalt say, Thus saith the LORD; Behold, I set before you the way of life, and the way of death.

Verses 3-7 were addressed to the king (v. 3). Now we read a message to the *people* besieged in Jerusalem. The Lord was giving them a choice between *the way of life, and the way of death*, much as Moses did centuries earlier (Deuteronomy 30:15). [See question #5, page 96.]

9. He that abideth in this city shall die by the sword, and by the famine, and by the pestilence: but he that goeth out, and falleth to the Chaldeans that besiege you, he shall live, and his life shall be unto him for a prey.

Jerusalem was going to be captured. That was certain (v. 10). Perhaps, however, this message was given soon after the Babylonian army arrived. The siege was going to last more than a year. The way of death (v. 8) was to stay in the doomed city. The food supply would be exhausted, and many people would die *by the famine*. In addition there would be a *pestilence*, an epidemic of disease. That would bring death to many. And when at last the invaders would breach the walls and force their way into the starving city, *by the sword* they would slaughter without mercy all who would seem inclined to resist them.

There was, however, another possibility: the people did not have to stay in the city and die there. The way of life (v. 8) was to go out and surrender *to the Chaldeans. (Chaldeans* is another name for the Babylonians.) One who chose to surrender would be taken to Babylon as a captive, but he would not die of starvation or be killed by the sword. He would be a part of the prey taken by the enemy, but *his life* would be *unto him for a prey:* The enemy might seize his goods and possessions as part of the spoils, but he himself would be kept alive.

As one might expect, such a message was not well received by the people of Jerusalem. Most of them considered Jeremiah's message unpatriotic and branded him a traitor (Jeremiah 26:8-11). He became the target of bitter opposition (37:11-15; 38:1-6). In the end, however, his words proved true, as God's words always do.

C. The Prophet's Explanation (v. 10)

10. For I have set my face against this city for evil, and not for good, saith the LORD: it shall be given into the hand of the king of Babylon, and he shall burn it with fire.

No longer was there any hope for Jerusalem, for the Lord himself was *against this city*. The time of reckoning had come. *The king of Babylon* was going to conquer the city and *burn it with fire*. The King of Heaven and earth had decreed it. If Zedekiah was hoping for a more positive word from God's prophet, he was sadly disappointed.

Home Daily Bible Readings

Monday, Nov. 9—I Went Down to the Potter's House (Jeremiah 18:1-11)
Tuesday, Nov. 10—I Will Bring Evil on This Place (Jeremiah 19:1-9)
Wednesday, Nov. 11—I Will Break This People and Their City (Jeremiah 19:10-15)
Thursday, Nov. 12—Jeremiah Is Placed in the Stocks (Jeremiah 20:1-6)
Friday, Nov. 13—Jeremiah's Complaint (Jeremiah 20:7-18)
Saturday, Nov. 14—I Myself Will Fight Against You (Jeremiah 21:1-10)
Sunday, Nov. 15—They Have Forsaken the Covenant of the Lord God (Jeremiah 22:1-9)

Conclusion

As we look back over the time spanned by the lessons of this quarter, two wonders stand out. They are God's patience and God's punishment.

A. God's Patience

God called the nation of Israel to keep His law and enjoy His blessing. He led that nation out of bondage in Egypt, but it was so rebellious that He thought of destroying it even before it reached the promised land (Exodus 32:9, 10). Yet His patience waited, and waited, and waited. We have seen in today's lesson how Judah finally reached a point when God's judgment could not be withheld. This was approximately eight hundred years after the deliverance of the people from Egypt.

Centuries later God sent His Son to establish a New Covenant with peoples around the world. Jesus laid the foundation for an eternal kingdom. Then He returned to Heaven, promising to come again. Even before that century was done, however, scoffers began to doubt His promise. Peter explained that Jesus is waiting patiently because God is "not willing that any should perish, but that all should come to repentance" (2 Peter 3:9). Nineteen centuries have passed, and He is still waiting—waiting for people to repent and be saved. What wonderful patience!

B. God's Punishment

God's punishment has always been as certain as His patience. He waited eight hundred years for His chosen people to become what He desired them to be; but then He sent the Babylonians to destroy His temple and carry thousands into captivity in a distant land.

Today we live under the New Covenant established by Jesus. Sometimes we hear people say, "God is love. God is merciful and gracious. He would never condemn anyone to Hell." But Jesus said that one day He will say, "Depart from me, ye cursed, into everlasting fire, prepared for the devil and his angels" (Matthew 25:41). Whom will you believe?

C. Prayer

Merciful Father, we are saddened by the doom that befell Jerusalem, and saddened yet more by the thought of everlasting fire. Give us courage, we pray, and keep us faithful until we stand in Your presence. Amen.

D. Thought to Remember

"I have no pleasure in the death of him that dieth, saith the Lord God: wherefore turn yourselves, and live ye" (Ezekiel 18:32).

Learning by Doing

This page contains an alternate lesson plan emphasizing learning activities.
Classes desiring such student involvement will find these suggestions helpful.

Learning Goals

As a result of studying this lesson, your students should be able to:

1. Summarize the warnings Jeremiah gave to Jerusalem in today's text.

2. List some of the false hopes that cause people to ignore God's warnings today.

3. Give thanks to God for Jesus, who gives us living hope in place of judgment.

Into the Lesson

Introduce the idea of false hopes and ignored warnings by posing the following situations and asking your students to suggest some false hopes that would cause people to persist in harmful and self-destructive behaviors in each situation:

• A doctor warns a smoker that his cigarettes are killing him, but he doesn't want to give up smoking. (False hope: "Other smokers may get cancer, but not me.")

• A neighbor with whom you have been sharing the gospel refuses to respond to its message, saying, "I'm just as good as So-and-so [a member of your church]. If he's going to Heaven, then I am, too." (False hope: "My good works can save me apart from Jesus.")

The people of Judah greeted Jeremiah's warning of divine judgment with the false hope that God would never destroy His own special people. In today's lesson we'll look at Jeremiah's prophetic messages and see how they apply to the false hopes we or people around us may have.

Into the Word

Provide some background information on the prophet Jeremiah. Using Jeremiah 1:1-3, do a brief lecture on who Jeremiah was and when he prophesied. Use a chronological chart (like the visual for lesson 2) to help you show when Jeremiah was prophesying and who the contemporary kings were. Note Jeremiah 1:13-19 and summarize his message and the general response God told Jeremiah to expect. Use Jeremiah 18:18 to illustrate how people responded to Jeremiah's message.

Now divide your class into groups to take a closer look at Jeremiah's prophetic message. Assign each group to find answers to one of the study questions below by studying Jeremiah 19:1-11; 21:1-10.

1. To whom was Jeremiah's message addressed? (See 19:1, 3; 21:3.)

2. What was the content of Jeremiah's message? (See 19:3, 6-9, 11; 21:8-10.)

3. What precipitated Jeremiah's message? What had the people done to call forth the message? (See 19:4, 5.)

Point out verses 1, 2 of Jeremiah 21. Ask, "What false hope is implied in the king's question?" (That God would deliver His people and not allow the Babylonians to take Jerusalem.) Ask whether anyone knows why the king would believe such a thing. (Refer the class to 2 Kings 19:14-19, 35-37 for the answer.)

The people of Judah believed that God would not send judgment on His own special people and His own special city. Ask your students to suggest some false hopes that cause people to ignore God's warnings today. For example:

• "God loves us too much to punish us."

• "Those stories about God's judgment in the Old Testament are myths. God doesn't work that way."

• "Other people are a lot worse than we are."

In contrast to attractive and appealing false hopes, God offers true and genuine hope through Jesus Christ.

Into Life

True and living hope—the hope that comes from God—is what makes life worth living. Hope in place of judgment is something to be thankful for. Ask a volunteer to read 1 Peter 1:3-5. Note that our hope, individually and personally, is in Jesus Christ. While the people of Judah hoped in their nation as God's chosen possession, we who are in Christ have a personal hope in Him.

In closing, hand a sheet of paper to each student and challenge each one to list five reasons for hope for which he or she would like to thank God. You can start them off by suggesting that we all can thank God for Jesus Christ. Without Jesus, none of us would have any hope.

When your students have compiled their lists, urge them to take the lists home and display them in a prominent place—perhaps fastened to the refrigerator with magnets. Every day they need to be reminded that God wants to give them hope rather than judgment. But if they reject the message of hope, judgment is sure.

Let's Talk It Over

The questions on this page are designed to encourage review of the lesson Scriptures and to promote discussion of the lesson by the class. The answers provided are only discussion starters. Let your class talk it over from there.

1. Jeremiah stood in a public place and declared "the word of the Lord" to the people of Judah. How can we deliver "the word of the Lord" to our own generation, to the people of our community?

Once in a while you will still see a preacher standing in a public square preaching to those who pass by. Most people do just that: they pass by without listening. Some other means is necessary to get people's attention. Some churches have found that large billboards on busy highways have attracted people to come and hear God's Word proclaimed. Other churches have found web pages on the Internet to be successful. Jesus encouraged us to let our behavior act as a beacon to God's love (Matthew 5:16). Whatever we do, we need to take advantage of the opportunities our own time and place offer us, and our behavior must be consistent with our message.

2. Jeremiah used the shattering of a clay jar as a means of symbolizing Jerusalem's approaching destruction. What are some symbols that could be used to visualize the corruption in our society and the dangers to which we have exposed ourselves?

Jeremiah used an image common to the people he was warning. Jesus used the same practice when He told parables about farmers and merchants and landowners. We need to show the same sensitivity to people's interests and experience. If we are talking to computer users, we might suggest sin is like a computer virus that will eventually destroy and shut down the system. If we are talking with people familiar with farming or gardening, we might compare the evils in the culture with weeds that will choke out what is wholesome. People living in earthquake-prone areas understand the danger of building on a fault line. We might suggest that sin has created a fault in the foundation of our society and the equivalent of a massive earthquake may be nearing.

3. The common reaction to Jeremiah's message was to ignore it or to belittle it. Then Zedekiah wanted Jeremiah to make inquiry of the Lord for him! Why do you think he did this? Why do you suppose he would be willing to believe Jeremiah at that time when he had not

before? What lesson do you see in this event for us today?

Perhaps the king had noticed over time that Jeremiah's prophecies were unfailingly accurate and he was, even if reluctantly, coming to faith. Such a case would suggest we need to keep on testifying for the Lord, for we never know when hearts might finally change and turn to Him.

The question suggests some wishful thinking on Zedekiah's part, however. Perhaps he was hoping to get Jeremiah to say what he was hoping to hear. There will always be those who want us to speak in behalf of the Lord what He has not said, but what they want to hear. We must speak the truth plainly and boldly as Jeremiah did.

4. What are some of the false hopes that people today cling to?

Like Judah in Jeremiah's time we may take comfort in God's past acts of deliverance on our behalf. Our society has survived wars, natural disasters, economic collapses, and other crises. But we have no guarantee that God will continue to preserve a society that ignores His laws.

Many people trust in technology and education to solve the ills of society. But technology is merely a tool. In the hands of a godless technician, this tool can do nothing to address the spiritual ills of society.

Many people have abandoned the God of the Bible. They have the false hope that God—if there is a God, they can never be quite sure—will surely save them if they are relatively good people. Their hope is not founded on Jesus Christ, and it is vain.

5. Through Jeremiah the Lord told the people, "Behold, I set before you the way of life, and the way of death." What significance, if any, do you see in this statement?

Though Jeremiah referred to a particular situation at a particular time, it is illustrative of God's dealings with man through the ages. In the garden He gave Adam and Eve the same choice. Moses' challenge to Israel in Deuteronomy 30:15 and Joshua's in Joshua 24:15 are similar. The New Testament echoes the same theme; see John 3:16, for example. The Lord's final invitation is, "Whosoever will, let him take the water of life freely" (Revelation 22:17).

Hope From God's Promise

DEVOTIONAL READING: **Revelation 21:1-7.**

LESSON SCRIPTURE: **Ezekiel 37.**

PRINTED TEXT: **Ezekiel 37:1-11a, 25-27.**

Ezekiel 37:1-11a, 25-27

1 The hand of the LORD was upon me, and carried me out in the Spirit of the LORD, and set me down in the midst of the valley which was full of bones,

2 And caused me to pass by them round about: and, behold, there were very many in the open valley; and, lo, they were very dry.

3 And he said unto me, Son of man, can these bones live? And I answered, O Lord GOD, thou knowest.

4 Again he said unto me, Prophesy upon these bones, and say unto them, O ye dry bones, hear the word of the LORD.

5 Thus saith the Lord GOD unto these bones; Behold, I will cause breath to enter into you, and ye shall live:

6 And I will lay sinews upon you, and will bring up flesh upon you, and cover you with skin, and put breath in you, and ye shall live; and ye shall know that I am the LORD.

7 So I prophesied as I was commanded: and as I prophesied, there was a noise, and behold a shaking, and the bones came together, bone to his bone.

8 And when I beheld, lo, the sinews and the flesh came up upon them, and the skin covered them above: but there was no breath in them.

9 Then said he unto me, Prophesy unto the wind, prophesy, son of man, and say to the wind, Thus saith the Lord GOD; Come from the four winds, O breath, and breathe upon these slain, that they may live.

10 So I prophesied as he commanded me, and the breath came into them, and they lived, and stood up upon their feet, an exceeding great army.

11a Then he said unto me, Son of man, these bones are the whole house of Israel.

. . . .

25 And they shall dwell in the land that I have given unto Jacob my servant, wherein your fathers have dwelt; and they shall dwell therein, even they, and their children, and their children's children for ever: and my servant David shall be their prince for ever.

26 Moreover I will make a covenant of peace with them; it shall be an everlasting covenant with them: and I will place them, and multiply them, and will set my sanctuary in the midst of them for evermore.

27 My tabernacle also shall be with them: yea, I will be their God, and they shall be my people.

GOLDEN TEXT: My tabernacle also shall be with them: yea, I will be their God, and they shall be my people.—Ezekiel 37:27.

God Calls a People to Faithful Living
Unit 4: God Judges and Renews
(Lessons 11-13)

Lesson Aims

After this lesson the student will be able to:
1. Retell the story of the dry bones.
2. Compare the condition of the Jewish exiles with that of the church today.
3. Suggest a way to apply at least one of God's promises of hope to the church.

Lesson Outline

INTRODUCTION
    A. Death of Hope
    B. Lesson Background
  I. PROPHECY OF LIFE (Ezekiel 37:1-6)
    A. Place of Death (vv. 1, 2)
    B. Question of Life (v. 3)
    C. Command to Prophesy (vv. 4-6)
 II. LIFE AS PROPHESIED (Ezekiel 37:7-10)
    A. From Bones to Bodies (vv. 7, 8)
    B. From Dead to Living (vv. 9, 10)
      "Things Go Better With Coke"
III. MEANING OF THE VISION (Ezekiel 37:11a, 25-27)
    A. Life for Dead Israel (v. 11a)
    B. A Home for the Exiles (v. 25)
    C. An Everlasting Covenant (vv. 26, 27)
      Restored Relationships
CONCLUSION
    A. Where Is Our Hope?
    B. Prayer
    C. Thought to Remember

Introduction

Mourning was great in the village, for a popular citizen was dead. Throughout his days of illness, hope had gleamed brightly; but now hope was gone as well. Day after day the bereaved home was thronged with friends bringing comfort, but the shadow of grief remained.

Several days after the funeral the family's best friend came to town and was led to the tomb. For a few moments He stood weeping as others had. Then suddenly, in an authoritative voice, He called, "Lazarus, come forth!"

Come forth? Lazarus was not only dead; he was also so tightly bound in his graveclothes that he could not move even if he were alive. But that command could not be ignored. Lazarus

did indeed "come forth." Willing hands quickly loosened the graveclothes, and grief was dethroned by gladness.

Thus was demonstrated the truth that is so often illustrated in Scripture and in our own experience: "With God all things are possible" (Matthew 19:26).

A. Death of Hope

Centuries earlier there was great mourning in another location—the colony of Hebrew captives in the land of Babylon. Perhaps, in the early stages of captivity, the people of Judah still clung to some hope of liberation. But in 586 B.C. most of the people of Judah were dragged into captivity as well. Jerusalem and the temple were destroyed. Hope appeared dead, for there no longer was a home to which to return. The captives could only sit in Babylon and weep (Psalm 137:1-6).

B. Lesson Background

We need to remember that the Hebrews' captivity in Babylon came in three phases.

Phase 1. When Babylonian troops first came to Judah in 605 B.C., they took captive only a few Jewish citizens. Among them were Daniel and his three famous friends—Shadrach, Meshach, and Abednego (Daniel 1:1-7). Judah continued its national life as before, but had to pay tribute to Babylon.

Phase 2. After some years Judah rashly rebelled against Babylon and refused to pay tribute. In 597 B.C., King Nebuchadnezzar and the army of Babylon returned. This time they took ten thousand captives, including the statesmen and politicians, the military leaders, and the craftsmen and smiths who made spears and swords. (It seemed unlikely that there would be another rebellion without either leaders or weapons.) The king of Babylon also took away the king of Judah (Jehoiachin), but he left another man of the royal family (Zedekiah) to rule the nation and pay the tribute (2 Kings 24:1-17).

Phase 3. For approximately eight years King Zedekiah obediently paid the tribute, but in the ninth year he too rebelled. Again the Babylonians returned, and in 586 B.C. they destroyed Jerusalem. They took most of the survivors to Babylon, leaving only a few of the poor people to cultivate the land (2 Kings 25:8-12).

The prophet Ezekiel was God's spokesman among the captives. He had gone to Babylon with the ten thousand who were taken during the second phase of the captivity, when King Jehoiachin was taken (Ezekiel 1:1-3). While others had hoped for an early release, Ezekiel foretold the end of Jerusalem. But now that Jerusalem was destroyed and the nation was in the throes of utter despair, Ezekiel became the voice of hope to God's people.

Visions were a prominent part of the ministry of Ezekiel. Each is introduced by the phrase, "the hand of the Lord was upon me." These visions occur in four sections of the book. At the beginning comes the vision of the glory of God (1:1—3:15), during which Ezekiel received his call to prophesy. Next comes a vision of the abominations that were taking place in the temple (chapters 8-11). Perhaps the most famous vision is the one that is recorded in today's printed text from Ezekiel 37. The book closes with a detailed vision of a future temple (chapters 40-48).

I. Prophecy of Life
(Ezekiel 37:1-6)

A. Place of Death (vv. 1, 2)

1. The hand of the LORD was upon me, and carried me out in the Spirit of the LORD, and set me down in the midst of the valley which was full of bones.

To be *in the Spirit of the Lord* is to be in a condition to receive His revelation, whether it is given in words, in a vision, or through tangible objects and visible events. *The hand of the Lord* represents His power in action. Ezekiel did not walk out to the valley; as he saw this happening, the Lord carried him there and put him down *in the midst of the valley which was full of bones.*

2. And caused me to pass by them round about: and, behold, there were very many in the open valley; and, lo, they were very dry.

Having placed Ezekiel on the ground, the Lord now led the prophet to walk *round about* the bones for a good look at them. Two facts caught his attention: *There were very many*, and *they were very dry.* Verse 9 describes them as "slain." It was as if there had been a terrible battle in the valley, killing countless thousands of men and leaving their bodies unburied until wild animals and vultures had torn away the clothing and stripped the flesh from the bones. Perhaps the bones had lain in the valley for many years, dried and bleached by the wind and the sun.

B. Question of Life (v. 3)

3. And he said unto me, Son of man, can these bones live? And I answered, O Lord GOD, thou knowest.

You or I might have answered, "Certainly not! These bones have been dead for years. There's no possibility of life in them." But this *son of man* was a prophet. He knew that all

things are possible with God. Wisely he waited for the Lord to reveal what the dried bones could do.

C. Command to Prophesy (vv. 4-6)

4. Again he said unto me, Prophesy upon these bones, and say unto them, O ye dry bones, hear the word of the LORD.

Prophesy to dry *bones*, long dead? Talking to them seemed like a waste of breath. But *the word of the Lord* is not like yours or mine. His power "quickeneth the dead, and calleth those things which be not as though they were" (Romans 4:17). [See question #1, page 104.]

5. Thus saith the Lord GOD unto these bones; Behold, I will cause breath to enter into you, and ye shall live.

It still sounded impossible, didn't it? Those bones had no lungs. How could *breath* get into them? The next verse mentions some details that needed to be addressed first before this could happen.

6. And I will lay sinews upon you, and will bring up flesh upon you, and cover you with skin, and put breath in you, and ye shall live; and ye shall know that I am the LORD.

Sinews most likely describes the ligaments or tendons that bring bones together at the joints. It is plain that the term *flesh* as used here includes organs such as the stomach, liver, and lungs, along with blood vessels, nerves, glands, and whatever else goes into forming a human body. God's plan was to add completed bodies to the bones, and then endow the bodies with life. They would become living human beings with minds, and they would know that the one who put them together was *the Lord*—the only one who can do something this magnificent.

II. Life As Prophesied
(Ezekiel 37:7-10)

A. From Bones to Bodies (vv. 7, 8)

7. So I prophesied as I was commanded: and as I prophesied, there was a noise, and behold a shaking, and the bones came together, bone to his bone.

Wise Ezekiel! He did what God told him to do, thus setting a good example for all of us. Whether we are prophets or not, God has commandments for us. Knowing they come from Him, we should obey without question.

Promptly, as Ezekiel *prophesied* to the lifeless *bones*, they began to obey. Ezekiel heard *a noise.* The Hebrew word can also mean a "sound" or a "voice." Then there was *a shaking.* This Hebrew word is often used to describe an earthquake; thus some students believe that the trembling of

How to Say It

ABEDNEGO. Uh-*bed*-nee-go.
EZEKIEL. E-*zeek*-yul or E-*zeek*-e-ul.
JEHOIACHIN. Jeh-*hoy*-uh-kin.
MESHACH. *Me*-shack.
NEBUCHADNEZZAR. *Neb*-uh-kad-*nezz*-er
   (strong accent on *nezz*).
RUAH (Hebrew). *rue*-ah.
SHADRACH. *Shad*-rack.
ZEDEKIAH. Zed-uh-*kye*-uh.

the ground brought the bones together. However, the *New American Standard Bible* translates it "a rattling." We cannot be sure exactly what Ezekiel meant by this Hebrew word; but it does seem probable that two dry bones coming together would produce a click, and that multiplied thousands of clicks would produce a rattling sound.

Whatever the sound was like, and whether there was an earthquake or not, the power of God brought the separated bones together. Miraculously each bone found *his bone*—the very one it needed to join in order to take its place in a complete skeleton.

8. And when I beheld, lo, the sinews and the flesh came up upon them, and the skin covered them above: but there was no breath in them.

Before his very eyes, Ezekiel saw the bones disappear from sight, encased in muscles, tendons, ligaments, and all the other components of human bodies. When the bodies were complete, *the skin covered them above: but there was no breath in them*. These people remained dead— dead as the dry bones had been. [See question #2, page 104.]

B. From Dead to Living (vv. 9, 10)

9. Then said he unto me, Prophesy unto the wind, prophesy, son of man, and say to the wind, Thus saith the Lord GOD; Come from the four winds, O breath, and breathe upon these slain, that they may live.

This verse presents a problem to translators, because the Hebrew word *ruah* can mean either *wind*, *breath*, or *spirit*. Most versions consider *the four winds* as a proper translation, symbolizing the four directions—north, south, east, and west. But in the other places where the *King James Version* has "wind," the *New American Standard Bible* has "breath." With either translation the meaning is the same, and it is quite clear. There were so many thousands of *these slain* that an abundance of air was needed to fill their lungs and start them breathing. Therefore the Lord summoned the wind, or

breath (or possibly God's Spirit as a source of life) to come from every direction. As it comes, it will bring air into every lung, and with that breath God will provide life.

10. So I prophesied as he commanded me, and the breath came into them, and they lived, and stood up upon their feet, an exceeding great army.

The *breath*, or wind, obeyed God's command as promptly as the bones had done. Pressing in from every direction, it filled the lungs of the dead; and suddenly the dead became alive. They *stood up upon their feet*. No estimate of their number is given, but they formed *an exceeding great army*.

"THINGS GO BETTER WITH COKE"

There was a time when the only remedies for colds or the flu were foul-tasting patent medicines. It's no wonder that there has long been a market for sweeter remedies to help us endure life's common ailments.

Coca-Cola was introduced in 1886 as one such medical advance. It was first sold as a "brain and nerve tonic" that would cure "all nervous afflictions—Sick Headache, Neuralgia, Hysteria, Melancholy, Etc."

Today the secret formula no longer includes cocaine. Still, the stimulative effect of the caffeine in Coke and other cola drinks causes many people to feel much better after drinking one, especially if they are accustomed to drinking several a day. So it does seem to many people that "things go better with Coke."

The house of Israel had more than a mere moral headache. The nation was dead, and Ezekiel's vision of dried bones scattered across a valley was an accurate depiction of its moral condition. But God offered hope to His people if they would take the remedy He offered. It was a remedy far better than Coke: the word of the Lord would bring life to a people whose spirits were dead. It did then; it does now!

—C. R. B.

III. Meaning of the Vision (Ezekiel 37:11a, 25-27)

A. Life for Dead Israel (v. 11a)

11a. Then he said unto me, Son of man, these bones are the whole house of Israel.

This metaphor is explained clearly in the rest of verse 11 and in the next three verses, which are omitted from the printed text. With Ezekiel in Babylon were others from Judah who had been brought there as captives. They were living and breathing, but they thought that their nation, *the whole house of Israel*, was dead—dead as those bones long bleached in the sun. Through His messenger Ezekiel, God assured them that the nation would be revived as the bones had been. Furthermore, the nation would be restored to its own land.

Note that the promise was made to *the whole house of Israel*, thus encompassing both Israel (the northern kingdom) and Judah (the southern kingdom). More than three centuries before the Babylonian captivity, the nation had divided. More than one century before the captivity, the northern kingdom had been crushed, and its people scattered among foreign lands. Now the people of the south were living in exile. But restoration would be experienced by the entire nation. This is clearly promised and illustrated in some of the verses omitted from our printed text (vv. 15-24). [See question #3, page 104.]

B. A Home for the Exiles (v. 25)

25. And they shall dwell in the land that I have given unto Jacob my servant, wherein your fathers have dwelt; and they shall dwell therein, even they, and their children, and their children's children for ever: and my servant David shall be their prince for ever.

See Psalm 137:1-6 for a powerful expression of the anguish of the captives in Babylon. Precious to those captives was the promise that they would live again in their own *land*, and that *their children* would live there *for ever*. We must remember, of course, that the promised land was never promised unconditionally. The people of Israel could live there if they were obedient to God. If they were disobedient, they would be "plucked from off the land" (Deuteronomy 28:63, 64). Just as God promised, the people were "plucked" and taken to Babylon for a time. Now they were to live in the land again, ruled by *my servant David*.

David himself had died long before the time we are studying, of course; but God had promised that members of his family would rule forever (2 Samuel 7:16). Thus the fulfillment of such promises as described here must be linked with the work of Jesus Christ. Jesus, the true Son of David, has provided a way for us to enter the true promised land of Heaven (Hebrews 9:24). Even Old Testament saints knew that this was the land where they desired to live (Hebrews 11:13-16). Forever Jesus stands at the head of the church—of Christians who by faith are children of Abraham (Galatians 3:7) and constitute the Israel of God (Galatians 6:16) under the New Covenant. Other blessings of the kind only Jesus can provide are described in the remaining verses of our printed text.

C. An Everlasting Covenant (vv. 26, 27)

26. Moreover I will make a covenant of peace with them; it shall be an everlasting covenant with them: and I will place them, and multiply them, and will set my sanctuary in the midst of them for evermore.

The *covenant of peace* is the New Covenant foretold in Jeremiah 31:31-34. Its crowning feature is this: "I will forgive their iniquity, and I will remember their sin no more." Today God's *sanctuary* is not a massive building of stone; He lives in each devoted Christian (1 Corinthians 6:19), and together these sanctuaries make up "a holy temple . . . built upon the foundation of the apostles and prophets, Jesus Christ himself being the chief corner stone" (Ephesians 2:19-22). This is the church that Jesus is building, "and the gates of hell shall not prevail against it" (Matthew 16:18). On such a foundation God places His people, and He has promised to *multiply* them as they go "into all the world, and preach the gospel to every creature" (Mark 16:15). This covenant is truly *everlasting*: it will never need to be replaced or amended.

27. My tabernacle also shall be with them: yea, I will be their God, and they shall be my people.

The word *sanctuary* in verse 26 means "holy place." The word *tabernacle* here refers to the same structure, but the meaning of the word, "dwelling place," is significant. Jehovah is not an occasional visitor; in the person of the Holy Spirit, He abides with us. He is our God: our Creator, our Ruler, and our Provider. We are His people: His creation, His obedient subjects, and the beneficiaries of His provisions. [See question #4, page 104.]

RESTORED RELATIONSHIPS

Interesting things happen in car pools—so interesting that several governmental agencies in southern California sponsored a contest to discover the most memorable car pool experience.

Visual for lesson 12

Today's visual reminds us of the promise in verse 27. Discuss how this finds fulfillment in the church and in eternity. (See Revelation 21:3.)

Kimberly Arguelles won the contest. Her mother and stepfather died in an auto accident in Mexico in 1974. For a while Arguelles and her sister lived with their father in southern California, but as she reached her teen years, Arguelles became rebellious and was sent to live in Mexico with her grandmother. She refused to respond to her sister's attempts to communicate with her, and they lost track of each other.

In 1987, Arguelles returned to California to work. Her car broke down, so she joined a car pool. By the second day of ride-sharing, she discovered that a strangely familiar woman in her car pool was her long-lost sister! In mature adulthood, both women were able to put the past behind them and rejoice in the restoration of their relationship.

Ezekiel foretold the day when Israel's immature rebellion against God would be past. They would have learned an important lesson through their exile in a strange land. Their relationship with God would be restored through a growing spiritual maturity.

The good news of the gospel is that God specializes in restoring our relationship with Him. Through Jesus, "old things are passed away; behold, all things are become new" (2 Corinthians 5:17).   —C. R. B.

Conclusion

This lesson is well titled, "Hope From God's Promise." After the tragic events of 586 B.C., Israel was no more, or so its captive people thought, as they wept by the streams of Babylon. They had no hope. Then came God's promise: Israel would live again. Hope was reborn in people who believed the Lord and His Word.

Throughout our survey of the Old Testament this quarter, mankind has failed repeatedly. With God, however, there is always reason to hope.

A. Where Is Our Hope?

When we look at the impact of God's people (the church) today, are we optimistic or pessimistic? Nearly two thousand years have passed since the church began, yet it still often seems weak, timid, and unsure of itself.

Is there hope for the church? Many believe that we are in a "post-Christian" age. The church and its message are believed no longer relevant. Critics claim that the church has failed miserably in its task and deserves to be replaced by something more productive.

Jesus, the Head of the church, acknowledged that His church would not be perfect. He warned His disciples of "false prophets, which

come to you in sheep's clothing, but inwardly they are ravening wolves" (Matthew 7:15). Later, Paul told the Ephesian elders, "Of your own selves shall men arise, speaking perverse things to draw away disciples after them" (Acts 20:30). Even in these days when the church was only a few years old, Paul knew that there would be threats against which the believers must guard. Yet he also wrote a letter to this same church, confidently declaring that the church is the body of Christ, "the fulness of him that filleth all in all" (Ephesians 1:23), and that the church is meant to be something "glorious" (5:27).

How can the church restore its "glory"? Does it seem to be in a condition similar to that of the dry bones? Then let us heed the Word of God and obey the Head of the church. To a lukewarm church, Jesus said, "Behold, I stand at the door, and knock: if any man hear my voice, and open the door, I will come in to him, and will sup with him, and he with me" (Revelation 3:20).

In a world where many voices clamor for the church's attention, only one voice matters. We must listen to Jesus. The Head of the church is the hope of the church. [See question #5, page 104.]

B. Prayer

In a world of turmoil, Father, we are grateful for Your promises and the hope they bring. By Your grace and by Your power, may each one of us be faithful unto death, and at last be crowned with life eternal. Amen.

C. Thought to Remember

"Now the God of hope fill you with all joy and peace in believing, that ye may abound in hope, through the power of the Holy Ghost" (Romans 15:13).

Home Daily Bible Readings

Monday, Nov. 16—The Spirit Entered Into Me (Ezekiel 3:22-27)
Tuesday, Nov. 17—The Spirit Lifted Me Up (Ezekiel 8:1-13)
Wednesday, Nov. 18—Can These Bones Live? (Ezekiel 37:1-14)
Thursday, Nov. 19—I Will Make Them One Nation (Ezekiel 37:15-23)
Friday, Nov. 20—My Servant David Shall Be Their King (Ezekiel 37:24-28)
Saturday, Nov. 21—In Visions of God (Ezekiel 40:1-4)
Sunday, Nov. 22—The Glory of the Lord Filled the Temple (Ezekiel 43:1-9)

Learning by Doing

This page contains an alternate lesson plan emphasizing learning activities.
Classes desiring such student involvement will find these suggestions helpful.

Learning Goals

As a result of this lesson, your students should be able to:

1. Retell the story of the dry bones.
2. Compare the condition of the Jewish exiles with that of the church today.
3. Suggest a way to apply at least one of God's promises of hope to the church.

Into the Lesson

Begin by showing students a bone or a picture of a bone. (It would be even better if you could get your hands on a skeleton—even a small novelty or toy skeleton.) Ask, "What hope does a bone (or skeleton) have? What possibilities and potentials does a bone (or skeleton) have?"

Obviously, the answer to both questions is "None." However, with God in the picture things are not always as they appear.

In today's lesson God took the prophet Ezekiel to a valley littered with the bones of warriors who had been killed in battle. God was using sun-bleached bones to illustrate that divine power can transform even a hopeless and desperate situation. There did not appear to be much hope for Judah and Israel in Ezekiel's day, but God was about to show his prophet—and His people—that He can bring hope even when there seems to be none.

This lesson is about finding hope in a seemingly hopeless situation. It is about seeing possibilities and potentials where none is apparent.

Into the Word

Today's lesson is based on a dramatic vision seen by the prophet Ezekiel. Ask a volunteer to read Ezekiel 37:1-11a aloud for the class. Pass out index cards and ask students to list the steps it took to transform a valley of old bones into a great army. (The old spiritual "Dry Bones" is based on Ezekiel's vision. If you can find a tape of the spiritual, play it while the students complete their cards.)

• First, the bones needed to be joined with other bones to form skeletons. See verse 7.

• Then they needed connecting tissue (sinews) and vital organs and muscle (flesh). See verse 8a.

• They needed to be covered with skin. See verse 8b.

• More than anything else, they needed the breath of life. See verses 9, 10.

Divide the class into three-person groups and tell the students to study Ezekiel 37:11, 12, 25-27. Pose the following questions:

• Why were the bones in Ezekiel's vision a good representation of Judah and Israel? (vv. 11, 12).

• What did God promise Judah and Israel in verses 25-27?

• In what ways could God's promise of hope in verses 25-27 be applied to today's church?

Into Life

Observe that there is not much of a difference between lifeless cadavers and professing Christians who do not demonstrate the fruit of the Spirit. Say, "The description in Ezekiel of the dry bones may remind us of dryness and lost vitality in our church or in our own spiritual lives. What can we do about this?"

As you discuss this issue, note that the "dead" church in Sardis in Revelation 3:1-6 was urged to "be watchful, and strengthen the things which remain." If our church seems dead and dry in any way, we need to offer the famous prayer, "Revive Thy church, beginning with me."

Very often, those who complain about their church's being dead have unrealistic expectations of the church. They may confuse spiritual with spirited; they may be looking more for entertainment than for edification. Before we complain about our church, we need to make sure it is not we ourselves who need to draw nearer to God, repenting of arrogance and pride and giving Him first place. Then, while we are praying for our own reviving, we can offer similar prayers for our minister, elders, teachers, and other members. If there is a problem with the church, nothing will help more than prayer and setting a good example of faithfulness and zeal.

Some of your students may especially need God's life-giving touch because of difficult situations in their lives. Maybe a loved one is ill. Financial problems may seem overwhelming. One may be bearing a load of emotional pain. Another's marriage may be falling apart. This lesson affirms that God's life-giving power is sufficient for even the most desperate and seemingly hopeless situation.

Close with a prayer that today will be a new beginning for your students—a transformation from despair to hope.

Let's Talk It Over

The questions on this page are designed to encourage review of the lesson Scriptures and to promote discussion of the lesson by the class. The answers provided are only discussion starters. Let your class talk it over from there.

1. "Hear the word of the Lord." Ezekiel's vision of the dry bones illustrates the power of the Word of God. How can we develop a deeper appreciation for this power?

We will not appreciate the power of God's Word unless we expose ourselves to that power. Merely listening to a weekly sermon and/or Bible lesson will not provide adequate exposure. It is when we devote ourselves to the personal reading and study of the Word that we see it as "the word of God, which effectually worketh also in [us who] believe" (1 Thessalonians 2:13). Another way in which we come to appreciate the power of God's Word is by learning of its mighty work in other believers' lives. One important aspect of our Christian fellowship should be a sharing of the Word's ministry in our lives. When we hear a brother or sister describing how the Word brought comfort, encouragement, or guidance during a time of critical need, it will surely build our confidence in the Bible.

2. Ezekiel's vision, with the bones coming together, taking on flesh, and becoming whole bodies was quite impressive. But still, Ezekiel said, "There was no breath in them." Sometimes we can look good on the outside, but there is no breath or spirit in us, no enthusiasm for the Lord or His work. How can we be energized, even as the lifeless bodies in the valley were?

Whether you translate the word "breath" or "Spirit" in verse 9, the source of life was God: "Thus saith the Lord God. . . ." If we are going to have spiritual vitality, then it, too, must come from the Lord. Too often we try to serve and function in the church on our own strength. We need to spend more time with the Lord in prayer, in Bible study, in meditation. We need to talk more of the Lord when we are together with our brothers and sisters. We need to be more purposeful about the Lord's kingdom and less concerned about how we look to others.

3. When the bones became bodies and came to life as "an exceeding great army," God said, "These bones are the whole house of Israel." How might the exiles have received this message?

The hopeless condition of the exiles was thus declared to be temporary—the nation would be brought to life again. And it would be the "whole nation"—not the fragmented Israel and Judah that had been since the death of Solomon. This should have brought great joy and hope to the exiles.

Of course, some may have received the message with skepticism, as many receive the Word of God today. Others may have placed undue emphasis on the fact that the bones became an "army" and looked for a military solution to their predicament. We must be careful to hear God's message as He intends and not read our own ideas into the text.

4. God promised Israel and Judah several blessings in Ezekiel 37. He promised reconciliation (vv. 11, 12), unity (v. 19), peace (v. 26), an everlasting covenant (v. 26), and His presence (v. 27). How can you apply each of these promises of hope to the church today?

You might want to consider the following Scriptures in your discussion: Ephesians 2:4, 5 (reconciliation); Ephesians 4:4-6 (unity); Philippians 4:6, 7 (peace); Hebrews 8:6-13 (New Covenant); and Matthew 28:20; Hebrews 13:5 (God's presence). Israel and Judah were promised reconciliation, unity, and peace, though it was a promise they had to accept or decline. Through Jesus' death and resurrection we now have this same option. We can accept God's promises or reject them.

5. Some days our hope seems strong and bright, and on other days it seems to grow dim. What causes our hope to dim? How can we be faithful to God even when hope seems dim?

We must never let our emotions dictate the level of our Christian discipleship. The most dedicated believers will experience times of sadness along with times of joy, turmoil along with peace, and dismay along with hope. Our hope in Christ, from the emotional standpoint, may wane during periods of physical suffering, economic uncertainty, and family crises. But our allegiance to Christ must be a matter of our will more than our emotions. We must say to ourselves, "I am determined to follow Jesus Christ, whatever happens to me." Remember that God has promised salvation to those who follow Him, and God always keeps His promises.

Renewal and Worship

DEVOTIONAL READING: Galatians 3:23-29.

LESSON SCRIPTURE: Nehemiah 8, 9.

PRINTED TEXT: Nehemiah 8:13—9:3.

Nehemiah 8:13-18

13 And on the second day were gathered together the chief of the fathers of all the people, the priests, and the Levites, unto Ezra the scribe, even to understand the words of the law.

14 And they found written in the law which the LORD had commanded by Moses, that the children of Israel should dwell in booths in the feast of the seventh month:

15 And that they should publish and proclaim in all their cities, and in Jerusalem, saying, Go forth unto the mount, and fetch olive branches, and pine branches, and myrtle branches, and palm branches, and branches of thick trees, to make booths, as it is written.

16 So the people went forth, and brought them, and made themselves booths, every one upon the roof of his house, and in their courts, and in the courts of the house of God, and in the street of the water gate, and in the street of the gate of Ephraim.

17 And all the congregation of them that were come again out of the captivity made booths, and sat under the booths: for since the days of Jeshua the son of Nun unto that day had not the children of Israel done so. And there was very great gladness.

18 Also day by day, from the first day unto the last day, he read in the book of the law of God. And they kept the feast seven days; and on the eighth day was a solemn assembly, according unto the manner.

Nehemiah 9:1-3

1 Now in the twenty and fourth day of this month the children of Israel were assembled with fasting, and with sackclothes, and earth upon them.

2 And the seed of Israel separated themselves from all strangers, and stood and confessed their sins, and the iniquities of their fathers.

3 And they stood up in their place, and read in the book of the law of the LORD their God one fourth part of the day; and another fourth part they confessed, and worshipped the LORD their God.

GOLDEN TEXT: Thou, even thou, art LORD alone; thou hast made heaven, the heaven of heavens, with all their host, the earth, and all things that are therein, the seas, and all that is therein, and thou preservest them all; and the host of heaven worshippeth thee.—Nehemiah 9:6.

God Calls a People to Faithful Living
Unit 4: God Judges and Renews
(Lessons 11-13)

Lesson Aims

After this lesson each student will be able to:
1. Describe the observances renewed by the former exiles in today's text.
2. Tell why the observances were significant to their identity as God's people.
3. Commit to worshiping in such a way that his or her observances become times of genuine renewal and identification with God's people.

Lesson Outline

INTRODUCTION
  A. This Backsliding World
  B. Return From Captivity
  C. Lesson Background
  I. LEARNING FROM THE LAW (Nehemiah 8:13-15)
    A. Searching the Scriptures (v. 13)
    B. Forgotten Custom (vv. 14, 15)
      Lost Treasures
  II. OBEYING THE LAW (Nehemiah 8:16-18)
    A. Building Booths (v. 16)
    B. Living in Booths (v. 17)
      Renewing a Great Tradition
    C. Earnest Bible Study (v. 18)
  III. HUMBLE WORSHIP (Nehemiah 9:1-3)
    A. Grief for Wrongs (v. 1)
    B. Separation and Confession (v. 2)
    C. Reading and Worshiping (v. 3)
CONCLUSION
  A. God's Faithful People
  B. God's Worshiping People
  C. Prayer
  D. Thought to Remember

Introduction

A. This Backsliding World

Edmund Burke wrote, "All that is necessary for the triumph of evil is that good men do nothing." How often that truth has been demonstrated in times ancient and modern!

In Israel there were times of exemplary goodness. A dynamic judge, prophet, or king would lead the nation in obedience to God's law, and peace and prosperity would result. But when that leader died and his influence was no longer present, the people would quickly drift back into selfishness and sin.

Because of its wrongdoing, the nation of Israel was split into two smaller countries. Because of its wrongdoing, the northern kingdom was captured by Assyria, and its people were scattered abroad. Because of its wrongdoing, the southern kingdom was taken in captivity to Babylon. Still, God did not abandon His people. He gave them an opportunity to resettle in the promised land. Liberation came about fifty years after Jerusalem was destroyed, and seventy years after the first captives were taken to Babylon.

B. Return From Captivity

Last week we noted that Israel's deportation to Babylon occurred in three phases. Now we note three phases in the return from captivity.

In 538 B.C., approximately fifty thousand of the captives traveled to Jerusalem. Enthusiastically they began to rebuild the temple. However, after they had laid the foundation, opposition to their project arose from some of the residents of the area. After nearly sixteen years of inactivity, two prophets, Haggai and Zechariah, stirred the people to move forward with the project. The temple was completed in 516 B.C. amidst great celebration (Ezra 1—6).

In 458 B.C., Ezra led another group from Babylon. He was a priest and a scholar, eager to teach God's Word. To his distress, he found that some of the people had intermarried with the pagan peoples of the land. Immediately he undertook to restore the purity of the nation (Ezra 7—10).

In 445 B.C., Nehemiah arrived with another group of Jews from Babylon, and with authority from the Persian king to rebuild the walls of Jerusalem. Vigorously he rallied the people to work, and the walls were finished in only fifty-two days (Nehemiah 1—6).

C. Lesson Background

The intensive work on the walls was completed on the twenty-fifth day of the sixth month (Nehemiah 6:15). The people were then quickly organized for purposes of worship and security (Nehemiah 7:1-3). By the first day of the seventh month they were prepared for a period of intensive Bible teaching. Ezra and his assistants taught them for half a day (Nehemiah 8:1-8), following a plan that is worthy of imitation by any Bible teacher: "They read in the book in the law of God distinctly, and gave the sense, and caused them to understand the reading" (v. 8). The people grieved because they realized that they had not been obeying that law. However, Ezra and Nehemiah told them to rejoice instead, because they now understood the law and could obey it (vv. 9-12).

I. Learning From the Law (Nehemiah 8:13-15)

Now that the people had renewed their acquaintance with the law and their allegiance to it, the next step was to lead them in actual and active obedience to it.

A. Searching the Scriptures (v. 13)

13. And on the second day were gathered together the chief of the fathers of all the people, the priests, and the Levites, unto Ezra the scribe, even to understand the words of the law.

As noted in the Lesson Background, the first day of the seventh month was a day of reading from the law and rejoicing (v. 2). *On the second day*, a smaller group of leaders gathered for another session with *Ezra the scribe*. The word *scribe* literally means "writer," but the professional writers who copied the Scriptures by hand naturally became well versed in what they copied. Thus the term *scribe* became a name for a scholar and teacher such as Ezra. *The fathers of all the people* were the heads of families; *the chief of the fathers* were likely the heads of clans, with each clan made up of several families. *The priests* were leaders of worship; *the Levites* were assistants to the priests. All these leaders met with Ezra in order *to understand* more adequately *the words of the law.* [See question #1, page 112.]

B. Forgotten Custom (vv. 14, 15)

14. And they found written in the law which the LORD had commanded by Moses, that the children of Israel should dwell in booths in the feast of the seventh month.

The feast of the seventh month is also called the Feast of Tabernacles. It should be noted that this word for *tabernacles* is not related to the word that describes God's dwelling place when the people were living in tents in the desert (Exodus 40:34-38). Instead, it describes the *booths*, or shelters, that the people were commanded to make from branches of trees; for this reason, this feast was also designated as the Feast of Booths. The feast lasted seven days, and on the day following it a special gathering of the Israelites was to take place (Leviticus 23:33-36). The people lived in booths in memory of the time when they had lived in tents before they reached the promised land (Leviticus 23:39-43). [See question #2, page 112.]

15. And that they should publish and proclaim in all their cities, and in Jerusalem, saying, Go forth unto the mount, and fetch olive branches, and pine branches, and myrtle branches, and palm branches, and branches of thick trees, to make booths, as it is written.

So that no one would forget, this feast and others were to be proclaimed publicly *in all their cities* (Leviticus 23:4). Usually the announcement would have to be made well in advance, of course, so that people would have time to travel to *Jerusalem*. In this case, however, the people were already assembled for the reading of the law (vv. 2, 3), so it was easy to let them know about the feast.

It seems that branches might be gathered from any kind of *trees* that were *thick* with foliage, in order to provide sufficient shade in the booth. The trees named are likely the kinds that grew in abundance near Jerusalem. The feast was nicely timed before the end of the dry season, so that rain would not be a problem.

Here, as in many other places, the word *mount* refers to a hilly area, not to one single mountain. The *New International Version* reads: "Go out into the hill country."

LOST TREASURES

We usually think of pawnshops as "other-side-of-the-tracks" establishments where hapless "down-and-outers" trade items of meager value for a bit of needed cash. Worse yet, pawnshops sometimes provide a venue where thieves can get money for stolen goods with no questions asked.

But in Beverly Hills, California—home of some of the world's most famous "up-and-outers"—a "Jewelry and Loan" shop trades in more precious commodities. One young woman, seeking to finance a trip to Europe, recently pawned a 1920 Cartier twenty-eight-carat diamond necklace and a matching Burmese sapphire bracelet for a total of $45,000. The dealer said that they were heirlooms of the family of the woman's husband: "It's old money. Sometimes young

---

How to Say It

ASSYRIA. Uh-*sear*-ee-uh.
BABYLON. *Bab*-uh-lun.
ELIJAH. Ee-*lye*-juh.
EPHRAIM. *Ee*-fray-im.
HAGGAI. *Hag*-ay-eye or *Hag*-eye.
JESHUA. *Jesh*-you-uh.
LEVITES. *Lee*-vites.
NEBUCHADNEZZAR. *Neb*-uh-kad-*nezz*-er (strong accent on *nezz*).
NEBUCHADREZZAR. *Neb*-uh-kad-*rezz*-er (strong accent on *rezz*).
NEHEMIAH. Nee-huh-*my*-uh.
ZECHARIAH. Zek-uh-*rye*-uh.

people don't care for this stuff. It's a shame, really." A shame indeed!

Israel was in much the same situation regarding the law of God. Not appreciating what the law had symbolized in the history of God's family, several generations had allowed the words of the law to become forgotten. They were more concerned with the pleasures of the present than with the treasures of the past.

But in Nehemiah's time, a new generation of leaders arose who acknowledged the value of their heritage. When the book of the law was read, they realized the significance of the Feast of Tabernacles and began again to observe it. A lost family treasure was redeemed. —C. R. B.

II. Obeying the Law
(Nehemiah 8:16-18)

The leaders became aware of the law regarding the Feast of Tabernacles on the second day of the seventh month (v. 13). The feast began on the fifteenth day of the same month (Leviticus 23:34). There was still plenty of time to prepare for it.

A. Building Booths (v. 16)

16. So the people went forth, and brought them, and made themselves booths, every one upon the roof of his house, and in their courts, and in the courts of the house of God, and in the street of the water gate, and in the street of the gate of Ephraim.

Probably every available open space in the city was used in constructing the *booths*. The flat *roof* of a *house* could support a booth. A big house might be built around a small courtyard or patio where a booth could be built. The large *courts of the house of God* (the temple) had room for many small booths.

The word *street* is rendered "square" in other versions. Inside each gate was a wide space where hundreds of men could be assembled to resist an invader who threatened to break down the gate and enter the city. These open spaces soon were green with booths. Two specific gates are mentioned: *the water gate*, on the east side of Jerusalem, and *the gate of Ephraim*, which was the main gate on the north side of the city.

B. Living in Booths (v. 17)

17. And all the congregation of them that were come again out of the captivity made booths, and sat under the booths: for since the days of Jeshua the son of Nun unto that day had not the children of Israel done so. And there was very great gladness.

The Hebrew verb rendered *sat* can also mean "lived," and is probably better understood that

way here. The verse simply says that the booths became living quarters for the Israelites who had come back from the *captivity* in Babylon.

The statement *since the days of Jeshua the son of Nun unto that day had not the children of Israel done so* does not mean that the Feast of Tabernacles had not been observed since Joshua's time. Scripture tells us it was celebrated following the dedication of Solomon's temple (2 Chronicles 7:8-10) and after the return of the captives from Babylon (Ezra 3:4), and it is likely that it was celebrated at other times as well. Most likely the statement means that the feast had not been celebrated with such joy. To the usual *gladness* of the feast was added the joy of keeping God's law more faithfully than it had been kept for some time.

It is clear that *Jeshua* refers to the Biblical Joshua. Compare the slight difference in spelling between Nebuchadnezzar and Nebuchadrezzar noted in lesson 11. [See question #3, page 112.]

RENEWING A GREAT TRADITION

Can you remember the days of the steam locomotives? There was something awesome about the sound of one huffing and puffing up a mountain pass, and something strikingly beautiful in the billowing clouds of smoke and steam rising into a clear blue winter's sky as a locomotive and its train streaked across a snow-covered plain.

Things are more efficient today. Gone are the gritty particles of coal ash that settled on fresh-washed clothes hung out to dry. In their place is the vaporous exhaust of the diesel-electric locomotive. A mechanical roar and electric hum has replaced the powerful puffing of steam that symbolized the industrial age.

Because diesels are cheaper, cleaner, and easier to maintain, they began replacing steamers some fifty years ago. Steam locomotives are museum pieces now; but in order that their link to a romantic past may not be lost, many railroad museums around the country are training people to run the steamers and thus keep alive this legacy.

In the days of Nehemiah, the people of God had allowed a legacy to die. By failing to observe faithfully the Feast of Tabernacles, they had lost touch with the exodus—the event that gave them their national identity. As they renewed the great tradition of the feast, they were reminded that they had been wanderers until God gave them a home.

When properly observed, traditions remind us of who we have been and what we have become. We need to cherish our traditions—as individuals, families, and churches. —C. R. B.

Visual for
lesson 13

Today's visual shows Jerusalem before and after the exile. Use the map on the right to locate places named in today's lesson.

C. Earnest Bible Study (v. 18)

18. Also day by day, from the first day unto the last day, he read in the book of the law of God. And they kept the feast seven days; and on the eighth day was a solemn assembly, according unto the manner.

Intensive Bible study was a daily part of the celebration, as *from the first day unto the last day* Ezra *read in the book of the law of God.* Probably he or his assistants added explanation as it was needed, according to the pattern described earlier in verse 8. The congregation *kept the feast seven days,* and then added *a solemn assembly* on the following day, *according unto the manner* prescribed in the law. See Numbers 29:12-39 for specific instructions about the sacrifices to be offered on each day of the feast.

III. Humble Worship (Nehemiah 9:1-3)

The feast covered the fifteenth through the twenty-first days of the seventh month, followed by a solemn assembly on the twenty-second. The people then had a day to prepare for a different kind of worship on the twenty-fourth day.

A. Grief for Wrongs (v. 1)

1. Now in the twenty and fourth day of this month the children of Israel were assembled with fasting, and with sackclothes, and earth upon them.

Wise Solomon spoke of "a time to weep, and a time to laugh" (Ecclesiastes 3:4). After listening to the law for half a day on the first day of the month, the people began to weep (Nehemiah 8:9). Probably they realized how far they had strayed from obeying the law. But now they knew what the law said. They could obey it instead of ignoring it. Their leaders encouraged them to rejoice (v. 10). Two weeks later the Feast of Tabernacles began. This was a joyous harvest festival that took place after the grapes

and other fruits were gathered. It was also a time to rejoice because the people now had comfortable houses in which to dwell instead of the tents or booths in which they had lived when they left Egypt (Leviticus 23:42, 43).

When the people met again on the *twenty and fourth day,* obviously they and their leaders had agreed that the time to weep had come. They *assembled with fasting.* They wore uncomfortable clothing of rough sackcloth. They threw dust on their heads. These were traditional ways of expressing deep mourning (Job 2:12; Daniel 9:3).

B. Separation and Confession (v. 2)

2. And the seed of Israel separated themselves from all strangers, and stood and confessed their sins, and the iniquities of their fathers.

Strangers refers to people who were not Jews. Perhaps we should read *had separated* instead of *separated,* for such a step had been taken when Ezra first began to teach in Jerusalem (Ezra 9, 10). If any unwise alliance with a pagan had been made since that time, it was now renounced.

Mingling with pagan foreigners had been a clear violation of the law (Deuteronomy 7:1-5). That specific prohibition was given because God knew that cordial associations with pagan peoples would turn His people away from Him. The nation's experience over many centuries proved that this was true.

Humbly and sorrowfully the people of Israel *confessed their sins and the iniquities of their fathers.* These included their dangerous associations with pagans, but there must have been other sins as well. Recently these people had been listening to the reading of the law (Nehemiah 8:1-8, 18). That must have called their attention to various acts of dishonesty and unkindness among themselves. [See question #4, page 112.]

C. Reading and Worshiping (v. 3)

3. And they stood up in their place, and read in the book of the law of the LORD their God one fourth part of the day; and another fourth part they confessed, and worshipped the LORD their God.

And they stood up in their place. The standing posture is mentioned repeatedly in this section (vv. 2, 3, 4, 5). Apparently it was a sign of respect for God and His Word, and of the people's active participation in praise and confession. For *one fourth part of the day,* or daytime (about three hours), they *stood* and *read in the book of the law of the Lord.* Probably Ezra and his assistants read aloud, while the people listened to the law and mourned their transgressions. Then they spent three more hours in prayer, confessing their own wrongdoing and praising God's goodness.

Most likely this meeting was held in the large outer court of the temple. In order to be seen and heard by the entire crowd, the worship leaders stood on the stairs that led up to an inner court (v. 4). [See question #5, page 112.]

The rest of chapter 9 records some of the words of praise and confession. These words also review the national history of Israel. It is a lengthy record of God's power and goodness, and of Israel's ingratitude and sin. Chapter 10 then notes the people's fervent pledge "to walk in God's law . . . and to observe and do all the commandments of the Lord our Lord, and his judgments and his statutes" (v. 29).

Conclusion

A. God's Faithful People

In every era God has had His faithful people—people who have done His will and enjoyed His favor. Noah was "a preacher of righteousness" (2 Peter 2:5) as he labored to build the ark, and he "found grace in the eyes of the Lord" (Genesis 6:8). Abraham heard the call of God and set out on a long journey, not even knowing where he was going (Hebrews 11:8); his faithful obedience brought blessing to all families of the earth (Genesis 12:1-3). Faithfully for over forty years Jeremiah gave God's word to an unbelieving people, and he lived to see God's word proved true. Mary said, "Behold the handmaid of the Lord; be it unto me according to thy word" (Luke 1:38); and she became the mother of God's Son and our Savior.

Home Daily Bible Readings

Monday, Nov. 23—All the People Gathered (Nehemiah 8:1-12)
Tuesday, Nov. 24—To Study Words of the Law (Nehemiah 8:13-18)
Wednesday, Nov. 25—They Confessed Their Sins (Nehemiah 9:1-5)
Thursday, Nov. 26—You Are the Lord! (Nehemiah 9:6-15)
Friday, Nov. 27—You Are Ready to Forgive, Gracious, and Merciful (Nehemiah 9:16-25)
Saturday, Nov. 28—You Have Been Just (Nehemiah 9:26-37)
Sunday, Nov. 29—Peace Be Within Your Walls (Psalm 122:1-9)

God's faithful people may feel lonely at times, for many unfaithful are choosing the wide road that leads to destruction (Matthew 7:13, 14). Elijah once thought that he was the only faithful one in Israel, but the Lord knew that there were seven thousand more (1 Kings 19:18).

Yes, God has His faithful people in the world today—people who not only do His will but also share His Word and help others do His will. In this world they may experience either prosperity or persecution, but in the world to come they will have joy forever.

B. God's Worshiping People

Today's lesson text provides some helpful insights on the subject of worship. Note the ingredients that made up the worship of those who gathered in Judah. There was Bible study: the leaders of the people assembled "to understand the words of the law" (Nehemiah 8:13). This was followed by obedience; when the leaders found that the law required the people to live in booths during the feast of the seventh month, they encouraged the people to keep the law (vv. 14, 15). There was also "very great gladness" once the people had followed the law's instructions (v. 17). Finally, there was an opportunity to confess sins and to demonstrate repentance through fasting, wearing sackcloth, and dealing decisively with sin (9:1, 2).

Let's take a close look at our worship today and raise some appropriate questions:

Is our time of worship characterized by a period of serious Bible study?

Do we challenge others to obey and apply the Scriptures?

Is there a spirit of gladness and joy as together we celebrate the Lord's goodness?

Is there a time for renewal through confession of sin?

We live in a day when worship is often designed to be convenient rather than convicting. The worship of those in Ezra and Nehemiah's day should challenge us who live under the New Covenant. Are we worshiping to please God or to please ourselves?

C. Prayer

Father eternal, how good You are to give Your Word to generation after generation, though often it is disregarded! By Your power may we have strength to remain among Your faithful people, and by Your grace may our failures be forgiven. Amen.

D. Thought to Remember

True worship takes us from the world in order that we may face the world on God's behalf.

Learning by Doing

This page contains an alternate lesson plan emphasizing learning activities.
Classes desiring such student involvement will find these suggestions helpful.

Learning Goals

As a result of this lesson your students should be able to:

1. Describe the observances renewed by the former exiles in today's text.

2. Tell why the observances were significant to their identity as God's people.

3. Commit to worshiping in such a way that their observances become times of genuine renewal and identification with God's people.

Into the Lesson

If you have married couples in your class, ask, "How do you like to celebrate your wedding anniversary?" (If you have singles, ask how their parents or married friends celebrate.) Discuss why such a celebration is important. How does celebrating reinforce the commitment made in the past? What does a celebration say about the value of the relationship?

Then ask, "What events do we observe as a church, and why?" Your church may celebrate some of the traditional holidays like Mother's Day and Father's Day, Thanksgiving, Christmas, and others. You may also celebrate some days that are special to you as a congregation, like the anniversary of the church's founding or the dedication of its first building. At some point, someone is sure to mention the Lord's Supper.

Observe that all of these remembrances are important to us as the people of God. They help to define who we are. The Jews had some special observances, too. But after seventy years in captivity in Babylon, many of these observances had been forgotten. Our lesson today shows how they renewed one of them.

Into the Word

Use the information in the Lesson Background to set the stage for the events of today's lesson. If there are two creative men in the church (not members of your class so they can visit briefly and then exit), ask them to assume the roles of Ezra and Nehemiah and dress up in period costumes. (Bathrobes, with towels on their heads, would be okay.) They can present the background information to the class in first person.

If your class is large enough, divide it into groups of five to eight members each. Each group is to prepare a news story on the events of Nehemiah 8:13-18. The story, like one broadcast on the evening news, should answer the famous questions "Who? What? When? Where? Why? and How?" Along with straight news ("just the facts"), the group could include a commentary feature, where one senior journalist explains the significance of the event. If the group members are creative, they could even choose some members to be residents of Jerusalem who are interviewed by news correspondents. Give them time to prepare the broadcast and, if there is enough time, an opportunity to perform it. (If there is not time for the performances in class, maybe the scripts could be used in an evening service or shared with a youth group.)

Then have a volunteer read Nehemiah 9:1-3. Ask the following questions:

1. The Feast of Tabernacles was concluded on the twenty-first day of the month and was followed on the twenty-second with a solemn assembly. What took place on the twenty-fourth?

2. How did the Israelites demonstrate their sorrow?

3. Why did they separate themselves from "strangers"?

4. What did they confess?

5. What role did the book of the law of the Lord play in their assembly?

Into Life

Point out that as soon as the returned exiles learned from the Scriptures about the Feast of Tabernacles (or Booths), they put their new understanding of the Word into practice by doing what the Word said.

We have a great advantage over the former exiles. Where they were dependent on public readings to hear God's Word, we have copies available for our own reading. Discuss, "What added responsibility do you think we have over the former exiles because of our added opportunity to know God's Word?"

For the exiles, the Feast of Tabernacles became a great opportunity to incorporate a commemoration of their past into a meaningful worship experience. Discuss how we can incorporate the observances of special past events into meaningful times of worship. Discuss ideas for special services as well as your weekly worship times. Then talk with the appropriate church leaders about implementing some of the better ideas.

Let's Talk It Over

The questions on this page are designed to encourage review of the lesson Scriptures and to promote discussion of the lesson by the class. The answers provided are only discussion starters. Let your class talk it over from there.

1. Our text describes the coming together of family leaders and religious leaders among the former exiles "to understand the words of the law." How can we better equip family heads and church leaders to understand and practice the teachings of the Scriptures?

Many parts of our church program should be designed to help *everyone* understand God's Word. Sunday school classes, small groups, and sermons should facilitate understanding. Leadership retreats, marriage and parenting seminars, and other special programs might prove helpful to specific groups in the congregation. The church could encourage families to spend time in the Word together, providing a reading plan coordinated with the preacher's messages or designed to go through the Bible in a year. Additional help could be offered to family heads to help them initiate the program in their homes.

2. The exiles had not been observing the Feast of Tabernacles—at least, not as they should have. When God's Word exposed their neglect, they set about to make things right. Do you think people today are as quick to make right a deficiency they find when they compare their lives with the Word? Why or why not? How can such a readiness be cultivated in people's lives?

People today don't like to be told they are not doing something right. The society as a whole has rejected the concept of absolute right and wrong, and some of that is evident in the church. We need to be committed to the concept of truth and that the Bible is true. Only from such a starting point will the Bible's rebuke of our neglect be effective. Such an attitude about the Bible is best developed early. We need to be sure our children and teens are being taught from a perspective that holds the Bible up as wholly true and incapable of error.

3. The Feast of Tabernacles was an occasion on which the Jews remembered the difficult times of living in tents in the wilderness. What kind of past events or difficulties do you think we should commemorate? How should we do it?

When we are successful and comfortable, we may forget what it took to reach our present status. Such forgetfulness can lead to our becoming lax and indifferent in our discipleship. The Feast of Tabernacles recalled, not just the difficulty of the exodus, but that God was leading. When we recall our own past difficulties, we need to focus on how God has led us in those times. That in turn can stir us to depend on Him in present times, for we still require His guidance. Whatever we do to commemorate the past, our emphasis must be on God's leading and provision, not on ourselves.

4. We must keep ourselves separate from the pagans of our time, but we must also seek to influence them with the gospel. How can we accomplish these seemingly contradictory aims?

Paul speaks strongly about the need for separation in 2 Corinthians 6:14-18. And yet, earlier in 1 Corinthians 5:9, 10, he says that, to remain completely separate, "then must ye needs go out of the world." So we must associate with unbelievers, but we dare not let them lure us into their value systems and lifestyles. We should be the influencers and not the influenced. As we have opportunity, we can boldly espouse our faith and take our stand for Christian values. If we discover that a non-Christian associate is influencing us with ungodly ideas and practices, we must end the association.

5. The people of Israel engaged in a public confession of their sins. Should we encourage the public confession of sins? Why or why not?

James does tell us to "confess your faults one to another, and pray one for another" (James 5:16), but this command does not specify that members must stand before the entire congregation to confess their sins. It seems rather to refer to a one-to-one sharing of confession and supportive prayer. Belonging to a small group or meeting regularly with an accountability partner can provide a believer with the means to obey the command in James.

In the case of a public sin, one that has affected the entire congregation, then perhaps a more public confession would be in order. If, for example, a minister or elder has been guilty of adultery or theft or some other breach of trust, confession before the church may be a step in mutual healing. The more public the sin, the more public the confession and repentance need to be.

Winter Quarter, 1998-99

God Calls Anew in Jesus Christ
(New Testament Survey)

Special Features

Lessons

Unit 1: The Good News of Jesus Christ

Unit 2: Good News for Daily Living

Unit 3: Good News for Changing Times

About These Lessons

Having completed last quarter's survey of the Old Testament, we delve this quarter into an overview of the New. The good news is that God has called each of us into a reconciled relationship with Him through the person of His Son Jesus. That truth comes through in each lesson of the quarter.

Dec 6
Dec 13
Dec 20
Dec 27
Jan 3
Jan 10
Jan 17
Jan 24
Jan 31
Feb 7
Feb 14
Feb 21
Feb 28

Quarterly Quiz

The questions on this page may be used in several ways: as a pretest at the beginning of the quarter; as a review at the end of the quarter; or as a review after each lesson. The questions are based on the Scripture text of each lesson (King James Version). **The answers are on page 115.**

Lesson 1

1. The writer of Hebrews states that Jesus has been made so much better than the *Angels*. *Hebrews 1:4*

2. What did Jesus say He would give Peter after Peter had made what is now called the Good Confession? *Matthew 16:19*

Lesson 2

Customary

1. Name the individual to whom Luke addresses his Gospel. *Luke 1:3*

2. What three facts about Jesus constituted the gospel that Paul had received and that he preached? *1 Corinthians 15:3, 4*

Lesson 3

1. Just before Jesus was born, who issued the decree that all the world should be taxed? *Luke 2:1*

2. Who was governor of Syria at the time of Jesus' birth? *Luke 2:2*

3. The angel said, "I bring you *good News* of *great Joy*, which shall be to all people." *Luke 2:10*

Lesson 4

1. What did the disciples give Jesus to eat when He appeared to them after His resurrection? *Luke 24:42*

2. Jesus told the disciples to wait in Jerusalem until they received *power* from on high. (a vision, power, or forgiveness?) *Luke 24:49*

Lesson 5

1. Who asked Jesus, "Which is the first commandment of all?" *Mark 12:28*

2. According to Jesus, how shall all men know those who are His disciples? *John 13:35*

Lesson 6

1. When a man asked Jesus to assist him with settling an inheritance, Jesus gladly helped him. T/F *Luke 12:13, 14*

2. Jesus' parable of the rich fool followed His warning to beware of *greed*. *Luke 12:15*

Lesson 7

1. Whom did Jesus call to Him to illustrate His view of greatness for His disciples? *Matthew 18:2-4*

2. Jesus said that the Son of man came to *Served* and to give His life a *ransom* for many. *Matthew 20:28*

Lesson 8

1. Who asked Jesus, "How oft shall my brother sin against me, and I forgive him? till seven times?" *Matthew 18:21*

2. How much did the unforgiving servant owe the king? *Matthew 18:24*

Lesson 9

1. In what city was Mars' Hill located? *Acts 17:22*

2. What was written on the altar that Paul had noticed? *Acts 17:23*

3. Some in the crowd on Mars' Hill mocked Paul when he spoke of the resurrection of the dead. T/F *Acts 17:32*

Lesson 10

1. Paul writes, "Let every soul be subject unto the _____ _____." *Romans 13:1*

2. We should owe no man anything except what? *Romans 13:8*

Lesson 11

1. When Jesus instituted the Lord's Supper, He described the cup as the _____ _____ in His blood. *1 Corinthians 11:25*

2. What should one do before eating of the bread and drinking of the cup? *1 Corinthians 11:28*

Lesson 12

1. Paul writes, "Knowing . . . the _____ of the Lord, we persuade men." (love, terror, or patience?) *2 Corinthians 5:11*

2. Anyone who is in Christ is a _____ _____. *2 Corinthians 5:17*

3. Christians have been given the ministry of _____. *2 Corinthians 5:18*

Lesson 13

1. Paul describes our attitude toward the second coming as "looking for that _____ _____." *Titus 2:13*

2. The writer of Hebrews says that we should serve God with reverence and godly fear, for He is a _____ _____. *Hebrews 12:29*

It Is Still Good News Today

by Johnny Pressley

"THE BEGINNING OF THE GOSPEL of Jesus Christ, the Son of God" (Mark 1:1). So begins the New Testament writer Mark as he introduces his readers to his main subject, Jesus Christ, and to the Biblical concept of a "Gospel." Today we often refer to the "good news" of Jesus Christ.

The New Testament records for us the good news of Jesus—the story of His life on this earth, the lessons He taught, and the spiritual legacy He left behind for His followers. These three items—the life, teaching, and legacy of Jesus—are the essence of the New Testament message. They comprise the truths that we have grown up with in the church. One might wonder if there is anything more to be said on such familiar themes, and the answer is an unqualified *yes*. There is such a rich depth to the gospel story that we can always go back and find nuggets of truth that we had not noticed before.

The lessons for this quarter form a survey of the New Testament. It is hoped that the thirteen lessons will stimulate the minds of your students with new ideas to consider. Never forget, however, that there is also great value in looking afresh at truths we already know, not so much to learn new ideas as to enjoy the familiar company of old ones. Just as a wife never tires of hearing her husband say that he loves her, so our souls are strengthened and renewed each time we hear again the Scripture passages we have grown to love. By them we continue to be challenged and encouraged. Our lessons may present an old familiar message, but it is still good news today.

The Life of Jesus

The first unit of four lessons, "The Good News of Jesus Christ," will review some of the stories from the life of Jesus and show how they should impact our lives in a practical way.

Lesson 1, "The Son of God," will focus on the divine nature of Jesus. Combining bold declarations from the opening verses of Hebrews with Peter's confession recorded in Matthew 16:16, this lesson reminds us that inside Jesus' human body was, as Paul says, "all the fulness of the Godhead" (Colossians 2:9).

Lesson 2, "The Gospel of Jesus Christ," will summarize some of what makes the church's message about Jesus so distinctive. Luke 1 represents the testimony of someone who did not see Jesus for himself, but who thoroughly researched the evidence and stated with confidence that the gospel story of Jesus is true. The opening verses of 1 Corinthians 15 give a succinct summary of the key elements of the gospel: Jesus' death, burial, and resurrection. The first four verses of 1 John present John's affirmation that he actually saw, heard, and touched Jesus.

Lesson 3, "The Birth of Jesus," will focus on one of the most cherished Biblical stories at the height of the Christmas season. The Luke 2 account will once again stir the heart with the familiar images of the "little town of Bethlehem," a baby in a manger, and angels announcing their "good tidings" to shepherds.

Lesson 4, "The Promise of Power," touches on the climax of Jesus' ministry on earth as He prepared to ascend to Heaven. The text from Luke 24 tells of a postresurrection appearance by Jesus that was typical of all those recorded in the Gospels. Those who saw Jesus alive doubted at first, but were led to believe by the convincing evidence at hand—a nail-pierced body that they could see and touch. Jesus then commissioned His disciples to be His witnesses to others, who would then follow their lead in taking the gospel to all nations. As Luke 24 affirms, the evangelistic success of the apostles as well as the church ultimately derives from the powerful ministry of the Holy Spirit in the lives of Jesus' followers.

Answers to Quarterly Quiz on page 114

Lesson 1—1. angels. 2. the keys of the kingdom of heaven. **Lesson 2**—1. Theophilus. 2. the death, burial, and resurrection of Jesus. **Lesson 3**—1. Caesar Augustus. 2. Cyrenius. 3. good tidings, great joy. **Lesson 4**—1. a piece of broiled fish and a honeycomb. 2. power. **Lesson 5**—1. one of the scribes. 2. if they have love one to another. **Lesson 6**—1. false. 2. covetousness. **Lesson 7**—1. a little child. 2. minister, ransom. **Lesson 8**—1. Peter. 2. ten thousand talents. **Lesson 9**—1. Athens. 2. "To the Unknown God." 3. true. **Lesson 10**—1. higher powers. 2. to love one another. **Lesson 11**—1. new testament. 2. examine himself. **Lesson 12**—1. terror. 2. new creature. 3. reconciliation. **Lesson 13**—1. blessed hope. 2. consuming fire.

The Teaching of Jesus

The second unit of lessons is entitled "Good News for Daily Living." These four lessons will focus on the teaching ministry of Jesus in the Gospels. Each lesson will develop a different theme that often recurred throughout Jesus' ministry, showing once again the practical implications of His words for our lives today.

Lesson 5, "Love One Another," will use texts from three different Gospels to illustrate a key theme of Jesus' teaching—that His disciples must learn to exhibit toward each other the same kind of self-sacrificing love that brought Him to earth to die for their sakes. As the final text from John 13 will note, this kind of brotherly love is to be the distinguishing mark of those who have become followers of Christ.

Lesson 6, "Follow Kingdom Priorities," will use Luke 12:13-21 to challenge our natural attraction to money and possessions. The parable of the rich fool illustrates how easy it is to be blinded by prosperity and to forget our first duty to God and to others. The lesson's intent will not be to paint material blessings as wrong, but to remind us of the priorities by which we are to handle that which God gives us to enjoy.

Lesson 7, "Reverse the World's Standard," will use two stories from Matthew that contrast the immature thinking of the apostles in their early years—when they argued about who was "the greatest"—with the servant-leader style required for ministry in the Lord's church.

Lesson 8, "Forgive One Another," will use Matthew 18 to teach a lesson on the grace and forgiveness we have received from God and are expected to show to others. Jesus' parable of the servant who was forgiven but failed to show forgiveness to another will challenge us to "do unto others" as God has so graciously done to us.

The Legacy of Jesus

The third unit of lessons is entitled, "Good News for Changing Times." These five lessons are taken from the book of Acts, the New Testament epistles, and Revelation. They are intended to represent how the early Christians applied in their own culture and context the ideas they learned from Jesus. It is hoped that their efforts will illustrate for us today how to apply the unchanging message of the gospel in a world that never ceases to change.

Lesson 9, "Knowing No Boundaries," will focus on an incident from Paul's missionary journeys that seems as fresh and relevant today as it was when it first happened. Acts 17 records the spread of the gospel into new territories, crossing previously untouched cultural and religious boundaries. As the world we know continues to "shrink" and we encounter firsthand a greater variety of peoples and cultures, we will appreciate the lesson we can learn from Paul's first "cross-cultural" experience on Mars' Hill.

Lesson 10, "Obeying Civic Authorities," will touch on issues of continuing interest to modern Christians. In democratic countries Christians can be intimately involved in the workings of government, with the right to vote and speak out on issues and even to seek political office—something impossible for most believers of the Biblical era. Of course, the greater our privileges, the greater our responsibilities. As Christians we have the greatest burden of all citizens: a command from God to give obedience and respect to all authorities, acknowledging their legitimacy from God. Romans 13 gives guidelines for our duty to government, even when we do not like the policies of that government.

Lesson 11, "Building a Caring Community," focuses on the observance of the Lord's Supper, using Paul's teaching in 1 Corinthians 11. Starting with the primary purpose of this ceremony as a "remembrance" of Christ's death, we will look at another dimension of the Lord's Supper—its message of unity among fellow believers who have also accepted the death of Christ for their salvation. The improper conduct of the church at Corinth teaches us not to partake "unworthily" and bring God's judgment upon us.

Lesson 12, "Reconciling the World to God," will pick up on one of the grandest themes in Scripture—the meaning of Christ's death at Calvary. From 2 Corinthians 5 we will view the cross as a work of "reconciliation," in which Christ restored a peace and a friendship between man and God that was disrupted because of our sin. And as Paul emphasizes, the blessing of Calvary also comes with a duty—to speak as ambassadors of Christ and let others know that they too can be reconciled to God.

Lesson 13, "Living in Hope," is an appropriate way to end this New Testament survey. The lesson will focus on Jesus' promise to return one day to gather the saints and take them home to Heaven forever. Titus 2 reminds us of the content of our hope, Hebrews 12 assures us of the security of our hope, while Revelation 1 reveals a heavenly vision of our hope. This will be a lesson of celebration and challenge, encouraging us to live out the hope of which we speak and sing.

The "good news" of Jesus Christ, demonstrated by His life on earth, proclaimed through His teachings, and living on in His spiritual legacy to the church, is indeed still good news today. Let us faithfully carry out our mission as Christ's ambassadors, declaring to a lost world, "Be ye reconciled to God!"

THE
NEW TESTAMENT
WORLD

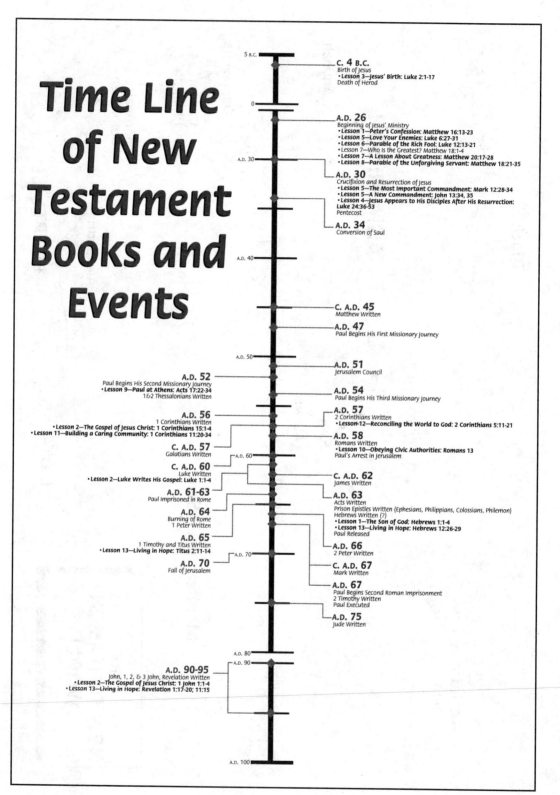

Time Line of New Testament Books and Events

5 B.C.

C. 4 B.C.
Birth of Jesus
• *Lesson 3—Jesus' Birth: Luke 2:1-17*
Death of Herod

0

A.D. 26
Beginning of Jesus' Ministry
• **Lesson 1—Peter's Confession: Matthew 16:13-23**
• **Lesson 5—Love Your Enemies: Luke 6:27-31**
• **Lesson 6—Parable of the Rich Fool: Luke 12:13-21**
• *Lesson 7—Who Is the Greatest? Matthew 18:1-4*
A.D. 30
• **Lesson 7—A Lesson About Greatness: Matthew 20:17-28**
• **Lesson 8—Parable of the Unforgiving Servant: Matthew 18:21-35**

A.D. 30
Crucifixion and Resurrection of Jesus
• **Lesson 5—The Most Important Commandment: Mark 12:28-34**
• **Lesson 5—A New Commandment: John 13:34, 35**
• **Lesson 4—Jesus Appears to His Disciples After His Resurrection: Luke 24:36-53**
Pentecost

A.D. 34
Conversion of Saul

A.D. 40

C. A.D. 45
Matthew Written

A.D. 47
Paul Begins His First Missionary Journey

A.D. 50

A.D. 52
Paul Begins His Second Missionary Journey
• **Lesson 9—Paul at Athens: Acts 17:22-34**
1&2 Thessalonians Written

A.D. 51
Jerusalem Council

A.D. 54
Paul Begins His Third Missionary Journey

A.D. 56
1 Corinthians Written
• **Lesson 2—The Gospel of Jesus Christ: 1 Corinthians 15:1-4**
• **Lesson 11—Building a Caring Community: 1 Corinthians 11:20-34**

A.D. 57
2 Corinthians Written
• **Lesson 12—Reconciling the World to God: 2 Corinthians 5:11-21**

C. A.D. 57
Galatians Written

A.D. 58
Romans Written
• **Lesson 10—Obeying Civic Authorities: Romans 13**
Paul's Arrest in Jerusalem

A.D. 60

C. A.D. 60
Luke Written
• **Lesson 2—Luke Writes His Gospel: Luke 1:1-4**

C. A.D. 62
James Written

A.D. 61-63
Paul Imprisoned in Rome

A.D. 63
Acts Written
Prison Epistles Written (Ephesians, Philippians, Colossians, Philemon)
Hebrews Written (?)
• **Lesson 1—The Son of God: Hebrews 1:1-4**
• **Lesson 13—Living in Hope: Hebrews 12:26-29**
Paul Released

A.D. 64
Burning of Rome
1 Peter Written

A.D. 65
1 Timothy and Titus Written
• **Lesson 13—Living in Hope: Titus 2:11-14**

A.D. 66
2 Peter Written

A.D. 70

A.D. 70
Fall of Jerusalem

C. A.D. 67
Mark Written

A.D. 67
Paul Begins Second Roman Imprisonment
2 Timothy Written
Paul Executed

A.D. 75
Jude Written

A.D. 80

A.D. 90

A.D. 90-95
John, 1, 2, & 3 John, Revelation Written
• **Lesson 2—The Gospel of Jesus Christ: 1 John 1:1-4**
• **Lesson 13—Living in Hope: Revelation 1:17-20; 11:15**

A.D. 100

Old and New, New and Old
Using Comparison and Contrast in Bible Teaching

by Ronald G. Davis

STRUGGLING TO DESCRIBE or define objects or concepts often elicits a comparison/contrast way of thinking. And rightly so. Noting similarities and differences is one way we make sense of our world. To describe is to "draw a line around"—to say what is inside and what is not. To define is to "set the limits of"—to say that something goes "this far" and no farther.

Comparison/contrast is always worthy of the teacher's consideration. Relating what students don't know to what they do know is good teaching. This quarter's study provides especially suitable content for this method of teaching/learning.

Texts from the Epistle to the Hebrews begin and end this quarter's lessons. Within this letter, we see the important similarities of the Old and New Covenants, but also the overwhelming difference: the absolute superiority of the New. The text for lesson 1 is a perfect example of the comparison/contrast strategy at work in teaching:

"God, who at sundry times and in divers manners spake in time past unto the fathers by the prophets, hath in these last days spoken unto us by his Son, whom he hath appointed heir of all things, by whom also he made the worlds; who being the brightness of his glory, and the express image of his person, and upholding all things by the word of his power, when he had by himself purged our sins, sat down on the right hand of the Majesty on high" (Hebrews 1:1-3).

God spoke "in time past"—when the Old Covenant was in force. He speaks "in these last days"—the era of the New Covenant. But now He is speaking not in words but in the *Word*. In the former days the speaking was of a temporary nature. In these last days the speaking is final: Jesus is God's last Word.

Using Similarities and Differences

Christianity is distinctively different from all the philosophies and pseudo religions of the world. The Christian has compared truth with lie, fact with theory, morality with pragmatism, evidence with supposition. He has concluded that Christian faith has superior answers to all of life's hard questions. True disciples persist in applying that same comparison/contrast mindset to a wide range of circumstances. The unit of study at hand lends itself to advance the disciple's faith through such analysis.

Such an approach to teaching and learning offers several possibilities for in-class activity. One is the variety of *pen-and-paper activities* normally associated with tests and testing, which can call attention to important comparison/contrast elements in a lesson. Another is the use of *tables and charts*, which are essentially efforts to show how two or more concepts are alike and how they are different by highlighting shared and nonshared characteristics. A third involves *role playing*, which enables students to respond to hypothetical situations. This method is useful to emphasize the difference between Christian and non-Christian lifestyles and ways of thinking.

How well does the teacher of adults want his learners to know the Bible and its life-directing truths? The Spirit has spoken: "Till we all come in the unity of the faith, and of the knowledge of the Son of God, . . . no more children, tossed to and fro, and carried about with every wind of doctrine, . . . but speaking the truth in love, may grow up into him in all things, which is the head, even Christ" (Ephesians 4:13-15).

Consider the following possibilities from the choices above and the lessons ahead:

True or False?

Tests generate thinking and demand choices. Thoughtful choice is at the heart of Christian faith. A lesson with narrative material such as lesson 4, "The Promise of Power," lends itself to a test activity. To get learners to focus on the important facts of the text and to generate discussion of relevant issues, even a simple true-false test will work. As an example, take these ten statements taken from the printed text for lesson 4 (Luke 24:36-53). The number in parentheses is the verse(s) where the answer to the statement can be found.

NEW FEATURE!

This quarter finds the introduction of another new feature in *Bible Teacher and Leader/Standard Lesson Commentary*: an article on methodology for teachers. Watch for other **Teacher Tips** in future quarters. Collect and save them for future reference.

___ Jesus claimed to fulfill Scripture. (44, true)

___ The resurrected Christ had a fully human body. (39, true)

___ Doubt is impossible for true believers. (38, false)

___ Jesus ate food before His disciples to show them that He was not a spirit. (42, 43, true)

___ At His appearance, Jesus fully empowered His disciples. (49, false)

___ The disciples were deeply saddened at Jesus' ascension. (52, false)

___ The core elements of the gospel are Jesus' death and resurrection, and repentance and forgiveness. (46, 47, true)

___ The disciples never really worshiped Jesus. (52, false)

___ Jesus' initial words when He appeared to His disciples were, "Why are you not believing?" (36, false)

___ Jesus' final earthly deed was to bless His disciples. (50, 51, true)

Such a test is not designed simply to review and reinforce facts. Ponder the discussion possibilities. Key Christian doctrines—the deity of Christ, His bodily resurrection, for examples—are involved. Consider how the fellowship between Jesus and the disciples offers true encouragement to all who would be His today: He is concerned about our peace of mind; He trusts us to be His witnesses; He provides the joy of worship.

Whatever format you choose, a test can stimulate serious and significant reflection. Comparing truth with falsehood will move your learners toward the goals stated in Ephesians 4:13-15.

Side by Side

One simple but sure way to see the likenesses and the differences between two (or more) items is to hold them up side by side (by side). *Tables and charts*—whether on paper, chalkboard, or overhead transparency—are designed to provide just such a view. In a vertical column, the items to be compared are named. In horizontal columns, the relevant characteristics are listed. Then the task is a simple: "Does this item have this particular characteristic or not?" Advertisers regularly use such a device to show the superiority of their product over comparable ones. They always highlight the advantages: "With the 1999 Moxie sedan, leather seats are standard; in the Blahmobile, they're $650 extra!"

Paul used the same method in his message at Mars' Hill in Athens (lesson 9, Acts 17:22-34). Picture an imaginary chart with two headings: "Greek Gods" and "The Unknown God." Run through Paul's checklist as you read his sermon: (1) Made the world; (2) Lives in man-made temples; (3) Needs service from men; (4) Made every nation; (5) Expects men to repent; (6) Will judge the world; (7) Raised one from the dead; (8) Wants fellowship with men; (9) Made by man's design and skill; (10) Determines history with purpose. Some Athenians saw this comparison and sneered. Some wanted to hear more. A few became believers. The gospel always gets these responses. Thoughtful choices, based on comparison and contrast, will vary, but God always allows people to make their own choices.

Self or Others?

In certain ways Christian thinking and non-Christian thinking are alike. But at one significant point they differ greatly. "To serve or be served"—that is the question. Christians exist to serve. Non-Christians exist to be served, so they think and act accordingly. The choice is self-centeredness or Christ-centeredness, being selfish or selfless. Jesus made it clear: "By this shall all men know that ye are my disciples, if ye have love one to another" (John 13:35). Non-Christians are likewise easily spotted: they love themselves.

The coming quarter has several studies designed to emphasize how the individual living under the New Covenant thinks and behaves differently from the ungodly. Lesson 7, "Reverse the World's Standard" (based on Matthew 18:1-4; 20:17-28), is probably the primary example.

Role playing is one activity that allows students to experience tough choices without the risks of reality. (If one chooses poorly in a role play, the consequences are irrelevant.) For lesson 7, class members might be assigned (or recruited!) to be the Christian or non-Christian in each of the following hypothetical situations:

You are driving carefully at the speed limit through a business district in the left lane, anticipating a left turn several blocks away. A car behind you accelerates, passes you on the right honking madly, and swerves dangerously close in front of you.

As you leave the office after dark one evening, on the way to your car you are approached by a dirty, gaunt beggar asking, "Do you have a dollar for something to eat, friend?"

Ask your role players to dramatize and verbalize their responses. Have the group discuss whether the responses chosen reflect what the students would like to do or what they would really do. Through such an activity your learners should be challenged to "grow up into him in all things, which is the head, even Christ."

And that is the point of it all: to attain "unto the measure of the stature of the fulness of Christ." What more worthy goal could a Christian teacher have for his students?

The Son of God

DEVOTIONAL READING: Isaiah 11:1-10.

LESSON SCRIPTURE: Hebrews 1:1-4;
Matthew 16:13-26.

PRINTED TEXT: Hebrews 1:1-4; Matthew
16:13-23.

Hebrews 1:1-4

1 God, who at sundry times and in divers manners spake in time past unto the fathers by the prophets,

2 Hath in these last days spoken unto us by his Son, whom he hath appointed heir of all things, by whom also he made the worlds;

3 Who being the brightness of his glory, and the express image of his person, and upholding all things by the word of his power, when he had by himself purged our sins, sat down on the right hand of the Majesty on high;

4 Being made so much better than the angels, as he hath by inheritance obtained a more excellent name than they.

Matthew 16:13-23

13 When Jesus came into the coasts of Caesarea Philippi, he asked his disciples, saying, Whom do men say that I, the Son of man, am?

14 And they said, Some say that thou art John the Baptist; some, Elijah; and others, Jeremiah, or one of the prophets.

15 He saith unto them, But whom say ye that I am?

16 And Simon Peter answered and said, Thou art the Christ, the Son of the living God.

17 And Jesus answered and said unto him, Blessed art thou, Simon Barjona: for flesh and blood hath not revealed it unto thee, but my Father which is in heaven.

18 And I say also unto thee, That thou art Peter, and upon this rock I will build my church; and the gates of hell shall not prevail against it.

19 And I will give unto thee the keys of the kingdom of heaven: and whatsoever thou shalt bind on earth shall be bound in heaven; and whatsoever thou shalt loose on earth shall be loosed in heaven.

20 Then charged he his disciples that they should tell no man that he was Jesus the Christ.

21 From that time forth began Jesus to show unto his disciples, how that he must go unto Jerusalem, and suffer many things of the elders and chief priests and scribes, and be killed, and be raised again the third day.

22 Then Peter took him, and began to rebuke him, saying, Be it far from thee, Lord: this shall not be unto thee.

23 But he turned, and said unto Peter, Get thee behind me, Satan: thou art an offense unto me: for thou savorest not the things that be of God, but those that be of men.

GOLDEN TEXT: Simon Peter answered and said,
Thou art the Christ, the Son of the living God.—Matthew 16:16.

> ### God Calls Anew in Jesus Christ
> Unit 1: The Good News of Jesus Christ
> (Lessons 1-4)

Lesson Aims

After this lesson a student should be able to:

1. Describe the unique character of Jesus, the Son of God, as illustrated in today's text.

2. Explain why Jesus must be accepted as Son of God or not at all.

3. Make a confession of faith in Jesus, the Son of God, and determine to share that confession with someone this week.

Lesson Outline

INTRODUCTION
    A. Christianity Is Jesus
    B. Lesson Background
I. CHRIST'S SUPREMACY DESCRIBED (Hebrews 1:1-4)
    A. The Word of God to Man (vv. 1, 2)
    B. The Image of God to Man (v. 3)
    C. The Salvation of God for Man (v. 4)
    The Floodlights Shine on Jesus
II. CHRIST'S SUPREMACY DECLARED (Matthew 16:13-23)
    A. A Probing Question (vv. 13-15)
    B. An Inspired Answer (vv. 16, 17)
    C. An Encouraging Promise (vv. 18-20)
    Search and Rescue
    D. A Solemn Warning (vv. 21-23)
CONCLUSION
    A. No Mere Man
    B. Prayer
    C. Thought to Remember

Introduction

A. Christianity Is Jesus

Consistently in surveys that address religious matters, more than ninety percent of the people in America report believing in God. Not nearly that many believe in Jesus. It is not enough to admire Jesus or proclaim Him to be a great teacher or prophet. What makes Christianity distinctive is its belief that Jesus is divine, and that He is uniquely the Son of God. Some people may describe themselves as Christians who do not hold these beliefs. They would not, however, meet the Biblical criteria. Christianity is founded upon Jesus—not just His teachings, but also His person and work.

Today's lesson is the first in a survey of the New Testament, and also the first in a unit on Jesus. Its contents go right to the heart of the matter: Who is Jesus? Matters of eternal significance will be determined by our answer.

B. Lesson Background

Our discussion today is based on two very different Biblical texts. The first is a selection from the opening verses of the book of Hebrews. The most difficult question surrounding this book is its authorship. Unlike other epistles or letters in the Bible, this one does not bear the author's name. This is appropriate, since the author wanted to lift up Christ. Some believe Paul to be the author. Others have speculated that the writer may have been John the apostle, Apollos the great preacher, Barnabas, Priscilla and Aquila, or a number of others. After all the speculation, we must conclude that we do not know with certainty who wrote the book. We do know that it appears to have been written to Jewish believers who were considering abandoning their Christian faith to return to Judaism. The author proclaims the superiority of Jesus and of the Christian faith.

The second part of the printed text comes from the Gospel of Matthew. It highlights a pivotal discussion between Jesus and His disciples, focusing particularly on Peter.

I. Christ's Supremacy Described (Hebrews 1:1-4)

A. The Word of God to Man (vv. 1, 2)

1. God, who at sundry times and in divers manners spake in time past unto the fathers by the prophets.

The author of Hebrews begins his treatise with a tribute to the majesty of Jesus. He recalls that *God* has always had a desire to communicate with His creation. He has, in fact, spoken in *sundry times and in divers manners* (at various times and in various ways) in the *past* through *the prophets*. These were inspired verbal messages. However, these men did not communicate all that God desired mankind to know. The author of Hebrews was eager to call attention to a message from God that was far superior—one to which many of the prophets pointed in their preaching (1 Peter 1:10).

2. Hath in these last days spoken unto us by his Son, whom he hath appointed heir of all things, by whom also he made the worlds.

Jesus has come in *these last days* as a unique messenger of God. He is not just another prophet; as God's *Son*, He embodies God's Word. The beginning of John's Gospel notes how the Word, which was "in the beginning with God" (John 1:2), "was made flesh, and dwelt among us" (v. 14).

The reference to Jesus' arrival in the *last days* should be interpreted in light of how the New Testament uses this phrase. It does not refer to the end of time, but rather to the final stage of God's redemptive plan. The Old Testament is considered the "former days," or "time past" (Hebrews 1:1). The New Testament era, beginning with Jesus' first coming and concluding with His return, is viewed as the *last days* (see also Acts 2:16, 17; 1 Peter 1:19, 20; 1 John 2:18).

In addition, Jesus is *heir of all things*. This is another way of saying Jesus is God's Son in a special sense—one not achievable by any human being. As the second person of the Godhead, He was also a participant in the creation of the world (John 1:3). The author does not use the most common word for *worlds* here. He uses a word that is often translated "the ages." It seems he is stressing in the most comprehensive term possible that Jesus was instrumental in creating not only this planet, but also the universe and all that is part of it, both seen and unseen.

B. The Image of God to Man (v. 3)

3. Who being the brightness of his glory, and the express image of his person, and upholding all things by the word of his power, when he had by himself purged our sins, sat down on the right hand of the Majesty on high.

The author continues to wax eloquent in his lofty tribute to Jesus. He describes Jesus as *the brightness of his [God's] glory* (John 1:14). He is also *the express image of his person*. The Greek word translated "express image" is a term that applied to an impression made by a seal or stamp, which left behind an image of itself. It was the kind of stamp used by a government official or person of wealth to seal a document. In other words, Jesus bears the stamp of the heavenly Father's image, and has revealed to us the Father's nature and character (John 14:9).

Jesus is also *upholding all things by the word of his power*. He holds the world together by His

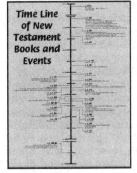

This visual will be useful throughout the quarter. It will help you place the events studied and the Biblical texts in chronological order.

Visual for lesson 1

powerful word; "by him all things consist," says Colossians 1:17.

The final half of this verse calls our attention to the cross, where Jesus *by himself purged our sins*. When He finished His redemptive work, Jesus *sat down on the right hand of the Majesty on high*. This signifies that His work is completed, and contrasts His accomplishment with that of the Old Testament priests, who "standeth daily ministering and offering oftentimes the same sacrifices, which can never take away sins" (Hebrews 10:11). [See question #1, page 128.]

C. The Salvation of God for Man (v. 4)

4. Being made so much better than the angels, as he hath by inheritance obtained a more excellent name than they.

In today's world, many have become fascinated by *angels*. We now have movies, television programs, books, and even a magazine devoted solely to angels. Certainly the angels who appear in the Scriptures are magnificent creatures, inspiring awe and wonder. But they are not worthy of worship. Only Jesus is worthy of worship because He is *much better than the angels*. He has a greater *inheritance* and a greater *name*. An angel is simply a messenger. The ministry of angels is significant, but their splendor pales in comparison with Jesus as God's Son. The writer elaborates on this point in the remainder of Hebrews 1. [See question #2, page 128.]

THE FLOODLIGHTS SHINE ON JESUS

We've all seen buildings that are surrounded by floodlights and beautifully illuminated at night. The owner of such a building may have spent thousands of dollars on the floodlights; yet no one ever says, "Wow! Look at those floodlights! Aren't those the most impressive floodlights you've ever seen?" Instead, people say, "Wow! Look at that building! Isn't it magnificent?" The lights draw attention to the building, not to themselves.

God's angels do not call attention to themselves. They simply point to Jesus. Don't give your worship and allegiance to the angels, but to the One on whom the angels shine their "floodlights." Only Jesus can give you truth, meaning, hope, and salvation.   —G. A.

II. Christ's Supremacy Declared (Matthew 16:13-23)

As we continue our study of Jesus as God's Son, we move not only from one book to another, but from one kind of literature to another. We leave Hebrews, an epistle or letter, and go to an eyewitness account of the life of Christ—the

Gospel according to Matthew. Here we'll find a critical teaching encounter between Jesus and His disciples.

A. A Probing Question (vv. 13-15)

13. When Jesus came into the coasts of Caesarea Philippi, he asked his disciples, saying, Whom do men say that I, the Son of man, am?

This encounter took place after heightened tensions had developed between Jesus and the Pharisees and after a series of miracles (Matthew 14:13—16:12). Jesus' *disciples* needed a lesson on how to interpret those events.

The incident recorded here took place in the *coasts* (or vicinity) of *Caesarea Philippi*. This city was built by Herod Philip, a son of Herod the Great who is called "tetrarch of Ituraea and of the region of Trachonitis" (Luke 3:1). Although Herod the Great had arranged to divide his kingdom among his sons upon his death, all the Herods ruled at the pleasure of Caesar (Tiberias), the Roman emperor. Herod Philip wanted to curry favor with Caesar, so he called this city Caesarea. His own name was attached to the city to distinguish it from the other Caesarea, which was near the Mediterranean Sea.

14. And they said, Some say that thou art John the Baptist; some, Elijah; and others, Jeremiah, or one of the prophets.

The disciples offered several answers to Jesus' question. *Some* believed Jesus to be *John the*

Baptist returning from the dead. The record of John's Gospel is clear that John the Baptist was not the Messiah (John 1:8, 19-27; 3:28).

The disciples also reported that some said that Jesus was *Elijah*. Elijah was a popular prophetic figure. The prophet Malachi (Malachi 3:1; 4:5, 6) declared that Elijah would be God's messenger, preceding the coming of the Messiah. Jesus explained that this prophecy was fulfilled in John the Baptist (Matthew 11:10-14). According to the words of the angel Gabriel, John came "in the spirit and power of Elijah" (Luke 1:17).

Still others claimed that Jesus was *Jeremiah*. Jeremiah was another great prophet who was revered because of his courage and his passion for God's truth. Jesus, however, was not any of these. He was no mere man or prophet.

15. He saith unto them, But whom say ye that I am?

Now Jesus made the question much more personal, directing it to the disciples and asking, "Who do you say I am?" This was a question they had to face, along with everyone who has ever heard of Jesus. It is one thing to report what others say; it is quite another to declare what *you* believe. [See question #3, page 128.]

B. An Inspired Answer (vv. 16, 17)

16. And Simon Peter answered and said, Thou art the Christ, the Son of the living God.

True to his personality, *Simon Peter* was the first to speak. In most cases, he said (or did) the wrong thing, but here he was right on target. He *answered* that Jesus is the *Christ*. The word *Christ* is a title. It is the Greek equivalent to the Hebrew word *Messiah*. It means "anointed one." Peter went on to say that Jesus is the *Son of the living God*. This went beyond a declaration of messiahship, for Peter could have had in mind a human Messiah. Peter was declaring his conviction that Jesus is no mere mortal. He is God in the flesh.

17. And Jesus answered and said unto him, Blessed art thou, Simon Barjona: for flesh and blood hath not revealed it unto thee, but my Father which is in heaven.

Jesus responded to Peter's answer by calling him *blessed*. This is the same word as that used in the Beatitudes, and it is not easy to translate into English. Some have suggested that "happy" or "joyful" are good translations.

The prefix "bar" in *Barjona* simply means "son." We see it in other names such as Bartholomew, Barabbas, and Barnabas. In this case, *Barjona* means "son of John" or "son of Jonah."

Why was Peter *blessed*? The confession he made was not one whose source was mere human reasoning. (The phrase *flesh and blood* was a common Jewish expression referring to

---

How to Say It

APOLLOS. Uh-*pahl*-us.
AQUILA. *Ack*-will-uh.
BARABBAS. Buh-*rab*-us.
BARJONAH. Bar-*jo*-nuh.
BARNABAS. *Barn*-uh-bus.
BARTHOLOMEW. Bar-*thahl*-uh-mew.
CAESAREA PHILIPPI. Sess-uh-*ree*-uh Fuh-*lip*-pie or *Fill*-uh-pie.
ELIJAH. Ee-*lye*-juh.
GABRIEL. *Gay*-bree-ul.
HADES. *Hay*-deez.
ITURAEA. It-you-*ree*-uh.
JEREMIAH. Jair-uh-*my*-uh.
MALACHI. *Mal*-uh-kye.
MEDITERRANEAN. *Med*-uh-tuh-*ray*-nee-un (strong accent on *ray*).
PETRA (Greek). *peh*-trah.
PETROS (Greek). *peh*-tross.
PRISCILLA. Prih-*sill*-uh.
SANHEDRIN. San-*heed*-run or *San*-huh-drin.
TIBERIAS. Tie-*beer*-e-us.
TRACHONITIS. Trak-o-*nye*-tus.

mortals or mortality.) It was a confession that required spiritual sensitivity and discernment. Peter was responding to a truth *revealed* by God through Jesus' words and works.

C. An Encouraging Promise (vv. 18-20)

18. And I say also unto thee, That thou art Peter, and upon this rock I will build my church; and the gates of hell shall not prevail against it.

The interpretation of this verse has been subject to much discussion. In responding to Peter's confession, Jesus declared, *Upon this rock I will build my church.* Was he talking about Peter? Or was he talking about the confession itself and the truth it contains? The latter seems to be the better answer. Would Jesus build His church on a human foundation? That is doubtful. On one level this might make sense, since the Bible teaches that the church was built on the foundation of the apostles and prophets (Ephesians 2:20). But can one man be the rock? Only one person deserves that designation: Jesus Himself.

Part of what makes this verse problematic is that Peter's name means "rock." However, when Jesus said, "Upon this rock I will build my church," He was using a Greek word (*petra*) that was slightly different from the Greek form of Peter's name (*petros*). The difference may be expressed as follows: "You, Peter, are just a small pebble; but on this bedrock [the truth of who I am] I will build my church." Jesus was using a play on words that was most appropriate in the language of the New Testament.

Furthermore, Jesus promised that *the gates of hell shall not prevail against* the church. The Greek word translated *hell* (*Hades*) is a general word for the abode of the dead, both good and bad. Other times it is taken to mean death or the powers of death. The latter is most likely its meaning here. Notice also that the church is pictured as on the march—not in a defensive mode. Jesus' description of the church is not one of the powers of death pounding on the gates of the church. It is the church pounding on the gates of death and prevailing over them. Jesus' church is a victorious church. [See question #4, page 128.]

19. And I will give unto thee the keys of the kingdom of heaven: and whatsoever thou shalt bind on earth shall be bound in heaven; and whatsoever thou shalt loose on earth shall be loosed in heaven.

This verse is part of Jesus' great promise, but it also is a bit problematic. Peter was told that he would be given *the keys of the kingdom of heaven.* Keys are used in opening doors, allowing people to enter buildings or rooms. Peter used the keys given to him when he outlined the

VISUALS FOR THESE LESSONS

The *Adult Visuals* packet contains classroom-size visuals designed for use with the lessons in the Winter Quarter. The packet is available from your supplier. Order No. 292.

terms of admission into the Christian life on the Day of Pentecost (Acts 2:38).

Jesus appears to say that any judgment Peter makes *on earth* will be acknowledged as binding *in heaven.* This reference to "binding" and "loosing" does speak of a special authority, but it is an authority to declare judgment, not to determine it. A better translation of Jesus' words (and one followed in the *New American Standard Bible*) might be, "Whatever you shall bind on earth shall have been bound in heaven, and whatever you shall loose on earth shall have been loosed in heaven."

20. Then charged he his disciples that they should tell no man that he was Jesus the Christ.

Jesus then gave *his disciples* what must have seemed a strange command. They were not to tell anyone that He was *the Christ.* Why not? Jesus would set His own time for the cross. He would lay His life down; it would not be taken from Him (John 10:18). Jesus did not want to arouse the crowds at this point, or give the authorities reason to question His ministry. This command was given for a specific occasion and a specific need. Today we are no longer under any obligation to keep the truth about Jesus quiet. Rather, we are obligated to share it wherever we go.

SEARCH AND RESCUE

Who can forget the heart-wrenching images in the aftermath of the bombing of the federal building in Oklahoma City in 1995? The scenes of grieving family members, dead children, and horrific destruction linger in our minds.

Among the scenes that few of us will ever forget are those involving the incredible rescue operations conducted by emergency personnel. For many days they kept reentering the fragile, collapsing structure at the risk of their own lives. Weren't they afraid it might collapse on them? Of course. Weren't they afraid there might be additional explosives that could yet be detonated? Of course. But the larger fear that they had for the ones still trapped overcame their fears for themselves.

It is true that Jesus did not want His disciples to tell anyone that He was the Christ, according to today's text (Matthew 16:20). However, His command to us is to be His witnesses "unto the uttermost part of the earth" (Acts 1:8).

We may have many fears about sharing our faith with our friends, family, and co-workers. Perhaps we're afraid that someone will be more intelligent than we are. Maybe we'll lose the respect of others. Maybe we've fumbled some attempts in the past.

What can keep us motivated to share with others in the face of these fears? A greater fear—the fear that if we don't keep sharing, others will spend eternity one day without Jesus Christ and thus without hope.

Christmas is just around the corner. Let's share the good news of this season with someone who needs Jesus.   —G. A.

D. A Solemn Warning (vv. 21-23)

21. From that time forth began Jesus to show unto his disciples, how that he must go unto Jerusalem, and suffer many things of the elders and chief priests and scribes, and be killed, and be raised again the third day.

Jesus followed up on this "mountaintop experience" with a disturbing announcement: the Messiah must die. Jesus knew the when, where, and how of His death. He even told them of His resurrection—a promise that (as their reaction shows) they appeared to ignore.

Jesus also told who would instigate His suffering. *The elders* was a general designation of the Jewish leaders. The *chief priests* were those in charge of the temple and its procedures. *Scribes* were also thought of as teachers of the Jewish law, or lawyers (Luke 11:45, 46, 52). These three groups made up the Jewish ruling council called the Sanhedrin.

22. Then Peter took him, and began to rebuke him, saying, Be it far from thee, Lord: this shall not be unto thee.

Peter, who had just spoken in such exemplary fashion, now returned to his characteristic rashness. He told Jesus that the scenario He had just described must not happen. His words constituted a *rebuke*—a strange way to talk to a person whom he had just affirmed to be Christ and Lord.

23. But he turned, and said unto Peter, Get thee behind me, Satan: thou art an offense unto me: for thou savorest not the things that be of God, but those that be of men.

In contrast to Jesus' earlier compliment of Peter's faith, we now see a bluntness in Jesus' response to Peter's folly. Jesus said, *Get thee behind me, Satan*. Earlier Jesus called attention to the meaning of Peter's name ("rock"). Now Peter has become a stumbling stone.

What did Jesus' addressing Peter as *Satan* mean? The word *Satan* means "adversary." When

it is used as a proper name, it signifies the ultimate adversary—the devil himself. Here, by calling Peter *Satan*, Jesus may have been saying that Peter was speaking and acting as an adversary of God's plan and purpose. Any attempt to stop Jesus from facing the cross was an attempt to oppose the will of God. [See question #5, page 128.]

Conclusion

A. No Mere Man

Napoleon was reported to have said that he knew men, and that Jesus was no mere man. As we study the text from Hebrews and the Good Confession of Peter, we see that the Bible does not give us the option of believing that Jesus is a mere man. Jesus is Lord, Christ, and so much more. He is beyond description. It is interesting that most world religions try to find some way to fit Jesus into their schemes, for such is the force of His powerful influence. Frequently, however, the emphasis that these religions place on Jesus is far less than what the Scripture says He must receive.

We must accept Jesus on His terms, not ours. We need to find a place for Jesus as He is, and He is no mere man.

B. Prayer

Above all else, dear God, I want to know Your Son. In Him I see You. In Him I understand Your grace. In Him I discover Your love. Thank You for putting a face on Yourself by sending us Jesus. Thank You for His sacrifice and suffering for us. We worship and serve a suffering Savior. In the name of Him who bears the scars. Amen.

C. Thought to Remember

Words cannot express or the mind fathom the majesty of Jesus.

Home Daily Bible Readings

Monday, Nov. 30—She Shall Name Him Immanuel (Isaiah 7:10-17)
Tuesday, Dec. 1—A Child Has Been Born to Us (Isaiah 9:1-7)
Wednesday, Dec. 2—A Vision of Peace (Isaiah 11:1-10)
Thursday, Dec. 3—He Was Wounded for Our Transgressions (Isaiah 53:1-12)
Friday, Dec. 4—Arise, Shine; for Thy Light Is Come (Isaiah 60:1-7)
Saturday, Dec. 5—God Has Spoken by His Son (Hebrews 1:1-4)
Sunday, Dec. 6—Thou Art the Christ! (Matthew 16:13-26)

Learning by Doing

This page contains an alternate lesson plan emphasizing learning activities.
Classes desiring such student involvement will find these suggestions helpful.

Learning Goals

After this lesson a student should be able to:

1. Describe the unique character of Jesus, the Son of God, as illustrated in today's text.

2. Explain why Jesus must be accepted as Son of God or not at all.

3. Make a confession of faith in Jesus, the Son of God, and determine to share that confession with someone this week.

Into the Lesson

Write the heading *"Bible Names and Descriptions of Jesus"* on a large poster or on the chalkboard. (Waxed butcher paper also works well.) Select a student to act as "scribe" to write the responses students give. A few ideas for names and descriptions include "Immanuel," "Almighty God," "the way, the truth, and the life," "the bread of life," etc.

At the end of this exercise, thank the students for the names and descriptions. Add the name "Son of God" to the list (or circle it if it is already there). Tell the class that today we will explore more descriptions with special attention given to the name "Son of God."

Into the Word

Explain that this quarter's study is a survey of the New Testament. The first four lessons highlight the basic gospel story, including Jesus' birth, life, death, and resurrection. Today, we see a wonderful snapshot of His character.

Ask the students to read Hebrews 1:1-4 and Matthew 16:13-23 and to list every title or description of Jesus they can find. This task may be accomplished in small groups, in pairs, or as a whole class. List the answers on another poster. Note: This exercise is included in the student book. (Answers should include His [i.e., God's] Son, heir of all things, He made the worlds, the brightness of His glory, the express image of His person, upholding all things, purged our sins, sits on the right hand of the Majesty, better than the angels, a more excellent name, Son of Man, Christ, Son of the living God, and Lord.)

Using the Scripture and the lesson commentary as your guides, ask the class to explain or clarify the significance of each of these names or descriptions. Then use the following discussion questions to deepen the probe of the text.

1. Why did some think Jesus was John the Baptist, Elijah, Jeremiah, or one of the prophets? (See Matthew 14:1, 2; Malachi 4:5, 6; John 3:2.)

2. Of all the descriptions of Jesus given in our text, why is Peter's response, "the Son of the living God," so special? What is the great significance of Jesus as God's Son? (As Son of God, He is divine—equal with God. His word is greater than that of the prophets; see Hebrews 1:1, 2.)

3. Within five hundred years of Jesus' ascension, distorted views of Jesus became a serious problem for the church. Some denied that Jesus was God, saying that He was only a man. Others denied that Jesus was human and insisted that He, being God, couldn't really have suffered and died. (Seeds of this heresy are seen as early as the *first* century—1 John 4:3.) What ramifications do these views have for the Christian faith? (If Jesus were a mere man, He was sinful as we are and could not atone for sin; see 2 Corinthians 5:21. If He were God and not man, He also could not atone for sin; see Hebrews 4:15.)

Our lesson commentator says that in Peter's confession, he affirmed that Jesus is no mere mortal. He is God in the flesh. Why would this become the premise upon which Jesus would build His church? (Jesus is God, but He was also fully human. He is fully God, having existed eternally and having the power and nature of God. He was also fully human, experiencing all human emotions and temptations. In order for Him to complete God's plan of salvation, He had to be both God and man.)

Into Life

Give each student a sheet of paper or an index card with the following question written on it: "Suppose you were asked by a non-Christian friend, 'Who is Jesus?' In light of today's study, what would you say? List five to ten key views you now hold about Jesus that are important for your friend to know." Ask class members to work on this project in pairs. After the project, allow a few students to share their answers with the whole class.

Challenge each class member to identify a friend with whom he/she will try to create an opportunity to share these convictions about Jesus.

Ask the pairs that worked together to share these names and pray for each other's commitment.

Let's Talk It Over

The questions on this page are designed to encourage review of the lesson Scriptures and to promote discussion of the lesson by the class. The answers provided are only discussion starters. Let your class talk it over from there.

1. God created humankind in his own image (Genesis 1:26). How does that relate to Jesus' being the "express image" of God?

Created in God's image, we humans display certain distinctives that separate us from the rest of what biologists call the "animal kingdom." These include the abilities to reason, create, and to communicate ideas. We are the only species able to make reasoned choices or to enter into contracts or commitments to be honored at or until some future date. This allows for the expression of love that is more than instinctual or hormonal. These qualities also enable us to have a special relationship with God. Since we are like God in some ways, we can relate to Him in ways the rest of creation cannot.

Jesus, however, is not just *like* God in some ways. He *is* God, and is thus like God in every way. Even if the image of God in us were not distorted by sin, it would still be limited. Jesus, as the "express image" of God's person, is not merely one who shares some features in common with God; He is God. And He is thus uniquely suited to restore in us the image of God as we are "conformed to [His] image" (Romans 8:29).

2. How is Jesus superior to angels?

Angels are "ministering spirits, sent forth to minister for them who shall be heirs of salvation" (Hebrews 1:14). The Bible depicts angels as serving at some important moments, generally as messengers (the literal meaning of "angels"). Jesus accomplished far more than conveying a message. The name Jesus means "Jehovah saves" (Matthew 1:21). Jesus was the atoning sacrifice for our sins. He provided the means for our forgiveness. None of the angels could do that. Though Jesus came "not to be ministered unto, but to minister" (Matthew 20:28), He is ultimately "King of kings" and "Lord of lords" (1 Timothy 6:15). Angels refuse worship (Revelation 19:10), but Jesus is worthy of the worship of men and angels (Revelation 4:11; 5:12-14).

3. What practical difference does it make whether Jesus was just one more great religious teacher or the Son of God?

Jesus was a great moral teacher, and in many ways His teaching established a new standard, and can be argued to be superior to other moral codes or religious formulas. If Jesus was only a religious teacher, however, He had no power or authority to back up His promise of forgiveness and eternal life. Only as the unique Son of God could He provide the remedy justice demands. He could sacrifice His perfect life for our sake. He is the only one in history with moral credit that He can apply to our account. No mere teacher can do that. And any teacher who claimed he could do what he could not do would be a liar, and not a good teacher or a good role model. If Jesus were just a good teacher, He was not God's Son; but if He were not God's Son, He was not a good teacher!

4. Jesus anticipates the church storming the gates of Hell. Where do you see our church waging the battle against the forces of evil and death? What evidence can you cite that the church is prevailing?

Unfortunately, many churches get into a defensive posture, simply trying to preserve previous gains or protect themselves from disappearing. Churches that begin to think and act that way generally do disappear in time. More creative and bold churches are finding ways to take the battle to the very gates of Hell. What form of evangelistic outreach have you and your church been trying? Are you demonstrating God's love by meeting any needs in your community? Are any lives being touched and changed by the practical application of grace and love through your hands?

5. Jesus told Peter that rejecting the way of suffering was thinking like men and not like God. Can you give any examples of believers today thinking like the world and not like God?

Following Jesus means choosing the way of the cross, the way of self-surrender. How are believers you know denying themselves in order to be more obedient to the will of God? Do they restrict their material wants in order to contribute to the church outreach project? Would they sacrifice a vacation in order to serve short-term with a foreign mission or work in Vacation Bible School? Unbelievers are interested in personal comfort, leisure, entertainment, and luxury. Are we controlled more by those thoughts, or by Jesus' motives?

The Gospel of Jesus Christ

DEVOTIONAL READING: Colossians 1:15-20.

LESSON SCRIPTURE: Luke 1:1-4; 1 Corinthians 15:1-4; 1 John 1:1-4.

PRINTED TEXT: Luke 1:1-4; 1 Corinthians 15:1-4; 1 John 1:1-4.

Luke 1:1-4

1 Forasmuch as many have taken in hand to set forth in order a declaration of those things which are most surely believed among us,

2 Even as they delivered them unto us, which from the beginning were eyewitnesses, and ministers of the word;

3 It seemed good to me also, having had perfect understanding of all things from the very first, to write unto thee in order, most excellent Theophilus,

4 That thou mightest know the certainty of those things, wherein thou hast been instructed.

1 Corinthians 15:1-4

1 Moreover, brethren, I declare unto you the gospel which I preached unto you, which also ye have received, and wherein ye stand;

2 By which also ye are saved, if ye keep in memory what I preached unto you, unless ye have believed in vain.

3 For I delivered unto you first of all that which I also received, how that Christ died for our sins according to the Scriptures;

4 And that he was buried, and that he rose again the third day according to the Scriptures.

1 John 1:1-4

1 That which was from the beginning, which we have heard, which we have seen with our eyes, which we have looked upon, and our hands have handled, of the Word of life;

2 (For the life was manifested, and we have seen it, and bear witness, and show unto you that eternal life, which was with the Father, and was manifested unto us;)

3 That which we have seen and heard declare we unto you, that ye also may have fellowship with us: and truly our fellowship is with the Father, and with his Son Jesus Christ.

4 And these things write we unto you, that your joy may be full.

GOLDEN TEXT: That which we have seen and heard declare we unto you, that ye also may have fellowship with us: and truly our fellowship is with the Father, and with his Son Jesus Christ.—1 John 1:3.

God Calls Anew in Jesus Christ
Unit 1: The Good News of Jesus Christ
(Lessons 1-4)

Lesson Aims

After this lesson a student should be able to:

1. Summarize the testimony of Luke, Paul, and John regarding the gospel.

2. Tell why the historical foundation of the gospel makes it worthy of our acceptance and belief.

3. Give thanks to God for the firm foundation of our faith.

Lesson Outline

INTRODUCTION
  A. Passing the Faith Along
  B. Lesson Background
I. LUKE'S TESTIMONY (Luke 1:1-4)
  A. Received From Eyewitnesses (vv. 1, 2)
    Where Are the Critics?
  B. An Orderly Account (vv. 3, 4)
II. PAUL'S TESTIMONY (1 Corinthians 15:1-4)
  A. The Power of the Gospel (vv. 1, 2)
  B. The Person of the Gospel (vv. 3, 4)
    Only Jesus Can Rescue
III. JOHN'S TESTIMONY (1 John 1:1-4)
  A. I Have Seen Him (v. 1)
  B. I Have Shared Him (v. 2)
  C. I Have Fellowship With Him and You
    (vv. 3, 4)
CONCLUSION
  A. He's the Real Thing
  B. Prayer
  C. Thought to Remember

Introduction

A. Passing the Faith Along

Have you ever watched a relay race? The most important part of the race is the passing of the baton. No matter how speedy the team members, a fumbled baton is almost certain to cost them the race. For this reason, relay teams spend hours practicing the passing of the baton.

Most of us have something we wish to pass on to our children. Perhaps it is property, money, or family heirlooms. The most important item to pass on is our faith. We owe much to the writers of the New Testament. They and their colleagues have given us a clear picture of Jesus. We can decide whether or not to believe them,

but we cannot say that we don't know what they believed. Even those who do not believe must come to the conclusion that these men believed in Jesus with all their hearts. They knew Jesus, they were certain of who He is, and they wanted others to know of their certainty. The job now belongs to us. We have to pass on the message to the next generation. Let's not drop the baton!

Last week's lesson dealt with the identity of Jesus as God's Son. This week we look at the substance of the apostolic preaching about Jesus. We will seek to learn what the early preachers told their audiences about Jesus. What was the message that "turned the world upside down" (Acts 17:6)?

B. Lesson Background

The New Testament writers were insistent on establishing the truth of their message. They wanted people to know that Jesus was real, not a creation of their imaginations. They wanted to confirm that people saw, heard, and touched Him. Today's lesson looks at three texts from three different writers, who each in his own way provided evidence of the reality of Jesus. The first witness is Luke. Known as "the beloved physician" (Colossians 4:14), Luke may have been a convert of the apostle Paul. In Philemon 24, he is listed among Paul's "fellow laborers." Luke is also the author of the book of Acts.

The second witness is the apostle Paul himself. Paul had been reared outside of Palestine but was well-educated in the Jewish faith and traditions. He was educated by the great rabbi Gamaliel (Acts 22:3), and was also a Pharisee (Philippians 3:5). Paul was not one of the original twelve apostles. In fact, he was at first violently hostile to the Christian cause (Acts 26:9-11). But Jesus called him to become an apostle to the Gentile (non-Jewish) world (Acts 26:12-18). Paul was eminently qualified for this task because he was well educated, knew the Scriptures well, and had lived in the Gentile world. He wrote more of the New Testament than any other writer.

Our third witness is the apostle John, known as the beloved apostle. He was one of the first of Jesus' disciples, along with his brother, James, and his fishing partners, Peter and Andrew. John was part of Jesus' "inner circle"; he, Peter, and James witnessed certain events that the other disciples did not (Luke 8:51; 9:28; Mark 14:33). He stood with Jesus' mother at the cross as Jesus was dying (John 19:25-27). It appears that he was the last of the apostles to die, yet we shall see that his writing reveals a knowledge of Jesus that had deepened, not diminished, over the years.

I. Luke's Testimony
(Luke 1:1-4)

Luke's testimony is found in the prologue to his Gospel, in which he validates the historical accuracy of his work.

A. Received From Eyewitnesses (vv. 1, 2)

1. Forasmuch as many have taken in hand to set forth in order a declaration of those things which are most surely believed among us.

While we generally think of four Gospels, Luke records that *many* in his day had *taken in hand to set forth . . . a declaration of those things* that are at the heart of our faith. Just what records did he have in mind? There is no way of knowing. Was he referring to the Gospels we have in our Bibles? They may be included, but Luke surely was also including some accounts that were not inspired and have not been passed down to us. The implication here is that not all the many accounts were trustworthy, so Luke took in hand to provide an orderly account so that Theophilus and others could "know the certainty" (v. 4) of the facts of the gospel.

Each of the four Gospels has its own theme and point of view. Each writer organized his material to make a specific point. While much of the information in Luke is also in Matthew and Mark, Luke had certain themes he wanted to explore and a particular method that he wanted to employ. The inspiration of Scripture does not mean that a writer could not use his own personality, or that his writing would not reflect his own style. Notice that in Luke's case (see verse 2), the Holy Spirit inspired him to talk to eyewitnesses. The doctrine of inspiration does not require that every word of Scripture be supplied by God directly. Inspiration is the process by which God guarded the words that were written, whether they came by revelation from God, from the author's memory or research, or from another source. Together, revelation and inspiration have produced for us a Bible that is reliable and trustworthy, completely inerrant in the original manuscripts. [See question #1, page 136.]

2. Even as they delivered them unto us, which from the beginning were eyewitnesses, and ministers of the word.

Who were the *eyewitnesses* to whom Luke refers? Surely the apostles must be included among them. In Acts 6 the apostles delegated the care of the needy widows to seven men of sterling character so that they could devote themselves to prayer and to the "ministry of the word" (Acts 6:4). They were, then, *ministers of the word.* No doubt there were other eyewitnesses as well. Luke could easily have spoken to Mary, the mother of Jesus, and others of the women who supported Jesus' ministry (Luke 8:2, 3). He could have talked to Jesus' brothers.

Those who view the stories of Jesus as legends or myths have to reckon with the brief period of time between when the events took place and when the written works began to appear. There were people alive who could verify the truthfulness of the accounts. Matthew, Mark, and Luke were written within about thirty years of Jesus' death. It takes much longer than thirty years to create a legend.

WHERE ARE THE CRITICS?

Imagine that you picked up the newspaper tomorrow and saw a headline that read, "Preacher Raises Dead Elephant Back to Life." Wouldn't you be a bit skeptical? Wouldn't you have doubts?

Well, then, imagine as you continued reading that you discovered that the person making the incredible claims was your preacher, and that this miracle was allegedly done in your home church at a time when you know you were present. Wouldn't you let the newspaper and everyone else know, "Hey, I was there! My preacher didn't raise a dead elephant back to life!" And if your preacher started appearing on talk shows and news programs, and people seemed to be buying his story, wouldn't you raise some strong objections? Of course you would!

An important part of the credibility of the life, miracles, and resurrection of Jesus is the absence of the critics. Eyewitnesses wrote down their records of Jesus' life, and these have been preserved for us in the Bible. These records circulated soon enough after the events themselves that others could have stepped forward and challenged these claims if they were not true. The silence of the critics testifies loudly to the accuracy of the eyewitnesses' reports.   —G. A.

B. An Orderly Account (vv. 3, 4)

3. It seemed good to me also, having had perfect understanding of all things from the very first, to write unto thee in order, most excellent Theophilus.

Luke claims *perfect*, or complete, *understanding of all things from the very first.* Most likely he is talking about the instruction he received from the apostles and other witnesses concerning the events of Christ's birth, life, death, and resurrection. Luke was also determined to write an account *in order.* We do not know if this means chronological order or thematic order. Slight differences in the arrangement of events in the Gospels make chronology difficult to determine with much precision. Luke's Gospel seems to be mostly chronological, with a few exceptions.

Luke was writing to a man named *Theophilus.* Who was he? The name *Theophilus* means "friend of God" or "lover of God." Thus, many Bible students believe this was a name for all friends and lovers of God wherever they may be. If these students are right, then *Theophilus* simply represents all Christians. Others suggest that Theophilus was an otherwise unknown Christian who was the recipient of Luke's accounts of Jesus' life (Luke) and of the early church (Acts). There is even a suggestion that Theophilus may have been a Roman official somehow connected with Paul's trial in Rome. Those who hold this position believe that Theophilus was involved in Paul's defense in court, and needed an orderly account of the life of Jesus in order to learn more about the Christian message. Luke uses the title *most excellent* in referring to Theophilus. Such a title would normally be used for an official (see Acts 23:26), or some other person of great prominence. Perhaps Theophilus was a benefactor who supported Luke in the production of his writings.

4. That thou mightest know the certainty of those things, wherein thou hast been instructed.

Here it appears that Theophilus knew something of Jesus but needed to be assured of *those things* about which he had *been instructed.* Perhaps he was a believer who needed an accurate standard by which to measure all that he was hearing about Jesus. In the Biblical records, we too have an accurate standard by which to measure the teachings of those who claim to be spiritual guides. [See question #2, page 136.]

II. Paul's Testimony (1 Corinthians 15:1-4)

Paul's testimony is found toward the end of his first letter to the church at Corinth. It is part of his teaching concerning the basic facts of the gospel, of which some Corinthians seemed unsure. This troubled church needed advice in many areas, but they needed special help with their doctrine.

How to Say It

CORINTH. *Kor*-inth.
CORINTHIANS. Kor-*in*-thee-unz.
DAMASCUS. Duh-*mass*-kus.
GAMALIEL. Guh-*may*-lee-ul.
GNOSTICISM. *Nahss*-tih-sizz-um.
GNOSTICS. *Nahss*-tiks.
PHARISEE. *Fair*-ih-see.
THEOPHILUS. Thee-*ahf*-ih-luss.

A. The Power of the Gospel (vv. 1, 2)

1. Moreover, brethren, I declare unto you the gospel which I preached unto you, which also ye have received, and wherein ye stand.

Paul reminds the Corinthians of *the gospel* he had *preached* to them. The word gospel means "good news" and is related to the Greek word from which our English word "evangelism" comes. Paul says that this is a gospel that had been *received.* In other words, the Corinthians had responded to the message about Jesus. It was also a gospel in which they could *stand.* It was something in which they had placed their total confidence. It was not a new message to the Corinthians, but they needed to be reminded of what it had accomplished in their lives.

2. By which also ye are saved, if ye keep in memory what I preached unto you, unless ye have believed in vain.

Here Paul describes the gospel as that which *saved* the Corinthians. However, their responsibilities were not completed; they were to *keep in memory* what Paul had *preached,* or else they will have *believed in vain.* Such warnings to saved people are found in other portions of the New Testament (Colossians 1:21-23; Hebrews 6:4-6; 2 Peter 1:10; 3:17).

B. The Person of the Gospel (vv. 3, 4)

3. For I delivered unto you first of all that which I also received, how that Christ died for our sins according to the Scriptures.

Not only had the Corinthians received the gospel (v. 1); Paul himself had *received* it. Paul was not one of Jesus' original twelve apostles. He was, however, qualified to be an apostle, since he had seen the resurrected Lord when Jesus appeared to him on the road to Damascus (Acts 9:1-9). Paul writes of receiving the gospel message "by the revelation of Jesus Christ" (Galatians 1:12). [See question #3, page 136.]

What is the substance of this gospel? First, it centers on the death of Jesus Christ on the cross. Paul says that this death happened *according to the Scriptures.* For Paul *the Scriptures* meant the Old Testament, particularly those portions that predicted the death of Jesus. No doubt he had in mind passages such as Isaiah 53 that foretold the suffering that Jesus experienced.

This death had a specific purpose: *Christ died for our sins.* The word translated *sins* comes from the world of archery, and pictures an archer missing the mark. Whether sins of omission or commission, all sins involve missing God's mark. Jesus, the perfect Lamb of God who never missed that mark, died in the place of all persons, who without exception have missed it (Romans 3:23). The cross thus allows God to be

Home Daily Bible Readings

Monday, Dec. 7—An Orderly Account (Luke 1:1-4)

Tuesday, Dec. 8—The Good News Paul Proclaimed (1 Corinthians 15:1-4)

Wednesday, Dec. 9—That Which We Have Seen and Heard (1 John 1:1-4)

Thursday, Dec. 10—Those Who Do God's Will (1 John 2:15-29)

Friday, Dec. 11—We Are Children of God (1 John 3:1-10)

Saturday, Dec. 12—We Should Love One Another (1 John 3:11-24)

Sunday, Dec. 13—God Is Love (1 John 4:13-21)

both loving (by saving lost mankind) and just (by punishing sin) at the same time.

4. And that he was buried, and that he rose again the third day according to the Scriptures.

Paul also stresses that Jesus was *buried*. Why would he bother with this detail? Perhaps he was countering some of the arguments that one sometimes hears today—that Jesus was not really dead, that perhaps He merely "swooned" on the cross. Of course, if there had never been an actual death and burial, then the resurrection loses its significance. This is the next important fact of the gospel: Jesus *rose again*.

This resurrection, notes Paul, was also accomplished *according to the Scriptures*. What Old Testament Scriptures speak of a resurrection? General references to this can be found in Job 19:25, 26; Psalm 16:10; and Isaiah 53:10, 11. As for being raised on the third day, Paul may have been thinking of the words of Hosea 6:2 or of Jonah 1:17. In subsequent verses (5-8), Paul lists six specific appearances of the risen Christ. Adding this information to the Gospels, we have a total of at least eleven separate appearances. That is far too many for the resurrection to be dismissed as the product of mere rumor, wishful thinking, or hallucination.

ONLY JESUS CAN RESCUE

If you were in a boat out on the open sea and fell overboard, but didn't know how to swim, what would you want your friends in the boat to do? Certainly their encouragement to "hang in there" and "stay above the water" would be welcome. They could even model for you how to swim or how to tread water. They could tell you stories about how they once fell overboard and survived. But sooner or later, wouldn't you hope that they would throw you a life preserver? At some point you would have to be rescued, because your situation is a matter of life and death.

In 1 Corinthians 15:1-4, Paul tells us that the substance of the gospel message is the death, burial, and resurrection of Jesus Christ. Yet many times in our witnessing it seems as if this message is noticeably absent. We may talk about the exciting church we're a part of and all that is happening there. We may talk about how Jesus' wisdom for living has helped us find meaning and significance as a single person, or in our marriage, or in our family. We may talk about how the power of Jesus Christ has helped us overcome addictive behaviors, or a sinful past, or a painful season of grief. And there's a time to talk about all of that.

But unless there is a time where we get down to basics and talk about the cross and the empty tomb, we are not sharing the true gospel. Sooner or later we've got to throw people a life preserver—because all that can save a person from drowning for eternity is the death, burial, and resurrection of Jesus Christ!   —G. A.

III. John's Testimony (1 John 1:1-4)

John's testimony concerning Jesus is taken from the first four verses of his first epistle. Although the name of the author does not appear in the letter, there are sufficient similarities in language and style between this letter and the Gospel of John to indicate that the apostle John was the writer.

A. I Have Seen Him (v. 1)

1. That which was from the beginning, which we have heard, which we have seen with our eyes, which we have looked upon, and our hands have handled, of the Word of life.

The opening of John's first letter is reminiscent of the opening of his Gospel. His Gospel begins with, "In the beginning was the Word," and his epistle commences with, *That which was from the beginning*. In both cases John is stressing the eternal nature of the Son of God. His Gospel also stresses that "the Word was made flesh, and dwelt among us" (John 1:14). Here in this letter he describes Jesus as *that . . . which we have heard, which we have seen with our eyes, which we have looked upon, and our hands have handled*.

One may ask, "What is the difference between saying *we have seen with our eyes* and *we have looked upon*?" The second phrase is more intense. A casual glance may account for the report, "We have seen Him," but a steady gaze is suggested by, "We have looked upon Him." It may carry the connotation of looking intently or looking with understanding. We sometime use the word "see" in this sense when we say, "I see," meaning "I understand."

John wants his readers to know assuredly that Jesus was no legend or myth. Just as Jesus is called "the Word" in John's Gospel, here John calls Him *the Word of life.* John's emphasis on seeing, looking upon, and handling Jesus may have been an attempt to counter an early form of false doctrine that came to be called Gnosticism. The Gnostics held many odd beliefs that challenged certain essentials of the Christian faith. Among their views was the idea that all flesh is absolutely evil, and that Jesus, if holy, could not have appeared in human flesh. John denies such teaching and reminds his readers that Jesus had a real body. He was not a phantom. [See question #4, page 136.]

B. I Have Shared Him (v. 2)

2. (For the life was manifested, and we have seen it, and bear witness, and show unto you that eternal life, which was with the Father, and was manifested unto us.)

Here Jesus is called *the life.* This is partly because of His resurrection, but also because He is the source of life. This life was *with the Father,* but has now been given to human beings. It is *eternal life,* inseparably connected to Jesus Himself. Just as Jesus is the Word made flesh, He is eternal life made flesh.

C. I Have Fellowship With Him and You (vv. 3, 4)

3. That which we have seen and heard declare we unto you, that ye also may have fellowship with us: and truly our fellowship is with the Father, and with his Son Jesus Christ.

The partnership, or *fellowship,* that we experience with other Christians is a result of the testimony concerning Jesus being passed from believer to believer. We who are alive today

Perfect Fellowship
1 John 1:3, 4, NIV

Visual for lesson 2

Use this visual to challenge your students to share their own testimony of Jesus to expand the fellowship of believers in your own community.

have not *seen and heard* Jesus as John did. We accept the testimony of eyewitnesses such as him, and this brings us into fellowship with the *Father,* the *Son,* and all others who have fellowship with them. [See question #5, page 136.]

4. And these things write we unto you, that your joy may be full.

John could never experience true and complete *joy* unless others shared in the knowledge he had of Christ. Those who know Jesus and have accepted His offer of salvation can always experience a joyous fellowship with each other (even when they are meeting for the first time!).

Conclusion

A. He's the Real Thing

Some people try to place Jesus in the same category with legends such as Robin Hood and King Arthur. Luke, Paul, and John will not let us do that. It takes hundreds of years to build a legend. All of the New Testament was written within the lifetime of those who had some knowledge of the events recorded therein. There were many who could have stepped forward to counter any false information that was included. Had there been any "cunningly devised fables" (2 Peter 1:16) within the early church's preaching, they surely would have been exposed, given the hostility of so many to the church's message.

Clearly something dramatic and wonderful happened to the disciples. Some may choose not to believe what Luke, Paul, and John have written, but no one should do so unless and until he has examined the testimony of men such as these. Jesus is a person rooted in history. Few if any modern scholars, no matter how skeptical, doubt that Jesus of Nazareth existed. They may argue over how much they trust the Biblical account of His life, or whether He was who He claimed to be. But there is no way to escape Him. Jesus has changed history. He has changed countless lives. He is "the real thing."

B. Prayer

Dear Father, help me not only to pass the faith along to the next generation, but to appreciate the great heritage that my spiritual ancestors have passed down to me. Although I have not seen Jesus with physical eyes, I have seen Him with the eyes of faith. May I never lose the vision. In Jesus' name. Amen.

C. Thought to Remember

Those who saw Jesus were greatly blessed, but Jesus said that there would be a greater blessing for those who "have not seen, and yet have believed" (John 20:29). That means you.

Learning by Doing

This page contains an alternate lesson plan emphasizing learning activities.
Classes desiring such student involvement will find these suggestions helpful.

Learning Goals

After this lesson each student will be able to:

1. Summarize the testimony of Luke, Paul, and John regarding the gospel.

2. Tell why the historical foundation of the gospel makes it worthy of our acceptance and belief.

3. Give thanks to God for the firm foundation of our faith.

Into the Lesson

Ask the class to suppose you had a book in which the author claimed to have seen a working time machine. "Time travel is no longer science fiction," the author claims. "It is here!" Ask, "What would it take for you to believe the story?" Different kinds of evidence probably will be demanded, but the basic source will be testimony from witnesses. Who else has seen it? What tests have been run to verify the performance of the machine? What credentials do the people testing it have that we can believe them?

People want the same thing when it comes to believing in Jesus. Who saw Him and can verify His existence? Who witnessed His actions, and what credentials do the witnesses have that we should believe them?

The Bible offers many witnesses to Jesus. Our lesson today will consider the testimony of three of them. One was an eyewitness and very close associate of Jesus. One was an unbeliever who became convinced when Jesus made a dramatic appearance to Him. And one was a careful historian who spoke with eyewitnesses and carefully researched the matter. (See if the class can identify the three witnesses from those descriptions before they know the texts for today's lesson.)

Into the Word

Choose three good readers to read aloud today's Scripture texts: Luke 1:1-4; 1 Corinthians 15:1-4; 1 John 1:1-4. Then provide the students with the following list of statements. Ask the class to read each statement and to match it with the witness (Luke, Paul, or John) who might likely have made the statement. (Answers are provided here for your convenience.) Have the students work on the activity individually or in small groups; then go over the list together. Use information from the commentary to explain or reinforce important points raised.

1. Many people have written about the life of our Lord, but some of those accounts are not accurate and may cause confusion. I wrote to establish a certain record, one that people could count on. (Luke)

2. We know what we're talking about. We saw Jesus; we heard Him; we touched Him. You can believe our testimony about Him. (John)

3. I wasn't there with Jesus, but I talked to a lot of people who were. (Luke)

4. My preaching is just what the Lord told me and what the Scriptures affirm was to happen: Jesus died, was buried, and rose again. (Paul)

5. Jesus was no mere man. He existed from the beginning. He was with the Father before, and then was made known to us in human form. (John)

6. The good news about Jesus has saving power when it is received and believed. (Paul)

7. I have a very clear understanding of the details of Jesus' life, so I have written an orderly account of it. (Luke)

8. I have not written a "Gospel," but I preach the gospel all over the world—just as I preached it to you in Corinth. (Paul)

9. Won't it be grand when our fellowship with one another and our fellowship with the Father and with Jesus are made perfect in Heaven? That is eternal life! (John)

Into Life

Remind the class that Luke tells us of many other testimonies and writers not included in the Scriptures. Many of these were not inspired, but were the natural expressions of believers wanting to share with others what they had come to believe.

That process continues to this day. Songwriters in particular write their testimonies, and we can enjoy them and use them to express something of our own faith. Ask the students to name some of their favorite songs about Jesus. (Sing a few of these hymns and choruses if you have time.)

One hymn that summarizes much of what we have been discussing is "How Firm a Foundation," by Norman J. Clayton. This hymn celebrates the certainty we can have for our faith because of the testimony of the Bible. Close the class period with prayers of thanks for the Scriptures and with a singing of this hymn.

Let's Talk It Over

The questions on this page are designed to encourage review of the lesson Scriptures and to promote discussion of the lesson by the class. The answers provided are only discussion starters. Let your class talk it over from there.

1. Luke notes that there were many accounts of Jesus' life. Four inspired ones are included in the New Testament. How does the presence of more than one Gospel encourage your faith?

The multiple witnesses to the life and work of Jesus are important in giving credibility to the story. If only one observer had made such fantastic claims about the life and work of Jesus, there would be reason to doubt. We also gain the advantage of different perspectives. Identify the material that is unique to each Gospel and you will discover how our appreciation and understanding is enriched by having four instead of one. For example, only Luke records the visit of the shepherds to the birthplace of Jesus, and only Matthew records the visit of the Magi. John includes very few parables, but he alone recounts the conversations of Jesus with Nicodemus and the woman at the well in Samaria.

2. We now know of several apocryphal gospels—spurious accounts of Jesus' life that contain obvious errors and exaggerations. What reasons can we give for trusting that the New Testament accounts of Jesus are believable?

Both Matthew and John were apostles and close companions of Jesus. They were present to witness much of what they retold in their Gospels. Mark was from Jerusalem and was an early disciple and close associate of the apostles. Luke, a companion of Paul, was a scholar and a careful historian, often adding references to the politics, culture, or geography pertinent to his writing. The Gospels were written and circulated while many eyewitnesses were still living who could verify or deny the claims made about Jesus. There is no way to explain the rapid spread of Christianity nor the ineffectiveness of its enemies if in fact the Christian message was based on lies and inflated legend. Of course, belief in the inspiration of Scripture (2 Timothy 3:16) settles the matter once and for all.

3. Luke spoke of "eyewitnesses" and "ministers of the word" who delivered the news of Jesus to others. Paul also speaks of delivering the gospel that he received. Delivery of the gospel seems as important as receiving it! How did you first receive the news of Jesus? Who delivered it to you? Why did you believe it to be accurate? What are you doing to deliver it faithfully to others?

For the first generation of Christians, the gospel had to be passed along orally. Any error or deficiency in the message told could result in many people being misled and the truth would be lost. Now we have the Bible as a standard by which we can test every teaching; but since many people rely upon what they hear about the Bible, or upon what they are taught, it is still important that we guard the message for accuracy and completeness. Care must be taken that Bible classes and small groups are led by people committed to the trustworthiness of the Bible. And the church must be aggressive in its outreach and support of world missions.

4. How does it add confidence to your faith to know that John and the other apostles were such close companions of Jesus in the flesh?

The apostles serve as the source of most of the information we have concerning Jesus. Because they were close companions of Jesus over a period of approximately three years, we know that they were not dealing in hearsay or speculation. They had the opportunity to assess the integrity and authenticity of Jesus through being with Him consistently through a variety of circumstances. Not only are the claims about Jesus coming from firsthand observers, but it is significant that virtually every one of the apostles went to a martyr's death defending the truth of those claims.

5. How would you describe the "fellowship" that is created when people believe the same things about Jesus? How does that fellowship relate to personal joy?

When a person believes in Jesus, it begins to affect his value system, personal standards, moral behavior, attitudes, choice of leisure activities, and spending decisions. Because they can be distinguished by these changes, believers form a kind of subculture in any society. We draw strength from identifying with one another and encouraging one another. There is joy in having friends who share so much in common and with whom we can give and receive encouragement. But there is even greater joy in knowing that this fellowship will extend into eternity!

The Birth of Jesus

DEVOTIONAL READING: Isaiah 9:2-7.

LESSON SCRIPTURE: Luke 2:1-20.

PRINTED TEXT: Luke 2:1-17.

Luke 2:1-17

1 And it came to pass in those days, that there went out a decree from Caesar Augustus, that all the world should be taxed.

2 (And this taxing was first made when Cyrenius was governor of Syria.)

3 And all went to be taxed, every one into his own city.

4 And Joseph also went up from Galilee, out of the city of Nazareth, into Judea, unto the city of David, which is called Bethlehem, (because he was of the house and lineage of David,)

5 To be taxed with Mary his espoused wife, being great with child.

6 And so it was, that, while they were there, the days were accomplished that she should be delivered.

7 And she brought forth her firstborn son, and wrapped him in swaddling clothes, and laid him in a manger; because there was no room for them in the inn.

8 And there were in the same country shepherds abiding in the field, keeping watch over their flock by night.

9 And, lo, the angel of the Lord came upon them, and the glory of the Lord shone round about them; and they were sore afraid.

10 And the angel said unto them, Fear not: for, behold, I bring you good tidings of great joy, which shall be to all people.

11 For unto you is born this day in the city of David a Saviour, which is Christ the Lord.

12 And this shall be a sign unto you; Ye shall find the babe wrapped in swaddling clothes, lying in a manger.

13 And suddenly there was with the angel a multitude of the heavenly host praising God, and saying,

14 Glory to God in the highest, and on earth peace, good will toward men.

15 And it came to pass, as the angels were gone away from them into heaven, the shepherds said one to another, Let us now go even unto Bethlehem, and see this thing which is come to pass, which the Lord hath made known unto us.

16 And they came with haste, and found Mary and Joseph, and the babe lying in a manger.

17 And when they had seen it, they made known abroad the saying which was told them concerning this child.

GOLDEN TEXT: Unto you is born this day in the city of David a Saviour, which is Christ the Lord.—Luke 2:11.

God Calls Anew in Jesus Christ
Unit 1: The Good News of Jesus Christ
(Lessons 1-4)

Lesson Aims

After this lesson students should be able to:

1. Retell the familiar story of Jesus' birth, as recorded in Luke.

2. Explain the significance of the details reported by Luke.

3. Commit themselves to telling others the good news of the Savior—as the shepherds did.

Lesson Outline

Introduction

A. Here We Are Again

Did you hear about the man who took his preacher to task for preaching on the same subjects over and over again? He said, "All I ever hear you talk about are the birth of Jesus and the resurrection of Jesus." The man quickly turned red when his wife said, "That's because the only times you come are on Christmas and Easter!"

Why do we need to talk about Jesus' birth again? It is probably the most familiar part of the Bible. We revisit it year after year at Christmastime. Nevertheless, there are many traditions that have grown up around Christmas that are not really Biblical. The story seems so familiar, but occasionally we discover that we do not really know it as well as we thought. It is important to remind ourselves of the significance of

Jesus' birth and its implications for today's confused world.

In an unassuming way, Luke tells us how God came down, not only in human form, but as a baby. Have we become so used to hearing this truth that it has lost some of its wonder? It is good for us to step back at this time of the year and take a fresh look at the Christmas story. Think of what it means: God on earth. God in Bethlehem. God in a manger. God on a cross. These are some of the mysteries of what we call the incarnation.

Besides being appropriate for this Sunday before Christmas, today's lesson is a fitting follow-up on last week's lesson, which stressed the trustworthiness of the New Testament record concerning Jesus. Today we return to that specific time and place in history when God entered our world in the person of Jesus.

B. Lesson Background

Virtually all we know about Jesus' birth comes from Matthew and Luke. Mark begins with a brief description of John the Baptist's ministry and jumps immediately to Jesus' baptism. John begins by considering Jesus' preexistence. It is Matthew and Luke who lead us to Bethlehem. Matthew gives us the story of the angelic appearances to Joseph, the visit of the wise men, and the journey of Mary, Joseph, and Jesus to Egypt. Luke records the birth of John the Baptist, the announcement to Mary by the angel Gabriel that she would become the mother of God's Son, and the account of the birth itself in Bethlehem.

Luke's is the only account that includes the visit of the shepherds near Bethlehem. One of the unique characteristics of Luke's Gospel is his interest in common people and those whom society regarded as outcasts. Only Luke mentions the parable of the good Samaritan (10:25-37), the parable of the prodigal son (15:11-32), the story of the rich man and Lazarus the beggar (16:19-31), the cleansing of the ten lepers (17:11-19), and Jesus' meeting with the despised tax collector Zaccheus (19:1-10). Shepherds were looked upon with disdain by many, because they tended to be a rather crude group of men. In addition, their work with animals often left them ritually unclean. Jesus had an effective ministry among such "common people" (Mark 12:37).

Even though many details in the Christmas story are very familiar to us, let us see if we can recapture what it would be like to hear this story for the very first time. Let us never lose our sense of wonder and celebration at the "good tidings of great joy," that unto *us* a Savior is born!

I. Setting of Jesus' Birth
(Luke 2:1-7)
A. The Rulers (vv. 1, 2)

1. And it came to pass in those days, that there went out a decree from Caesar Augustus, that all the world should be taxed.

As a careful historian, Luke fixes the birth of Jesus in a particular historical context. He places the event during the reign of *Caesar Augustus*, who was the first emperor of Rome. The word *Caesar* means "ruler" and became the title used by subsequent Roman rulers. The name *Augustus* means "exalted"; thus the first Roman emperor was designated "exalted ruler."

That *all the world* was *taxed* refers to a census of the population that was taken for taxation purposes. *The world* would have included any territories under Rome's control. Some skeptics have claimed that Luke is in error because such an empire-wide census is not recorded in Roman history. But this is not a valid reason to conclude that it never happened. Such a practice would have been consistent with Roman policy in occupied territory. In fact, there is a reference to another census, taken later than the one mentioned here, which Luke also notes in Acts 5:37.

Isn't it ironic that as renowned as Caesar Augustus was, and as important as he thought he was, he is probably most famous for what is said about him in connection with the birth of Jesus in a remote part of his empire? Truly, "God hath chosen the weak things of the world to confound the things which are mighty" (1 Corinthians 1:27). [See question #1, page 144.]

2. (And this taxing was first made when Cyrenius was governor of Syria.)

Some say that Jesus could not possibly have been born *when Cyrenius was governor of Syria*, for there are non-Biblical records of his being governor later. However, there is evidence that suggests Cyrenius held the office of governor for two terms, and the first coincides with the time of Jesus' birth. We must keep in mind that Luke's account was written within a generation of the event itself. Luke, who has already spoken of his concern for historical accuracy and careful research (Luke 1:1-4), would not likely have included this detail if he did not have a sound basis for doing so. Justin Martyr in A.D. 140 claimed to have documentation to prove that Jesus was born under Cyrenius.

B. The Couple (vv. 3-5)

3, 4. And all went to be taxed, every one into his own city. And Joseph also went up from Galilee, out of the city of Nazareth, into Judea, unto the city of David, which is called Bethle-hem, (because he was of the house and lineage of David).

Joseph lived in a region called *Galilee*, a name that means "circle." The word describes a cluster of small towns that formed a rough circle near the Sea of Galilee. *Nazareth* was a small town in Galilee, covering probably no more than seven acres in Jesus' day.

From Nazareth, Joseph and Mary traveled approximately eighty miles to *Bethlehem*, a small town just five miles south of Jerusalem, for the census. Such a trip normally took about three days, perhaps longer for one in Mary's condition. The journey was necessary since Mary and Joseph were both descendants of David, and Bethlehem—being King David's hometown (1 Samuel 16:1, 13)—was considered *the city of David*. Perhaps this journey also served as a means of escaping the wagging tongues of those in Nazareth who may have had their own theories of the cause of Mary's pregnancy.

Bethlehem means "house of bread." It was a fitting birthplace for one destined to become the Bread of Life.

5. To be taxed with Mary his espoused wife, being great with child.

Mary is described as Joseph's *espoused wife*. An espousal was considered much more binding than an engagement. If an espoused woman's husband died, she was considered a widow. The problem for Joseph, of course, was Mary's pregnancy during the espousal period. If not for angelic intervention, he would have "put her away privily" (Matthew 1:19).

By now Mary was *great with child*. Just how far along she was at the time of the trip to Bethlehem is uncertain. The text simply describes her as pregnant, with nothing to suggest how many months remained until the time of birth. The context implies that the time was fairly close.

C. The Time (vv. 6, 7)

6. And so it was, that, while they were there, the days were accomplished that she should be delivered.

While in Bethlehem, Mary gave birth. This is just what had been prophesied about the birth of

---

How to Say It

CAESAR AUGUSTUS. *See*-zer Aw-*gus*-tus.
CYRENIUS. Sye-*ree*-nee-us.
GABRIEL. *Gay*-bree-ul.
IMMANUEL. Ih-*man*-you-el.
SYRIA. *Sear*-e-uh.
ZACCHEUS. Zack-*key*-us.

the Messiah (Micah 5:2). The "fulness of the time" (Galatians 4:4) had come.

7. And she brought forth her firstborn son, and wrapped him in swaddling clothes, and laid him in a manger; because there was no room for them in the inn.

When Jesus was born, He was wrapped in *swaddling clothes*. These were bands of cloth in which a newborn baby was tightly wrapped to provide the infant with warmth, protect his extremities, and provide a sense of security. Thus Jesus was treated like any other infant in His day. Unlike any other newborn, He was *laid . . . in a manger*, which describes a feeding place for the animals. We usually assume that this feeding place was in a stable. Quite possibly it was in a cave.

The reason that Mary and Joseph found themselves in such lowly surroundings was that *there was no room for them in the inn*. Sometimes the innkeeper is treated in Christmas pageants as though cruel and heartless. Notice that Luke says nothing of any innkeeper, although most likely there was one. If so, perhaps he should be commended for finding a quiet, out of the way place where Mary could give birth. Ancient inns were often crowded, noisy places that at times could be dangerous as well. This may have been especially true on this occasion, given the circumstances that had forced many to make the journey to Bethlehem in compliance with the emperor's decree. [See question #2, page 144.]

Jesus is referred to as Mary's *firstborn son*. This implies that Mary had other children after Jesus. In fact, the Gospels do tell us that Jesus had brothers and sisters (Matthew 13:55, 56; Mark 6:3).

GOD AS A MAN

Radio commentator Paul Harvey says that the story he is most often asked to repeat is about a farmer, his wife, and their young daughter. The mother and little girl attended church, but the father did not. He said he refused to believe in God because it just wasn't reasonable that God would come down from Heaven and become a man.

On the Sunday night before Christmas, the farmer's wife and little girl asked him to attend the children's Christmas program at the church, but he declined. It was bitterly cold when they left, so the farmer sat by the fire in the living room and read the newspaper. Before long he started hearing little thuds on the big picture window—first one, then another, and then another. He went to the window and realized that some birds were trying to get in where it was warm.

So the farmer went out and opened the barn doors so that the birds could get out of the cold, but the birds ignored him. He did all he could to entice them and even drive them in, yet nothing worked. He asked himself, "How can I get those birds into the barn?" Then he thought, "You know, if I could just become a bird, I could lead them in." Just as that thought came to him, the church bells began ringing, and he realized what he had said. He fell to his knees in the barn and prayed, "Oh, dear God, I believe now, because I understand."

God became a little baby wrapped in swaddling clothes so He could lead human beings like us into Heaven.   —G. A.

II. Announcement of Jesus' Birth (Luke 2:8-17)

A. The Recipients (v. 8)

8. And there were in the same country shepherds abiding in the field, keeping watch over their flock by night.

The story now moves to a *field* near Bethlehem, where *shepherds* were *keeping watch over their flock by night*. Some people believe that the birth of Jesus could not have happened anywhere near December 25 because that would be in the rainy season, and shepherds would not be out in the field that time of year. It is possible, however, that these sheep were being raised for use in the temple sacrifices in Jerusalem (since Bethlehem was not far from Jerusalem). In that case these shepherds may well have needed to be in the field throughout the year. Still, the critics may be right. We simply do not know what time of year Jesus was born. Let's just praise God that He was born—of that we can be certain!

It is fascinating to note that God chose to make the announcement of His Son's birth to humble people, not to the wealthy, the powerful, or the famous. Had we been in charge of planning this event, we might have arranged for the Messiah to be born into a king's family, a priest's family, or at least a family of significant wealth and influence. We might have sent angels to announce the birth in Herod's palace or the temple in Jerusalem.

God's ways, however, are not like man's ways (Isaiah 55:8). He had His own plan, and according to that plan it was necessary that Jesus be born to humble people and then announced to humble people. As noted earlier, shepherds were not high on the social ladder and were treated by most as outcasts. The announcement of the gospel came first to the down and out, rather than the high and mighty. [See question #3, page 144.]

B. The Messengers (vv. 9-14)

9. And, lo, the angel of the Lord came upon them, and the glory of the Lord shone round about them; and they were sore afraid.

The quiet night was dramatically interrupted by *the angel of the Lord*. Perhaps this was the same angel (Gabriel) who made other significant events relevant to the birth of Jesus (Luke 1:19, 26). The immediate response to such an angelic messenger was often fear (Judges 6:22; Mark 16:5, 6; Acts 10:3, 4). The shepherds are described as being *sore afraid*. The Greek text literally says, "They feared a great fear."

10. And the angel said unto them, Fear not: for, behold, I bring you good tidings of great joy, which shall be to all people.

It makes sense that the angel's first words were *Fear not*, thus responding to the shepherds' terror. The angel had *good tidings*, not bad, to convey. Furthermore, this good news is for *all people*. This implies that Jesus will be a universal Savior, sent not for Jews alone, but for the whole world.

11. For unto you is born this day in the city of David a Saviour, which is Christ the Lord.

Here is the essence of the good news: the world has a *Saviour*. He is *Christ the Lord*. The word *Christ* means "Messiah" or "anointed one" and would have been understood by any Jew. The word *Lord* was a title with greater meaning to Gentiles, who would have had no concept of the Jewish Messiah. Once again, Bethlehem is called *the city of David*, because it was King David's hometown. Here in David's town the greatest Son of David *is born*. [See question #4, page 144.]

THE SIGNIFICANCE OF THE INSIGNIFICANT

In 1809 Napoleon was sweeping across Europe with blood, destruction, and French rule in his wake. Nothing else that year seemed as significant in the scope of world events as his exploits.

This visual illustrates the angel's message that a Savior has been born. His light is not just for the little town of Bethlehem, but for the whole world.

Visual for lesson 3

In that year of 1809 many babies were born, but who had time to notice when history was being made by Napoleon? However, during that year William Gladstone and Alfred Tennyson were born in England. Oliver Wendell Holmes and Edgar Allan Poe were born in Massachusetts. A young physician and his wife named their infant son Charles Robert Darwin. And in a Kentucky log cabin Abraham Lincoln was born.

Today only those who are true history buffs can name more than two or three of the battles of Napoleon. But these seemingly insignificant births that so few noticed had an impact that is still felt.

Twenty centuries ago the world was watching Rome in all of its splendor. The Roman Empire stretched from the Atlantic to the Euphrates, and from the Rhine to the Sahara. All eyes were on Caesar Augustus as he demanded a census in order to raise taxes. Who would have even noticed a young Jewish couple making their way to Bethlehem? But while Rome was making history, God was about to arrive. Most of the world would miss this birth of the King of kings.

Today, in the midst of all that we think is so important, let us not overlook the significance of this humble birth.   —G. A.

12. And this shall be a sign unto you; Ye shall find the babe wrapped in swaddling clothes, lying in a manger.

The angel gave the shepherds a *sign*. The newborn is *wrapped in swaddling clothes, lying in a manger*. The swaddling clothes were not particularly unusual (this was the customary practice with infants), but being in a manger was quite out of the ordinary. Only one baby in Bethlehem would fit that description.

13. And suddenly there was with the angel a multitude of the heavenly host praising God, and saying.

The one *angel* was then joined by a *multitude of the heavenly host*. We often think of them as singing their message, but the Bible simply reports that they said it. The angels were *praising God* for the wonderful news that they were privileged to tell the shepherds.

14. Glory to God in the highest, and on earth peace, good will toward men.

The angels' message proclaimed *glory to God in the highest*, focusing on Heaven's response to God's wondrous gift. The phrase *on earth peace, good will toward men* is rendered in more recent translations as "peace to men on whom his favor rests" (*New International Version*) and "peace among men with whom He is pleased" (*New American Standard Bible*). Either interpretation emphasizes the *peace* that the Messiah has come to bring—a peace "not as the world giveth" (John 14:27). [See question #5, page 144.]

C. The Response (vv. 15-17)

15. And it came to pass, as the angels were gone away from them into heaven, the shepherds said one to another, Let us now go even unto Bethlehem, and see this thing which is come to pass, which the Lord hath made known unto us.

Immediately the *shepherds* determined to travel to *Bethlehem* and investigate the sign given them. They showed admirable discernment in recognizing that what they had witnessed was not a dream or hallucination; it was something *the Lord* had *made known* to them.

16. And they came with haste, and found Mary and Joseph, and the babe lying in a manger.

The shepherds *came with haste*, signifying how important they thought the good news was. It did not take long for them to find *Mary*, *Joseph*, and *the babe*. Many of us procrastinate in telling others about Jesus (and we know far more about Him than the shepherds did!). Such good news should set our feet running.

17. And when they had seen it, they made known abroad the saying which was told them concerning this child.

These shepherds became evangelists and witnesses as they *made known abroad* what they had *seen* and heard. If it is true that these shepherds were responsible for keeping watch over the temple lambs, then there is truly something special about their being given the first opportunity to visit the Lamb of God who would one day take away the sins of the world.

Home Daily Bible Readings

Monday, Dec. 14—John the Baptist's Birth Foretold (Luke 1:5-17)
Tuesday, Dec. 15—Gabriel Visits Mary (Luke 1:24-38)
Wednesday, Dec. 16—"My Spirit Hath Rejoiced in God My Saviour" (Luke 1:39-55)
Thursday, Dec. 17—The Hand of the Lord Was With Him (Luke 1:57-66)
Friday, Dec. 18—The Child Grew and Became Strong in Spirit (Luke 1:67-80)
Saturday, Dec. 19—Joseph Went From Nazareth to Bethlehem (Luke 2:1-7)
Sunday, Dec. 20—Good Tidings of Great Joy (Luke 2:8-20)

Conclusion

A. I Wonder

Christmas has been so overtaken by the secular dimensions of the holiday that it is easy to lose the sense of wonder that should be associated with it. Even Christians can get caught up in the commercialism of the season, allowing spiritual priorities to take a back seat. Perhaps it would help if we could capture the spirit of the old Christmas carol that says,

> I wonder as I wander out under the sky,
>   How Jesus, the Savior, did come for to die
> For poor, ornery people like you and like I—
>   I wonder as I wander out under the sky.

We must never allow the Christmas story to be reduced to the level of a fairy tale. If we grasp its reality and its glory, as Luke wanted us to, then we cannot help but be caught up in the wonder of it all. Christmas is a wonderful time of the year, but the most wonderful part about it is what God was doing for us.

B. Moving in at Christmastime

On Christmas Eve in 1908, a young seminary student named Toyohiko (Toy-o-*hee*-ko) Kagawa (Kuh-*gah*-wuh) moved into the worst slums of Kobe (*Ko*-bee), Japan. He felt that he could never understand the people and minister to them unless he shared their lot. Soon he was taking in the poor and homeless. Eventually he had to acquire more houses in order to take care of the expanding needs of others. In time Kagawa became synonymous with Christian charity.

It is fitting that Kagawa moved in at Christmastime to minister to the needs of others, for it was at Christmas that God came down to the "slums" of earth to minister to our needs. Who, knowing the joys of Heaven, would voluntarily leave it to live on this planet? The answer is: Someone who loved us more than we can ever comprehend.

C. Prayer

Gracious God, clear away the clutter of this season and close our ears to the sound of the cash register, so that we may truly thank You for the gift of Your Son. We thank You for the way in which You sent Him. We thank You for those who were the first witnesses. Help us never to lose our sense of awe and wonder at what this season really means. We pray in the name of our Savior, Christ the Lord. Amen.

D. Thought to Remember

Christ needs to be born twice. He was born in Bethlehem, and He wants to be born again in your heart.

Learning by Doing

This page contains an alternate lesson plan emphasizing learning activities.
Classes desiring such student involvement will find these suggestions helpful.

Learning Goals

After this lesson students should be able to:

1. Retell the familiar story of Jesus' birth, as recorded in Luke.

2. Explain the significance of the details reported by Luke.

3. Commit themselves to telling others the good news of the Savior—as the shepherds did.

Into the Lesson

As soon as students arrive, ask each one to complete a worksheet as described below (or refer the student to the appropriate page in the *Adult Bible Class* student book). The worksheet should have these instructions at the top: "Read Matthew 1:18—2:23 and Luke 1:26-56; 2:1-20. Identify which author tells about the events and people listed below by initialing them as 'M' (Matthew) or 'L' (Luke). If the person or event is not mentioned in the Bible but there is a traditionally held belief about it, mark it 'T' (Tradition)."

Below the heading, list the following (without the answers that are in parentheses): wise men (M), Herod (M), Caesar Augustus (L), the innkeeper (T), Emmanuel (M), Mary's donkey (T), the names of the wise men (T), the flight to Egypt (M), an angel appears to Joseph (M), Gabriel appears to Mary (L), swaddling clothes (L), the manger (L), the star over a stable (T), Mary's visit with Elisabeth (L), the announcement to the shepherds (L), the little drummer boy (T).

Give the students a few minutes to work; then review the lists for accuracy. Explain that the accounts in Matthew and Luke are the only records we have of Jesus' birth. We need to pay careful attention to what they say so that our celebration of the Lord's birth focuses on the spiritual significance first and foremost.

Into the Word

Read the printed text, asking the students to listen for words or events they do not understand or would like clarified. An alternative to reading the text would be to have an "honored guest" read it by way of an audio or video recording. After the reading, invite the students to ask questions about this text.

Using the lesson commentary, provide clarification on some of the details of the text. The following should be discussed and/or explained:

a. The significance of Caesar Augustus's name.

b. The dating of Jesus' birth.

c. First-century marriage customs, especially the "espousal" (v. 5).

d. The purpose of "swaddling" clothes.

e. Why God chose to announce His Son's birth to humble shepherds rather than the rich or the power brokers.

f. The significance of the title "Christ."

Into Life

Explain that the significance of the incarnation of Jesus is often lost in the celebration traditions of Christmas. Ask the class to call out all the Christmas celebration traditions and symbols they can recall (e.g., Christmas tree, fruitcake, gifts). Have a class member list these on a visual. Then review the list and ask the class to cite items on the list that are distinctly related to the incarnation.

Remind the class of the importance of remembering the reason for the celebration. In his novel, *The Screwtape Letters,* C. S. Lewis's devil, Screwtape, wrote to his nephew: "I shudder to think what might happen if too many Christians should suddenly remember what Christmas is all about."

Ask the class members to take three or four minutes to write an answer to the question, "What would be the situation of our world if Jesus had not come? Why?" After the project has been completed, ask volunteers to share their thoughts with the entire class.

Next, issue this challenge: "Suppose you were asked to explain the significance of Christmas to a friend. What would you say to him or her?" Ask each student to share his or her thoughts with one other class member.

Remind the students that such an opportunity may present itself in the next few days before Christmas. However, in many situations, we need to create a window of opportunity to speak with a friend or family member about this important subject. Ask each class member to identify someone who needs to know the good news the shepherds heard. Then, ask for ideas on how to create a window of opportunity to share the significance of the incarnation with that person.

In closing, challenge your students to open that window and share the joy of Christ's coming with the persons they have identified.

Let's Talk It Over

The questions on this page are designed to encourage review of the lesson Scriptures and to promote discussion of the lesson by the class. The answers provided are only discussion starters. Let your class talk it over from there.

1. In Caesar's decree we see a human explanation for why Jesus was born in Bethlehem. Of course, we know God's providence was at work to arrange for His prophecies to be fulfilled. How should we view the interaction of the human and the divine in the events of life?

Many in your class can probably tell amazing stories of when they or people they knew were in just the right place at just the right time. Skeptics see these as coincidence and dismiss the idea of God's providence. Believers, however, accepting the Bible's claim that God is always at work to accomplish His will and to work all things together for good for them that love God, are certain that His hand is present. This is a result of faith, however, and not the source of it. We probably cannot convince the skeptic with what we believe, but cannot prove, to be providence. Better to lead one to Christ on the solid evidence of the resurrection, and then help the new believer to appreciate God's providence.

2. Mary laid the infant Jesus in a manger. Apparently, Jesus was born in some kind of stable or corral close to animals. If we had been in charge of choosing the setting for the birth of a Savior, surely we would have chosen some place comfortable, or even spectacular—or at least sanitary! Why do you think God did not intervene to provide a "better" setting for the birth of the Savior?

Several suggestions might be offered. Perhaps the humble beginning was to help us realize that Jesus came not just for the elite, who live in fine palaces and have all the luxuries of life at their disposal, but for everyone. Perhaps God wanted to show how vulnerable Jesus was. The setting for Jesus' birth suggests that God would not shelter His Son from adversity or hardship in life, but would allow Him to suffer all sorts of human difficulty, common and uncommon.

3. Who would be the modern-day equivalent of shepherds (in terms of socioeconomic class)? What efforts are you or your church making to reach them with the good news?

Shepherds existed on one of the lower rungs of the social ladder. They were foul smelling because of their association with the sheep, and they were often suspected of being thieves. As a

result, they were alone much of the time. You can probably name several categories of people in our culture who are not socially welcomed and who are held in low regard. To take the good news to the "shepherds" of our culture, we will have to leave our comfort zones and make a special effort. We may have to leave our neighborhoods or work through the agency of a group already engaged in ministering to such people. Many churches give baskets of food to the needy at Christmas, but is that the extent of what we could or should do to reach the "shepherds"?

4. The message that a "Savior" has been born is good news only if one recognizes a need to be saved. What do you think most people believe about their need for a Savior or of salvation?

People today rationalize or otherwise excuse so much behavior that few of them feel a need to be saved because of moral guilt. They just do not believe that they stand condemned before a holy God. People are much more likely to recognize their need to be saved after experiencing some personal failure or loss. In the face of their own human frailty or vulnerability, people often grasp for a savior. Some look to wealth as a solution: "If I am wealthy I can insulate myself from the various things that threaten me and I can provide a secure life." Others look to education, to therapy, to physical training, to other forms of "self-help," to friendships, and to various philosophies and religions. The question is, how can we help people see a need to be saved from sin? When we do, we can show them the Savior!

5. How did Jesus bring "peace on earth"?

The birth of Jesus did not bring an end to wars, conflict, or disagreement. Jesus Himself said, "Do not suppose that I have come to bring peace to the earth. I did not come to bring peace, but a sword" (Matthew 10:34, *New International Version*). The birth of Jesus was the beginning of a new era of peace between God and mankind. Between the last prophet of the Old Testament, Malachi, and the birth of Jesus, 400 years had passed. It was a time when God seemed distant and estranged from earth. Now it was clear that God had not forgotten us, but was taking the initiative to establish a new relationship between us and Himself. Peace with God would be restored.

The Promise of Power

DEVOTIONAL READING: John 16:1-11.

LESSON SCRIPTURE: Luke 24:13-53.

PRINTED TEXT: Luke 24:36-53.

Luke 24:36-53

36 And as they thus spake, Jesus himself stood in the midst of them, and saith unto them, Peace be unto you.

37 But they were terrified and affrighted, and supposed that they had seen a spirit.

38 And he said unto them, Why are ye troubled? and why do thoughts arise in your hearts?

39 Behold my hands and my feet, that it is I myself: handle me, and see; for a spirit hath not flesh and bones, as ye see me have.

40 And when he had thus spoken, he showed them his hands and his feet.

41 And while they yet believed not for joy, and wondered, he said unto them, Have ye here any meat?

42 And they gave him a piece of a broiled fish, and of a honeycomb.

43 And he took it, and did eat before them.

44 And he said unto them, These are the words which I spake unto you, while I was yet with you, that all things must be fulfilled, which were written in the law of Moses, and in the prophets, and in the psalms, concerning me.

45 Then opened he their understanding, that they might understand the Scriptures,

46 And said unto them, Thus it is written, and thus it behooved Christ to suffer, and to rise from the dead the third day:

47 And that repentance and remission of sins should be preached in his name among all nations, beginning at Jerusalem.

48 And ye are witnesses of these things.

49 And, behold, I send the promise of my Father upon you: but tarry ye in the city of Jerusalem, until ye be endued with power from on high.

50 And he led them out as far as to Bethany, and he lifted up his hands, and blessed them.

51 And it came to pass, while he blessed them, he was parted from them, and carried up into heaven.

52 And they worshipped him, and returned to Jerusalem with great joy:

53 And were continually in the temple, praising and blessing God. Amen.

GOLDEN TEXT: Behold, I send the promise of my Father upon you.—Luke 24:49.

God Calls Anew in Jesus Christ
Unit 1: The Good News of Jesus Christ
(Lessons 1-4)

Lesson Aims

After this lesson each student will be able to:

1. List some of the proofs Jesus provided for His resurrection when He appeared to the disciples.

2. Explain how those proofs answer those who doubt Jesus' resurrection.

3. Determine to fill each day with worship and joy in the power of the risen Christ.

Lesson Outline

INTRODUCTION
  A. Anyone Here Need Power?
  B. Lesson Background
I. JESUS COMFORTS HIS FRIENDS (Luke 24:36-43)
  A. He Invites Investigation (vv. 36-40)
    From Sadness to Joy
  B. He Shares Fellowship (vv. 41-43)
II. JESUS CONFIRMS HIS RESURRECTION (Luke 24:44-46)
  A. He Opens the Scriptures (v. 44)
  B. He Opens Their Minds (vv. 45, 46)
III. JESUS COMMISSIONS HIS DISCIPLES (Luke 24:47-49)
  A. He Issues a Challenge (v. 47)
  B. He Issues a Promise (vv. 48, 49)
IV. JESUS COMPLETES HIS MISSION (Luke 24:50-53)
  A. He Ascends Into Heaven (vv. 50, 51)
  B. The Disciples Obey (vv. 52, 53)
CONCLUSION
  A. The Wrong Side of Easter
  B. Feel the Power
  C. Prayer
  D. Thought to Remember

Introduction

A. Anyone Here Need Power?

Jesus' resurrection had a lasting impact on the church and the world. The risen Christ turned His disciples from doubters to doers. He turned fearful men into forceful men. This He did by convincing them of His victory over death. They realized that if Jesus had power over death, then He had power over any circumstance they would face.

Many people today feel that they lead powerless lives. They are unable to meet the demands placed on them. To the disciples, taking the gospel to "all the world" (Mark 16:15) must have seemed impossible. (It seems overwhelming to us today.) Nevertheless, they undertook the task with great vigor and determination. They fearlessly proclaimed their faith in Jesus wherever they went. This they could not have done without the power that the resurrected Christ provided. Today, if we find ourselves continually overwhelmed by life's challenges, our primary problem may be a lack of power.

A preacher was traveling through Tennessee not long after the Tennessee Valley Authority started building the great hydroelectric dams. These dams produced huge amounts of electricity for the rural inhabitants of that state. As he traveled, the preacher noticed a small house that was located near a dam but was still using kerosene lamps. The residents were close to the power source, but they were not plugged into it. So it is with many who are near Jesus but are not plugged into His power. Jesus' resurrection provided power for the early church. He can provide power for today's church as well.

Last week's lesson considered the beginning of Jesus' earthly life. This week we look at the end of His earthly life and the effect of His resurrection on His disciples. Last week we focused on the baby in the manger, this week on the risen Lord.

B. Lesson Background

Today's lesson examines one of the accounts of Jesus' appearances following His resurrection. Usually we consider this subject only at Easter, but it is beneficial to consider at any time the blessing of what it means to serve a living Savior. And it is appropriate, as we prepare to leave an old year and enter a new one, to remind ourselves that our Savior is the same "yesterday, and today, and for ever" (Hebrews 13:8).

All four Gospels (along with 1 Corinthians 15:5-8) tell about Jesus' postresurrection appearances. Whatever differences exist in the accounts are minor and do not pose any significant problems. In fact, newspaperman Louis Cassels once said that the small differences we encounter in the Gospels are the mark of a true testimony. If every account were exactly alike, one would suspect some measure of collusion. With careful study, all accounts of the resurrection can be harmonized.

What impact did Jesus' postresurrection appearances have on His disciples? This is the question we want to consider in today's lesson. What did Jesus accomplish through these appearances? And what does He want His disciples—both then and now—to do?

I. Jesus Comforts His Friends
(Luke 24:36-43)

The disciples were in despair. They had lost a friend; but more than that, they had lost the leader on whom they had pinned all their hopes. They had come to believe that He was the Messiah—and now He was gone. It is not hard to imagine their sorrow.

Jesus' first order of business was to comfort His disheartened disciples. He may have appeared to them in the same room in which He shared the Last Supper with them. That supper spoke of Jesus' impending death. The meal soon to be shared will celebrate His life.

A. He Invites Investigation (vv. 36-40)

36. And as they thus spake, Jesus himself stood in the midst of them, and saith unto them, Peace be unto you.

This is the third appearance of the risen Christ recorded by Luke and apparently the same one mentioned by John in John 20:19-23. If so, we should note that John records that "the doors were shut where the disciples were assembled" (v. 19). Jesus was not restricted by closed doors, even though, as we shall see, He was not a spirit.

Luke does not tell of Jesus' appearance to Mary Magdalene (John 20:11-17) or to the other women (Matthew 28:8-10). The first appearance in Luke is to an otherwise unknown disciple named Cleopas and his companion on the way to Emmaus (Luke 24:13-32). Upon recognizing the Lord, the two returned to Jerusalem, where they learned Jesus had also appeared to Simon Peter (Luke 24:33, 34). Luke is the only Gospel writer to mention the appearance to Peter, though Paul confirms it in 1 Corinthians 15:5.

At this point, story after story was beginning to confirm that Jesus had indeed risen from the dead. While Cleopas and his companion were talking, *Jesus himself stood in the midst of them*. His greeting was, *Peace be unto you*. This was a common first-century greeting among the Jews. Variations of it are still used today.

37. But they were terrified and affrighted, and supposed that they had seen a spirit.

In spite of Jesus' greeting of peace, the disciples were *terrified*. This word in the Greek text comes from a word that is the source of our English word "phobia." The disciples thought that they had seen a *spirit*, or ghost.

If this story were a fictitious account, it probably would not portray the disciples as still entertaining doubts about Jesus' resurrection. But the Bible is an honest book. It reveals these people as they really were. This should not *dis*courage us; it should *en*courage us. These men, who became leaders of the New Testament church, were people just like us. [See question #1, page 152.]

38. And he said unto them, Why are ye troubled? and why do thoughts arise in your hearts?

Jesus asked the disciples why they were *troubled*. He Himself had predicted these events (Mark 8:31; 9:31; 10:34); thus they should not be so surprised that His words had been fulfilled. Furthermore, at this point they had ample evidence for the resurrection: the empty tomb; the testimonies of Mary Magdalene, the two on the road to Emmaus, and Peter; and Jesus' own presence with them now.

39. Behold my hands and my feet, that it is I myself: handle me, and see; for a spirit hath not flesh and bones, as ye see me have.

Jesus then allowed the disciples to *handle*, or touch, Him. Jesus wanted to assure the disciples of the truth of His resurrection. They needed to know that He was, in fact, the same individual who had died on the cross. The crucified Savior was now the living Lord. That is the reason He still bore the scars of Calvary in His *hands* and *feet*. The disciples were not hallucinating. This was not a *spirit*; this was someone with *flesh and bones*. Later, Jesus invited doubting Thomas to touch Him in order that he too could be assured that Jesus was alive (John 20:27).

Reading this passage, some have wondered about the resurrection body that is promised to Christians. Will our resurrection bodies still show scars and physical handicaps? It is important to distinguish between Jesus' experience and ours. Regarding the resurrection, Paul writes in 1 Corinthians 15:44, "It is sown a natural body, it is raised a spiritual body." Yet Jesus' resurrection body, as He took care to demonstrate, was not "spiritual." Jesus' resurrection was followed by numerous "flesh and blood" appearances meant to convince His disciples that He was alive. Such will not be the case with our resurrection; for when Jesus comes, those believers who have died will be raised from the dead and will "meet the Lord in the air" (1 Thessalonians 4:17). We will then receive the kind of "spiritual body" that Jesus received following His ascension, in order to dwell with His Father where "flesh and blood" cannot be present (1 Corinthians 15:50).

40. And when he had thus spoken, he showed them his hands and his feet.

Having offered the invitation to touch Him, Jesus showed the disciples the wounds in *his hands and his feet*. These were consistent with those received on the cross. Sometimes people who were crucified were simply tied to the cross, but we know Jesus was nailed to His. Seeing the wounds settled any doubts that the disciples may have had concerning the individual standing before them. This was without question Jesus—the crucified One, now risen from the dead.

FROM SADNESS TO JOY

In December a few years ago, Frank and Bet Forest were getting ready for their daughter to come home from college. Page was a freshman and their only child. It seemed as though the college she attended in Oklahoma was a million miles from their California home. The thought of her being home for Christmas filled every moment with anticipation.

Frank and Bet headed for the airport and couldn't help but laugh at themselves when they realized they were a full hour early. About thirty minutes before Page's flight was due to arrive a voice announced, "Will persons waiting for flight number . . ." The rest of the announcement was a blur. Frank and Bet were escorted to another room where a representative of the airlines explained that there had been an accident. Page's flight had crashed on takeoff from Denver. All the passengers were believed to have been killed.

Frank and Bet made their way back home. Standing in their living room they hugged and cried, unsure what to do. A few minutes later the phone rang. The voice at the other end said, "This is Mrs. Hastings with the airline. Your daughter missed the plane. She's all right."

If you can imagine how those parents felt upon hearing such news, then you know something of how the disciples must have felt when Jesus came and stood among them and they realized, "He is alive!"   —G. A.

B. He Shares Fellowship (vv. 41-43)

41-43. And while they yet believed not for joy, and wondered, he said unto them, Have ye here any meat? And they gave him a piece of a broiled fish, and of a honeycomb. And he took it, and did eat before them.

Then Jesus said something that must have appeared just as curious as the invitation to touch Him. He asked the disciples if they had any *meat* (or food). Certainly Jesus could have provided

---

How to Say It
ALEXANDRIA. Al-iks-*an*-dree-uh.
CLEOPAS. *Klee*-uh-pass.
EMMAUS. Em-*may*-us.
MAGDALENE. *Mag*-duh-leen or
Mag-duh-*lee*-nee.
PTOLEMY. *Tahl*-uh-me.
ZECHARIAH. Zek-uh-*rye*-uh.

---

food miraculously, for Himself and the disciples. No doubt this action served as yet another proof that He was the same person who had been crucified. A "spirit" would not be able to partake of such food. [See question #2, page 152.]

II. Jesus Confirms His Resurrection (Luke 24:44-46)

Having provided a series of "infallible proofs" (Acts 1:3) that He was the resurrected Jesus, Jesus now demonstrated the significance of the resurrection by pointing to the testimony of the Old Testament Scriptures.

A. He Opens the Scriptures (v. 44)

44. And he said unto them, These are the words which I spake unto you, while I was yet with you, that all things must be fulfilled, which were written in the law of Moses, and in the prophets, and in the psalms, concerning me.

Jesus moved from the realm of personal experience to the Scriptural support for His resurrection. He spoke specifically of *the law of Moses*, *the prophets*, and *the psalms*. This was a characteristic way to summarize the entire Old Testament. The Jews in Jesus' day usually referred to the categories of the Law, the Prophets, and the Writings; but since the book of Psalms is the first book found in the Writings, it was sometimes used to designate this third category.

Jesus also reminded the disciples that He had spoken to them of these matters before. Now, with the evidence of the resurrection before them, they were capable of a greater understanding of God's master plan. That plan included events, foretold in the Scriptures, that *must be fulfilled*. [See question #3, page 152.]

B. He Opens Their Minds (vv. 45, 46)

45. Then opened he their understanding, that they might understand the Scriptures.

What does the phrase *then opened he their understanding* mean? Most likely this refers to the understanding that came with Jesus' explanation of what the Old Testament Scriptures taught concerning Him. It was the same method that He used with the men on the road to Emmaus, as He "expounded unto them in all the Scriptures the things concerning himself" (Luke 24:27). Such understanding was also provided when Jesus taught His disciples "of the things pertaining to the kingdom of God" during the forty days between His resurrection and ascension (Acts 1:3).

46. And said unto them, Thus it is written, and thus it behooved Christ to suffer, and to rise from the dead the third day.

Again, Jesus emphasized that His death and resurrection were part of a plan. *It behooved Christ to suffer*; this was something that had to happen. A suffering Messiah had not been easy for the disciples to accept (Matthew 16:21, 22). This is why so many failed to recognize Jesus as the Messiah, and why many saw the cross as a "stumblingblock" (1 Corinthians 1:23).

Jesus specifically mentioned the prophecies of the resurrection on *the third day*. This has troubled some students of the Bible, because they cannot account for three full days in the Scriptural record. But in the normal speech of that time, a span of "three days" could cover any portion of any of those days. Jesus was crucified on Friday; therefore, He spent part of Friday, all of Saturday, and part of Sunday in the tomb. The expression would have made perfect sense to the disciples. [See question #4, page 152.]

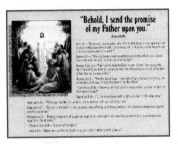

Visual for
lesson 4

Today's visual illustrates Jesus' promise to send the Holy Spirit to empower the apostles (verse 49).

III. Jesus Commissions His Disciples (Luke 24:47-49)

Jesus' next concern was to prepare the disciples for the challenge of world evangelism. This must have seemed an impossible task to them, yet Jesus did not issue the command without also promising adequate help.

A. He Issues a Challenge (v. 47)

47. And that repentance and remission of sins should be preached in his name among all nations, beginning at Jerusalem.

Here Jesus alludes to what will happen on the Day of Pentecost. In *Jerusalem*, Peter will preach a sermon emphasizing *repentance and remission of sins* (Acts 2:38). Following the *beginning* of its proclamation on that day, the message was then to go out to *all nations*. We must not hear these words without considering their fulfillment in Acts 2 and without accepting the challenge in our day to take the gospel to *all nations*.

B. He Issues a Promise (vv. 48, 49)

48, 49. And ye are witnesses of these things. And, behold, I send the promise of my Father unto you: but tarry ye in the city of Jerusalem, until ye be endued with power from on high.

Jesus did not command these men to be His *witnesses* without supplying the necessary *power* for such a mission. This power *from on high* was the Holy Spirit (Acts 1:8). Sending the disciples out to win the world without the power of the Holy Spirit would have been like sending a child out in the wilderness to trap his own food with just a pocketknife. The equipment would not be appropriate for the task. Jesus promised that the disciples would be *en-*

dued, or clothed, with the Holy Spirit. He would surround and envelop them like a robe.

However, all of this would not take place immediately; the disciples were to *tarry . . . in the city of Jerusalem*. It almost seems as if Jesus is telling them, "Hurry up . . . but wait." Yet the waiting will be worthwhile, for the work Jesus has commissioned these men (and us) to do cannot be done without the aid and assistance that the Holy Spirit brings.

IV. Jesus Completes His Mission (Luke 24:50-53)

Even though Jesus appeared to His followers several times, the appearances could not continue indefinitely. The promised Spirit could not come until Jesus went away (John 16:7). The stage was being set for Jesus' ascension.

A. He Ascends Into Heaven (vv. 50, 51)

50. And he led them out as far as to Bethany, and he lifted up his hands, and blessed them.

This event took place near the city of *Bethany*, which was located on the south side of the Mount of Olives. Bethany was the home of Mary, Martha, and Lazarus (John 11:1).

While Luke's account reads as though the ascension immediately followed the events described in verses 36-49, we know from the book of Acts that Jesus spent forty days instructing His disciples prior to His ascension (Acts 1:3). Since there were fifty days between Passover and Pentecost, this left ten days between Jesus' ascension and the Day of Pentecost.

Prior to His ascension, Jesus *lifted up his hands, and blessed them*. The Greek word for *blessed* is a word that gives us the English word "eulogy." Literally it means "to speak well of." But when Jesus gave this blessing to His disciples, it meant much more than well-wishing. It carried the impact of His full authority as Lord and Christ.

51. And it came to pass, while he blessed them, he was parted from them, and carried up into heaven.

Jesus then ascended *into heaven*. A fuller account of this is found in Acts 1:9-11. Jesus was *parted from them*, "and a cloud received him out of their sight" (v. 9). Then "two men . . . in white apparel" (apparently angels) reminded the disciples that "this same Jesus . . . shall so come in like manner as ye have seen him go into heaven" (vv. 10, 11).

B. The Disciples Obey (vv. 52, 53)

52, 53. And they worshipped him, and returned to Jerusalem with great joy: and were continually in the temple, praising and blessing God. Amen.

The disciples obeyed Jesus immediately and *returned to Jerusalem*. Notice that the attitude of terror with which our text began (v. 37) has now been replaced with *great joy*. [See question #5, page 152.]

It is interesting that Luke's Gospel ends in about the same place it begins. After his opening remarks (1:1-4), he takes his readers to the temple where Zechariah heard the news regarding the birth of his long-awaited son. Now, at the conclusion, the disciples of Jesus go to the temple to worship the Son of God.

Luke's account may seem to end somewhat abruptly, since it does not record the coming of the promised Holy Spirit. That is because Luke's Gospel is only part one of his writing. Luke will continue his account in part two: the book of Acts. This tells the story of how the disciples fulfilled what Jesus commanded them to do following His resurrection. The risen Christ provided them with the peace, the proof, and the power to take the gospel "unto the uttermost part of the earth" (Acts 1:8).

Conclusion

A. The Wrong Side of Easter

James Stewart, the great Scottish preacher, once declared that this world is living on the wrong side of Easter. What did he mean by that? He meant that most people act as if Jesus had never risen from the grave. They are as solemn and discouraged as the disciples were before they saw the risen Lord. The sad fact is that many people live as if there were no resurrection. The mood of some churches would cause some to think that the Savior is not alive. Nothing has done the Christian cause a greater disservice than the grimness that sometimes accompanies Christian commitment. Who would want to be part of such an organization?

The existence of the church is one proof of the resurrection. Let's resolve that our attitude as part of the church will be another.

When Julius Caesar came to Alexandria, Egypt, the residents showed him the coffin of Alexander the Great. They then asked him if he wanted to see the coffin of the Egyptian ruler Ptolemy. He replied, "I came to see a king, not a corpse." When we come to church, we come to see a King, not a corpse! We need less mourning and more celebration, less fear and more confidence, less apathy and more commitment.

B. Feel the Power

Some time ago, a television ad promoting professional football featured people talking about their passion for football. The ad concluded with a player looking into the camera and saying with great intensity, "I feel the power." When it comes to our Christian commitment, we should ask, "Do we feel the power?" Jesus calls and equips us to carry out the glorious task of fulfilling His Great Commission. How committed are we to doing this? Are we placing ourselves at His disposal to accomplish His mission?

Now that you have considered the challenge of this lesson, do you "feel the power"?

C. Prayer

Father, help us to recognize that, until we call on Your power, we have not used all our power. Thank You for making us partners in Your great enterprise of taking the gospel to the world. Like the disciples of old, may we accept Your mission and depend on Your power to accomplish it. Through the powerful name of Jesus, amen.

D. Thought to Remember

"Ye shall receive power" (Acts 1:8).

Home Daily Bible Readings

Monday, Dec. 21—Jesus Himself Drew Near (Luke 24:13-27)

Tuesday, Dec. 22—Abide With Us; for It Is Toward Evening (Luke 24:28-35)

Wednesday, Dec. 23—Peace Be Unto You (Luke 24:36-43)

Thursday, Dec. 24—Everything Must Be Fulfilled (Luke 24:44-53)

Friday, Dec. 25—I Will Not Leave You Comfortless (John 14:15-24)

Saturday, Dec. 26—The Holy Spirit Promised (John 14:25-31)

Sunday, Dec. 27—Sorrow Will Turn to Joy (John 16:12-28)

Learning by Doing

This page contains an alternate lesson plan emphasizing learning activities.
Classes desiring such student involvement will find these suggestions helpful.

Learning Goals

After this lesson each student will be able to:

1. List some of the proofs Jesus provided for His resurrection when He appeared to the disciples.

2. Explain how those proofs answer those who doubt Jesus' resurrection.

3. Determine to fill each day with worship and joy in the power of the risen Christ.

Into the Lesson

Prepare and display a very large poster with the word "Power" printed at the top. If possible, also attach a picture (perhaps from a comic book cover) of a superhero. Ask the class members to recall the names of comic book, television, or mythological heroes who had super powers (e.g., Superman, the "bionic woman," or Hercules). After listing some heroes, remind the class that these are fictional. But the supernatural resurrection of Jesus is historical fact. The resurrection also turned Jesus' disciples from fearful doubters into forceful doers. But they had to tap into the power of the Holy Spirit, whom He promised to send them.

Use the illustration of the TVA dams that is given on page 146. Point out that knowing *about* Jesus is not enough. We must be plugged into the power He has promised. This study will help us tap into that power.

Into the Word

Briefly review the Lesson Background; then read today's printed text. Have the class form groups of four or five people each, and give each group one of the following tasks. (Print each assignment on an index card to be given to the appropriate group. You will also need to make available information from the commentary section of this lesson to give to groups 1 and 3.) Each group should select a spokesperson to report its work to the class. If you have a large class, more than one group can do the same assignment. Just allow each group to report and contrast their findings. Of course, if you choose not to use groups, these assignments may be used for discussion items for the entire class.

Group 1. Jesus Comforts His Disciples.

Read Luke 24:36-43. Tell how the disciples' fear and doubt can actually encourage us today. (They had to be convinced Jesus was alive, so we also can be convinced.) Cite and comment on the evidences Jesus offered that He is alive. (Physical presence; they saw Him; they heard Him; He ate with them.)

Group 2. The Resurrection Is Part of God's Plan!

Read Luke 24:44-46. Use a concordance to find some Scriptures from the Law (Genesis—Deuteronomy), the Prophets (this includes the books we call "history"), and the Psalms that foretell Jesus' death and resurrection. Check Peter's sermon in Acts 2:22-36 for some ideas.

Group 3. Jesus Commissions His Disciples.

Read Luke 24:47-53. Describe Jesus' simple strategy for spreading the gospel. (See also Acts 1:8.) How was that task accomplished in the early church? How was the "promise of my Father" to give "power from on high" accomplished? (See Acts 2:1-21.) How does that promise to the apostles help us today? (The Spirit inspired the Scripture, 2 Peter 1:21; the Spirit is still active, living in Christians, Acts 2:38; He equips us for spiritual ministry, 1 Corinthians 12:4; He intercedes for us, Romans 8:26, 27).

Allow each group to work for ten or twelve minutes. Then ask the spokesperson from each group to report the results of the group's work.

Into Life

Tell the class that the record makes it apparent that the resurrection of Jesus transformed the lives of the disciples. Write the words "Living on the Wrong Side of Easter" on a visual, explaining that James Stewart, a great Scottish preacher, once declared that this world is living on "the wrong side of Easter." Ask them, "Why would he say that? What do you suppose he meant?" Use the lesson commentary (page 150) to guide the discussion. Additional questions may include, "If people choose to live on the right side of Easter, how will that affect their worship?" "How does living on the right side of Easter affect one's lifestyle and witness?"

Distribute index cards (and pens, if needed). Ask each student to write, "I will live on the right side of Easter this week by. . . ." Have each student complete the sentence with some way he or she will fill each day with worship and joy in the power of the risen Christ. If there is time, ask volunteers to share their responses. Close with prayer.

Let's Talk It Over

The questions on this page are designed to encourage review of the lesson Scriptures and to promote discussion of the lesson by the class. The answers provided are only discussion starters. Let your class talk it over from there.

1. By the time Jesus appeared to the disciples in today's text, He had already appeared to Mary Magdalene (John 20:11-17), the other women (Matthew 28:8-10), two on the road to Emmaus (Luke 24:13-33), and Simon Peter (Luke 24:33, 34). Why, then, do you suppose the disciples were so afraid and slow to believe when Jesus appeared to them?

John tells us that Jesus appeared in the midst of the disciples in spite of the doors' being locked (20:19). The sudden appearance must have been startling, and it explains why they thought Jesus may have been a ghost instead of "flesh and bones." The disciples were not unlike people today. Once their minds were made up, it took a tremendous amount of persuasion to change them. Unbelievers need to hear the facts again and again to help them move from unbelief to acceptance of the evidence.

2. Luke says the disciples "believed not for joy" (v. 41). In other words, they found it hard to believe Jesus was alive because it was too good to be true. Do you think some people today do not believe because the idea is "too good to be true"? Why or why not? How can we help people believe that, in this case, something too good to be true really is true?

The presence of so many con artists in our world has given rise to the belief that if something seems too good to be true, then it's probably not true. Jesus made several significant promises to His followers, including eternal life. Those promises might seem to be too good to be true, and that may be one reason some people reject them. The overwhelming evidence for the resurrection must be shared to help people realize it is true. Jesus' ability to keep His promise to rise from the dead gives credibility to His other promises. We can believe that Jesus can forgive sins and give new birth. We can believe that He hears and answers our prayers. We can believe that He is preparing a home for us that will be forever. We can believe that He is with us always through the Holy Spirit.

3. The text suggests that the disciples could have had a better understanding of what was happening if they had had a clearer understanding of the Scriptures. (See vv. 44, 45.)

What are we doing to make sure that people in our church have a good understanding of the Scriptures so they can understand what God's plan is and work in harmony with it?

The best way to understand the Bible is to read it and study it. Too many Christians spend little or no time in personal Bible study. Thus they are open to deception and misunderstanding when false teachers come along peddling their heresies. The church needs to promote both corporate and private Bible study by all ages. Sunday school must be encouraged as well as small group Bible studies. Children can be encouraged to participate in fun activities that promote Bible study, like memorization contests or Bible quiz games. Fathers need to be encouraged to lead out in some kind of family devotional time that emphasizes the key role of the Bible.

4. Jesus made clear that His suffering and death were part of God's plan. How does that help us understand suffering in our lives?

In order to release you and me from the condemnation of our sin, God was willing that Jesus surrender His morally perfect life to a cruel death on the cross. Our spiritual need was a greater priority than Jesus' personal comfort. We may conclude that, at least in some cases, suffering accomplishes some higher purpose. There are times when the welfare of others, or even our own character development, requires that we suffer. In every case we are promised that God can redeem some good even out of extreme adversity (Romans 8:28).

5. After Jesus ascended, the disciples "returned to Jerusalem with great joy." How can we cultivate that same kind of joy in the lives of believers today?

The disciples had finally come to realize that there was something better than Jesus' physical presence with them. They knew Jesus would return and renew their fellowship with Him, and that they would be in His presence forever. In the meantime, they had a job to do to let others know they could be part of that fellowship. When we change our focus from the physical and temporal to the eternal, we will find joy in our lives in spite of whatever physical and temporary difficulties we might encounter.

Love One Another

DEVOTIONAL READING: 1 John 4:7-12.

LESSON SCRIPTURE: Mark 12:28-34; Luke 6:27-36; John 13:31-35.

PRINTED TEXT: Mark 12:28-34; Luke 6:27-31; John 13:34, 35.

Mark 12:28-34

28 And one of the scribes came, and having heard them reasoning together, and perceiving that he had answered them well, asked him, Which is the first commandment of all?

29 And Jesus answered him, The first of all the commandments is, Hear, O Israel; The Lord our God is one Lord:

30 And thou shalt love the Lord thy God with all thy heart, and with all thy soul, and with all thy mind, and with all thy strength: this is the first commandment.

31 And the second is like, namely this, Thou shalt love thy neighbor as thyself. There is none other commandment greater than these.

32 And the scribe said unto him, Well, Master, thou hast said the truth: for there is one God; and there is none other but he:

33 And to love him with all the heart, and with all the understanding, and with all the soul, and with all the strength, and to love his neighbor as himself, is more than all whole burnt offerings and sacrifices.

34 And when Jesus saw that he answered discreetly, he said unto him, Thou art not far from the kingdom of God. And no man after that durst ask him any question.

Luke 6:27-31

27 But I say unto you which hear, Love your enemies, do good to them which hate you,

28 Bless them that curse you, and pray for them which despitefully use you.

29 And unto him that smiteth thee on the one cheek offer also the other; and him that taketh away thy cloak forbid not to take thy coat also.

30 Give to every man that asketh of thee; and of him that taketh away thy goods ask them not again.

31 And as ye would that men should do to you, do ye also to them likewise.

John 13:34, 35

34 A new commandment I give unto you, That ye love one another; as I have loved you, that ye also love one another.

35 By this shall all men know that ye are my disciples, if ye have love one to another.

GOLDEN TEXT: By this shall all men know that ye are my disciples, if ye have love one to another.—John 13:35.

God Calls Anew in Jesus Christ
Unit 2: Good News for Daily Living
(Lessons 5-8)

Lesson Aims

After completing this lesson, a student should be able to:

1. Describe love according to what Jesus taught in today's text.

2. Tell why loving God first and one's neighbor as himself is the essence of the law.

3. Look for a practical way to express love to God and for a neighbor.

Lesson Outline

INTRODUCTION
   A. You're Going to Love This
   B. Lesson Background
  I. THE GREATEST COMMANDMENTS (Mark 12:28-34)
   A. Loving God (vv. 28-30)
   B. Loving Others (vv. 31-34)
 II. LOVE YOUR ENEMIES (Luke 6:27-31)
   A. How to Respond to Them (vv. 27-30)
   B. How to Treat Others (v. 31)
    The Hazards of Hatred
III. LOVE YOUR FRIENDS (John 13:34, 35)
   A. Jesus' Example (v. 34)
   B. The Christian's Trademark (v. 35)
    The Iron, Silver, and Golden Rules
CONCLUSION
   A. In a Nutshell
   B. Prayer
   C. Thought to Remember

Introduction

A. You're Going to Love This

Perhaps there are no greater words that a person can hear than, "I love you." As children we felt a sense of security when parents and teachers expressed their love to us. In our courting days many of us freely spoke these words as our affection for another grew. Later as parents our hearts seemed to melt when we heard our own children say these magic words to us. Some of us are blessed with hearing them spoken by a grandchild or great-grandchild.

Unfortunately, our affinity toward love has also led to a certain amount of unclarity regarding the meaning of the word. We talk about how much we *love* a good pizza or an ice cream treat,

how we *love* to play basketball or watch a baseball game, or how we would *love* to have someone come visit us sometime. We *love* sunny days and walking on the beach and would *love* to stay and talk some more if only we had the time. We introduce a program by telling our audience, "You're going to *love* this." Is it any wonder that we have trouble arriving at a clear, simple definition of the word *love*?

In several passages in the Gospels, Jesus teaches us the true meaning of love. He describes the nature of love and gives practical examples of how it should be expressed. And to motivate us toward this kind of love, He reminds us of how He Himself demonstrates love to us. Anyone confused about the meaning of love would do well to learn from Jesus what love truly is and how it is expressed.

B. Lesson Background

It was nothing new for the Jews of Jesus' day to hear one of their teachers talk about love. The Old Testament contains many verses that speak of God's love for us and our duty to love others (Leviticus 19:18, 34; Deuteronomy 6:5; 7:8, 9; Joshua 22:5; 1 Kings 10:9; Psalm 146:8). But first-century Judaism was also keenly interested in the concepts of wrath and vengeance. Throughout their history the Jews had suffered much at the hands of invading armies and oppressive overlords. In the first century they were chafing under the political restraints of Rome's domination of their country. Thus it is not surprising that Jews of that day often spoke of their feelings of anger toward their enemies. In addition, one of the frequent themes of the book of Psalms is the prayer that God would bring vengeance upon the enemies of His oppressed people (Psalms 6:10; 18:3, 40; 56:9; 66:3; 72:9; 132:18; 139:19-22). This mind-set was so pervasive that the work of the promised Messiah was typically viewed from this perspective. As John the Baptist's father, Zechariah, put it, the Messiah was to come that Israel might be "saved from our enemies, and from the hand of all that hate us" (Luke 1:71).

It is against this background that Jesus' teaching on love stood out. He elevated love to the high status that God intended it to have from the beginning, even going so far as to maintain that God expects us to love our enemies rather than wish them harm. Jesus placed our God-given duty to love in settings that seemed awkward to His contemporaries (and probably seem that way for many of us today!). God's kind of love will test the boundaries we have erected in our thinking, and will challenge us to reach out much farther than we have imagined.

I. The Greatest Commandments
(Mark 12:28-34)
A. Loving God (vv. 28-30)

28. And one of the scribes came, and having heard them reasoning together, and perceiving that he had answered them well, asked him, Which is the first commandment of all?

The discussion found in Mark 12 occurred on Tuesday of Jesus' final week, just three days prior to His crucifixion. On this occasion Jesus sought to teach in the temple, but He was constantly interrupted by His enemies. The chief priests, scribes, and elders (Mark 11:27), the Pharisees and Herodians (12:13), and the Sadducees (12:18), all took turns sending representatives to challenge Jesus with a supposedly difficult question. They hoped that Jesus would give a weak or offensive answer that would turn the crowds against Him and give the religious leaders an occasion to arrest Him. Each time, however, Jesus responded with an answer that challenged the hypocrisy of the religious leaders and left the crowd even more supportive of Him.

The question in our text was put forward by *one of the scribes*, one of a group of scholars who were experts in the intricacies of rabbinical law. [See question #1, page 160.] Perhaps he originally approached Jesus as part of those who came to trap Him (Mark 11:27), yet there was something that set him apart from the others. Or perhaps he was passing by when he *heard them reasoning together* and stopped to listen.

This scribe thought that Jesus *had answered them well*. His motive was not the deep animosity felt by his colleagues. Instead, he possessed a sincere appreciation for Jesus' wisdom and a curiosity about His views on Jewish law.

29. And Jesus answered him, The first of all the commandments is, Hear, O Israel; The Lord our God is one Lord.

Both the scribe's question and Jesus' answer reflected a long-standing debate among Jewish scholars of that day over the question of which was *the first of all the commandments*. First-century Judaism had systematized the instructions written by Moses and created a list of approximately 613 commands, with 248 of them positive ("do this . . .") and 365 negative ("thou shalt not . . ."). According to the rabbinical literature now available to us, much fervor was applied to the debate over which of the 613 commands was to be given priority by a Jew.

For those scheming to undermine Jesus' ministry, this multiple-choice question looked promising. No matter which command Jesus suggested as the *first*, His enemies could argue for other possibilities, thereby suggesting that

Jesus was not as wise as He claimed or even implying that He may not really care about the commandments He passed over in His answer. What they did not count on was Jesus' proposing an answer that would make so much sense that it would be impossible to refute.

In His statement of the most important commandment, Jesus quoted Deuteronomy 6:4, 5. Jewish tradition referred to verse 4 as the *shema*, a Hebrew word that means "hear," because this is the first word in the Hebrew text of this passage (*Hear, O Israel . . .*). The *shema* was held in such high esteem that it was quoted as the invocation for every synagogue service (and is still used as such in Jewish services today).

The reason this passage was so highly valued by the Jews was that it succinctly expressed the monotheism (belief in one God) that formed the foundation of the Jewish faith. Though the tendency in ancient times was to worship many gods, Judaism held the distinctive view that there is only one God. The *shema* was treasured as a clear, concise summary of this view.

30. And thou shalt love the Lord thy God with all thy heart, and with all thy soul, and with all thy mind, and with all thy strength: this is the first commandment.

By quoting the verse that followed the *shema*, Jesus proposed that the *entire* passage be treated with great esteem, not just the first part. That is, one's priority should be not only to believe that there is just one God, but also to *love* that one God. The Scripture text that defined one's most important belief also supplied his most important command.

It is possible to take the different terms Jesus uses (*heart, soul, mind, strength*) and treat them as distinct aspects of man's nature, thereby drawing several implications about the way in which we are to love God. However, knowing the Jewish penchant for speaking in "parallelism" (that is, repeating an idea several times with phrases that are roughly synonymous), we cannot say for certain whether Jesus intended

---

How to Say It

AGAPE (Greek). uh-*gah*-pay.
CONFUCIUS. Con-*few*-shiss.
HERODIANS. Heh-*roe*-dee-unz.
MONOTHEISM. *mah*-nuh-thee-ih-zum (*th* as in *thin*).
PHARISEES. *Fair*-ih-sees.
SADDUCEES. *Sad*-you-sees.
SHEMA (Hebrew). shih-*mah*.
ZECHARIAH. Zek-uh-*rye*-uh.

for us to make such fine distinctions. What we can reasonably conclude from Jesus' statement is that our love for God should spring from our entire being, impacting every aspect of life. [See question #2, page 160.]

B. Loving Others (vv. 31-34)

31. And the second is like, namely this, Thou shalt love thy neighbor as thyself. There is none other commandment greater than these.

Jesus had not been asked to list the *second* greatest commandment, but He took this opportunity to teach a more complete view of our primary duty to God. This second quotation is taken from Leviticus 19:18. In first-century Jewish thought, this was recognized as a legitimate command; however, its full force was often blunted by attempts to limit the scope of the word *neighbor*. Recall one man's attempt to "justify himself" by asking Jesus, "Who is my neighbor?" (Luke 10:29).

There is none other commandment greater than these. Loving God and loving our neighbor are God's highest expectations for mankind. Why should these two loves be so closely linked? Because the latter logically follows from the former. One who truly loves God cannot help but love those who carry within them the image of God.

32. And the scribe said unto him, Well, Master, thou hast said the truth: for there is one God; and there is none other but he.

This is not the kind of admission that we would expect from one working within the ranks of those attempting to discredit Jesus. But then, sometimes truth is so powerful that an honest man cannot deny it, no matter how much he may dislike the source of that truth.

33. And to love him with all the heart, and with all the understanding, and with all the soul, and with all the strength, and to love his neighbor as himself, is more than all whole burnt offerings and sacrifices.

It is not uncommon for Christians to assume that Old Testament saints were saved by lawkeeping and sacrifices, whereas we under the New Covenant are saved by grace and faith. However, animal sacrifices could not atone for sin (Hebrews 10:1-4). Furthermore, all who were saved in the Old Testament age were saved by faith in God and His promises (as noted in Romans 4; Galatians 3:6-9; and Hebrews 11:13-16, 39, 40). Therefore it should not surprise us to discover that the prophets often stated the principle that the attitude of the heart is much more important to God than the sacrifices offered on an altar (see Hosea 6:6; Micah 6:8). The scribe's words were an insightful summary of the message of the Old Testament. It is no wonder that Jesus was pleased with his answer. [See question #3, page 160.]

34. And when Jesus saw that he answered discreetly, he said unto him, Thou art not far from the kingdom of God. And no man after that durst ask him any question.

Here was a man who was not yet in full stride with God's Messianic plan, but he was *not far* off. Perhaps he was like the chief rulers John mentions (12:42, 43), who believed in Jesus but would not admit it because "they loved the praise of men more than the praise of God." Or perhaps he was moving in the right direction but just had not come to faith yet. We don't know any more about him, but we can hope that he was one of those who later accepted Jesus as the promised Messiah, perhaps on Pentecost.

II. Love Your Enemies
(Luke 6:27-31)

A. How to Respond to Them (vv. 27-30)

27, 28. But I say unto you which hear, Love your enemies, do good to them which hate you, bless them that curse you, and pray for them which despitefully use you.

Earlier in His ministry, Jesus explained the true nature of love in His teaching. The "sermon on the plain" (Luke 6:17) recorded in Luke 6 may have been delivered on a different occasion from the famous Sermon on the Mount (Matthew 5—7), but the two texts are very similar in style and content. In both sermons, Jesus declared that the love God manifests and commands is unconditional, acting with kindness even to those who are anything but kind.

How is it possible to feel love toward those who would hurt us? The answer is that we have not been commanded to *feel* love, but to act in a loving manner. The love described by the Greek word *agape* involves a decision of the will, not a feeling of the heart. It is a decision to treat others in a kind and considerate way, regardless of how we actually *feel* about them. [See question #4, page 160.]

29. And unto him that smiteth thee on the one cheek offer also the other; and him that taketh away thy cloak forbid not to take thy coat also.

Our natural tendency (and the accepted practice of modern society) is to say, "If you hit me, I will hit you back." But *agape* love says, "I will not stoop to your level; I will not hit back." In many situations we could retaliate quite strongly, but *agape* love chooses not to do so. Thus Jesus said that He could have called upon twelve legions of angels to destroy His enemies (Matthew 26:53); instead, He allowed them to arrest Him and literally strike his *cheek* without reprisal (John 18:22). He felt free to challenge the actions of those who slapped Him (v. 23), but He did not strike back at them.

30. Give to every man that asketh of thee; and of him that taketh away thy goods ask them not again.

Does Jesus want us to be doormats for people to step on and trample? Do we always have to stand by and let others hurt us and take advantage of us? Not necessarily. For example, Paul was not opposed to Christians seeking restitution when they have been wronged; but if the manner in which we seek redress damages our public witness for Christ, then he would rather that we choose to "be wronged" and "be cheated" for the sake of the gospel (1 Corinthians 6:1-7, *New International Version*). Perhaps the key question is: "What is at stake if I exercise my rights?" In other words, will the cause of Christ suffer loss in order for me to gain, or will my loss serve to advance the cause of Christ?

Sometimes the most *agape* thing we can do is to let people know that we could seek retaliation for their unkindness, but for the sake of Christ we choose not to do so. Thus the position of strength is not found in beating your enemy, but in letting him know that today he is a beneficiary of your grace. By this reaction, a gospel seed can be planted within a sinful heart.

B. How to Treat Others (v. 31)

31. And as ye would that men should do to you, do ye also to them likewise.

From childhood most of us have memorized some version of Jesus' Golden Rule: "Do unto others as you would have them do unto you." Something similar to this has been expressed by most ancient philosophers and religions. Perhaps that is because this principle is built within the nature of man by God. We do seem to have a natural instinct toward self-preservation, and we soon learn from experience that how we treat others has implications for how we will be treated in turn.

Our tendency is to oppose rules restricting what we can do, and we will do evil if we think we can get away with it. But given the possibility that someone might follow our evil lead and retaliate by doing evil to us, we recognize the value of restraint. Jesus' "do as you would have others do to you" rule makes sense, in many cases even to an unbeliever.

THE HAZARDS OF HATRED

It was a very old twelve-gauge shotgun, passed down through the family for three generations. Its owner wouldn't let anyone shoot the

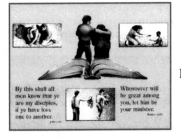

Visual for
lessons 5 and 7

Use this visual to illustrate the truth that love must be demonstrated with action. Only active love can declare our discipleship.

gun. "It kicks so bad," he said, "it can kill at both ends." No doubt that was not literally true of the old shotgun, but it is literally true of hatred. It wounds the hater as much as the one hated.

Some time ago, newspapers reported that a terrorist in the Middle East had blown himself up with the bomb he intended for others. If we allow ourselves to hate someone, we do him great harm; however, we do ourselves more harm. Harry Emerson Fosdick said, "Hating people is like burning down your house to get rid of a rat."

During the Civil War, Abraham Lincoln once referred publicly to the people of the Confederacy as erring human beings, not as foes to be exterminated. An older woman criticized him for speaking kindly of his enemies, when, according to her, he ought to be thinking of destroying them. "Why, Madam," said Lincoln, "do I not destroy my enemies when I make them my friends?"

The great American poet Edwin Markham stated it well in this little verse:

He drew a circle that shut me out—
  Heretic, rebel, a thing to flout.
But Love and I had the wit to win:
  We drew a circle that took him in.

—R. C. S.

III. Love Your Friends
(John 13:34, 35)

A. Jesus' Example (v. 34)

34. A new commandment I give unto you, That ye love one another; as I have loved you, that ye also love one another.

Agape love requires that we treat others with kindness and consideration. It does not allow us to act with rudeness or meanness or spite. In this passage, we also learn that *agape* demands even more than this: we must *love one another* the way Jesus has *loved* us. That kind of love is a self-sacrificing love that ultimately led Him to die on the cross for our sakes.

The occasion for Jesus' *new commandment* was the Last Supper in the upper room on the Thursday evening prior to His death. With Calvary just hours away, Jesus went on to explain what it means to love as He has loved us: "Greater love hath no man than this, that a man lay down his life for his friends" (John 15:13). More than a warm feeling, more than kindness and consideration, love is ultimately a willingness to help someone else, no matter what it may cost you to do so.

B. The Christian's Trademark (v. 35)

35. By this shall all men know that ye are my disciples, if ye have love one to another.

When a friend betrays your confidence or hurts your feelings, the test of Christian character will be whether you seek revenge or choose to overlook how he or she has wronged you. When a husband no longer has feelings of love toward his wife, the test of Christian character will be whether he abandons his wife or chooses to continue to treat her in an honorable way, regardless of his feelings. When members of the church disagree with each other over a decision, the test of Christian character will be whether they alienate themselves from each other or choose to continue to regard one another as brothers and sisters in Christ. *Agape* love is the distinguishing mark of a heart that has truly been changed by the love of Christ. [See question #5, page 160.]

THE IRON, SILVER, AND GOLDEN RULES

Even people who know very little about the Bible can quote the Golden Rule in some form: "Do unto others as you would have them do unto you." This rule stands in contrast to two other rules. One we may call the Iron Rule. It is stated as follows: "Whatever others do to you, do you also to them." This is the rule of retribution. Many live by this rule, but Jesus taught us that we should never try to get even.

The second rule we may call the Silver Rule. It is a great improvement over the Iron Rule; for it says, "What you do not want done to yourself, do not do to others." This was the rule of Confucius. It is a good rule, but it is entirely negative. It demands only that we refrain from doing wrong, but it requires nothing in terms of positive action.

The Golden Rule, however, stands far above both of these. It is positive. It requires far more of us than the Silver Rule, for it goes beyond not doing evil to doing good. It demands that we go beyond the minimum. We cannot say, "I am as good as my neighbors." We have to be better than they. We have to be like Christ! —R. C. S.

Conclusion

A. In a Nutshell

Legal contracts can be long and tedious. Logical arguments in the realms of science and philosophy can become rather complex. Explanations and excuses for wrong behavior can meander aimlessly. Usually, when all is said and done, what we need is a succinct summary of the key issues at stake. As we sometimes say, "Here it is in a nutshell.".

The Bible is filled with hundreds of commandments and guidelines, which could seem overwhelming. However, the key commandments can be put "in a nutshell." To love God and to love one's neighbor are the greatest and second greatest commandments. Echoing Jesus' teaching, the apostle Paul writes: "For this, Thou shalt not commit adultery, Thou shalt not kill, Thou shalt not steal, Thou shalt not bear false witness, Thou shalt not covet; and if there be any other commandment, it is briefly comprehended in this saying, namely, Thou shalt love thy neighbor as thyself" (Romans 13:9).

The people of the world need to see our Christianity demonstrated, not by lengthy and detailed explanations of our beliefs, but, "in a nutshell," by our love.

B. Prayer

Heavenly Father, help us to love one another even as You and Your Son have expressed Your love toward us, through the bounty of Your creation and the blessings of Your redemption. In Jesus' name, amen.

C. Thought to Remember

Love should be the trademark of the Christian. Is your trademark easy to read?

Home Daily Bible Readings

Learning by Doing

This page contains an alternate lesson plan emphasizing learning activities. Classes desiring such student involvement will find these suggestions helpful.

Learning Goals

After this lesson, a student should be able to:

1. Describe love according to what Jesus taught in today's text.

2. Tell why loving God first and one's neighbor as himself is the essence of the law.

3. Look for a practical way to express love to God and for a neighbor.

Into the Lesson

Before the students arrive, arrange the chairs in circles or around tables, with four or five chairs per group. At each group supply a worksheet as described below. (Or refer the groups to the Learning by Doing page in the student book, *Adult Bible Class.*)

Write the heading "Confusing Definitions of Love" at the top of the worksheet. Then write the following instructions: "Define *love* as the word is used in each of the following expressions." Follow that with a list of expressions, including but not necessarily limited to these:

I love classical music. Puppy love. Forty serving love (a score in tennis). I love my country. We'd love to have you visit us. We love a sunny day. I love my husband. "Love thy neighbor."

Allow six or eight minutes for the groups to discuss their definitions; then share answers quickly. Observe that our many uses and definitions of the word *love* have produced some confusion. When Jesus says, "Love God," or, "Love your neighbor," what does He mean? That is the focus of our lesson today.

Into the Word

Early in the week, ask a class member to read the lesson commentary notes on the *shema*. The class member should be ready to give a very brief report to the class on the history and significance of the *shema*. Call for the report just before group 1 reveals the results of their discussion of question 2.

Keep the class in the groups formed earlier (at least three groups) and give each group one of the following assignments:

Group 1. Love Your Neighbor (Mark 12:28-34)

1. Do you think the scribe asked this question because of animosity he had learned from his colleagues, appreciation for Jesus' wisdom, or curiosity about Jesus' view on Jewish law. Why?

2. In citing the most important commandment, Jesus quoted Deuteronomy 6:4, 5. Why do you think Jesus connected the concept of the one God to the command to love God first and foremost? How is that relevant to us?

3. Jesus was asked to cite only one commandment, but He added a second commandment: "Love thy neighbor." Why do you think He added this commandment to answer the scribe's question? Consider these options: It teaches a more holistic view of our primary duty to God; these two commands comprise a summation of all God's commands; if we love our neighbor, we are being like God, who loves all people.

Group 2. Love Your Enemies (Luke 6:27-31)

1. Which of the following best defines "love" as it is expressed toward our enemies? Why? (a) a feeling or emotion, (b) a decision of the will, (c) an idealistic but unattainable goal.

2. What is the primary benefit of loving our enemies? (a) peacemaking, (b) demonstrating how to be a doormat that people can walk on, (c) frustrating our enemies, (d) demonstrating Christ's love.

3. Who benefits most when we love our enemies—we, the enemies, or God? Why?

Group 3. Love Your Friends (John 13:34, 35)

1. Do you think the emphasis of Jesus' new commandment is on (a) our feelings, (b) our determination or will, or (c) our behavior?

2. What is distinctive about the love practiced by Christians? How does it tell people that we are Jesus' disciples, and not just "nice people"?

Allow fifteen minutes for discussion; then review the questions and expand the discussion to include the whole class. Use the lesson commentary to fill in the gaps and answer any questions.

Into Life

To allow this lesson to become personal, ask each student to write on an index card the words "I will better express my love for God by. . . ." Allow thirty seconds for the students to write their answers; then ask one student to pray and ask God to bless this commitment. Do a similar exercise with the words "I will express love to a neighbor by . . ." and "I will express love to an 'enemy' by. . . ." Close with a prayer of thanks for God's love and ask His help in expressing love.

Let's Talk It Over

The questions on this page are designed to encourage review of the lesson Scriptures and to promote discussion of the lesson by the class. The answers provided are only discussion starters. Let your class talk it over from there.

1. Do you think the scribe who questioned Jesus was interested in increasing knowledge or increasing obedience? Why? What is the difference? What kind of knowledge should we strive for in the church today, and how can we do it?

As a scribe this man was a religious professional. Perhaps he had been engaged often in debating this question, and he may have been genuinely interested in Jesus' view. His question is academic in the sense that it seemingly had nothing to do with the practical matter of obedience. It is possible to be filled with knowledge about a subject, but fail to translate knowledge into behavior.

Of course, obedience is difficult without knowledge. We have to know what the Bible teaches in order to practice it. So we need to teach in the church so people increase their knowledge of the Bible, but we also need to teach and model a lifestyle that challenges the learners to obey as well. Jesus said the scribe was "not far from the kingdom" (v. 34). Perhaps he simply needed to translate his knowledge into action.

2. What does wholehearted love for God look like in terms of everyday life?

Even though many have trouble keeping them, the demands of monogamous marriage seem fairly well agreed on in our culture. There is an expectation that love will be expressed in loyalty, devotion, honor, and companionship. A wholehearted marriage relationship may be hard to define, but we recognize it when we see it.

That may help our understanding of a wholehearted love toward God. We recognize the evidence in terms of sincere worship, generous service, faithful obedience, and a reverent, humble spirit, even though these can take many forms. It is a dangerous thing to assume we know the condition of another's heart toward God, but we know our own hearts. Are we committed to God wholeheartedly, or does the evidence point to divided loyalty?

3. Why do the commands to love God and to love our neighbor stand above all the other commands of God?

These commands are positive; they are not prohibitions. Rather than set boundaries, they establish direction. They are progressive—never completed. When have you finished loving? It can be argued that all the other commands are simply commentary on these two (Matthew 22:40). The commands of God give definition to what it is to love Him and our neighbor. To disobey any of the commands is to fail to love.

4. Does Jesus really expect us to love our enemies, or is this some kind of hyperbole? If He means it, how can we honestly do it? Suggest some practical ways of loving one's enemies.

We first have to understand what love is and what it is not. Love is not a warm feeling of affection. Love is a decision, a commitment, an action. To love another is to work for that person's best interests in spite of how that person may respond. God sent Jesus to die for all people, even though He knew that most would reject His salvation. Still He loved—and loves—them all.

We can practice love first by what we do not do. We can refuse to retaliate when we are wronged. Returning evil for evil only escalates the conflict. But we need to look for active ways to express love as well. Can we speak well of a work associate who has wronged us, perhaps helping that person to advance in the company? Can we help someone with yard work even if the person has been rude to us or criticized us unfairly? If a person who has injured us repents and comes to the Lord, can we accept that person as a brother or sister in Christ?

5. Christians are to be known by their love for one another. How are you showing love among your Christian friends? How could you do more?

Some believe they have obeyed the law of love because they have not done anything rude or mean to another. But passive politeness will hardly distinguish Christians from the rest of the population. It is a sad thing when the Elks Lodge, the Kiwanis Club, or a bowling league has a greater reputation for love than the local church. Jesus expected that His followers would be known for their love. For that to happen, it must be a remarkable love, a love that takes action and leaves evidence. When is the last time you went out of your way or made any kind of sacrifice to show love to someone in need—especially to another in the Christian family?

Follow Kingdom Priorities

DEVOTIONAL READING: Habakkuk 3:17-19.

LESSON SCRIPTURE: Luke 12:13-34.

PRINTED TEXT: Luke 12:13-21.

Luke 12:13-21

13 And one of the company said unto him, Master, speak to my brother, that he divide the inheritance with me.

14 And he said unto him, Man, who made me a judge or a divider over you?

15 And he said unto them, Take heed, and beware of covetousness: for a man's life consisteth not in the abundance of the things which he possesseth.

16 And he spake a parable unto them, saying, The ground of a certain rich man brought forth plentifully:

17 And he thought within himself, saying, What shall I do, because I have no room where to bestow my fruits?

18 And he said, This will I do: I will pull down my barns, and build greater; and there will I bestow all my fruits and my goods.

19 And I will say to my soul, Soul, thou hast much goods laid up for many years; take thine ease, eat, drink, and be merry.

20 But God said unto him, Thou fool, this night thy soul shall be required of thee: then whose shall those things be, which thou hast provided?

21 So is he that layeth up treasure for himself, and is not rich toward God.

GOLDEN TEXT: Take heed, and beware of covetousness: for a man's life consisteth not in the abundance of the things which he possesseth.—Luke 12:15.

God Calls Anew in Jesus Christ
Unit 2: Good News for Daily Living
(Lessons 5-8)

Lesson Aims

This lesson will encourage each student to:
1. Tell the setting for, and the significant details of, Jesus' parable of the rich fool.
2. Contrast the world's materialistic view of wealth with what it means to be "rich toward God."
3. Assess his or her own priorities and make a commitment to put God first, being content with the blessings He gives.

Lesson Outline

INTRODUCTION
  A. A Fool and His Money
  B. Lesson Background
 I. SEEK AFTER TRUE RICHES (Luke 12:13-15)
  A. An Inappropriate Request (vv. 13, 14)
  B. A Warning Against Greed (v. 15)
II. HAVE CONCERN FOR OTHERS (Luke 12:16-19)
  A. A Time of Blessing (vv. 16, 17)
  B. Ruined by Selfishness (vv. 18, 19)
    Use Your Head
III. BE THANKFUL TO GOD (Luke 12:20, 21)
  A. The Giver of All We Have (v. 20)
  B. Worthy of All Our Gratitude (v. 21)
    How Much Did He Leave?
CONCLUSION
  A. "You May Be Our Next Winner"
  B. Prayer
  C. Thought to Remember

Introduction

A. A Fool and His Money

Many of the fairy tales and fables that we learned as children cautioned us against those who would try to cheat us out of our money. Remember the story of "Jack and the Beanstalk"? Jack's mother called the young boy foolish because he let a crafty charlatan talk him into trading the family cow for a handful of beans. Fortunately for Jack, the beans turned out to be valuable after all. But then, fairy tales often have magical endings. In real life, a trade like that would not lead to a chest of gold, but to an overwhelming sense of how foolish we have been. The con man's credo is our word of warning: "A fool and his money are soon parted."

In Luke 12 Jesus tells a parable about a fool and his money. In this case, the story is not about a man who foolishly loses his money; it is about a man who saves his money in a foolish way. Neither problem is desirable, but the latter is more serious. The first scenario is often a matter of foolish judgment. However, the man in Jesus' story exhibited a foolishness that derives from an ungodly attitude, and ultimately will result in divine condemnation.

B. Lesson Background

Luke 12 presents a collection of highlights from Jesus' teaching ministry. All of the incidents could have occurred on the same day, but it is likely that Luke is presenting a summary of the kinds of topics that Jesus often spoke about as He traveled from town to town. Jesus probably spoke these teachings in about the middle of His three-and-a-half-year ministry. During this period Jesus spent most of His time in the region of Galilee and was regularly confronted with crowds likely numbering in the thousands. Luke 12:1 describes the crowd gathered on this occasion as "an innumerable multitude."

Chapter 12 begins with Jesus rebuking the hypocrisy of the Pharisees. He then proceeded to challenge His hearers concerning their perspective on life. Jesus taught that godly people should not worry about how they will protect and care for their lives because God is concerned about their welfare and is ready to come to their aid. What a disappointment it must have been for Jesus then to hear someone in the crowd petition Him to help him get more money! Jesus used this opportunity to teach a lesson on true riches.

I. Seek After True Riches
(Luke 12:13-15)

A. An Inappropriate Request (vv. 13, 14)

13. And one of the company said unto him, Master, speak to my brother, that he divide the inheritance with me.

Here is a familiar sight for our day and time: family members squabbling over an *inheritance*. Many of us can tell "horror stories" about brothers and sisters fussing over the terms of a will, arguing for why they deserve to get certain items, and eyeing each other's "take" to see whether anyone is getting more than his or her share. How sad that at a time when family members need to pull together, they can be so easily pulled apart over material property.

The Mosaic law had given certain instructions regarding inheritance disputes, such as the provisions in Deuteronomy 21:15-17 for a fair distribution to a son whose mother had fallen into disfavor with his father. By the time of Jesus, rabbinical law had created an elaborate system of guidelines for the distribution of an estate among the heirs.

We are not given enough information in this verse to know why the man who spoke up felt that he was being cheated out of his portion of the family inheritance. It may be that an older brother acting as executor was not honoring his father's wishes, perhaps cutting his younger brother out of the distribution, or giving him a smaller share than his father had stipulated. On the other hand, it could be that this man only imagined that he was being cheated, because he thought he deserved more than the will actually provided. Regardless of who was at fault, Jesus used the occasion to discuss the evils of covetousness and greed.

14. And he said unto him, Man, who made me a judge or a divider over you?

Why did Jesus refuse this man's request? It was obviously not because He lacked a knowledge of Jewish law or the wisdom to make such a judgment. Most likely Jesus saw this as an unwelcome diversion from His divinely appointed ministry. After all, it was not His mission to serve as a financial consultant or to resolve legal matters. Jesus' calling was to a work of much greater significance than redistributing money and property. His greatest desire was the redemption of the world from sin.

This is the reason Jesus put limits on the healing miracles He performed. He was pleased on many occasions to heal the sick in order to provide supernatural credentials for His claim to be the Messiah and the Son of God. In such cases His healings furthered His ministry. But when the crowds tried to dominate His time by demanding more healings, He had no qualms about slipping away from a town so that He could resume teaching somewhere else (Luke 4:42-44). Jesus understood that He had not been sent by the Father simply to be a doctor for physical ills. As important as such work is, it was not His primary calling. Jesus remained focused on His divinely ordained purpose.

Could He not, however, make one exception here and help this man without upsetting His ministry? Jesus knew the Galilean multitude well. Once they got a taste for what He could do, they always wanted more. So it was with His miraculous feeding of the five thousand. The crowd repaid His act of compassion by trying to block His departure, and then later demanding that He continue to provide them with bread (John 6:14-27). Jesus knew when it was best for the sake of His ministry to "just say no." [See question #1, page 168.]

Would this man suffer an injustice because Jesus refused to assist him? No; there were sufficient legal venues for resolving inheritance issues. There were courts that would hear his case. If this man had a legitimate complaint, he should have gone there. Either he had been rejected already by the courts or he was attempting to circumvent the process by taking advantage of the authority the crowds ascribed to Jesus. Whatever the case, Jesus simply affirmed that this was not a matter appropriate for His attention. [See question #2, page 168.]

B. A Warning Against Greed (v. 15)

15. And he said unto them, Take heed, and beware of covetousness: for a man's life consisteth not in the abundance of the things which he possesseth.

The tension that characterized this situation prompted Jesus to issue a warning against *covetousness*, or greed. The Greek word that is used here has an interesting etymology. The word literally means "to thirst for more." The imagery is that of a person who has finished a drink and yet still feels thirsty. Water is ideal for quenching thirst, but some beverages such as soft drinks can feel satisfying for the moment, only to leave you wanting a refill. Salty peanuts and potato chips have a similar effect on our hunger, drawing us back to them until we realize too late that we have eaten much more than we should have. A lust for material possessions can be just as strong or stronger. [See question #3, page 168.]

Is it wrong, then, for us to desire our fair share from an inheritance, or to expect to be treated fairly in a business deal, or to ask for an honest wage for an honest day's work? Not necessarily. The problem Jesus is addressing is the matter of priorities. He is concerned about a heart that

Home Daily Bible Readings

Monday, Jan. 4—Be on Guard Against All Kinds of Greed (Luke 12:13-21)

Tuesday, Jan. 5—Do Not Worry About Your Life (Luke 12:22-34)

Wednesday, Jan. 6—Greed Takes Away Life (Proverbs 1:8-19)

Thursday, Jan. 7—Money Alone Does Not Satisfy (Ecclesiastes 5:1-10)

Friday, Jan. 8—Amassing Wealth Unjustly Is Hazardous (Jeremiah 17:5-11)

Saturday, Jan. 9—Beware the Sin of Covetousness! (Micah 2:1-5)

Sunday, Jan. 10—Greed Is Self-Defeating (James 5:1-6)

cares more about accumulating material wealth than about seeking after spiritual treasure. Isn't that what this man has done? When out of a crowd of thousands he had the privilege to speak to Jesus, he missed the opportunity to seek spiritual guidance and blessing. Instead, his thoughts were focused on things that satisfy for a short while on this earth and then are no more. We can seek a good income on behalf of our families with a clear conscience as long as we do not allow such concerns to interfere with our devotion and service to God. [See question #4, page 168.]

II. Have Concern for Others
(Luke 12:16-19)

A. A Time of Blessing (vv. 16, 17)

16. And he spake a parable unto them, saying, The ground of a certain rich man brought forth plentifully.

This story is identified by Luke as a *parable*, which means that it is not a description of an actual event, but a realistic story of an experience that could happen often enough that Jesus' listeners could easily imagine it.

17. And he thought within himself, saying, What shall I do, because I have no room where to bestow my fruits?

This rich farmer was enjoying a bumper crop. By God's providence he was being blessed with a higher return than he had anticipated. This raises the question: Was there anything wrong with this man's being rich? The Bible does not condemn the possession of riches. It is more concerned with our attitude toward material things, the means by which we attain them, and the way we use our abundance. Many godly men such as Abraham and Job possessed material wealth, and there is no indication in the Bible that this was unacceptable.

The classic statement that links money with evil actually says that it is "the *love* of money" that is "the root of all evil," not necessarily the possession of money (1 Timothy 6:10). As this lesson will demonstrate, there is nothing inherently wrong with enjoying the blessings God has given us, as long as we follow His rules and avoid the kind of foolish mistakes illustrated by the farmer in this parable.

B. Ruined by Selfishness (vv. 18, 19)

18. And he said, This will I do: I will pull down my barns, and build greater; and there will I bestow all my fruits and my goods.

What a problem to have! More income than you anticipated and no place to put it all! Some have wondered why this man would not simply build additional *barns* rather than *pull down* the

old ones and put new ones in their place. It may be that he was acting out of pride and just wanted to trade in the old models for the new ones he could now afford. But it is more likely that he was working with a limited amount of nonfarming land that would support a structure like a barn; thus, to have bigger barns he had to use the space occupied by the smaller barns. We can give him the benefit of the doubt on this issue, because his problem was not so much the new barns as the motive behind the new barns.

19. And I will say to my soul, Soul, thou hast much goods laid up for many years; take thine ease, eat, drink, and be merry.

Here is the slogan often associated with the pleasure-seeking, hedonistic mind-set: *eat, drink, and be merry*. Now, to be fair to this rich man, our text does not imply that he was seeking sensual pleasure or drunkenness. His sin was his self-centered attitude that gave no thought to how his blessings could be used to bless others.

Many a commentator has noted how this man's brief speech is overrun with first-person pronouns. "What shall *I* do because *I* have no room where to bestow *my* fruits? . . . This will *I* do: *I* will pull down *my* barns . . . there will *I* bestow all *my* fruits and *my* goods. . . . *I* will say to *my* soul. . . ." Why would this man need more storage? He was already a rich man. At no time did he consider that there might be a better way to use his surplus than to simply hoard it all for himself. It was not his enjoyment of wealth that was the problem; it was his failure to acknowledge God or to consider the needs of others.

Some wonder whether this parable implies that planning for retirement is inappropriate for a Christian. To some it appears that this man might not have been punished by God if he had continued working with his hands, rather than living off the wealth he had set aside for retirement. It has also been argued by some that laying aside money for retirement implies a lack of trust that God will provide for His people.

None of these arguments will stand up under careful scrutiny. Scripture never encourages us just to sit back and wait for God to do everything for us. Rather, it commends those who are industrious. "Go to the ant, thou sluggard; consider her ways, and be wise" (Proverbs 6:6). The "virtuous woman" who engages in a variety of projects to provide for her family "can laugh at the days to come" because of the preparations she has made (Proverbs 31:25, *New International Version*). The Bible portrays Joseph in Egypt as a wise man because he heeded God's forewarning regarding the future and filled the storehouses with grain to be reserved for the years of famine (Genesis 41:25-36).

Occasionally we Christians can come up with ideas that have the appearance of being very spiritual but in fact are lacking in common sense. Jesus sometimes gives us a gentle rebuke regarding such matters. For example, after commending a shrewd manager for using his master's money in a way that profited himself, Jesus noted that "the children of this world are in their generation wiser than the children of light" (Luke 16:8). In a different context, He stated a principle that contains some relevance to our question: "Be as shrewd as snakes and as innocent as doves" (Matthew 10:16, *New International Version*). We want to be innocent of wrongdoing, but this does not mean that we have to be foolish. The person who makes no plans whatsoever for the future because he believes God will supply all he needs is likely to find himself coming up short.

USE YOUR HEAD

A minister once told of discussing with his leaders his need for life insurance. One of the men objected. He said that a minister should not worry about such things. He claimed that the minister's concern demonstrated a lack of faith. He told the minister, "Don't you believe that God will take care of you?" The minister wisely replied, "I believe God already took care of me when He put a head on my shoulders."

To use Jesus' words in Luke 12:15 as an excuse not to plan for the future is to misunderstand Him completely. There is no sin in life insurance. There is no sin in saving. The problem with this rich farmer was that when he thought he was prepared for the future, he was thinking only of his short-term future. He completely ignored his long-term future.

While it is commendable to plan for our future on this earth, we ought to be all the more concerned that we prepare for our ultimate future in eternity. We are not fools when we look ahead. But we are certainly as foolish as the man in our lesson if we prepare only for the body and make no preparation for the soul.

Therefore, when you use your head to plan for your retirement, which you *may* live long enough to experience, also use your head to prepare for the one thing that we all will certainly experience: eternity.　　　—R. C. S.

III. Be Thankful to God
(Luke 12:20, 21)

A. The Giver of All We Have (v. 20)

20. But God said unto him, Thou fool, this night thy soul shall be required of thee: then whose shall those things be, which thou hast provided?

This humorous poster will provide fuel for discussion as your class considers the plight of those who are not "rich toward God."

Visual for lesson 6

[See question #5, page 168.] Preoccupied with himself, the rich farmer in this parable rejoiced in his blessings without any recognition of the source of those blessings. In his words there is no acknowledgment of the providence of God. There is no consideration for what God's will might be regarding his abundance. There is no mention of any word of thanks. Thus the God who is the giver of all the rich man's wealth reminded him of another great truth: God is the giver of his life as well. On the very *night* in which the farmer uttered his self-serving speech, God took away his life and canceled his dreams.

We have all heard the expression, "You can't take it with you." We know it is true that when we die we must leave behind all of our possessions. What an irony it would be should death come sooner than we anticipated, and many of the things we accumulated for our own pleasure are actually used by someone other than ourselves. This is the question that the rich farmer in our parable had not yet considered. If death unexpectedly interfered with his long-range plans, *then whose shall those things be, which thou hast provided?* David's words offer a similar perspective: "Surely every man walketh in a vain show: surely they are disquieted in vain: he heapeth up riches, and knoweth not who shall gather them" (Psalm 39:6).

B. Worthy of All Our Gratitude (v. 21)

21. So is he that layeth up treasure for himself, and is not rich toward God.

Herein lies a summary of the sin of our rich farmer. He was so focused upon his own desires as he amassed *treasure for himself* that he gave no thought to how he might use his blessings to benefit others. God was nowhere to be found in his plans, because his self-centered attitude had blinded him to the need to be *rich toward God*.

Today's lesson is intended to prompt all of us to assess our attitude toward material things. This is an evaluation we need to do periodically, because we know that the love of money can be very seductive. But let us be careful not to draw erroneous conclusions from this parable. Scripture does not teach that it is wrong to have money and possessions, or to take pleasure in the good things we can attain through our labor. Life is to be enjoyed as long as we do so with a spirit of thankfulness, and act according to the moral guidelines of God's Word. "For everything God created is good, and nothing is to be rejected if it is received with thanksgiving, because it is consecrated by the word of God and prayer" (1 Timothy 4:4, 5, *New International Version*). [See question #6, page 168.]

It is legitimate for Christians to seek to better themselves, advance in their jobs, and work for promotions. It is wrong to pursue such goals with a heart of covetousness. What is required is an attitude of *contentment*. Biblical contentment does not mean that we must stay as we are and must never seek advancement. It means that we will continue to be happy with how the Lord is blessing us, regardless of whether or not we advance any further. Contentment sees items that would be nice to possess, but acknowledges that we do not have to have them to be happy. "For we brought nothing into this world, and it is certain we can carry nothing out. And having food and raiment, let us be therewith content" (1 Timothy 6:7, 8).

Contentment never forgets the priority of spiritual riches over material possessions. When there is a conflict between the two, we know what has the greatest value for us in the long run. "Lay up for yourselves treasures in heaven, where neither moth nor rust doth corrupt, and where thieves do not break through nor steal" (Matthew 6:20).

HOW MUCH DID HE LEAVE?

Those of us who were fortunate enough to grow up in small towns had a great advantage. We had the chance to sit around the country store and listen to the conversations of people older and wiser. A lot of wisdom was exchanged on those worn benches outside the crossroads store. On one occasion the men in a certain town were discussing a recent death in the community. "How much did he leave?" asked one. Some speculated that the amount was quite large. Others thought it was modest. One old man hit the nail on the head. "How much did he leave? He left it all." And so will we.

You cannot cash a check or use your *Visa* card in the world to come. Job said it well: "Naked came I out of my mother's womb, and naked shall I return thither" (Job 1:21). But while we must leave all our treasure behind and can take nothing with us, we *can* send it on ahead. Jesus spoke of laying up treasures in Heaven (Matthew 6:20). How do we do that? We do it by investing our treasure in people who are going to Heaven! Much of the money that we make we lose. All of the money we have made and kept we will leave. The only money that we can really keep is the money we give away in God's service. Then we are being "rich toward God," as Jesus said.

It matters little the amount of your net worth here. It matters terribly, and it matters for all eternity, whether or not you are rich toward God.

—R. C. S.

Conclusion

A. "You May Be Our Next Winner"

The end of December has many traditions associated with it. It is a time to put away the Christmas decorations, close out the year's financial records, make New Year's resolutions—and open a pile of sweepstakes letters. Who has not dreamed at some time or another about what it would be like to win a sweepstakes or inherit a vast fortune? We imagine what we could do with all that money: the debts we would pay off, the luxuries we could buy, or the assistance we could give to our families. Some of us may even dream about how we could use some of that wealth for our favorite ministries and missions. We like to think that we would be wise stewards of our new-found riches if we ever received such a windfall.

Of course, we know better than to expect money to fall into our laps. Most of us will never have an income that provides great wealth (although we know that by the standards of many in the world, we in our society are in most ways "rich"). Even so, whatever amount of material blessings we are able to accumulate will come to us with a God-given responsibility: to cultivate a godly attitude that focuses on spiritual priorities, seeks opportunities to be generous with others, and always maintains a spirit of gratitude to God for His many blessings.

B. Prayer

Our heavenly Father, who watches over our every moment and provides what Your wisdom knows is best, help us to be faithful servants and wise stewards of all the blessings You have given to us. In Jesus' name, amen.

C. Thought to Remember

"Seek ye first the kingdom of God, and his righteousness; and all these things shall be added unto you" (Matthew 6:33).

Learning by Doing

This page contains an alternate lesson plan emphasizing learning activities.
Classes desiring such student involvement will find these suggestions helpful.

Learning Goals

Today's lesson should enable each student to:

1. Tell the setting for, and the significant details of, Jesus' parable of the rich fool.

2. Contrast the world's materialistic view of wealth with what it means to be "rich toward God."

3. Assess his or her own priorities and make a commitment to put God first, being content with the blessings He gives.

Into the Lesson

Before class begins, write on the chalkboard, "A fool and his money are. . . ." Provide paper and pens or pencils and ask the students to complete the sentence in as many ways as they can. Give them about three minutes (or use the time while they are arriving and proceed when everyone is present), and then ask for volunteers to share their answers.

Option: Sometime before class take a survey of elementary children who may not be familiar with the popular expression about a fool and his money and ask them to complete the statement. Report on the results as you begin class.

Make the transition to Bible study by noting, "We're all familiar with the proverb, 'A fool and his money are soon parted.' But it's not always true. As our lesson today reveals, sometimes it is not reckless *spending* that makes one a fool; it may be reckless *hoarding.*"

Into the Word

Begin the Bible study by reading the printed text. Then ask, "What is the purpose of a will?" Use the lesson commentary notes on verses 13 and 14 to guide the discussion. Conclude by telling the class that there are two key thoughts in today's text that will guide the remainder of the study. They precede and conclude Jesus' parable. The first thought tells us what life is not: "a man's life consisteth not in the abundance of the things which he possesseth" (v. 15). The concluding statement defines a fool and implies who is wise: "So is he [a fool] that layeth up treasure for himself, and is not rich toward God."

1. Verse 15 tells us to beware of covetousness. What is the danger of covetousness?

2. What earned this man the title "fool"? Was he wrong in planning for early retirement? Why or why not?

3. Compare today's parable with the story of the rich young ruler in Luke 18:18-25. Do you think Jesus condemns riches? (Teacher: play devil's advocate on this one. The easy answer is, "No, Jesus doesn't condemn riches," but the temptations of the rich are great and Jesus' warnings about them can sound like a condemnation of wealth itself. Make sure the students are thinking through the warnings carefully and not just saying no because they hope to be rich someday!)

Point out to your students that the rich fool's error was not in acquiring wealth. He erred in giving the wealth a higher priority than God and by taking full credit for its acquisition. It is not a sin to acquire wealth. It is a sin to deem that wealth more important than God. The *love* of money is the root of evil (1 Timothy 6:10).

Ask your students to list aloud several earthly indicators of great wealth and success (fancy cars, summer homes, and the like). Next, ask your students to list items that make one rich toward God. Ask, "What is the difference between these two lists?" The major difference is the immortal maxim, "You can't take it with you."

Conclude this section by having verses 15 and 21 read aloud by two good readers. Observe that these verses summarize the key points of the Bible study.

Into Life

Ask the class to suggest one-word descriptions of the life of this fool. Words such as *selfish* and *godless* should surface. Explain that these are qualities we do not want in our lives if we are to be rich toward God.

Ask a couple of volunteers to read Philippians 4:11-13, 19 and 1 Timothy 6:6-10. Ask the class to contrast the attitude Paul urges in these verses with the attitude of the farmer in Jesus' parable. What new insights do these verses give about the concept of being "rich toward God"?

Probably all of us would like to be "rich." Most of us, however, will not be—at least, not by the standards we usually employ to measure worldly wealth. But all of us can be rich toward God. Close with prayer, confessing that we all yield occasionally to the temptation of covetousness and asking that your students will find the joy that comes from generosity, contentment, and putting God first in their lives.

Let's Talk It Over

The questions on this page are designed to encourage review of the lesson Scriptures and to promote discussion of the lesson by the class. The answers provided are only discussion starters. Let your class talk it over from there.

1. Jesus refused to arbitrate a dispute over an inheritance. Our lesson writer says to do so "was not His mission," that His calling was "to a work of much greater significance." We, of course, share Jesus' calling of bringing redemption to man. How do we respond to that greater calling? How can we encourage our young people to take that calling seriously?

The response to Jesus' calling leads some into vocational Christian ministry. Youth need to be challenged to consider that option when thinking about college and their future careers. Parents and counselors need to put serving the Lord first when they advise young people who are making choices that will affect their futures.

For many others, however, the response to Jesus' call is expressed from within a secular vocation. A well-paying job may allow for more financial generosity, or a skill learned on the job may be useful in a volunteer ministry at the church. Whatever vocation best allows a person to express his or her ministry gifts is the vocation that person should choose.

2. If two church members asked the church to settle a financial dispute, should the church follow Jesus' precedent or decide the case? Why?

Just as Jesus had a work of greater significance than arbitrating legal disputes, so the church has a greater work as well. However, the church leadership is responsible for helping the members get along and minister together. Paul suggests the church is a better place to settle disputes within the body than the secular courts (1 Corinthians 6:1-8). If both parties agreed to have the church leadership arbitrate a matter, then the church could probably handle it. But if one person came to the church and insisted that the other party be forced into a settlement, perhaps Jesus' response would be best. If the issue could divide the church, the mature response is still that it is better to suffer the wrong (1 Corinthians 6:7) than to seek worldly wealth.

3. Who do you think is more prone to give in to the temptation of covetousness, the rich or the poor? Why?

It's common to believe this is a problem for the rich. After all, they have tasted the benefits of wealth and may find themselves hungering for more. The poor, however, see the rich in their luxury and may well covet what they have. In thinking this is a problem of the rich, we usually excuse ourselves as not rich. The real issue is not whether the rich or the poor are more prone to covetousness, but that *I* am prone to covetousness. That is what *I* need to be concerned about!

4. Why are possessions a poor measure of a person's life or worth? What other measure may be more revealing?

The possessions a person enjoys may have nothing to do with character or the contribution of work performed. Wealth and possessions may be inherited or won in a sweepstakes. Possessions may reflect only a greedy and selfish attitude, or even the result of dishonest activity. A lack of possessions may be the result of a charitable spirit or investment in some noble pursuit that provides rewards that are not material. However wealth is accumulated, it remains temporal. The true measure of a man or woman is how well he or she has prepared for eternity.

5. Why was the rich farmer in the parable called a fool? What do you think he would have done differently if he had been wise?

The rich farmer was not foolish because he was rich or because his crops produced so well. The man was foolish because he made no provision for any but himself, and even for himself he failed to plan for eternity. A wise farmer might have distributed his surplus to the needy or made a special gift to the synagogue (or we would say, "the church"). Perhaps he would have stopped farming and lived off his surplus while he gave himself to ministry.

6. How does one become "rich toward God"? What are the benefits of this kind of wealth?

Being "rich toward God" includes being generous to God in giving possessions to godly works, but it is more. Believers should be rich in the currency of Heaven, that is, the things that matter to God. We should seek to be rich in faith, obedience, worship, love for God and for others, holiness of character, and witness for Christ. It is a matter of priorities and values. As we apply our energies toward seeking God and His will, we will become rich toward Him.

Reverse the World's Standard

DEVOTIONAL READING: Galatians 5:13-15.

LESSON SCRIPTURE: Matthew 18:1-4; 20:17-28.

PRINTED TEXT: Matthew 18:1-4; 20:17-28.

Matthew 18:1-4

1 At the same time came the disciples unto Jesus, saying, Who is the greatest in the kingdom of heaven?

2 And Jesus called a little child unto him, and set him in the midst of them,

3 And said, Verily I say unto you, Except ye be converted, and become as little children, ye shall not enter into the kingdom of heaven.

4 Whosoever therefore shall humble himself as this little child, the same is greatest in the kingdom of heaven.

Matthew 20:17-28

17 And Jesus going up to Jerusalem took the twelve disciples apart in the way, and said unto them,

18 Behold, we go up to Jerusalem; and the Son of man shall be betrayed unto the chief priests and unto the scribes, and they shall condemn him to death,

19 And shall deliver him to the Gentiles to mock, and to scourge, and to crucify him: and the third day he shall rise again.

20 Then came to him the mother of Zebedee's children with her sons, worshipping him, and desiring a certain thing of him.

21 And he said unto her, What wilt thou? She saith unto him, Grant that these my two sons may sit, the one on thy right hand, and the other on the left, in thy kingdom.

22 But Jesus answered and said, Ye know not what ye ask. Are ye able to drink of the cup that I shall drink of, and to be baptized with the baptism that I am baptized with? They say unto him, We are able.

23 And he saith unto them, Ye shall drink indeed of my cup, and be baptized with the baptism that I am baptized with: but to sit on my right hand, and on my left, is not mine to give, but it shall be given to them for whom it is prepared of my Father.

24 And when the ten heard it, they were moved with indignation against the two brethren.

25 But Jesus called them unto him, and said, Ye know that the princes of the Gentiles exercise dominion over them, and they that are great exercise authority upon them.

26 But it shall not be so among you: but whosoever will be great among you, let him be your minister;

27 And whosoever will be chief among you, let him be your servant:

28 Even as the Son of man came not to be ministered unto, but to minister, and to give his life a ransom for many.

GOLDEN TEXT: Whosoever will be great among you,
let him be your minister.—Matthew 20:26.

God Calls Anew in Jesus Christ
Unit 2: Good News for Daily Living
(Lessons 5-8)

Lesson Aims

As a result of this lesson, a student should:
1. Summarize what Jesus said about humility and greatness in today's Scripture texts.
2. Contrast the world's standards of greatness with Jesus' standards.
3. Identify someone who models Jesus' standard of greatness, and express his or her appreciation to that individual this week.

Lesson Outline

INTRODUCTION
    A. Feeling Young Again
    B. Lesson Background
I. A HUMBLE SPIRIT (Matthew 18:1-4)
    A. Not Seeking After Honor (v. 1)
    B. Becoming As a Child (vv. 2-4)
II. A DETERMINED WILL (Matthew 20:17-23)
    A. Jesus' Warning (vv. 17-19)
    B. Not Seeking Positions (vv. 20, 21)
        The Right-Hand Man
    C. Following Jesus' Example (vv. 22, 23)
III. A SERVANT'S HEART (Matthew 20:24-28)
    A. Not Controlling Others (vv. 24-27)
        The Greatest in the Kingdom
    B. Imitating Our Leader (v. 28)
CONCLUSION
    A. "I Quit"
    B. Prayer
    C. Thought to Remember

Introduction

A. Feeling Young Again

Why is it that the older we get the more we appreciate the beauty of childhood? Judging by some of our popular expressions, you would think that we adults have a fascination with our long-lost childhood years. We speak of a grown man enjoying a hobby or game with great enthusiasm as going through his "second childhood." When ridiculed for being an "overgrown kid" or "acting like a child," many of us are having so much fun that we consider the remark a compliment. It was an adult author who wrote the fantasy story of Peter Pan and the children living in a Never-Never Land, where one could always remain a child. We observe the innocence of a boy and a girl in love, and with longing we think, "Oh, to be young and in love again." And many of us have been heard to joke, "I would not mind being a child again as long as I could skip the teenage years." Childhood certainly looks inviting to those of us who can no longer experience it.

Perhaps this nostalgic feeling can help us appreciate those occasions when Jesus used children to illustrate the nature of the Christian life. Not only does the imagery of childhood easily draw our attention, but it also portrays important spiritual lessons that we all must heed.

B. Lesson Background

Today's lesson places us in the period of the final six months of Jesus' ministry. During this time, Jesus began to speak more plainly to His disciples regarding the nature of His mission, telling them details about His imminent arrest, trial, and execution. He also gave increased attention to the more difficult themes of His message: the full commitment, hardship and sacrifice, and radical changes in thinking and acting that following Him requires.

It was time for Jesus' followers to learn that being His disciple meant more than just enjoying companionship with Jesus. Discipleship still demands that we move away from the world's standard and become someone different, someone Christlike.

I. A Humble Spirit
(Matthew 18:1-4)

A. Not Seeking After Honor (v. 1)

1. At the same time came the disciples unto Jesus, saying, Who is the greatest in the kingdom of heaven?

The twelve *disciples* were men with great potential for service and leadership in Jesus' *kingdom*. Otherwise, Jesus would not have selected and trained them for such important work. Even so, during these early years of training for their future ministry, the disciples were often very immature and foolish. On more than one occasion, the Gospel writers record how they argued among themselves about what ranking each one of them deserved in the kingdom that Jesus was preparing to establish. This would not be something they would want to admit aloud to others, especially to Jesus. Matthew's account of this episode simply says that they put the question of *who is the greatest* to Jesus. The parallel account in Mark 9:33, 34 fills in what we might have guessed: the disciples refused to admit to Jesus that they "had disputed among themselves, who should be the greatest."

Such petty fussing must have been a great disappointment for Jesus. According to the two previous chapters of Matthew, He had begun to reveal to His disciples the dangers that awaited Him in Jerusalem (Matthew 16:21; 17:22, 23). They should have been focusing more on His words and how they could encourage and support Him. Instead, they were more concerned about how they might attain advancement and honor within the ranks of Jesus' followers. [See question #1, page 176.]

B. Becoming As a Child (vv. 2-4)

2, 3. And Jesus called a little child unto him, and set him in the midst of them, and said, Verily I say unto you, Except ye be converted, and become as little children, ye shall not enter into the kingdom of heaven.

Jesus declared that His disciples must *become as little children* if they wished to be admitted into *the kingdom of heaven*. There are so many good qualities that children possess that are worthy of our imitation: the simplicity of their lives and priorities, the way they can speak with frankness and unabashed truthfulness, and their unconditional trust in and dependence on those who watch over them. While all of these traits are exemplary, the next verse indicates the particular quality Jesus had in mind at this time.

4. Whosoever therefore shall humble himself as this little child, the same is greatest in the kingdom of heaven.

Humility was the virtue that the apostles needed to learn, especially on this occasion when they were arguing over who among them was the *greatest*. The *little child* does not succumb to such foolishness. At that stage in life, he or she is filled with an unpretentious spirit that feels no need to have one's ego stroked. Competition may occur at this age over a desirable toy or a parent's affection, but there is little concern for building up one's own self-esteem while putting others in their place. The simple feeling of being loved and valued for being oneself is satisfaction enough.

All of this changes as we grow older and are told that we live in a "dog-eat-dog" world where in order to survive we must "look out for number one." We readily adapt to this new way of thinking, and childhood innocence is quickly lost. Jesus challenges us to reach back into our past and retrieve the humble spirit that we once exhibited as a child. To do so we must stop casting a competitive eye on those around us. When others do well and are honored and rewarded, we should wish them our best rather than envy their success. We should rejoice in the thought

that we have family and friends, as well as a heavenly Father, who love us for who we are and not on the basis of how we measure up against others. [See question #2, page 176.]

II. A Determined Will (Matthew 20:17-23)

A. Jesus' Warning (vv. 17-19)

17. And Jesus going up to Jerusalem took the twelve disciples apart in the way, and said unto them.

Matthew 20 moves us a few months after the previous episode in chapter 18 to the final days of Jesus' ministry. Jesus is going up to Jerusalem for the Passover celebration that will also be the occasion for His arrest and crucifixion. He is apparently just days away from His journey to Jericho, where He healed two blind men (Matthew 20:29-34), followed immediately by His triumphal entry into Jerusalem on a donkey (Matthew 21:1-11). Jesus took the twelve disciples apart so that He could tell them some information not intended for the general populace.

18. Behold, we go up to Jerusalem; and the Son of man shall be betrayed unto the chief priests and unto the scribes, and they shall condemn him to death.

This is the third recorded occasion in Matthew where Jesus gave His disciples a clear and specific description of the *death* that awaited Him. Throughout most of Jesus' ministry, He had used symbolic language and parables to describe the nature of His ministry. Only during the final six months following Peter's famous confession near Caesarea Philippi did He begin to speak "openly," or plainly, regarding this matter (Mark 8:31, 32).

In His first prediction, Jesus declared that He would be killed in Jerusalem. He identified His assailants as the "elders and chief priests and scribes," also known as the Sanhedrin, the ruling body of the Jewish people. He also affirmed that He would be "raised again the third day" following His death (Matthew 16:21). The second prediction repeated much of this information, but added one detail: He would be delivered by one of His companions ("betrayed") into the hands of His enemies (Matthew 17:22, 23). This third prediction also included many of these same details.

19. And shall deliver him to the Gentiles to mock, and to scourge, and to crucify him: and the third day he shall rise again.

At this point, Jesus' third prediction of His death gave some new information to the disciples. While the Jewish leaders had already been designated as playing a significant part in His death, Jesus here indicated they would *deliver*

How to Say It

CAESAREA PHILIPPI. Sess-uh-*ree*-uh Fuh-*lip*-pie or *Fill*-uh-pie.
GETHSEMANE. Geth-*sem*-uh-nee.
JERICHO. *Jair*-ih-co.
JOSES. *Joe*-sez.
MAGDALENE. *Mag*-duh-leen or Mag-duh-*lee*-nee.
PATMOS. *Pat*-mus.
SALOME. Suh-*lo*-me.
SANHEDRIN. San-*heed*-run or *San*-huh-drin.
ZEBEDEE. *Zeb*-uh-dee.

him to the Gentiles in order to accomplish the execution. This agrees with the political realities of that day. The Jews were under the rule of the Roman Empire and did not possess the authority to execute a criminal. If the Jews wanted to see a criminal executed, they would need to convince the Roman governor that a Roman capital law had been violated.

This third prediction also included the additional information that Jesus would be mocked and scourged prior to His death. And then, in perhaps the most amazing detail of all, Jesus specifically identified the means of His death: crucifixion. The disciples did not grasp any of this information at the time. They assumed that Jesus was still speaking in symbols; thus they were completely caught off guard, even as they watched the predicted events unfold one by one.

Consider how this episode demonstrates Jesus' strength of will. He did not walk into a trap unwittingly. He possessed a full knowledge of the horrible suffering that awaited Him in Jerusalem. The average man would probably flee from such danger if given the opportunity, but not Jesus. He knew that mankind's eternal destiny depended on Him. He later shuddered in the Garden of Gethsemane as the decisive moment approached. But He did not depart from carrying out the will of His heavenly Father. [See question #3, page 176.]

B. Not Seeking Positions (vv. 20, 21)

20. Then came to him the mother of Zebedee's children with her sons, worshipping him, and desiring a certain thing of him.

The woman in this story is called *the mother of Zebedee's children*, who were James and John (Matthew 4:21; Mark 10:35). She is referred to one other time in the Gospels as one of three women who watched "beholding afar off" as Jesus died (Matthew 27:55, 56). It seems likely that she is the "Salome" mentioned in Mark's account of the women who witnessed the crucifix-

ion (Mark 15:40). Both Gospels name "Mary Magdalene" and "Mary the mother of James and Joses," but where Matthew refers to "the mother of Zebedee's children," Mark names "Salome." Even more intriguing is the possibility that in John's listing of the women at the cross, this woman could be the one described as the sister of Jesus' mother (John 19:25). It is not certain that any of the lists includes everyone who was present, so we cannot be sure about this identification; but if it is correct, then James and John would have been Jesus' cousins.

21. And he said unto her, What wilt thou? She saith unto him, Grant that these my two sons may sit, the one on thy right hand, and the other on the left, in thy kingdom.

It should not surprise us to see a mother looking out for what she perceives to be the best interests of her children. We should understand, though, that she was not acting alone. According to Mark's account of this incident, James and John actually expressed this request (Mark 10:35-37). Most likely the mother put the initial request to Jesus, and then Jesus insisted that James and John speak up for themselves. Which one of the three first came up with the idea cannot be determined, but Jesus' response was specifically directed to the two disciples.

THE RIGHT-HAND MAN

Because the majority of people are right-handed, it has become proverbial to say that someone who is most important to your work or success is called your "right-hand man." The Bible even uses this figure of speech when it says that Jesus "sat down on the right hand" of God (Hebrews 1:3).

However, there are some books on the subject of gaining influence and power that suggest just the opposite. They claim that if you are present at a corporate board meeting, the most powerful place to sit is on the *left* of the chairman. (Of course, to those facing the chairman the one on *his left* is actually on *their right*!) But Jesus' disciples were not aware of all this. They regarded the person on the right as the most powerful and influential, and the one on the left as the second most powerful and influential.

If Jesus had granted the request of James and John, would that have brought the discussion to an end? Don't you suppose that the two of them would then have gotten into an argument over which one got to sit on the right side? Likely they would have. But Jesus refused to be drawn into such controversy over positions. Such debates are part of the devil's strategy. He used it with James and John, and he still uses it today: get people thinking about power and position.

Then they will forget about the church's real task, and its progress will come to a screeching halt.   —R. C. S.

C. Following Jesus' Example (vv. 22, 23)

22. But Jesus answered and said, Ye know not what ye ask. Are ye able to drink of the cup that I shall drink of, and to be baptized with the baptism that I am baptized with? They say unto him, We are able.

Jesus' statement *ye know not what ye ask* was true in more ways than one. First, there was apparent in this request a misunderstanding of the nature of Jesus' kingdom. The disciples' thinking was being influenced by the traditional Jewish understanding of an earthly kingdom with thrones to sit on and armies to command. It was not until after Pentecost that these men finally grasped the idea of a spiritual kingdom that focuses on hearts committed to the lordship of Jesus.

James and John also had no idea of how much trouble they were asking for. They saw sitting next to Jesus as a position of honor. But they failed to take into account the opposition that Jesus had been facing throughout His ministry, and the suffering and death that He had recently predicted. To stand next to Jesus is to stand at the "ground zero" of hardship and persecution. [See question #4, page 176.]

Jesus challenged James and John's request because He knew their motive was self-serving. He wanted them to take a more realistic view of what it means to serve Him and stand by His side. There is certainly a heavenly glory awaiting those who follow Jesus, but to follow Him there we must first be willing to follow Him in the path of suffering (Luke 24:25, 26).

23. And he saith unto them, Ye shall drink indeed of my cup, and be baptized with the baptism that I am baptized with: but to sit on my right hand, and on my left, is not mine to give, but it shall be given to them for whom it is prepared of my Father.

We are so accustomed to associating the word *cup* with the Lord's Supper and *baptism* with water that we could easily read the wrong idea into this passage. Jesus' *cup* was the suffering associated with Calvary, as He Himself indicated when in the Garden of Gethsemane He prayed that this "cup" be taken away if possible (Matthew 26:39). His distress would not be that which courageous men are accustomed to handling, for He would be completely "immersed" (which is the meaning of the word *baptized*) into an agony beyond our comprehension.

Certainly James and John did not realize all of this when they asked to be seated next to Jesus.

They were rebuked for their selfish motives, and rightly so. But it is to their credit that Jesus also commended them. He knew that one day they would change their attitudes and become humble servants who would walk the path of suffering, not for their own glory, but for the praise and glory of their Master. Eventually James would be executed for his Christian faith (Acts 12:2), while John would be exiled to the island of Patmos (Revelation 1:9). They would ultimately be welcomed into glory, but only after they first learned humility.

III. A Servant's Heart
(Matthew 20:24-28)

A. Not Controlling Others (vv. 24-27)

24. And when the ten heard it, they were moved with indignation against the two brethren.

Were the other *ten* disciples filled with a righteous *indignation* because the selfish request of James and John was unbecoming for a disciple of Jesus? More likely they were upset that the two brothers had presumed to place themselves above the rest. No doubt each of them had reasons why he himself should be seated at Jesus' side instead of one of the other disciples. Jesus' ensuing rebuke indicates that all of these men still had much to learn about the heart of a true disciple of Jesus.

25. But Jesus called them unto him, and said, Ye know that the princes of the Gentiles exercise dominion over them, and they that are great exercise authority on them.

The power model of leadership used by *authority* figures in politics, military life, and business uses coercion, intimidation, and the threat of stiff penalties to achieve desired goals. Decisions are often unilateral, dictated from the top to those on the bottom. In such a system, a person learns to play by the rules and advance, or eventually be trampled on by everyone else.

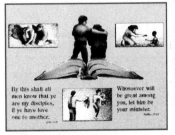

Visual for
lessons 5 and 7

This visual reminds us of today's golden text, that whoever wants to be great must achieve that status through humble acts of loving service.

26, 27. But it shall not be so among you: but whosoever will be great among you, let him be your minister; and whosoever will be chief among you, let him be your servant.

In contrast, the *servant* model of leadership guides people along by persuasion, wisdom, and godly example. Decisions are made, not to advance the leader's own interests and wealth, but for the good of those he leads. This is noticeably different from the way the world operates. But if the world's standard had been acceptable to God, Jesus would not have shown us a better way. [See question #5, page 176.]

The Greatest in the Kingdom

The story is told of a king who was very successful and well known. He had defeated all his enemies, and his people lived in peace and prosperity. To honor the king, they held a great banquet. Many attended and paid tribute to the king with their gifts.

That night one of the king's trusted counselors awakened him, greatly worried. "I've just dreamed a terrible dream," he told the king. "I dreamed that the greatest man in the kingdom is going to die tonight." Immediately the king stationed guards at the door to his room, in the corridors, and at the door to the palace. He could not sleep. The next morning, however, he felt fine. He told the counselor, "You had me scared for no reason at all," and put him in chains.

Later that day, the king went on a tour of his capital city. All the people cheered him until he reached the poorest part of the city. Crowds were present, but they were not cheering. They told the king, "It's not that we don't wish you well, but a man in our neighborhood died last night. You wouldn't have known him, but he was a slave in your palace. He didn't have much

money, but if anyone was in need he managed to help. He had a hard life, but he was always cheerful and happy. He died last night."

The king stopped his tour. He released his counselor. He told his advisers, "I am going on a long journey. I may never come back. My son will rule in my stead." The king never returned. But some noticed a new slave in the palace, doing what the old slave had done. The man looked remarkably like the king. —R. C. S.

B. Imitating Our Leader (v. 28)

28. Even as the Son of man came not to be ministered unto, but to minister, and to give his life a ransom for many.

There is no question that as our Creator and Redeemer, Jesus has absolute authority over all. He has the right and power to demand anything He wishes, and to treat us any way He chooses. Yet the example that He set for us in the incarnation was that of a humble servant who was fully dedicated to doing the will of God, even to the point of suffering on a cross. This is still the standard for anyone who would be His disciple.

Conclusion

A. "I Quit"

Many times I have spoken with students or friends who have quit their jobs before finding other employment. When I ask why they would quit before they had another job lined up, they say, "I just could not stand to work another day being treated like that!"

I may question the wisdom of my friends' timing, but I understand their frustration in working for an employer who uses his authority in a manner that breaks morale. The world's approach to authority may seem to get results; but it is demeaning to those on the bottom, and ultimately unfulfilling for those on the top.

The lesson for today challenges us to "reverse the world's standard." If we are going to "quit" anything, let us quit playing by the world's rules and follow the model of Jesus. Let us develop a servant's heart.

B. Prayer

Our Father in Heaven, break down within us the remnants of worldly pride and selfishness, so that we may serve You and those around us in a humble manner, for Your glory and honor. In the name of Jesus. Amen.

C. Thought to Remember

"The Son of man came not to be ministered unto, but to minister, and to give his life a ransom for many" (Matthew 20:28).

Home Daily Bible Readings

Monday, Jan. 11—A Child Among Them (Matthew 18:1-4)

Tuesday, Jan. 12—Not to Be Served, But to Serve (Matthew 20:17-28)

Wednesday, Jan. 13—I Have Given You an Example (John 13:1-15)

Thursday, Jan. 14—The Strong Ought to Help the Weak (Romans 15:1-6)

Friday, Jan. 15—I Am Not Worthy (Genesis 32:3-12)

Saturday, Jan. 16—Humility Goes Before Honor (Proverbs 15:25-33)

Sunday, Jan. 17—Humble in Spirit (Isaiah 57:15-21)

Learning by Doing

This page contains an alternate lesson plan emphasizing learning activities. Classes desiring such student involvement will find these suggestions helpful.

Learning Goals

As a result of this lesson, a student should:

1. Summarize what Jesus said about humility and greatness in today's Scripture texts.

2. Contrast the world's standards of greatness with Jesus' standards.

3. Identify someone who models Jesus' standard of greatness, and express his or her appreciation to that individual this week.

Into the Lesson

Before class, prepare enough slips of paper to tape one to the bottom of every chair in the classroom. On a third of the slips write, "I became a Christian through the influence of _____." On the second third write, "_____ is someone who has helped me in my Christian walk." On the remaining third write, "Someone who has given freely of himself or herself for the sake of the Lord is _____."

Ask each person to reach under his seat, remove the slip of paper he or she finds there, and write the name of an individual who fits the description on the slip of paper. Give the students about two minutes, and then instruct them to pair up with another person with the same assignment. Once each student has a partner, ask the group to spend five minutes telling each other why the individuals named fit the descriptions. Then ask volunteers to share their responses with the whole class.

Tell the class that the definition of greatness varies with different people's perspectives and goals. Some would name people of power. Some would name people of authority. But the people your class has named are better examples of what Jesus meant by "greatness." The beauty of His definition is that every person can become great in the grandest kingdom of all.

Into the Word

Ask a volunteer to read Matthew 18:1-4; 20:17-28. (Or use a VCR to show a video dramatization of the text. Some very good ones are available.)

Use a flip chart or a couple of sheets of poster board to help the students follow the movement of the text and remember the principles gleaned in this study. Put this heading on the first page of the flip chart or poster board: "Lessons From Little Children About Greatness." After reading or viewing Matthew 18:1-4, give a brief lecture

about why Jesus would use children for illustrations. (The commentary section of this book will help you prepare the lecture.) Then ask and discuss the following questions:

1. Why do you suppose the disciples asked, "Who is the greatest in the kingdom of heaven?"

2. What did Jesus mean by, "Except ye be converted, and become as little children, ye shall not enter in the kingdom of heaven"?

3. What did Jesus teach us about humility in verse 4?

4. What are the specific lessons you learn about greatness and humility from this teaching? (Make a list of the students' answers on the flip chart or poster board.)

On the second page of the flip chart or poster board, print this heading: "Lessons From Grown-up Kids About Greatness." After reading or viewing Matthew 20:17-28, do a short lecture on the specific details Jesus was giving about His future in verses 17-19. Then, from verse 20, explain "sons of Zebedee." These "grown-up kids" presented another opportunity for Jesus to teach a lesson on greatness.

Ask these discussion questions:

1. Why would this mother ask such a bold favor of Jesus?

2. What was Jesus saying to James and John with His questions about His "cup" and "baptism"? What was He implying about their future?

3. What was Jesus telling them—and what does He say to us—about greatness?

4. Contrast the model of the "princes of the Gentiles" with Jesus' model of greatness in verses 25-27.

Into Life

When a person strives for greatness in the world, he strives to better himself. Often he is oblivious to how his pursuit damages those around him. Jesus' model starts with helping others first. What personal greatness we achieve is awarded us by God, our Father.

In closing, ask each student to think of a person he considers great by Jesus' standard. Ask your students to think of a way to thank this person for services rendered. Often, this thanks can take the form of a letter, a prayer, a phone call, or even a service rendered in return. Close the class with prayer, and challenge the students to appreciate those who are great by Jesus' standard.

Let's Talk It Over

The questions on this page are designed to encourage review of the lesson Scriptures and to promote discussion of the lesson by the class. The answers provided are only discussion starters. Let your class talk it over from there.

1. The disciples argued about who was the greatest among them. We don't like to admit it, but many of our disputes are, at heart, an argument about who is greatest. How does this ancient argument find expression in the church today, and how can we pursue the way of humility that Jesus modeled?

Whenever issues of personal opinion or taste become divisive in the body of Christ, we are insisting our way is better just because it is our way. When titles and offices become more important to us than ministry, we have succumbed to the temptation of seeking "greatness." No doubt, your students can think of many other examples, both specific and general.

One way we can fight this temptation is to remember where we have come from. We are sinners saved by grace. Another way to follow Jesus is to practice the way of love—actively seeking ways to express love and honor to others instead of seeking honor for ourselves. (See also Romans 12:10 and Philippians 2:3-5.)

2. Jesus said we need to "become as little children." But in Ephesians 4:14 Paul said we are to "be no more children." How would you respond if a friend said this was evidence of contradictions in the Bible?

Rather than a contradiction, these statements comprise a complementary package, like two sides of the same coin. Children can be very humble and freely accept direction from those in authority, such as their parents. But children can also be stubborn and choose to do things their own way, even though they don't have the experience or training to do the job right. This is the kind of behavior Paul warns against in Ephesians 4. Paul himself finds application for both the positive and negative characteristics of children in 1 Corinthians 14:20: "Be not children in understanding: howbeit in malice be ye children."

3. The lesson writer notes that it took great strength of character for Jesus, knowing what awaited Him in Jerusalem, to go there. In what situations do Christians need similar strength? How can we find it?

Jesus knew His mission was to "give his life a ransom for many" (Matthew 20:28). That knowledge, as well as frequent prayer and communion with the Father, strengthened Him for the task. Of course, He was God in the flesh also; so He had divine power unlike anything available to humans. Still, His example is instructive. If, even with His divine power, Jesus needed to spend time in prayer, how much more do we?

4. James and John did not understand what it would mean to "drink of the cup" Jesus would drink, but they would learn. What have you learned about discipleship that you did not know before you began to follow Jesus?

James and John believed that Jesus was the Messiah and that, as promised, He would reign on the throne of David. They wanted positions of honor and power in His kingdom. They did not comprehend that establishing the kingdom would require so much from Jesus, and that being near Him would be so dangerous for them. Jesus continues to demand everyone who would be His disciple to "deny himself, and take up his cross, and follow" Him (Matthew 16:24). Some who accept Jesus have overlooked or underestimated how rigorous or even dangerous it can be to remain loyal to Him. Jesus warned, "If they have persecuted me, they will also persecute you" (John 15:18-21). At the same time, many have found the joy of following Jesus to be beyond their imagination. This discussion may turn into a praise time before it's over!

5. Jesus' definition of greatness is very different from the world's. Do you think it is appealing to the world or repulsive? Why?

Those who are power hungry will surely not be impressed by Jesus' standards. But those who have been abused and mistreated by some in power over them will surely find Jesus' way a welcome relief. Leaders and would-be leaders may be threatened by the thought that greatness does not automatically accompany authority, but is attributed on the basis of actual contribution to the well-being of others. However, those who are more interested in the advance of the kingdom than they are in advancing their own interests will find Jesus' way a happier road to travel. Worldly leaders often have to pretend and exaggerate their importance to hold on to their power, but such pretense is unnecessary if holding on to power is not one's goal.

Forgive One Another

DEVOTIONAL READING: Psalm 103:6-14.

LESSON SCRIPTURE: Matthew 18:5-35.

PRINTED TEXT: Matthew 18:21-35.

Matthew 18:21-35

21 Then came Peter to him, and said, Lord, how oft shall my brother sin against me, and I forgive him? till seven times?

22 Jesus saith unto him, I say not unto thee, Until seven times: but, Until seventy times seven.

23 Therefore is the kingdom of heaven likened unto a certain king, which would take account of his servants.

24 And when he had begun to reckon, one was brought unto him, which owed him ten thousand talents.

25 But forasmuch as he had not to pay, his lord commanded him to be sold, and his wife, and children, and all that he had, and payment to be made.

26 The servant therefore fell down, and worshipped him, saying, Lord, have patience with me, and I will pay thee all.

27 Then the lord of that servant was moved with compassion, and loosed him, and forgave him the debt.

28 But the same servant went out, and found one of his fellow servants, which owed him a hundred pence: and he laid hands on him, and took him by the throat, saying, Pay me that thou owest.

29 And his fellow servant fell down at his feet, and besought him, saying, Have patience with me, and I will pay thee all.

30 And he would not: but went and cast him into prison, till he should pay the debt.

31 So when his fellow servants saw what was done, they were very sorry, and came and told unto their lord all that was done.

32 Then his lord, after that he had called him, said unto him, O thou wicked servant, I forgave thee all that debt, because thou desiredst me:

33 Shouldest not thou also have had compassion on thy fellow servant, even as I had pity on thee?

34 And his lord was wroth, and delivered him to the tormentors, till he should pay all that was due unto him.

35 So likewise shall my heavenly Father do also unto you, if ye from your hearts forgive not every one his brother their trespasses.

Jan 24

GOLDEN TEXT: If ye forgive men their trespasses, your heavenly Father will also forgive you: but if ye forgive not men their trespasses, neither will your Father forgive your trespasses.—Matthew 6:14, 15.

Lesson Aims

Today's lesson should encourage each of your students to:

1. Tell how Jesus illustrated the limitless grace of God and the duty that believers have to imitate His grace.

2. Explain the relationship between receiving God's grace and showing grace to others.

3. Attempt this week to resolve a conflict in such a way as to demonstrate God's grace at work in his/her life.

Lesson Outline

INTRODUCTION
  A. Animal Psychology
  B. Lesson Background
  I. FORGIVE AS OFTEN AS ASKED (Matthew 18:21, 22)
  A. A Reasonable Plan (v. 21)
  B. Grace Explained (v. 22)
      Losing Count
 II. FORGIVE REGARDLESS OF THE COST (Matthew 18:23-27)
  A. A Staggering Debt (vv. 23-25)
  B. Grace Bestowed (vv. 26, 27)
III. FORGIVE AS YOU HAVE BEEN FORGIVEN (Matthew 18:28-35)
  A. A Lesson Forgotten (vv. 28-31)
  B. Grace Denied (vv. 32-35)
      Frequent Forgiver Points?
CONCLUSION
  A. Three Strikes—You're Out
  B. Prayer
  C. Thought to Remember

Introduction

A. Animal Psychology

Those who devote their lives to animal behavioral studies have made some interesting observations. They tell us that animals have within them an instinct for "learning" from their experiences. If a dog is hit with a rolled-up newspaper each time he jumps up onto a sofa, he will soon be conditioned to stay off the sofa. A cat that is sprayed with water each time she scratches the side of a chair quickly learns to stay away from that chair. A mouse that bumps his nose a few times on a barrier placed in the middle of a maze will soon learn not to go down that portion of the maze.

Mankind approaches the experiences of life with certain God-given advantages over the animals. We have greater reasoning abilities, we can devise a plan in our minds and determine to see it through, and we can make freewill decisions. In short, we possess the image of God.

Why is it, then, that we are so often slower than the animal kingdom to learn from our mistakes? Too often we repeat the same errors that brought us trouble before, forgetting the lessons learned from previous experiences. As for positive reinforcement, we readily feel appreciation for those who show kindness to us; but then we fail to see the logical implication: people would appreciate us in like manner if we showed them the same kindness that we have received. Life's classroom has much to teach us, but we have to pay attention.

B. Lesson Background

Poor Peter! In the Gospel accounts, he tries so hard to come up with clever things to say; but more often than not, his great ideas end up looking pretty lame. We read the incidents recorded in the Gospels and talk about Peter's penchant for "putting his foot in his mouth." In today's text he attempts to make a perceptive observation regarding forgiveness, and then finds himself on the receiving end of a short sermon.

But just think how easy it would be for any of us to make the mistake Peter made. Jesus had just finished giving instructions regarding a brother who "shall trespass against thee," explaining how to discipline someone who refuses to deal responsibly with his sin when confronted with it (Matthew 18:15-20). It would be natural to assume that certain people may not deserve to be forgiven, especially if they keep repeating the same sin.

What Peter failed to consider in his thinking was that immediately before He gave the "sinning brother" instructions, Jesus had told the parable of the lost sheep (Matthew 18:12-14). Here Jesus painted a beautiful picture of the heart of God. As our Shepherd, He understands how easy it is for sheep to get lost; but because He values us so much, He does not abandon us to our folly. Instead, He does whatever He can to rescue even one sheep and restore it to the fold. True, there are appropriate times for tough measures when discipline should be applied, but even that should be done in harmony with a grace that desires an individual's restoration. Judgment should not begin until grace has had a hearing.

I. Forgive As Often As Asked
(Matthew 18:21, 22)
A. A Reasonable Plan (v. 21)

21. Then came Peter to him, and said, Lord, how oft shall my brother sin against me, and I forgive him? till seven times?

There is nothing in this text to indicate how Peter arrived at the number *seven* as his limit. Some have theorized that there may have been a rabbinical tradition of requiring forgiveness up to three times. With this in mind, Peter is said to have generously doubled the minimum number and then added one more for good measure. Whatever the reason for Peter's choosing the number seven, it is clear that he desired to set some kind of limit on forgiveness.

Apparently Peter was thinking that a person does deserve a second chance, but only so many "second chances." A person who continues to do the same wrong over and over is evidently not very serious about quitting, and not very sincere when he says, "I'm sorry." To keep on forgiving such a person unconditionally might very well tempt a sinful heart to take advantage of one's goodness. Clearly stated ultimatums and limits could serve as a much-needed wake-up call. What Peter proposed was not unreasonable.

B. Grace Explained (v. 22)

22. Jesus saith unto him, I say not unto thee, Until seven times: but, Until seventy times seven.

Jesus did not question Peter's logic, but He challenged him to consider a better plan: grace. The Biblical idea of grace is to treat a sinner better than he deserves to be treated. It is the nature of grace to go beyond what is reasonable and fair to something that is admittedly undeserved. Grace does not ask us to do something that is less than fair; rather, it challenges us to be more than fair.

Grace is not an easy path to take. In fact, it requires a substantial measure of spiritual maturity in order to maintain such a posture. After all, it is possible that a sinful heart may try to take advantage of your gracious disposition. And it is not easy to watch a person do wrong and yet go unpunished.

Perhaps grace would be an easier course of action if we also saw its positive aspects. A sinner who knows that we have forgiven him and will not pay him back could walk away feeling smug about his sin; however, being the beneficiary of grace has a way of stirring up a guilty conscience and melting a sinful heart (Romans 12:17-21). That is the reason it can be beneficial, when we forgive someone, to make it clear that we are doing so as a gracious choice, and not out of weakness or necessity. Forgiveness done well can be an opportunity for a persuasive gospel witness. As for someone's taking advantage of us, we can rest assured that God will one day "balance the scales" so that those who abuse us will pay, while we will be blessed with so much more than we ever lost. [See question #1, page 184.]

Let us not then read Jesus' number *seventy times seven* as a replacement limit for Peter's suggestion. Jesus was making a play on words based on Peter's comment. He used a large number that does not lend itself to record keeping; for it is not His intent that we keep count of the wrongs we have forgiven, but that we forgive indefinitely.

LOSING COUNT

The man has collected clocks for years. He has hundreds of them—small clocks, large clocks, old clocks, new clocks. Every room of the house has at least a dozen or two. If someone asks, "How many clocks do you have?" his answer is: "I don't know. My grandchildren try to count them every time they come to visit. They get up to about eight hundred, and then they can't remember which ones they've counted and which ones they haven't. They lose count."

Isn't this what Jesus had in mind when He gave His reply to Peter's generous offer to forgive seven times? Seventy times seven is 490. No one could possibly keep account of wrongs up to 490 without losing count somewhere along the way. The *New English Bible* translates 1 Corinthians 13:5 as follows: "Love keeps no score of wrongs." Keeping score is exactly what we often do. And after our enemy has run up the score to a certain point, we decide that it is time for us to get even.

Sometimes people have missed the point of Jesus' words in the Sermon on the Mount: "Whosoever shall smite thee on thy right cheek, turn to him the other also" (Matthew 5:39). They claim, "Jesus said to turn the other cheek, but He didn't say what to do after that!" But of course, Jesus *did* say what to do after that; He said it in today's lesson. Keeping score demands that we keep on remembering. Forgiving demands that we also try to forget. That may be the hardest part of forgiving, but it is also the most rewarding.

—R. C. S.

How to Say It

DENARII. dih-*nair*-ee or dih-*nair*-eye.
DENARIUS. dih-*nair*-ee-us.

II. Forgive Regardless of the Cost (Matthew 18:23-27)

A. A Staggering Debt (vv. 23-25)

23. Therefore is the kingdom of heaven likened unto a certain king, which would take account of his servants.

Parables are stories that are taken from real life and used to illustrate spiritual truths. The most frequently used imagery in Jesus' parables for representing the interaction of God and mankind is that of a *king* and his subjects.

The *servants* in this parable should not be thought of as slaves who worked for minimal compensation or nothing at all. It is more accurate to view them as managers who were commissioned by the king to invest his resources in projects that would bring a handsome return. For the king to *take account* involved a periodic summoning of each manager to the court to report on his investment of the king's money.

24. And when he had begun to reckon, one was brought unto him, which owed him ten thousand talents.

There is no way to put an exact dollar figure on *ten thousand talents* and expect it to remain accurate in an age when monetary values change daily. But we can come up with a rough idea that will enable us to appreciate the message of Jesus' parable. A denarius in New Testament times was equal to one day's wages, that is, what a person would be paid for one day's work on a typical manual labor job. One talent was worth approximately six thousand denarii, or six thousand days of labor. Ten thousand talents would thus be the equivalent of the income from sixty million work days! Once such a sum of money was lost, it would be virtually impossible to repay the debt. The only viable option was to sentence the debtor to prison. [See question #2, page 184.]

25. But forasmuch as he had not to pay, his lord commanded him to be sold, and his wife, and children, and all that he had, and payment to be made.

Both Jewish and Roman law contained certain provisions for dealing with loan defaults and financial mismanagement. A debt repayment plan was a possibility if the size of the debt was manageable. When repayment was not feasible, a person had the option of recouping some of his losses through the sale of the debtor's property and family. While this seldom, if ever, covered the full debt, it at least provided the satisfaction of seeing the debtor receive a stiff punishment.

It may seem strange and cruel to us to include the *wife* and *children* in such a penalty. This reflects the view (common in ancient cultures) that the head of a household acted in behalf of the rest of the household; thus, when he was guilty, so were they to a certain extent.

B. Grace Bestowed (vv. 26, 27)

26. The servant therefore fell down, and worshipped him, saying, Lord, have patience with me, and I will pay thee all.

This debtor's plea was totally unrealistic. No amount of *patience* would enable him to *pay . . . all.* The only hope that remained was that his king might bestow grace upon him.

27. Then the lord of that servant was moved with compassion, and loosed him, and forgave him the debt.

The *lord*, or king, is the hero of this parable. He is the model of grace in action. We have no way of knowing how much this loss affected him financially. No matter how you look at it, to lose the equivalent of millions of dollars had to hurt! To forgive a *debt* this size could happen only at a great cost to the king. Grace is not an easy course to follow.

Jesus would have us learn to forgive no matter what the cost. After all, is that not the way God has dealt with us? By His grace He has arranged a plan of redemption that allows us to be forgiven of our debt of sin, but only at the unthinkable cost of the life of His Son.

The king's action teaches us something else about grace: it cannot be demanded; it can only be requested. No one can require that you forgive them. No one who owes you a debt can obligate you to write off that debt. It is the nature of grace that it must be a gift freely given, or it is not really grace. The king in Jesus' parable was under no obligation to the debtor. He acted out of *compassion*, not necessity. [See question #3, page 184.]

III. Forgive As You Have Been Forgiven (Matthew 18:28-35)

A. A Lesson Forgotten (vv. 28-31)

28. But the same servant went out, and found one of his fellow servants, which owed him a hundred pence: and he laid hands on him, and took him by the throat, saying, Pay me that thou owest.

In the Greek text the phrase *a hundred pence* is "one hundred denarii," or as we noted earlier, the money an average worker would earn for one hundred days of manual labor. Sometimes a teacher today who wants to emphasize the contrast in the size of the two debts will liken the second debt to a few pennies or a few dollars. To view the debt in this way actually damages the credibility of the story, for no court of law,

Jewish or Greek, would imprison a man for such a small amount. However, one hundred denarii was an amount significant enough to call for legal action.

In modern terms, the difference in the two debts would be equivalent to the difference between owing a few thousand dollars and owing several million. The latter is beyond hope of repayment, while the former is manageable and could be resolved with a little patience. Our *servant*, however, was not in the mood for any patience or grace.

29. And his fellow servant fell down at his feet, and besought him, saying, Have patience with me, and I will pay thee all.

One would think that this plea would have had a familiar ring to our servant, since he himself had uttered these same words not long before. The old expression is true: "How quickly we forget!"

30. And he would not: but went and cast him into prison, till he should pay the debt.

How could a person *pay* a *debt* while sitting in a *prison*? One way was through a system by which the prison farmed its inmates out as slave labor. A prisoner would then be credited with a small amount of money that could be applied directly to his debt. Obviously it would take a long time to pay off a debt in this manner, but it could be done after several years.

A faster way for a prisoner to repay a debt was to call upon his family and friends to rescue him from his dire circumstances and pay his debt for him. These people might act out of compassion, or they might simply desire to remove an embarrassment to the family. The person who forced a debtor into imprisonment would not care by which means he got his money, just as long as he got it.

31. So when his fellow servants saw what was done, they were very sorry, and came and told unto their lord all that was done.

The *fellow servants* would be other men whom the king considered responsible enough to serve as managers of his large estate. As we might expect, men working the same job would naturally form a fraternal relationship, perhaps with some mutual assistance and even friendly competition for honors. And as this story indicates, over time they would develop a concern for the welfare of each other that would prompt them to stick up for one of their own who was not treated properly.

B. Grace Denied (vv. 32-35)

32, 33. Then his lord, after that he had called him, said unto him, O thou wicked servant, I forgave thee all that debt, because thou

Visual for lesson 8

This visual puts the words of the king of the parable (vv. 32, 33) in the mouth of Jesus. On the cross He forgave us so much— can't we forgive our brothers and sisters?

desiredst me: shouldest not thou also have had compassion on thy fellow servant, even as I had pity on thee?

The king did not argue on the basis of what the law demanded, because legally the servant was not required to cancel a debt (even though he had just had his own debt canceled). This was simply a matter of common courtesy, evident to the king, the fellow servants, and (Jesus apparently assumed) to His hearers as well. No law was required in this matter. It should be natural for a person who has received a grace in the "millions" to demonstrate a similar grace with a much lesser debt. Rightly so is this man called a *wicked servant*.

34. And his lord was wroth, and delivered him to the tormentors, till he should pay all that was due unto him.

The cancellation of the ten thousand-talent debt was rescinded and the wicked servant sent to prison. One might wonder how a debt earlier forgiven could legally be reinstated. Perhaps there was some stipulation in Roman law that allowed for putting conditions on a debt cancellation. Perhaps this was simply a matter of royal prerogative. In the case of God's forgiveness, however, we know how this works. The justification for sin that we enjoy now is always conditioned upon whether or not we continue to live by faith (Colossians 1:21-23; Revelation 2:10). Those of us who do not live by grace could one day lose the grace we now enjoy (Galatians 5:4). [See question #4, page 184.]

To say that the wicked servant would suffer until he could *pay all that was due unto him* was not to imply that repayment was possible. This debt was too great to be repaid. Jesus was saying that this person would not be released from his torment as long as any debt remained—and we know that there will always be a debt remaining. This was actually a creative way of referring to an eternal suffering, thus providing a good analogy to Hell.

35. So likewise shall my heavenly Father do also unto you, if ye from your hearts forgive not every one his brother their trespasses.

Forgiveness seems to work by a variation of the Golden Rule: "Whatsoever ye would that men should do to you, do ye even so to them" (Matthew 7:12). It is appropriate to practice forgiveness, so that those you forgive will in turn be gracious with you when you do them wrong. But our greater concern is not the forgiveness of man, but the forgiveness of our *heavenly Father*. We "do unto others" as we would have God do to us.

Jesus' warning is clear. We who refuse to forgive others jeopardize our status with God. To refuse to forgive after we have been forgiven of so much is a "slap in the face" of Almighty God. It suggests a lack of appreciation for what God has done, perhaps even an insincerity in our appeal for mercy. We dare not be cheap with a grace that cost God so much. [See question #5, page 184.]

FREQUENT FORGIVER POINTS?

All the major airlines now offer their passengers "frequent flyer points." Sometimes one can also accumulate points by using a certain credit card or long distance service. If you accumulate enough points, you can get a free ticket to fly on the participating airline.

At first glance this concluding verse in today's printed text sounds like a plan for "frequent forgiver points." This is especially true if we combine it with the portion of the Lord's Prayer that says, "Forgive us our debts, as we forgive our debtors" (Matthew 6:12). It sounds as if each time we forgive someone, we earn the forgiveness of one of our sins. (If that were true, we'd better hope that others do a lot of harm to us, so we can build up enough points to get forgiveness for all our sins!)

But Jesus was not talking about a one-for-one exchange. His meaning is this: when we are unforgiving, we build a shell around our hearts that even the grace of God cannot penetrate. If, having been forgiven by God, we do not forgive others, we show that we have not realized the magnitude of God's forgiveness of us. When we have done so, we will want to treat others as God has treated us.

This is not a merit system. We earn no merit badges. We accumulate no points. We do show what kind of persons we are and whether we understand what it means to be saved by grace.

—R. C. S.

Conclusion

A. Three Strikes—You're Out

Even those of us who do not play baseball know the expression "three strikes—you're out." In all sporting activities such as baseball, there are rules and boundaries and time limits. So also in life. We have deadlines for turning in school assignments and filing income taxes. We have limits on the number of trips we can make to the salad bar. We have honor codes at military academies that require immediate expulsion for violations. We learn to play by the rules, or "we're out." This is the way most of life needs to be in order to work effectively. After all, how is the outfield ever going to get a time at bat if there are no limits on strikes?

Not so with forgiveness. As Peter learned, there are no limits on how often we are to forgive others. We who have received an immeasurable amount of grace from God have a responsibility to be as gracious as we can with others. For if we cannot forgive the lesser debts against us, why should we expect God to forgive our eternal debt of sin? Three strikes . . . seven strikes . . . seventy times seven strikes . . . let us not think of limits, but rather let us think of, and rejoice in, God's abounding grace!

B. Prayer

Our Father in Heaven, help us to comprehend more fully the amazing grace that You have applied to our sin. May we be so overwhelmed by what You have done for us that we cannot help but share that same grace with any who have done us wrong. In Jesus' name, amen.

C. Thought to Remember

"Forgive us our debts, as we forgive our debtors" (Matthew 6:12).

Home Daily Bible Readings

Monday, Jan. 18—No Stumbling Blocks! (Matthew 18:6-14)
Tuesday, Jan. 19—Dealing With a Sinning Brother (Matthew 18:15-20)
Wednesday, Jan. 20—How Often Must I Forgive? (Matthew 18:21-35)
Thursday, Jan. 21—Restore Transgressors! (Galatians 6:1-5)
Friday, Jan. 22—"Be Ye Kind . . . Tenderhearted, Forgiving" (Ephesians 4:25-32)
Saturday, Jan. 23—God Forgives; So Should We (Psalm 103:6-14)
Sunday, Jan. 24—I Will Remember Their Sins No More (Hebrews 10:11-25)

Learning by Doing

This page contains an alternate lesson plan emphasizing learning activities.
Classes desiring such student involvement will find these suggestions helpful.

Learning Goals

Today's lesson should encourage each of your students to:

1. Tell how Jesus illustrated the limitless grace of God and the duty that believers have to imitate His grace.

2. Explain the relationship between receiving God's grace and showing grace to others.

3. Attempt this week to resolve a conflict in such a way as to demonstrate God's grace at work in his/her life.

Into the Lesson

Write the following open-ended sentences on poster board to display before students arrive.

"A time an acquaintance offered forgiveness that I did not deserve was. . . ."

"One time I really struggled with forgiving someone was. . . ."

"The biggest barrier to forgiving someone is. . . ."

Prepare three cans or baskets, each labeled with one of the three open-ended sentences above. Ask each person to jot an answer on a piece of paper. Do not sign names. Ask the students to drop the papers into the appropriate can or basket. At random, draw three slips of paper from each can and read the answers.

Make the transition from this activity to Bible study by admitting to the class that forgiveness is not an easy thing to do. Forgiveness is unnatural. But Jesus forgave us, and He expects us to forgive each other. In today's lesson, Jesus illustrates the grace of God and the duty believers have to imitate His grace.

Into the Word

Distribute handouts as described below (or refer the students to the proper page in the *Adult Bible Class* student book). Have a transparency or poster prepared with the same information.

On the handout, write the following headings across the top: *Person, The Offender, The Debt,* and *Action.* Under *Person* write the following in a vertical column: Peter, King (first time), Servant, King (second time), and Heavenly Father.

Have a volunteer read Matthew 18:21-35 aloud. Then ask the students to work in groups of two or three to complete the handouts. Next to each "person" listed in column 1, the students should write who offended the person ("offender"), how ("debt"), and what the person did about it ("action"). After the groups have completed their work, review the parable with the whole class by completing the chart on the overhead transparency or poster as volunteers give you information. As you complete the chart, comment on how the events of the parable illustrate God's forgiveness of our debts or sins. For example, the servant could not repay his debt, and we do not have any way to repay our debt for sin.

Ask the class, "Do you think Jesus' primary objective was to answer Peter's question about forgiving someone or to teach about God's grace? Why?" (Note: Jesus accomplished both objectives with this parable.)

Discuss the lesson writer's statement: "The Biblical idea of grace is to treat a sinner better than he deserves to be treated." How does that define God's grace toward us?

Do a brief summary, stressing that the king is a model of grace in action. (See the commentary on verses 27 and 35.) Jesus wants us to learn to forgive, no matter what the cost.

Into Life

Questions that will make the lesson personal include:

a. Would there be forgiveness of the debt or forgiveness of our sins without asking for it or without repentance? Why or why not? (See the notes on verse 27.)

b. The definition, "Grace is to treat a sinner better than he deserves to be treated," can also be applied to our relationship with persons who have offended us. What are the positive aspects of this kind of behavior? What kind of impact could forgiveness have on the offender? (See the commentary on verse 22.)

c. Why is practicing forgiveness good for the one who forgives? List the answers to this question on a chalkboard or poster board.

To conclude the lesson, ask the class to recall persons they've forgiven or have not yet forgiven. Remind them forgiveness is not easy, but God expects it of us. Challenge them to resolve at least one conflict this week in such a way as to demonstrate God's grace. Just before the closing prayer, ask someone to lead the class in singing the chorus, "Change My Heart, O God."

Let's Talk It Over

The questions on this page are designed to encourage review of the lesson Scriptures and to promote discussion of the lesson by the class. The answers provided are only discussion starters. Let your class talk it over from there.

1. The lesson writer says that when we forgive, we should communicate that we are doing so "as a gracious choice, and not out of weakness or necessity." How can we do that?

Sometimes what appears to be forgiveness is simply an inability to take revenge. Those who like to pick on smaller people count on that. They "get away with it" because their victims are unable to retaliate.

Sometimes forgiving Christians will seem to be in this position, and there is little we can do about it. Other times we'll be like David in the cave with King Saul (1 Samuel 24). Revenge will be within our grasp, but we must refuse to take it. Consistently refusing to take revenge when we can is the only way to have credibility with forgiveness when we can't take revenge.

2. The parable of the unforgiving servant is built on the premise that we owe a huge debt to God. That is not a universally accepted notion today. By and large, people believe that, if they have sinned at all, their offenses are "no big deal." How can we communicate the fact that there is a vast difference between us and our holy God and get people to act on that fact?

As long as Christians display, consciously or unconsciously, the attitude that they are saved because they have somehow earned that blessing, it will be impossible to communicate the overwhelming need for God's grace. We need to talk openly about our appreciation for God's grace, frankly admitting our own shortcomings and need for God's forgiveness. We need to be quick to forgive and to point out that we have been forgiven so much more by God that we can do nothing else but forgive. Even as we take a stand against the terrible moral excesses of society, we must clearly demonstrate our belief that God can forgive murderers, homosexuals, adulterers, and the rest as easily as He has forgiven us.

3. The master was moved by compassion to forgive his servant. How can we develop compassion as a motivation to be more forgiving?

Literally, compassion means to "feel with" or to "suffer with" another. It is not only to be aware of another's distress, but to have the desire to relieve it. To be moved with compassion for someone requires that we imagine how it must feel to be in their condition—to see things from their perspective. We may be moved to forgiveness if we can understand how forgiveness will lessen the distress of the offender. To exercise compassion means overcoming the desire to inflict more pain, and, instead, acting to relieve pain.

4. The "unforgiving servant" had a legal obligation to repay his debt. He failed but was treated as if he had done right. Later he had a legal right to demand repayment of the debt owed to him. But when he did so, he was treated as an evildoer. Do you think some might find this irony to be unfair? Why or why not? How would you explain it to a friend who was struggling with the concept of God's justice?

This is the irony of grace. Only one person ever kept the law perfectly and committed no sin. Yet He suffered the penalty. On the other hand, we who have sinned find justification through grace. It seems backward; it's not fair. No, it's more than fair, and it's our only hope. If we demand justice, we'll have to pay the penalty for our own sin.

That is what the unforgiving servant did—he demanded justice. And since he demanded justice, the king gave it to him.

5. Jesus speaks of forgiving "from your hearts." Is it possible to forgive but not "from your heart"? If so, how—what's the difference? How can you tell forgiveness from the heart from any other kind?

Anything less than forgiveness from the heart is not forgiveness. When we say we'll forgive but we won't forget, we're still keeping score. That is the very thing Jesus was telling Peter and us not to do. Sometimes we will forgive externally— someone owes us money and we tell him "not to worry" about it—but we don't really forgive from the heart. We keep bringing the matter up in order to secure some favor from the person: "After all I've done for you, I'd think you'd be more grateful!" Eventually the person begins to wish we had simply demanded repayment—it would have been cheaper in the long run! All he can do is "worry about it" because he never knows when we will use it against him. This is not forgiveness the way Jesus taught. In fact, it's just not forgiveness.

Knowing No Boundaries

DEVOTIONAL READING: Psalm 96.

LESSON SCRIPTURE: Acts 17:16-34.

PRINTED TEXT: Acts 17:22-34.

Acts 17:22-34

22 Then Paul stood in the midst of Mars' hill, and said, Ye men of Athens, I perceive that in all things ye are too superstitious.

23 For as I passed by, and beheld your devotions, I found an altar with this inscription, TO THE UNKNOWN GOD. Whom therefore ye ignorantly worship, him declare I unto you.

24 God that made the world and all things therein, seeing that he is Lord of heaven and earth, dwelleth not in temples made with hands;

25 Neither is worshipped with men's hands, as though he needed any thing, seeing he giveth to all life, and breath, and all things;

26 And hath made of one blood all nations of men for to dwell on all the face of the earth, and hath determined the times before appointed, and the bounds of their habitation;

27 That they should seek the Lord, if haply they might feel after him, and find him, though he be not far from every one of us:

28 For in him we live, and move, and have our being; as certain also of your own poets have said, For we are also his offspring.

29 Forasmuch then as we are the offspring of God, we ought not to think that the Godhead is like unto gold, or silver, or stone, graven by art and man's device.

30 And the times of this ignorance God winked at; but now commandeth all men every where to repent:

31 Because he hath appointed a day, in the which he will judge the world in righteousness by that man whom he hath ordained; whereof he hath given assurance unto all men, in that he hath raised him from the dead.

32 And when they heard of the resurrection of the dead, some mocked: and others said, We will hear thee again of this matter.

33 So Paul departed from among them.

34 Howbeit certain men clave unto him, and believed: among the which was Dionysius the Areopagite, and a woman named Damaris, and others with them.

**Jan
31**

GOLDEN TEXT: God . . . commandeth all men every where to repent: because he hath appointed a day, in the which he will judge the world in righteousness by that man whom he hath ordained; whereof he hath given assurance unto all men, in that he hath raised him from the dead.—Acts 17:30, 31.

God Calls Anew in Jesus Christ
Unit 3: Good News for Changing Times
(Lessons 9-13)

Lesson Aims

As a result of studying this lesson, a student should be able to:

1. Summarize the content and the results of Paul's message on Mars' Hill.

2. Compare the methods of Paul in trying to reach a Greek audience with current methods of reaching our secular culture.

3. Suggest one specific way to reach beyond his comfort zone to share the gospel with someone whose religious and cultural backgrounds are different from his own.

Lesson Outline

INTRODUCTION
    A. One Leg at a Time
    B. Lesson Background
  I. OUR CREATOR GOD (Acts 17:22-25)
    A. Evident to All Men (vv. 22, 23)
    B. Bigger Than We Imagine (vv. 24, 25)
      A Temple Made With Hands
 II. OUR RELIGIOUS DUTY (Acts 17:26-29)
    A. To Seek After God (vv. 26-28)
      Blood Types
    B. To Think of Him Correctly (v. 29)
III. OUR FINAL JUDGMENT (Acts 17:30-34)
    A. All Will Be Judged (vv. 30, 31)
    B. A Mixed Response (vv. 32-34)
CONCLUSION
    A. But Was It Worth It?
    B. Prayer
    C. Thought to Remember

Introduction

A. One Leg at a Time

It is our natural tendency to feel anxious and ill at ease when unfamiliar situations arise. For example, we are easily intimidated when we first encounter someone who is distinguished or famous because of personal achievements, power and prestige, or education and expertise. We wonder if we can handle our end of a conversation with such an individual without looking awkward and foolish.

Yet what a pleasant surprise to discover, after getting to know a person, that he or she is not that different from us. In fact, most people whom we hold in high esteem turn out to be ordinary people just like us. As the saying goes, "They put their pants on one leg at a time just as we do."

In Acts 17 the apostle Paul stepped out of his "comfort zone" as he moved from preaching the gospel to his Jewish brothers and sisters to discussing religion with "professional" Greek philosophers in Athens. Luke (the writer of Acts) does not record how Paul felt about this new experience; but if he was like most of us, he probably felt a certain amount of "fear and trembling." Yet Paul found the courage to stand before these highly intelligent scoffers and speak to them in a way that actually challenged their thinking.

How did he do it? We will note in today's study that Paul identified some ideas and concerns that he and the Athenians shared. Both believed that they were made by a divine Creator, that they had a religious duty to seek out this Creator, and that they needed to find a way to appease Him for the wrongs they had done. Paul came to realize that these new people in a strange culture were not much different from himself. This sense of identity allowed him to break through the cultural and intellectual boundaries that tend to intimidate, in order that he might present to them the gospel that they needed to hear.

B. Lesson Background

As the story of Acts 17 unfolds, we find Paul in the early stage of his second and longest missionary trip. His ministry thus far had been primarily in Asia Minor (what we know today as Turkey). But evangelistic boundaries began to crumble in Acts 16:9 and 10, when Paul received a heavenly vision challenging him to go to Macedonia (modern-day Greece). There was great significance in this move, because it represented the advancement of the gospel from beyond its Middle Eastern beginnings to a European culture. It marked Paul's entrance into the world of cross-cultural evangelism.

Once in Macedonia, Paul continued to use his proven evangelistic strategy of first seeking out the Jewish synagogue in a new town and using his own Jewish identity as a point of contact for preaching the gospel of Jesus Christ. When he finally arrived in Athens, Paul quickly made contact with the local synagogue (Acts 17:17). He also witnessed about Christ in the open marketplace, and it was here that he encountered the philosophers of Athens. Two different schools of Greek philosophy, the Epicureans and the Stoics, began to challenge Paul in open debate. They resisted his teaching, calling him a "babbler" who was a "setter forth of strange gods" and "certain strange things" (vv. 18-20).

A lesser man might have been frightened away by such a challenge, back to the familiar comfort of the Jewish synagogue. But Paul saw an opportunity to present the gospel here; for as skeptical as they were, the Greek philosophers were also very much intrigued by new ideas (v. 21). Paul accepted their invitation to speak in a more formal setting. He took the unchanging gospel and presented it in a way best suited to challenge the hearts and minds of a different kind of hearer, thereby showing us how the good news can penetrate the boundaries that often separate us from others.

I. Our Creator God
(Acts 17:22-25)

A. Evident to All Men (vv. 22, 23)

22. Then Paul stood in the midst of Mars' hill, and said, Ye men of Athens, I perceive that in all things ye are too superstitious.

The location for Paul's address was known as *Mars' hill*, also called the Areopagus. This was an open-air court on an elevated plateau in the middle of Athens. It was the place where the Athenian Supreme Court deliberated, as well as one of several locations where public disputations were held. [See question #1, page 192.]

Paul was able to *perceive* something about the religious character of the people of Athens by observing their public idols and temples. It has been estimated that first-century Athens may have had two to three thousand idols on display. This would have been overwhelming to a Christian who was a first-time visitor. Perhaps that was part of what Luke meant when he said Paul was "greatly distressed" (Acts 17:16, *New International Version*) at the sight of the idols.

We are not certain how best to understand Paul's statement that the *men of Athens* were *too superstitious*. The Greek word rendered *superstitious* can convey this idea, in which case Paul would be giving the Athenians a sharp rebuke for letting irrational emotions cloud their good judgment regarding religion. But the word can also refer to someone who is a seeker after religious truth (in which case Paul would be saying, "I perceive you are very religious"). If this was Paul's meaning, then he would be using a mild compliment to "soften up" his audience, so that they might give him a fair hearing. Some have even suggested that Paul intended to be ambiguous. Thus, by making the Athenians wonder whether they had just been complimented or criticized, Paul would have given them further reason to listen carefully to what else he had to say.

23. For as I passed by, and beheld your devotions, I found an altar with this inscription, To
THE UNKNOWN GOD. **Whom therefore ye ignorantly worship, him declare I unto you.**

The word rendered *devotions* refers to those items that were the objects of the Athenians' devotion or worship (their idols). The word is translated "objects of worship" in the *New International Version*.

We do not know the occasion for setting up an anonymous *altar*, but we can imagine how it was used thereafter. The city of Athens apparently intended to pay tribute to every religious personage that existed, without slighting even one. This would be a daunting challenge if one did not know for certain how many gods there are. An undesignated altar, however, could serve as a "miscellaneous" object of worship to cover any god that may have been inadvertently missed.

It is interesting that Paul could take something evil (a pagan altar) and turn it into an occasion for teaching the truth. Here is a principle worthy of note: to commend someone for a good thing he is doing does not necessarily imply you approve of everything he does. Sometimes Christians will refuse to acknowledge anything good in churches or religions different from their own for fear that it will appear that they have compromised their convictions. However, to recognize *both* strengths and weaknesses in another is not only the honest thing to do, but, as Paul demonstrates, it can also pave the way for further dialogue and teaching. [See question #2, page 192.]

How to Say It

ARATUS. *Air*-uh-tus.
AREOPAGITE. Air-ee-*op*-uh-gite.
AREOPAGUS. Air-ee-*op*-uh-gus.
ATHENA. Uh-*thee*-nuh (*th* as in *thin*).
ATHENIANS. Uh-*thin*-ee-unz.
CLEANTHES. Clee-*an*-theez.
CORINTH. *Kor*-inth.
DAMARIS. *Dam*-uh-ris.
DIONYSIUS. Die-oh-*nish*-ih-us.
EPICUREANS. Ep-ih-*cure*-ee-unz.
EPIMENIDES. Ep-ih-*men*-ih-deez.
HENOTHEISM. *heh*-nuh-thee-ih-zum (*th* as in *thin*).
MACEDONIA. Mass-uh-*doe*-nee-uh.
MONOTHEISM. *mah*-nuh-thee-ih-zum (*th* as in *thin*).
NEBUCHADNEZZAR. *Neb*-uh-kad-*nezz*-er (strong accent on *nezz*).
PARTHENON. *Par*-thuh-non.
PERICLES. *Pair*-ih-kleez.
STOICS. *Stoh*-iks.
ZEUS. Zoose.

B. Bigger Than We Imagine (vv. 24, 25)

24. God that made the world and all things therein, seeing that he is Lord of heaven and earth, dwelleth not in temples made with hands.

As Paul looked for some common ground with the Athenians from which he could present the gospel, he began with the most fundamental of beliefs: the existence of a divine Creator. As Paul explains in Romans 1, mankind has always sensed that someone wise and powerful must have put together all that we see (Romans 1:20). All of nature, from living beings to inanimate objects to the heavenly bodies, possesses an intricacy and beauty that testifies to an intelligent Designer. In theology we speak of this concept as "general revelation," that is, the testimony that creation gives on behalf of its Creator.

The Athenians had demonstrated their acknowledgment of the existence of a Creator (though their method left much to be desired). Now Paul was testing them to see if there was a genuine desire to know more about this God who was yet unknown to them.

25. Neither is worshipped with men's hands, as though he needed any thing, seeing he giveth to all life, and breath, and all things.

The city of Athens contained several pagan temples. In fact, Mars' Hill was located within sight of the most important worship center of that time—the Parthenon. This view provided Paul with the perfect occasion to present the idea that the Creator does not dwell "in temples made with hands" (v. 24), nor does He require the services or gifts of man in order to maintain His existence. Anyone capable of creating a universe is obviously too big to fit inside a building suited for man, and is far too powerful to require assistance from someone as small as man.

Such an argument as this would sound reasonable to the Greek philosophers whom Paul was addressing. In fact, by the first century many of the educated Greeks and Romans no longer believed the ancient pagan myths, though they retained a belief that there was some kind of divine Creator. Paul's description of the Creator was meant to appeal to the thinking of the "modern" philosopher of the first century.

A Temple Made With Hands

We do not know how many hands it took to build the magnificent temples in Athens to which Paul could easily point as he spoke on Mars' Hill. We do know that it took fifteen years (from 447 to 432 B.C.) to build one of them: the Parthenon. This temple to Athena, the Greek goddess of wisdom, required countless quarrymen, haulers, carpenters, stonecutters, sculptors, goldsmiths, workers in ivory, and painters. On a frieze located between the temple's outside columns and its walls, workmen carved and painted 350 figures of men and women and 125 horses. Thousands of tons of marble were hauled from a quarry ten miles away. The cost was astronomical. A little over two years after it was built, Pericles, the ruler who inspired and commissioned it, died. Soon after that the worship of Athena died as well.

We marvel that such effort went into building a temple for a god that never has existed. Our God is the living God, and as Paul told the Athenians, no temple "made with hands" is adequate to house Him. How humbling the thought that *we* are the only temple where God longs to dwell (1 Corinthians 3:16; 6:19)!   —R. C. S.

II. Our Religious Duty
(Acts 17:26-29)

A. To Seek After God (vv. 26-28)

26. And hath made of one blood all nations of men for to dwell on all the face of the earth, and hath determined the times before appointed, and the bounds of their habitation.

Without mentioning the name of Adam, Paul declared that the human race originated from one man (*one blood*). Greek philosophy did not typically speak this way; and yet the philosophers could readily grant that humanity had to begin somewhere small, then grow to the size it had now become.

As for Paul's description of God's involvement in political affairs, the Old Testament declares that God's hand is "stretched out upon all the nations" (Isaiah 14:26). To King Nebuchadnezzar, Daniel declared, "He [God] changeth the

Home Daily Bible Readings

Monday, Jan. 25—"God . . . Commandeth All Men Every Where to Repent" (Acts 17:16-34)

Tuesday, Jan. 26—Cornelius Is Instructed by an Angel (Acts 10:1-8)

Wednesday, Jan. 27—Peter's Vision (Acts 10:9-16)

Thursday, Jan. 28—Peter Welcomes the People From Cornelius (Acts 10:17-23a)

Friday, Jan. 29—No One Is Profane or Unclean (Acts 10:23b-33)

Saturday, Jan. 30—God Shows No Partiality (Acts 10:34-48)

Sunday, Jan. 31—Salvation Is for Everyone (Romans 1:8-17)

times and the seasons: he removeth kings, and setteth up kings" (Daniel 2:21).

All of this is in keeping with Paul's statement to the Athenians that God determines how long He will allow each nation to stand, and how far each nation may advance in conquest. Exactly how He does all of this is not certain to us, because from our perspective the workings of God in the world are very discreet. Even so, we must pray about social and political issues, believing that God is actively involved in the affairs of mankind, though we may not always know how.

BLOOD TYPES

Most people have one of four blood types: A, B, AB, and O. Until quite recently you could not put type A blood into a type B person, or vice versa. Blood donors who were type O could give blood to anyone.

Just recently, however, scientists have come up with a substance that can coat the molecules of blood so that one need not find a donor with the same type of blood that he has. Is Paul correct, then, when he says that God has "made of one blood all nations" (Acts 17:26)? Yes, he is, for the blood types do not divide along any racial or ethnic lines. The pigment of your skin has no bearing on the type of blood you have in your veins. The color of your hair or eyes has nothing to do with the type of blood you have. The land of your family's origin has no bearing on the type of blood you have.

Of course, Paul was not giving a lecture on biology or human anatomy. He was talking about the fact that we are all human and that we all have a common ancestry in our Creator. No race is superior to another, and no ethnic group is better than another. God does not honor such distinctions, and we should not take notice of them. We are all made in the image of God. Jesus died for all of us. —R. C. S.

27. That they should seek the Lord, if haply they might feel after him, and find him, though he be not far from every one of us.

Once one realizes that a Creator exists, he should naturally desire to know more about this Creator—who He is, what He is like, and how one can please Him. Paul expresses a similar idea in Romans 1 when he explains why God is angry with pagans who have seen His general revelation, yet refuse to *seek* Him. "That which may be known of God is manifest in them; for God hath showed it unto them. For the invisible things of him from the creation of the world are clearly seen, being understood by the things that are made . . . when they knew God, they glorified him not as God, neither were thankful"

(Romans 1:19-21). This is religious duty in its most elementary form, something with which Paul's philosophy-minded listeners could agree.

28. For in him we live, and move, and have our being; as certain also of your own poets have said, For we are also his offspring.

Paul tells us something about his own education by citing two statements from ancient Greek literature. These quotations were meant to highlight man's special relationship to his Creator. *In him we live, and move, and have our being* was apparently written by a poet from Crete named Epimenides, who lived around 600 B.C. *For we are also his* [God's] *offspring* was first recorded by the third-century B.C. Greek philosopher Cleanthes in his "Hymn to Zeus," and then later repeated by the poet Aratus (at around 270 B.C.) in a poem entitled, "Phenomena."

Why would Paul quote material from pagan sources? To do so would enhance his credentials in the eyes of this critical and skeptical audience. By showing that he was well versed in their literature, Paul would appear to them as a learned man worthy of their time and attention. By giving the Greek poets credit for knowing some truth about God, he would more likely be judged an honest and fair-minded man by the Athenians. And, in fact, Cleanthes' "Hymn to Zeus" is recognized as a pivotal work in influencing Greek thought toward an acceptance of monotheism—a belief in one god rather than in many.

Christians need to be acquainted with the literature, music, art, and other elements of their surrounding culture. Often we can use these to illustrate the futility of life without Christ and the need of the world for the abundant life that only Jesus can give. [See question #3, page 192.]

B. To Think of Him Correctly (v. 29)

29. Forasmuch then as we are the offspring of God, we ought not to think that the Godhead is like unto gold, or silver, or stone, graven by art and man's device.

Having established some intellectual rapport with his audience, Paul could present a more direct criticism of their position. Bowing to an idol does not make sense, and men as intelligent as these philosophers should have known better.

III. Our Final Judgment
(Acts 17:30-34)

A. All Will Be Judged (vv. 30-31)

30. And the times of this ignorance God winked at; but now commandeth all men every where to repent.

Even when linked with good intentions, idolatry is always an offense against God. All through the Old Testament age, God was gracious enough to restrain His anger at such *ignorance* and not bring the fury of Hell upon the nations at that time. But whereas He *winked at* (overlooked) that disobedience, He will not do so forever. There will be a day of judgment in which those who have offended Him will pay dearly, unless they *repent* of their sin.

31. Because he hath appointed a day, in the which he will judge the world in righteousness by that man whom he hath ordained; whereof he hath given assurance unto all men, in that he hath raised him from the dead.

The Athenian philosophers would readily grant that a Creator exists. They could concede the logic of Paul's description of man's religious duty to that Creator (though they might not have appreciated his criticism regarding idols). And if they were honest, they would have to admit that they had considered the possibility that one day they may have to give an account to this Creator regarding how they have treated Him. Paul builds upon this natural instinct and declares with certainty: you will be condemned by the Creator whom you have offended, if you do not respond to His plan of salvation.

Some are troubled that the name of Jesus is not mentioned in this account. But this is obviously a summary of Paul's message. (We assume that he preached longer than the five minutes it takes to read these verses in Acts.) It may be that during the complete sermon, Paul mentioned Jesus several times. It was Paul's preaching of "Jesus and the resurrection" (v. 18) that led to his being invited to speak on Mars' Hill. That Jesus' name is not mentioned in this brief summary should not concern us.

B. A Mixed Response (vv. 32-34)

32, 33. And when they heard of the resurrection of the dead, some mocked: and others said, We will hear thee again of this matter. So Paul departed from among them.

Today's visual is a dramatic reminder that the Lord Jesus will one day judge the whole world. Display it as you begin to discuss verse 31.

Visual for lesson 9

For some of the philosophers, Paul lost his credibility as a logical thinker when he spoke of a *resurrection of the dead*. "Perhaps he is the one who is 'too superstitious,'" they may have thought. Others were interested in hearing Paul defend his case for the resurrection, but assumed they had plenty of time to debate this new issue later. What a tragedy to see people put off until a more "convenient season" a decision with eternal implications (Acts 24:25)! This should challenge us to make sure that we are ready today to face the One who will pass eternal judgment on us. [See question #4, page 192.]

34. Howbeit certain men clave unto him, and believed: among the which was Dionysius the Areopagite, and a woman named Damaris, and others with them.

We know nothing about *Dionysius the Areopagite* (apparently meaning that he was a member of the court of the Areopagus) or *Damaris*, except what is said in this passage. We would do well just to focus on the facts we know: Dionysius, Damaris, and some unnamed friends came to Mars' Hill to hear a man present a new philosophy, but went home having received new life through Jesus Christ the Savior.

Conclusion

A. But Was It Worth It?

Your local theme park opens a new ride. For the first few weeks the line is two or more hours long, and yet the ride lasts no more than five minutes. As much fun as it may be, was it worth the trouble you went through to get on?

The cultural and intellectual boundaries confronting Paul at Mars' Hill put his ministry skills to the test. The pressure would have been great; the results, somewhat disappointing. Was it worth the effort, Paul? Absolutely, he would say. A new mission field was breached, a nucleus of believers was formed, and the seed of truth was planted in a pagan land. From such a small beginning as this, great things can happen in God's kingdom. From such small steps as these, boundaries once thought impenetrable by the gospel are removed. [See question #5, page 192.]

B. Prayer

Father, grant us the courage to reach out beyond where we feel safe and secure, and to touch people we have never imagined touching before. In Jesus' name, amen.

C. Thought to Remember

"Go ye into all the world, and preach the gospel to every creature" (Mark 16:15).

Learning by Doing

This page contains an alternate lesson plan emphasizing learning activities.
Classes desiring such student involvement will find these suggestions helpful.

Learning Goals

As a result of studying this lesson, a student should be able to:

1. Summarize the content and the results of Paul's message on Mars' Hill.

2. Compare the methods of Paul in trying to reach a Greek audience with current methods of reaching our secular culture.

3. Suggest one specific way to reach beyond his comfort zone to share the gospel with someone whose religious and cultural backgrounds are different from his own.

Into the Lesson

Before class begins, prepare letter-sized posters to be hung from the ceiling in various parts of the room. Print one of these religious or secular groups on the front and back of each poster: *Mormons, Jehovah's Witnesses, Muslims, Jews, New Agers, Humanists, Secular Scientists.* Feel free to add any other group to this list. As the students enter the classroom, ask them to select a sign that identifies a group with which they are at least somewhat familiar and stand under that sign. Make sure the class is evenly dispersed. If too many people choose a particular sign, ask a few students to join one of the other groups.

Ask the groups to sit together and give each group a poster board and this assignment: "Identify (1) some good practices or beliefs of people in this group and (2) some faults in their beliefs. Write your information in large print on the poster and select one person to report your information to the class."

After you have allowed each group to report its findings, remind the class how intimidating it is to share our faith with someone whose belief system is very different from our own. Yet the apostle Paul models a method of doing so. He identifies something good about the belief and uses this as a way to introduce the truth. Say, "Each of you knows something about one of the beliefs we have posted about the room. You have shared the good and the bad about them. How can we use this knowledge to introduce the Lord? Let's see how Paul did this."

Into the Word

Use the information in the commentary section to develop a brief lecture on the background

for this magnificent teaching event. Explain that this event is a practical model of cross-cultural teaching, one of the most intimidating challenges we may face as we try to share Christ.

Prepare a poster or transparency with the following information on it. (Do not include the material in italics.)

Paul's Model of Evangelism

What did Paul observe in Athens? (vv. 16, 22, 23)
Idols and pagan altars.

How did he capture attention? (vv. 22, 28)
He dubbed the Athenians "superstitious," referred to the altar to the unknown god, and cited Greek poets.

Paul's Message
- The common ground (vv. 24, 25)
  The existence of a divine Creator. (Be sure to explain "general revelation" from the lesson commentary notes on vv. 24-27.)
- Who is God? (vv. 24-26, 29)
  He is not an idol, and He is not dependent on man. He is the Creator.
- What has God done? (vv. 24-26)
  He has given life and breath to all men. He has created the many nations and has determined their place and time in history.
- God's expectation (vv. 30, 31)
  God expects all men to come to repentance.

The Mixed Response (vv. 32-40)
Various Athenian responses included rejection, procrastination, and acceptance.

After reading the text, ask the class members to help you complete the outline. Use the information in italics to assist you.

Note that Paul's trip to Athens was not a comfortable experience. He was "put on the spot" by some of the greatest thinkers in Athens. Paul performed well, however. Rather than attack his audience's beliefs, he identified the strengths and weaknesses of the Athenian religion and used that as a springboard into a discussion of Christ.

Into Life

Turn to the posters created in the lesson introduction and ask how we could use Paul's model to reach people in these groups. Ask each student to think of one person who falls into one of the categories posted. Encourage your students to implement Paul's model and introduce that person to the gospel.

Let's Talk It Over

The questions on this page are designed to encourage review of the lesson Scriptures and to promote discussion of the lesson by the class. The answers provided are only discussion starters. Let your class talk it over from there.

1. Athens in Paul's day was the crossroads of philosophical thought. (See Acts 17:21.) Planting a gospel seed in that soil was an important step. What forum in our community or nation might be comparable? How can we gain a hearing for the gospel in such an important field?

The major universities might be the field most comparable to Mars' Hill. There the thinking of the next generation is shaped. Christians who can gain a hearing on the university campus are in a position to influence the future of the church and the world for years to come. Such a hearing might be obtained by a professor or administrator on campus, by a notable leader invited to the campus as an expert in some field or another, or by students well prepared for the challenges and opportunities present on the college campus.

Note also, however, that before Paul was invited to speak to the philosophers on Mars' Hill, he was preaching in the synagogue and in the marketplace (v. 17). Sow the seed in the fields that are available, and if God should open the door to such a pivotal field as Mars' Hill, then you can respond to that opportunity.

2. The Athenians were a very "religious" people. What issues must Christians address in sharing the gospel with "religious" people today?

Missionaries to Islamic countries have said that the worst way of introducing Christianity is to deface the Muslim faith. Paul's message on Mars' Hill is a good model for such instances. Paul commended the Athenians for their interest in spiritual matters and for points about which they were right. Only after that did he identify points at which his religion and theirs disagreed. Paul remained firm in the truth without becoming offensive. People today are interested in spiritual matters—though their understanding is often weak and flawed. Still, if we are careful, we can use their interest to lead them to the truth.

3. Paul displayed both a thorough understanding of Scripture and a familiarity with the Greek culture and literature of the day. To what extent is that a precedent for Christians today to follow, and how much of that reflects Paul's unique role in the early church?

Paul was a "chosen vessel," called by the Lord to take the gospel to the Gentiles. Thus, not everything Paul did is something we can imitate. Still, we should take care that we appear credible with those to whom we speak on behalf of Christ, and that requires some study and effort on our part. Evangelical Christians, one skeptic said a few years back, are "ignorant" and "easily led." We should make sure that such a description does not rightly apply to us but, rather, "be ready always to give an answer" for our faith (1 Peter 3:15).

4. Many of the Athenians practiced "henotheism": they worshiped one god but acknowledged that there were other gods worshiped by others. They seem to have had little or no concept of judgment, and certainly not of the resurrection. What similarities do you find between Athens and our culture?

"Tolerance" is the key word today. One person can have one belief system and someone else another, and both must be accepted as equally valid. "We all worship the same God," this line of thinking says, "we just know Him by different names." This is politically correct but morally bankrupt! Like Paul, we are distressed by this situation (v. 16, *New International Version*), and we must introduce the hope of the gospel—not as another choice, but as the only choice.

5. Paul's message on Mars' Hill was largely rejected. Still, his visit there should not be considered a failure. (Note the benefits cited on page 190 under "But Was It Worth It?") How should we evaluate church programs and evangelistic efforts—especially in resistant fields?

Paul did not spend a long time in Athens, perhaps because it was a relatively resistant field. In his next two stops, Corinth and Ephesus, Paul's preaching met with greater results, and there he spent much more time. The lesson in strategy here may be to invest greater energy and time where the harvest is more plentiful, without neglecting to provide a witness to resistant fields.

When we evaluate our efforts, we must be good stewards of the opportunities and resources at our disposal. Sometimes we plant and sometimes we harvest. If a field is not being reached, we should make an effort to introduce the gospel there. But most of our time and effort must be put to use where they have the most impact.

Obeying Civic Authorities

Devotional Reading: 1 Peter 2:13-17.

Lesson Scripture: Romans 12:9—13:14.

Printed Text: Romans 13.

Romans 13

1 Let every soul be subject unto the higher powers. For there is no power but of God: the powers that be are ordained of God.

2 Whosoever therefore resisteth the power, resisteth the ordinance of God: and they that resist shall receive to themselves damnation.

3 For rulers are not a terror to good works, but to the evil. Wilt thou then not be afraid of the power? do that which is good, and thou shalt have praise of the same:

4 For he is the minister of God to thee for good. But if thou do that which is evil, be afraid; for he beareth not the sword in vain: for he is the minister of God, a revenger to execute wrath upon him that doeth evil.

5 Wherefore ye must needs be subject, not only for wrath, but also for conscience' sake.

6 For, for this cause pay ye tribute also: for they are God's ministers, attending continually upon this very thing.

7 Render therefore to all their dues: tribute to whom tribute is due; custom to whom custom; fear to whom fear; honor to whom honor.

8 Owe no man any thing, but to love one another: for he that loveth another hath fulfilled the law.

9 For this, Thou shalt not commit adultery, Thou shalt not kill, Thou shalt not steal, Thou shalt not bear false witness, Thou shalt not covet; and if there be any other commandment, it is briefly comprehended in this saying, namely, Thou shalt love thy neighbor as thyself.

10 Love worketh no ill to his neighbor: therefore love is the fulfilling of the law.

11 And that, knowing the time, that now it is high time to awake out of sleep: for now is our salvation nearer than when we believed.

12 The night is far spent, the day is at hand: let us therefore cast off the works of darkness, and let us put on the armor of light.

13 Let us walk honestly, as in the day; not in rioting and drunkenness, not in chambering and wantonness, not in strife and envying:

14 But put ye on the Lord Jesus Christ, and make not provision for the flesh, to fulfil the lusts thereof.

Feb 7

Golden Text: Let every soul be subject unto the higher powers. For there is no power but of God: the powers that be are ordained of God.
—Romans 13:1.

God Calls Anew in Jesus Christ
Unit 3: Good News for Changing Times
(Lessons 9-13)

Lesson Aims

After today's lesson, students will be able to:

1. Summarize Paul's teaching on good citizenship in Romans 13.

2. Explain why a Christian should show respect to civic authorities even when their views and actions are questionable.

3. Suggest at least one way to be a better Christian citizen, and begin to implement it in the coming week.

Lesson Outline

INTRODUCTION
  A. Patriotism
  B. Lesson Background
 I. OBEDIENT CITIZENS (Romans 13:1-7)
  A. For God's Sake (vv. 1, 2)
  B. For Your Own Sake (vv. 3, 4)
  C. For Conscience' Sake (vv. 5-7)
 II. LOVING NEIGHBORS (Romans 13:8-10)
  A. Giving What Is Due (v. 8)
    Debts and Debtors
  B. Never Doing Harm (vv. 9, 10)
III. GODLY SAINTS (Romans 13:11-14)
  A. Nothing to Hide (vv. 11-13)
    Night Creatures
  B. Living for Christ (v. 14)
CONCLUSION
  A. What Do I Owe You?
  B. Prayer
  C. Thought to Remember

Introduction

A. Patriotism

Every country in the world has a flag, its own banner that identifies not just a political and geographical boundary, but a people. Bound together by history and tradition, and often by ethnic ties, this people takes its place among the many peoples of the world. When many of the flags of the world hang together, as they may during the Olympic Games or other international athletic competition, one can always pick out his own country's flag. Its unique colors or striping or emblem always stands out. We are proud of our flag because we are proud of our country.

We feel a similar pride—a surge of patriotism—each time we see a military parade, with soldiers decked out in their dress uniforms and marching proudly to a patriotic tune. When our national anthem begins to play, we are instantly on our feet, standing proudly, perhaps searching for that flag of which we are so proud. As the music comes to an end, a tear may trickle down our cheek. An impartial observer of all of this would conclude that we must possess a great respect for our country.

So why is it, then, that crime persists, with citizens hurting their fellow citizens? Is not every violation of the law an affront to the country in which we take such pride? Why do average citizens, including Christians, feel that there is no real harm in violating certain laws—like speed limits, for example? Since we Christians should strive to be genuine in all things, perhaps it is time that we brush up on the basics of citizenship.

B. Lesson Background

The apostle Paul addressed the epistle from which today's text is taken to a church living in the most important city of his day—the imperial city of Rome. Paul shared with so many others a fascination with Rome, expressing in this letter his long-standing desire to one day visit and minister in this city (Romans 1:10-13). His dream was fulfilled just a few years later (in a way he likely did not anticipate), when he was taken to Rome as a prisoner (Acts 28).

The epistle to the Romans does not reveal a specific occasion that prompted Paul to write. It does not indicate that there was any previous communication between Paul and the Romans. There do not seem to be any controversial issues that Paul has been called on to address. The letter reads more like a doctrinal treatise in which Paul uses twelve chapters to examine the grand theme of salvation by grace.

Chapter 13, from which our Scripture text comes, likewise does not indicate that it was occasioned by a previous question or problem. Perhaps Paul decided to develop the subject of a Christian view of government and citizenship, because he assumed that Christians living in the capital of the Roman Empire would have a great interest in this. Whatever their concerns with such matters may have been, we know that subsequent generations of Christians have struggled with the issue of what is the proper way to relate to a secular government, especially when that government is hostile to our religious convictions. What Paul tells the church at Rome has abiding relevance for church-state relationships in today's world as well.

I. Obedient Citizens
(Romans 13:1-7)

A. For God's Sake (vv. 1, 2)

1. Let every soul be subject unto the higher powers. For there is no power but of God: the powers that be are ordained of God.

The Christian's primary duty to civic laws and officials is to *be subject*, or obedient. This is a God-given responsibility of every person without exception. Note, as other translations indicate, that *soul* is used here to refer to the whole person, not just his spiritual nature. Paul is saying, "Let everyone . . ."

There is a problem, though. Could Paul really be saying that God is responsible for oppressive dictators and regimes that persecute the church? Perhaps he is best understood as saying that God has ordained the *principle* of civic government. The heart of man is so sinful that he will repeatedly take advantage of his neighbor if he thinks he can get away with it. That is why it is in the best interest of all of us to have some kind of civic authority over us, to keep us in check when we consider hurting each other. No one form of government has been established in God's Word as the ideal, but the legitimacy of governing authority has been *ordained*. [See question #1, page 200.]

None of this should be thought to imply that God condones the wrong actions of a government. The prophet Daniel, for instance, informed kings such as Nebuchadnezzar and Belshazzar that God would hold them responsible for the misuse of their God-given authority (Daniel 4:19-28; 5:18-23). Whether the individual is good or bad, we remain obligated to submit to legitimate authority, even if he is as bad as the infamous persecutor Nero—the ruler of the Roman Empire when Paul penned these words.

2. Whosoever therefore resisteth the power, resisteth the ordinance of God: and they that resist shall receive to themselves damnation.

To *resist* a civic authority is an implicit resistance of the God who gives authorization to all rulers. It is quite likely that a person defying an earthly power would have no intent to oppose God. His complaint would be solely against the ruler he perceives as undeserving of his submission. Regardless of what we intend, however, we

will be judged on the basis of what God perceives. Respect for authority, even bad authority, is necessary simply because it is what God expects of us.

B. For Your Own Sake (vv. 3, 4)

3. For rulers are not a terror to good works, but to the evil. Wilt thou then not be afraid of the power? do that which is good, and thou shalt have praise of the same.

Rulers are not a terror to good works. An honest citizen should not be *afraid* of government officials. After all, if their job is to punish lawbreakers, then we who are not lawbreakers have nothing to fear when we see them or when they drive through our neighborhood. [See question #2, page 200.]

4. For he is the minister of God to thee for good. But if thou do that which is evil, be afraid; for he beareth not the sword in vain: for he is the minister of God, a revenger to execute wrath upon him that doeth evil.

We are accustomed to thinking of a *minister* as someone involved in Christian service, such as a preacher or youth minister. Thus it can be puzzling to see Paul refer to a government official as a *minister of God*. The older idea of a minister is someone who performs a service in behalf of a superior. Government officials are God's ministers because they are the human instruments He uses to effect justice on earth. [See question #3, page 200.]

Paul notes that God uses an earthly ruler to be a *revenger to execute wrath upon him that doeth evil.* In Romans 12:17-19 Paul teaches that individuals are not permitted to repay anyone "evil for evil." Should you hurt me, I am not to strike you back, curse you back, or shoot you back. We as individuals have no authority, from the state or from God, to take vengeance on someone who has done us great harm. "Vengeance is mine; I will repay, saith the Lord." We are to allow God to administer vengeance as He sees best.

However, God's plan is not always to wait until Judgment Day. Just six verses after Paul's declaration of God's vengeance (12:19), we are told that even on this earth He will avenge some of the wrong done to us. His agent of justice is government. Criminal penalties by a human court are a God-appointed means for getting some relief from the injustices we suffer from criminal activity. Paul himself was not averse to using the legal system of his day to avoid being mistreated (Acts 16:35-39; 22:22-29).

One of the ongoing debates within society and the church is just how much vengeance is appropriate for a fallible, human government to take. Some are opposed to the use of deadly

---

How to Say It

BELSHAZZAR. Bel-*shazz*-er.
NEBUCHADNEZZAR. *Neb*-uh-kad-*nezz*-er
(strong accent on *nezz*).

force in law enforcement, the execution of murderers, and even the support of one's country in warfare. Those who take such a position believe that only God has the right to take a human life —even that of a hardened criminal. This position has the appearance of taking the moral high ground, but it fails to take into account the clear teaching of Scripture about government's role as God's appointed avenger.

When God started creation all over again with Noah and his family, He not only authorized the practice of execution, but also the agent. "Whoso sheddeth man's blood, by man shall his blood be shed: for in the image of God made he man" (Genesis 9:6). The nation of Israel fought many wars under the authorization and guidance of divine revelation. Soldiers such as Cornelius were told how to receive remission of sins (Acts 10:43), but no soldier was told in Scripture to discontinue his military service. When Paul was on trial in a Roman court, he did not challenge the state's right to execute him if they found him guilty of a capital crime; he only insisted that he was not guilty (Acts 25:11).

Christians should support a government's pursuit of justice. Anyone who serves as an agent of government is doing something not only legitimate, according to Biblical precedent, but also honorable. Of course, any Christian who does not feel comfortable using an instrument of deadly force should refrain for the sake of conscience. But he should not thereby expect that everyone else must do as he, for God has declared that human governments are to "bear the sword" as His servant.

C. For Conscience' Sake (vv. 5-7)

5. Wherefore ye must needs be subject, not only for wrath, but also for conscience' sake.

Paul has made the theological case that it is our duty to *be subject* to civic authorities lest we show disrespect to God, who ordained such authority. He has given the pragmatic reason that it is wise to obey our authorities so that we will not have to face their *wrath* as punishment for our disobedience. Now he points out the personal reason that we must obey lawful authority: *for conscience' sake.*

Whenever we violate or take lightly the rules of those who have authority over us, we know deep within ourselves that we are wrong. Do you want to have a good feeling about yourself? Then do what is right. Do it because God commands it, but also because deep within yourself, you know it is right.

6. For, for this cause pay ye tribute also: for they are God's ministers, attending continually upon this very thing.

If we are to be obedient to our governing authorities, we must do so even when they demand *tribute* or taxes. Few of us enjoy parting with our money, especially when we have reason to believe that it will not be used wisely. But we cannot justify resisting authority at any point, including the payment of taxes. Jesus Himself spoke clearly to this issue when He said, "Render therefore unto Caesar the things which are Caesar's; and unto God the things that are God's" (Matthew 22:21).

Though Christians have a duty to pay whatever taxes are demanded, we may find it necessary in some cases to challenge the amount of taxes required and the way our tax money is used. As noted earlier, it is helpful to consider the occasions in Paul's ministry when he protested questionable acts of the civic authorities. In a representative form of government, in which there are legitimate means for citizens to express their views, Christians should feel free to offer their perspective, though always through proper means and always in a Christlike spirit.

7. Render therefore to all their dues: tribute to whom tribute is due; custom to whom custom; fear to whom fear; honor to whom honor.

Here is a good summary of our responsibility toward our civic leaders. There is some repetition of concepts here for the sake of emphasis. For instance, *tribute* and *custom* are essentially the same thing—taxes. The same is true of *fear* and *honor.* The *fear* Paul has in mind here is not the fear of being punished, as in verses 3 and 4, but a respect for the legitimate authority that someone has by virtue of the office he holds. [See question #4, page 200.]

II. Loving Neighbors
(Romans 13:8-10)

A. Giving What Is Due (v. 8)

8. Owe no man any thing, but to love one another: for he that loveth another hath fulfilled the law.

Some have understood the Bible to forbid Christians from either loaning money with interest or borrowing money from others. It is true that the Law of Moses did have regulations regarding "usury" (interest), but with guidelines for fair dealings, not a total prohibition of interest on loans (Exodus 22:25; Deuteronomy 23:20). It is also true that Jesus taught that we should "lend . . . without expecting to get anything back" (Luke 6:35, *New International Version*); however, the context was not business dealings, but confrontational situations where we are to love our "enemies" and show kindness to people who do not deserve kindness from us.

As for borrowing money, the New Testament does not prohibit this. Someone might argue, "But is that not what Paul is saying in this passage: *owe no man any thing*"? In the context of this chapter, the "owing" Paul has in mind has to do with our civic duty—such matters as obedience, civic service, taxes, and respect. He has not mentioned financial issues. Still, it is good advice to try and stay as free from financial debt as possible—not because Paul commands it but because it is wise stewardship of the resources that God has given us.

When it comes to giving the obedience and respect due to those who have authority over us, we should never come up lacking. To our neighbors we have a duty as well: to show them love and kindness each time we interact with them.

DEBTS AND DEBTORS

Debt is something we all understand. The national debt of the United States changes daily, but at the time of the writing of this illustration it was well over five *trillion* dollars! Often we hear news reporters talking about the credit card debt of consumers in this country. It, too, has reached astronomical proportions. Perhaps you are concerned about your personal debt. Without debt, however, there would be no banks; for banks cannot exist without borrowers.

What did Paul mean when he said, "Owe no man any thing" (Romans 13:8)? Did he intend for the entire world of banking and finance to collapse? No—the meaning is that we should incur no debt that we cannot repay. In fact, we should repay every debt but one. That is a debt that can never be repaid: the debt to *love one another.*

It is interesting that the same Paul who said, "Owe no man" also said, "I am debtor" (Romans 1:14). Paul recognized a spiritual obligation that can never be completely "paid in full." While as Christians we must be honest, must pay our bills, and must not take on debts we cannot repay, we will never be able to repay the debt of love. As Isaac Watts wrote in his great hymn, "At the Cross":

But drops of grief can ne'er repay
  The debt of love I owe:
Here, Lord, I give myself away,
  'Tis all that I can do!

—R. C. S.

B. Never Doing Harm (vv. 9, 10)

9, 10. For this, Thou shalt not commit adultery, Thou shalt not kill, Thou shalt not steal, Thou shalt not bear false witness, Thou shalt not covet; and if there be any other commandment,

Visual for lesson 10

What kind of witness are this driver's bumper stickers yielding now? This visual draws a practical application to today's lesson title.

it is briefly comprehended in this saying, namely, Thou shalt love thy neighbor as thyself. Love worketh no ill to his neighbor: therefore love is the fulfilling of the law.

Here Paul lists the last five of the Ten Commandments (Exodus 20:13-17), treating them as *neighbor* commandments. Apparently he sees the first four Commandments as focusing upon God, the fifth as honoring parents, and the remainder as dealing with how to treat our neighbors. Each one of these five prohibitions represents an action that is unkind and unloving, bestowing *ill* on one's neighbor. Thus, Paul declares, all of the "neighbor commandments" of Scripture can be summed up in a simple rule: *Thou shalt love thy neighbor as thyself.*

III. Godly Saints
(Romans 13:11-14)

A. Nothing to Hide (vv. 11-13)

11. And that, knowing the time, that now it is high time to awake out of sleep: for now is our salvation nearer than when we believed.

It was Paul's concern that Christians begin acting like the Christ whose name they wear. Why such urgency? The answer: *Our salvation is nearer than when we* first *believed.* Some see this as a reference to the second coming of Christ, and then wonder why Paul mistakenly assumed that it would occur soon ("the day is at hand," v. 12). It is good to remember that New Testament writers could speak of Christ's return as "soon," and yet understand this as being from God's perspective and not necessarily ours (as in 2 Peter 3:8, 9).

However, what Paul more likely had in mind was not the end of all time, but of our individual timetables. Each one of us has a limited amount of time to "work out" our salvation (Philippians 2:12). Those who are not taking seriously their duty to pursue godly living had better "wake up" before their time runs out.

12, 13. The night is far spent, the day is at hand: let us therefore cast off the works of darkness, and let us put on the armor of light. Let us walk honestly, as in the day; not in rioting and drunkenness, not in chambering and wantonness, not in strife and envying.

The best way for a Christian to live in a secular world is to practice a godly lifestyle that can be displayed boldly for all to see. Christians are encouraged not to cultivate any of the *works of darkness,* such as sexual orgies (*rioting*), *drunkenness,* sexual infidelity (*chambering*), degrading behavior (*wantonness*), *strife,* and *envying.* Instead, we must *put on the armor of light* and *walk honestly,* being authentic in our conduct and unashamed of what others will see.

NIGHT CREATURES

Many of God's creatures are seen only at night: the bat, the possum, the raccoon, and the owl, to name a few. The psalmist recognized that night is the time that God has arranged for certain creatures to be active: "Thou makest darkness, and it is night: wherein all the beasts of the forest do creep forth" (Psalm 104:20).

In the moral and spiritual realms, night is associated with evil. Deeds are done in darkness that would never be done by day. Many do not feel a need to lock their doors during the daytime, but almost everyone locks the doors at night. If you have ever been in a bar or a liquor lounge, you may have noticed that such places are always dark. Darkness is associated with the penalty for evil (2 Peter 2:17; Jude 6, 13).

Jesus, on the other hand, is always associated with light and with day (John 1:5; 3:19; Ephesians 5:13, 14). He is the Light of the world (John 8:12), and He calls His people to be lights

in the world (Philippians 2:15). To be "light creatures" (not "night creatures") means that we do nothing of which we would be ashamed. Our lives are open books. We have nothing to keep in secret. In the words of an old gospel song, we are "stepping in the light."   —R. C. S.

B. Living for Christ (v. 14)

14. But put ye on the Lord Jesus Christ, and make not provision for the flesh, to fulfil the lusts thereof.

The secret to living a life others will respect is to live the way Jesus lived. It is true that His enemies nailed Him to a cross. But the opposition was always against His Messianic teaching, not His personal conduct. You cannot go wrong if you choose to ignore the *lusts* of *the flesh,* and instead *put . . . on the Lord Jesus Christ* and follow His leading. [See question #5, page 200.]

Conclusion

A. What Do I Owe You?

Have you ever been in the following situation: Your car breaks down while you are traveling out of town, and you feel helpless. Then comes a total stranger who offers to look under your hood, or change your flat tire, or take you to get some gas. When he has your car running again, there is a question that you naturally ask: "What do I owe you?"

This is the question that Paul wants us to ask of our government, our community, and our neighbors. Do we Christians have any special responsibilities as citizens and neighbors? The answer is a firm *yes.* We are to obey our civic authorities, regardless of whether or not we like them. We are to treat our neighbors with kindness, regardless of how they treat us. We are to live such decent lives in our communities that people will respect us, even if they do not care for our faith. We have a duty to be the best citizens and neighbors we can be, for that is what God has called us to be.

B. Prayer

Our Father in Heaven, the Ruler above all earthly authorities, help us to practice in our relationships and our daily contacts the kind of love and respect that we owe to each other, knowing that it will be a tribute to our love and respect for You. Amen.

C. Thought to Remember

"Render therefore to all their dues: tribute to whom tribute is due; custom to whom custom; fear to whom fear; honor to whom honor" (Romans 13:7).

Home Daily Bible Readings

Monday, Feb. 1—Hate What Is Evil; Hold Fast the Good (Romans 12:9-21)

Tuesday, Feb. 2—Be Subject to the Governing Authorities (Romans 13:1-7)

Wednesday, Feb. 3—Love Does No Wrong to a Neighbor (Romans 13:8-14)

Thursday, Feb. 4—Walking Blamelessly (Psalm 15:1-5)

Friday, Feb. 5—Accept the Authority of Every Human Institution (1 Peter 2:11-17)

Saturday, Feb. 6—Everything Needed for Life and Godliness (2 Peter 1:2-11)

Sunday, Feb. 7—A Living Sacrifice (Romans 12:1-8)

Learning by Doing

This page contains an alternate lesson plan emphasizing learning activities.
Classes desiring such student involvement will find these suggestions helpful.

Learning Goals

After today's lesson, students will be able to:

1. Summarize Paul's teaching on good citizenship in Romans 13.

2. Explain why a Christian should show respect to civic authorities even when their views and actions are questionable.

3. Suggest at least one way to be a better Christian citizen, and begin to implement it in the coming week.

Into the Lesson

Before class begins, hang a long sheet of butcher paper (several large poster boards will also work) on the wall with these words printed at the top, "Patriotism means. . . ." As students arrive, provide them with markers and ask each person to write an answer or draw a symbolic picture to express his or her definition of patriotism. Be sure you have enough space that three or four students may be writing at the same time. This activity is often called a "graffiti wall."

Begin the session with a review of the "graffiti wall." You may need to ask some students for clarification of their responses or pictures. Note the variety of understandings of and feelings about patriotism. Using the Introduction of the commentary section (page 194), briefly comment on the irony between our expressions of patriotism and our sometimes unpatriotic behavior.

Remind your students that it is easier to be patriotic when all is well. How would their view of patriotism change if they did not live in a free country? How would they respond to a government that persecuted Christians? Should we obey the laws of our land? If so, then why do so many Christians violate speed limits? Today's text drills right into the core of the Christian's relationship with the government. And, for some, its teachings may be uncomfortable.

Into the Word

Using the lesson commentary, begin with a brief lecture on the background of today's text.

Prepare a handout with the following tasks and questions. Ask the class members, in groups of three, to answer the questions quickly and briefly. (Several groups may be given the same task.)

1. Write a paraphrase of verse 1, making its principles clear to contemporary Christians.

2. According to Paul, why should Christians be obedient to secular governments? (vv. 2-5)

3. Why are governing officials called "ministers" in verses 4 and 6?

4. What is the meaning of Paul's statement that the ruler is "a revenger to execute wrath upon him that doeth evil"? (v. 4)

5. What are some practical applications of good citizenship that Paul cites in verses 7-14?

Allow ten minutes; then call for reports. Observe that this teaching raises some tough questions. Discuss the following issues:

1. Does verse 1 suggest God is responsible for oppressive regimes that assault basic human rights or even persecute the church? Explain. Can and will God use evil or oppressive governments to accomplish His will? Why or why not?

2. Does verse 2 suggest that such efforts as the failed resistance at Tiananmen Square in China (1989) or the American Revolution were wrong? Can you cite any Biblical justification for rebellion against a corrupt government? To what extent, or in what cases, is lesser "resistance" like protests, demonstrations, or blocking access to public buildings justified? (See also question #1, page 200.)

3. Paul's concern in verses 11-13 is that Christians begin acting like Christ even though oppressed. What are some of the major behavioral concerns that Christians are facing in today's free world? What advice would you offer to parents about how to live as Christians in a free society? To teens?

These issues may require more study than you have time for. If some students have strong opinions but cannot support them Biblically now, suggest they do some research during the week and come prepared to support them next week.

Into Life

Remind the class that patriotism is more than a feeling of pride or allegiance. It involves understanding God's ordination of the concept of government and His expectations for living as good citizens. And it involves everyday practical behavioral issues—like obeying the speed limit. Ask the class to share other everyday practical applications to good citizenship. List these on a chalkboard. Conclude by asking students to identify and implement at least one principle of good citizenship they have discussed today.

Let's Talk It Over

The questions on this page are designed to encourage review of the lesson Scriptures and to promote discussion of the lesson by the class. The answers provided are only discussion starters. Let your class talk it over from there.

1. What is the result when citizens refuse to "be subject unto the higher powers"—i.e., governing authorities? When, if ever, is civil disobedience in order?

The benefits of government depend on the co-operation of the citizens or subjects. Rebellion undermines the ability of authorities to govern and maintain peace, resulting in anarchy. We all have heard the reports from nations whose governments have faltered or been overthrown. It seems even poor government is better than none.

The only cases when civil disobedience was condoned in the New Testament were those when Christians were forbidden to practice what God had commanded. Peter preached the Word even when Jewish and Roman authorities forbade him to do so. Still, he counsels Christians to "submit . . . to every authority instituted among men" (1 Peter 2:13, *New International Version*). Even religious persecution does not justify total rebellion.

2. If it is the duty of governments to be a terror to the evil, how is that best accomplished?

To keep evil in check requires diligence and strong measures on the part of government, law enforcement, and the justice system. It should be obvious that to be a terror to the evil, the government must first agree on what behavior is evil. Unfortunately, there seems to be a failure of moral courage and conviction on the part of many governments today, even those that were at one time founded on Christian principles. To be effective in its role against evildoers, the government must enact unambiguous laws that uphold a clear standard of what is right and then vigorously and consistently enforce those laws. Violators must receive swift and certain punishment.

3. Does the concept that those in government and the justice system are "God's ministers" (vv. 4, 6) invalidate the concept of a "separation of church and state"? If so, what are the practical implications for government? If not, how can the two function together?

The "separation principle," as first expressed by the third President of the United States, Thomas Jefferson, is a hands-off policy by the government as regards the church. It was not originally intended to secularize government, but to keep the church free of government interference.

Thus, it is valid—not only in American government but in any free society—and in harmony with the concept that government's authority is from God. While many officials do not recognize their roles as divinely appointed, God still uses them, as He used pagan rulers like Cyrus (Isaiah 45:1), to effect His plans and purposes. Christians in government, appreciating their God-given roles, can act with a sense of divine purpose.

4. What if we believe a public official has done things that make him/her unworthy of honor? How should we regard that official?

Unfortunately, not all public officials have the upright character we would desire. Some are guilty of crimes that cause them to be removed from office. Others may be guilty of moral lapses or indiscretions that either cannot be proven or do not constitute a crime, so they continue to serve, usually pretending innocence. That may cause us to lose respect for the individual, but we should distinguish between the individual and the position. If the office is worthy of honor, we must give proper honor to the office or position, even though the individual is of questionable character. The law of love demands that we not enter into slander or gossip, though we may press for investigation and use proper channels to call for removal or replacement.

5. What does making "provision for the flesh" have to do with submission to the government?

Whoever said you can't legislate morality simply did not know what he was talking about! Virtually all laws are based on moral principles. Stealing, murder, assault, and other crimes are violations of moral order first and violations of the law second. Thus, Christians who "make not provision for the flesh" accomplish the goals of the law and of the officials who enforce the law. Immoral persons, who seek only to gratify the flesh, are the ones who engage in prostitution, theft, burglary, pornography, abusive behavior, illegal drug use, and murder. While some governments are lowering the standards and removing legislation against some of these evils, the Christian continues to live by a higher standard. He will have no trouble abiding by the moral standards of law if he walks "in the Spirit" (Galatians 5:16-25).

Building a Caring Community

DEVOTIONAL READING: 1 Corinthians 12: 14-27.

LESSON SCRIPTURE: 1 Corinthians 11:17-34.

PRINTED TEXT: 1 Corinthians 11:20-34.

1 Corinthians 11:20-34

20 When ye come together therefore into one place, this is not to eat the Lord's supper.

21 For in eating every one taketh before other his own supper: and one is hungry, and another is drunken.

22 What! have ye not houses to eat and to drink in? or despise ye the church of God, and shame them that have not? What shall I say to you? shall I praise you in this? I praise you not.

23 For I have received of the Lord that which also I delivered unto you, That the Lord Jesus, the same night in which he was betrayed, took bread:

24 And when he had given thanks, he brake it, and said, Take, eat; this is my body, which is broken for you: this do in remembrance of me.

25 After the same manner also he took the cup, when he had supped, saying, This cup is the new testament in my blood: this do ye, as oft as ye drink it, in remembrance of me.

26 For as often as ye eat this bread, and drink this cup, ye do show the Lord's death till he come.

27 Wherefore whosoever shall eat this bread, and drink this cup of the Lord, unworthily, shall be guilty of the body and blood of the Lord.

28 But let a man examine himself, and so let him eat of that bread, and drink of that cup.

29 For he that eateth and drinketh unworthily, eateth and drinketh damnation to himself, not discerning the Lord's body.

30 For this cause many are weak and sickly among you, and many sleep.

31 For if we would judge ourselves, we should not be judged.

32 But when we are judged, we are chastened of the Lord, that we should not be condemned with the world.

33 Wherefore, my brethren, when ye come together to eat, tarry one for another.

34 And if any man hunger, let him eat at home; that ye come not together unto condemnation. And the rest will I set in order when I come.

Feb 14

GOLDEN TEXT: Let a man examine himself, and so let him eat of that bread, and drink of that cup. For he that eateth and drinketh unworthily, eateth and drinketh damnation to himself, not discerning the Lord's body.—1 Corinthians 11:28, 29.

God Calls Anew in Jesus Christ
Unit 3: Good News for Changing Times
(Lessons 9-13)

Lesson Aims

After this lesson students will be able to:

1. Tell what Paul said about the meaning and purpose of the Lord's Supper, and how the Corinthians' behavior violated that.

2. Explain the relationship between the Lord's Supper and the spirit of community that should characterize a church.

3. Make a commitment to partake of the Lord's Supper in a manner worthy of Christ and the community of believers.

Lesson Outline

INTRODUCTION
  A. I Couldn't Care Less
  B. Lesson Background
 I. WORSHIPING AS ONE (1 Corinthians 11:20-22)
  A. Acting as One Body (vv. 20, 21)
  B. Loving Each Other (v. 22)
II. FOCUSING ON CHRIST (1 Corinthians 11:23-26)
  A. His Broken Body (vv. 23, 24)
  B. His Shed Blood (v. 25)
    The Cup of Blessing
  C. His Redemptive Death (v. 26)
III. EXAMINING OUR HEARTS (1 Corinthians 11: 27-34)
  A. To Remove Unworthy Motives (vv. 27-32)
    Self-Examination
  B. To Practice Consideration (vv. 33, 34)
CONCLUSION
  A. Bad Dog
  B. Prayer
  C. Thought to Remember

Introduction

A. I Couldn't Care Less

It is interesting to track the ever-changing lingo of the youth culture. Sometimes the new expressions make sense, sometimes they are absurd, but always they are interesting. Many popular expressions go through a process of change, often taking on a new form and yet retaining something of the old. Take, for instance, the old standard, "I couldn't care less." Its meaning is clear: "I have no interest in what you are saying or thinking; my interest level is at zero." The shorter version, "I could care less," is generally

understood to mean the same thing; however, it actually says the opposite: "I *could* have less interest than I have." And if economy of words is desirable, there is always the succinct, "So?" No matter how the child says it, the message comes through loud and clear to the parent or teacher: here is an attitude that needs adjustment!

Christians must not be people who "couldn't care less." We should have a genuine interest in others that listens when they speak and gives their ideas a fair hearing—even when we disagree. We should hear their concerns and seek appropriate ways to respond. We are not permitted to "tune out" others because we do not care. We are called to be a community that cares.

B. Lesson Background

The church at Corinth has maintained a reputation throughout church history as a congregation with lots of problems. And no wonder. They had the unique "privilege" of receiving a letter from the apostle Paul, in which every one of its sixteen chapters addressed something that these people were doing wrong. Paul knew them well, having ministered with them for a year and a half (Acts 18:11) and having kept in touch with them by means of letters and through reports from others who informed him of certain situations (1 Corinthians 1:11; 5:1; 7:1; 11:18).

Paul viewed the Corinthians' problems as very serious and potentially damaging to the stability of their fellowship and their relationship with God. Even so, he did not "write off" the Corinthians. He still considered them among "them that are sanctified in Christ Jesus" (1 Corinthians 1:2). As we read Paul's admonitions in chapter 11, let us humble our hearts and be prepared to change where change is needed.

I. Worshiping as One
(1 Corinthians 11:20-22)

A. Acting as One Body (vv. 20, 21)

20. When ye come together therefore into one place, this is not to eat the Lord's supper.

The church at Corinth regularly gathered *together* for corporate worship. According to 1 Corinthians 16:2, this took place on "the first day of the week," or, every Sunday (see also Acts 20:7). The apostle John notes the special regard the early Christians had for Sunday when he refers apparently to it as "the Lord's day" (Revelation 1:10). This is an "apostolic precedent" that most churches still maintain today.

Paul claimed that what the Corinthians were doing during their worship service was *not . . . the Lord's supper*. This is evidence that the Lord's Supper was a regular weekly feature in New

Testament worship. Had eating the Lord's Supper not been expected when they would *come together*, the fact that they didn't would have warranted no comment from Paul. The obvious implication is that observing the Lord's Supper was expected each week when they came together—that they were, in fact, going through the motions of observing it with the bread and the juice—but they were doing it in such a way that their observance did not deserve to be called "the Lord's Supper." [See question #1, page 208.]

21. For in eating every one taketh before other his own supper: and one is hungry, and another is drunken.

The church at Corinth apparently had a practice of *eating* the Lord's Supper in conjunction with a fellowship meal. After all, it is hard to imagine why Paul would speak of some going *hungry* and some being *drunken* with just the small portions used during the Lord's Supper.

Probably the practice of having a larger meal with the Lord's Supper was followed to imitate the original institution of the ceremony by Jesus during His final Passover supper in the upper room. Churches who did this would either have the Lord's Supper at some point during their meal, or shortly thereafter. This is a practice that could be done today if a church so desired, because there is Biblical precedent. However, there is no Biblical evidence that *every* church in the apostolic age did this. Corinth is the only first-century church we know that observed the Lord's Supper in the context of a larger meal.

The error of the Corinthians is implied in verse 21 but more precisely stated in verse 18. The church was divided into groups or cliques that would not fellowship with each other. Thus, in the eating of church meals, believers would share their food only with their friends. As a result, some were overlooked, while others overindulged. The unity for which Jesus prayed (John 17:20, 21) and the love of one another that He taught (John 13:34) were apparently nonexistent at Corinth.

B. Loving Each Other (v. 22)

22. What! have ye not houses to eat and to drink in? or despise ye the church of God, and shame them that have not? What shall I say to you? shall I praise you in this? I praise you not.

When Paul asked, *have ye not houses to eat and to drink in?* he was not condemning the practice of serving the Lord's Supper with a meal, but the uncaring manner in which the Corinthians ate their meal. He questioned whether the Corinthians intended to *despise . . . the church of God* and put each other to *shame*. The attitude he was condemning was the very opposite of the love he

will define in chapter 13. Love would not be so rude and inconsiderate, nor would it hurt and offend. [See question #2, page 208.]

II. Focusing on Christ (1 Corinthians 11:23-26)

A. His Broken Body (vv. 23, 24)

23. For I have received of the Lord that which also I delivered unto you, That the Lord Jesus, the same night in which he was betrayed, took bread.

For I have received of the Lord. Paul could not give firsthand testimony regarding the institution of the Lord's Supper, because he had not been one of the apostles present in the upper room. His information had been given to him by divine revelation, perhaps during the three-year period that he spent by himself in Arabia in preparation for his ministry (Galatians 1:15-18).

24. And when he had given thanks, he brake it, and said, Take, eat; this is my body, which is broken for you: this do in remembrance of me.

At some point during the Passover supper, Jesus paused and broke a piece of bread. We know it would have been bread made without yeast because it was required that there be no yeast anywhere in a Jewish house during the whole week leading up to the Passover celebration. [See question #3, page 208.] Most churches today have chosen to use unleavened bread for the Lord's Supper, not only because that is what Jesus would have used, but because of the appropriateness of the symbolism. Since leaven is often used in Scripture to represent sin (Luke 12:1; 1 Corinthians 5:6-8), unleavened bread is a good reminder of what we want our lives to be in Christ.

The purpose for the broken piece of bread is that it serves as a *remembrance* of how Jesus' body was "broken" on the cross of Calvary. The bread itself is not the body of Christ, but it represents or symbolizes the body of Christ. After all, the first piece of bread used by Jesus could not literally have been His body; His body was still alive and holding the bread.

What brings Calvary to our minds during the Lord's Supper is not the bread itself, but the fact that we eat a *broken* piece of bread. That is the

---

How to Say It

AGAPE (Greek). uh-*gah*-pay.
ARABIA. Uh-*ray*-bee-uh.
CORINTH. *Kor*-inth.
CORINTHIANS. Kor-*in*-thee-unz.

reason some churches prefer to serve a larger loaf for Communion. Each worshiper breaks off a piece of bread in order to participate personally in the symbolism. However, even the use of precut wafers can carry the symbolism when we remember that each little piece was "broken" from a larger portion.

B. His Shed Blood (v. 25)

25. After the same manner also he took the cup, when he had supped, saying, This cup is the new testament in my blood: this do ye, as oft as ye drink it, in remembrance of me.

During the institution of the Lord's Supper, the bread and the juice were not given to the disciples at the same time. The bread was broken during the meal, but the cup was presented after they *had supped*. The probable reason for this was that Jesus wanted to wait and use the "third cup" of the Jewish Passover meal for His Lord's Supper memorial. In a traditional Passover service, there were four occasions when the participants would drink a cup of the fruit of the vine. Each cup had a distinctive theme, often accompanied by prescribed words, songs, and prayers. The first two cups were taken prior to the main meal, and the latter two cups were taken after the meal. The third cup was called the Cup of Redemption, which celebrated the fact that God had redeemed Israel from bondage in Egypt and that He continues to redeem His people in times of distress. It is likely that this was the cup Jesus used for the Lord's Supper, giving it a new and richer meaning than before—a celebration of the ultimate redemption that God would give His people through the death of His Son on the cross.

The message of the cup is much the same as that of the bread. The broken body of Jesus produced blood—the blood that ushered in a *new testament*, or covenant (Hebrews 9:11-15), by which sins can be forgiven and forgotten (8:12). Just as many churches prefer to use unleavened bread for the observance of the Lord's Supper, they prefer unfermented grape juice.

THE CUP OF BLESSING

In his series of poems *Idylls of the King*, Alfred Lord Tennyson told a story that had in some form already circulated in England as one of the legends surrounding King Arthur. Sir Galahad saw a vision of the very cup that Jesus used when He instituted the Lord's Supper. It was called "the Holy Grail." He and the other knights embarked on a long and fruitless search to find this cup.

Suppose the cup had been found. Would Communion then mean more to us than it already does? Would that enhance our observance of the Lord's Supper? Not at all. However, we *do* have something from the upper room. We have the presence of Jesus Himself. That is enough to make Communion holy, no matter the kind of cup we use. It is His presence and our reverence, humility, and prayerful attitude, that give meaning to the Supper. The kind of table on which the emblems rest, the kind of utensil from which they are poured or into which they are poured, the kind of building in which we meet—all of these are really unimportant. What is in our hearts is most important. And what happens in our lives as a result is essential.

Let the cup then stand for what it symbolizes: Jesus' sacrifice for us and our response of loving remembrance to Him.   —R. C. S.

C. His Redemptive Death (v. 26)

26. For as often as ye eat this bread, and drink this cup, ye do show the Lord's death till he come.

The simple ceremony that Jesus instituted in the upper room was intended to be observed by His disciples until the day that He will *come* to take us to our heavenly home. It is meant to insure that every Sunday that we gather for worship, we will give at least a few minutes to remembering Christ's death—the most important event in history, the key to our salvation, and the reason we are gathered as a church.

This fundamental meaning of the Lord's Supper has some practical implications for us. Our thoughts should not wander to other concerns; rather, we should make a serious effort to reflect on Calvary and its significance for us. Likewise, those who present a "Communion meditation" should refrain from discussing other subjects or

Home Daily Bible Readings

Monday, Feb. 8—Not for the Better, But for the Worse (1 Corinthians 11:17-22)

Tuesday, Feb. 9—Do This in Remembrance of Me (1 Corinthians 11:23-26)

Wednesday, Feb. 10—Origin of the Passover (Exodus 12:1-13)

Thursday, Feb. 11—A Day of Remembrance (Exodus 12:14-28)

Friday, Feb. 12—The Passover for the Whole Congregation of Israel (Exodus 12:43-51)

Saturday, Feb. 13—Remember This Day (Exodus 13:1-16)

Sunday, Feb. 14—One Body, Many Members (1 Corinthians 12:14-27)

telling entertaining stories. They should seek to direct our thoughts where they belong for the next few moments—to the redemptive death of Jesus our Savior.

III. Examining Our Hearts (1 Corinthians 11:27-34)

A. To Remove Unworthy Motives (vv. 27-32)

27. Wherefore whosoever shall eat this bread, and drink this cup of the Lord, unworthily, shall be guilty of the body and blood of the Lord.

Paul raises an issue that has puzzled many readers and troubled the consciences of some as they have approached the Lord's Supper. What is an *unworthy* manner of partaking of the *bread* and the *cup*? While we could list a number of sinful thoughts that no Christian should be entertaining during this most solemn occasion, the immediate context is focused upon one problem in particular. The church at Corinth was in a state of division, yet had the gall to partake of a ceremony that symbolizes the unity of the body of Christ!

While the primary focus of the Lord's Supper is upon Calvary, Paul also notes a secondary imagery in 1 Corinthians 10:17: "For we being many are one bread, and one body: for we are all partakers of that one bread." My individual piece of bread was broken from a larger, single loaf, just as was yours. I may partake of the Lord's Supper in a quiet meditation of my own, but the small piece should remind me that I am a member of a larger fellowship. Thus to participate in a sacred ceremony that symbolizes unity, while willfully being at odds with my Christian brother or sister, is an act of hypocrisy. Of course, the same can be said for meeting with the body at all while willfully at odds with a brother or sister.

Some people wonder if they should stay away from the Lord's Supper while they are wrestling with sinful issues in their lives, lest they be guilty of partaking in an "unworthy manner." It was not Paul's intention here to keep people away from the Lord's Supper. Believers with a genuine concern for the sin in their lives benefit from being at the Lord's Supper and seeing afresh the sacrifice that will remove their sins entirely if they repent of them. The Lord's Supper does not push sinners away; rather, it draws repentant sinners to it so that their thinking can be challenged and their lives renewed.

28. But let a man examine himself, and so let him eat of that bread, and drink of that cup.

Rather than abstinence, Paul urges examination. Every time we prepare to partake of the Lord's Supper, we should first *examine* ourselves

and ask whether there is any fellow believer from whom we are estranged, or toward whom we have bitterness, or against whom we hold a grudge. If such is the case, we must immediately release that bitterness and repent of it. Some would even suggest that we should not partake until we have first made an effort at reconciliation, though their appeal to Matthew 5:23, 24 is not conclusive.

Paul's purpose was not to tell when we should and when we should not partake of the Lord's Supper. Rather, he was giving directives for a proper observance, in a right spirit and in full fellowship with the body. As long as we seek to partake in such a manner, we can have a clear conscience at the Lord's Supper.

SELF-EXAMINATION

With cancer so prevalent, health care professionals are urging both men and women to do careful self-examinations. They publish literature that tells you what signs to look for. News reports on television provide relevant information. They claim that many lives can be saved by careful self-examination.

The Lord's Supper is an occasion for spiritual self-examination. What danger signs should we look for? Pride is one. Selfishness is another, along with harboring a divisive spirit. So is self-indulgence, even in something otherwise good and proper. We need to detect these early warning signs before the cancer of sin destroys us.

Certainly no one can come to Communion, conduct a self-examination, and not find something. This does not mean that we should not partake. It does mean that we should recognize our weaknesses, repent of our sins, and resolve to do better and to be better. To diagnose our own condition is to go a long way toward curing that condition.

Often cancer in the human body can be cured. Always cancer of the soul can be cured if we follow the prescriptions of the Great Physician. To ignore what we discover in our self-examination would be more dangerous than to ignore the signs of malignancy in the human body. To recognize signs of spiritual sickness, confess them, repent of them, and find forgiveness for them can lead us to full recovery and renewed spiritual health.   —R. C. S.

29. For he that eateth and drinketh unworthily, eateth and drinketh damnation to himself, not discerning the Lord's body.

It is a sin to partake of the Lord's Supper when we are at odds with a Christian brother or sister. To do so will make us "guilty" (v. 27) before God and liable for divine *damnation*.

This understanding helps us to grasp what Paul means when he speaks of *not discerning the Lord's body*. The *body* refers to the church. To "discern the Lord's body" means to envision the unity of all believers and to realize that our alienated brother or sister is still a partner with us in Christ's church. We are under obligation to do our part to reestablish unity where we have allowed it to lapse. [See question #4, page 208.]

30. For this cause many are weak and sickly among you, and many sleep.

Here Paul mentions additional consequences of disregarding the unity of the body of Christ. His reference to becoming *weak, sickly*, and going to *sleep* could describe a weakening of our moral character. But it is also possible that Paul is referring to physical ailments that may be used in our lives as disciplinary measures to break down our complacency and lead to repentance. This would be consistent with verse 32, which refers to the Lord chastening us. He wants to see us reform our sinful attitudes before it is too late and we receive the eternal condemnation that He has planned for the rest of the world.

31, 32. For if we would judge ourselves, we should not be judged. But when we are judged, we are chastened of the Lord, that we should not be condemned with the world.

How can we avoid being *judged* by God and receiving the accompanying penalties, spiritual and otherwise? We must *judge ourselves* (recall the exhortation to "examine" ourselves in v. 28) and then seek reconciliation where we find it is needed. [See question #5, page 208.]

B. To Practice Consideration (vv. 33, 34)

33, 34. Wherefore, my brethren, when ye come together to eat, tarry one for another. And if any man hunger, let him eat at home; that ye come not together unto condemnation. And the rest will I set in order when I come.

Visual for lesson 11

Display today's visual as you discuss v. 29. Discuss the implications of "discerning the Lord's body" in a proper observance of the Lord's Supper.

From now on, when the Christians at Corinth *come together*, for a fellowship meal or any other purpose, they are advised to show consideration for each other. Anyone at a fellowship meal who thinks he is too hungry to wait for others to arrive should have eaten something *at home*.

To build a strong church, the members must learn to exercise love and patience *one for another*. This was practical advice for a church whose thinking was not only foolish, but sinful. The Corinthians now knew what they had to do to address this particular problem; if other matters remained unresolved, Paul promised to set them *in order* when he returned to Corinth.

Conclusion

A. Bad Dog

Have you ever had to discipline a dog for doing something wrong, such as jumping up on your furniture or chewing on your shoes? You know the routine. You hit him with a rolled-up newspaper and tell him "bad dog." The dog's typical response is to run away with his head down, his ears hanging low, and his tail tucked between his legs. It is a sight so pitiful that it can make you wonder if you did the right thing. But God designed a dog so that he rebounds quickly. As soon as you summon him back, he comes running with head up and tail wagging, eager for your affection. He acts as if you never touched him, yet in the future he will be more cautious around your furniture and your shoes. A lesson has been learned, and the friendship remains intact.

Paul's second epistle to the Corinthians indicates that the church at Corinth did make some changes after Paul's first hard-hitting letter. They felt the sting of his rebuke and humbly repented (2 Corinthians 7:8, 9). Of course, they could have responded with a bitterness that would have aggravated their problems within the church. However, they made the better choice; and Paul's second letter expressed the confidence he had in them (7:16).

Whenever we are challenged by our study of God's Word, may we have the strength to respond as well as the church at Corinth.

B. Prayer

Heavenly Father, help us to grow in our concern for each other so that we can truly be one body in Christ, in whose name we pray, amen.

C. Thought to Remember

"For we being many are one bread, and one body: for we are all partakers of that one bread" (1 Corinthians 10:17).

Learning by Doing

This page contains an alternate lesson plan emphasizing learning activities.
Classes desiring such student involvement will find these suggestions helpful.

Learning Goals

After this lesson the student will be able to:

1. Tell what Paul said about the meaning and purpose of the Lord's Supper, and how the Corinthians' behavior violated that.

2. Explain the relationship between the Lord's Supper and the spirit of community that should characterize a church.

3. Make a commitment to partake of the Lord's Supper in a manner worthy of Christ and the community of believers.

Into the Lesson

Before the students arrive, write the words "A Very Special Communion Service" on the chalkboard or on a large poster at the front of the classroom. As the students arrive, ask them to be thinking of Communion services that particularly impressed them with the significance of the Lord's Supper. Perhaps it was a special service in your own church, or perhaps some of your students have participated in special observances while they were traveling.

When it is time to begin, ask for some volunteers to share their experiences. Write down some key features of these services on the chalkboard or poster.

Move into Bible study by explaining that there are many forms of sharing the Lord's Supper. Some of the differences are minor variations of procedure. Other differences, rooted in a theology of Communion, are more significant. Today's lesson will introduce us to a church that had drifted into a Lord's Supper tradition that was divisive to the local church and was offensive to the Lord. In it we will discover principles for our Communion observances.

Into the Word

Form study groups of no more than five people in each group. Larger classes can have more than one group doing the same project. Give each group a written copy of one of the following tasks. Note: the tasks may also be used as discussion guides for the class as a whole.

Group 1. Read 1 Corinthians 11:18, 20, 21. Create a detailed verbal picture of how you visualize the Corinthian church sharing in the Lord's Supper. Detail all the problems and obstacles to a rich fellowship and experience in this church's Communion service.

Group 2. Read 1 Corinthians 11:24-26. Explain the rich symbolism in the Lord's Supper. Compare the Biblical symbolism with the special features noted earlier. (See "Into the Lesson.")

Group 3. Read 1 Corinthians 11:27-34. Make a presentation on the significance of church fellowship in the Lord's Supper, and the idea of partaking "unworthily" or in an "unworthy manner."

Allow each group adequate time to discuss their tasks and formulate their presentations. After they have made their presentations, use the "Bad Dog" illustration on page 206 to demonstrate the changes in the Corinthian church before Paul sent his second and more accepting letter to them.

Into Life

Ask each group to work together again to write a Communion meditation that reflects their research. If there is not enough time to write the meditation, ask them to simply make a few notes about what they would stress in their presentation.

Group 1. Please write a three- or four-minute Communion meditation that begins with, "What might Paul say if he were writing to our church about our Communion practices?"

Group 2. Please write a three- or four-minute Communion meditation that begins with, "The impact of Communion lies, partly, in the symbols of the bread and the cup. . . ."

Group 3. Please write a three- or four-minute Communion meditation that begins with, "The words 'unworthily' or 'unworthy manner' are words for every Christian to heed. . . ."

Ask a spokesman from each group to read the meditation that the group has prepared. You might also submit these meditations to your church newsletter to be adapted for a series of instructional articles celebrating the richness of the Lord's Supper.

Conclude the lesson by asking for testimonies from volunteers about what they learned that will impact how they celebrate the Lord's Supper. The closing prayer time can be done in the same small groups used earlier. Ask each person to make a silent or oral commitment to share in the Lord's Supper in a worthy manner that honors the Lord and brings credit to the fellowship of believers.

Let's Talk It Over

The questions on this page are designed to encourage review of the lesson Scriptures and to promote discussion of the lesson by the class. The answers provided are only discussion starters. Let your class talk it over from there.

1. The Corinthians' problem with the Lord's Supper could be called one of putting form over function. They went through the *form* of observing the Lord's Supper, but they were not keeping its *function* intact. How does that happen? How can we keep our worship from becoming empty and devoid of legitimate function?

Any form or ritual accepted uncritically can become empty and lifeless. Each worshiper must participate "in spirit and in truth" for a rite or ceremony to have real meaning. Reading Scriptural explanations of the function and purpose of the rituals is helpful. Participating in a prayerful attitude is also important.

Perhaps it would be helpful to take your morning bulletin and review each item. Ask for suggestions on how each item can be practiced with sincerity and purpose.

2. Some believers think that Paul's words in verse 22 condemn the practice of having fellowship meals in the church building. How would you respond to a brother who expressed such a belief?

First, we should note that the word *church*, to Paul, did not mean a church *building*, but the people of the church. The early church met in homes or in whatever large facilities they were able to secure, like the temple in Jerusalem, or the school of Tyrannus in Ephesus (Acts 19:9). If Paul is forbidding church dinners, then he is condemning all church dinners, in or out of the so-called church building.

Second, note that Paul was correcting an abusive practice in Corinth. There the believers were partaking of what was called the *agape* feast in connection with the Lord's Supper—only they were not showing any *agape* (love). Paul said it was better to skip the meal than to do what they were doing. In other cities, where the *agape* feast enhanced the observance of the Lord's Supper, Paul would not likely have forbidden its practice.

3. How important, if at all, do you think it is that the church follow the precedent of using *unleavened* bread in the Lord's Supper? Why?

The Lord's Supper was instituted at Passover, so we know it was unleavened bread that Jesus used. At Passover, the unleavened bread recalled the haste with which Israel left Egypt (Deuteron-

omy 16:3). Since haste is not a part of the Lord's Supper observance, some feel the fact that the bread was unleavened is merely an attendant circumstance and not part of the precedent. However, leaven is often used as an illustration of influence (usually negative influence), and many believers feel the use of unleavened bread is significant. Paul speaks of Christ as "our Passover" and says we must get rid of the "leaven of malice and wickedness" (1 Corinthians 5:7, 8). It seems best to observe the Lord's Supper with the same emblems as Jesus used whenever possible. But if for some reason unleavened bread is not available, we should observe the Supper with whatever materials are on hand and focus on the meaning and importance more than the materials.

4. Who is qualified to participate in the Lord's Supper? Who is responsible to determine who may partake?

The invitation of Jesus, "this do in remembrance of me," was issued to disciples. The act assumes that the participant has a reverence for the body and blood of Christ. Since the cup is the "cup of the new covenant," it assumes one has entered into that covenant relationship with Jesus as Lord and Savior. We are invited to the Lord's Supper, not because we are sinless, but because He is. We must come with a repentant heart, ready to acknowledge our need for forgiveness. We must come with proper regard for the rest of the body of Christ, the believers with whom we worship. Our text puts the burden upon each individual to "examine himself" before partaking. No authority was delegated to another to guard the Lord's Supper against any who should not partake.

5. How should one properly prepare for the Lord's Supper?

The key words are in verses 28 and 31: "examine himself" and "judge ourselves." It seems clear that Christians should give attention to personal assessment in anticipation of the Lord's Supper. Do you recognize sin in your life? Have you confessed that with a repentant heart and asked the Lord's forgiveness? The promise of Scripture is, "If we confess our sins, he is faithful and just to forgive us our sins . . ." (1 John 1:9).

Reconciling the World to God

DEVOTIONAL READING: 1 Peter 2:18-25.

LESSON SCRIPTURE: 2 Corinthians 5:11-21.

PRINTED TEXT: 2 Corinthians 5:11-21.

2 Corinthians 5:11-21

11 Knowing therefore the terror of the Lord, we persuade men; but we are made manifest unto God; and I trust also are made manifest in your consciences.

12 For we commend not ourselves again unto you, but give you occasion to glory on our behalf, that ye may have somewhat to answer them which glory in appearance, and not in heart.

13 For whether we be beside ourselves, it is to God: or whether we be sober, it is for your cause.

14 For the love of Christ constraineth us; because we thus judge, that if one died for all, then were all dead:

15 And that he died for all, that they which live should not henceforth live unto themselves, but unto him which died for them, and rose again.

16 Wherefore henceforth know we no man after the flesh: yea, though we have known Christ after the flesh, yet now henceforth know we him no more.

17 Therefore if any man be in Christ, he is a new creature: old things are passed away; behold, all things are become new.

18 And all things are of God, who hath reconciled us to himself by Jesus Christ, and hath given to us the ministry of reconciliation;

19 To wit, that God was in Christ, reconciling the world unto himself, not imputing their trespasses unto them; and hath committed unto us the word of reconciliation.

20 Now then we are ambassadors for Christ, as though God did beseech you by us: we pray you in Christ's stead, be ye reconciled to God.

21 For he hath made him to be sin for us, who knew no sin; that we might be made the righteousness of God in him.

GOLDEN TEXT: God was in Christ, reconciling the world unto himself, not imputing their trespasses unto them; and hath committed unto us the word of reconciliation.—2 Corinthians 5:19.

God Calls Anew in Jesus Christ
Unit 3: Good News for Changing Times
(Lessons 9-13)

Lesson Aims

As a result of participating in this lesson, students should:

1. Explain what Paul said about the means and message of reconciliation with God.

2. Compare and contrast the way sinners are reconciled to God with other types or occasions of reconciliation.

3. Accept God's offer of reconciliation or plan to share His offer with someone else who needs to accept it.

Lesson Outline

INTRODUCTION
  A. It's for a Worthy Cause
  B. Lesson Background
  I. A MISSION TO ACCOMPLISH (2 Corinthians 5:11-15)
  A. Not for Personal Gain (vv. 11-13)
  B. Compelled by Love (vv. 14, 15)
 II. A MOTIVE TO INSPIRE (2 Corinthians 5:16, 17)
  A. Not Limited by What We See (v. 16)
  B. Seeing What We Can Become (v. 17)
  New Creatures
III. A MESSAGE TO PROCLAIM (2 Corinthians 5:18-21)
  A. Nothing Else God Can Do (vv. 18, 19)
  Shuttle Diplomacy
  B. An Offer to Accept (vv. 20, 21)
CONCLUSION
  A. I Want to Come Home
  B. Prayer
  C. Thought to Remember

Introduction

A. It's for a Worthy Cause

Do you remember the floods of 1997? Maybe you live in an area that was not affected, so for you the floods were nothing more than a story on the news several evenings. But for many people in the Ohio River Valley and the northern plains the spring floods were a life-changing experience. Some of the older residents in those areas could tell stories of earlier floods, but for most of them it was a "once in a lifetime" event. Property loss was high, and loss of life was tragic. However, what may be remembered longer than the devastation of the floods is the volunteer aid that responded to the need.

In both areas volunteer relief assistance arrived with great haste and abundance. Churches and civic groups collected donated supplies and shuttled them to the flood areas for distribution. Groups of people drove in from great distances to spend a few days cleaning and rebuilding. Sometimes the volunteers and supplies came in faster than organizers could manage them, prompting appeals to wait until a call was issued for more. Such a response is what happens time and time again when a heart-touching need is presented to the public. People will rally together for what they believe to be a worthy cause.

Paul devoted his adult life to the ministry of the Word. He preached the gospel all over the known world, establishing new churches and then nurturing them through visits and letters. But Paul knew there was a limit to how much one man could do, so he recruited people he had converted to join him in ministry. He wrote in his epistles of the world's great need—of people alienated from God and from each other, in danger of being lost for eternity. He hoped that Christians would respond to a spiritual need as well as they do to a natural disaster. He believed that if followers of Jesus could get a vision of a lost and dying world, they would rally together for the worthiest of all causes.

B. Lesson Background

As noted in last week's lesson, Paul's first epistle to the church at Corinth gave a stinging rebuke for many sinful attitudes and practices there. While most of the Corinthians accepted Paul's rebuke and repented (2 Corinthians 7:8, 9), some of them apparently took offense at Paul's tone and words. Some were asking, in effect, "Who does Paul think he is, talking to us like that?" Considering how strongly Paul defends his apostleship in 2 Corinthians, some of the scoffers must have been challenging his credentials, perhaps noting that he was not one of the original twelve, or that he had once been a persecutor of the church. In some cases, Paul does go on the defensive in behalf of himself and his ministry. See, for example, 2 Corinthians 3:1, 2; 4:1, 2; 6:3; 7:2; 10:7—11:33; 12:17-19.

However, in chapter 5 (from which today's text is taken), Paul takes the offensive. He challenges friend and foe at Corinth to put aside their bruised feelings and petty fussing in order that they might concentrate upon the higher calling that God has put before all Christians. Paul challenges the Corinthians, not to fight him, but to join him as partners in the ministry of reconciliation.

I. A Mission to Accomplish
(2 Corinthians 5:11-15)

A. Not for Personal Gain (vv. 11-13)

11. Knowing therefore the terror of the Lord, we persuade men; but we are made manifest unto God; and I trust also are made manifest in your consciences.

In response to his critics at Corinth who challenged his authority and his motives, Paul begins this section of 2 Corinthians by explaining his devotion to preaching. He has taken on an evangelistic ministry of trying to *persuade men* to accept Christ. He does this, not for his own sake, but for the sake of those whom he persuades.

In the preceding verse Paul has mentioned that all must "appear before the judgment seat of Christ." For those outside of Christ, that will be a *terror*, but for those in Christ it will be a reward. Paul did not want the judgment to be a terror for anyone, so he worked to persuade everyone to come to Christ.

The charges being made against Paul were patently false. He had no ulterior motives or insatiable ego behind his ministry. Paul declared that his whole life was *made manifest* for both God and man to see and examine. [See question #1, page 216.]

12. For we commend not ourselves again unto you, but give you occasion to glory on our behalf, that ye may have somewhat to answer them which glory in appearance, and not in heart.

We commend not ourselves again unto you. Several times in 2 Corinthians, Paul provides details regarding his ministry, his background, and his apostolic authority. But Paul insisted that he was not providing any new information to the Corinthians; instead, he was simply reminding them of what they already knew. He hoped that his reminder would *give you occasion to glory on our behalf*; that is, it would encourage them to speak up for him when his critics became especially spiteful.

Paul's critics are described as those who *glory in appearance, and not in heart.* Apparently some of their criticism of Paul was grounded in certain external matters that they found objectionable. Perhaps there was something about Paul's appearance that they did not like. Some believe that Paul's "thorn in the flesh" (2 Corinthians 12:7-10) was a physical abnormality, though this is only speculation. Perhaps there was something about Paul's speaking style that his critics found wanting, since he himself acknowledged that he did not speak with the "excellency of speech or of wisdom" that some valued so highly (1 Corinthians 2:1-5).

Whatever their specific complaints may have been, Paul charged his critics with being superficial. The true measure of a person is not found in outward appearances, but in the character of the heart.

13. For whether we be beside ourselves, it is to God: or whether we be sober, it is for your cause.

Apparently Paul's mental stability was also being challenged. Paul's response was to turn the charge around and make it look ridiculous. Are we *beside ourselves*? Am I out of my mind? Then it would be because I am "crazy" about God. Of course, Paul was not admitting any incompetence; he was simply responding "tongue in cheek" to the critics' charge. The second part of the verse expresses what was closer to reality. Paul saw himself as of sound mind (*sober*), which was evident in the way he had devoted his life to serving the *cause* of others rather than himself.

B. Compelled by Love (vv. 14, 15)

14. For the love of Christ constraineth us; because we thus judge, that if one died for all, then were all dead.

Paul develops a logical argument in this verse and the next. It actually begins with the premise *if one died for all*, a reference to Christ dying on the cross for all sinners. If this is true (and we know it is), then it implies that *all were dead*. How so? Paul is picturing Christ's death as a substitutionary atonement. We sinners had a penalty we owed to God because of our sin. Christ was willing to pay that penalty for us as our substitute. We would expect the penalty that He paid to be the same as the penalty we owed. Therefore, Paul is reasoning, if what Christ did for us was to die, then this reveals the condition that Christ came to remedy as our substitute: *all were dead*.

Why such clever reasoning here? Paul was simply explaining his motive for ministry. Since he along with everyone else was once "dead in sin" until Jesus paid his penalty for him, he felt a great burden in his heart to find some way to "repay" Jesus for loving him enough to do what He did at Calvary. As Paul says, *the love of Christ constraineth us.*

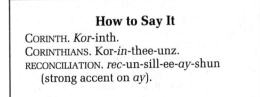

How to Say It

CORINTH. *Kor*-inth.
CORINTHIANS. Kor-*in*-thee-unz.
RECONCILIATION. *rec*-un-sill-ee-*ay*-shun
   (strong accent on *ay*).

15. And that he died for all, that they which live should not henceforth live unto themselves, but unto him which died for them, and rose again.

Now Paul completes his logical progression by arguing that every person for whom Christ died should feel in his heart the same constraint that Paul feels toward his preaching. All who have been saved by the death of Christ should feel compelled to serve with full devotion the One who saved them. [See question #2, page 216.]

II. A Motive to Inspire (2 Corinthians 5:16, 17)

A. Not Limited by What We See (v. 16)

16. Wherefore henceforth know we no man after the flesh: yea, though we have known Christ after the flesh, yet now henceforth know we him no more.

Paul had come to realize that the physical matters, those of *the flesh*, were temporary. Even Jesus had been *known . . . after the flesh* only for a short time. His disciples had known and related to Him in physical form, but since His return to Heaven the believers no longer related to Him in that way. Still, He is real, and our spiritual fellowship with Him is even more significant than was the physical relationship of His disciples with Him.

If that is the case with *Christ*, then there is a spiritual dimension in all people that we should strive to see, and not relate to them *after the flesh* only. We need to learn to appreciate that everyone is created in God's image and seek to relate to one another on that basis. [See question #3, page 216.]

B. Seeing What We Can Become (v. 17)

17. Therefore if any man be in Christ, he is a new creature: old things are passed away; behold, all things are become new.

When a person is *in Christ*, he or she still looks the same "after the flesh" as before. But in spirit, the person *is a new creature*. Those we can persuade to yield to Christ in faith will have their inner character completely reworked. When we who have been radically changed by Christ consider what a difference He could make with our family and friends, how could we not make every effort to persuade each of them to let Christ make him a *new creature* as well?

The Corinthians could easily have testified to the dramatic change that being *in Christ* could produce. Some of them had been sordid characters of the worst kind (1 Corinthians 6:9-11). But they had been "washed" in the blood of the Lamb, "sanctified," and "justified in the name of the Lord Jesus, and by the Spirit of our God" (v. 11). In other words, they were "in Christ."

NEW CREATURES

When Europeans first came to Australia, they found many new creatures that they had never seen before. We can imagine their excitement when they first saw the kangaroo! Here also they found the emu, the kiwi, and the duck-billed platypus. It was a continent filled with new creatures.

Christians are new creatures never seen before the coming of Christ. And it is still true that when a sinner becomes a Christian, he becomes a new creature. His physical appearance may be the same, but if you watch his life, you will know that something has happened. He is not the person he used to be!

A minister was at a gas station when one of the newer members of his church walked in. The minister said to the man who owned the gas station, "Do you know Fred?"

The owner answered, "Yes, I know him."

Then the minister asked, "Do you know anything good about him?"

The owner replied, "I know that he made a great change in his life."

That man had become a new creature, and it was obvious to all who knew him! If you become a Christian and no one can tell the difference, you have to wonder whether anything really happened.

Of course, the gas station owner was not entirely correct. It was not the man himself who had made such a radical change in his life. Only the Lord can make new creatures. They come from His hand, not from our best efforts. What God did at creation He does again in conversion.

—R. C. S.

III. A Message to Proclaim (2 Corinthians 5:18-21)

A. Nothing Else God Can Do (vv. 18, 19)

18. And all things are of God, who hath reconciled us to himself by Jesus Christ, and hath given to us the ministry of reconciliation.

To understand *the ministry of reconciliation*, we must first understand the concept of *reconciliation*. The basic idea is to take two persons who are in disagreement and help them resolve their differences so that they can resume their normal relationship. For example, when management and labor are in a contract dispute, their normal working relationship is interrupted. When negotiations reach an impasse, a mediator is brought in to help them resolve their differences. The mediator's job is essentially to listen as each side states his case, determine where each has legitimate claims against the other, and then help the two sides work out a reasonable solution to which both can agree.

At Calvary Jesus Christ acted as the mediator between God and sinful man. We had no legitimate charge against a holy God, for He has never done us wrong. But because of our sin against God, He did have just cause for punishing us with death. The mediator's judgment against us would have been devastating, but He graciously offered to pay the penalty for us in order to bring a resolution to this dispute. This offer was above and beyond the duty of a mediator; but then, Christ is no ordinary mediator. So it is that all sinners who agree to these terms and allow Christ to pay their death penalty for them can be *reconciled* to God, restored to a peaceful relationship with the One our sins have alienated.

We who have been reconciled to God by Christ are not to rest comfortably in our new standing. We have been given *the ministry of reconciliation*. We have a duty to announce to others what they need to do if they want to be reconciled to God as we have been. [See question #4, page 216.]

19. To wit, that God was in Christ, reconciling the world unto himself, not imputing their trespasses unto them; and hath committed unto us the word of reconciliation.

No one should ever imagine that God was a bystander at Calvary, observing what went on, then deciding how to respond. The cross was part of God's "set purpose and foreknowledge" (Acts 2:23, *New International Version*). It was God who was *reconciling the world unto himself*. Reconciliation was neither our idea nor our doing; it was entirely of God.

Because of the work of Christ on behalf of His people, God is no longer *imputing their trespasses unto them*. We need to understand that our biggest obstacle to a relationship with God is the guilt of our sin. The idea of being guilty means to deserve punishment because one has done wrong. Sin makes us guilty in the eyes of God and deserving of His punishment. (It should be noted that we do not always feel guilty, but we are in fact guilty just the same.) For those of us who through faith claim the death of Christ for our sins, God will not "impute" the guilt of our sins to our record; instead, He will mark our debt "paid."

SHUTTLE DIPLOMACY

It is only since the advent of the jet airplane that diplomats have been able to engage in what is called "shuttle diplomacy." Now it is quite common. Two nations are at odds. They're about to go to war—or may already be at war. A diplomat from a third nation undertakes to be the peacemaker. He flies back and forth between the warring countries. In some instances, he is able to bring the two nations to the peace table, where at least some dialogue can begin.

Our Lord Jesus did not need to engage in shuttle diplomacy to reconcile man and God. He came only once from Heaven to earth and accomplished that reconciliation—not by skillful negotiation, but by His sacrificial death. This is the amazing truth of the gospel.

Today we who have been reconciled to God serve as Christ's ambassadors, or "diplomats," in order to bring others into the same reconciliation. He did it with His death. We do it with our lives. We do it when we tell of His death and how it brings us from sin into salvation. All Christians have been called to the ministry of reconciliation. —R. C. S.

B. An Offer to Accept (vv. 20, 21)

20. Now then we are ambassadors for Christ, as though God did beseech you by us: we pray you in Christ's stead, be ye reconciled to God.

Here is one way to summarize our gospel message to the world: *be ye reconciled to God*. Paul's phrasing is intended to add one more thought to the picture of two disputing parties in mediation. After a mediator works out a plan for reconciliation, each party in negotiation must then decide whether or not to agree to the terms. Usually as one party agrees to the terms, he reaches his hand out across the table for a handshake that will "seal the deal." He has decided that he is ready to be reconciled to his adversary. He now asks his adversary to do the same, to "be reconciled" to him.

Home Daily Bible Readings

Monday, Feb. 15—The Love of Christ Urges Us On (2 Corinthians 5:11-15)
Tuesday, Feb. 16—There Is a New Creation! (2 Corinthians 5:16-21)
Wednesday, Feb. 17—Justification and Life for All (Romans 5:18—6:4)
Thursday, Feb. 18—Alive to God in Christ Jesus (Romans 6:5-11)
Friday, Feb. 19—God's Gift Is Eternal Life (Romans 6:12-23)
Saturday, Feb. 20—Instructed by Law; Saved by Grace (Romans 7:1-13)
Sunday, Feb. 21—Thanks Be to God! (Romans 7:14-25a)

In a spiritual sense, God stands even now with His hand reaching out across the table. He has agreed to the terms of Christ the mediator. He has accepted His substitutionary death at Calvary. He is ready to shake hands and "seal the deal." Through our preaching, He is pleading with sinful man: *be ye reconciled to God*. There is nothing more that God needs to do for our salvation. It now remains for each individual to decide whether or not to accept the terms of reconciliation.

This wonderful news will not be communicated unless those who have already been reconciled do so. Thus we Christians are Christ's *ambassadors* or royal representatives. We speak in His behalf a message He has given. We are not permitted to modify or compromise it, for it is not our message. We speak what Christ has told us to say. It is the same message that was once delivered to us: *be ye reconciled to God*. [See question #5, page 216.]

21. For he hath made him to be sin for us, who knew no sin; that we might be made the righteousness of God in him.

The pronouns of this verse should first be identified in order to grasp the meaning. The one *who knew no sin* is Jesus Christ. His sinless character is clearly affirmed in Scripture (Hebrews 4:15; 7:26) and supported by the Gospel accounts of His life.

At Calvary Jesus was *made . . . to be sin for us*. This is another reference to the substitutionary atonement, by which Jesus assumed the guilt of our sins and paid their penalty. This should not be read so as to imply that Jesus actually became a real sinner. He took the place of sinners, and He was punished as a sinner should be punished; but He will always be the one who in reality *knew no sin*.

The one who made all of this happen was God Himself. God was the *he* who *hath made* [Jesus] *to be sin for us*. Once again we are reminded that Calvary was ultimately God's plan,

a program of redemption "foreordained before the foundation of the world" (1 Peter 1:20).

And never forget the other side of the substitution. Christ took on the guilt of our sins so that *we might be made the righteousness of God in him*. We could never pass the judgment bar of God on the basis of our own record of good deeds; for no matter how much good we could show, it would never be enough to make up for our sins against God. That is why God's grace allows us to assume Christ's perfect record even as He assumes our guilt. We stand before God fully reconciled to Him, not on the basis of our good deeds, but because He allows us to wear the righteousness of Christ.

Conclusion

A. I Want to Come Home

Have you ever noticed the advertisements for the Runaway Teen Hotline? It is a free service for youth who have run away from home, but now desire help in contacting their parents to find out if they can come back home. If you are a parent and have noticed the ads, you probably also have felt somewhat ill at ease. A runaway child is a parent's worst nightmare. Were it to happen to any of us, our days would be filled with anxiety, and our nights would give little relief. Each time the phone rang, we would pray to hear a familiar voice say the words, "I want to come home."

Jesus told a parable of a "prodigal son" who, after leaving his family and squandering his father's money, wondered whether he would be welcomed back home. He prepared a speech to win over his father. He was ready and willing to admit his mistakes and to plead for a second chance. But what he found at home surprised him—a father running to him, having anxiously watched for his son's return. All along the father had been ready for a reconciliation. It was just a matter of waiting for the son to decide to come back home.

This is the gospel message that the world needs to hear. The Father loves us. He longs for us to stop running and come home.

B. Prayer

Our Father in Heaven, we thank You for Your mercy and grace, for loving us so much that You would give us the privilege of coming back home to You. Thank You, in Jesus' name. Amen.

C. Thought to Remember

"We implore you on Christ's behalf: Be reconciled to God" (2 Corinthians 5:20b, *New International Version*).

Visual for lesson 12

The visual for today's lesson illustrates our need for Jesus to act in our behalf to pay the debt we could not pay.

Learning by Doing

This page contains an alternate lesson plan emphasizing learning activities.
Classes desiring such student involvement will find these suggestions helpful.

Learning Goals

As a result of participating in this lesson, students should:

1. Explain what Paul said about the means and message of reconciliation with God.

2. Compare and contrast the way sinners are reconciled to God with other types or occasions of reconciliation.

3. Accept God's offer of reconciliation or plan to share His offer with someone else who needs to accept it.

Into the Lesson

Option 1. If your class sits around tables, have enough cutouts of butterflies on the tables for each student to have one. As students enter, ask them to decorate the butterflies with markers or crayons you provide. Explain that, because of the way a butterfly is transformed from a caterpillar, it has become a symbol of new life. Ask each student to print the words, "If any man be in Christ, he is a new creature," on his or her butterfly. Point out that our new life in Christ becomes a reality when our relationship with God changes. The key word in today's study is "reconciliation."

Option 2. Begin by asking the following question: "Suppose you could be appointed an ambassador to any nation you chose. What nation would you choose and why?" Allow each student to share his or her answer with one other student. Then ask, "What would be your job? What does an ambassador do?" Discuss this briefly with the entire class.

Tell the class that our text calls us to be ambassadors. But we will have to read the text to discover our target group and discover our task.

Into the Word

Prepare a handout with two columns. In column one print the text in four sections: 2 Corinthians 5:11-13; verses 14 and 15; verses 16 and 17; and verses 18-21. Place the heading "Personal Notes" over column 2.

Begin this section by distributing the handouts and giving a brief lecture on the background of the text. (See page 210.)

Ask a class member to read the first section, verses 11-13. Then ask the following discussion questions and encourage the students to make notes on their handouts during the discussion.

1. What is Paul's motive for ministry?

2. Why does Paul offer an opportunity for his readers to take pride in him?

3. Can you paraphrase verse 13 to clarify Paul's thoughts?

Ask another volunteer to read verses 14 and 15. Using the commentary, lecture on the logical progression in these verses. Emphasize the substitutionary atonement Christ offers for our sins. Also emphasize Paul's call to service in verse 15.

Ask a third volunteer to read verses 16 and 17; then ask why Paul would say, "We once regarded Christ . . . from a worldly point of view." What was in Paul's background that would make him say this about himself? Also ask how a person becomes a "new creature" (v. 17).

Read verses 18-21. Make a few comments about the basic concept of reconciliation and the concept of a mediator (see pages 212, 213). Ask, "How does Jesus act as a mediator between God and man?"

Clarify verse 21 by placing these words on the chalkboard to identify the pronouns:

He = God
Him = Jesus
Who = Jesus

Then reread the text, substituting the names for the pronouns: "For God hath made Jesus to be sin for us, [even though] Jesus knew no sin." Also read Isaiah's wonderful description of Christ's substitutionary atonement from Isaiah 53:4, 5. Conclude this section by explaining the term "the righteousness of God" (page 214).

Into Life

Summarize the text by explaining that there are two important messages in today's study. The first is to "be reconciled to God," to get our relationship with God resolved. God has done His part with Jesus' substitutionary sacrifice. He now waits for our response. (Invite class members who want to talk more about this to tell you. Meet with them after class to discuss this.)

The second message is a reminder that we are ambassadors of God. Ask class members to affirm their commitment to be ambassadors in closing prayer groups.

If you used the butterfly option in the lesson introduction, ask class members to post this on the bathroom mirror for one week as a joyful reminder of their new life.

Let's Talk It Over

The questions on this page are designed to encourage review of the lesson Scriptures and to promote discussion of the lesson by the class. The answers provided are only discussion starters. Let your class talk it over from there.

1. We are often cautioned about being too pushy in evangelism, about "cramming the gospel down people's throats." Yet Paul said, "We persuade men." What is the difference between persuasion and being too pushy? How can we follow Paul's example without becoming offensive?

It is possible to persuade without becoming offensive. Showing courtesy and respect toward people will give us much more latitude in trying to persuade them than if we fail in those common graces. Having a clear, well-reasoned testimony for our faith will also be more persuasive than expressing mere feelings and impressions. Of course, some people will be offended by any expression of faith. For them, any kind of testimony is probably being "pushy." Paul, too, was opposed on many occasions. Most of us need to work, not on being too pushy, but too timid.

2. What examples can you give where the love of Christ compelled you to action, when you did something you would not have done except in response to Christ's love?

Perhaps there are members in your class who have donated time to work in Christian service camp or a homeless shelter or a crisis pregnancy clinic. Perhaps some have assisted in foreign mission work. These activities pay nothing except in spiritual terms, as one is rewarded to see the love of Christ expressed in tangible ways. Others may have risked their relationships with friends or family members in order to share the gospel with them. Being compelled by Christ's love will lead us to a variety of activities, but they will always require stepping out of one's comfort zone. If some in your class cannot think of occasions when they have stepped out of their comfort zones because of the love of Christ, you might suggest that they need to do some self-examination and draw nearer to the Lord so they can begin to express His love in tangible ways.

3. If we see people through spiritual eyes rather than the eyes of the flesh, what difference will it make in what we notice?

The eyes of the flesh will notice matters of physical appearance: height, weight, complexion, racial features, hair color and style, clothing, posture, etc. The eyes of the flesh are also quick to notice signs of wealth, education, status, and accomplishment. From those appearances we may draw conclusions that are completely contrary to the discernment of the spirit. We may discover that one who appears comfortable or successful actually has a troubled heart and is in desperate need of the forgiveness and the peace of God. One who appears in need may actually be rich toward God and full of joy. We must train ourselves to see deeper than the surface.

4. It is hard for some people to recognize that sin has put them at enmity with God and in need of reconciliation. How can we who are charged with the "ministry of reconciliation" expose their need and effect reconciliation?

One familiar use of the word *reconciliation* pertains to bringing two disagreeing or offended parties back together. Another application is from the banking or accounting world. When I reconcile my bank statement, I make sure that my record of deposits and withdrawals matches with what is actually in the bank. Because of sin, each of us falls short of God's righteous standard (Romans 3:23). Nearly everyone will admit he or she is not "perfect"; perhaps the accounting illustration will help some to see that they cannot by their own goodness make up the shortfall. Just as a manager whose books do not balance finds himself in trouble with the auditors or, worse yet, government regulators, one finds himself at enmity with a holy God when his "books" don't balance. The account can be reconciled only because Jesus Christ makes up the lack. When one accepts Christ as Savior and Lord, He applies His righteousness to the account.

5. How is our role as Christians in the world like that of an ambassador?

An ambassador is a delegate from another government. We are in this world representing the kingdom of Heaven. An ambassador does not create policy; he or she only announces it and conforms to it. We announce the good news of our King and act according to His directives. People may draw conclusions about a government based upon the character and demeanor of its ambassador. People may draw conclusions about the kingdom of Heaven based upon our representation of it.

Living in Hope

DEVOTIONAL READING: 1 Peter 1:3-9.

LESSON SCRIPTURE: Titus 2:11-14; Hebrews 12:18-29; Revelation 1:14-20; 11:15-19.

PRINTED TEXT: Titus 2:11-14; Hebrews 12:26-29; Revelation 1:17-20; 11:15.

Titus 2:11-14

11 For the grace of God that bringeth salvation hath appeared to all men,

12 Teaching us that, denying ungodliness and worldly lusts, we should live soberly, righteously, and godly, in this present world;

13 Looking for that blessed hope, and the glorious appearing of the great God and our Saviour Jesus Christ;

14 Who gave himself for us, that he might redeem us from all iniquity, and purify unto himself a peculiar people, zealous of good works.

Hebrews 12:26-29

26 Whose voice then shook the earth: but now he hath promised, saying, Yet once more I shake not the earth only, but also heaven.

27 And this word, Yet once more, signifieth the removing of those things that are shaken, as of things that are made, that those things which cannot be shaken may remain.

28 Wherefore we receiving a kingdom which cannot be moved, let us have grace, whereby we may serve God acceptably with reverence and godly fear:

29 For our God is a consuming fire.

Revelation 1:17-20

17 And when I saw him, I fell at his feet as dead. And he laid his right hand upon me, saying unto me, Fear not; I am the first and the last:

18 I am he that liveth, and was dead; and, behold, I am alive for evermore, Amen; and have the keys of hell and of death.

19 Write the things which thou hast seen, and the things which are, and the things which shall be hereafter;

20 The mystery of the seven stars which thou sawest in my right hand, and the seven golden candlesticks. The seven stars are the angels of the seven churches: and the seven candlesticks which thou sawest are the seven churches.

Revelation 11:15

15 And the seventh angel sounded; and there were great voices in heaven, saying, The kingdoms of this world are become the kingdoms of our Lord, and of his Christ; and he shall reign for ever and ever.

GOLDEN TEXT: Looking for that blessed hope, and the glorious appearing of the great God and our Saviour Jesus Christ.—Titus 2:13.

Lesson Aims

As a result of today's lesson students should:

1. Summarize what today's texts tell us about the return of Jesus and how that gives us hope.

2. Compare the Christian's perspective on living in hope with the secular concept of living to "make a difference" in the present world.

3. Tell one activity or behavior each of them practices—or will begin to practice—because of the hope he or she has in Christ Jesus.

Lesson Outline

INTRODUCTION
    A. Practice What You Preach
    B. Lesson Background
  I. PRACTICING A GODLY LIFESTYLE (Titus 2:11-14)
    A. The Way Grace Demands (vv. 11, 12)
    B. The Way God Intended (vv. 13, 14)
      Living With Hope
  II. SERVING A HEAVENLY KINGDOM (Hebrews 12:26-29)
    A. Never to Be Destroyed (vv. 26, 27)
    B. Our Duty as Citizens (vv. 28, 29)
  III. TRUSTING AN ALMIGHTY SAVIOR (Revelation 1:17-20; 11:15)
    A. Power Over Death (1:17, 18)
      The Keeper of the Keys
    B. Presence With the Church (1:19, 20)
    C. Final Triumph (11:15)
CONCLUSION
    A. "Time's Up"
    B. Prayer
    C. Thought to Remember

Introduction

A. Practice What You Preach

Can you picture the irony of this scene? Inside a barber shop is a man getting a haircut. Leaning against the wall outside is the sign he has been carrying around on the street: "The world will end today." You have to wonder if the man is serious about what he is preaching.

This probably sounds like possible subject matter for a cartoon. Surely no one would actually do this—would he? How about the preacher who uses Scriptures and charts to predict an immediate date for Christ's return while at the same time putting away funds into a retirement plan for the future? (Some actually do!) What is lacking in both illustrations is consistency. The time-honored adage, "Practice what you preach," surely applies.

We need to ask ourselves how well we "practice what we preach" regarding the second coming. We say we believe that Christ will return one day to judge the world. Have we done everything we need to do to be ready to stand before the Judge? We say we want to live forever in the presence of God. But are we preparing now for that kind of existence by saying no to our sinful habits (since we cannot practice them there), by spending as much time as we can in personal devotion and corporate worship (since we will be worshiping continually there), and by actively participating in Christian service (since we will be serving our King forever)?

We need to do more than just talk and sing about the return of Christ. We need to live in a way that shows that we are serious about our hope for the future.

B. Lesson Background

The Old Testament prophets spoke often of a coming Messiah who would bring salvation and judgment to the world. The common assumption by Jews in the time of Christ was that all of this would occur in one Messianic appearance. But as the Gospels tell us, Jesus explained that He had come primarily "to seek and to save that which was lost" (Luke 19:10). Later, He would return to carry out judgment upon the lost as well as the saved (Matthew 25:31-33).

The New Testament epistles (such as Titus and Hebrews) provide the clearest picture of how the original Messianic plan is to be understood. Their purpose is to instruct all Christians, who are already enjoying the blessings of Christ's first coming, how to prepare for the remaining Messianic work of the second coming.

The book of Revelation is well known as a book of prophetic themes; however, its primary purpose should never be overlooked. Like the epistles, it encourages those who live between the first and second comings of Christ, not to set dates for His return but to set their lives in order.

I. Practicing a Godly Lifestyle (Titus 2:11-14)

The letter to Titus was written by the apostle Paul. Titus was a young preacher serving on the island of Crete (Titus 1:5). The epistle is filled with practical guidelines for life in the church, regarding both its organization (elders and their qualifications) and the proper conduct of individual members.

A. The Way Grace Demands (vv. 11, 12)

11. For the grace of God that bringeth salvation hath appeared to all men.

Some of the grandest Biblical themes regarding our *salvation* are summarized in this verse. Salvation derives from the work of *God*, not from our initiative. Salvation is made possible by the *grace* and mercy of God, not because we deserved it. The offer of salvation is intended for *all men* and not just for a select few. However, though freely given, this salvation includes certain responsibilities that cannot be ignored.

12. Teaching us that, denying ungodliness and worldly lusts, we should live soberly, righteously, and godly, in this present world.

The grace of God obligates us to *live* a *godly* lifestyle, not in order to earn our salvation, but because we are compelled to express our gratitude in this way. A heart truly changed by God's grace will reflect that change by *denying ungodliness*, that is, saying no to any temptation to do something that violates God's standards.

Paul also warns against the influence of *worldly lusts.* This calls to mind John's counsel to "love not the world, . . . for all that is in the world, the lust of the flesh, and the lust of the eyes, and the pride of life, is not of the Father, but is of the world" (1 John 2:15, 16). Though we live *in this present world*, we are called to live differently. [See question #1, page 224.]

This passage also lists three of the many virtues that should be developed in the life of a Christian. First, we should strive to be sober. The basic idea of the Greek word is of someone who has so much self-control and discipline that he does not allow other people or things to push him around or to dictate his agenda. He makes decisions with a clear head and rational thinking, not because of emotions or coercion. The Greek word behind *righteously* refers to being upright, fair, and above board in one's dealings. A *godly* person is someone who seeks to imitate the moral qualities of God emphasized in Scripture, such as holiness, love, mercy, patience, and faithfulness. These virtues and many others like them are the distinguishing marks of a person who has been changed by God's grace.

B. The Way God Intended (vv. 13, 14)

13. Looking for that blessed hope, and the glorious appearing of the great God and our Saviour Jesus Christ.

The second coming of Christ is our *blessed hope* in that it is the one event in the future toward which we have directed our lives. While the death and resurrection of Christ are the essence of our faith, the return of Christ is the essence of our hope.

The phrasing of this passage in the Greek text poses some difficulties for us in translation and interpretation. It is not typical to speak of God's *appearing* when referring to the second coming, but the idea is not inappropriate. Most likely, Paul is referring to Jesus by a divine title, as *the great God and our Saviour.* This is consistent with Paul's teaching that in Jesus "dwelleth all the fulness of the Godhead bodily" (Colossians 2:9; see also Romans 9:5; Philippians 2:6).

LIVING WITH HOPE

The Talmud is a commentary on the Old Testament Scriptures and is regarded highly by Jews. It teaches that the first question we will be asked at the judgment will be, "Did you live with hope?" However, the question about hope is properly a question for life now, not judgment in the future: "Are you living with hope now? What is the basis for your hope?"

In common usage, hope has come to mean a rather vague wish that we do not really expect to be fulfilled. But hope in the Bible is not vague, nor is it just wishful thinking. Biblical hope is something strong and resilient. It is "an anchor of the soul, both sure and steadfast" (Hebrews 6:19). It is able to sustain us in any circumstance we face.

During the days of Communist rule, people in Romania used to greet one another by asking, "How are you today?" The typical answer was, "Better than tomorrow!" But Christians in that country sang and believed the words of the old hymn: "My hope is built on nothing less than Jesus' blood and righteousness." In a situation that seemed politically hopeless and economically hopeless, Christians found their hope in Jesus to be of supreme value.

Whatever our circumstances may be, we can rejoice that our lives are never hopeless. In

Visual for lesson 13

Today's visual is both a good illustration of our Golden Text (Titus 2:13) and a helpful reminder of the hope we have in Christ.

Christ we have help for the present and hope for the future. —R. C. S.

14. Who gave himself for us, that he might redeem us from all iniquity, and purify unto himself a peculiar people, zealous of good works.

Note how this passage affirms that God's purpose in saving us is not simply to get us out of trouble, but to change us into a new kind of people. We are expected to sever ties with *all* practices that involve *iniquity*, or sin. We are to be a pure people, cleansed from both the guilt and the moral contamination of sin. We are to join with others who have also been saved, thus forming *a peculiar people*. The word *peculiar* here does not mean "strange" or "odd," but that we are God's exclusive property (peculiar to Him), to be used in any way He chooses. We are to be *zealous* in practicing *good works* that help others and glorify God. [See question #2, page 224.]

II. Serving a Heavenly Kingdom (Hebrews 12:26-29)

The book of Hebrews was written by an unknown yet inspired author to a community of Jewish Christians who were considering abandoning the Christian faith and returning to Judaism (Hebrews 10:35). Chapter 12 (vv. 18-22) likens Judaism to Mount Sinai, where Moses received the Ten Commandments and the Law. The appearance of Sinai was terrifying, marked by fire, dark clouds and smoke, thunder and lightning, and an earthquake (Exodus 19:16-18). It is the nature of Judaism, the writer argues, that it instills within its adherents a sense of separation from God; because it reminds them of their sin and their guilt, yet offers no real solution (Hebrews 10:1-4).

The Christian faith, on the other hand, is like Mount Zion, the mountain upon which the city of Jerusalem was built. (Mount Zion is one of several Biblical symbols for Heaven.) In contrast to Judaism, Christianity proclaims a sacrifice that will remove our guilt (Hebrews 10:11-14), thus opening the way for us to move one day to the "heavenly Jerusalem" (Hebrews 12:22).

A. Never to Be Destroyed (vv. 26, 27)

26. Whose voice then shook the earth: but now he hath promised, saying, Yet once more I shake not the earth only, but also heaven.

The writer observes that God's *voice . . . shook the earth* when Moses received the law at Sinai. The next time God speaks such a powerful word will be at the end of time. His voice will then *shake* everything—the earth as well as the heav-

enly bodies. The writer refers to a portion of the Old Testament in this verse (Haggai 2:6) in order to strengthen his appeal to his readers, whose background, as we have noted, was in Judaism.

27. And this word, Yet once more, signifieth the removing of those things that are shaken, as of things that are made, that those things which cannot be shaken may remain.

When the ultimate shaking comes, the *things that are made,* that is, the material universe, will collapse. Everything we value from this life will exist no longer. All that will *remain* will be *those things which cannot be shaken.*

Spiritual realities cannot be touched by an earthquake. Our relationship with Christ, our brotherhood within the church, the fruit of our service—these and other blessings will continue after the end of time. They are secure on the heavenly Mount Zion.

B. Our Duty as Citizens (vv. 28, 29)

28, 29. Wherefore we receiving a kingdom which cannot be moved, let us have grace, whereby we may serve God acceptably with reverence and godly fear: for our God is a consuming fire.

Once again we see a familiar theme. Reflecting on the heavenly life that we hope to inherit one day has implications for how we should live our lives now on this earth. The thought of *receiving a kingdom* in Heaven should move us to *have grace* (perhaps better rendered "have gratitude"). We should want to *serve* God actively and faithfully because we appreciate how much He has done for us.

Note also how this passage brings in another motive for our godly lives and service: the reality of Hell. We should serve God *with reverence and godly fear,* not only because we appreciate His grace, but also because we do not want to face the *consuming fire* of His wrath. [See question #3, page 224.]

III. Trusting an Almighty Savior (Revelation 1:17-20; 11:15)

The apostle John wrote the book of Revelation while in exile on the island of Patmos (Revelation 1:9). It is usually dated at sometime near the end of the first century.

A. Power Over Death (1:17, 18)

17. And when I saw him, I fell at his feet as dead. And he laid his right hand upon me, saying unto me, Fear not; I am the first and the last.

While in a state of worship one Lord's day (1:10), John received a vision of Jesus. He saw the Lord adorned in glorious garments that were symbolic of His great power and authority (1:12-16). The sight was beautiful, yet terrifying at the same time. John *fell at his feet as dead.*

Jesus tried to calm John's fears with a gentle touch and encouraging words. He called John's attention to His eternal nature, identifying Himself as *the first and the last* of everything, the One who has no beginning and no ending.

18. I am he that liveth, and was dead; and, behold, I am alive for evermore, Amen; and have the keys of hell and of death.

John well knew that at one time Jesus *was dead;* he had been present at the crucifixion (John 19:26, where John is described as the disciple whom Jesus loved) and had seen Him die. John knew where to go to find Jesus' tomb, so we assume he saw Him buried as well (John 20:1-4). John was also one of the first witnesses to the resurrection of Jesus (John 20:5-8, 19). Now, as John's life and ministry were threatened by a hostile emperor, he received a vivid reminder that the One whose church the emperor sought to destroy was *alive* and well.

Jesus is described as having *the keys of hell and of death.* The Greek text does not say "Hell" (i.e., *Gehenna*), the place of eternal suffering, but *Hades,* which is a general term referring to the place where the dead go when they die while they await the judgment. Jesus had been there for three days and had broken free, taking with Him the keys that lock a person into death permanently. Such imagery implies not only that Jesus is the Conqueror of death, but that He has the power to release us from death's grip after we die. In other words, this vision dramatized the Christian's hope that one day Jesus will resurrect the saints to everlasting life so that they may live with Him in Heaven. [See question #4, page 224.]

THE KEEPER OF THE KEYS

A man once told how during his youth, his father was the janitor of the high school he attended. There were some disadvantages to that; for example, often the father had to stay and work after school. But there was one great advantage. If the boy and some of his friends wanted to get into the gym and play basketball on weekends, they could go right to the boy's father. Why? Because he had the keys! To have the keys is to have power. So we should be encouraged by today's lesson when we learn that Jesus has "the keys of hell and of death."

A Sunday school teacher who had never been to Bible college or seminary saw to the heart of this verse. He said, "So the devil doesn't even have the keys to his own house." That's a very helpful insight. It reassures us that Christ al-

ways has more power than Satan. It tells us which side is going to win. It also reminds us that in Christ we become stronger than Satan. "Greater is he that is in you, than he that is in the world" (1 John 4:4).

We should be alert to the influences of Satan, but we should not be afraid of his power. He doesn't even have the keys to his own house!
—R. C. S.

B. Presence With the Church (1:19, 20)

19. Write the things which thou hast seen, and the things which are, and the things which shall be hereafter.

John was not given this vision simply that he might watch and learn. He was explicitly commissioned to record it all (Revelation 1:11) and then send it to seven specific churches in Asia Minor (modern western Turkey). This is an area where, according to the early church fathers, John served (particularly in Ephesus) during the later years of his life.

John's writing was to consist of three parts (not of equal length). *The things which thou hast seen* referred to the vision he had just witnessed in chapter 1. *The things which are* referred to the messages Jesus was about to give to the seven churches (chapters 2 and 3). *The things which shall be hereafter* designated the visions John was yet to see—in other words, the remainder of the book (chapters 4–22).

20. The mystery of the seven stars which thou sawest in my right hand, and the seven golden candlesticks. The seven stars are the angels of the seven churches: and the seven candlesticks which thou sawest are the seven churches.

Determining the meaning of the symbolism in the book of Revelation can be challenging. Perhaps the best place to find clues is the Old Testament, because most of the figures in Revelation have clear parallels in the Old Testament prophets. We may not be certain regarding our conclusions, but a person who studies this background thoroughly can make some reasonable suggestions.

Of course, the best interpretations are those that are given to us by John himself. In the verse before us, he records Jesus' explanation of the meaning of two of the symbols in the vision he had seen. The *seven stars* were the *angels of the seven churches*, while the *seven candlesticks* were the *seven churches* of Asia Minor. Understanding the seven churches presents no difficulty for us, since we have already been given their names (v. 11). However, it would be more accurate not to picture candlesticks, but, as the Greek word indicates, "lampstands" with oil lamps sitting upon them.

Seven angels still presents some confusion because we are not sure what kind of "angels" a church has. Some assume this refers to guardian angels, but then we wonder why Jesus would send a letter to guardian angels. The Greek word used here literally means "messengers," which could designate either a heavenly messenger (an angel) or an earthly messenger (such as an elder or a preacher). Perhaps the seven messages were to be sent to the preacher of each congregation, who would then read the letter aloud.

Regardless of what the stars symbolize concerning the seven churches, the meaning of this stirring vision is clear. Jesus appears "in the midst of the seven candlesticks" (1:13). Thus, He is present with His people—the churches. In dramatic form John's vision teaches what Matthew 28:20 declares: "Lo, I am with you alway, even unto the end of the world."

C. Final Triumph (11:15)

15. And the seventh angel sounded; and there were great voices in heaven, saying, The kingdoms of this world are become the kingdoms of our Lord, and of his Christ; and he shall reign for ever and ever.

Home Daily Bible Readings

Monday, Feb. 22—The Blessed Hope (Titus 2:11-14)
Tuesday, Feb. 23—What Cannot Be Shaken Remains (Hebrews 12:18-29)
Wednesday, Feb. 24—Do Not Be Afraid (Revelation 1:12-20)
Thursday, Feb. 25—He Will Reign Forever and Ever (Revelation 11:15-19)
Friday, Feb. 26—A Living Hope (1 Peter 1:3-9)
Saturday, Feb. 27—The Hope to Which God Has Called Us (Ephesians 1:15-23)
Sunday, Feb. 28—A New Heaven and a New Earth (Revelation 21:1-8)

The book of Revelation is filled with action—seven seals being broken, seven trumpets being sounded, seven bowls of plagues being poured out, along with a host of other symbolic actions. We cannot always be certain about how to interpret what is happening, but usually we can see enough to learn a valuable lesson.

As a case in point, we may not understand as fully as we would like the meaning of the first six trumpets and all the disasters that are associated with them. However, when the seventh *angel* blows the last of the trumpets, we know without a doubt of the final triumph of Christ and His people.

Many will not read the words of the verse before us without thinking of the majestic "Hallelujah Chorus" that is part of Handel's *Messiah*. Let us endeavor to make certain that we are part of the heavenly kingdom of Christ, so that we can one day join the great voices of the "Hallelujah Chorus" in Heaven. [See question #5, page 224.]

Conclusion

A. "Time's Up"

Most of us know what it is like to take a test in school. Often the teacher passes out the test questions face down, and then, when every student has a copy, she announces, "Begin!" The test may seem to go well for a while; however, there is usually a sense of panic whenever students realize that the allotted time is nearing an end. Eventually they are either relieved or terrified to hear the teacher say, "Time's up!"

The above scenario provides us with an appropriate way to look at the second coming of Christ. Your life and mine may be considered a kind of "test." We cannot know for certain when the day of "grading" (Judgment Day) will take place. We must live each day, as one of our texts for today puts it, "looking for that blessed hope." We need to be secure in our knowledge that whatever comes first (our death or Jesus' return), we belong to Jesus. For the Christian, "time's up" means that eternal life has just begun!

B. Prayer

Father in Heaven, thank You for the promise that You will one day send Your Son back to earth to gather His people. Help us to be ready for that day. In Jesus' name, amen.

C. Thought to Remember

"Since everything will be destroyed in this way, what kind of people ought you to be? You ought to live holy and godly lives" (2 Peter 3:11, *New International Version*).

Learning by Doing

This page contains an alternate lesson plan emphasizing learning activities.
Classes desiring such student involvement will find these suggestions helpful.

Learning Goals

As a result of today's lesson students should:

1. Summarize what today's texts tell us about the return of Jesus and how that gives us hope.

2. Compare the Christian's perspective on living in hope with the secular concept of living to "make a difference" in the present world.

3. Tell one activity or behavior each of them practices—or will begin to practice—because of the hope he or she has in Christ Jesus.

Into the Lesson

Divide the class into small groups of three to five persons and give each group one or two hymnbooks and a piece of poster board. Ask the groups to look for songs about Heaven (often found under "Eternal Destiny, Heaven, Everlasting Life" in the index). Ask them to list every word or phrase used by hymn writers to describe Heaven (e.g., pearly gates, mansions, glory, beyond the river, etc.). Hang their posters in front of the class when they are finished. You may highlight the variety of descriptive phrases. Allow volunteers to tell which descriptions particularly touch them and why.

Comment that many hymns, while describing the joy of Heaven, also remind us we have something to do while we are waiting for this fantastic place. A good example is "When We All Get to Heaven." List the words and phrases from this hymn that tell us how to live while here on earth.

Point out that the hymn writers simply reflect the writers of Scripture. The Scriptures remind us of our wonderful goal, yet they also remind us how to live while we are waiting.

Into the Word

Place three poster boards with the following headings at the front of the class: "How to Live," "Our Hope," and "Characteristics of Our Almighty Savior."

Copy the printed text on handouts to give to each class member. Tell the class to listen when the text is read for what the Scriptures tell us about how to live (mark these on their handouts with an "L"), words that describe our hope (mark these "H"), and words that describe our Savior ("S").

Read Titus 2:11-14 and give the students time to mark their texts. Ask one student to write each word or phrase on the corresponding poster as class members recite them.

Use the commentary section to define or clarify the phrases "denying ungodliness," "worldly lusts," "soberly," "righteously," "godly," "blessed hope," "great God," "redeem," and "peculiar people." Emphasize that while the death and resurrection of Jesus are the essence of our faith, the return of Christ is the essence of our hope.

Read Hebrews 12:26-29, giving the students time to mark their texts and entering their answers on the posters. Use the commentary to explain the background to and significance of this text. Ask for definitions of "a kingdom which cannot be moved," "grace" (see page 220), and "consuming fire."

Do the same exercise with Revelation 1:17-20 and 11:15. Ask why John would fall at the Lord's feet "as dead." Comment on the significance of the word "liveth." Then ask the class to help you define "the keys of hell and of death" and the sevens (stars, candlesticks, churches, and angels). Conclude by emphasizing the transfer of power and the eternal reign of the Lord in 11:15.

Into Life

Point to the three posters you have just completed. Tell the class that God wants us to enjoy the assurance that He will conquer death and has created an eternal kingdom for us. That assurance gives us a hope that should change our values, our lifestyles, and our commitments.

Write on the chalkboard "Living in Hope" and "Living to Make a Difference." Observe that there are many good non-Christian people who want to "make a difference" in this world. Ask the class to suggest differences in the Christian's perspective on "living in hope" and the secular view of "making a difference." Note their responses under the headings on the chalkboard. Then use the "Time's Up" illustration on page 222. This is an appropriate way to think about the second coming of Christ.

Give each class member a three-inch by five-inch card with these words printed on it: "Because I am Heaven bound, I will. . . ." Ask each student to identify one activity or behavior pattern he or she needs to change or strengthen in order to bring glory to God. Close the class session by asking God to hear and bless each commitment.

Let's Talk It Over

The questions on this page are designed to encourage review of the lesson Scriptures and to promote discussion of the lesson by the class. The answers provided are only discussion starters. Let your class talk it over from there.

1. How has receiving God's grace taught you to say no to ungodliness? With all the temptations around us, how can we stay motivated to live "soberly, righteously, and godly, in this present world"?

It is only by God's grace that we are forgiven of our sins. This "unmerited favor," as some define grace, and the realization of what it cost Jesus to redeem us from bondage to sin, does "teach us" to live in a different way. Our gratitude for what God has done to provide for our forgiveness and salvation should motivate us. We also have a wonderful hope that encourages faithfulness and obedience: Jesus has promised that He will return. Certainly Christians who are looking forward to Jesus' return, and who consider themselves citizens of His eternal kingdom, have a desire to honor their Lord by following Him and learning to live "soberly, righteously, and godly." To learn such in this present world means we will be prepared for the next, where righteousness and godliness will be the rule.

2. Who impresses you as being "zealous of good works"? What makes this person so eager for doing good? What can we learn from such a person?

That it seems unusual enough that one or two persons might stand out as zealous is a pity, but too often we have cowed to our culture, which despises "religious fanatics." Such eagerness comes from putting the needs of others ahead of one's own interests—another oddity in today's culture. What we learn from such a person is to focus on the eternal instead of the temporal. People who look out for Number One are always looking for a way to make material gain and to polish their image. People zealous of good works are always looking for ways to help others and to exalt the name of Christ.

3. The writer of Hebrews contrasts the things that can "be shaken" with those that can't. Why do so many people trust in the shaky things like material wealth or temporal power? How can we persuade them to put their faith in the eternal and almighty God?

If there were one answer to this question, what a different world this would be! How much easier would be our role as evangelists! Of course,

this is exactly our mission, and there are many methods we may employ. Perhaps one of the most essential is a clear demonstration that our own faith is not in riches or reputation or any other thing that will be shaken. Our example must be consistent with our message, however we communicate the message.

4. How have your values and behavior changed since you came to faith in the promise of eternal life with Christ? What has been the result of such a change?

Some of your students may have dramatic testimonies of lives turned around "one hundred eighty degrees" when they came to know the Lord. Such testimonies are exciting, but they are not the only demonstrations of God's grace at work. Many of your students probably grew up in the church, and their stories are not as dramatic. Still, perhaps they can recall a time when their faith became their own, and not just something they did because Mom and Dad had faith. Perhaps they got caught up in worldly pursuits in an effort to be popular at one time, but then returned to the faith of their childhood. "There is none righteous, no, not one" (Romans 3:10). However "dramatic" anyone's story might seem, each one of us is dependent on the amazing grace of God.

5. How does the vision of Jesus as the Lord who will "reign for ever and ever" enrich your worship?

When the Son of God took on flesh and dwelt on the earth in the form of a servant, His identity was not always apparent. His glory was concealed. When we see Him next there will be nothing ambiguous about His authority, His position, or His glory. John got a glimpse of the glorified Christ and "fell at his feet as dead." As we imagine what it will be like to stand in the throng before the throne of Christ in His glory, it should stir feelings of awe and wonder. We may worship today in anticipation of joining the heavenly chorus of angels who sing, "Worthy is the Lamb that was slain . . ." (Revelation 5:11-14). We will join the grand voices in Heaven singing the "Hallelujah Chorus" and other praises to our Lord, who "shall reign for ever and ever" (Revelation 11:15).

Spring Quarter, 1999

That You May Believe
(Gospel of John)

Special Features

Lessons

Unit 1: Jesus' Coming Calls for Faith

Unit 2: Jesus Is Raised to Life

Unit 3: Jesus Declares God's Message

Unit 4: Jesus Prepares His Followers

About These Lessons

This quarter will be a faith builder. These thirteen lessons from the Gospel of John will remind your students of some of the reasons they have placed their faith in Jesus Christ and will equip them to share that faith with others.

Mar 7
Mar 14
Mar 21
Mar 28
Apr 4
Apr 11
Apr 18
Apr 25
May 2
May 9
May 16
May 23
May 30

Quarterly Quiz

The questions on this page may be used in several ways: as a pretest at the beginning of the quarter; as a review at the end of the quarter; or as a review after each lesson. The questions are based on the Scripture text of each lesson (King James Version). **The answers are on page 231.**

Lesson 1

1. John the apostle states that "the _____ was made _____, and dwelt among us." *John 1:14*
2. Whereas the law was given by Moses, ____ and _____ came through Jesus Christ. *John 1:17*
3. John observes that Jesus did many other signs that are not written in his Gospel. T/F *John 20:30*

Lesson 2

1. John the Baptist described his ministry using words from which prophet? (Isaiah, Jeremiah, or Ezekiel?) *John 1:23*
2. John the Baptist called Jesus "the _____ of God, which taketh away the _____ of the _____." *John 1:29*

Lesson 3

1. Nicodemus was a member of which Jewish sect? (Zealots, Pharisees, or Sadducees?) *John 3:1*
2. Jesus told Nicodemus that one must be born of the _____ and of the _____ to enter the kingdom of God. *John 3:5*
3. Jesus compared His being lifted up with what Old Testament incident? *John 3:14*

Lesson 4

1. The woman at the well wondered why a ____, like Jesus, would ask a drink of a _____. *John 4:9*
2. How long did Jesus stay with the Samaritans? *John 4:40*

Lesson 5

1. The "place of a skull" where Jesus was crucified was called by the Hebrew name _____. *John 19:17*
2. When Jesus first spoke to Mary Magdalene after His resurrection, she thought that He was the _____. *John 20:15*

Lesson 6

1. The disciples had assembled with the doors shut for what reason? *John 20:19*
2. What was the other name by which the apostle Thomas was called? *John 20:24*
3. What did Thomas say after the resurrected Christ appeared and spoke to him? *John 20:28*

Lesson 7

1. Jesus said, "Him that cometh to me I will in no wise _____ _____." *John 6:37*
2. Jesus compared Himself as the living bread with the _____ that the Israelites ate in the wilderness. *John 6:49, 50*

Lesson 8

1. When Jesus spoke of going where the Jews could not come, they wondered if He was going to kill Himself. T/F *John 8:21, 22*
2. The Jews defended themselves before Jesus by claiming to be whose seed? *John 8:33*

Lesson 9

1. When God spoke to Jesus from Heaven, what two explanations did the people nearby give for what had happened? *John 12:29*
2. Whom did Jesus say would be "cast out"? *John 12:31*
3. Though some of the Jewish leaders believed on Jesus, they were afraid to confess Him. Of whom were they afraid? *John 12:42*

Lesson 10

1. Who told Jesus, "Thou shalt never wash my feet"? *John 13:8*
2. Jesus told the disciples, "The _____ is not greater than his _____." *John 13:16*

Lesson 11

1. Jesus called Himself the true ____ and His Father the _____. *John 15:1*
2. Complete this statement: "Greater love hath no man than this, ..." *John 15:13*

Lesson 12

1. Jesus referred to the Holy Spirit as another _____ and as the Spirit of _____. *John 14:16, 17*
2. Jesus promised that the Spirit would reprove the world of three things. What were they? *John 16:8*

Lesson 13

1. In His prayer, Jesus said that He had _____ the work that the Father had given Him to do. *John 17:4*
2. Jesus prayed that believers might be one. What grand result did He say would come from the unity of believers? *John 17:21*

The Business of Believing

by Edwin V. Hayden

I WAS FILLING OUT A POSITION questionnaire from the political party that gets most of my support. The first part was easy: what did I believe about each of several issues being contested between "our" party and "theirs"? A penciled mark in the proper box would record my position on each point. On most questions, I knew my responses would please the pollsters.

Then the party's questions became more difficult. Would I support my opinions with a financial contribution at this or that level? Substantial sums were suggested to indicate a substantial degree of support. Then I was asked if I would campaign for the party in my neighborhood and represent it as a poll watcher in the forthcoming election. Now the issue had become not only what I believed, but how far I was willing to follow my belief. Later mailings would present the party's position in a way designed to strengthen my faith in its principles and increase my commitment to it.

A Gospel With a Goal

In his Gospel, John deals in a better way with our faith in Jesus Christ as Lord. John doesn't begin by asking questions; he starts with a firm declaration of Jesus as the bodily revelation of God—the Word who "was made flesh, and dwelt among us" (John 1:14). He then continues with a factual account to establish his claim. He doesn't make repeated demands on the reader for increasing commitment; he sets forth Jesus' own claims concerning who He is and what He demands of His followers. Innumerable blessings are promised for those who believe and irreparable loss for those who will not. In conclusion John makes plain his plan and purpose for writing. He has told what is most important about Jesus, "that ye might believe that Jesus is the Christ, the Son of God; and that believing ye might have life through his name" (John 20:31).

Who are the *ye* to whom John's Gospel is addressed? He doesn't say. The approach and appeal are so general that it might have been directed to "Dear Reader" or "To Whom It May Concern." Yet the contents are so personal that John might have called each reader by name. What, moreover, is meant by *believing*? Obviously the word includes all that was suggested by my political opinion poll, but much more. It involves life and living, for now and eternity. It invites the first-time reader to consider and

acknowledge the truth of what John has written. It also challenges the lifelong follower of Jesus to a higher and deeper commitment.

Four Dimensions of Faith

Scripture uses *belief*, or *faith*, in four distinct but related ways. In the phrase *the faith* it signifies that which is believed. For the Christian, that embraces the truth embodied in Jesus Christ and revealed through Him and His chosen apostles. It is "the faith which was once delivered unto the saints" (Jude 3). That belief is to be kept, defended, and proclaimed, in full recognition that those committed to other beliefs (or faiths) will resist its claims and will need to see a consistent, patient demonstration of Christlike living before they are likely to believe in Him.

Second, *believing* is an act of the will—a voluntary response to evidence. For the Christian, "faith cometh by hearing, and hearing by the word of God" (Romans 10:17). John's Gospel sets forth God's Word with the purpose of persuading its readers that Jesus is indeed God's Son and the promised Messiah (John 20:31).

Next, *faith* describes a trust and commitment that is built on one's conviction of what is truth. It causes one to think, feel, and act on the basis of his belief. So Jesus insisted that those who *believe* (trust) in God will not be unduly concerned about material security (Luke 12:28), frightened by troubling circumstances (Mark 4:40), or upset by the prospect of death (John 14:1).

A fourth aspect of *faith* is better known as faithfulness, a steadfastness in doing as belief directs. We sometimes call it "keeping the faith." Jesus once told some wavering followers that they did not believe, and John adds, "Jesus knew from the beginning who they were that believed not, and who should betray him" (John 6:64). The Lord's grand assurance in Revelation 2:10 must not be neglected here: "Be thou faithful unto death, and I will give thee a crown of life." We can be sure that He will be faithful to that promise!

Our lessons for the forthcoming quarter are designed to build a steadfast *faith* in Jesus Christ as Lord. They are arranged in four units according to four different emphases. The texts, taken from thirteen of John's twenty-one chapters, begin with the first chapter of John and proceed through its contents, though not always consecutively.

Believe!

Unit 1 ("Jesus' Coming Calls for Faith") occupies the four weeks in March. Texts are taken primarily from John 1, 3, and 4.

Lesson 1 ("The Word Became Flesh") ties John's introduction (John 1:1ff) with his statement of purpose (20:30, 31). His Gospel is designed to establish the fact that Jesus, the eternal Word made flesh, is God's Son and the Messiah.

Lesson 2 ("John the Baptist Testifies of Jesus") is taken from John 1:19-34. It presents the ministry and message of the man who came preaching and baptizing to prepare the way for Jesus.

Lesson 3 ("Nicodemus Visits Jesus"), from John 3:1-17, sets forth Jesus' demand for a new birth "of water and of the Spirit." The lesson text includes the Golden Text of the Bible (John 3:16), with its grand announcement of salvation for believers in God's only begotten Son.

Lesson 4 ("A Woman Brings Her Village to Jesus"), recounts Jesus' conversation with a woman of Samaria by Jacob's well (John 4). When He identified Himself as the Messiah, the enthusiastic woman brought her neighbors to meet Jesus, and many came to believe in Him.

Believe What?

Unit 2 ("Jesus Is Raised to Life") provides lessons for the first two weeks in April (Resurrection Sunday and the week following). These lessons present the facts described in 1 Corinthians 15:1-4 as the essence of the gospel: the death, burial, and resurrection of Jesus.

Lesson 5 ("Jesus Is Crucified and Resurrected") is from John 19 and 20, including the touching account of Jesus' resurrection appearance to Mary Magdalene. Read the full account of Jesus' arrest, crucifixion, and resurrection in John 18–20.

Lesson 6 ("Jesus Appears to His Disciples"), from John 20:19-29, recounts two events a week apart from each other. Thomas, who was absent on the first occasion, was present to see the risen Christ on the second and to voice his faith. Jesus declared that those who believe in Him without having seen Him are "blessed."

Believe in Whom?

The theme of **Unit 3** ("Jesus Declares God's Message") provides lessons for two weeks in April and one in May. It describes qualities and characteristics in Jesus that demand our faith in Him as God's Son and our Lord.

Lesson 7 ("Jesus, the Bread of Life"), from John 6, depicts the feeding of more than five thousand persons with five small loaves and two fishes, and follows that with Jesus' presentation of Himself as the Bread of life eternal for all mankind.

Lesson 8 ("Truth That Sets People Free") comes from John 8:12, 21-36. It highlights teaching that Jesus gave in the heat of controversy in Jerusalem during the Feast of Tabernacles. He is the Light of the world. He is God's eternal Son. His way is the way of truth. He is God's appointed means by which mankind can be freed from slavery to falsehood, sin, and death.

Lesson 9 ("Death That Gives Life"), from John 12, presents material from Jesus' last public teaching session. He was soon to die, but that was necessary in order to provide the life that He came to give to others. Tragically, many still refused to believe in Jesus, and some who believed were afraid to admit it.

Believe and Do

Unit 4 ("Jesus Prepares His Followers") will cover the last four weeks in May. All texts for this unit come from Jesus' final evening with His disciples before His betrayal and arrest. Jesus instructed them, and through them all believers, in the kind of life that is lived by faith in Him.

Lesson 10 ("Jesus Teaches Servanthood") is taken from John 13:1-17. It tells of Jesus' object lesson on servanthood, when He washed His disciples' feet.

Lesson 11 ("Jesus, the True Vine"), from John 15:1-17, calls attention to another vivid object lesson. Just as the fruit-bearing branch of a grapevine cannot live and bear grapes unless it maintains a vital connection with the trunk, so spiritual life and usefulness are impossible without a constant, vital connection with Jesus. Love is cited as an example of Christian fruitfulness.

Lesson 12 ("The Spirit Empowers Loving Obedience") is based on texts from John 14 and 16. The Comforter, sent to be with the apostles after Jesus' departure, would remind them of all He had taught and would guide them in all truth. Such a promise assures us of the trustworthiness of the New Testament Scriptures.

Lesson 13 ("Jesus Prays for His Disciples"), from John 17, focuses on what has been called Jesus' high priestly prayer. First, He prayed to be glorified so that His Father would be glorified. Then He prayed for the apostles to be kept united in Him, strong in faith, and untainted by the world. Finally, Jesus prayed for unity among future believers so that others would also believe.

Here, then, is a series of lessons in which we draw near to the center of the apostles' (and the Holy Spirit's) purpose in giving us the Bible; the center of Jesus' purpose in coming to earth; and the center of God's purpose for all creation! What we do with these lessons will make a difference, not only to those we teach, but to God Himself! What an awesome thought!

Jesus' Ministry
in the Gospel of John

Mediterranean

Sea

GALILEE

Capernaum •

Site of
Feeding 5000

*Sea of
Galilee*

SAMARIA

▲ Mt. Ebal

• Sychar

Jordan River

PEREA

▲
Mt. Gerizim

• Arimathea

• Jericho

• Bethabara

Jerusalem ★
Bethlehem •

Dead

1

JUDEA

Sea

2

1. Three-fourths of John's Gospel tells of Jesus in Judea, with Jerusalem as its center.
2. Less than one-fourth tells of Jesus in Galilee, with Capernaum as its center.
   The remainder tells of Jesus in generally non-Jewish territory (e.g., Samaria).

John: Journey to Faith

*John does not specifically mention this as a Passover, but most agree that the "feast" mentioned in John 5:1 was the Passover.

"That Ye Might Believe"

Making Your Case in the Classroom

by Ronald G. Davis

AS A WRITER, THE APOSTLE John follows a time-honored strategy: a clear-cut theme and purpose, supported with carefully chosen example after example. His theme? "Jesus is the Christ, the Son of God!" His purpose? To convince all of that one grand truth, so that all may receive life in Him. This treatise, from John's pen and by the power of the Spirit, is a thorough and convincing argument of his central thesis. Beginning with a resounding affirmation of Jesus' preexistence and full Godness, John furnishes testimony upon testimony, miracle upon miracle, insight upon insight.

Such a writer is overwhelmed by the vastness of his material—so much so that he is led to conclude, "If I had written it all down, I suppose the whole world would not have room for the books!" And he wants his readers to know that he has carefully chosen, from a wealth of possibilities, a selective but more than adequate sampling to prove his point: Jesus is the Christ, the Son of God!

The teacher who leads in a study of the Gospel of John must share John's purpose and strategy: to convince, to convince with evidence, and to convince with overwhelming evidence. Discussion and debate can serve as the heart of the teacher's instructional plan. Students should be unequivocal in affirming: "Jesus is the Christ, the Son of God!" They should be more fully "ready . . . to give an answer to every man that asketh . . . a reason of the hope" they possess in Jesus "with meekness and fear" (1 Peter 3:15).

Determining who a person is can be achieved by posing three questions: (1) What do others say about him? (2) What does he say about himself? and (3) What do his deeds say about him? John uses all three of these lines of testimony in his Gospel, and this series of studies does as well. Consider three lessons from the upcoming quarter, each emphasizing one of these three questions, and consider how you as a teacher can "argue your case" that Jesus is the Christ, the Son of God.

What Others Say

Lesson 2 examines the text that immediately follows John's grand opening statement declaring Jesus to be the Word, who "was made flesh, and dwelt among us" (John 1:14). It highlights

John the Baptist's testimony to who Jesus is. In a court of law, a witness's testimony is both heard and evaluated. For any lesson dealing with someone's personal testimony (see also Lessons 3, 4, 5, and 6), the following learning activity could be used effectively.

Recruit three class members to play these "courtroom" roles: prosecutor, defense attorney, and John the Baptist (or the "witness" in the specific lesson chosen). The prosecutor is playing the role of one of the "priests and Levites from Jerusalem" who came to interrogate John (John 1:19). The defense attorney is speaking on behalf of God. Establish a courtroom scene before your class, and tell the class members that they are to serve as the jury.

If your "actors" are willing and able, let them write their own questions. But if not, prepare and assign a few. For example, for the prosecutor: "John, tell this court exactly who you are." "Who do you claim Jesus to be?" "Don't you have some personal doubts about who He is?" "Who gave you authority to preach?" "Where did you get your training—if any—in the law and its interpretation?" "Why should we believe your word above that of those specially trained in religious matters?" "John, wouldn't you characterize your lifestyle as just a bit . . . well . . . eccentric?" "Don't you claim to hear voices—such as that of God—on a regular basis?"

For the defense attorney, suggest such questions as these: "How would you characterize your parents?" "Tell the court about the strange nature of your birth, John." "What was your father told about you before your conception?" "Are some still alive who can testify of seeing your awestruck and mute father when he came out of the temple? What of those who were present when his voice returned?" "Are you doing all of this preaching simply to draw attention and fame to yourself?" Your "John" may want to examine these references to prepare himself: Luke 1:5-23, 57-80; Matthew 3:1-17; Mark 1:1-11; Luke 3:1-22; John 1:19-27; 3:25-30.

After the question and answer period, charge the "jury" to decide whether John the Baptist is a credible witness. Ask them to explain why they accept his testimony.

You may choose to study one of the other "personal testimony" lessons in a similar manner. Imagine how the Samaritan woman could impress a courtroom! Picture Nicodemus or Thomas on the stand! The witnesses speak. Let them speak!

What He Says of Himself

One is always justified—even compelled—to determine who a person is by examining what he says of himself or what he claims himself to be. Jesus' claims are astounding; if they are true, they cannot be ignored.

When you come to Lesson 7, where Jesus claims to be "the bread of life" (John 6:35), you will have a good opportunity with your students to analyze Jesus' claims and decide why believing in Him is both reasonable and essential.

Divide your class into groups of four or five and give each group the following list of texts from John. In each, Jesus affirms who He is: 4:25, 26; 6:35, 38; 8:58; 10:9, 30; 11:25, 26; 14:6, 9; 17:5. Ask each group to survey the texts, list the affirmations, and then arrange them in order of magnitude or significance. Assure students that this is not intended to lessen any of the truths; it is simply a way to consider the impact of each claim. Have the groups share and defend their choices.

Such a procedure could also be used with Lesson 11, where Jesus characterizes Himself as "the true vine" (John 15:1), or in Lesson 4, where He avows, "Whosoever drinketh of the water that I shall give him shall never thirst; . . . [it] shall be in him a well of water springing up into everlasting life" (John 4:14).

Some skeptics, wanting to discredit Jesus at every opportunity, have said Jesus never claimed to be deity. Help your class members to see the above passages from John as obvious and irrefutable evidence to the contrary. Jesus clearly claimed to be fully God. Are those who question this willing to give the evidence a fair hearing?

What His Deeds Say

A tree is known by its fruit. Seeing what fruit issues from a life is the best confirmation of the character and quality of that life. Words without deeds are inadequate. Thus, to say finally and conclusively that Jesus is the Christ, the Son of the living God, necessitates an examination of His deeds. Do His deeds reveal divine character? Do His deeds demonstrate divine power?

The studies in this quarter offer proof to substantiate both answers in the affirmative. Jesus does personify the character and the power of God. Full insight into new acquaintances such as Nicodemus and the Samaritan woman reveal His omniscience. Feeding a multitude with a small amount of food demonstrates His power to supersede the "laws of nature." Jesus can do this because He is God—He wrote the "laws"!

Lessons 5 and 6 declare the crowning truths of these studies: Jesus is Savior, giving His life on the cross to redeem mankind in love and grace; and Jesus is Lord, conquering death by His resurrection. Consider handing each class member an index card as he or she enters one of these two sessions. Use equal numbers of *believer* and *doubter* cards. At some point in the lesson, have the class form pairs, with a believer and a doubter in each pair. The believer should ask the doubter, "How could you doubt?" and the doubter should ask the believer, "How could you believe?" Point out that some of the early followers of Jesus accepted news of His resurrection with ease and confidence (for example, Mary Magdalene in John 20:18), while others were much more resistant (the classic example is Thomas in John 20:24, 25). As your students identify before the class what they believe are the most cogent reasons for each position, ask them, "In what ways are these first-century reasons demonstrated in the lives of people today?"

Reaching Conclusions

Every court case comes to an end. The person indicted must be freed or punished; he must be declared innocent or guilty. Either Jesus is the Christ, the Son of the living God, or He is not. What does the evidence show? What conclusion will your students reach? Of what truths will they be able to convince others? These are the primary issues—in any Bible study.

The Word Became Flesh

DEVOTIONAL READING: 1 John 4:1-6.

LESSON SCRIPTURE: John 1:1-18; 20:30, 31.

PRINTED TEXT: John 1:1-18; 20:30, 31.

John 1:1-18

1 In the beginning was the Word, and the Word was with God, and the Word was God.

2 The same was in the beginning with God.

3 All things were made by him; and without him was not any thing made that was made.

4 In him was life; and the life was the light of men.

5 And the light shineth in darkness; and the darkness comprehended it not.

6 There was a man sent from God, whose name was John.

7 The same came for a witness, to bear witness of the Light, that all men through him might believe.

8 He was not that Light, but was sent to bear witness of that Light.

9 That was the true Light, which lighteth every man that cometh into the world.

10 He was in the world, and the world was made by him, and the world knew him not.

11 He came unto his own, and his own received him not.

12 But as many as received him, to them gave he power to become the sons of God, even to them that believe on his name:

13 Which were born, not of blood, nor of the will of the flesh, nor of the will of man, but of God.

14 And the Word was made flesh, and dwelt among us, (and we beheld his glory, the glory as of the only begotten of the Father,) full of grace and truth.

15 John bare witness of him, and cried, saying, This was he of whom I spake, He that cometh after me is preferred before me; for he was before me.

16 And of his fulness have all we received, and grace for grace.

17 For the law was given by Moses, but grace and truth came by Jesus Christ.

18 No man hath seen God at any time; the only begotten Son, which is in the bosom of the Father, he hath declared him.

John 20:30, 31

30 And many other signs truly did Jesus in the presence of his disciples, which are not written in this book:

31 But these are written, that ye might believe that Jesus is the Christ, the Son of God; and that believing ye might have life through his name.

GOLDEN TEXT: The Word was made flesh, and dwelt among us, (and we beheld his glory, the glory as of the only begotten of the Father,) full of grace and truth.—John 1:14.

Lesson Aims

After this lesson a student should be able to:

1. State the identity and mission of Jesus as the incarnate Word.

2. Compare Jesus' mission with John's purpose for writing his Gospel.

3. Express a commitment to living in harmony with Jesus' identity and mission.

Lesson Outline

INTRODUCTION
   A. "Show Me"
   B. Lesson Background
 I. THE ETERNAL WORD (John 1:1-5)
   A. The Word and God (vv. 1, 2)
     What Does This Word Mean?
   B. The Word and Creation (v. 3)
   C. Light in the Darkness (vv. 4, 5)
 II. THE FAITHFUL WITNESS (John 1:6-13)
   A. God's Man for the Work (vv. 6-8)
   B. God's Light for the World (v. 9)
   C. The Light Rejected (vv. 10, 11)
   D. The Light Received (vv. 12, 13)
III. THE WORD MADE FLESH (John 1:14-18)
   A. "Full of Grace and Truth" (vv. 14-16)
   B. Superior to Law (vv. 17, 18)
IV. JOHN'S PURPOSE FOR WRITING (John 20:30, 31)
CONCLUSION
   A. Convincing Demonstration
   B. Prayer
   C. Thought to Remember

Introduction

A. "Show Me"

A man in our town liked to tell why he was an atheist. He recalled walking one day through a wooded area when his mind turned to thoughts of God. "Is there really a God?" he wondered. He sat down on a convenient log to ponder the question and considered how he could settle the matter once and for all. He decided to ask God (if indeed there were a God) to show Himself in some convincing demonstration, now!

Nothing happened. The man was left among the trees with no recognizable voice or vision. So he got up and went on, a confirmed atheist. God had failed to provide the proof the man ordered.

From earliest times men have wanted to see God or witness special proofs of His existence. The Pharisees pestered Jesus with demands for miraculous signs (Matthew 12:38, 39; 16:1-4). Near the close of His earthly ministry, even one of Jesus' own disciples pleaded, "Show us the Father" (John 14:8).

That, however, was exactly what Jesus had been doing throughout His earthly ministry. It may not have been the kind of revelation of God that people were looking for, but it was an infinitely better demonstration than they could have imagined. Today's lesson deals with this subject of how "the Word became flesh."

B. Lesson Background

Today's printed text includes portions of both the introduction and the conclusion to the fourth Gospel. The writer does not identify himself by name. However, by comparing material in this Gospel with that in the other three, we conclude that the writer was the apostle John, son of the fisherman Zebedee (Matthew 4:21). This "disciple whom Jesus loved" (John 13:23; 19:26; 20:2; 21:7, 20), along with his brother James, were among the Lord's first disciples. It is generally assumed that John was directed to Jesus by John the Baptist, whom he and Andrew had followed earlier (John 1:35-40).

Jesus nicknamed James and John "sons of thunder" (*Boanerges*) from their highly temperamental personalities (Mark 3:17; 9:38-41; Luke 9:49-55). Nevertheless, John was so completely transformed by his acquaintance with Jesus that he came to be known as the apostle of love—a theme that permeates his writings, particularly his three epistles. Along with Simon Peter (another temperamental fisherman!), the sons of Zebedee became Jesus' closest followers, sharing with Him significant experiences not shared by the other disciples (Mark 5:37; 9:2; 14:33). John seems to have done his writing—his Gospel, his three brief epistles, and the book of Revelation—later in a long life. Most students date these writings toward the end of the first century.

John's Gospel is different from the other three in several respects. It says nothing of Jesus' birth or early life; it tells more of His ministry in Judea and less of His work in Galilee; it focuses on Jesus' discourses rather than His parables; it includes more of Jesus' one-on-one encounters; and it highlights strong contrasts—life and death, light and darkness, spirit and flesh, truth and falsehood, love and hate. John's prologue, the text for today's lesson, is also unique. Nothing in the other Gospels (or elsewhere in Scripture) compares with the description of God's revelation of Himself found in these verses.

I. The Eternal Word
(John 1:1-5)

A. The Word and God (vv. 1, 2)

1, 2. In the beginning was the Word, and the Word was with God, and the Word was God. The same was in the beginning with God.

The beginning echoes the thought of Genesis 1:1. God has always been. He is without beginning, without end, and without change. Many in the scientific world can see nothing before time except more time. John declares plainly what they cannot even imagine: God's *Word*, who was Jesus (v. 14), is before and beyond all of it!

The term *word* was important in Hebrew thought as God's vehicle of creation. He spoke, and things came into being (Psalm 33:6). *Word* also designated His command; the term "Ten Commandments" is literally, in the Hebrew text, "ten words." Prophets often introduced God's messages with "Hear the word of the Lord."

To first-century Greeks the term *logos*, which is the Greek term rendered *word*, signified thought and reason, as well as a unit of speech or writing. It is difficult to determine whether John had a specific idea in mind by his use of this concept. Perhaps he simply chose a term that people had been using for years and declared its true meaning and fulfillment in Jesus.

The Word was with God. The Word was God's companion before anything else existed. A distinct being is recognized, as Genesis 1:26 indicates: "Let *us* make man in *our* image." The Word was with God—not only in His presence but with Him in the sense of agreeing with all His purposes and doings. Jesus speaks of "the glory which I had with thee before the world was" (John 17:5).

The Word was God. Scripture consistently affirms the deity of Him who came to earth as Jesus of Nazareth (John 20:28; Acts 20:28; Romans 9:5; Colossians 2:9; Hebrews 1:1-4). [See question #1, page 240.]

WHAT DOES THIS WORD MEAN?

In the marvelous opening phrases of his record of the "good news" of Jesus, the apostle John uses the word *logos*—a word of profound significance to the Greeks. Several words reflected the Greek view of the universe. For example, *chaos* was believed to be the primary and original state of the universe. *Logos* was the divine principle that imposed order and arrangement upon this wild confusion.

The concept of the *logos* as that which organizes and systematizes reality is seen in the large number of our English words by which we characterize various disciplines of knowledge.

We speak of psycho*logy*, bio*logy*, ornitho*logy*, archaeo*logy*, etc. All these words contain the element of *logos* to describe an ordered, systematized study of some area of our universe.

John defines the *logos*, not as a concept, but as a person. He declares that the *logos* "was made flesh, and dwelt among us" (John 1:14). Genesis tells us that the original creation was "without form, and void" until God spoke (Genesis 1:2). It was His *Word* that brought order out of chaos. Jesus is the divine *Word*, who brought order not only in the beginning, but brings it to all human chaos now.   —J. G. V. B.

B. The Word and Creation (v. 3)

3. All things were made by him; and without him was not any thing made that was made.

Some philosophers in John's day thought matter was evil; they did not believe a righteous God could have created anything material. John insists that *all things*, including material items, were brought into being by the Word of God and are to be used with thanksgiving to His glory. As the agent of creation, the eternal Word brought into orderly existence the world and all that is in it (Colossians 1:16, 17; Hebrews 1:2). Our universe with its design and order is no accident!

C. Light in the Darkness (vv. 4, 5)

4. In him was life; and the life was the light of men.

Life and *light* are terms used often and meaningfully by the apostle John—more than by any other writer of Scripture. The living Word of God is the source of the human life that was breathed into Adam, so that he became a living soul (Genesis 2:7). Eternity is part of the life that God intended for mankind, and Jesus came to make such eternal life possible.

Light was the first item spoken into existence (Genesis 1:3). This light was intended to benefit mankind by dispelling darkness. There is also a moral light of goodness and purity dispelling the kind of darkness that is loved by wicked men because their deeds are evil (John 3:19). Only in Jesus, however, is there "the light of the knowledge of the glory of God" (2 Corinthians 4:6).

How to Say It

BOANERGES. Boe-uh-*nur*-geez.
GABRIEL. *Gay*-bree-ul.
LOGOS (Greek). *law*-goss.
PHARISEES. *Fair*-ih-seez.
ZEBEDEE. *Zeb*-uh-dee.
ZECHARIAH. Zek-uh-*rye*-uh.

5. And the light shineth in darkness; and the darkness comprehended it not.

The deeper the *darkness*, the brighter a light will shine (even the small light of a candle will seem bright in the deep darkness of a cave). The light of Christ continues to shine amidst the moral and spiritual darkness of our times, just as it did in the darkness of first-century paganism. If His light is not dispelling the darkness around it, it is because its handlers have kept it hidden!

Two meanings may be found in the phrase *comprehended it not*. Both are captured in the translation "apprehended" (*American Standard Version*), which can describe either a physical or a mental activity. The darkness has never been able to overcome or understand the light of Jesus. That light will lead men to salvation as long as there are men to lead, despite the failures of its followers and the attacks of its foes.

II. The Faithful Witness
(John 1:6-13)

A. God's Man for the Work (vv. 6-8)

6. There was a man sent from God, whose name was John.

Having introduced the Word as eternal with God, and having touched on the impact of the Word's earthly ministry, John calls attention to the messenger who prepared men to receive the Word. That was another *man* named *John*, son of a priest named Zechariah and his wife Elisabeth. The angel Gabriel had appeared to Zechariah, assigning the name *John* to the child not yet conceived and describing his ministry (Luke 1:8-17). John the Baptist was thus indeed *sent from God*, and he lived up to his appointed mission. Jesus once described him as "a prophet . . . and more than a prophet." He declared, "Among them that are born of women there hath not risen a greater than John the Baptist" (Matthew 11:7-11).

7, 8. The same came for a witness, to bear witness of the Light, that all men through him might believe. He was not that Light, but was sent to bear witness of that Light.

John the Baptist's primary purpose was "to make ready a people prepared for the Lord" (Luke 1:17). In doing so he preached and prac-

ticed the baptism of repentance and remission of sins (Luke 3:3). His hearers were told to *believe* in Jesus *through* John the Baptist's testimony. When asked to identify himself and explain his mission, John answered with a firm negative: "I am not the Christ" (John 1:20).

B. God's Light for the World (v. 9)

9. That was the true Light, which lighteth every man that cometh into the world.

Jesus said of John the Baptist, "He was a burning and a shining light: and ye were willing for a season to rejoice in his light" (John 5:35). Jesus, however, is the *true Light*, whose influence is worldwide. *World* is another of John the apostle's powerfully inclusive words. It can designate the universe, the earth, the people on the earth, most people, or the human system opposed to God's purposes. Here it signifies the population of the earth, including all those multitudes yet to be born into the world. The Light of life had come to save all by giving His life for "the sins of the whole world" (1 John 2:2). [See question #2, page 240.]

C. The Light Rejected (vv. 10, 11)

10, 11. He was in the world, and the world was made by him, and the world knew him not. He came unto his own, and his own received him not.

In spite of the fact that the *world* had come into being through Jesus, He was not recognized when He came to it. "No room . . . in the inn" (Luke 2:7) describes how Jesus was treated not only as a baby, but throughout His life. For the most part, *his own* people (the Jews) did not acknowledge Him—a fact Pilate noted when Jesus stood before him (John 18:35).

What about us? Do our words and works always recognize Jesus for who He really is? Or have we treated Him as if He were a stranger? [See question #3, page 240.]

D. The Light Received (vv. 12, 13)

12, 13. But as many as received him, to them gave he power to become the sons of God, even to them that believe on his name: which were born, not of blood, nor of the will of the flesh, nor of the will of man, but of God.

John the Baptist was among the first and most influential of those who gladly welcomed Jesus as "the Lamb of God, which taketh away the sin of the world" (John 1:29). Those who follow in doing so receive the privilege of becoming what no one can become in any other way—members of God's family. Until then, although they are creatures of God and beloved by God, they are not His children.

VISUALS FOR THESE LESSONS

The *Adult Visuals* packet contains classroom-size visuals designed for use with the lessons in the Spring Quarter. The packet is available from your supplier. Order No. 392.

To *believe on* the *name* of Jesus is to recognize and confess by word and deed the sonship, saviorhood, and lordship implied in His name. "There is none other name under heaven given among men, whereby we must be saved" (Acts 4:12). Full commitment to Him brings much to celebrate: "Behold, what manner of love the Father hath bestowed upon us, that we should be called the sons of God" (1 John 3:1).

This family relationship comes through a process parallel to, but very different from, the birth that makes us members of human families. That birth is physical and takes place in accordance with the willing participation of the parents. The new birth from above (John 3:3-6) is spiritual and is the product of the work of God through His Word (1 Peter 1:23).

III. The Word Made Flesh (John 1:14-18)

A. "Full of Grace and Truth" (vv. 14-16)

14. And the Word was made flesh, and dwelt among us, (and we beheld his glory, the glory as of the only begotten of the Father,) full of grace and truth.

Here is one of Scripture's most definitive statements of the incarnation: *the Word was made flesh.* (See also Philippians 2:5-8.) He *dwelt among us* (literally, "pitched His tent among us"). Jesus' stay on earth was temporary, as though in a tent instead of a permanent dwelling.

John includes himself as one who *beheld his glory.* Along with Peter and James, John saw certain incidents that the others did not, such as Jesus' transfiguration (Matthew 17:1-8). With the other disciples, John saw the risen Lord ascend to Heaven (Luke 24:51; Acts 1:9-11).

Jesus demonstrated a perfect balance of tender mercy and moral perfection (*full of grace and truth*). Since He who dwelt for a time *among* us now dwells within us (Colossians 1:27), we must demonstrate a similar balance in our daily conduct and our dealings with others. Paul introduced his passage about the incarnation by saying, "Let this mind be in you, which was also in Christ Jesus" (Philippians 2:5). It's a big order, but eternally worth working on!

15. John bare witness of him, and cried, saying, This was he of whom I spake, He that cometh after me is preferred before me; for he was before me.

Again John the apostle calls attention to the *witness* of *John* the Baptist, who was assured when he baptized Jesus (by a voice from Heaven and a dove) that this was God's beloved Son (Matthew 3:16, 17; John 1:32-34). The first two verbs in this verse are properly in the present

Visual for lesson 1

The visual for this lesson illustrates verse 14. Display it as you begin to discuss section III (The Word Made Flesh).

tense: "bears witness" and "cries out." John the Baptist's testimony was not meant to be a one-time event; it still speaks to all who will listen.

Jesus is the eternal Word, infinitely greater than the great man who introduced Him. John the Baptist was six months older than Jesus in the flesh (Luke 1:24-31), but he knew that the Word was *before* either of them was born (see John 1:30).

16. And of his fulness have all we received, and grace for grace.

Here the apostle speaks for himself and countless other followers of the Lord. All have gained measureless blessings from humble acceptance of Jesus' overflowing goodness and mercy. That has been a continual source of blessings, one after another, to every Christian. Some versions render the final phrase of this verse in a way that emphasizes the ceaseless nature of Jesus' provisions. The *New International Version* reads, "From the fullness of his grace we have all received one blessing after another." [See question #4, page 240.]

B. Superior to Law (vv. 17, 18)

17. For the law was given by Moses, but grace and truth came by Jesus Christ.

This continues the subject of *grace and truth* that was begun in verse 14. John is not downplaying *Moses* or *the law* that was given through him; however, Jesus is the divine means by which God conveys what was impossible through the law. The law provided God's directives and indicated the consequences of following or disobeying them. Jesus provides the example of perfect obedience, the means of cleansing and forgiveness for the transgressor, and the power to live a daily life of godliness.

18. No man hath seen God at any time; the only begotten Son, which is in the bosom of the Father, he hath declared him.

Exodus 33:20 records God's statement to Moses: "There shall no man see me, and live." It is impossible for the mortal to comprehend that which is eternally divine. But as there is one God, there is also "one mediator between God and men, the man Christ Jesus" (1 Timothy 2:5). He is (literally) *the only begotten Son*—the divine Son of God who entered the world by birth, interrupting an eternity of being in the very presence of God. Thus He could describe and demonstrate the Father, and declare, "He that hath seen me hath seen the Father" (John 14:9; see also Colossians 1:14, 15; 1 Timothy 6:14-16; Hebrews 1:1-4).

IV. John's Purpose for Writing (John 20:30, 31)

We come now to a summary statement of the apostle's pattern and purpose for writing his Gospel. He has just told of Jesus' meeting with His disciples a week after His resurrection. Thomas, absent from an earlier and similar meeting, was firmly convinced by seeing for himself the proofs of the resurrection. In reverent faith he declared, "My Lord and my God" (John 20:26-29).

30. And many other signs truly did Jesus in the presence of his disciples, which are not written in this book.

Present with Thomas on this occasion were the other *disciples*, chosen to observe and bear witness to this and other "infallible proofs" (Acts 1:3) of Jesus' deity. John's *book* includes other *signs* observed by the disciples, with others also present on most occasions. *Many other* similar pieces of evidence could have been set forth, but what is included is sufficient for the sincere seeker after truth.

31. But these are written, that ye might believe that Jesus is the Christ, the Son of God;

Home Daily Bible Readings

Monday, Mar. 1—In the Beginning Was the Word (John 1:1-5)
Tuesday, Mar. 2—The Witness of John the Baptizer (John 1:6-9)
Wednesday, Mar. 3—John Baptizes Jesus (Mark 1:1-11)
Thursday, Mar. 4—To All Who Received Him (John 1:10-13)
Friday, Mar 5—Believe on the Lord Jesus (Acts 16:25-34)
Saturday, Mar. 6—The Word Became Flesh and Lived Among Us (John 1:14-18)
Sunday, Mar. 7—Before the Foundation of the World (Ephesians 1:3-14)

and that believing ye might have life through his name.

John's purpose in writing is clear. *Ye* are the readers of his Gospel. Not having seen the risen Christ, they must come to *believe* through the word of those who have seen. Their faith will be especially blessed (John 20:29).

What are they to believe? Faith must have an object, and in this case the object is *Jesus* (John 3:16). But notice also that one must believe a specific truth about Jesus: that He is *the Christ, the Son of God,* as Peter confessed earlier (Matthew 16:16) and converts were to confess later (Acts 8:37). In other words, faith must have content. One who possesses such faith must then accept the truth about Jesus and make a commitment of his life to Him. *Believing* in this manner brings to the believer new *life* (Romans 6:1-11)—life that continues beyond the grave.

Let us never forget that the purpose of every gospel presentation is to lead another person from death to life. [See question #5, page 240.]

Conclusion

A. Convincing Demonstration

The apostle John has said that the eternal Word became flesh in the person of Jesus. The life of Jesus provided a convincing demonstration that this was so. John has also declared that he wrote his Gospel in order that you, the reader, might believe and find life in Christ. A reading of the Gospel will provide a convincing demonstration that this also is true. But how well do *you* know that demonstration? Have you read the Gospel of John lately? The next few weeks will provide an excellent opportunity to study selected passages from John. Why not go a step further and read his account completely and repeatedly for yourself during this quarter? Give John a chance to demonstrate the worth of his writing. Each journey through John will take no longer than sitting through an ordinary baseball game. Let John demonstrate his purpose for writing to *you*!

B. Prayer

You have given us more than we can imagine, dear God, in sending Your Son as Your Word and Your way to life eternal. May our thanks include an eager acceptance of Your gift, and a joyous sharing of it with others. In Jesus' name. Amen.

C. Thought to Remember

"These are written, that ye might believe that Jesus is the Christ, the Son of God; and that believing ye might have life through his name" (John 20:31).

Learning by Doing

This page contains an alternate lesson plan emphasizing learning activities.
Classes desiring such student involvement will find these suggestions helpful.

Learning Goals

After this lesson students should be able to:

1. State the identity and mission of Jesus as the incarnate Word.

2. Compare Jesus' mission with John's purpose for writing his Gospel.

3. Express a commitment to living in harmony with Jesus' identity and mission.

Into the Lesson

Review briefly the theme of the new quarter: that we may believe that Jesus is Lord. Mention the four units that are included, especially the second one—the death, burial, and resurrection of Jesus, which comprise the essence of the gospel (cf. 1 Corinthians 15:1-4). The other three units explore Jesus' call to faith, His declaration of God's message, and His concern for His followers as His death drew near.

Distribute index cards or small slips of paper, each with one of the following expressions written on it: "I give you my *word*." "The *word* on the street." "I need a *word* with you." "Wait until I give the *word*." "He is a man of his *word*." "That's the final *word* on the subject." "Put in a good *word* for me." "Send us *word* when you arrive." If you have a large class, ask people with the same expressions to get together and discuss the significance of the word *word* in their expressions; then discuss them together as a class. If your class is smaller, have individuals read their expressions and tell what is significant about *word* in each one. Discuss the expressions together.

Next, do a similar activity based on the word *light*. Use expressions like the following: "Significant facts were brought to *light*." "I saw the *light*!" "This will shed some *light* on the situation." "She is the *light* of his life!" "He saw things in a different *light* today." "In *light* of the circumstances." "Turn on the *light*."

Note that these terms are important to understanding Jesus' identity and mission. We'll see how in today's lesson.

Into the Word

Ask, "What is needed for us to have faith in something or someone?" As the class discusses this question, the idea should emerge that faith requires knowledge; it cannot be groundless or completely emotional. Then have someone read John 20:30, 31. Observe that John recognized the

need for a solid foundation of evidence for faith to develop. He attempts to provide that foundation in his Gospel. Take a minute or two to explain how the Gospel of John differs from others. (See the introductory material on pages 234 and 235.)

Ask a volunteer to read John 1:1-18. Discuss, "Why is Jesus called the 'Word'?" Prompt the discussion by having students read Psalm 33:6; Isaiah 55:11; 1 John 1:1; Revelation 19:13. Observe that John identifies Jesus as eternal, one with God and yet distinct in personality, the Creator of all things, the One who leads us to the Father, and the One who became like us in order to do that but was not recognized by the world.

Discuss also the *work* of the "Word." Compare the concept here with the different expressions using the term *word* that you discussed earlier. Note how Jesus' role as the "Word" suggests that He is God's ultimate revelation (cf. Hebrews 1). He brings a message from God, but He is more than a mere messenger. He Himself is the Word.

Note that Jesus is also described as the "Light," the "true Light." Discuss the significance of Jesus as light. Again, use ideas from the introductory activity to help. Ask volunteers to read the following Bible verses and explain what they mean regarding Jesus: Psalm 119:105; Proverbs 4:18; Isaiah 9:2; 1 Corinthians 4:5.

Into Life

Recall again John's purpose for writing (John 20:30, 31). Ask, "In view of John's purpose, what is significant about where John starts with his Gospel?" As you discuss, note the importance of identifying Jesus' identity and mission as the incarnate Word in order to give substance to the readers' faith. Our faith is not merely in a great teacher or good moral example, but in the eternal God who took on human flesh to save us!

Ask, "How does Jesus' identity and mission make a difference in your own life?" Encourage believers to make a statement of their own faith in Jesus and their own involvement in ministry in His behalf. If there are non-Christians in your class, challenge them to consider seriously the faith messages of John over the next twelve weeks of your study together. His purpose is as valid at the close of the twentieth century as it was in the first!

Let's Talk It Over

The questions on this page are designed to encourage review of the lesson Scriptures and to promote discussion of the lesson by the class. The answers provided are only discussion starters. Let your class talk it over from there.

1. Some people will admit that Jesus was a tremendous teacher or a bold crusader for social reform or a compassionate humanitarian, but they balk at the idea of His being the Son of God. John leaves no room for such unbelief. At the outset he makes the reader aware that the human Jesus he is about to describe was present "In the beginning"—at creation and even before. How could you use this text to help someone who believes Jesus was merely a great teacher to come to faith in Him as the Son of God?

If such a one is willing to accept the Bible's record as true, then a simple reading of John's Gospel, without any presuppositions or predetermined conclusions, should be effective. It is exactly for the purpose of producing such faith that John wrote (John 20:30, 31). If the person does not accept the Bible, then from where did he or she get the idea that Jesus was a good teacher? Evidence of the trustworthiness of the Bible, along with the evidence of what the Lord has done for you, may help you to convince your friend that John's affirmation about Jesus is true.

2. When John calls Jesus the "true Light," he suggests there were other so-called lights in the world, claiming to provide enlightenment but failing. The same is true today. What are some of the false lights in our world, and how can we shine the true light in such a way as to expose them as mere darkness?

Your class should be able to suggest several. We might immediately think of competing religious systems (New Age, humanism, cults) as false lights. But there are others. Some people believe enlightenment will come through education, and others look to politics. Always there have been people who believed wealth could buy anything, including enlightenment.

Are there false lights in the church? It is possible to focus on the mechanics of "doing church" and find ourselves looking for light in our methods instead of in the message: "Jesus Christ, and him crucified" (1 Corinthians 2:2).

3. John notes that even Jesus' own people did not receive Him. In what ways may Christians sometimes be guilty of treating Jesus "as if He were a stranger"? How can we guard from doing so?

Jesus' own people, particularly their leaders, refused to accept Jesus because He did not fit their idea of a Messiah, or because they feared they would lose their own power, or because they "loved the praise of men more than the praise of God" (John 12:43). Seeking acceptance from our peers, we may sometimes keep silent about our faith. Confronted with Biblical teaching that challenges our opinions or behavior, we may cling to our own way of thinking instead of making the proper adjustments. More than additional teaching is probably needed to change such behavior. We need to spend more time in prayer and to make ourselves accountable to another believer who can help us to follow the Lord more closely.

4. John says we have received "grace for grace"—or "one blessing after another" (*New International Version*). What are some of the blessings you have received as a follower of Jesus? How can you use these blessings to testify of Jesus?

Of all the blessings your students will mention, surely the gift of salvation will be one of the first mentioned. Consider also the church, the Bible, and one's family. Some may be able to tell of answered prayer in regard to recovery from an illness or rescue from harm. Help the students to see that all of these can be used to testify of the grace of God and lead our unbelieving neighbors to faith.

5. John's purpose for writing his Gospel was to lead his readers to faith in Jesus Christ. How does his Gospel help your faith? How can you use it to lead others to faith?

John frequently mentions that, as a result of Jesus' actions, someone believed in Him. (See page 230 for several examples.) These same events can produce faith in our own hearts.

John's Gospel, though it is "the old, old story," is quite current. Demographers tell us that the new generation responds best to stories and pictures. John has both. He tells the story of Jesus' life as well as stories Jesus told. He also includes vivid word pictures: "I am the bread of life"; "I am the door"; "I am the good shepherd." John's Gospel will communicate well if we combine it with sincerity and honesty in our own lives.

John the Baptist Testifies of Jesus

DEVOTIONAL READING: Ephesians 4:25—5:2.

LESSON SCRIPTURE: John 1:19-42.

PRINTED TEXT: John 1:19-34.

John 1:19-34

19 And this is the record of John, when the Jews sent priests and Levites from Jerusalem to ask him, Who art thou?

20 And he confessed, and denied not; but confessed, I am not the Christ.

21 And they asked him, What then? Art thou Elijah? And he saith, I am not. Art thou that Prophet? And he answered, No.

22 Then said they unto him, Who art thou? that we may give an answer to them that sent us. What sayest thou of thyself?

23 He said, I am the voice of one crying in the wilderness, Make straight the way of the Lord, as said the prophet Isaiah.

24 And they which were sent were of the Pharisees.

25 And they asked him, and said unto him, Why baptizest thou then, if thou be not that Christ, nor Elijah, neither that Prophet?

26 John answered them, saying, I baptize with water: but there standeth one among you, whom ye know not;

27 He it is, who coming after me is preferred before me, whose shoelatchet I am not worthy to unloose.

28 These things were done in Bethabara beyond Jordan, where John was baptizing.

29 The next day John seeth Jesus coming unto him, and saith, Behold the Lamb of God, which taketh away the sin of the world!

30 This is he of whom I said, After me cometh a man which is preferred before me; for he was before me.

31 And I knew him not: but that he should be made manifest to Israel, therefore am I come baptizing with water.

32 And John bare record, saying, I saw the Spirit descending from heaven like a dove, and it abode upon him.

33 And I knew him not: but he that sent me to baptize with water, the same said unto me, Upon whom thou shalt see the Spirit descending, and remaining on him, the same is he which baptizeth with the Holy Ghost.

34 And I saw, and bare record that this is the Son of God.

GOLDEN TEXT: The next day John seeth Jesus coming unto him, and saith, Behold the Lamb of God, which taketh away the sin of the world!—John 1:29.

That You May Believe

Unit 1: Jesus' Coming Calls for Faith

(Lessons 1-4)

Lesson Aims

After this lesson students should be able to:

1. Identify and explain the mission of John the Baptist.

2. Compare John's mission with that of Christians today.

3. Determine one way to be a better witness of Christ and seek to implement it in the coming week.

Lesson Outline

INTRODUCTION

    A. Who Are You, Anyway?

    B. Lesson Background

  I. JOHN THE ANNOUNCER (John 1:19-23)

    A. Identification Demanded (v. 19)

    B. Messiahship Denied (vv. 20-22)

    C. Purpose Declared (v. 23)

      A Voice in the Wilderness

 II. JOHN THE BAPTIZER (John 1:24-28)

    A. Pharisees' Question (vv. 24, 25)

    B. Pointing to Jesus (vv. 26, 27)

      Bearing Witness

    C. Placing the Event (v. 28)

III. JOHN THE WITNESS (John 1:29-34)

    A. "Here He Is!" (vv. 29, 30)

    B. "He Is Why I Baptize" (v. 31)

    C. "This Is How I Know Him" (vv. 32, 33)

    D. "Now I Tell You" (v. 34)

CONCLUSION

    A. What About Tomorrow?

    B. Prayer

    C. Thought to Remember

Introduction

A. Who Are You, Anyway?

An amusing television commercial showed a young man chatting with his mother in his place of work. After a brief time she mentioned some business she had come to transact. "Do you have any identification?" he demanded. The rules required documentary proof that she was who she claimed to be, and not even her son could allow her to conduct her business without it!

This raises a more complicated question that disturbs many insecure persons: Who are you, anyway? The answer may take any of several forms, depending on the viewpoint of the questioner. It was even asked of Jesus. Neighbors identified Him by family as son of Joseph and Mary, or by occupation as a carpenter. Judeans identified Him by residence as a Nazarene or Galilean. He became widely known as teacher, prophet, healer, and friend of tax collectors and other disreputable people. None of these labels, however, came close to His true identity as Messiah, Son of God, and Savior of mankind.

How, then, is any of us to be identified concerning his or her innermost character, purpose, and program in life? How, indeed, except in relation to Him who makes life meaningful and eternal? *Christian* or *non-Christian* is the real "ID."

John the Baptist was way ahead of us in choosing that focus for his own identity (though *Christian* would not be used for some time yet). He possessed an unshakable conviction that his calling in life was to glorify Jesus and point others to Him.

B. Lesson Background

Matthew 3:1—4:11; Mark 1:1-13; and Luke 3:1-22; 4:1-13 lay important foundations for today's lesson. They recount the ministry of John the Baptist as he preached to multitudes and baptized many who came to the wilderness along the Jordan River to hear him. Some even speculated that John could be the Messiah (Luke 3:15). Matthew, Mark, and Luke detail John's demand for repentance and the practical application of godliness. They tell how Jesus came from Galilee to be baptized by John, who hesitated at first but finally yielded. They report that when Jesus was baptized, the Holy Spirit in the form of a dove came down upon Him and a voice from Heaven acknowledged Jesus as God's beloved Son. Then Jesus retired into the wilderness for forty days of fasting and temptation, ending with victory over the tempter.

Today's text from John's Gospel tells of events that most likely accompanied Jesus' return to the area around the Jordan after His temptation. John 1:19-42 tells what happened there during three successive days.

I. John the Announcer
(John 1:19-23)

John 1:18 says that the eternal Word, having been "made flesh" (v. 14) as the only begotten Son of God, proceeded to reveal the nature of God. The Son was then made known through the testimony of John the Baptist. Our printed text begins with the solemn testimony given by John the Baptist under persistent questioning.

A. Identification Demanded (v. 19)

19. And this is the record of John, when the Jews sent priests and Levites from Jerusalem to ask him, Who art thou?

Here John speaks of *the Jews*, not as a body of people, but as a designation of the religious rulers in *Jerusalem*. There the Sanhedrin sat as a ruling body of seventy men, including the chief priests, elders, and scribes (the high priest served as president). Its duty was to oversee religious practices and activities among the people. The Sanhedrin became increasingly resistant to Jesus during His ministry. Its opposition is reflected in the approximately seventy times that *the Jews* are mentioned in John's Gospel.

These rulers were understandably concerned at news of the popular response to the preaching of John the Baptist. This new development in matters where they were the authorities called for investigation. The delegation included *priests*, who conducted worship and offered sacrifices, and *Levites*—members of the tribe of Levi who were usually temple helpers, but occasionally assisted in teaching (Nehemiah 8:7-9).

Who art thou? It is to their credit that they went to the right place with their question. They may, however, have exhausted other sources in their previous investigations of the matter.

B. Messiahship Denied (vv. 20-22)

20. And he confessed, and denied not; but confessed, I am not the Christ.

John the Baptist seems to have been aware of the rumors that he might be the *Christ* (Luke 3:15)—the "anointed One," empowered with divine authority beyond that of other anointed individuals, including kings (1 Samuel 16:13) and priests (Exodus 40:13-15). The preacher at the Jordan silenced immediately any suggestion of his being the Messiah. The structure of his statement emphasizes the *I*. The anticipated Christ was not he, but one immeasurably greater. Jesus was the One he wanted to talk about.

21. And they asked him, What then? Art thou Elijah? And he saith, I am not. Art thou that Prophet? And he answered, No.

The Baptizer's replies became increasingly brief as the questions continued. The first answer had addressed the examiners' primary concern. What was left?

Students of the Scriptures knew that the prophet *Elijah* had been taken to Heaven without dying (2 Kings 2:1) and that Malachi (Malachi 4:5) had predicted Elijah's return before "the coming of the great and dreadful day of the Lord." Zechariah was told that his son's ministry would demonstrate the "spirit and power of Elijah" (Luke 1:17). Jesus testified that John the Baptist fulfilled Malachi's prophecy (Matthew 17:10-13). However, the popular expectation was for a literal return of Elijah, and John the Baptist was not that. He answered the question as it was asked.

Moses had predicted the coming of a *Prophet* like himself, who was to be given a most respectful hearing (Deuteronomy 18:15). John the Baptist was not that Prophet; Jesus was (Acts 3:19-23). Neither was John or any of the other prophets who had been expected to return in the Messianic age (Matthew 16:14). The investigators were wrong on all counts.

22. Then said they unto him, Who art thou? that we may give an answer to them that sent us. What sayest thou of thyself?

These committeemen were in an embarrassing situation. They had been sent to get information, and all they had thus far was disappointment in their expectations and denial of their allegations. At this point, they had to let the object of their investigation speak for himself.

C. Purpose Declared (v. 23)

23. He said, I am the voice of one crying in the wilderness, Make straight the way of the Lord, as said the prophet Isaiah.

In answer to the investigators from Jerusalem, John needed only to declare himself a herald proclaiming the King's arrival. He was content with nothing more. Such a response from the Jordan was not likely to satisfy the Sanhedrin in Jerusalem. For us, however, it glows with the singleness of purpose that we need to establish our own self-identity and sense of worthwhile living. Thank God for John the Baptist!

A VOICE IN THE WILDERNESS

With words taken from Isaiah 40:3, John the Baptist identified himself as "the voice of one crying in the wilderness" (John 1:23). He was preaching in the arid, inhospitable land along a stretch of the Jordan River. It seemed a forlorn

This visual will help you locate for your class the sites mentioned in this lesson and throughout the quarter.

Visual for lesson 2

How to Say It

BETHABARA. Beth-*ab*-uh-ruh.
BETHANY. *Beth*-uh-nee.
ELIJAH. Ee-*lye*-juh.
GALILEAN. Gal-uh-*lee*-un.
ISAIAH. Eye-*zay*-uh.
LEVITES. *Lee*-vites.
MALACHI. *Mal*-uh-kye.
NATHANAEL. Nuh-*than*-yull.
NAZARENE. *Naz*-uh-reen.
PHARISEES. *Fair*-ih-seez.
SANHEDRIN. San-*heed*-run or *San*-huh-drin.
ZECHARIAH. Zek-uh-*rye*-uh.

and unlikely place to draw crowds, yet many came to hear John.

It was in the late 1890s that Dr. Susie Rijnhart (*Rine*-hart) and her husband went as missionaries of the churches of Christ to the faraway desolate land of Tibet. After a brief time there, her husband was murdered, and her only child died and was buried in a small box at the foot of the Dang-La Mountains. Such sacrifices as these inspired others to follow in Dr. Rijnhart's steps.

In 1908 Dr. Zenas S. Loftis left the United States as another witness to "cry" in the vast wilderness of Tibet. He began working as a medical missionary with Dr. A. L. Shelton. Dr. Loftis died of typhoid fever and smallpox on August 12, 1909. Through these dedicated missionary lives, voices were calling out in a remote "wilderness" to point to the Redeemer.

Amidst the rising tide of secularism, negativism, and false religions around us, we too are seemingly in a "wilderness" that is alien to the Christian faith. However, if we, like John, lift our voices in faith and dedication on behalf of the Christ, transformed and obedient lives will be the result.

—J. G. V. B.

II. John the Baptizer
(John 1:24-28)

A. Pharisees' Question (vv. 24, 25)

24, 25. And they which were sent were of the Pharisees. And they asked him, and said unto him, Why baptizest thou then, if thou be not that Christ, nor Elijah, neither that Prophet?

Pharisees, not mentioned previously in our text, are introduced here to provide background for their question about John's baptism. They were eager guardians of the Law of Moses and the traditions of the elders. They seem to have been rather persistent in their interrogation of John.

The *Christ*, or even a returning prophet, would have recognizable authority to introduce a new religious practice (such as John's baptism seemed to be) or even to require a ceremonial cleansing of those who were already good Jews. But what right had a mere proclaimer of another's arrival to practice such an invasion of lawful and traditional procedure? This was a question that resurfaced during the ministry of Jesus: did John's practice of baptism have divine authority, or was it a human invention (Matthew 21:23-27)? The Sanhedrin could not answer, but Jesus accepted John's testimony. He knew that John was not the Messiah, but he did speak God's message.

B. Pointing to Jesus (vv. 26, 27)

26, 27. John answered them, saying, I baptize with water: but there standeth one among you, whom ye know not; he it is, who coming after me is preferred before me, whose shoelatchet I am not worthy to unloose.

What kind of answer was this to the Pharisees' question? They had asked why John baptized; he admitted that he did indeed *baptize*, but there was a larger issue. The Pharisees still needed to become acquainted with the greater One whom he had come to introduce. The baptism *with water* (literally, "in water") was a purposeful part of the introduction. It provided a link with Christian baptism, which symbolizes the death, burial, and resurrection of Jesus—the events that form the core of the gospel (1 Corinthians 15:3, 4).

Jesus had been *among* the people who came to John to be baptized, and He would be among the crowds again on the following day. Until now, however, they had no idea of His real identity. Jesus came *after* John the Baptist, being six months younger (Luke 1:24-26) and just now entering His public ministry when John was at the height of his popularity. *Preferred before me* speaks of Jesus' higher standing and worthiness. It also hints at the Lord's being in glory with the Father before being born on earth.

To loosen or tighten another man's *shoelatchet* (actually a sandal rather than a shoe) was regarded as the most menial of services, to be done only by slaves. But John considered himself *not worthy* of even that degree of contact with the magnificent One whom he proclaimed. [See question #1, page 248.]

BEARING WITNESS

In spite of the adulation of crowds and the great success that John the Baptist enjoyed in leading many to be baptized in the river Jordan, he still kept his task in perspective. He remembered that he was testifying of another greater than he was. We need to evaluate our own Christian service and to understand that we are not seeking honor and glory for ourselves, but for our Savior.

One of the most famous biographers in English literary history was James Boswell (1740-1795). He dedicated himself to the recording and transcribing of the deeds, writings, and above all the "table talk" and conversational remarks of Samuel Johnson. Johnson was a novelist, biographer, and lexicographer. His *English Dictionary* was a landmark achievement. Boswell preserved so many of Johnson's interesting and perceptive observations that his *Life of Samuel Johnson* became a classic. His dedication to the presentation of Johnson's wisdom made Boswell famous as well.

In the same way, our testimony to Jesus also enlarges and ennobles our lives. We seek to make His words known. We remind others of His deeds of mercy and power, and we do what we can to enlist others as His followers. James Boswell simply sought to make Samuel Johnson known and loved. This is exactly what we seek to do in our presentation of Jesus—to make Him known and loved.   —J. G. V. B.

C. Placing the Event (v. 28)

28. These things were done in Bethabara beyond Jordan, where John was baptizing.

Most of the oldest Greek manuscripts have "Bethany" rather than *Bethabara*. Since it was located *beyond Jordan*, or east of the river, it should not be confused with the Bethany near Jerusalem, where Mary, Martha, and Lazarus lived. Apparently it was one of several places along the Jordan Valley where John the Baptist was preaching and *baptizing* (John 3:23).

We can only wonder what the investigating committee reported to the Sanhedrin when they returned home.

III. John the Witness
(John 1:29-34)

A. "Here He Is!" (vv. 29, 30)

29. The next day John seeth Jesus coming unto him, and saith, Behold the Lamb of God, which taketh away the sin of the world!

It was now *the next day*, but enough of the same audience remained for John to address them with a reference to previous comments. Note the timing of Jesus' coming: the committee from Jerusalem was gone. Having dealt with their questions, John could now freely and enthusiastically point to the promised One.

The Lamb of God! What a treasure of meaning that opens! In faith Abraham had assured Isaac

that "God will provide himself a *lamb*" as an alternative to the sacrifice of Isaac (Genesis 22:8). A *lamb* had been a part of the annual Passover observance for each family in Israel as the nation celebrated its deliverance from bondage in Egypt (Exodus 12:1-11). The sacrifice of a *lamb* was part of the daily ritual, morning and evening, in the tabernacle and the temple (Exodus 29:38, 39). Isaiah spoke of the sacrificial *lamb* in his prophecy of the Suffering Servant (Isaiah 53:7). The final book of the Bible pictures the glorified *Lamb*, standing though looking as if it had been slain, and recognized in Heaven as the only one worthy to open the book of secrets of life and eternity (Revelation 5). John the Baptist was indeed "a prophet . . . and more than a prophet" (Matthew 11:9). [See question #2, page 248.]

30. This is he of whom I said, After me cometh a man which is preferred before me; for he was before me.

Jesus, the living Word, was unquestionably and immeasurably *before* John, by virtue of both His pre-incarnation existence in eternity and His standing as God's Son on earth. John could not say that often enough, or strongly enough. But how did John know all that? Keep reading. [See question #3, page 248.]

B. "He Is Why I Baptize" (v. 31)

31. And I knew him not: but that he should be made manifest to Israel, therefore am I come baptizing with water.

John had told his hearers the previous day that they did not recognize the One standing among them (v. 26). Now he admits that except for his commission to baptize *with water* (or "in water," as in verse 26), he himself would not have known Jesus as God's Son.

This son of Zechariah was "sent from God" (John 1:6) to preach and baptize. When Jesus came to be baptized, the occasion revealed His true identity to John. Then and only then did John the Baptist understand why he had been commissioned to conduct his ministry as he did.

C. "This Is How I Know Him"
(vv. 32, 33)

32, 33. And John bare record, saying, I saw the Spirit descending from heaven like a dove, and it abode upon him. And I knew him not: but he that sent me to baptize with water, the same said unto me, Upon whom thou shalt see the Spirit descending, and remaining on him, the same is he which baptizeth with the Holy Ghost.

God, who had brought John into the world to be the forerunner of the Christ, revealed to him that the Christ would be identified as the one on *whom thou shalt see the Spirit descending, and remaining on him.* As the other three Gospels clearly show, this sign occurred when Jesus was baptized (Matthew 3:16, 17; Mark 1:9-11; Luke 3:21, 22). This visible sign included spoken testimony from the Father concerning His Son. [See question #4, page 248.]

In addition, God revealed to John that as he had baptized *with water,* the Christ would baptize *with the Holy Ghost.* Jesus made such a promise specifically to His chosen apostles (Luke 24:49; Acts 1:5) and fulfilled it on the Day of Pentecost (Acts 2:3, 4). Later Peter reflected on this fulfillment when he first brought the gospel to Gentiles (Acts 10:45-47).

D. "Now I Tell You" (v. 34)

34. And I saw, and bare record that this is the Son of God.

Having seen and heard the evidence that God had promised to provide him, John the Baptist began immediately to testify to the fact established by that evidence. He was delighted to become known for all time as the voice announcing *the Son of God.* That sonship became the theme, not only of the preaching of John the Baptist, but also of the writing of John the apostle, as noted in the previous lesson: "These are written, that ye might believe that Jesus is the Christ, the Son of God; and that believing ye might have life through his name" (John 20:30).

Conclusion

A. What About Tomorrow?

There was still a third day for the testimony of John the Baptist to be heard. Following the

Home Daily Bible Readings

Monday, Mar. 8—John's Testimony (John 1:19-23)

Tuesday, Mar. 9—I Baptize With Water (John 1:24-28)

Wednesday, Mar. 10—Here Is the Lamb of God (John 1:29-34)

Thursday, Mar. 11—What Seek Ye? (John 1:35-42)

Friday, Mar. 12—Jesus Must Increase (John 3:22-36)

Saturday, Mar. 13—Jesus Commends John (Luke 7:18-28)

Sunday, Mar. 14—John Is Beheaded (Mark 6:14-29)

day of *announcement* in response to the committee from Jerusalem, and the day of *introduction* when Jesus Himself came near, there was a day of *direction* when John led some of his disciples to follow Jesus (John 1:35-42). Among these were the brothers Andrew and Simon (Peter), and one not named who almost certainly was John, the author of this Gospel. On "the day following" (v. 43) Philip and Nathanael, who also became apostles, were added to the group. Obviously John the Baptist meant it when he said of Jesus, "He must increase, but I must decrease" (John 3:30).

The steps just observed are natural, coming logically one after the other, yet seldom in so brief a span. Most of us can recall the day when we chose to be known as *Christian.* Then came the time when we had the opportunity to introduce Jesus to a friend, and a friend to Jesus, saying, "He is the really important One in my life; He is the reason I choose as I do among the daily options of saying and doing and spending." [See question #5, page 248.]

A more difficult day may follow, when we face the full implications of the question, "How far am I willing to go in my commitment to Jesus as God's Son?" Perhaps we must say to a friend or family member, "Follow and serve Jesus, no matter where that may take you, or how far you must travel from the close associations and frequent contacts we have so greatly enjoyed. Your love for Christ is not complete until you love Him more than you love me." We need have no fear that the choice we have recommended will lead someone to abandon the responsibilities of caring for family members or friends in need. Genuine love of the Lord will, in fact, make one increasingly attentive to those responsibilities.

For how many of these days, then, have we walked with John the Baptist? Is it our continuing desire that Jesus "increase" while we "decrease"?

B. Prayer

Thank You, Father, for sending Your faithful forerunner to prepare the way for Jesus. May we follow the example of John the Baptist, so that we too will become instruments through which others come to know Jesus. May we develop the degree of commitment that will say, "Jesus is more important to me than anything or anyone else." Grant us grace to introduce Jesus as we know Him to friends who have not yet made His acquaintance. In His name. Amen.

C. Thought to Remember

Who am I? The answer to that question depends on my relationship to Jesus Christ.

Learning by Doing

This page contains an alternate lesson plan emphasizing learning activities.
Classes desiring such student involvement will find these suggestions helpful.

Learning Goals

After this lesson a student should be able to:

1. Identify and explain the mission of John the Baptist.

2. Compare John's mission with that of Christians today.

3. Determine one way to be a better witness of Christ and seek to implement it in the coming week.

Into the Lesson

In advance ask someone to give a short talk on what it means to be a witness in a court of law. Have that person point out the importance of eyewitness testimony as opposed to hearsay.

Invite two more class members to portray John the Baptist on the witness stand and a lawyer who questions him about his ministry and its purpose. Assist these two students in preparing a script. A brief sample follows. (For more ideas on this concept see Ron Davis's "Teaching Tips" article, "That Ye Might Believe," on page 231.)

Lawyer: What is your name?

J. B.: John the Baptist.

Lawyer: Your occupation?

J. B.: Prophet and advance preparer.

Lawyer: Who is your employer?

J. B.: God.

Lawyer: Where do you work?

J. B.: In the wilderness.

Lawyer: What is your purpose?

Add other appropriate questions. Conclude by noting that there is a "John the Baptist" in the life of every one of us who is led to the Lord. Someone acted as a witness for the Lord, and we accepted his or her testimony. Perhaps there were several witnesses. Ask for accounts of who played that role in the lives of class members. What qualities made these people point to the Lord? Was it encouraging, teaching, helping, example? (A good way to get this discussion going is to tell who led you to the Lord. What qualities made the testimony of this person—or these people—credible?)

Into the Word

Begin with a brief description of John the Baptist, tying in last week's text with this, and noting information from the Introduction to the lesson commentary (page 242). Then, citing Malachi 4:5, ask for a comparison of John with Elijah, in appearance, in the nature of their ministries, in their messages, in where they preached, and in how they lived.

Have class members read through John 1:19-34 to identify the testimonies of John. (I am not the Christ; I am the voice; compared to the Christ I am the lowliest; Jesus is the Passover Lamb.)

Arrange two columns on the chalkboard with the headings "A Witness" and "John." Referring back to the material in "Into the Lesson," ask for the characteristics of each. Bring out the unique role of John in calling God's people to repent, baptizing them, and identifying Jesus as the One for whom they had been waiting.

Into Life

John the Baptist had a clear sense of his identity, of his mission and purpose. Discuss, "In what ways is a clear sense of identity important to us as followers of Christ?" If your church has a published "Mission Statement," read it and discuss it together. What demands does it make on the members? What Biblical support can be found for such demands? In what ways was John's mission similar to that of your church?

If your church does not have a mission statement, discuss the concept together. Say, "If we had been asked by the elders to write a mission statement, what would it include?"

Write what class members have to say on a chalkboard and then use the notes to frame a statement about your church's sense of identity. Compare your mission with that of John the Baptist. How is it alike? How is it different? (You might take a little time to contrast John's baptism with Christian baptism. See Acts 19:1-5.)

You might conclude with a challenge to each Christian to become a John the Baptist and introduce others to Jesus. To make this concept more concrete, ask students to do the following:

1. Think of one person to whom you could give your testimony about Jesus this week—someone who is not a Christian.

2. Write some things you might say as part of your testimony.

3. When will you make contact with this person to share your testimony of the Lord?

Close with prayer that the Spirit of the Lord will be with your "John the Baptists" as they give their testimonies this week.

Let's Talk It Over

The questions on this page are designed to encourage review of the lesson Scriptures and to promote discussion of the lesson by the class. The answers provided are only discussion starters. Let your class talk it over from there.

1. One prominent characteristic of John the Baptist was his humility. How important do you think humility is in being an effective witness for Christ? How can that characteristic be cultivated in one's life? (vv. 26, 27)

There will be little disagreement that humility is important; perhaps you and your students will be able to share examples of the effectiveness of humble servants of the Lord. The question of "how" seems to be more problematic.

John maintained a clear sense of his purpose. When some of John's disciples pointed out how Jesus' popularity was growing, while John's own popularity was apparently waning, he responded, "He must increase, but I must decrease" (John 3:30). If we will focus on our purpose—to disciple people to *Jesus*—then we'll have an easier time maintaining humility.

2. For John to call Jesus "the Lamb of God" would have attracted Jewish hearers in his time. Is that title one that attracts hearers today? Why or why not? (v. 29)

We still use the expression "innocent as a lamb" today, so the image still communicates that Jesus is innocent, pure, and sinless—though that by itself falls short of the full implications of the Passover Lamb. The idea of the "sacrificial lamb" is also contemporary with our society, though it is used in a variety of ways and not with the fullness of meaning it would have for Jewish observers of Passover.

While the image maintains some value to people today, believers need to be instructed in the full implications of the term to appreciate it adequately. And to attract unbelievers, perhaps your class can come up with some new images that will communicate in this age with the freshness and fullness with which John communicated to his contemporaries when he called Jesus "the Lamb of God."

3. Though John had his own disciples, his mission was to point them and everyone else to Christ. His followers could have followed him instead of Christ, but John would not allow it. To what extent is it a problem for some to follow a religious leader instead of the Christ to whom that leader intended to point? What can such a leader do about it? (v. 30)

This is a problem that any leader may face. His or her own personality may be so attractive that it becomes the thing that the disciple follows instead of Christ. Parents especially face this as their young children adopt the form of the faith even before they are able to appreciate its content. Like John we must always point to Christ. We must be open and transparent, freely admitting our human weaknesses and mistakes. Leaders need to allow themselves to be held accountable so that they do not give into the temptation to accept another's allegiance, which rightly belongs only to Christ.

4. John saw the dove descend upon Jesus and was assured that He is the Son of God. What gives you assurance that Jesus is the Son of God? How would you answer a doubter in order to give him assurance? (vv. 32, 33)

If we accept the New Testament as reliable, then there is sufficient evidence for us to be sure of Jesus' identity. But what of those not convinced of the reliability of the New Testament? Then they need to examine the evidence. A good place to start is the resurrection. If one examines all the explanations for the empty tomb without any preconceived bias, the resurrection rises to the top as the best. Look also at the lives of believers, both in the New Testament and today—their lives are a testimony to the power of the risen Christ!

5. What are the benefits of thinking about our witness as a matter of introducing Jesus as a friend? What problems might there be in that approach?

Introducing Jesus as a friend probably means we will avoid using theological terms that may be meaningless to non-Christians. Such an approach makes our faith seem more a natural part of life, not merely a ritual. It allows us to establish an attraction between Jesus and our human acquaintance. Then later we may have opportunity to impart more detailed teaching.

Of course, some people expect a "friend" to be someone visible and tangible. Speaking of Jesus as a friend may remind them of children with imaginary friends that no one else can see. We must use careful discernment about how to testify of Jesus in a way that is both credible and understandable.

Nicodemus Visits Jesus

DEVOTIONAL READING: 1 Corinthians 15:17-22.

LESSON SCRIPTURE: John 3:1-21.

PRINTED TEXT: John 3:1-17.

John 3:1-17

1 There was a man of the Pharisees, named Nicodemus, a ruler of the Jews:

2 The same came to Jesus by night, and said unto him, Rabbi, we know that thou art a teacher come from God: for no man can do these miracles that thou doest, except God be with him.

3 Jesus answered and said unto him, Verily, verily, I say unto thee, Except a man be born again, he cannot see the kingdom of God.

4 Nicodemus saith unto him, How can a man be born when he is old? can he enter the second time into his mother's womb, and be born?

5 Jesus answered, Verily, verily, I say unto thee, Except a man be born of water and of the Spirit, he cannot enter into the kingdom of God.

6 That which is born of the flesh is flesh; and that which is born of the Spirit is spirit.

7 Marvel not that I said unto thee, Ye must be born again.

8 The wind bloweth where it listeth, and thou hearest the sound thereof, but canst not tell whence it cometh, and whither it goeth: so is every one that is born of the Spirit.

9 Nicodemus answered and said unto him, How can these things be?

10 Jesus answered and said unto him, Art thou a master of Israel, and knowest not these things?

11 Verily, verily, I say unto thee, We speak that we do know, and testify that we have seen; and ye receive not our witness.

12 If I have told you earthly things, and ye believe not, how shall ye believe, if I tell you of heavenly things?

13 And no man hath ascended up to heaven, but he that came down from heaven, even the Son of man which is in heaven.

14 And as Moses lifted up the serpent in the wilderness, even so must the Son of man be lifted up:

15 That whosoever believeth in him should not perish, but have eternal life.

16 For God so loved the world, that he gave his only begotten Son, that whosoever believeth in him should not perish, but have everlasting life.

17 For God sent not his Son into the world to condemn the world; but that the world through him might be saved.

GOLDEN TEXT: For God sent not his Son into the world to condemn the world; but that the world through him might be saved.—John 3:17.

Lesson Aims

After this lesson students should be able to:

1. Summarize what Jesus said to Nicodemus about the new birth.

2. Explain from this and related texts what it means to be "born again" or "born from above."

3. Thank God for the privilege of being born again and commit himself or herself to a pattern of consistent growth.

Lesson Outline

INTRODUCTION
   A. Incredible? Not With God
   B. Lesson Background
 I. THE NEEDY VISITOR (John 3:1, 2)
 II. THE NEW BIRTH (John 3:3-8)
   A. Necessity of the New Birth (v. 3)
   B. Nature of the New Birth (vv. 4-6)
      "Born Again"
   C. Mystery of the New Birth (vv. 7, 8)
 III. THE VISITOR'S PROBLEM (John 3:9-12)
 IV. DIVINE PROVISION (John 3:13-17)
   A. God's Son (v. 13)
   B. God's Sacrifice (vv. 14, 15)
   C. God's Salvation (vv. 16, 17)
      Condemnation or Salvation?
CONCLUSION
   A. How Far Did It Lead?
   B. Prayer
   C. Thought to Remember

Introduction

A. Incredible? Not With God

Incredible bargains! Incredible values! Unbelievable quality! These and other phrases are dinned into our ears and blazoned before our eyes as advertisers try to make us believe and buy on the basis of what they have just told us is past belief! I tend to accept their acknowledgment of reckless exaggeration and keep my money in my pocket, believing the maxim: "If it seems too good to be true, it probably is."

The Bible, on the other hand, speaks with unrestrained enthusiasm about God's *amazing* grace, His *marvelous* power, and His *indescribable* gift of love in Christ Jesus. It does not call it unbelievable, though, and then ask us to believe

it. In fact, the word *incredible* appears only once in the Bible: "Why should it be thought a thing incredible with you, that God should raise the dead?" (Acts 26:8). What God says and does is not incredible! We can believe it!

Before us in today's printed text is a truth that appeared unbelievable to Nicodemus. Twice he asked *how* what Jesus was telling him could happen. Jesus' words, however, were not too good to be true; on the contrary, they describe a truth that is too important to ignore.

B. Lesson Background

The first chapter of John's Gospel tells us of Jesus' coming to earth as God's eternal Word in human form. It also tells of the introductory ministry of John the Baptist, and of John's directing some of his own disciples to follow Jesus. The second chapter tells of Jesus' first miracle at a wedding feast in Cana of Galilee, then of His going to Jerusalem for the Passover. There Jesus saw the way in which some were using the temple as a marketplace, and He drove them out. Certain Jews who were present demanded a sign demonstrating Jesus' authority to do such a thing, and He told them that if they destroyed the temple (meaning His body) He would restore it (by rising again) in three days. Jesus' disciples did not understand the meaning of this statement until after His resurrection. But they did recall the Scripture that said, "The zeal of thine house hath eaten me up" (Psalm 69:9).

While in Jerusalem, Jesus worked a number of miracles and "many believed in his name." They were so shallow in their belief, however, that Jesus did not proceed any further in revealing Himself to them (John 2:23-25). One observer among the Jews considered the matter seriously enough that he determined to learn more from Jesus Himself about Him and His teaching. He may have been especially interested in Jesus' statement: "The time is fulfilled, and the *kingdom of God* is at hand" (Mark 1:15). We meet that observer, Nicodemus, in our lesson today.

I. The Needy Visitor
(John 3:1, 2)

1. There was a man of the Pharisees, named Nicodemus, a ruler of the Jews.

Pharisees (a term meaning "separated ones") were known for their strict interpretation of the law of Moses and their rigid adherence to the traditions surrounding it. Unfortunately, their zeal for the law resulted in an obsession with outward conformity rather than a concern "to do justly, and to love mercy, and to walk humbly with thy God" (Micah 6:8).

As we saw in last week's lesson, certain Pharisees had already queried John the Baptist about his baptism (John 1:24, 25). They would clash frequently with Jesus about His nonconformity to their regulations and traditions, particularly regarding the Sabbath. A Pharisee tended to take great pride in what he saw as his own assured position in the kingdom of God.

That *Nicodemus* was *a ruler of the Jews* indicates that he was a member of the Jewish ruling council, or Sanhedrin. This was composed of seventy priests, scribes, and elders who exercised authority over the religious community. Yet, in spite of his distinguished position, Nicodemus recognized a deficiency in his understanding of spiritual matters. He was curious about what Jesus had to say.

2. The same came to Jesus by night, and said unto him, Rabbi, we know that thou art a teacher come from God: for no man can do these miracles that thou doest, except God be with him.

Many Pharisees brought questions designed to trap Jesus to make statements in public that could be used against Him. Not Nicodemus. He sought a private and leisurely conversation with Jesus to find out more about His teaching. *Rabbi* and *teacher* are terms that were precious to the Pharisees (Matthew 23:1-10). Nicodemus's use of the terms appears to have been a sincere attempt at showing respect.

Evidently Nicodemus had discussed Jesus' miracles and teaching with some of his peers. His assertion *we know* indicates that he was not alone in his beliefs about Jesus. (Perhaps he intended to report this conversation to his peers.) The teaching aspects of Jesus' ministry would be important to a Pharisee, but he would also consider the working of genuine *miracles* as evidence that God was *with him*. Jesus acknowledged the value of miracles as credentials of His authority (John 10:37, 38). [See question #1, page 256.]

So what did this God-sent teacher have to offer a God-fearing Pharisee? Nicodemus had not yet asked any questions of Jesus. He did not have to. Jesus knew what the man needed to know and what was on his mind. (See John 2:25.)

II. The New Birth
(John 3:3-8)

A. Necessity of the New Birth (v. 3)

3. Jesus answered and said unto him, Verily, verily, I say unto thee, Except a man be born again, he cannot see the kingdom of God.

The double use of *verily* (*amen* in the Greek) is sometimes translated *truly, truly*. It appears twenty-five times among the words of Jesus

recorded in John's Gospel and always introduces a statement of extraordinary importance.

The kingdom, or reign, of *God* was a theme familiar to the Pharisees. Daniel 2:44 and 7:27 spoke of an eternal kingdom that God would establish, and John the Baptist had declared that "the kingdom of heaven is at hand" (Matthew 3:2). Now Jesus was claiming that God's kingdom could not be perceived without a radical change from the viewpoint of the natural man. That change meant beginning an entirely new life, so new that Jesus described it as being *born again* or "born from above" (both meanings are possible renderings of the Greek term). Paul would later write, "If any man be in Christ, he is a new creature" (2 Corinthians 5:17).

B. Nature of the New Birth (vv. 4-6)

4. Nicodemus saith unto him, How can a man be born when he is old? can he enter the second time into his mother's womb, and be born?

Nicodemus took Jesus' language literally and materially. This was the natural response to many of Jesus' statements. See other examples in John 2:18-21 and Matthew 16:5-7, 12. [See question #2, page 256.]

5. Jesus answered, Verily, verily, I say unto thee, Except a man be born of water and of the Spirit, he cannot enter into the kingdom of God.

Water and *Spirit* had been dramatically linked in the baptism of Jesus, when the Spirit's visible presence testified to God's acceptance of Jesus' baptism in *water* (Matthew 3:13-17). The same linking appears in the events of Pentecost, inaugurated by the Spirit (Acts 2:1-4) and completed with the promise that the Spirit would be given in response to believers' baptism into Christ (Acts 2:37-41). Titus 3:5 makes a similar connection between the water and the Spirit: "according to his [God's] mercy he saved us, by the washing of regeneration, and renewing of the Holy Ghost."

Romans 10:17 and 1 Peter 1:23 tell us that the means through which the Spirit begets new life is the Word of God. Romans 6:3-6 indicates that the moment of entering "newness of life" comes when in baptism we reenact Jesus' burial and resurrection.

"BORN AGAIN"

Twice Jesus told Nicodemus about the necessity of a new birth. The moment of birth ushers us into this world as separate, breathing individual beings. Of course, we are living before the time of birth, but not as persons separate from our mothers. Jesus was saying that we must come into the world of spiritual life by the process of birth, just as by physical birth we come into the world of breathing, eating, seeing, hearing, and other experiences.

Occasionally there are certain events or circumstances that lead us to think in terms of a "new birth." So it was that in his famous "Gettysburg Address," Abraham Lincoln spoke of his hope "that this nation, under God, may have a new birth of freedom." From the old system that allowed millions of Americans to be held as slaves, we were challenged to become a society where all were free, with none treated as the property or the chattel of another.

Sometimes we witness the rise of new modes of thought or expression in art, literature, politics, world views, or religion, which seem to be so revolutionary as to be called a new birth. Such a movement took place in western Europe between 1450 and 1550, and came to be called the *renaissance*. In essence, this means a new birth, a renewal, a completely new beginning.

Just as there is in physical birth a passage from life in the mother's womb to a new and different life in the world, so in spiritual birth we pass into a new and different life in Christ. As Paul describes it, "Behold, all things are become new" (2 Corinthians 5:17).   —J. G. V. B.

6. That which is born of the flesh is flesh; and that which is born of the Spirit is spirit.

Here was Jesus' answer to Nicodemus's question regarding the repetition of physical birth. Physical birth and bodily life are God-given and they are good, but they are material and temporal; they are not spiritual and eternal. The latter qualities must come from another source. "Flesh and blood cannot inherit the kingdom of God" (1 Corinthians 15:50). John 1:12, 13 emphasizes the spiritual source of the spiritual life: "As many as received him [Christ, the living Word], to them gave he power to become the sons of God, . . . which were born, not of blood, nor of the will of the flesh, nor of the will of man, but of God."

C. Mystery of the New Birth (vv. 7, 8)

7, 8. Marvel not that I said unto thee, Ye must be born again. The wind bloweth where it listeth, and thou hearest the sound thereof, but canst not tell whence it cometh, and whither it goeth: so is every one that is born of the Spirit.

Marvel not—do not be surprised or amazed, as though something wholly unreasonable is being presented. All around us are commonly accepted happenings for which we have no ready explanation.

The words are addressed *unto thee*—Jesus was speaking to Nicodemus alone. But the obligation to be *born again* is stated in the plural: ye—all of you—in the Sanhedrin, in Israel, and throughout the world!

Since *wind* and *spirit* are both translations of the same Greek word, *pneuma*, this passage offers a fascinating play on words. We should not be surprised that we cannot grasp all the intricacies of spiritual truth as well as we would like. We cannot fully understand the movements of natural phenomena such as the wind, since we hear its *sound* and see its impact, we do not doubt that it is real. In the same way, we cannot observe the Spirit at work or actually see the processes of faith and repentance taking place, but we can see the Spirit's influence in the transformed lives of *every one that is born of the Spirit*.

A person can welcome and yield to the Spirit, or he can stifle and "quench" the Spirit (1 Thessalonians 5:19), just as one can erect barriers against the wind. The new life generated by God's Spirit must not be aborted before it comes to fruition in the new birth. [See question #3, page 256.]

III. The Visitor's Problem (John 3:9-12)

9. Nicodemus answered and said unto him, How can these things be?

Nicodemus did not understand Jesus' words, but he was not giving up. He still asked *how*.

10. Jesus answered and said unto him, Art thou a master of Israel, and knowest not these things?

In the Greek text the definite article appears before the word *master* ("*the* master of Israel"), calling attention to Nicodemus's standing as a highly respected scholar. However, there are things that even a presumed expert does not know, especially if he has allowed form to take precedence over substance—as the Pharisees so often did. Nicodemus should not have found this information so amazing. After all, Ezekiel had announced God's promise: "A new heart also will I give you, . . . and will put my Spirit within you" (Ezekiel 36:26, 27). Was a new birth more amazing than that?

11. Verily, verily, I say unto thee, We speak that which we do know, and testify that we have seen; and ye receive not our witness.

We most likely includes Jesus' disciples. *Ye* refers to the group of which Nicodemus is a part. Most of the Jewish leaders rejected Jesus' claims and teachings. Thus they were refusing Heaven's ambassador and His authoritative *witness* concerning the kingdom of God.

12. If I have told you earthly things, and ye believe not, how shall ye believe, if I tell you of heavenly things?

Jesus had spoken, as He did in His parables, of common and familiar items—birth, wind, and water. These *earthly things* receive their permanent value from heavenly and spiritual concepts, such as love, mercy, faith, truth, and goodness. A fuller understanding of *heavenly things* would have to await Nicodemus's further observation of Jesus' ministry. [See question #4, page 256.]

IV. Divine Provision
(John 3:13-17)

A. God's Son (v. 13)

13. And no man hath ascended up to heaven, but he that came down from heaven, even the Son of man which is in heaven.

John and the other Gospel writers did not use quotation marks to indicate words spoken by a certain person at a certain time. So we don't know whether Jesus spoke these and the following words to Nicodemus that night or whether John added them as additional explanation. In any case they provide additional insights into what is needed for entrance into God's kingdom.

Man's only hope of salvation was for God to provide it. We could never have reached Heaven on our own merit or effort. As the *Son of man* who *came down from heaven,* Jesus justified the claim of verse 11 that He bore witness to what He knew. Ephesians 4:9, 10 speaks both of Jesus' coming from Heaven and His returning to Heaven after His resurrection.

B. God's Sacrifice (vv. 14, 15)

14. And as Moses lifted up the serpent in the wilderness, even so must the Son of man be lifted up.

Numbers 21:4-9 recounts the occasion when God punished the children of Israel in the wilderness for their thankless complaints by sending serpents whose bite proved fatal. Penitent prayer followed, and God commanded Moses to set up a brass serpent on a pole, directing those bitten by the serpents to look upon it and live.

This unusual incident became a symbol of Jesus' crucifixion, which brings salvation from the venom of sin to those who look in obedient faith upon the uplifted Christ. Jesus said, "I, if I be lifted up from the earth, will draw all men

The visual for today's lesson portrays Jesus pleading for the defense of those who by faith have accepted Him and received the new birth.

Visual for lesson 3

unto me" (John 12:32). And the explanation follows: "This he said, signifying what death he should die" (v. 33). That prediction of Jesus' atoning death was an immediate part of the "heavenly things" that Nicodemus was not yet able to understand.

15. That whosoever believeth in him should not perish, but have eternal life.

The term *whosoever* means that the benefits of Jesus' death are available to all persons everywhere. All sinners are invited to faith—belief and trust in the uplifted One—and thus to faith in the Father who provided His Son as our sacrifice. The *eternal life* to which the obedient faith leads begins with the knowledge of Jesus as Savior (John 17:3); it has no end, for death is merely the means of passage into the presence of God.

C. God's Salvation (vv. 16, 17)

16. For God so loved the world, that he gave his only begotten Son, that whosoever believeth in him should not perish, but have everlasting life.

Jesus' crucifixion was not the tragic murder of a good man. His death was the result of the fact that God is love (1 John 4:8). His love looked in compassion on the world of mankind, created in His own image as the climax of all His creation (Genesis 1:26-28). His love was so great that *he gave his only begotten Son* for man's redemption. Before Jesus came we were doomed to *perish;* now we can *have everlasting life.*

John 3:16 is properly called the Golden Text of the Bible. In it every word is stretched to the full capacity of its meaning: *God . . . loved . . . the world . . . whosoever believeth . . . perish . . . everlasting . . . life.* You cannot grasp this on the run. You have to linger and let its truth soak in. And you must take the time to substitute your own name in place of the word *whosoever.*

17. For God sent not his Son into the world to condemn the world; but that the world through him might be saved.

Since the law of Moses was not perfectly kept by anyone, it became a tool of condemnation, an agency of divine judgment. Jesus, on the other hand, was God's expression of love and grace, providing a way by which *the world* could be *saved*. He was sent on a rescue mission to live among the inhabitants of earth for the purpose of removing their condemnation.

However, condemnation has not been entirely set aside. Some persons are not interested in the salvation that God has offered, and so by their own choice they judge themselves as unsuited to receive it. Paul said to some of that kind, "Ye put it [the word of God] from you, and judge yourselves unworthy of everlasting life" (Acts 13:46). John 3:18-21 (not included in our printed text) announces freedom from condemnation for the believer in Christ, but condemnation "already" for the unbeliever. He has rejected the "true Light" (John 1:9). [See question #5, page 256.]

CONDEMNATION OR SALVATION?

Probably John 3:16 is the most familiar verse in all the Bible. It has been quoted and lauded as "the New Testament in miniature," a succinct summary of the essence of Christianity. It may come as a surprise, then, to learn about a preacher who, given liberty to choose whatever text he pleased as the basis for what would surely be a once-in-a-lifetime sermon, chose John 3:17 instead of John 3:16. It was on June 2, 1850, that Alexander Campbell spoke from John 3:17 to both houses of the United States Congress in the chamber of the House of Representatives. Although he spoke for some ninety minutes, it was said that during this time, Campbell held his audience "in the most fixed attention."

How vital to know that God did not send Jesus to *condemn* the world, but to *save* it. It is such a temptation to attack the grossness, the insensitivity, and the moral decay of the world. It seems its many sins need to be itemized and denounced. But Jesus came to save men. To declare Jesus' love, His grace, His sacrifice, and His salvation is the true task of those who are His. As Dora Greenwell wrote:

He did not come to judge the world,
  he did not come to blame;
He did not only come to seek—
  it was to save He came;
And when we call Him Saviour,
  then we call Him by His name.

The message of the gospel is not bad news about human failures (we get enough of that from the world every day!). No, the gospel is good news about God's love in Jesus. It is the loving appeal of a Father, who longs for the wanderer to come home. —J. G. V. B.

Conclusion

A. How Far Did It Lead?

Whatever happened to Nicodemus after that memorable night visit with Jesus? John's Gospel mentions Nicodemus twice more, identifying him as the one who "came to Jesus by night." In the first of these, Nicodemus cautioned his fellow rulers in the Sanhedrin not to condemn Jesus before they heard His teaching. That comment was not well received (John 7:45-52). On the other occasion, Nicodemus and Joseph of Arimathea claimed and cared for the body of Jesus after His crucifixion (John 19:38-42). That was expensive, and it required some courage. A tradition says that Nicodemus later became a part of the church in Jerusalem. The Holy Spirit, however, did not provide the rest of the story in the record of Scripture, so we do not really know just how far Nicodemus's admiration for Jesus led him. A more important issue for you and me is how far our admiration for Jesus will lead us.

B. Prayer

Thank You, Father, for our Savior Jesus, who used this personal conversation with Nicodemus as an opportunity to teach eternal truth to all of us. Help us to be faithful in following that truth by living the new life in Christ for time and eternity. Help us in leading others to their own experience of the new birth. Amen.

C. Thought to Remember

"Except a man be born of water and of the Spirit, he cannot enter into the kingdom of God" (John 3:5).

Home Daily Bible Readings

Monday, Mar. 15—Nicodemus Comes to Jesus (John 3:1-10)
Tuesday, Mar. 16—God So Loved the World (John 3:11-21)
Wednesday, Mar. 17—Nicodemus Takes a Stand (John 7:45-52)
Thursday, Mar. 18—Joseph and Nicodemus Claim Jesus' Body (John 19:38-42)
Friday, Mar. 19—A Contrasting Response to Jesus (Matthew 19:16-22)
Saturday, Mar. 20—Another Contrasting Response (Acts 24:22-27)
Sunday, Mar. 21—God Cares for All (Psalm 91:1-16)

Learning by Doing

This page contains an alternate lesson plan emphasizing learning activities.
Classes desiring such student involvement will find these suggestions helpful.

Learning Goals

After this lesson students should be able to:

1. Summarize what Jesus said to Nicodemus about the new birth.

2. Explain from this and related texts what it means to be "born again" or "born from above."

3. Thank God for the privilege of being born again and commit himself or herself to a pattern of consistent growth.

Into the Lesson

Before class prepare a poster with a large question mark [?] in the middle. Across the top write, "You Have Questions." Across the bottom write, "Who Has Answers?"

Post this in a conspicuous place in the classroom. When it's time to begin, ask, "How do you go about getting answers to difficult questions?" Allow everyone who wants to suggest answers to do so. Write each one without evaluation on the chalkboard or on the poster. Responses such as seeking experts, looking in reference books, or using a computer network may be expected.

Observe that in today's lesson we shall meet a man with questions. He went to the best source of all for answers. He went to Jesus.

Into the Word

Assign a class member to prepare in advance a background check on Nicodemus. A good Bible dictionary should provide sufficient information. Start the Bible study with that report. You might also have someone prepared to provide some information about the sect of the Pharisees, who they were, what they believed and practiced, and how influential they were in Jesus' time.

Next, have a volunteer read John 3:1-17. Make some brief remarks about the passage, noting three metaphors in Jesus' discourse: new birth, the wind, and the serpent in the wilderness. Divide the class into at least three small groups and ask each group to explore the meaning of each metaphor. (If you have more than eighteen members in your class, make more groups, giving duplicate assignments as needed.) Give the groups about six or eight minutes, then call for reports. Below are some suggestions for what the groups should report.

Group 1: New Birth. As birth marks a great new beginning for the child who has been living in his mother's womb, so life in Christ is radically new and different from one's life before becoming a Christian.

Group 2: The Wind. As the wind is invisible and yet obvious in its power and effect, so the Spirit works in ways unseen by the human eye yet producing visible and powerful results.

Group 3: The Serpent. This is a reference to an historical event from the wilderness wanderings. See Numbers 21:4-9. As the people of Israel could not save themselves from the serpents, so no one today can save himself from the guilt of sin. But God has raised up a Deliverer!

After the groups report, move into a study of Scriptures having to do with being born again. Begin with Romans 6:3-11. Draw out ideas of what this rebirth means, what is involved in the process, and what the distinction is between born "of water" and born "of the Spirit." (Use information from the lesson commentary to clarify this concept.)

Have a Bible drill aimed at clearing up why Jesus said Nicodemus should know about the new birth. Begin with the following: 1 Samuel 10:6; Isaiah 32:15; Jeremiah 31:33; Ezekiel 36:25-27; Joel 2:28, 29. These passages will reveal that, for many centuries, God's people were taught to expect a new heart and new spirit, that it would come from on high, that it would be for all humanity, and that it would be part of a personal covenant that stressed individual responsibility.

Into Life

Nicodemus asked a good question: "How can a man be born [again] when he is old?" Studies show that, if a person does not make a decision for Christ by the time he or she turns eighteen, it is rare that the person does so at all! Discuss how your class can reach adults with the message of Jesus and the new birth. If you have some students who came to the Lord as adults, ask them what attracted them to the Lord. Suggest ways you and your class can make this a more common experience.

Discuss also what your church is doing to nurture new converts—and long-time believers as well. How well are most people taking advantage of these opportunities? Challenge your class members to commit themselves to taking advantage of every opportunity that will help them develop a pattern of consistent growth. Close with a prayer of thanks for the new birth available in Christ Jesus.

Let's Talk It Over

The questions on this page are designed to encourage review of the lesson Scriptures and to promote discussion of the lesson by the class. The answers provided are only discussion starters. Let your class talk it over from there.

1. Some students think Nicodemus came to Jesus by night out of fear. Others think he chose a time when he could have an uninterrupted and meaningful discussion with Jesus. They find him noble. What do you think? What does he teach us in this matter?

Nicodemus is associated with Joseph of Arimathea in John 19:38-42. There John says that Joseph was "a disciple of Jesus, but secretly for fear of the Jews" (v. 38). Perhaps Nicodemus shared his fear, and his nighttime visit is evidence of that. At the same time, Nicodemus spoke up on Jesus' behalf on at least one occasion (John 7:45-52). And neither Jesus nor John give any condemnation of Nicodemus for coming at night. So many believe his intentions were noble.

Whatever his reasons, we see in Nicodemus a desire to learn. His manner was sincere and open. These are traits we can emulate, however strong or weak his faith may have been when he first came to see Jesus.

2. One commentator says there was a longing in Nicodemus's question, "How can a man be born when he is old?" He wanted a new birth, a fresh start, but he did not know how to attain it. How much do you think people today long for a "new birth" or a fresh start? How can we use that longing to win them to Christ?

Anyone who feels he or she has failed in some way surely would welcome a fresh start. Today's high suicide rate suggests that many people are completely dissatisfied with the way their lives are heading. To them, a new life is probably what they are really looking for. But since they don't know where to find it, they simply choose to cancel the life they have.

The church must make its presence known in a way that will attract such seekers. Perhaps your church could begin a suicide hotline. Ask the class for other ideas on how to identify people especially longing for a fresh start but unable to find it—until you introduce them to Jesus!

3. What comparisons and contrasts can we make between physical birth and spiritual rebirth?

We had no control over the time and circumstances of our physical birth. But we are born again as a matter of choice—God does not force

this new birth upon us. Our physical birth resulted from an act of love between our parents. Our spiritual birth is possible because of God's love. At the time of our physical birth, we required nourishment and nurture from others. Newborn Christians need teaching and guidance from those who are older in the faith. After our birth in this world, we began a process of growth and development into mature beings. Infant believers must also experience growth, so that they can develop into mature servants of Christ. It is tragic when Christians remain immature and undeveloped in the faith. (See 1 Corinthians 3:1-4; Hebrews 5:12-14.)

4. Jesus almost chided Nicodemus—a teacher of Israel—for not understanding what He was saying. Why is it that those who ought to have spiritual insight often seem not to have any? How can such insight be gained?

The Pharisees had become so enamored with the form of the law that they had lost sight of its substance. They liked the power their current structure gave them, so they wanted to preserve it at all costs. What Jesus was talking about required Nicodemus to perceive the essence of God's plan for "a new covenant . . . not according to the [old] covenant" (Jeremiah 31:31-34).

It is always easier for us to adapt to the way things are than to cause things to be the way they ought to be. Those in the most privileged positions in the current structure have the most to lose if the structure changes. Their insight is hindered by their comfort. Church leaders must always ask, "What will make the most impact for Christ?" and not be concerned so much with their own positions, authority, and comfort.

5. It is not God's desire to condemn the world. How clearly are we communicating this truth? How can we do it better?

God's intentions are clear. (See 1 Timothy 2:4; 2 Peter 3:9.) Too often, His people act as if they would be glad to see some people condemned. When we become better known for what we are against than what we are for, we fail to convey the Lord's desire that "whosoever believeth in him" should have eternal life. It is a good exercise to remind ourselves regularly that every person we meet is someone whose salvation God desires.

A Woman Brings Her Village to Jesus

DEVOTIONAL READING: Revelation 7:13-17.

LESSON SCRIPTURE: John 4:1-42.

PRINTED TEXT: John 4:7-15, 28-30, 39, 40.

John 4:7-15, 28-30, 39, 40

7 There cometh a woman of Samaria to draw water: Jesus saith unto her, Give me to drink.

8 (For his disciples were gone away unto the city to buy meat.)

9 Then saith the woman of Samaria unto him, How is it that thou, being a Jew, askest drink of me, which am a woman of Samaria? for the Jews have no dealings with the Samaritans.

10 Jesus answered and said unto her, If thou knewest the gift of God, and who it is that saith to thee, Give me to drink; thou wouldest have asked of him, and he would have given thee living water.

11 The woman saith unto him, Sir, thou hast nothing to draw with, and the well is deep: from whence then hast thou that living water?

12 Art thou greater than our father Jacob, which gave us the well, and drank thereof himself, and his children, and his cattle?

13 Jesus answered and said unto her, Whosoever drinketh of this water shall thirst again:

14 But whosoever drinketh of the water that I shall give him shall never thirst; but the water that I shall give him shall be in him a well of water springing up into everlasting life.

15 The woman saith unto him, Sir, give me this water, that I thirst not, neither come hither to draw.

. . . .

28 The woman then left her waterpot, and went her way into the city, and saith to the men,

29 Come, see a man, which told me all things that ever I did: is not this the Christ?

30 Then they went out of the city, and came unto him.

. . . .

39 And many of the Samaritans of that city believed on him for the saying of the woman, which testified, He told me all that ever I did.

40 So when the Samaritans were come unto him, they besought him that he would tarry with them: and he abode there two days.

GOLDEN TEXT: Whosoever drinketh of the water that I shall give him shall never thirst; but the water that I shall give him shall be in him a well of water springing up into everlasting life.—John 4:14.

That You May Believe

Unit 1: Jesus' Coming Calls for Faith

(Lessons 1-4)

Lesson Aims

This study should help the class member to:

1. Tell how the Samaritan woman's life and village were changed by an encounter with Jesus.

2. List several principles for evangelism demonstrated by Jesus and the woman.

3. Form a specific plan to tell others of Jesus, using one or more of the principles from this text.

Lesson Outline

INTRODUCTION

    A. Just Between the Two of Us

    B. A History of Hostility

    C. Lesson Background

  I. TALKING ABOUT WATER (John 4:7-15)

    A. Jesus Asks for Water (vv. 7-9)

    B. Jesus Offers Living Water (vv. 10-14)

    A Spring Welling Up

    C. The Woman Asks for Water (v. 15)

 II. TALKING ABOUT JESUS (John 4:28-30)

    A. "Come and See" (vv. 28, 29)

    Everything I Ever Did

    B. Invitation Accepted (v. 30)

III. TALKING WITH JESUS (John 4:39, 40)

CONCLUSION

    A. Keep Talking

    B. Prayer

    C. Thought to Remember

Introduction

A. Just Between the Two of Us

Trivial!

You meet by chance in the shopping mall and you "pass the time of day." What do you talk about? The weather? Last night's ball game? Probably nothing very important, thus the origin of our word *trivial*. This word is derived from a Latin word that means "three ways." It described a place where paths intersected and neighbors paused to engage in small talk. When the conversation is "just between you and me," we may not feel as responsible for what we say.

It was not so with Jesus, who dealt with every conversation as an opportunity to bring someone closer to His Father in Heaven. The third and fourth chapters of John's Gospel provide notable examples, one with a religious leader who came to Him by night, and the other with a woman whom He met by a well in Samaria. In each person He saw a need, and with each He addressed that need through teaching that went far beyond the hearer's immediate understanding. Now all of us have the opportunity to learn from those one-on-one conversations. We met Nicodemus in last week's lesson. Today we meet the woman of Samaria.

B. A History of Hostility

A business establishment in our city operates a "Samaritan van," which patrols streets and highways and offers help to travelers who need it for any reason. This service is named for the unlikely hero of Jesus' parable about a man who helped the victim of robbers on the road from Jerusalem to Jericho (Luke 10:25-37).

The Jews in Jesus' day did not consider Samaritans as heroes. A succinct statement of relations between the two groups is found in John 4:9: "The Jews have no dealings with the Samaritans." Tensions between the two can be traced to events that occurred some seven hundred years earlier. In 722 B.C., when the Assyrians conquered the northern kingdom of Israel and its capital of Samaria, they scattered its people to other parts of the empire, replacing them with foreigners. The people who resulted from this mixture of populations came to be called Samaritans.

Years later in 538 B.C., following seventy years of captivity in Babylon, the Jews from Judah were allowed to return to Jerusalem and rebuild their temple. Samaritans in the area expressed an interest in helping with the temple, but their offer was refused because they did not worship Jehovah exclusively. Eventually the Samaritans established their own religious practices, based on the five books of Law (Genesis to Deuteronomy). They built their own temple on Mount Gerizim, located within sight of "Jacob's well." That temple was destroyed during the period between the Old and New Testaments, but the site continued to be considered holy ground by the Samaritans. (A Samaritan group worships at the base of Mount Gerizim to this day!)

By the time of Christ, mutual resentment between Jews and Samaritans had intensified. Jesus, however, refused to be a part of it, taking notable occasions to show that God's love and mercy included Samaritans. One of these occasions is the subject of today's lesson.

C. Lesson Background

Jesus' conversation with Nicodemus was a significant event in His early ministry in Judea, where He is said to have baptized some of His hearers (John 3:22). Soon the disciples of John the Baptist began to express their concern that Jesus was gaining a larger following than John (v. 26). John was pleased to see this happening, saying, "He must increase, but I must decrease" (3:30). Certain Pharisees were eager to transfer their criticism and opposition of John to Jesus, but Jesus knew the time was not right for that. So Jesus and His disciples headed north to Galilee (4:1-3). Instead of following the Jews' popular detour around Samaritan territory (traveling east and crossing the Jordan River, then crossing again north of Samaria), He went directly northward through Samaria. At "about the sixth hour" (noon by Jewish reckoning) the group arrived "near to the parcel of ground that Jacob gave to his son Joseph" (v. 5; see Genesis 33:18, 19; Joshua 24:32). Jacob's well, still usable, was a familiar landmark.

Jesus was not one to seek favors, but at this point He was "wearied with his journey" (John 4:6). He sat to rest by the well while His disciples went to buy food in the town of Sychar, about half a mile away.

I. Talking About Water
(John 4:7-15)

It was time for refreshment, physical and spiritual. Both kinds were on the agenda.

A. Jesus Asks for Water (vv. 7-9)

7. There cometh a woman of Samaria to draw water: Jesus saith unto her, Give me to drink.

The *woman* was a citizen of the region, not the city, *of Samaria*. (To come from the city would have required about a two-hour walk.) She had come *to draw water*. From verse 28 we gather that she was carrying a "waterpot," either on her head or her shoulder.

Jesus saw this woman as a person having more than one kind of thirst. He could help her with her spiritual thirst, and the best possible opportunity to do this was through asking her to help Him with His physical thirst. He would put Himself in debt to her for a kindness that she could easily render. What could be more natural than for a thirsty person to ask for a *drink*? But under the social circumstances, what could be more startling?

8. (For his disciples were gone away unto the city to buy meat.)

We can only guess how many disciples were with Jesus on this journey, and why or whether they all went *unto the city*. The rift between Jews and Samaritans did not prevent their doing business on commercial levels, but it might limit what *meat* (here meaning food of any kind) a Jew would buy in a Samaritan market.

9. Then saith the woman of Samaria unto him, How is it that thou, being a Jew, askest drink of me, which am a woman of Samaria? for the Jews have no dealings with the Samaritans.

The *woman* did not refuse the request, but she was in no hurry to grant it. She was puzzled and curious. This stranger's Jewishness would have been evident from His physical appearance, His clothing, and His speech, at least. Jews did not fraternize with Samaritans, and Jewish men did not talk in public places with women at all! What Jew would acknowledge a need that a Samaritan could supply? Yet Jesus had asked her for a *drink*!

We are left to wonder when or whether the woman actually drew water from the well and supplied the drink that Jesus had requested. The conversation moved swiftly to more important matters. [See question #1, page 264.]

B. Jesus Offers Living Water (vv. 10-14)

10. Jesus answered and said unto her, If thou knewest the gift of God, and who it is that saith to thee, Give me to drink; thou wouldest have asked of him, and he would have given thee living water.

The woman's need was greater than Jesus' need, and He lost no time in pointing this out. Her need was spiritual, and it would be met by God's provision rather than by her ability. The phrase *gift of God* is not used elsewhere in John's Gospel, but John 3:16 carries the same idea when it describes God's love as a love that "gave his only begotten Son." He is the source of the *living water* that He was offering to the woman. But it was too early in the conversation for her to recognize this link.

Living water should be understood as a fresh, flowing stream (as from a spring or artesian well), in contrast to the standing and stagnant water in a pond or cistern. The water that Jesus offers is as necessary to spiritual life as water is to physical life. It is *living* water in a double sense, in kind and in movement: "If anyone is thirsty, let him come to me and drink. Whoever believes in me, as the Scripture has said, streams of living water will flow from within him" (John 7:37, 38, *New International Version*). [See question #2, page 264.]

11. The woman saith unto him, Sir, thou hast nothing to draw with, and the well is deep: from whence then hast thou that living water?

Just as Nicodemus had found difficulty with the idea of being born again (John 3:4), so this woman found it hard to think beyond the difficulties related to providing water from a deep *well* without a rope and a bucket. (The well at this site has been measured at more than a hundred feet in total depth.)

This visual illustrates our Golden Text, John 4:14.

Visual for lesson 4

Nevertheless, the woman had observed qualities in Jesus that commanded her respect, and she addressed him as *Sir* (the Greek form is *kurie*, frequently translated as "lord"). Perhaps His courtesy toward her had something to do with her respect of Him. Still, she obviously suspected this man of promising more than He could deliver. Did she dare to think that He had another source for the *water* that He offered?

12. Art thou greater than our father Jacob, which gave us the well, and drank thereof himself, and his children, and his cattle?

The patriarch *Jacob* was acknowledged as *father* by both Jews and Samaritans. He had shown remarkable resourcefulness in providing a dependable source of water for his family and his flocks. Was this Jewish stranger suggesting that He could outdo the respected ancestor of both Jew and Samaritan?

13, 14. Jesus answered and said unto her, Whosoever drinketh of this water shall thirst again: but whosoever drinketh of the water that I shall give him shall never thirst; but the water that I shall give him shall be in him a well of water springing up into everlasting life.

The woman had suggested a comparison between Jacob and Jesus. Jesus chose instead to contrast the kinds of water that each was able to provide. The water from Jacob's well could satisfy a physical thirst for a time, but that thirst would return to make repeated demands. And that water could never slake the spiritual thirst that was even now tormenting the woman who came to draw from the well.

There is something better about the water of life, however, than simply providing a permanent supply that keeps a person going and going indefinitely. Ordinary water satisfies the person who drinks it, and no one else. Christ's water of life is a constantly renewed and overflowing supply, affecting not only the believer in Christ, but also those with whom the believer comes in contact. That quality was to be demonstrated

within the hour as the Samaritan woman's enthusiasm for Jesus spilled over to her neighbors and brought them to meet Him too.

A SPRING WELLING UP

It was at Jacob's well that Jesus met and conversed with the woman of Samaria. Despite their many differences, both Jews and Samaritans obtained water from this well (the well can still be visited and used).

Jesus told this woman that the "living water" He could give her would be "a well of water springing up into everlasting life"—always refreshing, enlivening, and never running dry! There is something mysterious and marvelous about everflowing springs of water. They gush forth from the earth, pouring forth constantly, day and night, year after year, in every season.

In Florida there are many such springs, which *every day* pour out over four billion gallons of water. Some of these seemingly inexhaustible springs are: Silver Springs, five miles northeast of Ocala, which emits 808 cubic feet of water per second; Rainbow Springs, four miles northeast of Dunnellon (699 cubic feet per second); and Ichatuckee Springs, near Hildreth (335 cubic feet per second).

Just as this abundance of water flows in a torrent of clear and continual freshness, so Jesus' presence and power constantly revives us within. Whatever the drabness and dreariness of the outer life, inwardly all is green and fresh and beautiful for the Christian.   —J. G. V. B.

C. The Woman Asks for Water (v. 15)

15. The woman saith unto him, Sir, give me this water, that I thirst not, neither come hither to draw.

Without hearing the words spoken, it is hard to say what the woman meant here. Perhaps she was sincere, not understanding yet what Jesus was talking about but liking what she heard. The idea of not having to draw water was very appealing. Her thirst for spiritual water, if recognized, was not yet on her mind. Or she may have been sarcastic with her remark. If she was thinking about physical water, Jesus' promise did sound too good to be true!

Whatever her intent, when Jesus raised the issue of her chaotic marital status (vv. 16-18), His insight convinced her that He was a prophet (v. 19). Probably embarrassed, especially if she had spoken rudely, she changed the subject from husbands to religion. For Jews and Samaritans, this raised the question of Jerusalem versus "this mountain" (Mount Gerizim, which would have been visible from where Jesus and the woman were) as the place of acceptable worship. Jesus promised the time when the spirit, rather than the location, would determine acceptable worship before God. The woman was willing to leave such matters to the Messiah at His sometime-in-the-future arrival. Jesus then told her plainly that He was that Messiah! (v. 26).

At this point the Lord's disciples returned. They were amazed, but politely silent, at finding their Master in conversation with this woman.

II. Talking About Jesus
(John 4:28-30)

A. "Come and See" (vv. 28, 29)

28, 29. The woman then left her waterpot, and went her way into the city, and saith to the men, Come, see a man, which told me all things that ever I did: is not this the Christ?

The disciples' arrival may have startled the woman into recognizing that others also needed to hear the remarkable things that she had just heard. Her priorities suddenly changed. She set aside her *waterpot* (perhaps still empty), for she had found something vastly more important than that for which she came. She did not return home, but went to where others were, to share with them her remarkable experience. Her first contacts happened to be with *men*, either on the road back to Sychar or in the town marketplace.

What was so exciting? She had met a *man* so wonderful that they must meet Him too. The quality that impressed her most was not that He spoke of giving the water of life, or of God caring more for the spirit of one's worship than the place where it was offered. No! This wonderful man understood *her*, and talked about *her*! He knew all about her and still respected her!

Could this be the long-anticipated *Christ*? Limiting their use of Scripture to the books of the Law, the Samaritans lacked the clear Messianic prophecies found in Isaiah and other writers; but they would have known, for example, what Moses had said about a Prophet whom God would one day "raise up" (Deuteronomy 18:15). The woman's question served well to stir curiosity in her hearers, who then wanted to find out about this remarkable individual for themselves. [See question #3, page 264.]

EVERYTHING I EVER DID

The Samaritan woman claimed that Jesus had told her everything "that ever I did" (John 4:29, 39). Of course, Jesus did not literally tell her about every act she had ever done. But He did tell her about her five husbands and the man with whom she was living who was not her husband (v. 18). These unhappy situations had probably been the repeated source of frustrated

hopes, days of discord, and nights of tension (perhaps even of terror).

Perhaps such a checkered past affected this woman's standing in the community and resulted in her alienation from her family. We do not know what children she may have borne to her various husbands, or what rifts might have occurred in her relationships with their families. In any case, Jesus had quietly touched on the things she had done, but had done so in such a way as to give her a sense of hope, not despair.

Have we not sometimes heard a teacher or preacher who seemed to "lay bare" for us our most basic fears and hopes and questions? Often we are not really aware of these until a speaker or writer seems to strike a certain key. Suddenly all the music of our life is revealed as more discordant than we realized. However, as the Samaritan woman came to discover, Jesus can bring harmony to even the most out-of-tune life. May we let similar moments of self-awareness lead us to Jesus as well.

> Let words of Jesus reach your heart,
> Let vision clear and healing start;
> All can be cleansed, but nothing hid,
> For He knows everything you did.
> —J. G. V. B.

B. Invitation Accepted (v. 30)

30. Then they went out of the city, and came unto him.

As the multitudes had gone out of Jerusalem to hear John the Baptist in the wilderness, so the men of Sychar "were coming" (a literal translation of the Greek text) to Jesus at the well. It is an amazing result from one single invitation. As an evangelist, this woman was an *amateur* in the best sense of that term (the word comes from a root meaning "to love"); for she was acting out of love for what she was doing, and not for any hope of gain. Her effectiveness came from her obvious passion rather than from the logic of her arguments.

The sight of many men coming out of Sychar toward Jesus became the basis for immediate

---

How to Say It

ASSYRIANS. Uh-*sear*-ee-unz.
GERIZIM. *Gair*-ih-zim or Guh-*rye*-zim.
JERICHO. *Jair*-ih-ko.
KURIE (Greek). *koo*-ree-eh.
NICODEMUS. Nick-uh-*dee*-mus.
SAMARIA. Suh-*mare*-ee-uh.
SAMARITANS. Suh-*mare*-uh-tunz.
SYCHAR. *Sigh*-kar.

discussion between Jesus and His disciples. The disciples wanted Him to eat of the food they had brought; He said He was enjoying a different kind of nourishment in doing God's will (vv. 31-34). The disciples saw prospects for a future harvest in the grainfields around them; He saw a spiritual crop ready for immediate harvest, and spoke of the need for laborers to work together in sowing, cultivating, and gathering the harvest (vv. 35-38). [See question #4, page 264.]

III. Talking With Jesus
(John 4:39, 40)

We turn now from the conversations of Jesus with the Samaritan woman and with His disciples to the reaction of the residents of Sychar after their encounter with Christ.

39. And many of the Samaritans of that city believed on him for the saying of the woman, which testified, He told me all that ever I did.

The woman's testimony to the townspeople had been convincing. Even allowing for some exaggeration that Jesus recounted *all that ever I did*, it is clear that they accepted her evaluation of Jesus as a prophet of God, and perhaps *the* prophet anticipated by Moses. Their faith is the more remarkable in light of the handicaps it had to overcome. It was a Jew—not a Samaritan—who just might be the Messiah, and the suggestion was coming from a person whose track record for dependability was less than perfect.

If this woman could be so effective in representing Jesus, who of us can say, "I could never bring anyone to Christ"? Perhaps we're simply not as excited about Him as she was.

40. So when the Samaritans were come unto him, they besought him that he would tarry with them: and he abode there two days.

Home Daily Bible Readings

Monday, Mar. 22—Jesus Goes Through Samaria (John 4:1-6)
Tuesday, Mar. 23—Jesus' Encounter With a Samaritan Woman (John 4:7-15)
Wednesday, Mar. 24—I Am the Messiah (John 4:16-26)
Thursday, Mar. 25—Jesus' Disciples Are Astonished (John 4:27-42)
Friday, Mar. 26—Even a Cup of Cold Water (Matthew 10:37-42)
Saturday, Mar. 27—Take the Water of Life As a Gift (Revelation 22:16-21)
Sunday, Mar. 28—Jesus Rides Into Jerusalem (Mark 11:1-11)

It seems that the *Samaritans* who came to see Jesus for themselves reached the same conclusion about Him that the woman had. They wanted to know more, and they insisted on His staying for a time among them.

The fruits of Jesus' brief two-day stay with the Samaritans were as remarkable as the events leading to it. They are reported briefly in the two verses immediately following our printed text: "And many more believed because of his own word; and said unto the woman, Now we believe, not because of thy saying: for we have heard him ourselves, and know that this is indeed the Christ, the Saviour of the world" (vv. 41, 42). But first, someone had to tell them about Jesus. The Samaritan woman had done her part in pointing others to Him. [See question #5, page 264.]

Conclusion

A. Keep Talking

Jesus talked, one-on-one, with a scholar named Nicodemus, whose acquaintance many would have sought. He also talked with an unnamed Samaritan woman, whose acquaintance many would have shunned. In each conversation He planted seeds of truth that the other was not yet prepared to understand, but which finally became intensely meaningful to countless generations.

Ironically, the results from the less promising conversation with the Samaritan woman were much more fruitful (at least immediately) than those from the conversation with the religious leader. What was the difference? Nicodemus pondered the matter and kept it to himself. The woman became excited about Jesus and told everyone she met about Him. They, in turn, inquired for themselves and came to believe for themselves, thus providing early evidence that the gospel was meant to break down the walls that had divided Jews and Samaritans for hundreds of years. And it all began with a conversation beside a well.

What conversations for Christ can you begin today?

B. Prayer

Father, we praise You for Your Son Jesus, who is to us the water of life, slaking our spiritual thirst now and forever. Thank You for faithful witnesses who brought the good news of the gospel to us. Grant us boldness to share it with others. In Jesus' name. Amen.

C. Thought to Remember

Come with me and see Jesus!

Learning by Doing

This page contains an alternate lesson plan emphasizing learning activities.
Classes desiring such student involvement will find these suggestions helpful.

Learning Goals

This lesson should equip students to:

1. Tell how the Samaritan woman's life and village were changed by an encounter with Jesus.

2. List several principles for evangelism demonstrated by Jesus and the woman.

3. Form a specific plan to tell others of Jesus, using one or more of the principles from this text.

Into the Lesson

Before class prepare a poster with the words, "I just have to tell you . . ." written in large letters. Add some pictures to the poster, either drawn or cut from magazines, of items that would suggest someone has great news to tell. You might include an engagement ring ("I'm getting married!"), a house ("We sold our house!" or "We've just bought/built a home"), a limousine (an important official is coming to town), money (got a scholarship, an inheritance, etc.), and several other items. Ask the students to guess what news each item might represent. Invite volunteers to tell about times they have had exciting news to tell. After some discussion, ask, "How excited are we to tell people about Jesus?" Discuss why we are sometimes not as excited about that as we are to tell other news. Make the transition to Bible study by noting that today's lesson introduces us to a woman who just had to tell the good news about Jesus.

Into the Word

At the outset, it is helpful to have someone brief the class on the Samaritans: who they were, what they believed. A Bible dictionary or a Bible encyclopedia should provide enough details for a quick survey.

It would also be informative to ask the class to read aloud the entire fourth chapter of John and then compare the Samaritan woman with Nicodemus. Two columns on the chalkboard can be used to visualize the reactions. For example, he was of high status in that society and she was of low. He was very "religious" and she was not. She was somewhat cynical and he was not. Their needs were not the same. What were they?

With the assistance of the entire class, outline the conversation between Jesus and the woman, as well as the results. Write the outline on a flip sheet or chalkboard.

- The request for a drink (v. 7)
- The cross-cultural communication (v. 9)
- The shift to "spiritual" water and to Jesus (vv. 10-15)
- A look at the woman's spiritual condition (vv. 16-18)
- Her change of subject to the appropriate place of worship (vv. 19-24)
- His revelation that He is the Messiah (vv. 25, 26)
- The woman shares the good news (vv. 27-30)
- Response of the city (vv. 39, 40)

Ask, "What made the woman want to tell others about Jesus?" After a brief discussion, ask, "How can we have the same desire and excitement to share the good news?"

Into Life

In order to make some applications to our lives today, review the conversation between Jesus and the woman, noting some timeless principles for evangelism that Jesus followed. Discuss how we can observe the same principles today. Some suggested principles follow:

1. Begin a conversation in a natural manner. (Jesus' request for a drink was natural enough, given the climate and the proximity of a well.)

2. Don't be afraid to cross cultural barriers. (What was unusual about Jesus' request was that it ignored the prejudice that existed between Jews and Samaritans.)

3. Appeal to felt needs. (Jesus' talk of living water appealed to the woman, as it seemed it would make her life easier.)

4. Stay focused. (When the woman tried to change the subject, Jesus kept the conversation focused on the message He had for her.)

5. Point to the Christ. (See vv. 25, 26.)

Compare how the woman followed some of the same principles in telling the people of her city about Jesus. For example, with the anticipation of the coming Messiah, her question, "Is not this the Christ?" appealed to their felt need for His arrival.

Ask the class to plan and organize some ways that Jesus can be shared today. Then distribute index cards and ask each student to get specific. Each one should write the name of someone who needs to know the Lord and write two or three steps that can be taken in the coming week to share Him with that person. Close with prayer.

Let's Talk It Over

The questions on this page are designed to encourage review of the lesson Scriptures and to promote discussion of the lesson by the class. The answers provided are only discussion starters. Let your class talk it over from there.

1. Jesus, a Jewish man, engaged in evangelistic discussion with a Samaritan woman. What are some principles to keep in mind when we have evangelistic contacts across racial and gender lines?

Obviously we must exercise discretion when we share the gospel with someone of the opposite sex. Jesus spoke with the Samaritan woman in a public place, and that should ideally be the case when a man shares the gospel with a woman, or *vice versa*. Also, whether we are crossing racial or gender lines, we must avoid any hint of a condescending attitude. A humble, loving manner will gain us the best hearing. Additionally, as Paul showed us in 1 Corinthians 9:19-23, we should find points of identification with the other person. It will help to know something about his/her family status, economic condition, level of education, religious background, and other personal factors. We will surely discover some areas of common interest that will aid us in establishing rapport.

2. It is amazing to see how Jesus was able to use everyday sights and experiences like water as vehicles for spiritual teaching. How can we turn casual conversation into opportunities to share Christ with our companions?

Some people seem to have a natural ability to carry on meaningful conversation while others struggle to put two sentences together. But each of us can improve in this area with planning. Jesus was deliberate about His task (see v. 34). We need to be more intentional about sharing the gospel, planning in advance what we will say (cf. 1 Peter 3:15). Marking a New Testament (underlining key verses and noting sequential references in the margin) is another aid, especially if memorizing is difficult. Paul's advice in Colossians 4:2-6 will also aid us in employing occasions of idle conversation as tools for evangelism.

3. What can we do to stimulate a spiritual thirst in the hearts of our friends and acquaintances?

One way that we can do that is by living in such a way as to demonstrate the love and power of Christ. This modeling of Christ will be particularly effective if people see that His love and power remain strong even when we are suffering.

We must be sure that people see that we have a positive faith. Too many people know only what Christians are *against;* they need to know what we are *for.* And we are for *them!*

Along with what we *can* do, you might discuss things we *must not* do: look down on people, be argumentative or insulting, and the like.

4. The Samaritan woman's excitement about Jesus stirred her neighbors to come hear Him. Jesus Himself said the harvest was ready (v. 35). How can we be more eager and effective in sharing the gospel and reaping this harvest?

Encourage your students to spend some time meditating on the great value of the gift of salvation. The more appreciative we are of what the Lord has done for us, the more eager we'll be to share it. Some success in sharing our faith will also energize us, so evaluate what you are doing as a church to reap this harvest.

Start with what you are already doing and suggest ways to improve. What are you doing to publicize your church and the ministries you offer, the needs you meet? What are you doing specifically for outsiders? If your church programming is predominantly for the convenience of the members, what can you do to change that? How are you training people for evangelism? How can you improve?

Discuss also some new fields in which your church can work. Is there a growing Spanish-speaking or other ethnic population nearby? How might you minister there? Is there an inner-city work that could use your help?

5. The Samaritans came out to investigate Jesus for themselves and were convinced. What do you think is the most convincing thing about who Jesus is today? How can we help people see that for themselves?

The Samaritan woman could bring her friends to the physical, human Jesus. We can bring people to the body of Christ, the church. Is our church a convincing demonstration of the love and power and deity of Christ? We can also point people to the Bible. Though some are skeptical of the Bible's veracity, those who will approach it with an open mind will find it convincing. Are we letting the Bible speak, or are we giving our own opinions?

Jesus Is Crucified and Resurrected

DEVOTIONAL READING: Acts 2:32-39.

LESSON SCRIPTURE: John 18:1—20:18.

PRINTED TEXT: John 19:16-18, 28-30; 20:11-18.

John 19:16-18, 28-30

16 Then delivered he him therefore unto them to be crucified. And they took Jesus, and led him away.

17 And he bearing his cross went forth into a place called the place of a skull, which is called in the Hebrew Golgotha:

18 Where they crucified him, and two others with him, on either side one, and Jesus in the midst.

. . . .

28 After this, Jesus knowing that all things were now accomplished, that the Scripture might be fulfilled, saith, I thirst.

29 Now there was set a vessel full of vinegar: and they filled a sponge with vinegar, and put it upon hyssop, and put it to his mouth.

30 When Jesus therefore had received the vinegar, he said, It is finished: and he bowed his head, and gave up the ghost.

John 20:11-18

11 But Mary stood without at the sepulchre weeping: and as she wept, she stooped down, and looked into the sepulchre,

12 And seeth two angels in white sitting, the one at the head, and the other at the feet, where the body of Jesus had lain.

13 And they say unto her, Woman, why weepest thou? She saith unto them, Because they have taken away my Lord, and I know not where they have laid him.

14 And when she had thus said, she turned herself back, and saw Jesus standing, and knew not that it was Jesus.

15 Jesus saith unto her, Woman, why weepest thou? whom seekest thou? She, supposing him to be the gardener, saith unto him, Sir, if thou have borne him hence, tell me where thou hast laid him, and I will take him away.

16 Jesus saith unto her, Mary. She turned herself, and saith unto him, Rabboni; which is to say, Master.

17 Jesus saith unto her, Touch me not; for I am not yet ascended to my Father: but go to my brethren, and say unto them, I ascend unto my Father, and your Father; and to my God, and your God.

18 Mary Magdalene came and told the disciples that she had seen the Lord, and that he had spoken these things unto her.

GOLDEN TEXT: He [the angel] saith unto them, Be not affrighted: ye seek Jesus of Nazareth, which was crucified: he is risen; he is not here: behold the place where they laid him.—Mark 16:6.

That You May Believe

Unit 2: Jesus Is Raised to Life

(Lessons 5, 6)

Lesson Aims

This lesson should equip the student to:

1. Recount the details of Jesus' death and His postresurrection appearance to Mary.

2. Explain why the death and resurrection of Jesus must continue to be the focus of the church's message to the world.

3. Suggest one or two ways the student or class can tell in a fresh way the good news of Jesus' resurrection.

Lesson Outline

INTRODUCTION
    A. Why Are You Crying?
    B. John and His Friends
    C. Lesson Background
  I. JESUS' CRUCIFIXION (John 19:16-18)
    The Scorned Becomes Sacred
 II. JESUS' DEATH (John 19:28-30)
III. MARY MAGDALENE SEES THE RISEN LORD (John 20:11-18)
    A. Angels Inquire (vv. 11-13)
    B. Jesus Makes Himself Known (vv. 14-16)
    Jesus Saith Unto Her, "Mary"
    C. Jesus Sends Mary (vv. 17, 18)
CONCLUSION
    A. Seeing, Hearing, and Telling
    B. Prayer
    C. Thought to Remember

Introduction

A. Why Are You Crying?

She was in college far from home, and in rehearsal for the prime dramatic event of the season. Today, however, she had learned that her mother's mysterious health problem appeared to be a long-term incurable disease. So between "takes" the girl was seeking quiet comfort in a darkened corner with a box of facial tissues. First to see her there was a seminary student with whom she shared a speaking acquaintance.

"Problems?" he wanted to know.

"You might say so," she replied.

"Do you want to talk about it?" he persisted.

"Not really," she said between sniffles.

But the young man was persistent. "Have you prayed about it?" This "preacher's kid" then brought out a clean handkerchief to replace the soggy tissues.

"I haven't done much else all day," she sobbed. She figured that if this pushy pest wanted a problem, she would lay it on him. So she did, and he listened and shed a few tears himself. The young man could at least weep with those who weep. Finally, with her permission, he laid it on the Lord.

A year or so later the girl's parents visited the college and had dinner with her and the "pushy preacher" student. They rejoiced together as an engagement ring went on the appropriate finger. Mother commented, "I'm so glad that someone could benefit from my illness."

"Why are you crying?" That's a good question to ask anyone in tears. Both angels and Jesus Himself asked the question of Mary Magdalene. The risen Christ then changed Mary's tears of sorrow to tears of joy—an experience that has been repeated numerous times in the lives of other followers of Jesus.

B. John and His Friends

When the apostle John wrote his inspired record of Jesus in the fourth Gospel, he was surely aware of what had been written earlier by his fellow apostle Matthew, by Peter's friend Mark, and by the careful historian Luke. Each had written in his own way for a special audience. John, the "disciple whom Jesus loved," could still supply important information as an intimate witness of Jesus' life and ministry. His focus on Mary Magdalene as the first witness of the risen Christ is a case in point.

Mary Magdalene is mentioned earlier by Luke as one of the women from Galilee who were blessed by Jesus' healing ministry and expressed their gratitude by supporting His work financially (8:1-3). The designation "Magdalene" distinguishes this Mary from other Marys mentioned in the Gospels. It probably indicates that she came from Magdala, a town located on the southwest shore of the Sea of Galilee. Luke specifically notes that Jesus cast out seven devils from Mary (Luke 8:2). It is fruitless to speculate about the nature of the devils or their influence on Mary, but her deliverance obviously identified her as one who had received much from the Lord and therefore loved much in return (Luke 7:47). That great love became increasingly evident during the events of Jesus' death and resurrection.

C. Lesson Background

Assigned for background reading this week are two and one-half chapters: John 18:1—20:18. These are important to the understanding of our printed text from John 19 and 20. Thus a brief survey of the events recorded within these chapters is in order. After Jesus' memorable Passover with His disciples in the upper room in Jerusalem, He led them to the Mount of Olives. There He engaged in intense prayer, after which Judas came with temple officers to arrest Him (John 18:1-11).

Jesus was then subjected to a series of "trials" before the high priest and Sanhedrin (who pronounced Him guilty of blasphemy against God), before Herod, and before Pilate, the Roman governor of Judea. Pilate, questioning Jesus privately, was quickly convinced of His innocence and made a series of efforts to set Him free. He sought to accomplish this by a Passover tradition of releasing one prisoner; however, Jesus' accusers "moved the people, that he should rather release Barabbas unto them" (Mark 15:11). When the Jewish leaders linked Pilate's desire to release Jesus with sedition against Rome (John 19:12-15), Pilate, whose position with Rome was rather shaky, gave in to their demands to put Jesus to death.

I. Jesus' Crucifixion
(John 19:16-18)

16. Then delivered he him therefore unto them to be crucified. And they took Jesus, and led him away.

Pilate *delivered* two prisoners to different fates: guilty Barabbas to freedom, and innocent Jesus *to be crucified*. The Romans executed the most despised criminals by fastening them to crosses, where they were exposed to maximum shame and pain before death. The Jewish leaders' fury against Jesus was so intense that they welcomed the opportunity to expose Him to the most degrading punishment. Since Rome did not permit the Jews to execute anyone, Jesus' sentence of crucifixion was carried out by the Romans.

17, 18. And he bearing his cross went forth into a place called the place of a skull, which is called in the Hebrew Golgotha: where they crucified him, and two others with him, on either side one, and Jesus in the midst.

[See question #1, page 272.] The victim of crucifixion was required to carry at least one beam of the *cross* to the place of execution. Luke 23:26 indicates that Jesus, apparently exhausted and unable to continue carrying the cross, was relieved of this duty. A bystander named Simon was seized from the crowd to finish the task.

Jewish law forbade executions within the walls of a city (Acts 7:58); thus Jesus was *crucified* outside Jerusalem at *Golgotha*, meaning *the place of a skull*. Such a name could indicate the

use of this site for executions, or it may have called attention to the appearance of the location. (A proposed site of the crucifixion, known as Gordon's Calvary, contains two hollow spaces on the side of the hill that resemble two eyes.) The Latin equivalent of the name, *Calvary* (Luke 23:33), is perhaps more pleasant to the ear than the harsh Hebrew *Golgotha*, and so *Calvary* appears more frequently in song and story. But there is nothing pleasing or appealing to the physical senses in what happened to Jesus at Golgotha.

That *two others*, called "thieves" by Matthew (27:38) and Mark (15:27) and "malefactors," or criminals, by Luke (23:32), should be crucified *on either side* of Jesus was an evident attempt to discredit Him by association. Instead, it fulfilled a Messianic prophecy (Isaiah 53:12) and provided an opportunity for Jesus, even in dying, to show the way of life to a penitent transgressor (Luke 23:39-43).

THE SCORNED BECOMES SACRED

When the idea was first suggested of building a memorial to honor the American military personnel who had been killed in the Vietnam War (more than fifty thousand of them), it was determined that a contest would be held to decide what type of memorial it should be. The winning idea was one presented by a young Chinese-American girl, Maya Lin, and selected over 1,420 other entries. Her proposal was to construct a wall on which would be engraved the name of every American serviceman or servicewoman who had lost his or her life during the Vietnam War.

At first the idea of a wall engraved with names seemed so ordinary that many thought it an insult to the soldiers rather than a tribute. Many bitterly objected to its construction. With the passing of time, however, the Vietnam Wall has become deeply revered and greatly respected. People now glory in what was once scorned.

How to Say It

BARABBAS. Buh-*rab*-us.
CLEOPAS. *Klee*-uh-pass.
EMMAUS. Em-*may*-us.
GOLGOTHA. *Gahl*-guh-thuh.
MAGDALA. *Mag*-duh-luh.
MAGDALENE. *Mag*-duh-leen or Mag-duh-*lee*-nee.
RABBI. *Rab*-eye.
RABBONI. Rab-*o*-nye.
SANHEDRIN. San-*heed*-run or *San*-huh-drin.
SEPULCHRE. *sep*-ull-kur.

Crucifixion was the most scorned and severe form of execution in the world of Jesus' day. However, Jesus' death on a cross for the sins of the world transformed something hideous and repulsive into an emblem of victory and freedom. Paul was unashamed to glory in the cross of Christ (Galatians 6:14), and so are Jesus' followers today. What was once despised and scorned remains a means of transformation, blessing, and renewal of life.   —J. G. V. B.

II. Jesus' Death
(John 19:28-30)

Verses 19-27, not included in our printed text, tell us that Pilate refused to change the inscription he had displayed above Jesus' head: "Jesus of Nazareth the King of the Jews." The attending soldiers divided Jesus' garments among them and cast lots for His cloak, as Psalm 22:18 said they would. Jesus consigned the care of His mother to "the disciple . . . whom he loved," apparently a reference to John. Thus Jesus was serving and thinking of others, even while He was dying for the sins of the world.

28. After this, Jesus knowing that all things were now accomplished, that the Scripture might be fulfilled, saith, I thirst.

From extreme loss of blood and sheer exhaustion, Jesus suffered a burning, ravishing *thirst*. Even now, *Scripture* continued to be *fulfilled*: "My strength is dried up like a potsherd; and my tongue cleaveth to my jaws; and thou hast brought me into the dust of death" (Psalm 22:15). No one would begrudge Jesus' giving a little attention to His own need at this point, but even His request for refreshment may have been not only for Himself. As He prepared for His victory cry (v. 30), it may be that He wanted to be sure it

was clear and understood. A little moisture in His mouth would help Him to speak more loudly and clearly. [See question #2, page 272.]

29. Now there was set a vessel full of vinegar: and they filled a sponge with vinegar, and put it upon hyssop, and put it to his mouth.

At hand was a container of *vinegar*—a cheap, sour wine possibly present for the soldiers' refreshment. This was not the mixture containing a pain-deadening drug that Jesus had earlier rejected (Mark 15:23). The present meager relief was made available by dipping a *sponge* in the wine, placing it on the tip of a reed or stalk from the *hyssop* plant, and lifting it to Jesus' *mouth*. Psalm 69:21 had said with prophetic foresight, "In my thirst they gave me vinegar to drink."

30. When Jesus therefore had received the vinegar, he said, It is finished: and he bowed his head, and gave up the ghost.

Jesus had laid down His heavenly glory to come to earth. He had laid down His rights and interests and concerns to serve and teach others. He could say to God His Father, "I have glorified thee on the earth: I have finished the work which thou gavest me to do" (John 17:4). Now that work—the work of saving lost humanity by bearing "our sins in his own body on the tree" (1 Peter 2:24)—was *finished*.

Seldom did a crucified person die in so short a time. For this reason the Roman authorities verified Jesus' death by piercing His side with a spear (John 19:31-37). This also fulfilled Scripture (Psalm 34:20; Zechariah 12:10). The Lord's body was taken from the cross and entombed by loving hands. His friends then dispersed to observe the Sabbath (John 19:38-42).

III. Mary Magdalene Sees
the Risen Lord (John 20:11-18)

The first ten verses of John 20 tell us that Mary Magdalene came to the tomb very early on the first day of the week and found the stone at the entrance of the sepulchre removed. (Other women accompanied her in this journey, but John does not mention them.) Mary Magdalene hurried to report the apparent grave robbery to Peter and John, who ran to the site and found the sepulchre empty except for the linen grave clothes. Then the men went home.

A. Angels Inquire (vv. 11-13)

11, 12. But Mary stood without at the sepulchre weeping: and as she wept, she stooped down, and looked into the sepulchre, and seeth two angels in white sitting, the one at the head, and the other at the feet, where the body of Jesus had lain.

Home Daily Bible Readings

Monday, Mar. 29—Judas Betrays Jesus (John 18:1-14)

Tuesday, Mar. 30—Peter Denies He Is a Disciple (John 18:15-27)

Wednesday, Mar. 31— Pilate Gives the People a Choice (John 18:28-40)

Thursday, Apr. 1—Jesus Is Condemned to Crucifixion (John 19:1-16a)

Friday, Apr. 2—Jesus Is Crucified (John 19:16b-30)

Saturday, Apr. 3—The Day of Preparation (John 19:31-42)

Sunday, Apr. 4—I Have Seen the Lord (John 20:1-18)

The *weeping* represented here is loud wailing, which might be expected of Mary Magdalene in her present grief and frustration. She had lost the one who had delivered her from a hopeless, demon-possessed existence and given meaning to her life. Now she had come to anoint His body and it was not to be found. Apparently she had not yet examined the interior of the tomb, so she *stooped down* to look through the low doorway. There on the shelf designed to accommodate the body were *two* individuals. John tells us they were *angels*, but he does not tell us whether Mary realized that fact or not.

13. And they say unto her, Woman, why weepest thou? She saith unto them, Because they have taken away my Lord, and I know not where they have laid him.

Why weepest thou? In reply Mary repeated what she had already told Peter and John (v. 2). She had expected to shed tears as she anointed the body. Now she sobbed in total frustration at finding no body to anoint.

They have taken away my Lord. It did not occur to Mary to speak of the "body" or the "remains" of one who had died. This was still the Friend whom she had known and loved.

B. Jesus Makes Himself Known (vv. 14-16)

14. And when she had thus said, she turned herself back, and saw Jesus standing, and knew not that it was Jesus.

We can only guess why Mary *turned* away from the angels. Was it a gesture of hopelessness to end the conversation? Did she sense that someone was behind her? Did the angels suddenly vanish from sight? And why did she not recognize Jesus when she saw Him? Were her eyes blurred with tears? Did she see Him indistinctly as she turned halfway around? We are reminded, however, that Jesus appeared "in another form" (Mark 16:12) to Cleopas and his companion on the way to Emmaus, and that "their eyes were holden" that they did not recognize Him (Luke 24:16).

While we may question why Mary could not recognize Jesus any sooner than she did, we should stop and ask: are any of us more prepared in times of major stress to recognize the presence of Jesus to help us overcome our difficulties? [See question #3, page 272.]

15. Jesus saith unto her, Woman, why weepest thou? whom seekest thou? She, supposing him to be the gardener, saith unto him, Sir, if thou have borne him hence, tell me where thou hast laid him, and I will take him away.

Again Mary Magdalene was asked to explain her distress. But this time Jesus' query went a step further: "You're looking for *someone*—who

is it?" That question is appropriate to address to anyone in trouble. Healing can come with the finding, not of some *thing*, but of some *one*; and that someone is always Jesus.

The questioner was obviously a friendly person, perhaps thought Mary, the *gardener*, or caretaker, of the grounds. (This indicates that the resurrected Christ had a common human appearance.) Mary addressed him respectfully as *Sir*. She assumed that he already knew the answer to the question he had just raised: that she was looking for the occupant of the tomb. Perhaps he knew where the body was. Perhaps it was he who had *borne*, or carried, it somewhere else. She would gladly take care of the body if he would simply *tell* her where it was. However, the promise found in Matthew 5:4 was about to be fulfilled: "Blessed are they that mourn: for they shall be comforted."

16. Jesus saith unto her, Mary. She turned herself, and saith unto him, Rabboni; which is to say, Master.

The sound of her name spoken in Jesus' familiar tones was all the identification Mary needed! The Good Shepherd, who had laid down His life for His sheep and then taken it again, had called one of His own by name (John 10:3, 14-17). Mary *turned* to look directly at Him, instantly calling out the affectionate title: *Rabboni*! While this meant the same as the more common *Rabbi* ("my teacher"), it was a more respectful form of address (in fact, it was often used in referring to God). Thus with audio-visual proof, Mary Magdalene became the first to see Jesus alive after His resurrection.

JESUS SAITH UNTO HER, "MARY"

This is one of the most tender and beautiful passages in the New Testament. When Mary did not recognize the risen Jesus, but mistook Him for a gardener, He spoke just one word to her— her own name, *Mary*. It is not hard to imagine the quick gasp of breath and the wonder of

Today's visual tries to express the love, awe, and complete amazement that were Mary's as she realized she was speaking to the risen Lord.

Visual for lesson 5

recognition in her eyes as she reverently addressed Him as *Rabboni*! or "Master!"

Most of us in the intimacy of family life give and receive "pet" names or nicknames. Examples are "Shorty," "Sunshine," "Pug," "Kiddo," and "Cutie." As the years go by, some of us may acquire titles or degrees and may be addressed by many as "Doctor," "Judge," or "Professor." Yet when we go back home and get back in touch with those who are nearest and dearest to us, we are still "Pug" or "Kiddo." And when we hear a certain person call us by one of those names, we know almost immediately who it is.

So it was with Mary. No one else had ever spoken her name in just the way Jesus did. Warm, tender, compassionate—*Mary*. So it will be when we hear our name spoken in the eternal city whose builder and maker is God. We will hear our name as our Savior knows it and, like Mary, we shall know fulfillment, reunion, and ecstasy as we reply, *Master*.   —J. G. V. B.

C. Jesus Sends Mary (vv. 17, 18)

17. Jesus saith unto her, Touch me not; for I am not yet ascended to my Father: but go to my brethren, and say unto them, I ascend unto my Father, and your Father; and to my God, and your God.

Jesus' command *touch me not* seems to contradict what occurred according to other passages. For example, Matthew 28:9 tells of an incident very shortly after this when some of the faithful women held Jesus by the feet and worshiped Him. Luke 24:39 says that Jesus invited the apostles to touch and feel His risen body.

This "contradiction" can be answered by noting the tense of the verb *touch* as it appears in the Greek text, where it implies continual action. Most recent versions thus translate Jesus' command to Mary as, "Do not hold on to me" (*New International Version*) or "Stop clinging to Me" (*New American Standard Bible*). Rather than to linger with Jesus, Mary was to go immediately and tell others that He had risen. Much was yet to be done in the days before Jesus ascended into Heaven.

The term *brethren* most likely refers to Jesus' disciples (Matthew 28:7). They were to be the primary witnesses of the good news of His resurrection (Luke 24:47-49). The word signaled the new and special relationship that followers of the living Lord are meant to have with Him (Psalm 22:22; Hebrews 2:11, 12).

Since Jesus and His followers are brethren, He can now refer to God as *my Father, and your Father*. However, God's relationship to Jesus as His Father is quite different from God's relationship to us in the same capacity. He is the Son of God by nature; we are sons of God by adoption (Romans 8:14-17; Galatians 4:4-7).

18. Mary Magdalene came and told the disciples that she had seen the Lord, and that he had spoken these things unto her.

In this summary statement is a vital link in the gospel chain from fact to faith, from Jesus to each of us. The first witness to the resurrection is identified as *Mary Magdalene*. In obedience to Jesus she came to His *disciples*, bearing witness that *she had seen the Lord*. Her report was faithful in fact and in word. John, the "disciple whom Jesus loved," kept in memory what Mary told and preserved, through the guidance of God's Spirit, the vivid details. He recorded them that others may read and believe and find eternal life in Christ (John 20:30, 31). [See question #4, page 272.]

Conclusion

A. Seeing, Hearing, and Telling

"Blessed are your eyes," said Jesus to His disciples, "for they see: and your ears, for they hear" (Matthew 13:16). Seeing eyes and hearing ears are exemplary faculties of the disciples and their companions, such as Mary Magdalene. They saw what Jesus did, they heard what He said, and they reported accurately what they observed. It was no ordinary experience that they talked about; it was the knowledge of the one and only Son of God. The object of their seeing and hearing and telling—Jesus, God's Son—is what made their report so effective in serving God and annoying His enemies. Men such as Peter and John, who saw and heard Jesus both before and after His death and resurrection, refused to yield to others' efforts to silence them: "We cannot but speak the things which we have seen and heard" (Acts 4:20). The "things" that they and Mary Magdalene saw and heard in Jesus demand and deserve telling again and again—until He returns. [See question #5, page 272.]

B. Prayer

We praise You, Father, for the privilege of weeping again with those who wept at Jesus' death, and of sharing in their joy at reporting the glorious news of His resurrection. Equip us with the courage and the willingness to tell this life-giving story to others. In Jesus' name. Amen.

C. Thought to Remember

"Christ died for our sins according to the Scriptures; . . . he was buried, and . . . he rose again the third day according to the Scriptures" (1 Corinthians 15:3, 4).

Learning by Doing

This page contains an alternate lesson plan emphasizing learning activities.
Classes desiring such student involvement will find these suggestions helpful.

Learning Goals

This lesson should equip the student to:

1. Recount the details of Jesus' death and His postresurrection appearance to Mary.

2. Explain why the death and resurrection of Jesus must continue to be the focus of the church's message to the world.

3. Suggest one or two ways the student or class can tell in a fresh way the good news of Jesus' resurrection.

Into the Lesson

Begin the lesson by asking one or more of the following questions: (1) What does it take for you to accept something as a fact? Explain how you decide that a statement is a fact. (2) What is required for you to accept a prediction as true?

The answers will vary, based as they are on personal experiences and viewpoint. Out of the responses, you may draw a distinction between fact and belief, pointing out that beliefs should be based on facts. (A similar activity appears in the student book.)

Observe that today's lesson involves the most "incredible" fact of history: the resurrection of Jesus Christ. Yet, in spite of the unbelievable nature of the report, the evidence is overwhelming. Jesus is alive! We'll look at some of the evidence for this fact in today's lesson.

Into the Word

Begin with a description of crucifixion as a form of capital punishment (a Bible dictionary will be useful). Distinguish it from other forms used in modern times (hanging, beheading, firing squad, electrocution, lethal injection, gas). All of these methods, if done properly, result in instant death, whereas crucifixion was a deliberately slow and brutally painful death. Establish the fact that the Roman soldiers were experts in death. No one came down off a cross alive!

Have a volunteer read John 19:16-18, 28-30. Ask the others to listen while the text is read and list all the details they can about Jesus' death; list these on the chalkboard as students report them after the reading. (Pilate turned Jesus over to the soldiers ["Then delivered he him therefore unto them"], v. 16; the order was "to be crucified," v. 16; the soldiers took Him as ordered, v. 16; Jesus carried His own cross—at least for a while, v. 17; He went to Golgotha,

v. 17; Jesus was crucified, v. 18; two others were crucified with Him, v. 18; Jesus said He was thirsty, v. 28; He was given wine vinegar, vv. 29, 30; Jesus declared His work "finished," v. 30; Jesus yielded up His spirit, v. 30.) Use the comments in the exposition section to note the significance of these details as they are reported.

Ask another volunteer to read John 20:11-18. This tells of Jesus' appearance to Mary Magdalene. Again, have the class list details as the text is read and then summarize. (Mary waited alone outside the tomb, v. 11; she was crying, v. 11; she saw two angels inside the tomb, v. 12; the angels asked her why she was crying, and she said Jesus' body had been moved to an unknown location, v. 13; when Jesus first appeared, Mary did not recognize Him, v. 14; Jesus repeated the angels' question, v. 15; Mary thought Jesus was the gardener and asked Him to direct her to Jesus' body, v. 15; at the sound of her name, Mary recognized Jesus, v. 16; she addressed Jesus as "Master," v. 16; Jesus would not allow Mary to touch—hold on to—Him, but told her to go to the disciples, v. 17; Mary obeyed and went to report the resurrection to them, v. 18.)

Into Life

Ask your students to cite some things they believe to be true that they have not verified by personal observation or experience. (They may suggest the existence of historical characters like national heroes; the presence of microscopic organisms like germs, viruses, and bacteria; historical events, etc.). Discuss why we believe in these. (Note the importance of eyewitness testimony.)

Observe that we have no living eyewitnesses today to testify of Jesus' resurrection. But we have the written record of eyewitnesses, like the ones we have noted today. (See also Acts 4:20 and 1 John 1:1-3.) Ask a volunteer to read 1 Corinthians 15:1-11. Note how Paul appealed to eyewitness testimony to plead for the truth of the resurrection. Discuss what Paul says about the importance of keeping the facts of the death, burial, and resurrection of Jesus central to the message we preach.

Divide the class into groups of four or five. Ask each group to develop a way to present the good news of Jesus' death and resurrection in a fresh and meaningful way. Share these ideas at the conclusion of your class time.

Let's Talk It Over

The questions on this page are designed to encourage review of the lesson Scriptures and to promote discussion of the lesson by the class. The answers provided are only discussion starters. Let your class talk it over from there.

1. Suppose, while studying this passage with a friend, your friend says, "Hey! This says Jesus carried His own cross. I thought one of the other Gospels said that they made a guy named Simon carry it. That's why I just can't believe the Bible: it's full of contradictions!" How would you respond?

Unbelievers often make the charge that *differing* testimony is *contradictory* testimony. That is simply not true. It is obvious from the accounts in Matthew 27:31, 32; Mark 15:20, 21; and Luke 23:26 that Jesus was bearing His own cross when the procession to Golgotha began. It is this time period that John describes. Somewhere along the way Simon of Cyrene was pressed into duty to carry the cross. We do not really know why— perhaps the common explanation that Jesus fell with the cross is correct, though the Bible never says so. But the fact remains that there is no contradiction between John's account and that of the other Gospels.

2. John notes in verse 28, as in other places, that Jesus' actions came "that the Scripture might be fulfilled." What significance do you find in this? How does it help your faith in Jesus?

The fulfillment of Scripture in Jesus' life is significant for several reasons. Fulfilled prophecy is one of the best witnesses to the identification of Jesus as the Christ. No one could have fulfilled all the Messianic prophecies by accident. No impostor could have read the prophecies and set about to fulfill them all, for some required actions by others.

Another point of significance is that the fulfillment of Scripture gives us confidence in the Bible. Yet another is that it reassures us that the crucifixion was no mistake. Some believe Jesus' death was not in God's plan, and the church is some kind of "Plan B" to make up for it. That is clearly not the case. Our redemption through Jesus' atoning death and our incorporation into His body, the church, is God's Plan A. There is no Plan B!

3. The lesson writer asks, "Are any of us more prepared [than Mary Magdalene] in times of major stress to recognize the presence of Jesus to help us overcome our difficulties?"

How can we be so prepared? How can we help others in difficult times to recognize the presence of our Lord?

Allow several students to share how God has seen them through difficult times. You might comment on the difference between quoting platitudes and giving sincere, heartfelt words of comfort. Allow the situation of Mary to instruct your class: the fact that she didn't recognize Jesus did not at all mean He was not there. We may not always recognize the presence of the Lord with us, but He is there!

4. The lesson writer calls John's summary in John 20:18 "a vital link in the gospel chain from fact to faith, from Jesus to each of us." How can we add more links to this chain—as a church and as individuals?

This metaphor illustrates the importance of evangelism. Review with your class what your church is currently doing to win the lost, both in your own community and worldwide through the support of missions. How can those efforts be improved, either through increased activity or through making the activities more effective? Are you targeting specific groups with methods that are likely to be effective with those groups, or are you trying to use the same approach with everyone? Does everyone feel welcome to join in those efforts, or do some feel that one has to be an "expert" to share the gospel? Is training available to help people know how to share their faith?

A chain ends when no more links are added. God has people He wants *us* to approach with the gospel, and He is counting on us to do it!

5. We are not eyewitnesses to the resurrection. We cannot, like Mary and Peter and John, "speak the things which we have seen and heard" (Acts 4:20) when we tell of Jesus' resurrection. So what can we tell?

If students are slow to respond, ask, "What did someone tell *you*, that caused you to believe?" Of course, we can tell what the New Testament witnesses saw and heard. That is the reason these things were written down (John 20:30, 31). But we, too, can "speak the things which we have seen and heard." Haven't we seen the change in our lives, and in the lives of others, that Jesus has produced? We can surely tell that!

Jesus Appears to His Disciples

DEVOTIONAL READING: **Mark 9:14-24.**

LESSON SCRIPTURE: **John 20:19-29.**

PRINTED TEXT: **John 20:19-29.**

John 20:19-29

19 Then the same day at evening, being the first day of the week, when the doors were shut where the disciples were assembled for fear of the Jews, came Jesus and stood in the midst, and saith unto them, Peace be unto you.

20 And when he had so said, he showed unto them his hands and his side. Then were the disciples glad, when they saw the Lord.

21 Then said Jesus to them again, Peace be unto you: as my Father hath sent me, even so send I you.

22 And when he had said this, he breathed on them, and saith unto them, Receive ye the Holy Ghost:

23 Whosesoever sins ye remit, they are remitted unto them; and whosesoever sins ye retain, they are retained.

24 But Thomas, one of the twelve, called Didymus, was not with them when Jesus came.

25 The other disciples therefore said unto him, We have seen the Lord. But he said unto them, Except I shall see in his hands the print of the nails, and put my finger into the print of the nails, and thrust my hand into his side, I will not believe.

26 And after eight days again his disciples were within, and Thomas with them: then came Jesus, the doors being shut, and stood in the midst, and said, Peace be unto you.

27 Then saith he to Thomas, Reach hither thy finger, and behold my hands; and reach hither thy hand, and thrust it into my side; and be not faithless, but believing.

28 And Thomas answered and said unto him, My Lord and my God.

29 Jesus saith unto him, Thomas, because thou hast seen me, thou hast believed: blessed are they that have not seen, and yet have believed.

GOLDEN TEXT: Blessed are they that have not seen, and yet have believed.—John 20:29.

That You May Believe
Unit 2: Jesus Is Raised to Life
(Lessons 5, 6)

Lesson Aims

As a result of this lesson each student should be able to:

1. Summarize the events of the two postresurrection appearances included in today's printed text.

2. Cite several "infallible proofs" for believing in Jesus' resurrection.

3. Give encouragement to someone this week who, like the doubting disciples, needs reassurance regarding his or her faith.

Lesson Outline

INTRODUCTION
  A. "He Is Risen"
  B. Lesson Background
I. JESUS AND THE DISCIPLES (John 20:19-23)
  A. Coming Among Them (v. 19)
  B. Convincing Proof (v. 20)
  C. Commission Given (vv. 21-23)
    Sent!
II. JESUS AND THOMAS (John 20:24-29)
  A. Skeptical Absentee (vv. 24, 25)
  B. Second Appearance (v. 26)
    Jesus' Greeting of "Peace"
  C. Seeing and Acknowledging (vv. 27, 28)
  D. Blessing of Believing (v. 29)
CONCLUSION
  A. Join the Rejoicing
  B. Prayer
  C. Thought to Remember

Introduction

A. "He Is Risen"

We sat enthralled for five hours in the great theater at Oberammergau in Bavaria, watching the village's dramatic presentation of the life and death of Jesus. The production was the renowned "Passion Play," emphasizing Jesus' suffering for our sins. It lingered on a scene not at all found in Scripture—Mary, Jesus' mother, holding and weeping over His body after it was removed from the cross. A hurried acknowledgment of Jesus' resurrection concluded the play, but the lasting impression was not a triumphant one. It lacked the angel's victorious announcement at the empty tomb: "Ye seek Jesus of Nazareth, which was crucified: he is risen; he is not here: behold the place where they laid him" (Mark 16:6).

A large segment of the "Christian" world still clings to its crucifixes—artistic representations of Jesus dying or dead on the cross—and bids us weep with them there. Today we join with the Lord's disciples in finding Him alive. Let us rejoice in the angel's glorious news: "He is risen; He is not here!"

B. Lesson Background

Early in His ministry, Jesus spoke of His eventual death and resurrection. He did this using symbolic language that the disciples did not grasp. The first record of such a warning was at the Passover in Jesus' first year of ministry (John 2:19). Another came midway through the Lord's ministry (Matthew 12:40). In the last months of His ministry, and following Peter's Good Confession, Jesus began to speak "openly" (Mark 8:32), or plainly, about these matters. Matthew 16:21 notes that Jesus told the disciples that He "must go unto Jerusalem, and suffer many things . . . and be killed, and be raised again the third day." This emphasis is also found in Matthew 17:22, 23; 20:17-19; Mark 8:31; 9:31; 10:32-34; Luke 9:22, 44, 45; 18:31-33. Yet the disciples seem to have rejected so vigorously the idea of Jesus' death that they did not even hear Him say He would rise again. In none of them do we find any trace of expectation that this would happen. Only after they saw Jesus alive after the crucifixion and were convinced by "many infallible proofs" (Acts 1:3) that He was indeed alive, did they recall His earlier predictions (John 2:22).

The risen Lord appeared first to Mary Magdalene and other women who came early to the tomb (Mark 16:1; Luke 24:1), then to Peter (Luke 24:34; 1 Corinthians 15:5), and to Cleopas and his friend on the road to Emmaus (Luke 24:13-35). These last two returned to Jerusalem to tell their news to the disciples. They found the group discussing the reports from the women and from Peter.

I. Jesus and the Disciples
(John 20:19-23)

A. Coming Among Them (v. 19)

19. Then the same day at evening, being the first day of the week, when the doors were shut where the disciples were assembled for fear of the Jews, came Jesus and stood in the midst, and saith unto them, Peace be unto you.

Resurrection Day was marked by important events from early dawn until *evening*. Ever since then, *the first day of the week* has been special to believers in the risen Lord. Gathered that evening—perhaps in the upper room where they had observed the Passover with Jesus (Luke 22:12, 13)—*the disciples* were concerned for their own safety. *The Jews* who had pursued Jesus to His death could be expected to press their campaign against any of His known companions. They had already tried to turn Rome's officers against the disciples by reporting the resurrection as a case of grave robbery (Matthew 28:11-15). The two from Emmaus and any others in the present gathering (Luke 24:33) must have been carefully identified before they were admitted. Security was of the utmost concern.

However, there was no need (and no possibility!) of securing the place against the risen Lord. Suddenly He *stood in the midst* of those who were discussing the reports of His resurrection. His familiar, reassuring greeting of *peace* was most timely. [See question #1, page 280.]

B. Convincing Proof (v. 20)

20. And when he had so said, he showed unto them his hands and his side. Then were the disciples glad, when they saw the Lord.

Luke 24:36-43 provides a more detailed account of this incident. At first the disciples were frightened, thinking they were seeing a ghost. To allay these fears Jesus said, "Behold my hands and my feet, that it is I myself: handle me, and see; for a spirit hath not flesh and bones, as ye see me have" (v. 39). Instead of Jesus' feet, John mentions Jesus' *side*, which was pierced by a spear in the hands of a soldier certifying Jesus' death. This is a detail of the crucifixion mentioned only by John (John 19:31-37). Luke also notes that, to remove any lingering doubts the disciples may have had, Jesus asked for food and ate it in their presence (Luke 24:42).

Many years later the apostle John wrote, "That which was from the beginning, which we have heard, which we have seen with our eyes, which we have looked upon, and our hands have handled, of the Word of life; . . . declare we unto you" (1 John 1:1-3). Thus the apostles *saw the Lord*, risen from the dead. Their eyes took in the details; their hands verified that they were not dreaming or hallucinating; their minds accepted the marvelous fact. This was indeed the same Jesus with whom they had walked and worked, and whom they had come to know as Lord and Master. They had reason to be *glad* to the ultimate degree!

C. Commission Given (vv. 21-23)

Jesus' Great Commission was given on a number of occasions following His resurrection. Here we see Him giving it in Jerusalem on the evening of Resurrection Day (Luke 24:46-49 notes this as well). In Mark 16:14-16 it appears immediately following the account of Jesus' appearances on Resurrection Day, but without indication of time or place. In Matthew 28:18-20, it is spoken to the apostles on a mountain in Galilee. In Acts 1:7, 8 it is given immediately before Jesus' ascension from the Mount of Olives.

21. Then said Jesus to them again, Peace be unto you: as my Father hath sent me, even so send I you.

Here were echoes and reinforcements of Jesus' Passover conversation with the disciples: "Peace I leave with you, my peace I give unto you: not as the world giveth, give I unto you. Let not your heart be troubled, neither let it be afraid" (John 14:27). Later Jesus prayed for the disciples: "As thou hast sent me into the world, even so have I also sent them into the world" (John 17:18).

An awesome responsibility accompanied the comparison of the disciples' commission from Jesus with the commission that *sent* Jesus from Heaven to earth! Their need for inner *peace* and practical courage would apply to matters far more important and more lasting than any immediate fear of trouble from the Jews.

SENT!

During one of Jesus' earliest postresurrection appearances, He commissioned His disciples to go forth carrying the message of forgiveness of sins. He told them, "As my Father hath sent me, even so send I you." (John 20:21).

In 1803 United States President Thomas Jefferson sent out Meriwether Lewis and William Clark on an expedition to the Pacific coast. They were to cross rivers, deserts, and mountains in a journey of many thousands of miles. They explored territory that no other white men had ever seen. They returned in 1806.

These men and their companions were sent out on a definite mission. The president who dispatched them had authority to do so and exercised it. In the same way, our Lord sent out His apostles—bound for a mission more difficult, but more rewarding and more vital than that of Lewis and Clark. Lewis and Clark wanted to extend the boundaries of their country. Jesus' apostles were to extend the boundaries of the kingdom of God.

Today are we not also sent? Does not the command to go forth to save men from sin also come to us? Jesus' church today is called to send His valiant disciples to every corner of the earth, however distant, difficult, or daunting, to bring under His sway every tribe and nation. We are sent to seek the lost and proclaim good news— just as Jesus was.

—J. G. V. B.

22, 23. And when he had said this, he breathed on them, and saith unto them, Receive ye the Holy Ghost: whosesoever sins ye remit, they are remitted unto them; and whosesoever sins ye retain, they are retained.

The act of breathing on the disciples seems to have been a symbolic gesture, reminiscent of God's bestowing on Adam the breath of life so that he became a living soul (Genesis 2:7). During Jesus' evening with the disciples in the upper room, He had promised that after His departure the Comforter (*the Holy Ghost*) would come to them (John 16:7). Now the promise was reaffirmed; however, its fulfillment awaited Jesus' departure into Heaven. Luke 24:49 records Jesus' command that the apostles remain in Jerusalem "until ye be endued with power from on high," and Acts 1:5 records His promise that this power would come "not many days hence." It came on the Day of Pentecost ten days after Jesus' ascension (Acts 2:1-4).

The Spirit-empowered apostles followed Jesus' instruction that "repentance and remission of sins should be preached in his name among all nations, beginning at Jerusalem" (Luke 24:47). On the Day of Pentecost the apostles (Peter specifically) preached Christ in Jerusalem in a way that caused hearers to ask what they could do to gain forgiveness for their sins. Peter's Spirit-led response was, "Repent, and be baptized every one of you in the name of Jesus Christ for the remission of sins, and ye shall receive the gift of the Holy Ghost. For the promise is unto you, and to your children, and to all that are afar off, even as many as the Lord our God shall call" (Acts 2:38, 39).

To *remit* (forgive) or *retain* (not to forgive) sins was not within the judgment of any man—even the apostles. These men were simply to announce and apply the conditions that were established by divine authority. God would not be bound by apostolic decree; apostolic decree would be bound by God's direction. The apostles were to announce what God had determined. And that is exactly what Peter did at Pentecost.

II. Jesus and Thomas
(John 20:24-29)

A. Skeptical Absentee (vv. 24, 25)

24. But Thomas, one of the twelve, called Didymus, was not with them when Jesus came.

Didymus is the Greek form of the Aramaic name *Thomas*, meaning "twin." Thomas had been chosen by Jesus as *one of the twelve* who were to share in His ministry and report it— especially His resurrection—as eyewitnesses (Mark 3:14-19; Acts 1:21, 22).

How to Say It

ARAMAIC. Air-uh-*may*-ick.
CLEOPAS. *Klee*-uh-pass.
CORNELIUS. Kor-*neel*-yus.
DIDYMUS. *Did*-uh-mus.
EMMAUS. Em-*may*-us.
MAGDALENE. *Mag*-duh-leen or Mag-duh-
   lee-nee.
SHALOM (Hebrew). shah-*lome*.

Thomas's absence on the evening of the resurrection is not rebuked, praised, or even explained in Scripture. It did give the others an opportunity to tell of Jesus' appearance to them, and it gave Thomas an opportunity to receive dramatic proof of the resurrection.

There are two other references to Thomas in the Gospels, both of which are found in John's record. One is found in John 11:16, where he believes (mistakenly) that Jesus is going to Bethany to die. Thomas suggests that the Twelve go with Jesus to face His enemies and "die with him." The other reference is in John 14:5, where we find Thomas asking Jesus, "Lord, we know not whither thou goest; and how can we know the way?" He asked this in response to Jesus' statement that He was going away to prepare a place for the disciples so that they might join Him there one day.

It appears from these incidents that Thomas was someone who desired facts, and, if given sufficient evidence, would give his total commitment to a cause. [See question #2, page 280.]

25. The other disciples therefore said unto him, We have seen the Lord. But he said unto them, Except I shall see in his hands the print of the nails, and put my finger into the print of the nails, and thrust my hand into his side, I will not believe.

The Greek verb rendered *said* indicates that this was not a one-time report. Literally, *the other disciples* "kept on saying" to Thomas, *We have seen the Lord*. Perhaps they spoke to him each day of the next week, trying to convince him that what they were claiming was true. But he had not experienced what they had; why should he share their conviction?

By the phrase *the print of the nails*, we know that Jesus was nailed, rather than bound with cords, to the cross. This also tells us that Jesus' wounds left a vivid impression on Thomas. Perhaps he remained at or near the cross until after Jesus died. He may have cringed at the size of the wound that was caused when Jesus' *side* was pierced by a Roman spear. Now Thomas wanted proof that the One whom his companions claimed was alive still bore the marks of His shameful treatment.

B. Second Appearance (v. 26)

26. And after eight days again his disciples were within, and Thomas with them: then came Jesus, the doors being shut, and stood in the midst, and said, Peace be unto you.

John seems to have employed the Jewish method of including the first and last days in reporting a given length of time (as musicians count both the first and last notes of the scale in counting an octave). Thus, *after eight days* was one week later, meaning that this second meeting with the *disciples*, like the first, was also on the first day of the week. The disciples had time to ponder, discuss, and investigate the events of Resurrection Day before those events were reinforced by this additional appearance.

Repetition characterized most of the details in this second meeting. The place was evidently the same, with the same concern for security. Jesus appeared again without announcement, suddenly standing among His friends and bidding them be at *peace*. Of course, there was one important difference. This time, *Thomas* was present.

JESUS' GREETING OF "PEACE"

John notes that after Jesus' resurrection, He greeted His disciples three times with the salutation, "Peace be unto you" (John 20:19, 21, 26). This was likely a form of the Hebrew greeting *shalom*, which means "peace." Certain standard words or phrases are used in many languages as a means of friendly expression when people meet. Usually the French say, *Bonjour*; the Spanish say, *Buenos dias*; the Italians say, *Ciao*; and those in Hawaii say, *Aloha*. Americans may

---

Home Daily Bible Readings

Monday, Apr. 5—Peace Be With You (John 20:19-23)

Tuesday, Apr. 6—Unless I See (John 20:24-29)

Wednesday, Apr. 7—On the Road to Emmaus (Luke 24:13-27)

Thursday, Apr. 8—Then Their Eyes Were Opened (Luke 24:28-35)

Friday, Apr. 9—Touch Me and See (Luke 24:36-43)

Saturday, Apr. 10—He Opened Their Understanding (Luke 24:44-52)

Sunday, Apr. 11—Jesus Showed Himself Again (John 21:1-14)

---

say, "How are you?" "Hello," or just "Hi!" The British often say, "Cheerio," and in Australia it's, "G'day, Mate."

Jesus' greeting of *peace* was particularly significant, since He came to make peace "through the blood of his cross" (Colossians 1:20). The angels over Bethlehem had spoken of peace as part of the purpose of His coming to earth (Luke 2:14). Jesus enables us to know peace with God and the peace of God as well. It is significant that in telling Cornelius the meaning of Jesus' coming, Peter said, "The word which God sent unto the children of Israel, preaching peace by Jesus Christ: (he is Lord of all:)" (Acts 10:36).

Peace is part of the greeting at the beginning of every one of Paul's letters. Let us give thanks that in the midst of a warring, restless, agitated world, Jesus not only brings the greeting, but the reality of *peace*!   —J. G. V. B.

C. Seeing and Acknowledging (vv. 27, 28)

27. Then saith he to Thomas, Reach hither thy finger, and behold my hands; and reach hither thy hand, and thrust it into my side; and be not faithless, but believing.

Earlier in his Gospel, John had noted that Jesus "knew all men, and needed not that any should testify of man; for he knew what was in man" (John 2:24, 25). Thus Jesus knew what Thomas had thought and said in response to the other disciples' report; and Jesus responded to all of it in precise detail.

The word *behold* clearly includes more than merely seeing something. It is an invitation to learn what one wants to know by every available means. Thomas had demanded to feel and examine the wounds in Jesus' *hands* and *side*. Now he was free to do so.

We should therefore note that the wounds that had been inflicted on Jesus at the crucifixion remained open and unhealed in His resurrection body. Some have proposed that this may be the case even in Heaven. The renowned hymn writer, Fanny Crosby, suggested this in one of her hymns: "I shall know Him by the print of the nails in His hand" ("My Savior First of All"). John's vision of Heaven does speak of "a Lamb as it had been slain" standing in the midst of God's attendants around His throne (Revelation 5:6).

28. And Thomas answered and said unto him, My Lord and my God.

Did Thomas actually touch and examine the Lord's hands and side as he had said he must do? If so, it is not recorded. He seems to have been convinced as much by Jesus' perfect knowledge of his inmost thoughts as he was by the physical evidence that this was indeed the

Lord whom he had followed in Galilee and Judea. Thomas left no doubt as to the deity of God's one and only Son. He was ready to concur with the introductory statement in John's Gospel: "In the beginning was the Word, and the Word was with God, and the Word was God. . . . And the Word was made flesh, and dwelt among us" (John 1:1, 14). He was also ready to echo John's conclusion: "These are written, that ye might believe that Jesus is the Christ, the Son of God; and that believing ye might have life through his name" (John 20:31).

Thomas was not easily convinced of Jesus' resurrection, but when he became fully convinced he was fully committed, never to be shaken. His kind will always be at the core of Christ's ongoing body, His church. [See question #3, page 280.]

D. Blessing of Believing (v. 29)

29. Jesus saith unto him, Thomas, because thou hast seen me, thou hast believed: blessed are they that have not seen, and yet have believed.

Thou hast seen me. As noted earlier, nothing is said here about Thomas's touching and feeling Jesus' resurrected body, as the other disciples had done. That may have been included in what was *seen*, but it is not necessarily so. In any case Thomas was now in the same situation as the rest of the disciples who had seen the risen Lord and were prepared to say so, even at the risk of their lives.

Jesus next turned His attention to those who would hear and accept the apostles' testimony concerning Him. These future believers would be especially *blessed*! In His Sermon on the Mount Jesus declared those *blessed* who reflect the character and actions they see in Him (Matthew 5:3-12). Here He used the same word to describe those who would believe in Him on the basis of the spoken and written Word, without demanding a special revelation to themselves. Don't

The visual for this lesson reminds us that Jesus' blessing is for all who come to Him by simple, trusting faith.

Visual for lesson 6

waste time envying Thomas and the other apostles, or even those latter-day mystics who claim miraculous visions. Jesus' special blessing rests with all those common people whom He welcomes as members of His family when they hear, believe, and follow Him as He is revealed in His Word. [See question #4, page 280.]

Conclusion

A. Join the Rejoicing

In a masterpiece of understatement, John 20:20 says, "Then were the disciples glad, when they saw the Lord." The *New International Version* renders that 20-20 vision in this manner: "The disciples were overjoyed." That sense of celebration swept onward, wave upon wave, over the followers of Jesus as they became convinced that "the Lord is risen indeed" (Luke 24:34). Later, when persecution came upon them, they were persistently and continuously joyous (Acts 5:41)

Followers of sporting events are familiar with "the thrill of victory and the agony of defeat," as successes and failures follow one another in the constant struggle to overcome various kinds of opposition. Something better is available in the blessings that come through steadfast faith in the risen Christ. Victory is offered, not sometimes or to some contestants, but consistently to all who look to Jesus in their wrestling not against flesh and blood, but against the forces of Satan in high places (Ephesians 6:12). They are blessed with the removal of guilt through Jesus' death for their sins at the cross. They are blessed with a clear purpose in life, focused on the goal of eternity with God. They are blessed with a warm family relationship with the children of God. Moreover, they can celebrate all these victories with a joy far greater and more lasting than the celebration of any sports championship, and without any letdown on the following day! "Rejoice in the Lord always: and again I say, Rejoice" (Philippians 4:4). [See question #5, page 280.]

B. Prayer

Father, we are thankful for the "many infallible proofs" by which the disciples were finally convinced and by which we are persuaded. We pray for courage to declare openly what they declared—that Jesus is the Christ, our Savior and Lord. Amen.

C. Thought to Remember

The living Lord, who appeared to His disciples after His resurrection, will appear to all mankind when He comes in judgment.

Learning by Doing

This page contains an alternate lesson plan emphasizing learning activities.
Classes desiring such student involvement will find these suggestions helpful.

Learning Goals

As a result of this lesson each student should be able to:

1. Summarize the events of the two postresurrection appearances included in today's printed text.

2. Cite several "infallible proofs" for believing in Jesus' resurrection.

3. Give encouragement to someone this week who, like the doubting disciples, needs reassurance regarding his or her faith.

Into the Lesson

Before class tape red, yellow, and blue index cards under the chairs where the students will sit, one card per chair. On the red cards, have this question written: "Have you ever feared for your life or for your safety? When?" On the yellow cards print the following: "We all have doubts about what to believe. What is your biggest doubt?" And on the blue cards should be written, "What was the biggest change of mind you ever experienced? What convinced you to change your mind?"

To begin the class, ask the students to retrieve the cards from under their chairs to form three groups by joining others with the same color cards as theirs. Have them discuss the questions on their cards in the groups and to choose which of the stories they will report to the class. Allow five minutes for discussion and then call for reports. (Don't spend too much time on this. You just want to introduce the concepts.)

Observe that the disciples of Jesus, just after the resurrection, experienced all of these: fear, doubt, and a great change of mind. Their experience will help us to put our faith unwaveringly in the risen Lord Jesus Christ!

Into the Word

Raise this question with the class: How would you prove something in a court of law? Legal procedures will be familiar enough to the class on the basis of courtroom dramas on television, both real and fictional.

Next, have a volunteer read John 20:19-25. As the class suggests items, list on the chalkboard the "evidence" for the resurrection, from a legal point of view. The following should be noted: physical evidence: the disciples saw and heard Jesus (19); they saw His wounds, so they knew this was not an impostor (20); eyewitness testimony: the ten disciples told Thomas about Jesus (25).

(If you have time, expand this activity by having the class examine what Luke 24:36-43 says about this same incident and adding to the evidence list what they find.)

Ask a volunteer to read the rest of today's text, John 20:26-29. Ask the following questions: 1. What evidence did Thomas receive? (The same as the other apostles, vv. 25-27.) 2. What was Thomas's response? (Confession of faith, v. 28.) 3. What blessing did Jesus pronounce? (Blessing on those who accept the testimony of those who did see Jesus, without seeing Him for themselves, v. 29.)

Into Life

Read Acts 1:1-3 to the class, then ask students to cite as many of the "many infallible proofs" of Jesus' resurrection as they can. (Several have already been noted in this lesson.) Ask, "What is significant about the variety of witnesses and occasions by which Jesus showed Himself alive?" (The accumulated evidence becomes impossible to explain away as hallucination, wishful thinking, or any other alternative except that it is the truth.)

Note Thomas's doubt. Remind the class that Thomas's need for conclusive evidence answers our need for evidence today. Thomas was not going to be swayed by sentimentality or wishful thinking. He demanded evidence and was convinced. Jesus really must have been present for Thomas to have made his confession of faith!

Discuss the problem of doubt in the church today. How does this passage help erase our doubts? How does it help us to encourage others who may be doubting? Note how the other apostles continued to fellowship with Thomas even as he was doubting. How is that a model for us when friends or loved ones have doubts? Ask the students to think of people who need some encouragement this week to help them come to a stronger faith. Ask each student to write the name of one person whom he or she could encourage to have greater faith in the risen Lord.

Close with prayer that your students will have greater faith in the risen Jesus, and that they will translate that faith into action by encouraging others to believe.

Let's Talk It Over

The questions on this page are designed to encourage review of the lesson Scriptures and to promote discussion of the lesson by the class. The answers provided are only discussion starters. Let your class talk it over from there.

1. Jesus' first word to the assembled apostles on resurrection evening was, "Peace." What significance do you find in this? What kind of peace does the risen Jesus give you?

While "Peace" (Hebrew *shalom*) was the traditional Jewish greeting, that surely is not the only reason for Jesus' using it on this occasion. The apostles were experiencing profound grief and great fear at the same time. They needed the "peace" that only Jesus could provide. This peace would also be significant to them in the future. In the midst of persecution and turmoil, they would be able to enjoy "the peace of God, which passeth all understanding" (Philippians 4:7). Some of your students will be able to share how the peace of Jesus saw them through times of grief, fear, or other troubles.

2. Thomas is best known for his doubt, but our lesson writer says, "It appears . . . that Thomas was someone who desired facts, and, if given sufficient evidence, would give his total commitment to a cause." How can we help modern believers to demonstrate the same kind of commitment?

Thomas knew that following Jesus was a life-or-death decision. In many parts of the world believers still appreciate this fact, and every year great numbers of them are martyred for their faith. In places where Christianity is accepted as one choice among many, commitment is often only halfhearted or weak.

We often measure commitment in terms of worship attendance, giving, and volunteering for ministry, but those are only symptoms. Somehow we need to target the cause—in the heart. Good examples of faithful witnesses may help, as well as clear calls to choose between the world and the Christ. What else can your class suggest?

3. Thomas was convinced of Jesus' resurrection and, in a dramatic moment, cried out, "My Lord and my God." Recall that dramatic moment in your life when you first acknowledged Jesus as Savior and Lord. What led you to that moment?

Many of your students probably grew up in Christian homes and may not remember a dramatic moment like Thomas's. Even so, perhaps they will recall a time when they realized they had to act on their faith—a time when their *parents'* faith was suddenly *their* faith. What triggered that realization?

For others, however, there may well have been a more dramatic time when they came to faith. Perhaps it was when a friend shared the gospel in a plain and understandable way. Perhaps one of them met a believer who shattered his negative stereotypes of Christianity. Perhaps another simply decided to read the Bible and see for herself what it said, and found it to be an amazing record she could not refuse.

4. We often say, "Seeing is believing." But Jesus pronounced a blessing on those who believe without seeing His resurrected body. How is it possible for us to believe without seeing?

Every day we practice belief without seeing. We accept as true the events described in the newspaper or in history books. We did not personally witness those events, but we regard the actual eyewitnesses and reporters as reliable. Even when we have discovered some of these reporters and witnesses to be biased, we still accept in large part the reports they give.

Our faith in the resurrected Christ is also based on eyewitness testimony. These witnesses impress us as honest and reliable. They were skeptical and yet were convinced. And once convinced, they were willing to die for proclaiming what they claimed to have witnessed. Through their eyes we see and believe.

5. The resurrection of Jesus Christ won the ultimate victory—the victory over death. How does that affect the defeats and disappointments we encounter?

Read John 16:33 and Romans 8:37. As you discuss this issue, do not minimize the trials believers face. In many places in the world the suffering is very great. Even in Western civilization, attacks on Christians are increasing, though they are usually made through false accusations, zoning ordinances, and legislation designed to silence the voice of believers in the public arena. But the class should conclude that the forces of evil can do no permanent harm; they can do no more than kill us, and then we'll be with the risen Lord!

Jesus, the Bread of Life

DEVOTIONAL READING: Isaiah 55:1-11.

LESSON SCRIPTURE: John 6:1-59.

PRINTED TEXT: John 6:10-14, 26, 27, 35-40, 47-51.

John 6:10-14, 26, 27, 35-40, 47-51

10 And Jesus said, Make the men sit down. Now there was much grass in the place. So the men sat down, in number about five thousand.

11 And Jesus took the loaves; and when he had given thanks, he distributed to the disciples, and the disciples to them that were set down; and likewise of the fishes as much as they would.

12 When they were filled, he said unto his disciples, Gather up the fragments that remain, that nothing be lost.

13 Therefore they gathered them together, and filled twelve baskets with the fragments of the five barley loaves, which remained over and above unto them that had eaten.

14 Then those men, when they had seen the miracle that Jesus did, said, This is of a truth that Prophet that should come into the world.

· · · · · · · · · · · ·

26 Jesus answered them and said, Verily, verily, I say unto you, Ye seek me, not because ye saw the miracles, but because ye did eat of the loaves, and were filled.

27 Labor not for the meat which perisheth, but for that meat which endureth unto everlasting life, which the Son of man shall give unto you: for him hath God the Father sealed.

· · · · · · · · · · · ·

35 And Jesus said unto them, I am the bread of life: he that cometh to me shall never hunger; and he that believeth on me shall never thirst.

36 But I said unto you, That ye also have seen me, and believe not.

37 All that the Father giveth me shall come to me; and him that cometh to me I will in no wise cast out.

38 For I came down from heaven, not to do mine own will, but the will of him that sent me.

39 And this is the Father's will which hath sent me, that of all which he hath given me I should lose nothing, but should raise it up again at the last day.

40 And this is the will of him that sent me, that every one which seeth the Son, and believeth on him, may have everlasting life: and I will raise him up at the last day.

· · · · · · · · · · · ·

47 Verily, verily, I say unto you, He that believeth on me hath everlasting life.

48 I am that bread of life.

49 Your fathers did eat manna in the wilderness, and are dead.

50 This is the bread which cometh down from heaven, that a man may eat thereof, and not die.

51 I am the living bread which came down from heaven: if any man eat of this bread, he shall live for ever: and the bread that I will give is my flesh, which I will give for the life of the world.

GOLDEN TEXT: I am the living bread which came down from heaven: if any man eat of this bread, he shall live for ever.—John 6:51.

Lesson Aims

This lesson should help each student to:

1. Tell the story of the feeding of the five thousand, and summarize Jesus' sermon on the bread of life, which followed.

2. Compare the people's desire for literal bread and an earthly kingdom with some of the wrong priorities of people today.

3. Make spiritual matters a higher priority in his or her daily choices.

Lesson Outline

INTRODUCTION
    A. What Do We Really Need?
    B. Lesson Background
 I. JESUS FEEDS A MULTITUDE (John 6:10-14)
    A. Directing the Crowd (vv. 10, 11)
    B. Saving the Surplus (vv. 12, 13)
    C. Reacting to Jesus (v. 14)
 II. JESUS OFFERS LASTING FOOD (John 6:26, 27)
III. JESUS SERVES GOD'S PURPOSE (John 6:35-40)
    A. He Is the Bread of Life (v. 35)
    B. Not All Accept Him (vv. 36, 37)
    C. He Does God's Will (vv. 38-40)
IV. JESUS IS THE TRUE BREAD (John 6:47-51)
    A. The Source of Life (vv. 47, 48)
    B. Superior to Manna (vv. 49-51)
    Bread and Life
CONCLUSION
    A. Making the "Cut"
    B. Prayer
    C. Thought to Remember

Introduction

A. What Do We Really Need?

Along with bright skies, birds' songs, and beautiful blooms, springtime occasionally brings some very turbulent weather. Tornadoes and torrential rains often inflict severe destruction, which, if we allow it to, can teach us a lesson about what we really need in the way of material possessions. When everything is lost and one is at the mercy of others for such basics as food and shelter, he or she comes to appreciate anew what most of us take for granted. "Give us this day our daily bread," Jesus taught His followers to pray (Matthew 6:11).

In every age, bread of one kind or another has been a basic food. In fact, the Hebrew word for *bread* is often used for food or sustenance of any sort. The New Testament word for *bread* indicates more definitely a loaf—usually about an inch thick and easily broken and shared—but this word is also used to describe food or nourishment in general. Today we still use the term in a general sense: we speak of a wage earner as a "breadwinner" or as someone who "keeps bread on the table."

How appropriate it is, then, that bread should appear in our text first as Jesus' miraculous provision for a hungry multitude and then as the symbol of Jesus Himself—the necessary and all-sufficient source of life eternal for mankind!

B. Lesson Background

Jesus' feeding of the five thousand with five loaves and two small fishes is the only one of His miracles (except His own resurrection) that is recorded by all four Gospel writers (Matthew 14:13-21; Mark 6:30-44; Luke 9:10-17; John 6:1-15). It took place at the height of His popularity in Galilee, when great crowds were following Him to witness His miracles and teaching. Matthew relates the event to John the Baptist's death by order of King Herod Antipas. Matthew 14:13 tells us that when Jesus heard of John's death, "he departed thence by ship into a desert place apart." Luke notes that this was a place "belonging to the city called Bethsaida" (Luke 9:10), on the northeast shore of the Sea of Galilee.

Despite Jesus' efforts to obtain privacy, multitudes from a wide area followed Him. He taught the crowds for the greater part of a day. Then the disciples suggested that He send the people home since "the day was now far spent" and there was nothing for them to eat (Mark 6:35, 36). Inquiry led to Andrew's discovery of a lad who had "five barley loaves, and two small fishes" (John 6:8, 9). That seemed hopelessly inadequate. But Jesus knew what was available and what He would do with it.

I. Jesus Feeds a Multitude (John 6:10-14)

A. Directing the Crowd (vv. 10, 11)

10. And Jesus said, Make the men sit down. Now there was much grass in the place. So the men sat down, in number about five thousand.

The people may have been standing in order to be near Jesus as He sat to teach (John 6:3). Now Jesus gave them the opportunity to be more comfortable. Mark 6:39, 40 says that the grass was green and that the people sat in "ranks, by hundreds, and by fifties." The result may have looked like a spring garden, with plots separated by paths to allow movement among the people. The mention of *men* leaves one to guess how many women and children may also have been present. (See Matthew 14:21.)

11. And Jesus took the loaves; and when he had given thanks, he distributed to the disciples, and the disciples to them that were set down; and likewise of the fishes as much as they would.

Mark 6:41 says that Jesus "looked up to heaven, and blessed, and brake the loaves, and gave them to his disciples to set before them." The giving of *thanks* was evidently similar to what was done by the head of each family at the Passover (John 6:4 notes that "the passover . . . was nigh"). It was likely a brief prayer, but with great meaning and power. The result was enough food to satisfy those with the healthiest appetites and others who seldom had enough to eat. [See question #1, page 288.]

B. Saving the Surplus (vv. 12, 13)

12. When they were filled, he said unto his disciples, Gather up the fragments that remain, that nothing be lost.

Nothing of God's provision is to be despised, but all of it at all times is to be treated with respect. *That nothing be lost* is a divine purpose to be applied most seriously to God's highest creation—persons made in His own image.

13. Therefore they gathered them together, and filled twelve baskets with the fragments of the five barley loaves, which remained over and above unto them that had eaten.

One fact is especially clear: the abundance of provision from meager beginnings. The Lord who had taken part in the original creation of "all things" (John 1:3) was fully able to multiply a small part of that creation in the fulfillment of His Father's purpose.

Most likely each of the *twelve* disciples was supplied with a basket, since the number of *baskets* matches the number of disciples. These *twelve baskets* were then used to collect the remaining *fragments* of the *loaves*. Nothing is said here about any leftover fish, but we know from Mark's account that there was some (Mark 6:43). Where they got the baskets and what they did with all those leftovers is not stated, but it would have been difficult and awkward for the disciples to have kept them. The Greek word used here most often refers to a large, heavy basket, not a small handbasket. Since the Lord's purpose in collecting the fragments was "that nothing be lost," and since the group of disciples probably could not have eaten that much food

before the fish spoiled, we may surmise the food was given to some nearby who were in need.

C. Reacting to Jesus (v. 14)

14. Then those men, when they had seen the miracle that Jesus did, said, This is of a truth that Prophet that should come into the world.

Those men were mostly Jews. They were familiar with Moses' promise that God would raise up a *Prophet* like himself, who would merit full attention (Deuteronomy 18:15). They saw in Jesus' miraculous provision of bread a similarity to Moses' bringing of manna from Heaven to feed the Israelites in the wilderness (Exodus 16). These people were on the right track in their thinking, but they were wrongly focused. The principal ministry of both Moses and Jesus was to make known God's covenant will for His people. The provision of emergency rations was a relatively small matter in both instances.

Jesus' observers were a prime example of zeal without knowledge (Romans 10:2). They planned to take Jesus by force and make Him their kind of king (John 6:15), probably hoping He would lead and supply an army to overthrow the Romans. Knowing their intentions, Jesus escaped into the nearby hills alone.

II. Jesus Offers Lasting Food (John 6:26, 27)

While Jesus went to the hills, the disciples set out to cross the Sea of Galilee. On the way, they encountered a severe storm, and as they struggled against it Jesus came to them walking on the water. Eventually the disciples landed and entered Capernaum. The next day they were approached by amazed crowds who had followed, looking for Jesus. "How did you get here?" they asked Him. Jesus responded to their need rather than to their question.

26. Jesus answered them and said, Verily, verily, I say unto you, Ye seek me, not because ye saw the miracles, but because ye did eat of the loaves, and were filled.

Jesus was more interested in addressing the people's motives than their questions about His mobility. In His miracles they had seen, not the

---

How to Say It

ANTIPAS. *An*-tih-pus.
BETHSAIDA. Beth-*say*-uh-duh.
CAPERNAUM. Kuh-*per*-nay-um.
NAZARETH. *Naz*-uh-reth.
ZACCHEUS. Zack-*kee*-us.

power and generous love of God, but only a free meal. They had eaten *loaves* without cost. They liked the sample, and they wanted more.

We may criticize the people's shortsightedness, but is our perception much better than theirs? When we quote Jesus' pattern prayer (Matthew 6:9-13), what gets the emphasis: God's name, kingdom, will, and glory, or our daily bread? And when we hear requests for prayer, do we give more attention to physical needs than we do to Jesus' own request that we pray for laborers to go into the harvest (Matthew 9:38)? [See question #2, page 288.]

27. Labor not for the meat which perisheth, but for that meat which endureth unto everlasting life, which the Son of man shall give unto you: for him hath God the Father sealed.

The people's energy would have been better spent, Jesus said, in following His teachings than in chasing after a free lunch. Any kind of *meat*, or food, eventually spoils if it is not eaten. And if it is eaten, it builds a physical body that is but temporary. The spiritual nourishment that Jesus came to give builds *unto everlasting life*.

The benefit Jesus offers must be received as a gift; it can never be earned by man's *labor*. So when Jesus told the crowd to *labor . . . for the meat which endureth*, He was not suggesting a regimen of works by which they could find *everlasting life*. The "works of God" that He was talking about was simply to put their faith in Jesus as God's Son (vv. 28, 29).

III. Jesus Serves God's Purpose (John 6:35-40)

Jesus had told His hearers to believe in Him. But why should they? What credentials did He offer? Could He provide anything similar to Moses' manna from Heaven? Jesus answered that God was now providing better bread from Heaven. That caught their attention, for it was just what they thought they wanted (John 6:34).

A. He Is the Bread of Life (v. 35)

35. And Jesus said unto them, I am the bread of life: he that cometh to me shall never hunger; and he that believeth on me shall never thirst.

Here is the grand, sweeping announcement to which the entire conversation had been leading. It begins as one of Jesus' seven great declarations of His divine being. Others, equally bold, are: "I am the light of the world" (John 8:12; 9:5); "I am the door" (John 10:7, 9); "I am the good shepherd" (John 10:11, 14); "I am the resurrection, and the life" (John 11:25); "I am the way, the truth, and the life" (John 14:6); and "I am the true vine" (John 15:1).

Jesus Himself is what He was offering to the people: *the bread of life.* [See question #3, page 288.] The two promises that follow emphasize one combined thought. Coming to Christ and believing in Christ belong together—in acceptance, trust, commitment, and action. One finds in Him a satisfaction of basic spiritual needs that can come through no other source. Thus is fulfilled the promise of Matthew 5:6: "Blessed are they which do hunger and thirst after righteousness: for they shall be filled." Their need will not go unmet. However, as Jesus proceeded to point out, some cannot claim that promise.

B. Not All Accept Him (vv. 36, 37)

36. But I said unto you, That ye also have seen me, and believe not.

Seeing is not always believing. In verses 26 and 27 are Jesus' earlier words of rebuke to those who had seen His miracles but had rejected His message. These people were not interested in learning and adjusting to the truth, but chose rather to twist the truth so as to support their own agenda. Let us pray that we may not yield to the same temptation.

In contrast to those unbelieving who have *seen* are those who are blessed for believing, even though they have not seen (John 20:29). That is good company in which to be included.

37. All that the Father giveth me shall come to me; and him that cometh to me I will in no wise cast out.

The bad news has been heard; now for the good news. In all places and all times there are those who with honest hearts hear the message of Christ, believe it, and commit themselves to following Him. *The Father* knows in advance who will accept Christ and follow Him faithfully. On this basis God gives such individuals to Jesus. That this does not do away with an individual's choice is clear from Jesus' reference to *him that cometh to me*. Each person must choose whether or not to be a part of what the Father has given to His Son. Watch the rich young ruler go sadly with his wealth rather than gladly with Christ (Mark 10:17-22). Watch Zaccheus make the opposite choice to part with his wealth and make Jesus his Master (Luke 19:8-10). Mark the destiny of those who change their minds and turn away after having followed Christ for a time (Hebrews 6:4-6).

C. He Does God's Will (vv. 38-40)

38. For I came down from heaven, not to do mine own will, but the will of him that sent me.

The only way we can understand or explain Jesus is by accepting His bold claim: *I came down from heaven.* Jesus pressed that claim five times in this context alone (vv. 33, 38, 50, 51, 58). The purpose of His coming provides a second emphasis in the Gospel of John: Jesus' commitment to the *will of him that sent me*. This was more important to Him than eating: "My meat is to do the will of him that sent me" (John 4:34). [See question #4, page 288.]

39. And this is the Father's will which hath sent me, that of all which he hath given me I should lose nothing, but should raise it up again at the last day.

This provides another aspect of Jesus' concern "that nothing be lost," spoken earlier of the miraculously multiplied loaves (v. 12). Here His emphasis is on people. This theme is sounded throughout the Bible, as in Ezekiel 33:11: "As I live, saith the Lord God, I have no pleasure in the death of the wicked; but that the wicked turn from his way and live." Compare 2 Peter 3:9: "The Lord is . . . not willing that any should perish, but that all should come to repentance."

However, *the Father's will* is not always fulfilled, because some are not willing to follow it. Some choose the path destined for punishment and will therefore perish. Even among Jesus' disciples was one who insisted on his own and opposite way: "Those that thou gavest me I have kept, and none of them is lost, but the son of perdition; that the Scripture might be fulfilled" (John 17:12).

The last day evidently refers to the time of Christ's coming in glory and judgment, when the dead in Christ will rise first and living saints will be caught up to meet and be with Him (1 Thessalonians 4:16, 17).

40. And this is the will of him that sent me, that every one which seeth the Son, and believeth on him, may have everlasting life: and I will raise him up at the last day.

Here the object of the divine *will* is described as *every one* (each individual) rather than "all" (the entire group of the saved), as in verse 37. *Everlasting life* is for those who both see and believe, in contrast to those whose seeing does not produce belief (v. 36). Attentive looking at God's revelation, and believing on the basis of what is seen, is required.

No matter how long the great *last day* may be delayed according to our calendar, the time will be as nothing from God's perspective (2 Peter 3:8). Jesus' promise is totally dependable.

IV. Jesus Is the True Bread (John 6:47-51)

Verses 41-46 tell us that some who knew Jesus' family in Nazareth were inclined to doubt that He came from Heaven. Their problem could be solved only by recognizing Jesus for what the evidence showed Him to be—the Son of God.

A. The Source of Life (vv. 47, 48)

47, 48. Verily, verily, I say unto you, He that believeth on me hath everlasting life. I am that bread of life.

The repeated *verily* (literally *amen, amen*) introduces a statement of utmost importance. Again Jesus insists on the personal application of His message. Believing, or faith, is at the core of any claim to God's eternal gifts. Faith has always been the key identifying mark in all God's heroes (Hebrews 11).

B. Superior to Manna (vv. 49-51)

49, 50. Your fathers did eat manna in the wilderness, and are dead. This is the bread which cometh down from heaven, that a man may eat thereof, and not die.

The eager eaters in Jesus' audience had earlier referred to how their *fathers* had been fed by *manna in the wilderness*. They had asked Jesus, "What sign showest thou then, that we may see, and believe thee?" (John 6:30, 31). Jesus pointed to the obvious fact that the manna eaters had died before or soon after they reached Canaan.

Moses had summarized the people's experience in these words: "[God] humbled thee, and suffered thee to hunger, and fed thee with manna, . . . that he might make thee know that man doth not live by bread only, but by every word that proceedeth out of the mouth of the Lord doth man live" (Deuteronomy 8:3). Jesus Himself was the Word of God who came *from heaven* to be the *bread* of life. He provides life that does not end. He could truly say, "I am the resurrection, and the life: he that believeth in me, though he were dead, yet shall he live: and

---

Home Daily Bible Readings

Monday, Apr. 12—There Is a Boy Here (John 6:1-15)

Tuesday, Apr. 13—"It Is I; Be Not Afraid" (John 6:16-21)

Wednesday, Apr. 14—Give Us This Bread Always (John 6:22-34)

Thursday, Apr. 15—I Am the Bread of Life (John 6:35-51)

Friday, Apr. 16—This Bread Came Down From Heaven (John 6:52-59)

Saturday, Apr. 17—Israel Was Given Bread From Heaven (Nehemiah 9:6-15)

Sunday, Apr. 18—Mortals Ate the Bread of Angels (Psalm 78:17-29)

Today's visual contrasts Jesus, "the bread of life," with the manna gathered by the Israelites in the wilderness.

Visual for lesson 7

whosoever liveth and believeth in me shall never die" (John 11:25, 26). [See question #5, page 288.]

51. I am the living bread which came down from heaven: if any man eat of this bread, he shall live for ever: and the bread that I will give is my flesh, which I will give for the life of the world.

Jesus built His whole discussion toward the climax found in this verse. The miracle of the loaves and fishes was not an end in itself; it was only a prelude to a greater spiritual reality to come. The *bread* of life, or *living bread . . . from heaven*, is Jesus Himself. Just as any food must be eaten, digested, and assimilated to build one's physical body, so Jesus—His teaching, life, and personality—must be assimilated as a part of oneself to build eternal life.

One startling fact was now added: the bread Jesus offers is not only Himself; it is His *flesh*! The fleshly body in which He lived (John 1:14) was to be offered as a sacrifice on the cross. His body became the gift, the basis of *life* for the believer—in time and eternity. This truth is etched in the believer's mind and memory at the Lord's table, where we recall Jesus' words at the breaking and presenting of the bread: "This is my body which is given for you: this do in remembrance of me" (Luke 22:19).

BREAD AND LIFE

Bread is one of the most basic necessities of life. Prepared and served in various ways, bread appears almost everywhere. One sees it in the shape of long, thin loaves in France, in a black color in Russia, and in a somewhat heavy white variety in England.

Jesus' description of Himself as "the bread of life" (John 6:35) is one to which most anyone can relate. He compared the "bread" of His salvation with the manna that the Hebrews ate during their wilderness wandering. Jesus also came down from Heaven (v. 38), but with the "true

bread" (v. 32). Whereas the Hebrews died, though they had eaten "bread from heaven" (v. 31), anyone who eats the bread Jesus provides "shall live for ever" (v. 51). Jesus also linked the provision of this bread to His death on the cross (v. 51). We recognize this link through the Lord's Supper, in which we partake of the bread that symbolizes Jesus' body given "for the life of the world" (v. 51).

We are to pray for our "daily bread" and eat it, as a way to continue our mortal life. Jesus gives us a bread with immortal life in it: "If any man eat of this bread, he shall live for ever."

"We taste thee, O Thou living Bread,
  And long to feast upon Thee still;
We drink of Thee, the Fountainhead,
  And thirst our souls from Thee to fill."
            —Anonymous
            —J. G. V. B.

Conclusion

A. Making the "Cut"

Many who want to play a particular sport never get into the game. They are cut from the squad before the team takes the field. John 6 is the account of a similar "cut" that took place among prospective followers of Christ. Thousands came, enjoyed eating of the food Jesus provided, and wanted more of the same. But the number dwindled rapidly during the follow-up coaching sessions; and when Jesus pressed the matter of accepting Him as the source of life, most of them left. The idea of eating His flesh and drinking His blood was too much for them, and they were not ready to consider words that were "spirit" and "life" (John 6:63).

The twelve apostles, though, stayed on. There was still much about Jesus that they did not understand, but faced with the alternatives they said, "Lord, to whom shall we go? thou hast the words of eternal life. And we believe and are sure that thou art that Christ, the Son of the living God" (John 6:68, 69). That should be enough to reassure any of us.

B. Prayer

We thank You, our Father, for Jesus, the Bread of life eternal. Thank You for the abundance of Your grace, which is limited only by our unwillingness to receive it. May we develop an ever-increasing appetite for Jesus and the life He provides. In His name. Amen.

C. Thought to Remember

Lord, evermore give us the living Bread—Jesus Himself for our nourishment and growth, for now and eternity.

Learning by Doing

This page contains an alternate lesson plan emphasizing learning activities.
Classes desiring such student involvement will find these suggestions helpful.

Learning Goals

This study should help each student to:

1. Tell the story of the feeding of the five thousand, and summarize Jesus' sermon on the bread of life, which followed.

2. Compare the people's desire for literal bread and an earthly kingdom with some of the wrong priorities of people today.

3. Make spiritual matters a higher priority in his or her daily choices.

Into the Lesson

On the chalkboard or on a large poster write *Hunger*. Ask the class to suggest characteristics of hunger. Write down these suggestions under the heading. Then write the headings *Physical* and *Spiritual* next to the word *Hunger*. Ask the class how each item you noted earlier applies to physical and/or spiritual hunger. Note these under the appropriate headings and next to the items listed under *Hunger*. You can expect such responses as pain, lethargy, weakness, and hallucinations. These are obvious in the physical realm; how does spiritual hunger induce such problems in a figurative way?

Make the transition to today's Bible study by noting the devastating effects of hunger on the human body. Observe that, in today's lesson, we'll see that the risks of spiritual hunger are even more frightening.

Into the Word

Ask in advance for four volunteers who will read today's text: John 6:10-14; 26, 27; 35-40; 47-51. Ask the first reader to read John 6:10-14 now. (This is the only miracle, outside Jesus' own resurrection, that is cited in all four of the Gospels. If you have time, have the records of Matthew, Mark, and Luke read also to provide fuller details of this miracle.)

Note the background events (see page 282), then ask a volunteer to provide a very brief summary of the feeding of the five thousand. Discuss the purpose of the miracle (meet the immediate need of hunger; demonstrate Jesus' power/authority—see v. 14). Note verse 15 (not in the printed text). The people saw only the physical and wanted to exploit Jesus' power by making Him an earthly king; but Jesus shunned their efforts.

Ask your second reader to read verses 26 and 27. Provide background to connect this event

with verses 10-15. Discuss, "Why did Jesus seem to be rebuking the crowd in this text?" (They were missing the point, focusing on physical bread.) Discuss how this still happens today. Ask, "How much of the trouble in the world is a result of people's pursuit of what satisfies their physical appetites instead of what satisfies their spiritual hunger?"

Ask your third reader to read John 6:35-40. This is the heart of Jesus' message. Divide the class into groups of five or six and ask each group to paraphrase this text. Give them five minutes, then ask each group to read its paraphrase. Compare the results and make any necessary comments based on the lesson exposition.

Note that this was not an easy sermon for the people to hear. Many were offended. But Jesus did not back down. Have your final reader now read verses 47-51. Ask your small groups to compare this section with verses 35-40. Ask half of the groups to list new information and the other half to list information that is repeated from the earlier section. Allow five minutes and then ask for reports.

Into Life

Ask, "Wouldn't it have been great to hear Jesus give this sermon? How do you think you would have reacted if you had been there?" Discuss briefly, then read verses 60-70. Most of the people abandoned Jesus after this, but the Twelve knew that He had "the words of eternal life."

Challenge the class, "This sermon presents a crisis for each of us. We, too, have to choose how we will respond to Jesus. Some of us have been too focused on material things: our jobs, money, our homes and cars and boats. Maybe we've been too focused on our families, wanting them to be happy and comfortable but not giving attention to their spiritual needs." Have a time of silent prayer, asking each student to ask God's help to make spiritual matters a higher priority in his or her daily choices.

After a few moments, point out that this text presents a crisis for our church too. The world, by and large, has abandoned the church, but the church still has Jesus' "words of eternal life." Discuss ways your church can reach out with renewed vigor to help your community hear the words of life.

Let's Talk It Over

The questions on this page are designed to encourage review of the lesson Scriptures and to promote discussion of the lesson by the class. The answers provided are only discussion starters. Let your class talk it over from there.

1. What would you say to a fellow Christian who said, "It was *easy* for Jesus to help people; He just did a miracle. But I can't do miracles! All these hurting, hungry, homeless people— and what can I do to help? It's hopeless"?

While Jesus did, indeed, work miracles, He also *worked!* Quite often he must have grown weary. In fact, before telling of this miracle, Luke records that Jesus had spent the day healing and teaching the people (Luke 9:11, 12), while Mark notes that He was seeking rest when the crowds approached Him (Mark 6:31-33). We are to be faithful according to what we have, not according to what we don't have. We cannot work miracles, but are we doing all we can? And considering the technology available to us, we can do many things that the people in Jesus' day would have thought miraculous! Are we using that technology to full advantage to help the hurting and to win the lost?

2. The lesson writer suggests that the content of our prayers demonstrates whether or not we allow physical and material concerns to override spiritual ones. How can we put more emphasis on spiritual matters?

Do we pray more for the healing of people's bodies than for the saving of their souls? Are our prayers geared more to the gaining of money for food, clothing, and other material needs than to growing "the fruit of the Spirit"? (Galatians 5:22, 23). As the lesson writer indicates, what we call "the Lord's prayer" (Matthew 6:9-13) offers us a proper pattern to follow in our prayers. By adhering to this pattern we will give priority to the honoring of God's name, the building of His kingdom, and the accomplishing of His will. Paul's prayers recorded in Ephesians 1:15-23; 3:14-21 are also useful in correcting our prayers. They guide us in seeking the exaltation of Christ and the spiritual growth of our fellow believers.

3. Jesus as the bread of life assures us that if we come to Him, we will never hunger. What kind of hunger does Jesus satisfy? How do we develop such a hunger in ourselves and others?

Certainly He was not speaking of physical hunger, which reminds us of our need for food to sustain our physical bodies. Jesus as the bread of life fulfills our deepest longings: the desire for a sense of purpose, the need to be loved and cared

for, the yearning for freedom from guilt, the quest for assurance of victory over death, and the like. Such a hunger must be cultivated with a focus on the things that last. Colossians 3:1-4 addresses this issue, though not with the "hunger" metaphor. We help others develop a greater yearning for spiritual satisfaction by demonstrating the satisfaction and contentment it gives us.

See also Matthew 5:6; Philippians 4:11-13; 1 Timothy 6:6-8.

4. In verse 38 Jesus emphasized His commitment to doing His Father's will. How can we demonstrate a similar commitment? What would happen if every Christian displayed a Christlike commitment to obeying the Father?

The record of Jesus' temptation in the wilderness (Matthew 4:1-11; Luke 4:1-12) reveals the importance of being able to recall Scripture to resist the temptation to stray from the Father's will. In Gethsemane Jesus prayed, "Not my will, but thine, be done" (Luke 22:42). On the same occasion He warned the disciples, "Pray that ye enter not into temptation" (Luke 22:40). Prayer— for ourselves and for one another—is another important tool in maintaining commitment.

We can only speculate what would happen if total commitment to God's will were more common. Imagine the possibilities in your church's own ministries. What is holding you back? Is it money, a shortage of volunteers, or what? Wouldn't total commitment by the entire congregation eliminate most or even all of them?

5. The Jews were proud that their ancestors in the wilderness had eaten manna, but Jesus declared Himself to be better than that manna. In what are people trusting today? How can we demonstrate that Jesus can satisfy more completely than anything else?

Your students should be able to suggest many things people trust in to make their lives better: education, politics, government programs, and science, to name a few. Discuss how these things have repeatedly failed to provide purpose or meaning in life, and have often made matters worse instead of better. Point out that for Jesus to be credible to people today, the Lord's people must be sincere and credible representatives in His behalf.

Truth That Sets People Free

DEVOTIONAL READING: Psalm 51:1-9.

LESSON SCRIPTURE: John 8:12-59.

PRINTED TEXT: John 8:12, 21-36.

John 8:12, 21-36

12 Then spake Jesus again unto them, saying, I am the light of the world: he that followeth me shall not walk in darkness, but shall have the light of life.

. . . .

21 Then said Jesus again unto them, I go my way, and ye shall seek me, and shall die in your sins: whither I go, ye cannot come.

22 Then said the Jews, Will he kill himself? because he saith, Whither I go, ye cannot come.

23 And he said unto them, Ye are from beneath; I am from above: ye are of this world; I am not of this world.

24 I said therefore unto you, that ye shall die in your sins: for if ye believe not that I am he, ye shall die in your sins.

25 Then said they unto him, Who art thou? And Jesus saith unto them, Even the same that I said unto you from the beginning.

26 I have many things to say and to judge of you: but he that sent me is true; and I speak to the world those things which I have heard of him.

27 They understood not that he spake to them of the Father.

28 Then said Jesus unto them, When ye have lifted up the Son of man, then shall ye know that I am he, and that I do nothing of myself; but as my Father hath taught me, I speak these things.

29 And he that sent me is with me: the Father hath not left me alone; for I do always those things that please him.

30 As he spake these words, many believed on him.

31 Then said Jesus to those Jews which believed on him, If ye continue in my word, then are ye my disciples indeed;

32 And ye shall know the truth, and the truth shall make you free.

33 They answered him, We be Abraham's seed, and were never in bondage to any man: how sayest thou, Ye shall be made free?

34 Jesus answered them, Verily, verily, I say unto you, Whosoever committeth sin is the servant of sin.

35 And the servant abideth not in the house for ever: but the Son abideth ever.

36 If the Son therefore shall make you free, ye shall be free indeed.

Apr 25

GOLDEN TEXT: If ye continue in my word, then are ye my disciples indeed; and ye shall know the truth, and the truth shall make you free.—John 8:31, 32.

Lesson Aims

After this lesson students should be able to:

1. Summarize Jesus' sermon at the Feast of Tabernacles.

2. Compare and contrast what Jesus said about truth and freedom with the way today's world views these concepts.

3. Tell how to counter the world's false views with the truth found in Jesus and the Scriptures.

Lesson Outline

INTRODUCTION
    A. What Do You Mean—"Free"?
    B. Lesson Background
  I. THE LIGHT OF THE WORLD (John 8:12)
 II. FURTHER DISCUSSION (John 8:21-30)
    A. Words of Warning (vv. 21-24)
    B. Words of Self-Revelation (vv. 25-27)
    C. Words of Promise (vv. 28-30)
III. THE WAY TO FREEDOM (John 8:31-36)
    A. By Knowing the Truth (vv. 31-33)
      "Never in Bondage"
    B. By Turning From Sin (v. 34)
    C. By Accepting the Son (vv. 35, 36)
      No Free Rides
CONCLUSION
    A. Keeping Freedom Alive
    B. Prayer
    C. Thought to Remember

Introduction

A. What Do You Mean—"Free"?

What is freedom? Try asking the kids.

"It's when you get into the movies without having to pay any money."

"It's when there's a lot of snow and no school."

"It's like when the young man in Jesus' story got his money from his dad and went a long way from home to do whatever he wanted to."

"It's like when slaves got away from their masters, and couldn't be brought back to be slaves anymore."

"It's when some dictator is thrown out of office, and the people get to vote for the leader they want."

However, the greatest liberty is enjoyed by numerous individuals who don't have any of the "freedoms" just described. They have a living relationship with Christ Jesus, who is the truth that sets people free. Because of His love, they choose to live in a better way than any law could compel them to live.

B. Lesson Background

The autumn Feast of Tabernacles brought Jesus to Jerusalem some six months before His crucifixion. It was a time of tension and controversy, as reported in John 7 and 8. The ruling hierarchy of the Jews had already determined that the troublesome preacher from Nazareth must be destroyed. Other Jews from many places, in Jerusalem for the feast and hearing Jesus for the first time, were astonished and impressed by Him. Many were even inclined to believe in Him as the Christ (John 7:31; 8:30).

John 8:12-59 tells of a discussion that took place soon after Jesus declared Himself to be the water of life (John 7:37-44; compare with John 4:10-15). Such a bold assertion created sharp differences of opinion among His hearers. A similar result could be expected from the discourse that followed.

I. The Light of the World (John 8:12)

12. Then spake Jesus again unto them, saying, I am the light of the world: he that followeth me shall not walk in darkness, but shall have the light of life.

Jesus began this discourse with another of His great "I am" declarations with which He had already shaken the religious community. Some commentators suggest that the lighting of four huge golden lampstands in the temple during the Feast of Tabernacles provided an appropriate background for His reference to Himself as *the light of the world.* [See question #1, page 296.]

From the dawn of creation, light has been recognized as essential to life and living (Genesis 1:3-5). The glory of God is essentially light (1 Timothy 6:16). The contrast between light and darkness is symbolic of the contrast between knowledge and ignorance, joy and sorrow, and good and evil. John 1:4 says of the eternal Word who became flesh in the person of Jesus, "In him was life; and the life was the light of men."

The Jewish establishment was not pleased with the idea of Jesus' being light for the entire *world.* They expected the Messiah to lead and serve the Jews, opposing and conquering their enemies. Yet Jesus expected His followers to reflect the light they found in Him without limitations of any kind. To them also He said, "Ye are *the light of the world*" (Matthew 5:14).

There is a twofold significance to living by *the light of life* rather than having to *walk in darkness*. First, he who walks in the light can see where he is going and can travel safely. Jesus is the ideal guide, providing continual light to lead our way. No one can stumble or be lost while following Him.

Second, he who walks in the light will be living daily according to Jesus' teaching and example. "If we say that we have fellowship with him, and walk in darkness, we lie, and do not the truth: but if we walk in the light, as he is in the light, we have fellowship one with another, and the blood of Jesus Christ his Son cleanseth us from all sin" (1 John 1:6, 7).

Pharisees in the temple charged Jesus with offering unsupported testimony about Himself. In response Jesus pointed to the testimony of His Father, as seen in His words and in the miracles that He enabled Jesus to do. However, as Jesus pointed out, the Pharisees did not know His Father (John 8:13-20).

II. Further Discussion
(John 8:21-30)

A. Words of Warning (vv. 21-24)

21. Then said Jesus again unto them, I go my way, and ye shall seek me, and shall die in your sins: whither I go, ye cannot come.

Jesus knew that His time was short. Only the presence of a friendly crowd prevented the Jewish establishment from arresting Him immediately—that and the fact that "his hour was not yet come" (John 7:30; 8:20; see also 7:6, 44; 8:59). Jesus would choose the time and would arrange the circumstances for His going to the cross. He had spoken earlier of going to a place where the Jews could not find Him, and they had speculated that He might be going to foreign lands to teach among the scattered Jews and their Gentile neighbors (John 7:34-36).

In bold contrast to Jesus' words *whither I go, ye cannot come* is His promise to His followers. He told them He was going to prepare a place for them and would come again to receive them. "And whither I go ye know, and the way ye know. . . . I am the way, the truth, and the life: no man cometh unto the Father, but by me" (John 14:4, 6).

22. Then said the Jews, Will he kill himself? because he saith, Whither I go, ye cannot come.

Just how would Jesus arrange His own departure so that He could not be found or followed? There was in His comment a note of finality that suggested death to His hearers. They were right to think of death, but it would not be at Jesus' own hand as they supposed.

23. And he said unto them, Ye are from beneath; I am from above: ye are of this world; I am not of this world.

Jesus said they misunderstood Him because they did not have the proper frame of reference by which to know—as we say today—"where He was coming from." The worldly interests, ambitions, and pride of the Pharisees clearly marked them as drawing from earthly sources and acting on an earthly level. In contrast, Jesus was *from above*, fully committed to the will and purpose of His Father.

24. I said therefore unto you, that ye shall die in your sins: for if ye believe not that I am he, ye shall die in your sins.

These scoffers would *die* in their *sins* because they did not *believe* in the only one who could save them from their sins. They were in the position of being "condemned already" because of their unbelief (John 3:18).

The Greek text does not include the word *he* in the statement, *Ye believe not that I am he*. It says only *that I am*. Perhaps Jesus was referring to His earlier declaration of Himself as the light of the world (v. 12). The statement may have been preparatory to Jesus' later and more controversial claim: "Before Abraham was, I am" (v. 58). The *New International Version* reads, "If you do not believe that I am the one I claim to be." Salvation from sin is possible only through a complete confidence and trust in Him who is the way, the truth, and the life, and whose claims are securely established by His resurrection from the dead: "If Christ be not raised, your faith is vain; ye are yet in your sins" (1 Corinthians 15:17).

B. Words of Self-Revelation (vv. 25-27)

25. Then said they unto him, Who art thou? And Jesus saith unto them, Even the same that I said unto you from the beginning.

Baffled by Jesus' refusal to identify Himself more clearly, the questioners demanded (literally), "You, who are you?" Again Jesus chose not to give a brief answer in plain words, lest they mistake the short phrase for the whole truth and never learn what they really needed to know. Instead, He chose to provide the means by which they could discover the truth for themselves, if they were willing. Besides, it was not yet time for Jesus to provide His enemies with a quotable declaration of His deity. That would come later when He was ready to die for what they would call "blasphemy." [See question #2, page 296.]

From the beginning of His ministry Jesus had been providing evidence that convinced His earliest followers that He was the Christ, the Son of the living God (Matthew 16:16). This continually drew others into the circle of faith. He had claimed to be the water of life, the bread of life, and the light of the world. Let these questioners draw their own conclusions from the evidence available to everyone else.

26. I have many things to say and to judge of you: but he that sent me is true; and I speak to the world those things which I have heard of him.

Jesus knew that the *things* He said and did would disturb and offend many. However, He also knew that He was not acting alone; God had *sent* Him to accomplish a particular task. Any unpopular deeds or words were a part of what the righteous and unchangeable Father in Heaven had commissioned Him to do and to say for the salvation of mankind.

27. They understood not that he spake to them of the Father.

The questioners had heard Jesus' insistence that His message had its source in the One who sent Him; but they did not, or would not, recognize that He was talking about God, and that His message was from God. The Pharisees revealed much about themselves by their slowness to recognize who Jesus is.

C. Words of Promise (vv. 28-30)

28. Then said Jesus unto them, When ye have lifted up the Son of man, then shall ye know that I am he, and that I do nothing of myself; but as my Father hath taught me, I speak these things.

The discussion continued, with Jesus speaking in parable-like terms and His hearers still not understanding what He was talking about. If they had understood, they likely would have demanded His death—at that very moment!

Home Daily Bible Readings

Monday, Apr. 19—"I Am the Light of the World" (John 8:12-20)
Tuesday, Apr. 20—Many Believed in Him (John 8:21-30)
Wednesday, Apr. 21—If You Continue in My Word (John 8:31-38)
Thursday, Apr. 22—Abraham's Children Do the Works of Abraham (John 8:39-47)
Friday, Apr. 23—Whoever Keeps My Word Will Never See Death (John 8:48-59)
Saturday, Apr. 24—Live As Children of Light (Ephesians 5:1-14)
Sunday, Apr. 25—Let Your Light and Your Truth Lead Me (Psalm 43:1-5)

The subject of *the Son of man* being *lifted up* was to recur some six months later during Jesus' last week in Jerusalem. At that time He said, "I, if I be lifted up from the earth, will draw all men unto me." John adds, "This he said, signifying what death he should die" (John 12:32, 33). Jesus' enemies would cause Him to be "lifted up" on the cross to die, but that was part of the eternal plan of God (Acts 2:23). Through Jesus' death and resurrection salvation for lost mankind would become possible.

The statement *then shall ye know that I am he* indicates that Jesus' death and resurrection would demonstrate that the controlling hand of God was in all Jesus had said and done. His critics would have all the evidence needed to conclude that Jesus was who He claimed to be. If not, they would forfeit any hope of salvation (Acts 4:10-12).

29. And he that sent me is with me: the Father hath not left me alone; for I do always those things that please him.

God was *the Father* who had both sent His Son into the world and constantly attended and empowered Jesus in His ministry. That truth would later be stated in even bolder terms: "I and my Father are one" (John 10:30). That is a source of contention to unbelievers, then and now. It was this very claim that moved the Sanhedrin to pronounce the death sentence on Jesus (Matthew 26:63-66).

Now, as then, Jesus' claims make it impossible for anyone to be neutral or indifferent in regard to Jesus. The serious thinker must either believe and follow Him, or disbelieve and reject Him.

30. As he spake these words, many believed on him.

Decision time had come, and a significant number decided in favor of Jesus. We are not told how many *believed,* or how the fact that they did so was expressed. At any rate, there were enough to pose a threat to the Jewish leaders in their determination to seize and do away with Jesus. They did not dare move against Him when too many people were around.

III. The Way to Freedom
(John 8:31-36)

A. By Knowing the Truth (vv. 31-33)

31. Then said Jesus to those Jews which believed on him, If ye continue in my word, then are ye my disciples indeed.

The previous discussion had been heavily influenced by the Pharisees' opposition to Jesus. Now Jesus addressed *those Jews which believed on him.* His teaching is appropriate to any stage of a believer's spiritual development. The beginning of discipleship, like the beginning of physical life, must be followed by nourishment and growth if it is to accomplish its purpose. It is one thing to follow Jesus with an initial burst of enthusiasm; it is another to *continue* in His teaching. Following Jesus is a never-ending learning process. [See question #3, page 296.]

32. And ye shall know the truth, and the truth shall make you free.

Here is an important step in the pathway of discipleship. The way of freedom, Jesus declared, is an intimate acquaintance with Him who is the *truth* (John 14:6). Truth is much more than mere facts or data; it is a Person. Pilate's cynical question, "What is truth?" (John 18:38), is answered by a *who*, and the who is Jesus.

Jesus' linking of truth with being *free* is significant, especially in today's world where freedom is often equated with not adhering to any kind of absolute truth. The knowledge of Christ frees one from ignorance, superstition, and bad habits; but more to the point, it frees from the slaveries of pride, self, and sin. These latter enslavements are more binding than any chains. Consider Paul and Silas, who did not let the restrictions of a maximum security prison silence their praise (Acts 16:25). In reality, they were free before their chains were broken!

Without Christ, on the other hand, the pursuit of philosophical "truth"—even within the mysteries of Scripture—can become an enslavement to self-centered pride. Paul writes of those who are "ever learning, and never able to come to the knowledge of the truth" (2 Timothy 3:7). [See question #4, page 296.]

33. They answered him, We be Abraham's seed, and were never in bondage to any man: how sayest thou, Ye shall be made free?

This question surprises us if it came from the believers whom Jesus urged toward a more mature discipleship (v. 31). Apparently the Pharisees were still present and were listening as Jesus addressed the new believers. We know Jesus was addressing them when He said that they were intending to kill Him (vv. 37, 40) and called them children of the devil (vv. 38, 41, 44). He stated clearly that they had refused to believe Him (vv. 45, 46). John's use of the term "the Jews" (vv. 48, 52, 57) is a reference to the disbelieving Jewish leaders, not to Jews in general. Probably it was these same leaders who challenged Jesus' statement, even though Jesus had been speaking to the ones who believed in Him.

Never in bondage? No Jew could be so ignorant of his national history as to deny Israel's slavery in Egypt, captivity in Babylon, or current

Today's visual illustrates our Golden Text. Discuss the kind of freedom that comes by the truth.

Visual for lesson 8

subjection to Rome. The Pharisees' claim reflected a fierce insistence that *Abraham's seed* might be enslaved politically, but they would never become voluntary slaves. From a religious standpoint, they would remain the chosen people and the "holy nation" that God had originally called them to be (Exodus 19:5, 6). To them, this was all the freedom they needed. What more could Jesus offer?

"NEVER IN BONDAGE"

The religious leaders who were listening to Jesus as He talked about freedom were curiously unaware of the relevance of what He was saying. They felt they were far from lacking in freedom—there was no way they could be called slaves.

As we read the account of the leaders' conversation with Jesus, we are amazed at their lack of perception. Were they not at that very moment under the control of imperial Rome? Furthermore, they claimed that as "Abraham's seed" they were "never in bondage to any man" (John 8:33). Had they forgotten the years of slavery in Egypt? Had they forgotten the years in Babylon? How inaccurate their answer was!

Today those who would venture to make a similar claim of having been "never in bondage" ought to stop and think. Have we lost sight of the great numbers who are actually enslaved to the use of tobacco? Are not millions held in bondage to alcohol? What about all who are becoming more and more addicted to the habit of gambling? What of those who are enslaved by drugs, such as cocaine, heroin, and other substances? Others are bound with chains of indebtedness due to credit card purchases or other forms of financial mismanagement.

Jesus still speaks to any who are bearing heavy chains of habits and attitudes that bind, imprison, and stifle. He alone can break such chains and set free those who are held captive.

—J. G. V. B.

How to Say It

PHARISEES. *Fair*-ih-seez.
SANHEDRIN. San-*heed*-run or *San*-huh-drin.

B. By Turning From Sin (v. 34)

34. Jesus answered them, Verily, verily, I say unto you, Whosoever committeth sin is the servant of sin.

Jesus' answer was introduced with the double amen (*verily, verily*), which to His hearers was a clear signal of its importance. These descendants of Abraham, like the Gentiles they despised, were in need of liberation because they really were in bondage—to sin. By serving sin they had made themselves its bondservants. Paul states the issue in these words: "Know ye not, that to whom ye yield yourselves servants to obey, his servants ye are to whom ye obey; whether of sin unto death, or of obedience unto righteousness?" (Romans 6:16). [See question #5, page 296.]

C. By Accepting the Son (vv. 35, 36)

35. And the servant abideth not in the house for ever: but the Son abideth ever.

He who has yielded himself in obedience to sin is not only in bondage, but until a more lasting relationship is established, he is without a home. A *servant* has no permanent place in the family whom he serves. He may be turned out at any time. But Jesus, as God's one and only *Son*, possesses an eternal claim on the rights and riches of Heaven; and He shares those freely with those who come to the Father in His name and thus become members of the family by adoption. "Behold, what manner of love the Father hath bestowed upon us, that we should be called the sons of God" (1 John 3:1).

36. If the Son therefore shall make you free, ye shall be free indeed.

Freedom is not living the way we want to live and doing what we want to do. Freedom is living the way we *ought* to live and doing what *God* wants us to do. By His life Jesus demonstrated this kind of freedom; by His death He made it possible for us to have it.

NO FREE RIDES

Jesus promises that those who yield to Him and become His disciples will be "free indeed." However, we must realize that being free does not mean a liberation from the regular responsibilities of daily life.

In August of 1947 India became free from Great Britain and was declared an independent state. Naturally this required some radical changes in thinking and living. For example, the British had always controlled the railroad, which was one of the most vital parts of the Indian transportation system. On becoming "free," many peasants believed that railroad passage was now free also. It was reported that within the first year of freedom, more than six million Indians were discovered to be traveling without tickets on the railroad! They had confused political liberty with freedom from responsibilities in general.

Surely we are made free in Jesus our Lord. No longer are we bound by Old Testament laws regarding sin offerings, fasts, or restrictions on the use of various foods. However, we are still governed by Jesus' example and by the commands He has given. Peter reminds Christians, "Live as free men, but do not use your freedom as a cover-up for evil; live as servants of God" (1 Peter 2:16, *New International Version*).

> Yes, free we are—forever free—
>   From sin's clogs brought to liberty!
> But Jesus' way of love and grace,
>   Steadfastly holds our lives in place.
>   —J. G. V. B.

Conclusion

A. Keeping Freedom Alive

Our world today is filled with those who like to boast of being free because they live in a country where a particular document declares that they are free, or whose brave men and women have fought and died to keep their freedoms alive. The Western world seems to have forgotten the God and the Bible that were once freely acknowledged as the basis of mankind's laws and liberties.

The New Testament gives its own directive for keeping alive the spiritual freedoms we treasure: "Brethren, ye have been called unto liberty; only use not liberty for an occasion to the flesh, but by love serve one another" (Galatians 5:13). Let us never forget the One who set us free and the tremendous price He paid for our freedom!

B. Prayer

Thank You, Father, for the love that willingly paid the price for our freedom from guilt and self and sin. Grant us courage to follow in the way lighted and led by Him who is the way of truth and life and liberty. Amen.

C. Thought to Remember

"If the Son therefore shall make you free, ye shall be free indeed" (John 8:36).

Learning by Doing

This page contains an alternate lesson plan emphasizing learning activities.
Classes desiring such student involvement will find these suggestions helpful.

Learning Goals

After this lesson students should be able to:

1. Summarize Jesus' sermon at the Feast of Tabernacles.

2. Compare and contrast what Jesus said about truth and freedom with the way today's world views these concepts.

3. Tell how to counter the world's false views with the truth found in Jesus and the Scriptures.

Into the Lesson

A few weeks before the lesson ask several children and/or teens the question, "What does it mean to be free?" Record their answers and make a poster with as many of them as you can. Display this poster in your classroom for today's lesson.

If you have several repeated answers, list the three most common answers in random order. Ask the class to guess which answer was the most common.

Option: If you aren't able to do the survey in advance, ask your class members the question and record their responses.

Review the list of answers (from your class or the earlier survey) and ask, "Why are there so many different answers for this question?" Discuss the variety of concepts of freedom: political freedom, freedom from responsibility, freedom from a habit, and others. Note that Jesus gives freedom of a sort that the world cannot match. It is that freedom which we will discuss today.

Into the Word

Ask someone to read John 8:12, 21-36. Divide the class into four study groups and assign the following topics: (1) What does Jesus teach us about light? (2) What does Jesus teach us about sin? (3) What does Jesus teach us about freedom? (4) What does Jesus teach us about truth?

The groups may want to use marginal notes in their Bibles or other references available to them to find related Scriptures and ideas about their topics. After ten minutes, allow some time for sharing what each group has uncovered. Use comments from the exposition section of the lesson to fill in any gaps you feel are left after the groups report.

Write this statement on the board: "What the world calls real is many times false." Ask the class to suggest examples that support the truth of this statement.

Option: If you have an amateur magician in your congregation, ask that person to be present and to perform one or two illusions for your class at this time to show that what seems real may not be.

Write the headings *Jesus* and *World* on the chalkboard. Have the students return to their study groups and ask two of the groups to compare and contrast what Jesus said about truth with the way today's world views it. The other two groups should make the same comparisons/contrasts regarding freedom.

Allow the groups about five minutes, then call for reports. (The second group reporting on each topic should report only new information and not repeat what the previous group has already stated.)

Observe that there is a clear difference between the world's view of truth and freedom and Jesus' view. Ask, "Is the church influencing the world on these issues more or less than the world is influencing the church? Why?" After some discussion ask the class to help you make a list: "In what ways have the world's views of truth and freedom infiltrated the church?" List as many answers as possible on the chalkboard.

Into Life

Have the class return once again to the study groups. Ask each group to come up with some ways to counter the world's intrusions on the church (the list referred to above). Assign one-fourth of the list to each group.

After a few minutes call for reports. Suggest ways to implement some of the more promising ideas that have been suggested. Are there some items that each group suggested in response to varying problems? Perhaps these should receive first priority.

Invite individuals to find and read these Scriptures: Deuteronomy 6:7; Ezra 7:10; Psalm 100:5; Galatians 3:26-29; and 4:22-31. The ensuing comments should include the following: (1) we must study, do, and teach God's Word; (2) we must teach our children God's Word; (3) God is faithful to all generations; (4) if we have put on Jesus, we are God's children and heirs of the promise of eternal life; (5) we are not the children of a bondservant, but of the free.

Close the lesson by having a volunteer read Psalm 119:159, 160 as a prayer.

Let's Talk It Over

The questions on this page are designed to encourage review of the lesson Scriptures and to promote discussion of the lesson by the class. The answers provided are only discussion starters. Let your class talk it over from there.

1. Some have suggested that Jesus used the lighting of the great lamps in the temple during the Feast of Tabernacles as an opportunity to declare Himself to be the true light of the world. What symbols can we use to demonstrate the superiority of Jesus today?

We need to be more eager to contrast Jesus with the things of the world and demonstrate that Jesus is far greater. The Christian football player might suggest that Jesus is the real "goal" in life. The Christian politician might suggest that Jesus is the ultimate "ruler." The Christian teacher can show that Jesus is the "Master Teacher."

Perhaps each of your students can suggest a metaphor particularly appropriate to his or her profession or situation in life. Discuss strategies for sharing these metaphors effectively.

2. When the woman at the well mentioned the Messiah, Jesus told her plainly that He was the Messiah (John 4:26). But with the Pharisees He was much less clear, forcing the hearers to think carefully about His words and leaving no opportunity for a charge of blasphemy. How can we know when to give someone a direct answer about Christ and when we need to be more cautious?

The woman at the well was ready to accept Jesus as the Christ; the Pharisees were not. This suggests a principle for us: give people what they are ready to hear. Accepting the Lord is a matter of both mind and heart, so we must be careful not to appeal to people on purely emotional grounds. It is proper to get people to think carefully about Jesus so that their faith has a foundation and will not collapse when the emotion of the moment passes. Knowing when to move from preparation to actual testimony must come from knowing the person involved and being sensitive to his or her understanding. Such knowledge comes only from deliberately cultivating a relationship with the person.

3. As disciples we must continue in Jesus' word. What are you doing that you would say is continuing in His teaching?

An obvious part of complying with what Jesus says here is being sure we know what Jesus' teaching is. How can we continue in it if we do not know it? Ask the class to share some methods of personal Bible study, then discuss available group Bible study opportunities, such as your Sunday School, small groups, and others.

Beyond that, this statement demands that we follow the Word wherever it leads us. It is easy to read the Scriptures and overlook passages that address habits or attitudes we do not want to give up or that contain other challenging teachings. If we are to be genuine, serious disciples, we must open our minds to such passages, and we must let the Word lead us where God wants us to go.

4. Many in our culture believe they have found freedom in the abandonment of the idea of absolute truth. Jesus, however, declared that it is the truth, not the absence of truth, that gives freedom. How can we communicate to people who do not believe in truth the concept that it is the truth which brings freedom?

No one can consistently hold to the idea that there is no absolute truth. Ask the class to suggest areas where everyone wants true standards adhered to, and they will think of several: the patient demands that the surgeon know the absolute truth about what is an appendix and what is not; the airline passenger wants the pilot to know the absolute truth about how to fly—and especially how to land—a jumbo jet. If there are true standards in the physical realm, then it is not unreasonable to expect true standards in the moral realm.

5. How can we get people to see that they are enslaved to sin and in need of the freedom Jesus offers?

Even people with addictions to substances such as alcohol, nicotine, or narcotics often deny that they have lost the freedom to act on their own. Often it takes a traumatic experience in which the person "hits bottom" to get one to recognize his true state. The same is true with the enslavement to sin. A person may have to hit bottom to see his or her true state. Perhaps the testimony of another who has had a similar problem will help to open someone's eyes. Certainly the Word of God must be part of the solution, as the Spirit who inspired the Word is the same Spirit who reproves the world of sin (John 16:8).

Death That Gives Life

DEVOTIONAL READING: Romans 5:1-11.

LESSON SCRIPTURE: John 12:20-50.

PRINTED TEXT: John 12:23-37, 42, 43.

John 12:23-37, 42, 43

23 And Jesus answered them, saying, The hour is come, that the Son of man should be glorified.

24 Verily, verily, I say unto you, Except a corn of wheat fall into the ground and die, it abideth alone: but if it die, it bringeth forth much fruit.

25 He that loveth his life shall lose it; and he that hateth his life in this world shall keep it unto life eternal.

26 If any man serve me, let him follow me; and where I am, there shall also my servant be: if any man serve me, him will my Father honor.

27 Now is my soul troubled; and what shall I say? Father, save me from this hour: but for this cause came I unto this hour.

28 Father, glorify thy name. Then came there a voice from heaven, saying, I have both glorified it, and will glorify it again.

29 The people therefore that stood by, and heard it, said that it thundered: others said, An angel spake to him.

30 Jesus answered and said, This voice came not because of me, but for your sakes.

31 Now is the judgment of this world: now shall the prince of this world be cast out.

32 And I, if I be lifted up from the earth, will draw all men unto me.

33 This he said, signifying what death he should die.

34 The people answered him, We have heard out of the law that Christ abideth for ever: and how sayest thou, The Son of man must be lifted up? who is this Son of man?

35 Then Jesus said unto them, Yet a little while is the light with you. Walk while ye have the light, lest darkness come upon you: for he that walketh in darkness knoweth not whither he goeth.

36 While ye have light, believe in the light, that ye may be the children of light. These things spake Jesus, and departed, and did hide himself from them.

37 But though he had done so many miracles before them, yet they believed not on him.

. . . .

42 Nevertheless among the chief rulers also many believed on him; but because of the Pharisees they did not confess him, lest they should be put out of the synagogue:

43 For they loved the praise of men more than the praise of God.

**May
2**

GOLDEN TEXT: And I, if I be lifted up from the earth,
will draw all men unto me.—John 12:32.

That You May Believe
Unit 3: Jesus Declares God's Message
(Lessons 7-9)

Lesson Aims

After this lesson students will be able to:
1. Explain what Jesus said in today's text about death and life.
2. Tell how Jesus' demands for His disciples imitate His own death and resurrection.
3. Conduct their lives in a way that demonstrates death to the world and life through Christ.

Lesson Outline

INTRODUCTION
    A. More Than Good-bye
    B. Lesson Background
I. LIFE FOUND THROUGH DEATH (John 12:23-26)
    A. Jesus' Coming Death (v. 23)
    B. An Illustration (v. 24)
       Many Seeds From One
    C. Jesus' Challenge (vv. 25, 26)
II. JESUS FACES DEATH (John 12:27-31)
    A. Commitment to the Father (vv. 27, 28a)
    B. Encouragement From the Father (vv. 28b-30)
    C. Judgment on Satan (v. 31)
III. PURPOSE OF JESUS' DEATH (John 12:32-36)
    A. His Death Is for All (vv. 32-34)
    B. He Is the Light (vv. 35, 36)
IV. RESPONSE TO JESUS (John 12:37, 42, 43)
    A. Unbelief Despite Evidence (v. 37)
       Still Unbelieving
    B. Secret Belief (vv. 42, 43)
CONCLUSION
    A. The Word Will Judge
    B. Prayer
    C. Thought to Remember

Introduction

A. More Than Good-bye

"Of all the dispositions and habits that lead to political prosperity, religion and morality are indispensable supports. . . . Whatever may be conceded to the influence of refined education in minds of peculiar structure, reason and experience both forbid us to expect that national morality can prevail in exclusion of religious principle."

Thus spoke George Washington, first President of the United States, in his thoughtful and thorough farewell address on September 19, 1796. That, rather than political or military accomplishments, was the contribution through which Washington chose to be remembered by future generations. When one has to say good-bye, it is the kind of gift that is more important than any material legacy.

Jesus is our perfect pattern for concluding a life of service with words of admonition. John 13–17 recounts His "family" conversation with His disciples just before His crucifixion. John 12:20-50, portions of which form today's printed text, records what apparently was Jesus' last public discourse. It served as a final appeal to a nation that, for the most part, had rejected Him.

B. Lesson Background

When Jesus raised Lazarus from the dead at Bethany, excitement about Him grew in nearby Jerusalem. He became immensely popular with the masses (John 11:45; 12:11) and intensely unpopular with the religious leaders of the Jews (11:53, 57). For a time Jesus stayed away from Jerusalem and "walked no more openly among the Jews" (v. 54). He returned, however, to a tumultuous welcome as he rode on a borrowed donkey into Jerusalem. By then Jews from near and far had crowded into Jerusalem for the Passover, and the enthusiasm regarding Jesus was intensifying (12:12-19). During the daytime Jesus taught in the temple area, where the presence of the multitudes protected Him from attack. At night He retired to Bethany.

Among those in the city for the Passover were some Greeks—worshipers who were denied certain temple privileges because they were not Jews. They wanted to meet Jesus and attempted to make arrangements to do so through the disciples Philip and Andrew. Scripture does not say what purpose they had in mind, nor does it indicate how or whether Jesus received them (John 12:20-22). His message may have been conveyed to the Greeks by Philip and Andrew. Jesus seems to have responded to these inquirers as was His custom—not in words directed to their questions, but in principles suited to their needs.

I. Life Found Through Death (John 12:23-26)

A. Jesus' Coming Death (v. 23)

23. And Jesus answered them, saying, The hour is come, that the Son of man should be glorified.

Son of man was Jesus' most frequently used title to describe Himself. Here the term possessed special significance. Jesus' messiahship involved taking on Himself "the likeness of men" (Philippians 2:7) with all its difficulties. Now He would be *glorified*. His disciples must have viewed recent events (particularly the triumphal entry) as long-overdue recognition of Jesus. But here He spoke of a very different kind of glory, attained by a very different means. The glory would come from God in response to Jesus' total self-sacrifice "unto death, even the death of the cross" (Philippians 2:8-11).

In previous references John noted that Jesus' enemies did not arrest Him because His *hour*, or time, had not yet come (7:6, 8, 30; 8:20; see also His words to Mary in John 2:4). Now we have reached a pivotal point: Jesus announces that *the hour is come*. He recognizes that His death is near and will speak in a similar manner in later settings (13:1; 16:32; 17:1).

B. An Illustration (v. 24)

24. Verily, verily, I say unto you, Except a corn of wheat fall into the ground and die, it abideth alone: but if it die, it bringeth forth much fruit.

As noted in previous lessons, Jesus' *verily, verily* gives emphasis to the words that follow. Here He uses an analogy of a *corn* (better understood as "kernel") *of wheat* that may be preserved indefinitely in a dry granary, but will produce life only when it "dies" in moist soil. There its potential is released and it grows into a stalk, with a head full of many kernels. [See question #1, page 304.]

MANY SEEDS FROM ONE

Jesus spoke of one seed dying and, through its death, producing many seeds. He was, of course, thinking of the vast influence that His death would have through the blessing of new life that would come as a result.

This principle also applies to our service for Jesus. In the latter part of the nineteenth century, a young preacher caught a vision of the need for a college where young men without much money could study to become preachers. With very little in financial resources, the young man began such an institution in a rural area of Tennessee. In spite of the setbacks he often encountered, the determined young preacher persevered and finally won support for his venture.

This young man, Ashley Johnson, gave his life—all his efforts and hopes—to develop a school that would advance the cause of Christ. Following his death the school was named after him: "Johnson Bible College." Today there are hundreds of students at the school. The campus is a beautiful one, including several buildings worth hundreds of thousands of dollars. Across

the world there have been and are hundreds of ministers and missionaries who owe their education to this institution. As a kernel of faith, hope, and love, Ashley Johnson gave his life, and much fruit has come from that gift.

Such an example challenges all of us to lose our lives for Christ's sake, knowing that the resulting blessings will be more than we could ever have imagined.   —J. G. V. B.

C. Jesus' Challenge (vv. 25, 26)

25. He that loveth his life shall lose it; and he that hateth his life in this world shall keep it unto life eternal.

The principle demonstrated in Jesus and illustrated by the grainfield is now expanded and applied to persons, one and all. The hate required by Jesus is best understood by comparing Luke 14:26 (which refers to one hating his family) with Matthew 10:37 (which speaks of one loving his family more than he loves Jesus). Jesus is saying that the disciple must hold his own life in comparative disregard, in view of the priority that he is to give to spiritual matters. In other words, the disciple is to follow the example of Jesus, who hated His own life in comparison with His desire to accomplish the will of God through His atonement for our sins.

It has been said that until one has something worth dying for, he does not really have anything worth living for. Christ is the only one ultimately worthy of total commitment.

26. If any man serve me, let him follow me; and where I am, there shall also my servant be: if any man serve me, him will my Father honor.

A disciple is one who learns from and follows his teacher. Jesus was going in the direction of death to accomplish the purpose for which He had come into the world. Were others willing to follow Him in the same path? To *follow* Jesus

---

How to Say It

ARIMATHEA. *Air*-uh-muh-*thee*-uh (*th* as in *thin*; strong accent on *thee*).

DAMASCUS. Duh-*mass*-kus.

GETHSEMANE. Geth-*sem*-uh-nee.

JAIRUS. *Jye*-rus or *Jay*-ih-rus.

LAZARUS. *Laz*-uh-rus.

NICODEMUS. Nick-uh-*dee*-mus.

PHARISEES. *Fair*-ih-seez.

SANHEDRIN. San-*heed*-run or *San*-huh-drin.

SYNAGOGUE. *sin*-uh-gog.

TARSUS. *Tar*-sus.

summarizes the *duty* of the disciple; to be with Jesus, now and forever, is the *reward* of the disciple (John 14:2, 3; 17:24; 1 Thessalonians 4:17; Philippians 1:23). [See question #2, page 304.]

II. Jesus Faces Death
(John 12:27-31)

Jesus had made it clear that life must come through death, and He knew that His own death—by crucifixion—was fast approaching. That was disturbing to Jesus, and it could be confronted only by calling upon His Father.

A. Commitment to the Father (vv. 27, 28a)

27, 28a. Now is my soul troubled; and what shall I say? Father, save me from this hour: but for this cause came I unto this hour. Father, glorify thy name.

The word *troubled* brings to mind the inner turmoil that Jesus experienced later in Gethsemane. Here we see foreshadowed the struggle between apprehension and commitment that would become the subject of fervent prayer.

For what should He pray? That God would *save* Him from suffering? He did pray, "Father, if thou be willing, remove this cup from me" (Luke 22:42). Yet the suffering for others' sins was the *cause* for which He had come to earth. Knowing this, the Lord prayed, "Not my will, but thine, be done." We should understand that as the same prayer Jesus here expressed by saying, *Father, glorify thy name.*

We, too, struggle between apprehension and commitment. When facing difficulty, it is proper to ask for relief, even as Paul prayed three times for his "thorn in the flesh" to be removed (2 Corinthians 12:7-10). May we learn to pray also, "Let this matter glorify You, Father; Thy will be done." Sometimes He will be glorified by our deliverance; at other times He will be glorified when we endure patiently through the grace He supplies. [See question #3, page 304.]

B. Encouragement From the Father
(vv. 28b-30)

28b. Then came there a voice from heaven, saying, I have both glorified it, and will glorify it again.

Jesus' voice lifted in prayer to Heaven was answered by the Father's assuring *voice from heaven.* Scripture records two other comparable events: at Jesus' baptism (Luke 3:21, 22) and at His transfiguration (Luke 9:28-36). Jesus was praying on both occasions.

The Father's name had been *glorified* in all that Jesus had said and done. It would be glorified especially in Jesus' suffering and death.

29. The people therefore that stood by, and heard it, said that it thundered: others said, An angel spake to him.

Voices from Heaven are apparently clearest to the ones addressed. Thus at Jesus' baptism it was not the words of God, but rather the lingering of the Spirit on Jesus (in the form of a dove) that revealed Him to John the Baptist as the promised Messiah (John 1:32-34). And when Jesus spoke from Heaven to Saul of Tarsus on the Damascus road, Saul's companions saw the blinding light but did not hear the spoken message (Acts 22:9). So here the voice was thought by many to be a coincidental sound from nature, and by others to be a heavenly message to Jesus. All, however, knew that something had happened in response to Jesus' prayer.

30. Jesus answered and said, This voice came not because of me, but for your sakes.

In certain instances the meaning of *not* is perhaps better understood as "not only." This is the case, for example, with Jesus' statement: "He that believeth on me, believeth not on me, but on him that sent me" (John 12:44). It was not only to encourage Jesus in His need that God's *voice came*, but especially to affirm Him in the presence of witnesses.

C. Judgment on Satan (v. 31)

31. Now is the judgment of this world: now shall the prince of this world be cast out.

The voice of God had expressed His approval of His Son in all His doings. That was an affirmative *judgment.* At the same time and with the same voice, it was a judgment that stood in condemnation of all that was opposed to Jesus, beginning with the source of such opposition—*the prince of this world* (John 14:30; 16:11; Ephesians 2:2).

The means by which Jesus' enemies thought they could destroy Him worked instead to glorify God and to destroy Satan and his reign. The essential judgment of the archenemy has occurred already. It is now up to each person to choose how he or she will be judged, whether with the redeemed or with the condemned.

III. Purpose of Jesus' Death
(John 12:32-36)

A. His Death Is for All (vv. 32-34)

32, 33. And I, if I be lifted up from the earth, will draw all men unto me. This he said, signifying what death he should die.

Jesus had centered thus far on His coming death; these words indicated the way in which it would happen. That Jesus was to be *lifted up* revealed *what death* He *should die*—the Roman

Today's visual illustrates the grand truth of verse 32. Discuss how your class can lift up Christ to your community.

Visual for lesson 9

procedure of fastening a victim to a cross, where he was lifted up and exposed to torture and ridicule as he died a slow and agonizing death.

Jesus spoke of the power of His death to *draw all men* to Himself. Through His sacrificial death Jesus is universally attractive, freeing from the guilt of the universal curse of sin. Why, then, do not all hearers of the gospel respond equally to its appeal? Consider that not all objects are equally drawn to the attraction of a magnet. The key factor is the resistance of the object drawn. The drawing power of Jesus does reach out to all, but some are held back by their wrong expectations of Jesus or their prejudices toward Him. Of course, the failure of Jesus' followers to lift Him up can constitute another reason why others are not attracted to Him. [See question #4, page 304.]

34. The people answered him, We have heard out of the law that Christ abideth for ever: and how sayest thou, The Son of man must be lifted up? who is this Son of man?

To those listening, there seemed to be a connection between Jesus' designation as the *Son of man* and the *Christ* (Messiah) who was prophesied in the Old Testament (here referred to as *the law*). Yet Jesus was predicting His death. How could this be, since Isaiah 9:7 said, "Of the increase of his government and peace there shall be no end," and Daniel 7:14 declared, "His dominion is an everlasting dominion, which shall not pass away"? There may have been nothing but honest inquiry in the minds of some who referred to the *Son of man*—the only time in the Gospels that this term is used by anyone except Jesus. Some, however, likely attempted to draw from Jesus a controversial statement that they could take to the Sanhedrin.

B. He Is the Light (vv. 35, 36)

35. Then Jesus said unto them, Yet a little while is the light with you. Walk while ye have the light, lest darkness come upon you: for he that walketh in darkness knoweth not whither he goeth.

Now Jesus issued a final appeal to the people to ponder what He had said, find understanding, and shape their behavior according to the teaching He had given. As the *light* of the world (John 1:4; 8:12), Jesus had shown the way. Let His hearers now use that light, lest nightfall find them stumbling and becoming lost.

36. While ye have light, believe in the light, that ye may be the children of light. These things spake Jesus, and departed, and did hide himself from them.

Trust in the *light* that is available to you! Depend on the guidance given by Jesus, the light of the world! To us the light of life is available through our personal knowledge of Jesus, and also through what we can learn of Him through further study of the Bible, prayer, and daily practice of His teachings.

IV. Response to Jesus (John 12:37, 42, 43)

A. Unbelief Despite Evidence (v. 37)

37. But though he had done so many miracles before them, yet they believed not on him.

Earlier the skeptics had demanded *miracles*, saying, "What sign showest thou then, that we may see, and believe thee?" (John 6:30). But their implied promise was worthless. John's Gospel describes fewer than a dozen miracles, but makes reference to *many* that Jesus did (John 2:23; 3:2; 4:45; 7:31; 20:30; 21:25). Unbelievers, however, remained adamant in their rejection of Jesus. In the case of Lazarus, for example, the Jewish leaders chose to try to destroy the evidence rather than be convinced by it (John 12:10, 11). And this in spite of the fact that they admitted, "This man doeth many miracles" (John 11:47)!

STILL UNBELIEVING

It seems impossible that people could see many of the miraculous works that Jesus performed and still not believe in Him as the promised Messiah. People will find every possible way to discount, minimize, evade, and explain away things supernatural and marvelous.

An incident that occurred some time ago illustrates this hardness of heart. Many of the students at a Christian college took courses at a state university located nearby. The philosophy department at the university had several professors who were in some cases indifferent and in other cases openly hostile to the Christian faith.

A debate, or at least a discussion, was arranged between a professor from the university's philosophy department and a professor from the Christian college. The philosophy professor presented arguments to prove that all "God talk" was meaningless, and that all ideas about God were part of man's search for meaning. He scoffed at any idea of God's revealing Himself to man.

When the Christian college professor gave a powerful argument for the resurrection of Jesus, affirming that this proved God's existence and Jesus' divinity, the philosophy professor remained unpersuaded. He said that even if someone were in fact to be raised from the dead, it would prove nothing!

Such was the attitude of many of those in Jesus' day who, despite the impressive array of evidence before them, "believed not on him."

—J. G. V. B.

B. Secret Belief (vv. 42, 43)

42. Nevertheless among the chief rulers also many believed on him; but because of the Pharisees they did not confess him, lest they should be put out of the synagogue.

Opposition to Jesus was not unanimous even among members of the Sanhedrin. Friends of Jesus included Nicodemus, who pleaded with his colleagues for fairness toward Jesus (John 7:45-52), and Joseph of Arimathea, who joined with Nicodemus in caring for the dead body of Jesus and placing it in Joseph's new tomb (John 19:38-42). Named also is Jairus, a synagogue ruler in Galilee whose daughter Jesus restored to life (Luke 8:40-56).

Most adamant in their opposition to Jesus were the *Pharisees*, eager guardians of the laws and traditions of the elders. They decreed that anyone who acknowledged Jesus as Messiah would be *put out of the synagogue* (John 9:22,

34). That meant ostracism from the Jewish community, socially as well as religiously. For *many* it was an effective deterrent.

43. For they loved the praise of men more than the praise of God.

A friend of Jesus among the membership of the Sanhedrin was a bit like a Christian on a city council representing a predominantly non-Christian constituency, or a Christian student in a class taught by a cynical atheist. God's will is clear enough in the Bible, but God doesn't vote in a local election or record this semester's grade. Often the *praise of men* carries much less personal risk than seeking the *praise of God*.

Jesus warned against doing even the most praiseworthy things, such as praying, fasting, and giving, for the purpose of pleasing the neighbors. What is done for human approval, He said, will bring no added honor from God (Matthew 6:1-18). If the purpose is to please and honor God, however, that should be evident to the neighbors as well (Matthew 5:16). God's opinion must come first, because His judgment is the one that matters! [See question #5, page 304.]

Conclusion

A. The Word Will Judge

Jesus' message in the temple concluded with His departure from the crowds in Jerusalem (v. 36). John notes disappointing responses to Jesus: rejection (v. 37) and a weak and timid faith (vv. 42, 43). In an appended paragraph (vv. 44-50) John records words of Jesus addressing those instances. What He had spoken was from God. It was final, and it would be the basis on which His hearers would be judged. His words would remain forever as the unchanging message of the unchanging God—to be considered, responded to, and applied as the basis of life everlasting.

God and His Word cannot change, conforming to us. By His grace we can change, conforming to Him, and live. Will we?

B. Prayer

We praise and thank You, heavenly Father, for Jesus, who endured a horrible death to give us a glorious life. We love You because You first loved us. We pray for wisdom and courage to choose the way of life eternal, no matter what it may cost in terms of this present world, for Jesus' sake. Amen.

C. Thought to Remember

Jesus died and rose, providing the way of eternal life. In Him we die to self and to sin, that we may live in Him and with Him forever.

Home Daily Bible Readings

Monday, Apr. 26—We Wish to See Jesus (John 12:20-26)

Tuesday, Apr. 27—For This Reason I Have Come (John 12:27-36a)

Wednesday, Apr. 28—Who Has Believed Our Report? (John 12:36b-43)

Thursday, Apr. 29—Whoever Believes in Me (John 12:44-50)

Friday, Apr. 30—The Same Mind That Was in Christ Jesus (Philippians 2:1-11)

Saturday, May 1—The Image of the Invisible God (Colossians 1:9-20)

Sunday, May 2—Knowledge of God's Mystery (Colossians 2:1-15)

Learning by Doing

This page contains an alternate lesson plan emphasizing learning activities.
Classes desiring such student involvement will find these suggestions helpful.

Learning Goals

After this lesson students will be able to:

1. Explain what Jesus said in today's text about death and life.

2. Tell how Jesus' demands for His disciples imitate His own death and resurrection.

3. Conduct their lives in a way that demonstrates death to the world and life through Christ.

Into the Lesson

Bring a few grains of wheat to class and give some to each student. Explain that these seeds, which seem to be dead, are actually full of life. Ask, "What is required for life to spring from these seeds?" Several answers should be given, such as being planted, light, warmth, and water. Tell the class, "Jesus used a grain of wheat as an example to teach that His own death was really the beginning of life. Included in His lesson was the concept that we, as His disciples, will also find life only when we are willing to lay down our lives—like seeds planted in a fertile field."

Into the Word

Ask a volunteer to read John 12:23-43. Then divide the class into four groups. Give each group one of the following assignments:

Group 1. Study verses 23-26 and explain how Jesus' parable of the corn (grain) of wheat applied to Jesus' own experience and how it applies to His followers—including us.

Group 2. Study verses 27-31 and explain how Jesus' death would bring glory to the Father. Suggest also how Jesus' prayer is a model for us as we face difficulty for the sake of Christ.

Group 3. Study verses 32-36 and explain the expression "lifted up" in both a literal and figurative manner. Tell what demands this passage puts on believers today.

Group 4. Study verses 37-43. Compare and contrast the different responses to Jesus that are described here. How are the same responses seen today?

Allow about ten minutes for study, then ask the groups to report. Supply additional information from the commentary pages as needed. Use the discussion questions on the next page to further explore the issues brought up in the reports. Be sure the following summaries are expressed in connection with the group reports:

Group 1. Jesus' death was followed by burial and resurrection, just as a seemingly dead seed is buried and then new life springs forth. As His disciples we must be willing to lay down our lives in service; He will raise us up.

Group 2. Jesus' death fulfilled God's plan of redemption. It proved God to be more powerful than death, and that brought God glory. See the commentary section to note how Jesus' prayer is a model for us (page 300).

Group 3. Literally, Jesus was talking about being "lifted up" on a cross to die. By doing so He opened the way for "whosoever will" to come to Him for salvation. Figuratively, He is "lifted up" when we tell what He has done so people may hear the Word and come to faith.

Group 4. The response to Jesus then was mostly negative (unbelief) even as it is today. Even those who believed were afraid to confess their faith. Are we as timid as they?

Into Life

Write this question on the board: "What areas of our lives should die?" As the ideas emerge, list them on the board. (Pride, selfishness, fear, fleshly lust, anger, disbelief and doubt, worldly ways of thinking, and others may be suggested.)

When the class seems to run out of ideas, ask the class to arrange the ones given in the order of importance. Then take the top three and ask for ways they can be accomplished. Call for a commitment to act, and ask for a report next Sunday of what was accomplished.

Ask the class, "Are you more or less vulnerable to peer pressure now than you were ten years ago?" We often think about the problems teens face with peer pressure, but we all wrestle with it to some extent. Ask, "What is something you have done because of peer pressure that you now wish you hadn't." (If possible, offer a humorous example about yourself.) Sometimes we get into trouble because of peer pressure, but none is worse than the peer pressure described in our text. Note verses 42 and 43 and ask how many of the students know of examples where believers have been afraid to express their faith because of other people. Discuss practical ways of resisting such peer pressure.

Close with a prayer circle, asking God for His strength to resist peer pressure and to take a stand of faith in the coming week.

Let's Talk It Over

The questions on this page are designed to encourage review of the lesson Scriptures and to promote discussion of the lesson by the class. The answers provided are only discussion starters. Let your class talk it over from there.

1. Jesus taught a spiritual lesson by referring to a seed's being planted in the soil. What are some ways in which the work of farming or gardening illustrates the kind of sacrifices we must make as Christians?

Farming metaphors are common in the Bible because the culture in which it was written was heavily dominated by agriculture. They teach us a variety of lessons. Hosea stresses the importance of tilling the soil (Hosea 10:12). That involves sacrificing our pride and self-sufficiency and approaching God in the spirit of humility and submissiveness. Planting requires the farmer to sacrifice grain he could use for food or fodder in anticipation of a greater quantity of grain at harvest (2 Corinthians 9:6). As our lesson Scripture shows, the seed that is planted is replaced by many seeds at harvest. Cultivating is another important agricultural activity. We must be diligent in weeding out of our lives those habits and attitudes that hinder our relationship with Christ.

2. Jesus commanded that we follow Him. But just what does it mean to follow Jesus? What is different about your life because you follow Jesus than would be true if you made no claim to follow Him?

In his famous novel, *In His Steps*, Charles Sheldon depicts a group of people who make no decisions without first asking, "What would Jesus do?" That is one way to picture the principle of following Jesus. Your students may be able to supply more personal examples. Perhaps one has made a job change because he felt his former employer required a behavior that was contrary to following Jesus. Another may tell of volunteer work she does—perhaps at personal expense or, at least, instead of pursuing more "profitable" activities—because she feels it is where Jesus is leading. Some may tell of habits they have conquered by following Jesus—habits to which they otherwise would be slaves today. Praise God for these reports of following Jesus.

3. The lesson writer notes that both Jesus and Paul faced situations when the Father was glorified, not by delivering them from trouble, but by enabling them to accomplish greater good through endurance. How have you found the same to be true in your own life?

Encourage your students to tell of occasions when they prayed for the Lord to act in one way or another—perhaps to deliver them from trouble —and how He responded. Was the Father glorified when one of them, or a loved one, was healed of a disease or an injury? Was He glorified by someone's patient endurance of a disabling injury or handicap? Was the Father glorified when one of your students found work quickly and easily after a layoff? Was His grace demonstrated in the life of one who was laid off and had to depend day to day on the Lord's providence for an extended period of time? Encourage all who have a story to share.

4. Our lesson writer suggests that the failure of Jesus' followers to lift Him up can constitute one reason why some people are not attracted to Him. What can we do to lift up Jesus in a more attractive manner?

Without criticizing any of the persons involved, evaluate your church's evangelistic efforts. Are services designed to appeal to the newcomer and visitor or only to the long-time members? What percentage of your programming is devoted to outreach, and how much is for the benefit of the membership? Does the community know you? Respect you? What can be done to increase your community exposure?

5. Still today some love "the praise of men more than the praise of God." What are some examples? Is this condition present in the church? If so, what can be done about it?

Certain prominent people in our time are more concerned about being politically correct than Biblically correct. Politicians, entertainers, and members of the news media are quick to endorse abortion, homosexuality, pornography, and the like because that will win the approval of their colleagues. And they sneer at Bible believers who label such matters as sin.

In the church, how many Christians in the workplace are silent about their faith in Christ because they fear losing the friendship of their fellow workers? Perhaps we need more emphasis on such passages as 1 John 2:15-17 to encourage timid believers. Role-playing in a friendly environment may also help them feel more comfortable in the more hostile one.

Jesus Teaches Servanthood

DEVOTIONAL READING: Matthew 25:31-40.

LESSON SCRIPTURE: John 13:1-35.

PRINTED TEXT: John 13:1-17.

John 13:1-17

1 Now before the feast of the passover, when Jesus knew that his hour was come that he should depart out of this world unto the Father, having loved his own which were in the world, he loved them unto the end.

2 And supper being ended, the devil having now put into the heart of Judas Iscariot, Simon's son, to betray him;

3 Jesus knowing that the Father had given all things into his hands, and that he was come from God, and went to God;

4 He riseth from supper, and laid aside his garments; and took a towel, and girded himself.

5 After that he poureth water into a basin, and began to wash the disciples' feet, and to wipe them with the towel wherewith he was girded.

6 Then cometh he to Simon Peter: and Peter saith unto him, Lord, dost thou wash my feet?

7 Jesus answered and said unto him, What I do thou knowest not now; but thou shalt know hereafter.

8 Peter saith unto him, Thou shalt never wash my feet. Jesus answered him, If I wash thee not, thou hast no part with me.

9 Simon Peter saith unto him, Lord, not my feet only, but also my hands and my head.

10 Jesus saith to him, He that is washed needeth not save to wash his feet, but is clean every whit: and ye are clean, but not all.

11 For he knew who should betray him; therefore said he, Ye are not all clean.

12 So after he had washed their feet, and had taken his garments, and was set down again, he said unto them, Know ye what I have done to you?

13 Ye call me Master and Lord: and ye say well; for so I am.

14 If I then, your Lord and Master, have washed your feet; ye also ought to wash one another's feet.

15 For I have given you an example, that ye should do as I have done to you.

16 Verily, verily, I say unto you, The servant is not greater than his lord; neither he that is sent greater than he that sent him.

17 If ye know these things, happy are ye if ye do them.

GOLDEN TEXT: Verily, verily, I say unto you, The servant is not greater than his lord; neither he that is sent greater than he that sent him.—John 13:16.

Lesson Aims

After this lesson students will be able to:

1. Tell the story of Jesus' washing the disciples' feet in the upper room.

2. Explain why it is difficult either to serve or to be served by another.

3. Resolve to do something each day this week in service to another, and to receive the service of others graciously.

Lesson Outline

Introduction

A. The Glory of Serving Jesus

The Slavic peoples of today make up many in Eastern Europe. During the early Middle Ages, these nations did not exist. There were only Slavic tribes, who were often in conflict with Germanic tribes from central Europe. When the Slavs lost, the captives were sold to other peoples as slaves. In fact, our word *slave* comes from the word *slav*. In the Slavic languages, however, the word *slav* means "glorious."

While we think of slavery and glory as two quite opposite ideas, they come together beautifully in Jesus Christ. As we will learn today, it is a glorious thing to be a servant (slave) of Jesus.

B. Lesson Background

John is the only Gospel writer to record the unforgettable demonstration of servanthood that occurred in the upper room—Jesus' washing of His disciples' feet. This visual aid served to reinforce what Jesus had been trying to teach His disciples all along about greatness in His kingdom. It was a lesson that the Twelve had been extremely slow to learn. Even in the upper room, with the cross fast approaching, "there was also a strife among them, which of them should be accounted the greatest" (Luke 22:24). The lesson Jesus taught them was one they desperately needed. It is one we must heed as well.

I. Setting the Scene
(John 13:1-5)

In any drama it is important to set the stage. The upper room where the events in our text took place did not look at all like the paintings of the Last Supper that we often see. In Jesus' day the second floor of a house was usually reached by an outside stairway. (One did not take up precious space inside the house with steps.)

We do not know who owned this upper room. Apparently he was a follower of Jesus not named by any of the Gospel writers. This may have been the same room where the disciples met after the resurrection and where the risen Christ appeared to them (John 20:19). Luke describes it as a large room (Luke 22:12). Appropriate preparations for the Passover had already been made by the disciples (Luke 22:12, 13). As was the custom in that time, they sat on couches or cushions arranged around a low table.

A. The Timing (vv. 1-3)

1. Now before the feast of the passover, when Jesus knew that his hour was come that he should depart out of this world unto the Father, having loved his own which were in the world, he loved them unto the end.

What does John mean by *before the feast of the Passover*? Most Bible students believe that this refers to the time just before the meal began. Some think that it means "before the day" of this Passover. They contend that Jesus died at the same time that Passover lambs were being killed on the temple altar (1 Corinthians 5:7). If this were the case, then Jesus and the Twelve shared an earlier meal as a substitute for the Passover. This may appeal to our poetic side; but it is not necessary to take this view, and most find the arguments for it unconvincing. Most likely the phrase simply means "before they sat down for the meal."

John's Gospel refers to three other Passovers besides this one. (See John 2:13; 5:1; 6:4; the feast mentioned in John 5:1 is generally considered to have been a Passover, though that is not specified.) From these feasts, we determine that the ministry of Jesus lasted between three and three and a half years. (See the chart on page 230.) Since Luke tells us that Jesus was "about thirty" at the beginning of His ministry (Luke 3:23), we deduce that He died at the age of thirty-three.

The Passover commemorated the Jews' departure from Egypt and their establishment as a nation. It is important to note that at the time when the most solemn Jewish ceremony was observed, Jesus instituted the most solemn Christian ceremony. Not only are the two alike in their solemnity, but both are also highly symbolic. Everything on the Passover table was symbolic of something that the Jews experienced during their exodus from Egypt. Everything on the Communion table is symbolic too. We must also remember that the Passover commemorated the Jews' deliverance from bondage in Egypt. Our Communion commemorates our deliverance from the bondage of sin.

We have noted in previous lessons the significance of the term *hour* in John's Gospel. On certain occasions during His ministry, Jesus stated (or John noted) that His hour had not yet come (2:4; 7:6, 8, 30; 8:20). In last week's lesson we saw how Jesus began to declare, "The hour is come" (12:23). Clearly *Jesus knew* what lay ahead. The cross was no surprise to Him. He said, "I lay down my life, that I might take it again. No man taketh it from me, but I lay it down of myself" (John 10:17, 18).

The expression *loved them unto the end* is a very beautiful description of the extent of Jesus' love for His disciples. The Greek word for *end* may also be translated "completion," so the expression may rightly be translated "loved them completely." The phrase rendered *unto the end* is translated "to the uttermost" in 1 Thessalonians 2:16. Thus these words are really saying that the love of Jesus was and is without end. A footnote in the *New American Standard Bible* has "loved them 'eternally.'"

Note the contrast between the words *his own* as used here and as they are used in the first chapter of John's Gospel (John 1:11). There the emphasis is on the rejection of Jesus by *his own*. Here *his own* describes the closeness that had developed between Jesus and the Twelve during the years of His ministry. They were truly His own; they belonged to Jesus in the strongest sense of the word because they had chosen to believe in Him, follow Him, and obey Him.

2. And supper being ended, the devil having now put into the heart of Judas Iscariot, Simon's son, to betray him.

Instead of *supper being ended*, the text at this point is better rendered "during the supper" or "as the supper was in progress." The events described here occurred after part of the Passover meal had ended but before it was finished.

The word *now* should not be understood to mean that at that very moment *the devil . . . put into the heart of Judas* the thought that he should *betray* Jesus. A more accurate reading is "already" (*New American Standard Bible, New International Version*). By this time Judas had begun the betrayal process, for he had already contacted and contracted with the enemies of Jesus (Matthew 26:14-16). He had only to decide on the proper time to carry out his plan and have Jesus arrested. It was obvious from the triumphal entry that Jesus was still immensely popular with the people. To try to arrest Him during the daytime could cause a disturbance. But on this night all the people were in their own homes for the Passover observance. It was the ideal moment to apprehend Jesus without incident. Later John notes that after Jesus gave to Judas the "sop" (the bread that had been dipped in a bowl of gravy or sauce), "Satan entered into him" (v. 27).

3. Jesus knowing that the Father had given all things into his hands, and that he was come from God, and went to God.

That someone who had been instrumental in the creation of the universe (John 1:3) and was one day to sit down at the right hand of God (Hebrews 1:3) should kneel to wash men's feet is amazing. Jesus knew that He was on His way to the cross, but He also knew that He was on His way to the crown. At a time when we might expect the greatest pride, we see instead the greatest humility.

That should not surprise us. It was Jesus' knowledge of who He was that freed Him to

This visual cites nearly all of today's printed text in a manner that reminds us that the full extent of Jesus' love was seen, not only in the upper room, but at Calvary.

Visual for lesson 10

How to Say It
ISCARIOT. Iss-*care*-ee-ut.
RABBI. *Rab*-eye.

serve His disciples. People whose sense of identity and self-worth come from externals are continually worried about what others think of them. They will not do anything that might make another think less of them. But Jesus knew He was God's Son and that He would soon rejoin His Father in Heaven. Washing His disciples' feet did not make Him any less divine.

We who follow Jesus can have the same freedom. We know that in Jesus we belong to God and will one day go to Him to live with Him forever. Such knowledge should fortify us against pride and temptation. It should never become a source of vanity. When we are so concerned about our own status and position that we are not willing to stoop to do common deeds for common people, we show how insecure we really are in our relationship to Christ. [See question #1, page 312.]

STOOPING TO SERVE
At a church I once served in Pittsburgh, Pennsylvania, it was customary for baptisms to be administered during the morning worship service. This required a quick change of clothing by the minister so he could prepare for the baptisms. An elder of the church went into the minister's dressing room and helped him don the boots that he wore while in the baptistery.

The elder who did this, often kneeling on the floor to help with this task, was the chief engineer with the Bell Telephone Company in Pittsburgh. Here was an important executive performing a humble task. He was doing it because he believed that the work of God at that time and place required this particular service.

This man probably made significantly more money than most people in the church. He had status, power, prestige—but he laid all of this aside so he could serve another. We should possess a similar dedication to any task that God may need us to accomplish.   —J. G. V. B.

B. Jesus' Preparation (vv. 4, 5)
4. He riseth from supper, and laid aside his garments; and took a towel, and girded himself.
As noted earlier, only John tells us about Jesus' washing of the disciples' feet. He is also the only Gospel writer who says nothing about Jesus' institution of the Lord's Supper in the upper room. In this case John (whose Gospel

was most likely the last of the four to be written) seems to be supplementing what Matthew, Mark, and Luke had already recorded.

The statement that Jesus *laid aside his garments* indicates that He took off His outer robe. Beneath this robe He would have been wearing a sleeveless tunic and a loincloth. Some believe He also removed the tunic, though that is not certain. Either way, He suddenly appeared before the disciples in the role of a servant instead of the host.

Jesus then *took a towel* (a long linen cloth). No doubt the towel and basin were provided by the owner of the upper room for use by his guests. That was customary. What was clearly not customary was for Jesus to wrap this towel around *himself* and do what He proceeded to do.

5. After that he poureth water into a basin, and began to wash the disciples' feet, and to wipe them with the towel wherewith he was girded.
In Jesus' day people did not wear shoes but open sandals. They walked in dust if the weather was dry and in mud if it was wet. Travelers generally arrived at a house with dirty feet. It was considered the responsibility of a household servant to wash the feet of the guests. But there was no servant in the upper room on this occasion, and none of the Twelve had been designated as such. So Jesus began to *wash the disciples' feet*.

We do not know to which of the Twelve Jesus went first, nor do we know the reaction of any except that of Peter. It is possible that one of them thought, "Why didn't someone think of that?" We hope that one of them may have said to himself, "Why didn't I think of that?" We must ask ourselves, "If I had been in that upper room, would I have volunteered for this task before Jesus did it? Would I have taken the towel from Him when He began to do it? Would I have accepted His service in silence, or would I have protested as Peter did?"

II. Exchange With Peter
(John 13:6-11)
A. Peter's Reluctance (vv. 6-9)
6. Then cometh he to Simon Peter: and Peter saith unto him, Lord, dost thou wash my feet?
Peter was astonished at what Jesus was doing, and he expressed his astonishment with a question: *Dost thou wash my feet?* He may have put the emphasis on the word *my*, especially if he was the last to have his feet washed. Or he may have put the emphasis on *thou*. Both pronouns are emphasized in the Greek text, and it is interesting to think of Peter stressing both in his question.

7. Jesus answered and said unto him, What I do thou knowest not now; but thou shalt know hereafter.

Jesus knew what He was doing and why He was doing it, but none of the Twelve did. He reassured them that they would *know hereafter.* After the crucifixion and the resurrection, they would understand what Jesus was really doing and what He wanted to teach them. Looking back on that night, the disciples would remember that they had been quarreling over who would be the greatest in Jesus' kingdom (Luke 22:24). Jesus had responded to their vain ambitions with an unforgettable gesture of service.

8. Peter saith unto him, Thou shalt never wash my feet. Jesus answered him, If I wash thee not, thou hast no part with me.

Perhaps others of the Twelve felt the same way as *Peter,* but he was always quick to speak up. His *Thou shalt never* sounds as harsh as his earlier "This shall not be unto thee" following Jesus' prediction of His death (Matthew 16:22). Jesus' reply to Peter was equally strict: if He did not wash Peter, Peter would have *no part with* Jesus. Obviously far more was involved than the mere washing of feet. On the surface Peter's words appeared to express an attitude of humility. In reality he was defying Jesus' authority, seeking to tell Him what to do. True fellowship with Jesus was impossible if Peter's attitude did not change. [See question #2, page 312.]

9. Simon Peter saith unto him, Lord, not my feet only, but also my hands and my head.

Peter still did not understand. He wanted to remain a devoted follower of Jesus. So, misunderstanding what Jesus had just said, he changed his reluctance to an eager acceptance: *not my feet only, but also my hands and my head.* Whatever blessing was involved, Peter wanted more of it. Again, his attitude may appear admirable, but Peter was still trying to tell Jesus what to do. This is a mistake we all make: trying to serve Jesus on our terms instead of accepting His.

B. Jesus' Response (vv. 10, 11)

10. Jesus saith to him, He that is washed needeth not save to wash his feet, but is clean every whit: and ye are clean, but not all.

Here Jesus shifted from physical cleansing to the more critical matter of spiritual cleansing (the phrase *clean every whit* means completely clean, or clean all over). But over against the promise of spiritual cleansing came these sad words: *but not all.* Obviously Jesus was referring to Judas Iscariot. Was he still present? It is difficult to tell from the accounts in the four Gospels at what specific point Judas left the group in the upper room. It is clear from John's Gospel that Judas did not leave the room until after Jesus had given him the sop (v. 30). If John's account is chronological, this would have been after the events related here. Many believe that Judas was present when Jesus washed the disciples' feet and that it was immediately after his departure that Jesus instituted the Lord's Supper with the remaining disciples. [See question #3, page 312.]

11. For he knew who should betray him; therefore said he, Ye are not all clean.

Again John notes that Jesus *knew who should betray him.* Yet Jesus not only sat at the same table with this man, but even offered him a special token of friendship. He took a piece of bread (the "sop") and gave it to Judas (v. 26). This was recognized in that time as a gesture of close, personal friendship—and Jesus extended it to his betrayer! Jesus' handing of the "sop" to Judas was an act that was every bit as remarkable as His washing of the disciples' feet.

III. Jesus' Application (John 13:12-17)

A. The Lord Is Also a Servant (vv. 12, 13)

12. So after he had washed their feet, and had taken his garments, and was set down again, he said unto them, Know ye what I have done to you?

This seems to be a strange question: *Know ye what I have done to you*? Certainly they knew what He had done—He had washed their feet! But they did not know the deeper meaning of Jesus' act, nor how it applied to them.

13. Ye call me Master and Lord: and ye say well; for so I am.

Home Daily Bible Readings

Monday, May 3—He Began to Wash His Disciples' Feet (John 13:1-11)

Tuesday, May 4—Do You Know What I Have Done? (John 13:12-20)

Wednesday, May 5—One of You Will Betray Me (John 13:21-30)

Thursday, May 6—I Am With You Only a Little Longer (John 13:31-35)

Friday, May 7—Here Is My Servant (Isaiah 42:1-9)

Saturday, May 8—The Greatest Among You Will Be Your Servant (Matthew 23:1-11)

Sunday, May 9—Follow in Christ's Steps (1 Peter 2:18-25)

The Greek word translated *Master* means "teacher." It is closely related to the term "Rabbi," as John 1:38 indicates. Rabbis were held in great respect among Jews of that day, even as they are today. *Lord* indicates authority or even ownership, as in a lord's relationship to a slave. Jesus did not condemn the Twelve for calling Him by either of these titles. He only intended to show that they had not yet fully grasped the meaning of either title.

B. An Example to Follow (vv. 14, 15)

14, 15. If I then, your Lord and Master, have washed your feet; ye also ought to wash one another's feet. For I have given you an example, that ye should do as I have done to you.

Did Jesus intend for us to take these words literally? Some believe that He did, and thus footwashing as a part of worship is practiced in some churches today. Those who do so maintain that Jesus instituted this ceremony as surely as He instituted the Lord's Supper in the upper room.

However, while there is further mention of the Lord's Supper in the letters of the New Testament, footwashing as a part of worship is never mentioned again. The only other time it is mentioned at all is in 1 Timothy 5:10, where it is one of several "good works" to be done for someone in need. Therefore, most believers understand Jesus' words as a challenge to follow His example of humility and service, not as the institution of an act of public worship. [See question #4, page 312.]

C. True Greatness (v. 16)

16. Verily, verily, I say unto you, The servant is not greater than his lord; neither he that is sent greater than he that sent him.

Jesus often encapsulated truth in memorable sayings like, *The servant is not greater than his lord.* His point was this: If He as Lord was willing to do the work of the lowest servant, then the men in that room must be prepared to do the same. They will be leaders in Jesus' church, of course. But they will fulfill that duty most effectively only if they are willing to be servants. Jesus remains the supreme example of servant leadership (Matthew 20:28; Philippians 2:5-8).

D. True Happiness (v. 17)

17. If ye know these things, happy are ye if ye do them.

To *know* what is right is commendable. However, knowledge alone, as Paul reminds us, puffs us up (1 Corinthians 8:1). To *do* what is right produces a sense of fulfillment and the blessing of true happiness. When we serve others, we for-get about ourselves, we forget all the things we ordinarily complain about, and we learn to count our blessings.

We should see more than a promise of happiness here, however. The word for *happy* is the same one used in the Beatitudes (Matthew 5:3-11), where it is more properly translated "blessed." Happiness is an emotion; as such, it is subject to change. But the blessings of obedience transcend emotion. God is concerned about our happiness, but He is more concerned about our faithfulness. When we are faithful to Him and to the example He has set for us to follow, then we will indeed be blessed. [See question #5, page 312.]

Conclusion

A. The Need for Humility

Humility is surely the most elusive of virtues. Just when we think we have attained it, we've lost it! Real humility is expressed in serving, in not insisting on our own way or supposing that we have all the answers, and in not insisting that we be given praise or preference. We should not be surprised that 1 John 2:16 places "the pride of life" alongside the lust of the flesh and the lust of the eyes as one of the taproots of sin.

B. Two Kinds of Humility

Whenever we read or study the incident recorded in today's text, we usually focus on Jesus, who was not too proud to wash men's feet. We also need to focus on Peter, who at first was too proud to allow Jesus to wash his feet.

In a monastery in Austria, at each end of a long colonnade is a wood carving. One shows Jesus kneeling to wash Peter's feet. The other shows a woman kneeling to wash Jesus' feet. Ordinarily we do not think of those two scenes together, but we should. It took as much humility for Jesus to permit that woman to wash His feet as it took for Him to wash the disciples' feet.

Certainly we need to develop a spirit of humility that is willing to serve in any capacity. At other times, however, we need the humility to allow others to serve us.

C. Prayer

O Lord, forgive the pride that robs us of the joy of service. Forgive as well the pride that makes us hesitate to accept the loving service of others. Keep ever before us the example of Jesus. We pray in His name. Amen.

D. Thought to Remember

Both in serving and in being served we follow the example of our Lord.

Learning by Doing

*This page contains an alternate lesson plan emphasizing learning activities.
Classes desiring such student involvement will find these suggestions helpful.*

Learning Goals

After this lesson students will be able to:

1. Tell the story of Jesus' washing the disciples' feet in the upper room.

2. Explain why it is difficult either to serve or to be served by another.

3. Resolve to do something each day this week in service to another, and to receive the service of others graciously.

Into the Lesson

Write on the chalkboard or a large poster the words, "Jobs I Hate to Do." Encourage students, as they arrive, to write answers under the heading. You'll probably get responses like "take out the garbage," "clean the toilet," or "scrub the floor." Parents of young children may add "changing diapers."

When it is time to begin, ask the class to vote on the worst job on the list. Ask, "Why are these jobs so distasteful?" Some of the jobs on the list will be difficult. Many will require handling or being near something dirty. But the worst thing about all—or nearly all—is that they are thankless jobs. Everyone expects them to get done, but the doing of them seems to be taken for granted.

Point out that, in New Testament times, people walked on dusty or muddy roads and streets in open sandals. They removed the sandals in Oriental fashion when they entered a home, but their feet were still dirty. So it was customary to greet one's guests with a footwashing to remove the soil. This job went to the lowest of servants. If a visitor from the first century had been present at the beginning of the class, "washing feet" is probably what he or she would have written on the "Jobs I Hate to Do" list. In today's lesson we'll see how Jesus used this thankless job to teach a valuable lesson.

Into the Word

Assign someone in advance to be prepared to read John 13:1-17. Distribute to the class a chart with the following headings across the top: Forget Yourself (vv. 1-5); How Can I Wash Your Foot When It's in Your Mouth? (vv. 6-11); I'd Rather See a Sermon Than Hear One (vv. 12-17). Ask the students to reflect on verses 1-5 and write how one's self-esteem is related to his or her willingness to serve. Ask them to write their thoughts in the first column.

After a few minutes, ask the class to look at verses 6-11 and write what was wrong with Peter's protest (v. 8) and his later exclamation (v. 9). Ask them to summarize what Jesus wanted the disciples to learn about serving and about being served.

Again allow a few minutes for the students to work; then ask them to consider the remaining six verses of the text. Ask them to suggest practical ways of following Jesus' example as He commanded, and to suggest at least one blessing that might result (v. 17).

Allow a few more minutes for the students to respond, then ask them to get into pairs to review their answers in column 1. Ask for volunteers to share some interesting items from their partner's answers. (No one may share his or her own answers.) Use information from the commentary section to supplement this discussion.

Repeat this same procedure to review the texts related to columns 2 and 3, asking the students to find new partners for each section.

Into Life

From the responses offered under column 3, make a list on the chalkboard of tasks that Christians can do to follow Jesus' example of humble service. Ask the class to think of others if the list seems short. (You need at least six.)

When your list is complete, distribute sheets of paper on which you have written the days of the week, Monday through Saturday, down the left side. Ask each student to write one activity from your list next to each day and to plan to do at least one act of loving service each day. Remind them to be ready to accept service from others as well.

Then ask the class to choose one item from the list that might make a good class project. Plan a time when your class can accomplish it. Perhaps "washing windows for an elderly person" was cited. Organize a time your class can get together and wash windows for several older members. You could meet at the church building and send teams of three or four people to different homes. Then meet back at the church building or a member's home for some fun and fellowship.

Conclude the class session by reading verses 14-17. Close with prayer that God would give you the grace to serve, and to accept the service of others, in the true spirit of Christ.

Let's Talk It Over

The questions on this page are designed to encourage review of the lesson Scriptures and to promote discussion of the lesson by the class. The answers provided are only discussion starters. Let your class talk it over from there.

1. Jesus' confidence in who He was freed Him to act as a servant and wash His disciples' feet. Why do we so often lack enough confidence in our standing in Christ to serve in menial ways? How can such confidence, and thus service, be encouraged?

It is a worldly concept that our importance is measured by what we will not do, but we often buy into the world's way of thinking. Perhaps we need to talk more about the confidence we have in Christ, using such passages as Romans 6: 3, 4; Philippians 3:4-14; Colossians 3:1-4; 1 John 5:13. Sometimes we talk of the "duty" of service; perhaps we should emphasize the "privilege" of imitating Christ in service. Sometimes we may unwittingly follow the world's standards even in the church when we recognize only highly visible servants and fail to give honor to those who serve in the lowliest roles.

2. Peter was initially resistant to the idea of Jesus' washing his feet. Have you ever tried to do something to help another, but that person resisted? Why do you think some people have so much difficulty in accepting service? How do you balance the need to be a servant and the need to allow another to serve you?

Certainly the lesson Jesus was teaching here was that we ought to be servants (see verse 14), and most of us have more trouble with serving than with being served. However, sometimes, in our zeal to play the servant, we resist when someone else tries to perform some service in our behalf. We need to be sure we are not just "playing" the servant in such matters. Some people refuse to accept another's service because they prefer to "play the martyr." This is not a wholesome attitude. If we are serving from a genuine attitude of love and concern for another, then we ought to serve. And if someone else is attempting to express a genuine attitude of love and goodwill toward us, we ought not to resist. The "Golden Rule" (Matthew 7:12) applies here: if we want our service to be accepted, we ought to accept graciously the service of another.

3. We do not know whether Judas Iscariot was present when Jesus washed the disciples' feet, but if he was, then Jesus washed his feet as well. What lessons does that suggest to you?

Imagine the scene as Jesus washed Judas's feet. Imagine the penetrating look Jesus must have had as He looked Judas in the eye. Did Judas have no shame? How could he continue with his plan? Yet do not we, who have been washed in the blood of the Lamb, sometimes act with equal callousness?

What does this scene teach us about our own level of service? Are we able to perform loving acts toward one we know has spread gossip about us or otherwise worked to our harm? Can we follow Jesus' example?

4. What are some modern-day counterparts to footwashing?

The washing of a guest's feet was a part of the welcome extended to him (see Luke 7:44-46). So we should be able to find some counterparts in the way we welcome one another in the church. Sometimes such a welcome begins in the church parking lot. Taking an umbrella to escort attendees on a rainy day is one example. Assisting persons who are wheelchair-bound or have difficulty walking is another.

This concept should not be limited to activities performed at the church building, however. There are many ways we can serve one another: taking in a meal to someone who is ill, visiting lonely people at a nursing home, or caring for a disabled person. In whatever way we put the needs of another ahead of our own status or comfort, we are following Jesus' example.

5. What blessings have you received from serving others?

Anyone who has from a pure heart rendered service in Jesus' name can surely tell of blessings received. One is the feeling of happiness that comes from knowing he or she has done what is right. Some of your students may tell of occasions when their acts of service were returned. Those who look after the needs of others find many eager to assist them when they find themselves in need. In some cases the actions of a believer to help an unbeliever in need may be the instrument by which that person is led to the Lord. Being part of God's effort to reach out and save the lost is surely among the greatest blessings we can receive. Encourage everyone to share how God has blessed his or her service.

Jesus, the True Vine

DEVOTIONAL READING: Psalm 1.

LESSON SCRIPTURE: John 15:1-17.

PRINTED TEXT: John 15:1-17.

John 15:1-17

1 I am the true vine, and my Father is the husbandman.

2 Every branch in me that beareth not fruit he taketh away: and every branch that beareth fruit, he purgeth it, that it may bring forth more fruit.

3 Now ye are clean through the word which I have spoken unto you.

4 Abide in me, and I in you. As the branch cannot bear fruit of itself, except it abide in the vine; no more can ye, except ye abide in me.

5 I am the vine, ye are the branches. He that abideth in me, and I in him, the same bringeth forth much fruit; for without me ye can do nothing.

6 If a man abide not in me, he is cast forth as a branch, and is withered; and men gather them, and cast them into the fire, and they are burned.

7 If ye abide in me, and my words abide in you, ye shall ask what ye will, and it shall be done unto you.

8 Herein is my Father glorified, that ye bear much fruit; so shall ye be my disciples.

9 As the Father hath loved me, so have I loved you: continue ye in my love.

10 If ye keep my commandments, ye shall abide in my love; even as I have kept my Father's commandments, and abide in his love.

11 These things have I spoken unto you, that my joy might remain in you, and that your joy might be full.

12 This is my commandment, That ye love one another, as I have loved you.

13 Greater love hath no man than this, that a man lay down his life for his friends.

14 Ye are my friends, if ye do whatsoever I command you.

15 Henceforth I call you not servants; for the servant knoweth not what his lord doeth: but I have called you friends; for all things that I have heard of my Father I have made known unto you.

16 Ye have not chosen me, but I have chosen you, and ordained you, that ye should go and bring forth fruit, and that your fruit should remain; that whatsoever ye shall ask of the Father in my name, he may give it you.

17 These things I command you, that ye love one another.

GOLDEN TEXT: I am the vine, ye are the branches. He that abideth in me, and I in him, the same bringeth forth much fruit; for without me ye can do nothing.—John 15:5.

That You May Believe
Unit 4: Jesus Prepares His Followers
(Lessons 10-13)

Lesson Aims

After this lesson students should be able to:

1. Summarize Jesus' message of the vine and the branches.

2. Explain the relationship that believers, as "branches," are to maintain with Jesus, the "Vine."

3. List one or two "fruits" that he or she is seeking to cultivate, based on a relationship with the Vine.

Lesson Outline

INTRODUCTION
  A. A Familiar Picture
  B. Lesson Background
I. CULTIVATING A FRUITFUL LIFE (John 15:1-6)
  A. The Vine (v. 1)
  B. The Branches (vv. 2, 3)
  C. Necessity of Abiding (vv. 4, 5)
  D. Cost of Not Abiding (v. 6)
    The Importance of Abiding
II. BLESSINGS OF A FRUITFUL LIFE (John 15:7-17)
  A. A Prayer-Filled Life (v. 7)
  B. A Purposeful Life (v. 8)
    Kinds of Fruit
  C. A Joyful Life (vv. 9-11)
  D. A Life of Friendship (vv. 12-15)
  E. A Life of Security (vv. 16, 17)
CONCLUSION
  A. Love and Hate
  B. Prayer
  C. Thought to Remember

Introduction

A. A Familiar Picture

Perhaps nothing in the landscape of Israel was more familiar to the Jews of Jesus' day than the vine. Vineyards could be seen almost everywhere. The vine was also prominent in their history. The twelve spies sent by Moses to explore the promised land spoke of clusters of grapes so large that it would take two men to carry them (Numbers 13:23). In addition the vine was prominent in the Jews' architecture: over the front of the temple in Jerusalem was a golden vine. And it was prominent in their Scriptures, for both the vine and the vineyard were often used in the Old Testament to represent the nation of Israel. So when Jesus called Himself the "vine," He was using a symbol quite familiar to His hearers.

B. Lesson Background

Last week's lesson focused on Jesus' washing of His disciples' feet in the upper room (John 13:1-17). At some point during the evening, Jesus made it clear to Judas that He knew of his plot to betray Him, and Judas left the group. Probably it was after Judas left that Jesus instituted the Lord's Supper.

Jesus then gave a lengthy discourse to His disciples, calming their fears, promising the Holy Spirit to aid them, and praying for both them and future believers (John 14–17). Some of these words were spoken in the upper room, but some may have been spoken on the way to Gethsemane, where Jesus prayed and was later arrested. (See Jesus' words, "Arise, let us go hence," in John 14:31.) If so, perhaps the disciples noticed on the way the golden vine on the temple or passed some growing vines. On the other hand, some believe that all the discourse was given in the upper room and that John 18:1 refers to the group's leaving the upper room. If that is so, perhaps they were simply preparing to leave at the end of chapter 14. In that case, the cup from which Jesus and the disciples had drunk of "the fruit of the vine" would have suggested the object lesson of the vine.

I. Cultivating a Fruitful Life
(John 15:1-6)

A. The Vine (v. 1)

1. I am the true vine, and my Father is the husbandman.

Often the Old Testament references to Israel as a vine are negative (Isaiah 5:1-7; Jeremiah 2:21; Ezekiel 15:1-6; Hosea 10:1). Jesus referred to Himself as *the true vine*, in contrast with disobedient Israel, which was an imperfect foreshadowing. Recall how elsewhere John records Jesus' statement that He is the "true bread" compared with the manna that God provided for the Israelites (6:31, 32). At the beginning of his Gospel, John calls Jesus the "true Light" compared with the light provided by John the Baptist (1:6-9).

Earlier in the week, Jesus had spoken a parable about a vineyard and the wicked husbandmen who abused their responsibility to care for it (Mark 12:1-12). He was speaking of the Jewish leaders. Here Jesus refers to His *Father* as the *husbandman*. Whatever the "wicked husbandmen" among the Jews may seek to do to Him, His Father's higher purpose will be fulfilled.

B. The Branches (vv. 2, 3)

2. Every branch in me that beareth not fruit he taketh away: and every branch that beareth fruit, he purgeth it, that it may bring forth more fruit.

Some claim that the branches that were removed were never really connected. However, the phrase *in me* indicates a connection to or relationship with Christ. Some say the unfruitful branch refers only to Judas, but what, then, of the word *every*?

Jesus was stating a principle by which God the husbandman continues to operate: as a gardener prunes away the dead branches, so God will cut off those who are unproductive. In addition, he also cuts back the good branches. This suggests the pruning away of all that would hinder us from wholesome Christian living. Thus does God trim and shape the fruitful branches so that they *may bring forth more fruit*. Note the importance of God's "chastening," or discipline, as described in Hebrews 12:5-11.

What is the fruit we are to bear? Sometimes the term *fruit* refers to converts to Christ (Romans 1:13). Here, however, it more likely refers to one's character, as it does frequently in the New Testament. (See, for example, Matthew 3:8; 7:16-20; 12:33; Galatians 5:22, 23.)

3. Now ye are clean through the word which I have spoken unto you.

The Greek word rendered "clean" comes from the same root as the verb meaning "to prune." Jesus says that we are made *clean*, or pruned, by *the word*. Concerning the church, Paul writes that it is Jesus' desire to "sanctify and cleanse it with the washing of water by the word" (Ephesians 5:26). [See question #1, page 320.]

C. Necessity of Abiding (vv. 4, 5)

4. Abide in me, and I in you. As the branch cannot bear fruit of itself, except it abide in the vine; no more can ye, except ye abide in me.

Jesus commands all followers to stay, or remain (*abide*), in Him. The *branch* that is cut off from the *vine* loses its source of life. In some countries where spring comes slowly, people will cut budding branches off fruit trees and bring them inside. The branches bloom in the indoor warmth, but they can never *bear fruit* as long as they are cut off from the parent stock.

5. I am the vine, ye are the branches. He that abideth in me, and I in him, the same bringeth forth much fruit; for without me ye can do nothing.

There is a mutual union stated in the words of verse 4: *Abide in me and I in you*. If we remain connected to Jesus, He will not sever the connection. But if we choose to disconnect our-

selves from Him, He will not force Himself on us. Here, of course, the illustration of the vine falls short (as all illustrations do). In the vineyard the branches have no choice. In life we "branches" do have a choice.

The result of abiding in Christ will be bountiful. It is not just that we will bring forth fruit, but that we will bring forth *much fruit*. No believer will ever be embarrassed that he connected himself to Jesus Christ.

As every coin has two sides, so every truth has a positive and a negative side. The negative side of this illustration is that without Christ we *can do nothing*. No real spiritual good can be accomplished without Him. [See question #2, page 320.]

D. Cost of Not Abiding (v. 6)

6. If a man abide not in me, he is cast forth as a branch, and is withered; and men gather them, and cast them into the fire, and they are burned.

When a *branch* is cut off from a vine, it becomes *withered* and dies. With certain plants one can cut off a branch, put it in water, and it will develop roots and become another plant. The vine is not like that. The follower of Jesus is not like that. If he cuts himself off from Christ, he withers and dies.

Branches pruned from a grapevine have no further use. One cannot build anything from them. He cannot carve anything out of them. They are simply worthless, so the best thing one can do is to see that they are *cast* in the *fire* and *burned*. Such a fate reminds us of the Scriptures' frequent warnings about the punishment of the wicked (Matthew 13:42, 50; Mark 9:48; Luke 16:24; 2 Thessalonians 1:8; Jude 7; Revelation 20:14, 15).

THE IMPORTANCE OF ABIDING

According to John 15, one of the most important aspects of bearing fruit is the need to

Today's visual illustrates verse 5 of the text. Discuss the kind of fruit Jesus expects of His followers today.

Visual for lesson 11

"abide" in Christ. It is obvious, as Jesus pointed out, that a branch separated from its vine quickly loses its life and becomes good for nothing except fuel for the fire.

While the illustration of a vine is not nearly as familiar to our society as it was to Jesus' audience, we can think of several modern examples that illustrate the importance of "abiding in," or remaining connected to, a source of power. When an electric wire is disconnected from a wall plug, it becomes useless. When something hinders the circulation of blood to a hand or finger, it becomes stiff, numb, and useless. If a telephone wire is cut, the phone will not work. Its connection has been severed. Sometimes a gas or an oil pipeline will be cut or broken; the result is that fuel cannot be carried to homes, schools, or factories.

Sometimes a Christian, through disobedience or apathy, loses his connection with Jesus. The consequences are far more tragic than those in the above illustrations of being "disconnected." Someone once observed, "If you are not feeling as close to God as you once did, who do you think moved?" In light of Jesus' words in John 15, we could alter the question to ask, "If you haven't been abiding in Christ, the true Vine, who do you think broke the connection?"

—J. G. V. B.

II. Blessings of a Fruitful Life
(John 15:7-17)
A. A Prayer-Filled Life (v. 7)

7. If ye abide in me, and my words abide in you, ye shall ask what ye will, and it shall be done unto you.

The little word *if* is a significant one: it tells us that it is possible for a believer to turn away

from Christ so that he does not *abide* in Him. We avoid this tragic condition by allowing His *words* to *abide* in us. Long ago David said, "Thy word have I hid in mine heart, that I might not sin against thee" (Psalm 119:11). Later, the apostle Paul wrote to the Colossians: "Let the word of Christ dwell in you richly" (Colossians 3:16).

Jesus gives an additional promise to those who remain in Him: *ye shall ask what ye will, and it shall be done unto you*. Whenever we read such promises as this (similar ones are found in Matthew 21:22; Luke 11:9; and John 16:23), we may immediately think of instances where our personal experience with prayer did not seem to confirm Jesus' promise. However, let us keep in mind the condition stated by Jesus: *if ye abide in me, and my words abide in you*. The petitions of those who abide in Christ will reflect His will and His purpose (note the promise in 1 John 5:14). Jesus was certainly not promising to satisfy each and every one of our whims. No wise and loving parent gives a child everything the child asks for—and God is our Father. Those occasions when we do not receive what we prayed for should strengthen our faith, not weaken it. [See question #3, page 320.]

B. A Purposeful Life (v. 8)

8. Herein is my Father glorified, that ye bear much fruit; so shall ye be my disciples.

Abiding in Christ enriches our own lives and brings glory to God. It should amaze us that our lives can be used to bring glory to God. We can understand how "the heavens declare the glory of God" (Psalm 19:1). We can understand how sacred music glorifies God. We can understand how certain forms of art, literature, and architecture glorify God. But God is *glorified* most of all through the holy lives of the *disciples* of Jesus.

KINDS OF FRUIT

In the first few verses of John 15, Jesus stresses how important it is for His disciples to "bear fruit." He speaks of "fruit" (vv. 2, 4), "more fruit" (v. 2), and "much fruit" (vv. 5, 8). Most likely the "fruit" of which He speaks includes the deeds of kindness, acts of love, and evidences of caring that His love inspires in us.

What kinds of fruit do we see in the world because Jesus' disciples are doing His will? Consider the hospitals, the orphanages, and the special schools for groups such as the blind, the deaf, and those who have mental retardation. Consider the people and organizations ministering faithfully to those in prison. Consider the soup kitchens and food pantries operated by churches in areas where few people care enough to get involved. Consider the nursing homes and retirement facilities that churches have started and staffed in order to provide adequate care and housing for the elderly.

If we desire a summary of the "fruit" that Jesus desires to see in His followers, we should examine Matthew 25:31-46. There we find a description of the conduct that Jesus will reward on Judgment Day. It includes feeding the hungry, giving hospitality to strangers, clothing the naked, looking after the sick, and ministering to prisoners. This is the kind of fruit that those who abide in Christ are to bear before a watching world.   —J. G. V. B.

C. A Joyful Life (vv. 9-11)

9. As the Father hath loved me, so have I loved you: continue ye in my love.

The coming crucifixion did not cause Jesus to think that God no longer *loved* Him. Nor should our suffering cause us to think that God does not love us. The love that God had for Jesus was the same *love* Jesus had for His disciples. They were to *continue* in that love. Of course, Jesus would continue to love them if they turned away from Him; but if they did, they would forfeit the blessings that walking in His love can bring. (By this time, Judas had already turned away from Jesus and resolved to carry out his plans of betrayal.)

The word translated *love* is a Greek word with which many are familiar—*agape*. It emphasizes the will more than the emotions and implies that love is shown by one's actions. That idea is developed in the next verse.

10. If ye keep my commandments, ye shall abide in my love; even as I have kept my Father's commandments, and abide in his love.

For all who follow Jesus Christ, the evidence of love is obedience. Jesus' question, "Why call ye me, Lord, Lord, and do not the things which I say?" (Luke 6:46), will not go away.

John records other instances where Jesus declared His obedience to the *Father's commandments.* "I seek not mine own will, but the will of the Father which hath sent me" (John 5:30). "The Father hath not left me alone; for I do always those things that please him" (John 8:29). In John 14:31 is recorded Jesus' words: "I do exactly what my Father has commanded me" (John 14:31, *New International Version*).

11. These things have I spoken unto you, that my joy might remain in you, and that your joy might be full.

Surely we have lived long enough and learned enough from the experiences of others to know that the world's *joy* can never *be full.* It is always shallow and superficial. It is always followed by regret and guilt. As Jesus wants us to have a more abundant life (John 10:10), so He wants us to have a fuller joy. [See question #4, page 320.]

D. A Life of Friendship (vv. 12-15)

12. This is my commandment, That ye love one another, as I have loved you.

If this love were simply an emotional feeling, we could hardly be commanded to *love one another.* But when we understand love as a commitment, then we can see how it can be commanded. Perhaps we can never love one another as much as Jesus loves us, but we can strive to demonstrate the same kind of love.

In John 13:34 Jesus called the *commandment* to love a "new commandment." It must have seemed to the disciples that there were already enough commandments. Why did they need another one? However, as Jesus had explained earlier (Matthew 22:34–40), two basic commandments embrace all the rest. When one loves God, and his neighbor as himself, keeping the other commandments naturally follows.

13. Greater love hath no man than this, that a man lay down his life for his friends.

In only a few hours Jesus will in fact *lay down his life.* The crucifixion was much more than the evil scheme of Jesus' enemies. He voluntarily allowed Himself to be put to death (John 10:18), and that remains the ultimate evidence of His love for mankind. John, who was present on this occasion, wrote in his first letter, "Hereby perceive we the love of God, because he laid down his life for us: and we ought to lay down our lives for the brethren" (1 John 3:16). (We ought to memorize 1 John 3:16 as well as John 3:16.)

14. Ye are my friends, if ye do whatsoever I command you.

In any friendship there are always mutual obligations. Jesus will fulfill His part by dying on the cross. His followers are to fulfill their part by doing *whatsoever* He commands them to do.

15. Henceforth I call you not servants; for the servant knoweth not what his lord doeth: but I have called you friends; for all things that I have heard of my Father I have made known unto you.

Jesus had indeed *called* His disciples *friends.* One of these occasions is recorded in Luke 12:4 (there may have been other times). Now He will explain the word and the relationship. The

---

How to Say It

AGAPE (Greek). uh-*gah*-pay.
GETHSEMANE. Geth-*sem*-uh-nee.

Greek word translated *servant* means "slave." A servant is not expected to maintain an intimate friendship with his *lord*. The relationship is strictly business; the servant's task is to carry out the master's orders.

Friends, however, make plans together and discuss matters that they would never talk about with someone else. Jesus' disciples would continue to serve Him, but they would share His mission of taking good news to a lost world. Thus the relationship would be far more intimate than that of servant to lord.

We should not suppose that the term *all things* means that the disciples knew everything that Jesus knew. Most likely it indicates that they understood all things necessary to carry out their work. Later, during this same discourse, Jesus promised to send the Holy Spirit, who would guide the disciples "into all truth" (John 16:13).

E. A Life of Security (vv. 16, 17)

16. Ye have not chosen me, but I have chosen you, and ordained you, that ye should go and bring forth fruit, and that your fruit should remain; that whatsoever ye shall ask of the Father in my name, he may give it you.

From among His many followers, Jesus had specifically *chosen* twelve. This choosing, or being *ordained*, refers to the specific calling to be an apostle. It does not refer to these men's original decision to follow Jesus. That is always a personal choice, made freely, both in Jesus' time and in our time.

The purpose to which these men were called was not an idle one. They were to *bring forth fruit*. They were also given the assurance that their fruit will *remain*. How that must have been a comfort to them! They may not succeed in every city or in every effort, but their cause would succeed. These words are also a great comfort to us. God's Word will not return to Him void; it will accomplish the purpose He has assigned to it (Isaiah 55:11). The apostle Paul had great confidence in the gospel as "the power of God unto salvation" (Romans 1:16).

Once again we have Jesus' promise that *whatsoever ye shall ask* shall be given. Here He adds the phrase *in my name*. It is common to close our prayers by saying "in Jesus' name" or similar words. This is a good way to pray and a proper thing to say. However, when we read the prayers of the New Testament, we find such language missing. Therefore, *in my name* must refer to something else besides the actual contents of a prayer. At the same time, it should warn us against praying for something that we cannot properly ask for in Jesus' name. The phrase thus limits our prayer requests to items that are consistent with a life of obedient faith.

Also, the word *name* usually suggests authority. Christ authorizes us to pray. He is our mediator, "bridging the gap" between us and God (1 Timothy 2:5; Hebrews 9:15; 12:24). It is good that we acknowledge this fact in the closing words of our prayers by praying "in Jesus' name." Were it not for His work on our behalf, we would not be able to approach God as our Father. [See question #5, page 320.]

17. These things I command you, that ye love one another.

In light of the jealous bickering that had gone on earlier in the upper room (Luke 22:24), this *command* was most appropriate. This was the third time during the evening that Jesus had given it (13:34, 35; 15:12).

Conclusion

A. Love and Hate

We have heard or sung the hymn, "Amazing Grace" so often that we can easily forget how "amazing" God's love and grace really are. We do not deserve the love of God. In fact, if we received from God what we truly deserved, condemnation for eternity would be the result. God loves us, not because of all the good we have done, but in spite of all the bad we have done. This is grace—unmerited favor—at work.

It is also important to read the four verses (18-21) that follow today's printed text. The love of Jesus for His followers and of His followers for one another is placed alongside the hate that both they and Jesus will experience in the world. Why did some people hate Jesus? The answer is that His perfect life served as a condemnation of their own. Similarly, the lives of genuine Christians stand in such contrast to the ways of the world that they too are sometimes hated by the world that both they and Jesus love.

While we should never lose our amazement at Jesus' love for us, neither should we ever be amazed when the world responds to it with hostility. As Jesus said, "The servant is not greater than his lord" (John 15:20).

B. Prayer

O Lord, we thank You for Your great love. We declare our love for You in return. Help us to love others as Jesus has loved us. May we abide in Him so that our lives will remain fruitful for the kingdom. Amen.

C. Thought to Remember

We can live fruitful Christian lives only when we let God do the gardening.

Learning by Doing

This page contains an alternate lesson plan emphasizing learning activities.
Classes desiring such student involvement will find these suggestions helpful.

Learning Goals

As a result of this lesson students should:

1. Summarize Jesus' message of the Vine and the branches.

2. Explain the relationship that believers, as "branches," are to maintain with Jesus, the "Vine."

3. List one or two "fruits" that he or she is seeking to cultivate, based on a relationship with the Vine.

Into the Lesson

Ask your students how many of them are making use of the Internet—that vast network of computers and file servers by which a person with a personal computer can access information, send electronic messages to other computer owners, and even make long-distance phone calls with the proper software. Ask those using the Internet, "How many of you have had problems getting connected or staying connected?"

Many Internet service providers have found demand for their services to be greater than they are able to deliver. Thus, several of your Internet users will probably say they have had some trouble. Busy signals, slow response, and loss of connection are frequent complaints. Ask, "What good is the Internet to you if you cannot connect or stay connected?" Obviously, it is of no value; it's as if the Internet were not there.

Tell the class, "Staying connected is the theme of our lesson today. But we're not talking about staying connected to the Internet. We're not even talking about staying connected to a vine—though that is the metaphor Jesus used to communicate the truth we want to explore today. We're talking about staying connected to Jesus Himself. It's frustrating when a computer user loses his or her connection with the Internet. But it's absolutely tragic when a believer loses the connection with Christ!"

Into the Word

Ask a volunteer to read John 15:1-17. Then divide the class into groups of three to five each. Give one-third of your groups one of the following assignments. (If you cannot form at least three groups, have the entire class work on all the activities together.)

Assignment 1: Read verses 1-6. Jesus used a metaphor familiar to people who knew about grape vines. What metaphor might He have used if He had been speaking to people of our time and place? Write a paraphrase of verses 1-6 with a different metaphor.

Assignment 2: Read verses 7-11. List all the promises Jesus gives in this section. If a promise is conditional, note the condition. Suggest at least one specific way a believer can comply with each condition you find. (The promises are as follows: "Ye shall ask what ye will, and it shall be done unto you" [conditioned on "If ye abide in me, and my words abide in you"]; "so shall ye be my disciples" [conditioned on "ye bear much fruit"]; "ye shall abide in my love" [conditioned on "if ye keep my commandments"].)

Assignment 3: Read verses 12-17. This section begins and ends with a command to "love one another." In between, Jesus emphasizes the themes of self-sacrifice, obedience, prayer, and bearing fruit. Explain how these themes are related to loving one another.

Allow about eight minutes for the groups to choose a reporter and to write their responses. Then ask each group to have its reporter summarize the group's findings. Supplement the reports with additional information from the commentary section as needed.

Into Life

Challenge the class to think of ways in which they can love and serve one another in the week ahead. Make a list of these suggestions on the chalkboard. Suggest that these activities comprise some of the "fruit" Jesus calls us to bear.

Ask, "Why do we not always demonstrate this kind of fruit in our lives?" Make a list on the board of the class's answers. Call for suggestions on how to reduce or remove each of these hindrances.

Use a full sheet of paper (eight and one-half by eleven inches) to draw a cluster of grapes. Write on the cluster, "I will bear fruit." Make a copy of this cluster for each member of the class. Distribute the copies and ask each class member to write on the back one or two "fruits" that he or she is seeking to cultivate, based on a relationship with the Vine, Jesus.

End the lesson with a circle prayer of thanksgiving and rejoicing that we can abide in the Vine and bear fruit for His glory.

Let's Talk It Over

The questions on this page are designed to encourage review of the lesson Scriptures and to promote discussion of the lesson by the class. The answers provided are only discussion starters. Let your class talk it over from there.

1. Jesus said that the Father not only cuts off the dead branches but also prunes the good ones. He does this, Jesus said, "through the word." How has the Word of God helped you to cut away unproductive attitudes and actions?

Students may share insights they have gained from their involvement in small group studies or from time spent each day in personal Bible study and prayer. Perhaps they will recall certain sermons or Bible lessons that challenged them to change their behavior. This would be a good opportunity to discuss the kind of attitude with which we must approach the hearing of a sermon or Bible lesson or our devotional reading of the Word. We are not to be on the alert merely for interesting facts or comforting promises. We must be prepared for the Word to reveal our hidden sins and challenge us to eliminate them. And we need to pray for the courage to respond properly to such challenges.

2. "Abide in me," Jesus said. That means to *remain* in Him, to *stay* with Him. What do you do to be sure you are abiding in Jesus? What are some things you will *not do* because doing them may make abiding in Him more difficult?

Many believers give this concept very little consideration. But Jesus clearly expected His followers to take this warning seriously, so we need to consider some specific ways to obey Him in this matter.

To remain with Jesus, we need to be sure that we have the same goals as He does. His desire is that no one should perish, but that all come to repentance. What are we doing to lead others to know the Lord? Jesus mentioned the importance of His words abiding in us (v. 7). What are we doing to be sure we know the Scriptures? If we would stay with Jesus, we cannot ignore His bride, the church. How faithful are we in our attendance and ministry involvement in the church? Encourage the students to be as specific as possible in their suggestions.

3. Suppose a Christian brother came to you and said, "What about this promise in John 15:7? I prayed that my wife and I would work out our problems, but we got divorced anyway. Why didn't God answer my prayers?" How would you answer?

If the divorce is not too recent, the brother might be able to look back and objectively determine whether or not his heart was in the right place when he prayed. The psalmist observed, "If I regard iniquity in my heart, the Lord will not hear me" (Psalm 66:18). James wrote, "Ye ask, and receive not, because ye ask amiss, that ye may consume it upon your lusts" (James 4:3). Peter spoke of how prayers could be hindered in an improperly ordered family (1 Peter 3:7).

One might also suggest that the wife had a responsibility in the matter. The Lord's promises do not take away our free will. If the wife was not determined to follow the Lord, that may be the reason the marriage failed.

The wise friend will not try to assess blame, however. This hurting brother needs encouragement. He should be allowed to assess his own heart and repent if he needs to, but he especially needs encouragement that God will work even this difficult situation for good in His time.

4. How can we attract people of the world, who believe they have joy without Jesus, to the fullness of joy Jesus offers?

The world's "joy" is shallow; it will eventually fail. The joy of the Lord sustains us even when we have trouble, just as it did Jesus at the cross (Hebrews 12:2). We need to be there for people when their worldly joy comes up short. To do that, we have to demonstrate the true joy of Jesus. Sometimes Christians seem as shallow as anyone else because they have not fixed their eyes on Jesus as they ought. We have to befriend the people who need what we have. We need to cultivate a relationship with them in order to have credibility in their time of need.

5. Jesus assured His disciples of "fruit [that] should remain" or "fruit that will last" (John 15:16, *New International Version*). How is this reassuring to you as you follow the Lord?

Everything about the world is temporary, and seems ever more so. The worker who has been laid off because his services were no longer required or the wife whose husband decided he no longer loved her will be encouraged to know that some things do last forever. Verses such as 1 Corinthians 15:58 and Galatians 6:9 are reassuring in this matter.

The Spirit Empowers Loving Obedience

DEVOTIONAL READING: Hebrews 2:10-18.

LESSON SCRIPTURE: John 14:15-31; 16:4b-15.

PRINTED TEXT: John 14:15-18, 24-26; 16:7-15.

John 14:15-18, 24-26

15 If ye love me, keep my commandments.

16 And I will pray the Father, and he shall give you another Comforter, that he may abide with you for ever;

17 Even the Spirit of truth; whom the world cannot receive, because it seeth him not, neither knoweth him: but ye know him; for he dwelleth with you, and shall be in you.

18 I will not leave you comfortless: I will come to you.

. . . .

24 He that loveth me not keepeth not my sayings: and the word which ye hear is not mine, but the Father's which sent me.

25 These things have I spoken unto you, being yet present with you.

26 But the Comforter, which is the Holy Ghost, whom the Father will send in my name, he shall teach you all things, and bring all things to your remembrance, whatsoever I have said unto you.

John 16:7-15

7 Nevertheless I tell you the truth; It is expedient for you that I go away: for if I go not away, the Comforter will not come unto you; but if I depart, I will send him unto you.

8 And when he is come, he will reprove the world of sin, and of righteousness, and of judgment:

9 Of sin, because they believe not on me;

10 Of righteousness, because I go to my Father, and ye see me no more;

11 Of judgment, because the prince of this world is judged.

12 I have yet many things to say unto you, but ye cannot bear them now.

13 Howbeit when he, the Spirit of truth, is come, he will guide you into all truth: for he shall not speak of himself; but whatsoever he shall hear, that shall he speak: and he will show you things to come.

14 He shall glorify me: for he shall receive of mine, and shall show it unto you.

15 All things that the Father hath are mine: therefore said I, that he shall take of mine, and shall show it unto you.

GOLDEN TEXT: The Comforter, which is the Holy Ghost, whom the Father will send in my name, he shall teach you all things, and bring all things to your remembrance, whatsoever I have said unto you.—John 14:26.

That You May Believe
Unit 4: Jesus Prepares His Followers
(Lessons 10-13)

Lesson Aims

After this lesson the students will be able to:
1. Summarize the Holy Spirit's role as companion, teacher, and evangelist.
2. Compare the apostles' need for "another Comforter" with our need for the Spirit.
3. Pinpoint aspects of their lives where they need to depend more completely on the Holy Spirit.

Lesson Outline

INTRODUCTION
   A. The Christian's "Coach"
   B. Lesson Background
 I. CONSTANT COMPANION (John 14:15-18)
   A. A Test of Love (v. 15)
   B. A Wonderful Promise (v. 16)
   C. Limitations of the Promise (v. 17)
   D. Assurance of the Promise (v. 18)
     Never Alone
 II. INSPIRING TEACHER (John 14:24-26)
   A. Authority of Jesus' Words (v. 24)
     The Priority of Obedience
   B. Authority of the Spirit (vv. 25, 26)
III. CONVINCING EVANGELIST (John 16:7-15)
   A. Following Jesus' Departure (v. 7)
   B. Reproving the World (vv. 8-11)
   C. Revealing the Truth (vv. 12, 13)
   D. Exalting Jesus (vv. 14, 15)
CONCLUSION
   A. With Us Always
   B. Prayer
   C. Thought to Remember

Introduction

A. The Christian's "Coach"

The next time you attend an athletic competition, keep your eyes on the coach. Whether the sport is being played on a high school, college, or professional level, good coaches pursue the same goals. They want their players to do their best and to perform at maximum efficiency. Whenever a player does something well or puts forth a particularly strong effort, the coach is enthusiastic in his praise. At other times, the coach may appear stern and demanding, wanting to know why a player failed to carry out an

assignment correctly. He may even "bench" the player and let him think about the error of his ways! But whatever the coach does, he does it with the player's best interests in mind.

Recognizing that all illustrations have limitations, we may compare the work of the Holy Spirit in the Christian's life with that of a coach. As we will see in today's text, the Spirit serves as the Christian's constant guide and companion, "coaching" him in the process of becoming more like Jesus. He provides encouragement in doing right, and conviction when the Christian is on the verge of embarking on the wrong path.

Whatever He does, the Holy Spirit wants only what is best for us. We need to learn the discipline of following our "Coach."

B. Lesson Background

Today's lesson is taken from another portion of Jesus' discourse with His disciples on the night before His arrest and crucifixion. Last week's text was taken from the part of the discourse concerning the vine and the branches (John 15:1-17). Today's text focuses on Jesus' promise of the Holy Spirit. Jesus made it clear to His disciples that He was going to leave them (John 14:1-4). However, He assured them that they would not be left alone, for He would send to them "another Comforter . . . the Spirit of truth" (vv. 16, 17). The Spirit would empower the disciples for the monumental task that they were to accomplish in Jesus' name. Such power would become especially important to them in light of the hostility that the world would demonstrate toward both them and their message (15:18-25; 16:1-4). It's a promise that still has application to Jesus' disciples today.

I. Constant Companion
(John 14:15-18)

A. A Test of Love (v. 15)

15. If ye love me, keep my commandments.

Someone once summarized the Bible's teachings as facts to be believed, commands to be obeyed, promises to be enjoyed, and warnings to be heeded. Here we see a command to be obeyed placed in the midst of promises to be enjoyed. The preceding verses include the promise of answered prayer (vv. 13, 14). In the succeeding verses we read Jesus' promise of the Holy Spirit.

In another portion of our printed text (v. 24), we will note words very similar to these about the importance of obedience to God. John stresses this theme in his first epistle: "Hereby we do know that we know him, if we keep his commandments. He that saith, I know him, and keepeth not his commandments, is a liar, and the truth is not in him" (1 John 2:3, 4).

B. A Wonderful Promise (v. 16)

16. And I will pray the Father, and he shall give you another Comforter, that he may abide with you for ever.

Jesus introduces the Holy Spirit by describing Him as a *Comforter.* The Greek word, *paraklete,* is difficult to translate. Besides *Comforter,* it is rendered in other translations as "Helper" and "Counselor." The word is used of Jesus in 1 John 2:1, where it is translated "advocate." The term actually means "one who is called alongside another." Imagine, by way of illustration, a person standing before a judge in the courtroom with his attorney standing alongside him. But the Spirit's presence is not limited to any one particular situation. He will be alongside the followers of Jesus *for ever*—in whatever situation they are facing. Such a promise would have been especially meaningful to the disciples, for Jesus had just told them He would be leaving them (v. 3).

Notice that Jesus described the Holy Spirit as *another Comforter.* The word for *another* does not mean a different kind of companion, but another of the same kind. While the disciples will miss the companionship of Jesus, the Spirit will be their unseen companion. He will be to them what Jesus was while He was present with them. [See question #1, page 328.]

C. Limitations of the Promise (v. 17)

17. Even the Spirit of truth; whom the world cannot receive, because it seeth him not, neither knoweth him: but ye know him; for he dwelleth with you, and shall be in you.

Earlier Jesus had declared Himself to be "the truth" (v. 6). Now He describes the Holy Spirit as the *Spirit of truth. The world,* referring to those who are under the sway of the "prince of this world" (John 16:11), or Satan, *cannot receive* the Spirit. As long as the "god of this world" blinds them to spiritual truth (2 Corinthians 4:4), the message of the Spirit will mean little or nothing to them.

The words *ye know him* call attention to the fact that the Holy Spirit is never referred to by the pronoun "it." Always He is described with the personal pronouns "he" and "him." The Holy Spirit is a person, just as God is a person and Jesus is a person. He has the characteristics of a person; for example, He can be grieved (Ephesians 4:30), vexed (Isaiah 63:10), and tempted (Acts 5:9).

Jesus' words also pointed to the intimate relationship between His followers and the Spirit: the Spirit would be *with* them and *in* them. The fact that the Holy Spirit dwells in believers receives constant emphasis in the New Testament (Acts 2:38; 5:32; Romans 8:9-17; 1 Corinthians 3:16; 6:19; 2 Corinthians 5:5; Ephesians 5:18; 1 Thessalonians 4:8; 2 Timothy 1:14; 1 Peter 4:14).

D. Assurance of the Promise (v. 18)

18. I will not leave you comfortless: I will come to you.

It is the universal experience of Christians that we are truly never left *comfortless.* The Greek word used here may be translated, "I will not leave you as orphans" (*New International Version*). Perhaps that is just how the disciples felt, knowing that Jesus would be leaving them.

Certainly Jesus did *come* to the disciples following His resurrection. This promise, however, is linked to His promise of the Holy Spirit. Through the presence of the Spirit, Jesus would be with His followers—"unto the end of the world" as He said (Matthew 28:20).

NEVER ALONE

Jesus promised that He would provide a *paraklete* for His followers. This Greek word means "someone who is called to stand beside another." It pictures someone who assists or encourages another. The term is translated "Comforter" in the *King James Version* and "Counselor" in the *New International Version.* One may think of the task of an attorney, an intercessor, a mediator, or anyone whose role involves being a helper to another. This is the work that the Holy Spirit has been sent to accomplish.

In promising the Spirit Jesus said, "I will not leave you comfortless" (John 14:18). The *New International Version* renders this, "I will not leave you as orphans." Just as an orphan is bereft of father and mother, and thus without an adult to offer comfort, consolation, and spiritual companionship, so we would be in this world without God's Spirit to indwell, bless, admonish, and encourage us.

This visual shows the breadth of meaning in the word Jesus used to describe the promised Holy Spirit. Discuss the significance of the different terms noted here.

Visual for lesson 12

The assurance of never being left "comfortless" is captured in this hymn, cherished by many:

I've seen the lightning flashing,
  I've heard the thunder roll,
I've felt sin's breakers dashing,
  Which almost conquered my soul;
I've heard the voice of my Savior
  Bidding me still to fight on;
He promised never to leave me,
  Never to leave me alone!
            (Author unknown)
                —J. G. V. B.

II. Inspiring Teacher
(John 14:24-26)

A. Authority of Jesus' Words (v. 24)

24. He that loveth me not keepeth not my sayings: and the word which ye hear is not mine, but the Father's which sent me.

Here we have the negative side of that which was presented positively in verse 15. As far as Jesus is concerned, the test of whether someone truly loves Him is always obedience. This is especially clear in Jesus' parable of the two sons (Matthew 21:28-32). Even in the Old Testament, God put a high premium on obedience (1 Samuel 15:22; Jeremiah 7:23). His concern in the New Testament era is no less. [See question #2, page 328.]

THE PRIORITY OF OBEDIENCE

In the first portion of today's printed text, Jesus speaks about the importance of keeping His commandments, or sayings (John 14:15). He repeats this theme in the second segment (v. 24). The primary test of our loyalty to Christ is our obedience to Him. Merely addressing Jesus as "Lord, Lord" is a waste of words if we do not treat Him as Lord in the way we live (Matthew 7:21; Luke 6:46).

The word *obey* may seem harsh or unfeeling to many. However, it is an essential element in many areas of our lives. What does a coach expect when he tells his team to execute a certain play in a specific situation? He wants them to *obey* his instructions. A parent tells a child that he wants him home for lunch at a certain time. The child's duty is to *obey*. When a teacher asks for a report to be prepared and turned in on a specific date, the student's duty is to *obey*. When a government says that a certain type of stamp is required for a first-class letter, the citizen's responsibility is to *obey*. Is the standard any lower concerning our relationship with God?   —J. G. V. B.

B. Authority of the Spirit (vv. 25, 26)

25, 26. These things have I spoken unto you, being yet present with you. But the Comforter, which is the Holy Ghost, whom the Father will send in my name, he shall teach you all things, and bring all things to your remembrance, whatsoever I have said unto you.

The term *Holy Ghost* is often used in the *King James Version* instead of the term "Holy Spirit." (Today the term *ghost* possesses certain negative or unpleasant connotations that it did not have when the *King James Version* was produced.) Some have suggested that we think of the Holy Ghost as a Holy Guest, for whom we must make room in our lives.

Jesus told His disciples that when the Spirit came, He would *bring* to their *remembrance* what Jesus *said*. Not one of us can remember completely the sermon he or she heard last Sunday. But the apostles were able to recall the teachings of Jesus many years after His earthly life, and could then write them down accurately. They could do this because of the inspiration of the Holy Spirit.

That the Spirit would *teach* the apostles *all things* is not to suggest that the apostles were omniscient. Only God knows everything. But they would be taught all that they needed to know, and they would thus convey to future generations all that they would need to know of Jesus and the way of salvation. We should keep in mind that this promise was given only to the apostles, in keeping with their role as part of the foundation of the church (Ephesians 2:20). Some have claimed to receive new revelations of truth through the Holy Spirit; but when these revelations contradict what the inspired writers of Scripture have taught, we must conclude that

Home Daily Bible Readings

Monday, May 17—If You Love Me, Keep My Commandments (John 14:15-24)
Tuesday, May 18—The Holy Spirit Will Teach You (John 14:25-31)
Wednesday, May 19—When the Spirit of Truth Comes (John 16:4b-15)
Thursday, May 20—The Spirit of the Lord Brings Freedom (2 Corinthians 3:12-18)
Friday, May 21—No Longer a Slave But a Child (Galatians 4:1-7)
Saturday, May 22—Strengthened With Power Through His Spirit (Ephesians 3:14-19)
Sunday, May 23—We Are Children of God (Romans 8:12-17)

the alleged revelations are false. Truth cannot contradict truth, nor can God contradict Himself.

This is not to diminish the importance of the measure of the Spirit that Christians receive, for we are to be "filled" with Him (Ephesians 5:18). However, we need the Holy Spirit, not to receive knowledge (which is found in the Scriptures), but to empower us to live lives of holiness (1 Thessalonians 4:7, 8).

III. Convincing Evangelist (John 16:7-15)

A. Following Jesus' Departure (v. 7)

7. Nevertheless I tell you the truth; It is expedient for you that I go away: for if I go not away, the Comforter will not come unto you; but if I depart, I will send him unto you.

It is expedient means "it is to your advantage." Jesus' departure did not seem to the disciples to be to their advantage; in fact, it appeared to put them at a serious disadvantage. What would they do without their Master? But Jesus' leaving would be a blessing in disguise, for it would be followed by the coming of the *Comforter*.

This is not to say that the Holy Spirit was not active prior to Jesus' departure into Heaven. The Spirit was present at creation (Genesis 1:2). The Spirit empowered men such as Moses (Numbers 11:17), Joshua (Deuteronomy 34:9), Gideon (Judges 6:34), Samson (Judges 14:6, 19; 15:14), David (1 Samuel 16:13; 2 Samuel 23:1, 2), and the Old Testament prophets (Nehemiah 9:30). John wrote of Jesus, "God giveth not the Spirit by measure unto him" (John 3:34).

However, Jesus' departure marked a new stage in the ministry of the Spirit. This is clear from John 7:39, which tells us, "This spake he of the Spirit, which they that believe on him should receive: for the Holy Ghost was not yet given; because that Jesus was not yet glorified." Only after Jesus was "glorified" in His ascension was the Spirit "given"—at Pentecost to the apostles (Acts 2:1-4, 33) and then as an indwelling source of power to all who choose to "believe on" Jesus and obey Him (v. 38).

B. Reproving the World (vv. 8-11)

8. And when he is come, he will reprove the world of sin, and of righteousness, and of judgment.

It is because of this verse that we can say that the Holy Spirit works in the role of an evangelist, for He is involved in the process of bringing people to Christ. The word *reprove* is often translated "convict." It used to be said that people whose conscience was bothering them and who were considering accepting Christ were "under conviction." Several translations use the word "convince" instead of "convict."

While human voices and personalities must do their very best to lead people to Christ, ultimately it is the Holy Spirit who convinces and convicts and brings a response to the gospel. This does not mean that we should remain passive in the area of evangelism. We must be untiring in our efforts to lead people to Christ, but we must also humbly recognize that the Spirit takes our efforts and uses them. [See question #3, page 328.]

9-11. Of sin, because they believe not on me; of righteousness, because I go to my Father, and ye see me no more; of judgment, because the prince of this world is judged.

Here Jesus elaborated on the threefold conviction that is brought by the Spirit. The first step is to convince people that they are guilty *of sin*. No one can be saved until he knows that he is lost. This may be the hardest task we have in evangelism, particularly in today's world where "tolerance" of one another often appears to be the noblest virtue. People will admit to making mistakes, but they find it hard to confess that they are sinners in need of a Savior.

The second step is to be convinced of the need for *righteousness*. People need to know that there is a better way to live than what the world offers. They need to see that life exemplified in Jesus. They must also realize that they have "come short" of God's standard of righteousness (Romans 3:23) and that they can never, by their own efforts, reach that standard. Their only hope of attaining it is through Jesus' efforts—His death for their sins (2 Corinthians 5:21).

Finally, people must be convinced of the reality of a coming *judgment*. Judgment is sometimes a neglected theme today (again, because of our excessively tolerant society), but it is a prominent theme in the New Testament (Matthew 25:31-46; Romans 14:12; 2 Corinthians 5:10; Hebrews 9:27; Revelation 20:12).

All of Jesus' references to *the prince of this world* (Satan) occurred during His final week, as the time of His crucifixion grew closer (John 12:31; 14:30). While we can indeed sing the great hymn, "This Is My Father's World," it is also true that Satan has usurped God's position as rightful ruler of this world. Jesus came in order to reclaim what was lost because of man's

---

How to Say It

GIDEON. *Gid*-ee-un.
PARACLETE. *pair*-uh-kleet.

sin. This is the significance of His description of someone who enters a house to "bind the strong man" (Matthew 12:29). First John 3:8 tells us, "For this purpose the Son of God was manifested, that he might destroy the works of the devil." Those who accept Christ as Savior choose to leave Satan's domain in order to follow Jesus as Lord.

C. Revealing the Truth (v. 12, 13)

12. I have yet many things to say unto you, but ye cannot bear them now.

The word *bear* means "grasp" or "understand." Just as one goes through different levels in obtaining an education, so the Master Teacher gradually revealed His truth to His followers. The same principle is noted elsewhere regarding Jesus' teaching method: "With many such parables spake he the word unto them, as they were able to hear it" (Mark 4:33). [See question #4, page 328.]

13. Howbeit when he, the Spirit of truth, is come, he will guide you into all truth: for he shall not speak of himself; but whatsoever he shall hear, that shall he speak: and he will show you things to come.

The Holy Spirit would not *come* with a different message from that which the disciples had received from Jesus. As the *Spirit of truth*, His message would be entirely consistent with what Jesus had taught. The word *guide* is most interesting here, for it is the first indication of the divine inspiration that the apostles would be granted in the writing of the New Testament Scriptures. 2 Peter 1:21 says that Biblical writers were "moved by the Holy Ghost." Paul claims that what he taught was what the Holy Spirit taught (1 Corinthians 2:13). He also declares in 2 Timothy 3:16 that "all Scripture is given by inspiration of God."

The phrase *things to come* could refer to the insights given to the apostles regarding events surrounding the second coming of Christ. (Consider, for examples, 2 Peter 3:1-13 and the book of Revelation.) It may also be describing the body of Christian truth and doctrine that the apostles, as part of the church's foundation, would be instrumental in communicating.

D. Exalting Jesus (vv. 14, 15)

14. He shall glorify me: for he shall receive of mine, and shall show it unto you.

Here Jesus says that the Spirit *shall glorify me*. The Spirit will not come to promote Himself. Often we hear some claim that there is not enough teaching on the Holy Spirit. The opposite may be the case. The Holy Spirit inspired Paul to write that in all things Jesus should have the preeminence (Colossians 1:18). [See question #5, page 328.]

15. All things that the Father hath are mine: therefore said I, that he shall take of mine, and shall show it unto you.

There is complete unity between the *Father*, the Son, and the Holy Spirit. The three are one; there is no rivalry. The best minds down through the ages have wrestled with the doctrine of the Trinity. Various illustrations have been used to explain it, though such illustrations must fall short of adequately explaining something so profound. However, we can believe in what Paul describes as "the mystery of godliness" (1 Timothy 3:16) without fully comprehending it.

Conclusion

A. With Us Always

The promise of today's lesson was repeated by Jesus after His resurrection. As the time neared for Him to leave His disciples, He promised never to leave them. "Lo, I am with you alway, even unto the end of the world," He said (Matthew 28:20). Believers down through the years are quick to confess that Jesus' promise has been kept in every era and in all places. This is one of the reasons Jesus had to leave this world and allow the Spirit to fulfill His appointed task. Jesus, because of His physical body, was limited in time and space. On the other hand, the Holy Spirit is not subject to such limitations and can dwell in believers throughout the world in any given period of history.

Many Christians have avoided the topic of the Holy Spirit because it tends to be so controversial. This is a tragic mistake, because the Spirit is meant to be the Christian's ever-faithful Friend and Companion—his "Coach." While we should never presume to claim for ourselves promises meant only for the apostles, we should be quick to claim for ourselves and all believers the promise that the Spirit will supply us with the power we need and the comforting presence we cherish.

B. Prayer

O Lord, thank You for the blessed assurance that we are not spiritual orphans in a lonely and sometimes friendless world. Thank You for keeping Your promise to be with us. May we welcome Your Holy Spirit as a Holy Guest and make room for Him in our lives. Amen.

C. Thought to Remember

"Greater is he that is in you, than he that is in the world" (1 John 4:4).

Learning by Doing

This page contains an alternate lesson plan emphasizing learning activities.
Classes desiring such student involvement will find these suggestions helpful.

Learning Goals

After this lesson the students will be able to:

1. Summarize the Holy Spirit's role as companion, teacher, and evangelist.

2. Compare the apostles' need for "another Comforter" with our need for the Spirit.

3. Pinpoint aspects of their lives where they need to depend more completely on the Holy Spirit.

Into the Lesson

Write the word *Good-bye* on the chalkboard or on a large poster. As students arrive, ask them to describe how they feel when they have to tell a loved one good-bye. The occasion may have been a death or alienation or a geographic separation. How do they deal with such a situation? Is there one good way to handle the situation or are there many good ways?

Have each student write on a card the hardest parting he or she ever faced. (These descriptions should remain anonymous.) Collect the cards and read three or four, asking for short reactions from the class.

Tell the class, "In our lesson today we'll look at a time when Jesus' disciples were facing the hardest separation of their lives: Jesus would soon be leaving them. While our circumstances are not the same, it is helpful to note how the hope that Jesus offered His disciples applies to us in our difficulties—not only in times of separation from loved ones, but in many similar situations. Jesus promised the Comforter—a Helper, the Holy Spirit—and He will help us to cope with whatever difficult times come our way."

Into the Word

Ask three volunteers to read these three passages without interruption: John 14:15-18; 24-26; 16:7-15.

Distribute sheets of paper to the class. Ask each student to write the headings *Role*, *Apostles*, and *Believers* at the top of his or her paper and to draw vertical lines separating the page into three columns. In the "Role" column, ask the students to write the word *Companion* near the top, *Teacher* about a third of the way down, and *Evangelist* about two-thirds down the page.

Have the students work individually or in small groups to note the promises connected with the Spirit's role as companion (John 14:15-

18), teacher (John 14:24-26), and evangelist (John 16:7-15), noting specific applications to the apostles and to believers generally by writing ideas in the two remaining columns. For example, in the "teacher" section, students should note verse 26. Under the "apostles" column they should note that this is a promise of inspiration so that the apostles could teach, preach, and write accurately and without error. Under the "believers" column they should note that we still have the benefit of this promise from what has been written in the New Testament. (See 2 Timothy 3:16, 17; 2 Peter 1:21.)

Allow time for the students to work—about five to seven minutes for each section. (If time is short, assign different sections to different groups.) Then discuss each section. Use information from the commentary section to help you sort out the differences between what Jesus promised the apostles and what applies to us.

Note that Jesus' farewell is much like many we face; separation from a loved one is always difficult. But His was unique in that He was able to promise "another Comforter." As your study has shown, we continue to benefit from that promise, but we need to depend on the Spirit for the promise to be of any help to us.

Into Life

Ask the students how the promise of a "Comforter" makes them feel. What about this promise is most significant to them? After a brief discussion, note the wider meaning of the word translated "Comforter" (see the commentary section or today's visual). How does this expanded meaning help them as they consider the Spirit's role in helping them to live for the Lord?

Distribute index cards to the class. Ask the students to use these cards to write down some of the things they are trying to do for the Lord. These might include breaking a bad habit, cultivating a closer relationship with a spouse, developing a better devotional time, serving in a ministry position in the church, or something else. Then ask each student to look at his card and to ask himself: "Am I depending on the power of the Spirit to help me with each of these items?" Encourage each student to choose one or two items where he or she needs to depend more completely on the Holy Spirit and to seek to do that this week.

Let's Talk It Over

*The questions on this page are designed to encourage review of the lesson
Scriptures and to promote discussion of the lesson by the class. The answers
provided are only discussion starters. Let your class talk it over from there.*

1. The literal meaning of the word "Comforter" in verse 16 is "one called alongside." It can refer to one called to help, to defend (as in a court of law), to rebuke, to encourage, or to comfort. All of these concepts fit the work of the Holy Spirit. Which do you find especially significant? Why?

All of these images make it clear to us that the Spirit is on our side—a companion who is with us constantly to help us in many ways. Those who have experienced great loss, as in the death of a spouse or child, will have found the comforting presence of the Spirit to be significant in a way others do not yet fully appreciate. Those who have undertaken a big task for the Lord and have found a strength not their own to accomplish it recognize the "Helper" as someone very special. Those who have been convicted of sin through reading the Word or hearing a sermon know the rebuke of the Spirit, yet they know His grace as well. Even when He rebukes, the Holy Spirit is still "on our side."

2. Some say that obedience is not important as long as one loves Jesus. "Obedience," they claim, "goes with the Old Covenant of law-keeping, but we live in the age of grace." How would you respond, based on today's text?

John 14:15, 24 make it clear that obedience is the evidence of love. Grace does not preclude the need for obedience; instead, the one who has experienced grace is more eager to obey. Legalistic obedience leads to the kind of self-justification of which the Pharisees were guilty. Obedience born of love is sincere. It does not look for loopholes; it looks for ways to please the One who is loved.

3. Since it is the Holy Spirit who reproves or convicts of sin, righteousness, and judgment, some people might assume that we need to do nothing to win the lost. What would you say about that?

Paul says, "I can do all things through Christ which strengtheneth me" (Philippians 4:13). Almost always God—and the Holy Spirit is God—does His work through people. He also works through the Word, which He inspired. That Word must be communicated by people. The New Testament was written by men who were

doing all they could to win the lost. There is no contradiction between the role of human evangelists and the role of the Spirit in evangelism.

4. Jesus knew that the apostles needed much more information than they had when He was speaking to them, but they were not ready for it. The Spirit would have to guide them later. What happens when we try to give people more spiritual information than they are ready for? How can we tell how much a person is ready and able to understand?

The apostles did not yet comprehend that Jesus was going to die and be raised again. There was no way, then, that they could understand the purpose for those events. Even so, many people today do not have a proper frame of reference to understand the gospel. For example, people who have been abandoned by their fathers have a difficult time appreciating God as a Heavenly Father. Speaking of our "Father" may fill their minds with negative images based on their own experience rather than on Scripture. We need to help these people know what a Father ought to be, or describe God with different Biblical models until they are ready to grasp the Fatherhood of God in a positive light.

Perhaps some of your students had to go through a growing process before they could accept certain Biblical truths. Allow them to share their journeys.

5. The Holy Spirit's ministry is to glorify Jesus. That should be our aim as well. How can we be sure that Jesus has the preeminence in all of our programs and personal efforts?

This will not happen by accident. We must be deliberate about our ministries and plan for Jesus to be exalted. We need to pray that His name will be glorified; we must speak of Him in ways that glorify Him. We must not adopt a program just because a larger church does it, or accept a plan just because a person of reputation suggests it. In our planning, we need to ask, "How will this glorify the Lord Jesus?" If we cannot give a reasonable answer, then we must either revise or reject the plan. Individually, we must take care not to act in order to be noticed or to make a name for ourselves. Instead, we must constantly seek to glorify the name of Jesus.

Jesus Prays for His Disciples

DEVOTIONAL READING: Ephesians 6:10-20.

LESSON SCRIPTURE: John 17.

PRINTED TEXT: John 17:1-5, 9-11, 15-24.

John 17:1-5, 9-11, 15-24

1 These words spake Jesus, and lifted up his eyes to heaven, and said, Father, the hour is come; glorify thy Son, that thy Son also may glorify thee:

2 As thou hast given him power over all flesh, that he should give eternal life to as many as thou hast given him.

3 And this is life eternal, that they might know thee the only true God, and Jesus Christ, whom thou hast sent.

4 I have glorified thee on the earth: I have finished the work which thou gavest me to do.

5 And now, O Father, glorify thou me with thine own self with the glory which I had with thee before the world was.

. . . .

9 I pray for them: I pray not for the world, but for them which thou hast given me; for they are thine.

10 And all mine are thine, and thine are mine; and I am glorified in them.

11 And now I am no more in the world, but these are in the world, and I come to thee. Holy Father, keep through thine own name those whom thou hast given me, that they may be one, as we are.

. . . .

15 I pray not that thou shouldest take them out of the world, but that thou shouldest keep them from the evil.

16 They are not of the world, even as I am not of the world.

17 Sanctify them through thy truth: thy word is truth.

18 As thou hast sent me into the world, even so have I also sent them into the world.

19 And for their sakes I sanctify myself, that they also might be sanctified through the truth.

20 Neither pray I for these alone, but for them also which shall believe on me through their word;

21 That they all may be one; as thou, Father, art in me, and I in thee, that they also may be one in us: that the world may believe that thou hast sent me.

22 And the glory which thou gavest me I have given them; that they may be one, even as we are one:

23 I in them, and thou in me, that they may be made perfect in one; and that the world may know that thou hast sent me, and hast loved them, as thou hast loved me.

24 Father, I will that they also, whom thou hast given me, be with me where I am; that they may behold my glory, which thou hast given me: for thou lovedst me before the foundation of the world.

GOLDEN TEXT: Holy Father, keep through thine own name those whom thou hast given me, that they may be one, as we are.—John 17:11.

That You May Believe
Unit 4: Jesus Prepares His Followers
(Lessons 10-13)

Lesson Aims

After this lesson students should be able to:
1. Tell what Jesus prayed for in John 17.
2. Explain why the unity of believers, for which Jesus prayed, must continue to be a priority for the church today.
3. Suggest steps that individuals and congregations can take to work for that unity.

Lesson Outline

Introduction

A. The True "Lord's Prayer"

It is often moving to listen to the public prayers of certain individuals. It can be especially moving to listen in on someone's private prayers, for they usually are offered with greater intensity and emotion. The prayer of Jesus found in today's lesson text was not a public prayer, but He meant for His disciples (both then and now) to overhear it. It is one of the most moving passages, not only in the Gospels but in the New Testament.

It is not wrong to call the prayer that Jesus taught us (which begins, "Our Father which art in heaven . . .") the Lord's Prayer. However, when we call it that, we must also realize that strictly speaking it is the disciples' prayer: "After this manner therefore pray *ye*," Jesus said (Matthew 6:9). John 17 records the true Lord's Prayer; for it is Jesus' own personal prayer, deliberately prayed in the hearing of His closest followers. In it we learn much about Jesus and about ourselves. When we examine its contents, we are truly walking on holy ground, like Moses before the burning bush. We should approach this lesson with a special measure of reverence.

B. Lesson Background

The lessons in this final unit of our studies from John's Gospel have all been drawn from the events that took place on the evening before Jesus' crucifixion. We have noted that of all the Gospel writers, only John records Jesus' words of warning and encouragement to His disciples and the prayer from which today's text is taken (chapters 14–17). At one point during His speaking, Jesus apparently left the upper room where He and the disciples had gathered (14:31). Somewhere along the way, before they crossed the brook Kidron (which ran between Jerusalem and the Garden of Gethsemane), Jesus offered the prayer recorded in John 17.

I. Jesus Faces Death
(John 17:1-5)

A. The Time Is Near (v. 1)

1. These words spake Jesus, and lifted up his eyes to heaven, and said, Father, the hour is come; glorify thy Son, that thy Son also may glorify thee.

Many of us are familiar with the hymn, "In the Cross of Christ I Glory." We should never forget what a strange thing that would have been to believe and profess in the first century. No cross was ever associated with being used to *glorify* someone until Jesus died on His cross. Crosses were instruments of abject humiliation and shame. But Jesus, who reversed the world's thinking in so many areas, reversed it here as well. Paul was not at all ashamed to glory in the cross (Galatians 6:14).

We have cited several occasions, earlier in Jesus' ministry, where John noted that Jesus' enemies did not make a move against Him because His *hour*, or time, had not yet come (7:30; 8:20). Then, as the cross drew near, Jesus began to change His language to say that His hour had come (12:23; 13:1; 16:32). This is how He speaks as He begins His prayer. We are reminded that the cross did not come as a surprise to Jesus. He knew that it was near. But He also knew that what men were plotting to do to shame Him would in fact bring glory both to Him and to His *Father*.

B. He Speaks of Life (vv. 2, 3)

2, 3. As thou hast given him power over all flesh, that he should give eternal life to as many as thou hast given him. And this is life eternal, that they might know thee the only true God, and Jesus Christ, whom thou hast sent.

Here Jesus speaks of Himself in the third person (*he* and *him*). (In the fourth verse He will switch back to the first person.) It is remarkable that Jesus, though facing certain death, speaks not of death at all, but of life—of *eternal life*. As Jesus shared in God's giving of physical life at creation (John 1:1-4), so here He is involved in the provision of eternal life.

Life is one of the most prominent themes in John's Gospel. Jesus declares Himself to be the source of "a well of water springing up into everlasting life" (4:14). He also describes Himself as the "bread of life" (6:35); the source of the "light of life" (8:12); "the resurrection, and the life" (11:25); and "the way, the truth, and the life" (14:6).

To experience this life, one must *know . . . the only true God*. It is not enough to know about God. One must have a personal acquaintance with Him. Notice that Jesus does not define eternal life in terms of endless years in Heaven. It is not a relationship with time, but with God. [See question #1, page 336.]

C. His Work Is Finished (vv. 4, 5)

4, 5. I have glorified thee on the earth: I have finished the work which thou gavest me to do. And now, O Father, glorify thou me with thine own self with the glory which I had with thee before the world was.

In one sense, of course, Jesus' work was not yet *finished*. The cross was still before Him. On the cross He would cry, "It is finished." However, at this point Jesus saw the cross not as a future event but as something already accomplished. His words indicate His readiness to proceed with this ultimate step in fulfilling the will of His *Father*. He was moving toward the last hours of His earthly work—the work God had given Him to do. That work *glorified* God. The Father did not have any reason to be ashamed of His Son Jesus.

A preacher once remarked that the cross was the greatest sacrifice imaginable. An older preacher later observed, "That may not be true. We don't know much about the glory of Heaven, but giving up the glory of Heaven for earth may have been a greater sacrifice than Calvary!" In any case, the *glory* that Jesus *had with* God *before the world was* would be given back to Him. When Jesus had completed everything necessary in fulfilling His Father's will, He would sit once again at God's right hand (Hebrews 1:3; 12:2).

GLIMPSES OF GLORY

Jesus begins His prayer of John 17 with a plea that God "glorify thy Son, that thy Son also may glorify thee" (v. 1). The words *glory, glorify,* and *glorified* appear eight times in this prayer (in the *King James Version*).

The glory of God is a prominent theme in both Old and New Testaments. The seraphim whom Isaiah saw in his vision of God in the temple cried out, "The whole earth is full of his glory" (Isaiah 6:3). When the temple of Solomon was dedicated, "the glory of the Lord filled the house. And the priests could not enter into the house of the Lord, because the glory of the Lord had filled the Lord's house" (2 Chronicles 7:1, 2). When the angel of the Lord appeared to the shepherds on the night of Jesus' birth, "the glory of the Lord shone round about them" (Luke 2:9); and the host of angels who soon appeared cried, "Glory to God in the highest" (v. 14). Paul tells us we have "the light of the knowledge of the glory of God in the face of Jesus Christ" (2 Corinthians 4:6).

Jesus prayed in John 17:24, "Father, I will that they also, whom thou hast given me, be with me where I am; that they may behold my glory." May we so give our lives to the Son of God, and to others in His name, that His petition may be answered. The fulfillment of this is found in the Holy City, which is described as "having the glory of God" (Revelation 21:11).   —J. G. V. B.

II. Jesus Prays for the Twelve (John 17:9-11, 15-19)

A. A Focused Prayer (vv. 9, 10)

9. I pray for them: I pray not for the world, but for them which thou hast given me; for they are thine.

Imagine how these disciples felt when they heard Jesus say, *I pray for them*. They did not know what dangers they would face in serving Him, but He did. Already one of them (Judas) had fallen prey to temptation and was even now carrying out his betrayal of Jesus.

Why did Jesus say, *I pray not for the world*? It was not that Jesus was unconcerned about the world (Jesus' mission was to the world, as John 3:16 clearly indicates). But in this particular portion of His prayer, He was concentrating more on those whom He would leave in the world to carry on His work. Only through their efforts would the world begin to hear the message of salvation. [See question #2, page 336.]

10. And all mine are thine, and thine are mine; and I am glorified in them.

When Jesus said *mine are thine, and thine are mine,* He was describing the complete unity that exists between the Father, the Son, and the disciples of the Son. There is no rivalry or division between Father, Son, and followers.

Jesus' statement *I am glorified in them* should be studied alongside earlier references to Jesus' prayer that God glorify Him (vv. 1, 5). God "glorified his Son Jesus" (Acts 3:13), ushering Him back to the glory of Heaven following His resurrection. Christians are called to live "that the name of our Lord Jesus Christ may be glorified" in us (2 Thessalonians 1:12). Are we seeking to fulfill such a noble calling?

B. A Prayer for Protection and Unity (vv. 11, 15-17)

11. And now I am no more in the world, but these are in the world, and I come to thee. Holy Father, keep through thine own name those whom thou hast given me, that they may be one, as we are.

Once again Jesus was looking ahead. The next day He will be crucified. After three days He will rise from the dead. He will appear to His followers for a period of forty days, then He will ascend to the Father and be *no more in the world.* Of course, Jesus meant that physically—in a visible, tangible form—He would no longer be in the world. Recall last week's lesson, which focused on Jesus' promise of the Holy Spirit. The Spirit is "another Comforter" (John 14:16), whose presence fulfills Jesus' promise, "Lo, I am with you alway" (Matthew 28:20).

Jesus continued His prayer for His disciples, knowing how vulnerable they would be by remaining *in the world.* He knew the hazards they would face, because that world would be, for the most part, as hostile to them as it had been to Him (John 15:18-21). The concern of Jesus for His own did not end with His departure from this earth. It continued—and it continues still.

The phrase *keep through thine own name* is rendered "by the power of your name" in the *New International Version.* Among Jews, the ideas of "name" and "power" were closely linked, as they are by us when we say, "in the name of the law." The word *keep* may be translated "protect." As we will see shortly (v. 15), Jesus did not intend for His followers to be secluded from the world, but to remain untarnished by the world's evil influences.

Jesus also prayed for His disciples *that they may be one, as we are.* At this point the unity of the group was fragile. Even in the upper room, they had been arguing as to "which of them should be accounted the greatest" (Luke 22:24). This temptation to place selfish interests above kingdom interests still surfaces. So Jesus' prayer for the unity of His followers remains relevant. It is sobering to consider that when we drive wedges of division between God's people, we are frustrating the prayer of Jesus!

15, 16. I pray not that thou shouldest take them out of the world, but that thou shouldest keep them from the evil. They are not of the world, even as I am not of the world.

The disciples will not be taken *out of the world.* To do so would be like taking the salt out of the food and the light out of the darkness. Jesus never meant for His followers to separate themselves physically from the world. He did want them to be spiritually separated from the world, or *from the evil,* which may refer to Satan as "the evil one." Thus are Christians to be in the world, but *not of the world.* [See question #3, page 336.]

17. Sanctify them through thy truth: thy word is truth.

The word *sanctify* means "to make holy" or "to set apart for a holy purpose." In the Old Testament, both objects and people were thus sanctified. Whenever we think of sanctification, two prepositions must follow. We are set apart *from* something—the world—and we are set apart *for* something—the service of God.

In only a few hours Pilate will cynically ask Jesus, "What is truth?" (John 18:38). Here is the answer: *thy word is truth.* Earlier Jesus had told the disciples, "I am . . . the truth" (John 14:6). In a world that has rejected the very idea of absolute truth, the church is called to proclaim without fear or hesitation where truth can be found: the written Word of God and the living Word of God.

C. A Prayer for Their Work (vv. 18, 19)

18. As thou hast sent me into the world, even so have I also sent them into the world.

The word *apostle* means "one who is sent." While we do not have exactly the same purpose or power that the apostles possessed, we too are *sent . . . into the world* by Jesus. Certainly we must gather faithfully in worship with other

---

How to Say It

GETHSEMANE. Geth-*sem*-uh-nee.
KIDRON. *Kid*-ron.

Use the visual from lesson 9 to illustrate today's lesson. It demonstrates Jesus' concern for the whole world, as expressed in John 17:23.

Visual for lesson 13

Christians (Hebrews 10:25), but we are not to remain isolated from those who need the salt and light that we can provide. Our lives have purpose and meaning only when we dedicate them to involvement in Christ's ministry. We are *sent* to continue the ministry that God began when He *sent* Jesus. It's an exciting thought—and a grave responsibility.

19. And for their sakes I sanctify myself, that they also might be sanctified through the truth.

Jesus was already sanctified in the sense of being set apart from the world. He was without sin and could not become holier in that sense. He could, however, *sanctify* Himself by committing Himself to the task that lay ahead—laying down His life in accordance with His Father's will (John 10:18).

III. Jesus Prays for Us
(John 17:20-24)
A. For Our Unity (vv. 20-22)

20. Neither pray I for these alone, but for them also which shall believe on me through their word.

Having prayed for those men who were to become His apostles, Jesus now focused His prayer on future followers. Certainly we who are Christians today are included among those who *believe* on Jesus *through their word*. "Faith cometh by hearing, and hearing by the word of God" (Romans 10:17). It is the testimony of the apostles, written for us in the New Testament, that brings us to faith in Christ as Savior and that forms the only foundation upon which genuine Christian unity can rest. The feelings or experiences of individuals or groups can never provide such a foundation; only the objective truth of the Scriptures will suffice. We should possess the confidence that Jesus had in the power and the priority of the apostolic message.

It is always touching and encouraging to know that someone is praying for us. How much

more so to know that Jesus prayed for us! How much more so to know that He prays for us still! He is at the right hand of God interceding for us even now (Romans 8:34; Hebrews 7:25).

21. That they all may be one; as thou, Father, art in me, and I in thee, that they also may be one in us: that the world may believe that thou hast sent me.

There is a purpose in Jesus' desire for the unity of believers: *that the world may believe that thou hast sent me.* Jesus saw the lack of unity as a hindrance to evangelism. We know from our own experiences that non-Christians often cite the division in the church as a reason for their lack of interest in the Christian message.

That we *all may be one* is not an organizational unity accomplished by man-made resolutions or the decisions of ecclesiastical bodies. Jesus describes our unity in this manner: *as thou, Father, art in me, and I in thee.* This unity is spiritual in nature—a oneness in mind, will, and purpose that is expressed in our love for God and for all who have accepted Christ and are therefore God's children. We need to recognize this oneness and seek to "keep the unity of the Spirit in the bond of peace" (Ephesians 4:3). [See question #4, page 336.]

"THAT THEY MAY BE ONE"

One of Jesus' most earnest petitions in His beautiful prayer was that those who would believe in Him in the future would be united— "that they all may be one" (v. 21). One of the major tragedies in the history of the church is the division among Jesus' followers and the sheer hatred that they at times have shown to one another.

An example of this may be seen in the reactions many church authorities had to the first complete translation of the Bible into English in the late 1300s under the influence of John Wycliffe. Wycliffe was viciously castigated by these leaders, being called (in the spelling of that era) "the Devells Instrument . . . Peoples Confusion, Hereticks Idoll."

How terrible that someone who was trying to put the Word of God into peoples' hands and in a language they could understand was considered an enemy of the God he loved and served. Several years after his death, Wycliffe was publicly condemned as a heretic, and his bones were dug up and burned. The ashes were then scattered in a nearby river.

Today the animosity between Christians is usually not as intense as that between Wycliffe and his critics. However, it does not have to be to have the effect of alienating a lost world that desperately needs Jesus.   —J. G. V. B.

22. And the glory which thou gavest me I have given them; that they may be one, even as we are one.

Jesus lived in heavenly *glory* before He came to earth (v. 5). Eventually He would return to that glory at the Father's right hand. This is the glory that Jesus wants to share with His followers, as verse 24 indicates. However, they must be willing to travel the path of humble service as Jesus did, realizing the glory of living in this manner. If all Christians sought such glory, rather than glory for themselves, how much greater the possibility that we would *be one*.

B. For Our Witness (v. 23)

23. I in them, and thou in me, that they may be made perfect in one; and that the world may know that thou hast sent me, and hast loved them, as thou hast loved me.

The word *perfect* means "mature" or "complete"; thus the *New International Version* renders Jesus' words, "May they be brought to complete unity." Such unity will be a powerful witness to *the world*—one that it cannot ignore. The world will then *know* that Jesus came from God. The world will also know that God loves those who commit their lives to Jesus. Many in our society today are starving for such love.

C. For Our Future (v. 24)

24. Father, I will that they also, whom thou hast given me, be with me where I am; that they may behold my glory, which thou hast given me: for thou lovedst me before the foundation of the world.

Jesus now looked beyond His departure from His disciples, beyond the days of their service, and into eternity. He has been with these men for three and a half years. But He wants to be with them forever! The rewards of Heaven are not grudgingly given. Jesus wants all His followers to spend eternity in *glory* with Him.

Then Jesus moved from thinking of the future to considering the distant past. He spoke of the Father's love for Him *before the foundation of the world*. These words about an eternal love deepen the mystery of creation in our minds. Why did God bother to create the world, knowing that the Son, whom He loved, would need to enter the world, live in it, and die for it? How could God love His Son and yet love the world so much that He gave His Son to die for it? This is a great mystery. It should give us reason to ponder the greatness of God's grace and the greatness of His desire to be loved by us.

Conclusion

A. Facing Death With Courage

The first part of today's lesson shows us how Jesus faced death with courage. The last part directs our minds to the glory of Heaven so that we too may face death with courage. Yet we are not to be so set on Heaven that we are discontent with earth. God wants us to live full, rich, and purposeful lives here. First Timothy 6:17 tells us, "God . . . giveth us richly all things to enjoy."

Sooner or later, however, all of us must face death. We need to face it with courage as Jesus did—looking forward with anticipation, not backward with regrets.

B. Working for Christian Unity

After reading of Jesus' burden for the unity of His followers, we need to ask, "What attitudes of mine hinder Christian unity? Do I have a divisive spirit that works contrary to the fervent prayer of our Lord?" We may not be able to work for unity in large ways, but we all can promote it in small ways. We can make sure that our spirit is gracious because we have been saved by grace, and that our attitude is loving because Christ first loved us—in our sins! [See question #5, page 336.]

C. Prayer

Dear God, we thank You for letting us listen to Jesus' prayer. Forgive us when anything we do or say frustrates the desires of Jesus or hinders the cause of world evangelism. In Jesus' name, amen.

D. Thought to Remember

Life must be lived upward and outward, not just inward. That upward and outward focus should be reflected in our prayers.

Home Daily Bible Readings

Monday, May 24—This Is Eternal Life (John 17:1-5)

Tuesday, May 25—I Have Made Your Name Known (John 17:6-10)

Wednesday, May 26—I Have Given Them Your Word (John 17:11-19)

Thursday, May 27—That They All May Be One (John 17:20-26)

Friday, May 28—I Have Prayed for You (Luke 22:24-32)

Saturday, May 29—Could You Not Stay Awake With Me? (Matthew 26:36-46)

Sunday, May 30—Nothing Can Separate Us From God's Love (Romans 8:31-39)

Learning by Doing

This page contains an alternate lesson plan emphasizing learning activities.
Classes desiring such student involvement will find these suggestions helpful.

Learning Goals

After this lesson students should be able to:

1. Tell what Jesus prayed for in John 17.

2. Explain why the unity of believers, for which Jesus prayed, must continue to be a priority for the church today.

3. Suggest steps that individuals and congregations can take to work for that unity.

Into the Lesson

Write the word UNITY vertically on the chalkboard. As students arrive, ask them to suggest a word or phrase that starts with each letter of *unity* and denotes a similar concept or a means of either achieving or maintaining unity. Here are some suggestions in case you get stuck:

Understanding

Not being selfish

In the world, but not of it

Truth

Yearning for harmony

Make a transition to the Bible study by noting that unity should not simply be a lofty ideal that we talk about but never achieve. At least in our own congregation we should be committed to achieving it. Whether that unity will spread beyond us is more than we can control, but we can do our part. Unity was the focus of Jesus' prayer in John 17, from which today's lesson is drawn. If unity was important to Jesus the last night that He was with His disciples before His crucifixion, then it must become important to us.

Into the Word

Review briefly the preceding events recorded in John 16 (Jesus warns the disciples of persecution, and He promises the Holy Spirit). Note that all the events in John 13–18 happened the same night and into the next morning. The events of John 13 and 14 occurred in the upper room where Jesus and the disciples observed the Passover. At the close of chapter 14 they began to make their way to Gethsemane, or at least to prepare to leave (see v. 31). The events of chapters 15–17, then, may well have occurred on the way to Gethsemane, though John 18:1 suggests that the group may not have left the room until after Jesus' prayer. Or perhaps they left the room and were still inside Jerusalem at the time described in John 18:1, when they "went forth" from the city and crossed the brook Kidron.

Have a volunteer read John 17:1-5, 9-11, 15-24. Ask the rest of the class to listen to the reading and to write down everything Jesus prayed for. (For the glorification of the Son and the Father [vv. 1, 5]; for the disciples [v. 9]; that the disciples be kept through God's name and that they be one [v. 11]; that they be protected from evil [v. 15]; that they be sanctified by the truth [vv. 17, 19]; for those who would believe in Jesus from the apostles' testimony [v. 20]; for the unity of believers with other believers and with God, in order that the world may believe in Jesus [vv. 21-23]; that believers may be with Jesus [v. 24].)

Review the lists the students develop, commenting on the significance of the items and discussing their importance. Use information from the commentary section as well as questions from the next page to assist in this.

Divide the class into groups of four or five, and ask each group to write a statement of the importance of unity in the church.

Into Life

Ask the class to name some characteristics of a united church. (This can be done as a class activity or in the small groups formed earlier.) What does a united church do that a church with division does not? What attitudes are apparent in a united church? Compile a list based on the students' responses and write it on the chalkboard.

Assign each of the small groups one or two of the items on the list. Ask them to decide whether each characteristic is a result of unity or a cause. That is, will unity result if the church works to develop this characteristic, or must the church have real unity before the characteristic can be present?

Ask the class to use the results of this activity, as well as any other insights they may have, to suggest specific ways a church or an individual Christian can work for unity in the church. Ask the students to make a commitment to implement at least one of the ideas suggested. Look also for an idea that might make a good class project so your class can take the lead in working for unity in the church.

Since this lesson is about Jesus' prayer for unity, it is especially appropriate that you close this session with a similar prayer.

Let's Talk It Over

The questions on this page are designed to encourage review of the lesson Scriptures and to promote discussion of the lesson by the class. The answers provided are only discussion starters. Let your class talk it over from there.

1. Jesus prayed that His disciples would experience eternal life in knowing Him and His Father. This suggests that eternal life is not merely something we anticipate in the "sweet by and by," but is a present reality for those who know Jesus. How does this concept of eternal life encourage you in your Christian walk?

Eternal life is, of course, a life that endures throughout eternity. It is not merely a better life on this earth. But it is eternal because it is in fellowship with the eternal God. Knowing we have that fellowship even now is an encouragement to endure until we have it perfectly in Heaven. Such knowledge also helps us to bear up under our earthly trials. See 2 Corinthians 4:16-18, where Paul contrasts his "present light and momentary troubles" with "an eternal glory that far outweighs them all" (*New International Version*).

2. In John 17:9 Jesus contrasted prayer for His disciples with prayer for the world. How are your prayers for non-Christians different from those you offer for Christian brothers and sisters?

Jesus' most famous prayer for unbelievers was the one He uttered on the cross: "Father, forgive them; for they know not what they do" (Luke 23:34). We may similarly ask for mercy on occasion for non-Christians. However, until they come to Jesus Christ, they can experience God's mercy in only a very limited way. How about our prayers on behalf of the sick and hurting? With believers we can pray for healing and for strength and patience in enduring whatever suffering remains. But surely in our prayers for unbelievers we will want to ask God to impress them during their physical suffering with the greater needs of their soul. Whenever we pray for people outside of Christ, our prayer should reflect John 16:8—we should pray that the Spirit will convict them of sin, righteousness, and judgment.

3. "In the world, but not of the world." How do you maintain the proper balance in that position? How do you maintain enough contact with the world to be a witness without becoming "of the world" yourself?

This is, indeed, a difficult line to walk, as evidenced by the high degree of worldliness among professing Christians. Echoing Jesus' prayer here is certainly one way to help in this. Pray for the unity of the church and the salvation of the lost (v. 21); then put your greatest efforts into those activities that will lead toward accomplishing those ends. Seek Christ's glorification more than your own (v. 10). Spend time in the sanctifying Word of God (v. 17). Pray for protection from the evil [one] (v. 15).

Perhaps some of your students can share specific practices that help them maintain a distance from worldliness without withdrawing from the world.

4. What difference do you think a greater measure of unity among Christians would make in an unbeliever's attitude about accepting Christ? Why?

The current state of denominationalism must certainly be confusing to unbelievers! Perhaps some of your students have been challenged with, "How can people who claim to follow the same Lord hold such differing views on things? And if they cannot get along with each other, what is so special about their faith anyway?" What did they say? What *could* they say?

But what if an unbeliever saw individual Christians loving one another rather than arguing and name-calling? Wouldn't they take notice of Christians who sacrifice for one another instead of stirring up scandals? Wouldn't genuine concern about meeting one another's needs be attractive to the unbeliever? Let us resolve to cultivate the unity for which Christ prayed, and thus to take away the barrier to faith that division places in the way of unbelievers.

5. What can we do to promote unity within our own congregation?

Paul wrote in Romans 12:18, "If it be possible, as much as lieth in you, live peaceably with all men." Unity needs to be more important to us than "winning" whatever argument or disagreement has brought separation. Encourage your students to suggest specific actions that will bring healing to whatever situation most threatens the unity of your congregation. Many divisions result from a lack of communication. What can be done to improve the lines of communication? What other issues can you address?

Summer Quarter, 1999

Genesis: Beginnings

About These Lessons

This quarter launches our chronological study of the Old Testament. Of course, we begin with that book of beginnings, Genesis. We'll see that, right from the start, God's people had their ups and downs, yet God was faithful through it all. May it encourage us to know that God is with us, too, through all of our own ups and downs.

Jun 6

Jun 13

Jun 20

Jun 27

Jul 4

Jul 11

Jul 18

Jul 25

Aug 1

Aug 8

Aug 15

Aug 22

Aug 29

Quarterly Quiz

The questions on this page may be used in several ways: as a pretest at the beginning of the quarter; as a review at the end of the quarter; or as a review after each lesson. The questions are based on the Scripture text of each lesson (King James Version). **The answers are on page 344.**

Lesson 1

1. In the beginning, who "moved upon the face of the waters"? *Genesis 1:2*

2. God gave the man and the woman this command: "Be _____, and _____, and _____ the earth, and _____ it." *Genesis 1:28*

Lesson 2

1. What two trees did God place in the midst of the garden of Eden? *Genesis 2:9*

2. God said that it was not good for the man to be _____. *Genesis 2:18*

Lesson 3

1. What were the occupations of Cain and Abel? *Genesis 4:2*

2. Where did God tell Cain that sin was lying? *Genesis 4:7*

3. Where did Cain go to dwell after he had murdered Abel? *Genesis 4:16*

Lesson 4

1. Noah is described as someone who found grace in the eyes of the Lord. T/F *Genesis 6:8*

2. How many of every clean animal was Noah to take on the ark? How many of every unclean animal was he to take? *Genesis 7:2*

Lesson 5

1. Identify the following members of Abram's family: father, wife, nephew. *Genesis 11:31*

2. Where did Terah die? *Genesis 11:32*

3. God promised Abram, "In thee shall all _____ of the earth be _____." *Genesis 12:3*

Lesson 6

1. Name the man who served as "steward" in Abram's house. *Genesis 15:2*

2. God told Abram to look at the _____ and told him, "So shall thy seed be." (sand, stars, stones?) *Genesis 15:5*

3. Of whom was God speaking when He said, "Twelve princes shall he beget, and I will make him a great nation"? *Genesis 17:20*

Lesson 7

1. Into what land did God tell Abraham to go to sacrifice Isaac? *Genesis 22:2*

2. Who asked, "Where is the lamb for a burnt offering?" *Genesis 22:7*

3. What did Abraham offer as a sacrifice instead of his son? *Genesis 22:13*

Lesson 8

1. The Scripture says that Esau _____ his birthright. (cherished, pondered, despised?) *Genesis 25:34*

2. Esau showed little emotion upon learning that Jacob had taken his blessing. T/F *Genesis 27:34*

Lesson 9

1. Jacob set out from _____ to go to Haran. *Genesis 28:10*

2. What did Jacob call the place where he slept and dreamed? *Genesis 28:19*

Lesson 10

1. What did Jacob call the place where he had wrestled with the angel all through the night? *Genesis 32:30*

2. How many men accompanied Esau when he came to meet Jacob? *Genesis 33:1*

Lesson 11

1. Which of Joseph's brothers protested the plan to kill him? *Genesis 37:21*

2. Which brother suggested that Joseph be sold into slavery? *Genesis 37:26, 27*

3. For how much was Joseph sold? *Genesis 37:28*

Lesson 12

1. When Joseph was brought before the Pharaoh, he was taken out of the _____. *Genesis 41:14*

2. Joseph told Pharaoh that first would come seven years of great _____, and that would be followed by seven years of _____. *Genesis 41:29, 30*

Lesson 13

1. Which of Joseph's brothers said, "God hath found out the iniquity of thy servants"? *Genesis 44:16*

2. When Joseph revealed himself to his brothers, he asked if his _____ were still alive. *Genesis 45:3*

3. According to Joseph, who had sent him to Egypt? *Genesis 45:7*

Roots

by John W. Wade

A LITTLE OVER TWENTY years ago, *Roots* became a popular television miniseries. Alex Haley, the author of the book on which the series was based, went back to Africa in an attempt to find the beginnings of his family and to trace its history down to the present time. In the course of the series, the evils of slavery were highlighted, along with some of the problems that faced the slaves after their emancipation. As a result of watching this program, many people became interested in their own roots and began to investigate the ancestry of their families.

The lessons in this quarter take us all the way back to the "roots" of humanity. They are drawn from Genesis—the book of beginnings.

In the Beginning

Unit 1 of this quarter consists of four lessons taken from the early chapters of Genesis. **Lesson 1**, based on the first chapter of Genesis, deals with the wonderful story of God's creation of the heaven and the earth, climaxing in the creation of human beings, both male and female, in the image of God (Genesis 1:27). Many people in our time have come to accept the hypothesis that the physical universe and all that is in it evolved out of nothing through the processes of blind chance. By contrast, the Genesis account in its sublime simplicity tells how everything was spoken into existence by an all-powerful, all-loving God. There are many applications of this truth that you as a teacher will want to emphasize to your class. In a world that seems increasingly hostile to more and more people, you will want to stress that God created human beings in order to have a wonderful and intimate fellowship with them. Stress that a person's view of origins has a significant impact on how he views the present and the future. If our beginning is shrouded in time and chance, then what gives the present any meaning? What does the future hold? Only God can give us clear and certain answers to these questions.

Lesson 2, based on Genesis 2, tells how God placed Adam in the garden of Eden, which he was to care for and enjoy. All the animals had companions, but Adam was alone. Then God created Eve to be Adam's helper and companion. You will want to stress how important marriage is in the plan of God, and how His directive in Genesis 2:24 provides a timeless definition of marriage (sorely needed in today's world!). In addition, emphasize the importance of relationships found through God's family—the church.

In **lesson 3** tragedy strikes. Genesis 3 tells how sin entered the garden of Eden. As a result Adam and Eve were forced to leave their beautiful home. Emphasize that the painful consequences of sin are not confined either to the sinners or the immediate time in which they live. In this lesson, we consider Cain's jealousy that eventually led him to kill his brother Abel. The irony of this incident is that the immediate occasion for the murder arose because of the sacrifices that the two brothers had presented to the Lord. Unfortunately, this is not the last time that differences over religious matters have led to violence. In presenting this lesson you will want to emphasize the importance of building strong family relationships. One reason for the high crime rates of our time is the breakdown of the family.

Lesson 4, "Judgment and New Beginning," relates the account of the flood—God's act of judgment upon a world that had turned away from Him. This was not the last time that God allowed judgment to fall on rebellious people. It is a pattern that has been repeated again and again. In your lesson presentation you will want to stress that nations today are not exempt from God's wrath, and that we have escaped only because God's mercy has delayed His judgment. You can end the lesson on a note of hope, however, for the closing verses of the text end with God's promise never to destroy the world again by water. Today He is "not willing that any should perish, but that all should come to repentance" (2 Peter 3:9).

The Beginnings of a People

Many of the most popular programs in the history of television have been those that have centered around the family. Most of these have examined (usually in a humorous manner) the predicaments and challenges involved in raising a family. Lessons five through thirteen of this quarter focus on a Biblical family—the family of Abraham and his descendants—that exhibited many of the problems that are quite common in modern families.

This family began approximately four thousand years ago in the city of Ur of the Chaldees, located in the southeastern part of modern Iraq.

In **lesson 5** we learn of God's call to Abraham (then known as Abram) to launch out on a venture of faith that led him first to Haran and then on to Canaan.

God had promised to bless Abraham and make of him a great nation (Genesis 12:2), but for a long time there seemed little hope that this promise would be fulfilled. **Lesson 6** tells how God gave Abraham and Sarah a child, Isaac, even though they were both advanced in years. A central theme of this lesson is that God fulfills His promises, though not always in the way we anticipate or at the time we may want them fulfilled.

The faith of those who trust God may at times be put to the test. **Lesson 7** tells how Abraham's faith was severely tested when God told him to offer his son Isaac as a sacrifice. While it is not likely that we today will ever face a test of this nature, we will face tests that are just as crucial. Help your students to understand that sometimes these tests come when we are confronted by situations in which the issues are clear and rather simple. But they must also recognize that more often the tests we face are temptations to cut corners, or to compromise our convictions just a little here or there.

Lesson 8, "Deceit and Blessing," deals with strife within the family of Isaac involving his two sons, Jacob and Esau. Sibling rivalries began with Cain and Abel and have recurred in almost every generation since. Parents and grandparents in your class will be able to identify with this problem. Use this as an opportunity to allow your students to share some ideas about how they have dealt with this issue in their own families.

A People Tested

The deceitfulness of Jacob toward Esau comes to a head in **lesson 9**. Jacob was forced to flee the wrath of his brother and to find refuge in the land where Abraham once lived. On the way there, God confronted Jacob in a dream and renewed the covenant that He had previously made with Abraham and Isaac. One idea you may want to discuss is the kind of people God can use—even a scheming deceiver like Jacob!

The Bible goes on to relate the story of the life of Jacob, who married, had a large family, and prospered in the land of his father-in-law Laban. A high point in **lesson 10** is Jacob's wrestling match with an angel, which symbolizes his long, hard struggle with God. Fearing what will happen when he finally meets Esau, whom he had not seen in twenty years, Jacob was relieved and happy to find that Esau no longer carried a murderous grudge against him.

Lesson 11 provides yet another illustration of family discord, with Jacob favoring his son Joseph over his ten older brothers. Such favoritism is almost certain to lead to some measure of tension. In this case, Joseph's brothers actually planned to kill him; however, his life was spared at the last minute when he was sold into slavery—a fate that in that day was only slightly better than death. Use this lesson as an opportunity to encourage your students to avoid favoritism and its harmful consequences in their own families. Encourage them to share some of the ways that they have dealt with this matter.

The events in **lesson 12** show God's hand at work in the life of faithful Joseph. Joseph was taken from prison and brought before the Pharaoh to interpret his dream. By the power of God, Joseph was able to do what none of the wise men of Egypt could—he provided Pharaoh with the answer for which he was looking. Pharaoh was so impressed that he placed Joseph in charge of collecting the grain during the coming seven good years and storing it for the seven years of famine that were to follow. The story may seem too good to be true except for one factor—God! Emphasize to your students how God still uses talented people in positions of leadership—if they are willing to surrender their talents to Him.

The final lesson of the quarter, "Forgiveness and Reunion," brings this series of lessons to a heartwarming conclusion. A famine forced Joseph's brothers to travel to Egypt to buy grain. Joseph immediately recognized them, but they were unaware of his identity. When the famine continued, they were forced to return for more grain, this time bringing their youngest brother Benjamin. Joseph devised a plan that was meant to test the brothers and to determine whether they were the same cruel, heartless men who had sold him into slavery. When the brothers passed this test, Joseph finally revealed his identity to them. What a beautiful scene it was when Joseph completely forgave their mistreatment of him! He was able to do this because through his unswerving faith in God he saw in his brothers' actions a part of God's plan to save a remnant of His people.

Our Sunday schools often suffer a "slump" during the summer months. Attendance may be down, and the attendance of the faithful members may be irregular because of vacations. In addition, many people seem to be "turned off" by lessons from the Old Testament. But don't let that happen in your class. These narratives can make for exciting teaching, and the applications can be just as contemporary as this morning's newspaper.

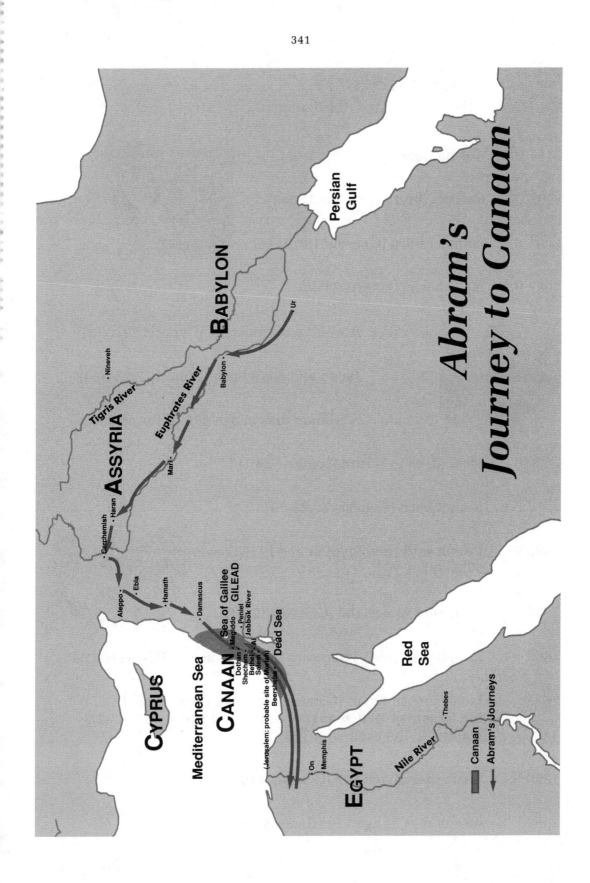

Abram's Journey to Canaan

Chronology of Genesis

From the Call of Abraham to the Death of Joseph

2167 B.C. **Abram born**

2092 B.C. **Call of Abram (Genesis 12:1-5)**

2081 B.C. **Ishmael born (Genesis 16:15, 16)**

2067 B.C. **Isaac born (Genesis 21:1-3)**

2050 B.C. **Abraham offers Isaac (Genesis 22:1-19)**

2007 B.C. **Jacob and Esau born (Genesis 25:24-26)**

1992 B.C. **Abraham dies at age 175 (Genesis 25:7)**

1930 B.C. **Jacob flees to Haran (Genesis 28:10)**

1916 B.C. **Joseph born (Genesis 30:22-24)**

1899 B.C. **Joseph sold into Egypt at age 17 (Genesis 37:2, 28)**

1887 B.C. **Isaac dies at age 180 (Genesis 35:28)**

1886 B.C. **Joseph interprets Pharaoh's dream at age 30 (Genesis 41:46)**

1877 B.C. **Jacob goes to Egypt (Genesis 46:5, 6)—Beginning of the Israelites' 430-year stay in Egypt (Exodus 12:40, 41), leading to the exodus in 1447 B.C.**

1860 B.C. **Jacob dies at age 147 (Genesis 47:28)**

1806 B.C. **Joseph dies at age 110 (Genesis 50:26)**

Real Places, Real Time

Putting Historical Events in the Correct Place and Time

by Ronald G. Davis

STUDYING HISTORY DEMANDS both a geographical and a chronological context. Such elements are part of what distinguish truth from fantasy. Real events happen at real places. Real people experience real events. And real events always happen in relationship to other real events. There is no "Once upon a time," no "East of the sun and west of the moon," and no "In a far, far kingdom where it was always summer."

The book of Genesis is real history. Real people. Real events. Real places. Real time. Its history is orderly and progressive. People are born, live, and die. Generation follows generation. The only constant is God, who began time with creation, set man into that time in a specific place, and allowed him the privilege and responsibility of choosing his own day-to-day events and thereby, in a sense, writing his own history.

This quarter's study traces the course of human history from two in a garden to a nation in Egypt. Generations and centuries pass, yet God is as present with Joseph at the end of Genesis as He is with Adam at the beginning. His expectations for the gardener are the same as they are for the governor. And both Adam and Joseph are free to make their own history—for good or for evil.

The wise teacher of history insists that his students know both the chronology and the geography of the material he teaches. Such information is essential, for the temporal and spatial elements confirm the reality of significant people and the events of which they are a part.

Teaching Places

The geography of Abraham's life is the geography of the Old Testament. The territory that includes Ur to Egypt, that stretches from the area of the Tigris and Euphrates Rivers to the land of the Nile River, became "center stage" for the unfolding of God's redemptive plan, culminating in the birth of His Son in an obscure but real Galilean town. Familiarity with this geographical framework is critical to a thorough understanding of God's revelation and activity.

Abraham's Place

Lessons 5-8 of this quarter's study cover the life of Abraham—the man with whom God established His covenant and through whom He intended to bless "all families of the earth" (Genesis 12:3). A map of Abraham's world on display throughout these four sessions (and the others preceding and following) will be an important part of your teaching strategy. And with maps, the general instructional principle is: "The larger, the more effective."

Even though the use of commercial maps can be beneficial, involving class members in the preparation and use of maps can be even more profitable. Look at the large open spaces available in your classroom: walls, tabletops, the floor, a bulletin board. Consider transferring a small outline of the land and water sites mentioned under "Teaching Places" to one or more of these spaces. If your congregation has an overhead projector, you can use an outline you have traced onto plastic to project a larger outline on the wall or on a large bulletin board. Masking tape (colored, if available) can be twisted to follow basic land lines. Or, for a bulletin board, yarn can be stapled into land shapes.

The traditional grid method of transferring an image can be used on any available surface. In this activity, the original small map is ruled into squares (one-inch squares should work). Then the large surface is also lined into squares in some fashion. Walls can be ruled with narrow masking tape; tabletops can be ruled with washable markers (or erasable pencil lines); in some cases, floors have the natural grid of square floor tiles. The idea is to make the squares on the larger surface proportionately larger and then put in the lines designating the land areas square by square. Most maps highlighting Abraham's geography that are found in the back of a Bible will be about 4" by 8" for the area covered. Thus, if your wall has a 4' by 8' area, the squares can be one-foot squares, and the resulting map will be 144 times the size of the original!

However you decide to do this project, recruit two or three class members to help you with the work. Recruit one or two others to letter appropriately sized place-name cards. During the class session in which a specific place is introduced, have someone stick the proper name on the map. (If you add map outlines to tabletops in the room where you assemble, you'll need place names for each table thus prepared. You might consider letting each table's "regulars" tape or draw the lines designating a certain area onto a grid that you have prepared in advance; if you do, give each table a small map already "squared.") Whatever map(s) you prepare, be certain to give the students a scale of miles: "one inch equals ____ miles." This will give students an appreciation of the rigors of Abraham's travels.

Cartographic precision is not your goal in this project, so don't be too concerned with details. General knowledge of bodies of water, cities, and the relationships of different areas to one another is what matters most. Abraham lived and moved in real places; your students need the ever-present reminder of what and where those real places were and are.

Teaching Time

Young children have often been taught the "big hand, little hand" method of telling time. (Today's students are probably more familiar with digital timepieces.) Genesis is a history of real people and real events. Those who study it need to be able to "tell time"—to know beginnings from middles and middles from ends. Chronology gives evidence of validity and believability. At every point during these studies from Genesis you, as a teacher, will want to emphasize the sequence of people and events. Once a student of the Bible learns to "tell time," he is much closer to grasping the sequence of events within God's master plan.

Early in the quarter you may find it helpful to give your students a list of the primary people of Genesis arranged in alphabetical order and ask

---

**Answers to Quarterly Quiz
on page 338**
Lesson 1—1. the Spirit of God. 2. fruitful, multiply, replenish, subdue. **Lesson 2**—1. the tree of life and the tree of the knowledge of good and evil. 2. alone. **Lesson 3**—1. Abel was a keeper of sheep; Cain was a tiller of the ground. 2. at the door. 3. the land of Nod, on the east of Eden. **Lesson 4**—1. true. 2. seven of every clean; two of every unclean. **Lesson 5**—1. his father was Terah; his wife was Sarai; his nephew was Lot. 2. Haran. 3. families, blessed. **Lesson 6**—1. Eliezer. 2. stars. 3. Ishmael. **Lesson 7**—1. Moriah. 2. Isaac. 3. a ram. **Lesson 8**—1. despised. 2. false. **Lesson 9**—1. Beersheba. 2. Bethel. **Lesson 10**—1. Peniel. 2. four hundred. **Lesson 11**—1. Reuben. 2. Judah. 3. twenty pieces of silver. **Lesson 12**—1. dungeon. 2. plenty, famine. **Lesson 13**—1. Judah. 2. father. 3. God.

---

them to put the names in chronological order. (You might use Abraham, Adam, Isaac, Ishmael, Jacob, Japheth, Joseph, Methuselah, Noah, and Terah.) One way of doing this would be to give each student a letter-sized sheet of paper divided into ten boxes, with one name in each box. Ask your class to tear the names apart and stack them up from earliest to latest. When you announce the correct order, each person can check his or her work.

With some lessons, you may choose to condense the main story to six to ten key events written as sentences on strips of paper. Ask your class to place these in the correct sequence. For example, lesson 4 surveys the four chapters (Genesis 6-9) given to Noah and the flood. Consider presenting the following ten sentences randomly to your class and asking the students to put them in correct order: (1) God tells Noah to build an ark. (2) Representative animals are gathered. (3) Rain falls for forty days and nights. (4) The flood covers the earth for one hundred fifty days. (5) The ark comes to rest on Ararat. (6) A raven is sent from the ark. (7) A dove is sent out twice. (8) Noah's family comes out of the ark. (9) Noah sacrifices to the Lord. (10) God provides the rainbow as a sign.

Joseph's Time

The life of Joseph is told in the final third of Genesis (chapters 37-50). When you come to lesson 11, where his story begins, use the following collection of objects to help give an overview of his life: a piece of bright plaid cloth, twenty pieces of silver (dimes), a torn robe or shirt, two sets of seven calendars, handcuffs or chains, a sack of flour, a silver cup, and a small doll wrapped in gauze (like a mummy). Display the objects randomly to your class, and ask them to decide in what order to put the items to represent Joseph's life.

Here are the answers: *cloth*=Joseph's coat of many colors; *twenty dimes*=the price of Joseph's slavery; *robe*=Potiphar's wife's act of lust; *chains*=imprisonment; *sets of calendars*=sets of seven years in Pharaoh's dream; *flour*=the plenty in Egypt; *cup*=Benjamin's sack of grain and silver; *doll*=embalmed Joseph.

Choose more or other objects if you think they will be more effective in telling the story.

Most students learn specific events best when they have an historic framework or overview. Most students learn history better when they can picture the geography of the area where the history takes place. Do all you can during this study of real history to aid your students in their understanding of the significant events and places of Genesis.

God's Good Creation

June 6
Lesson 1

DEVOTIONAL READING: Psalm 104:24-35.

LESSON SCRIPTURE: Genesis 1:1—2:4.

PRINTED TEXT: Genesis 1:1, 2, 20-31.

Genesis 1:1, 2, 20-31

1 In the beginning God created the heaven and the earth.

2 And the earth was without form, and void; and darkness was upon the face of the deep. And the Spirit of God moved upon the face of the waters.

. . . .

20 And God said, Let the waters bring forth abundantly the moving creature that hath life, and fowl that may fly above the earth in the open firmament of heaven.

21 And God created great whales, and every living creature that moveth, which the waters brought forth abundantly, after their kind, and every winged fowl after his kind: and God saw that it was good.

22 And God blessed them, saying, Be fruitful, and multiply, and fill the waters in the seas, and let fowl multiply in the earth.

23 And the evening and the morning were the fifth day.

24 And God said, Let the earth bring forth the living creature after his kind, cattle, and creeping thing, and beast of the earth after his kind: and it was so.

25 And God made the beast of the earth after his kind, and cattle after their kind, and every thing that creepeth upon the earth after his kind: and God saw that it was good.

26 And God said, Let us make man in our image, after our likeness: and let them have dominion over the fish of the sea, and over the fowl of the air, and over the cattle, and over all the earth, and over every creeping thing that creepeth upon the earth.

27 So God created man in his own image, in the image of God created he him; male and female created he them.

28 And God blessed them, and God said unto them, Be fruitful, and multiply, and replenish the earth, and subdue it: and have dominion over the fish of the sea, and over the fowl of the air, and over every living thing that moveth upon the earth.

29 And God said, Behold, I have given you every herb bearing seed, which is upon the face of all the earth, and every tree, in the which is the fruit of a tree yielding seed; to you it shall be for meat.

30 And to every beast of the earth, and to every fowl of the air, and to every thing that creepeth upon the earth, wherein there is life, I have given every green herb for meat: and it was so.

31 And God saw every thing that he had made, and, behold, it was very good. And the evening and the morning were the sixth day.

GOLDEN TEXT: God saw every thing that he had made, and, behold, it was very good.—Genesis 1:31.

Genesis: Beginnings
Unit 1: In the Beginning
(Lessons 1-4)

Lesson Aims

After this lesson the students will be able to:

1. Summarize the account of God's creative activity in Genesis 1.

2. Explain why the Biblical record of creation is superior to other explanations of man's origin.

3. Give thanks that he or she is not an "accident," but an individual created in the image of God.

Lesson Outline

INTRODUCTION

  A. Creation Commotion

  B. Lesson Background

I. IN THE BEGINNING (Genesis 1:1, 2)

  A. Creation Introduced (v. 1)

  B. Initial Chaos (v. 2)

II. DAY FIVE (Genesis 1:20-23)

  A. God Creates (vv. 20, 21)

  B. God Blesses (vv. 22, 23)

III. DAY SIX (Genesis 1:24-31)

  A. Land Animals Created (vv. 24, 25)

  B. Man Created (vv. 26, 27)

  C. A Mandate Given (v. 28)

    Top of the Line

  D. God's Provision (vv. 29-31)

    God Through Glass

CONCLUSION

  A. You and the Creation Debate

  B. Prayer

  C. Thought to Remember

Introduction

A. Creation Commotion

"In the beginning God created the heaven and the earth" (Genesis 1:1). The first verse of the Bible is so strikingly simple. Yet things can get awfully confusing when one ventures to investigate various aspects of the creation-evolution controversy, theories about the duration of the days of creation, and other related issues that surface in the early chapters of Genesis. Brilliant students and scholars, coming from opposing viewpoints, make impressive, persuasive, and often highly technical arguments to try to support their ideas. At times the scientific, philosophical, and linguistic arguments

can be bewildering, to say the least. What is the student of God's Word to do?

Not everyone feels comfortable with the often complicated discussions surrounding God's creative activity. Certainly these should not be allowed to overshadow the basic simplicity of the Biblical record, nor should they minimize the necessity of faith. "Through faith," the writer of Hebrews reminds us, "we understand that the worlds were framed by the word of God, so that things which are seen were not made of things which do appear" (Hebrews 11:3).

At the same time, we must seek to develop the discernment necessary to be able to distinguish truth from error. Creation and related issues constitute an area where we should "be ready always to give an answer to every man that asketh you a reason of the hope that is in you" (1 Peter 3:15). Our defense should include a concern for Christlike character and communication, avoiding the harsh words that can accompany such an often controversial subject. It should also include a sensitivity for how best to reach the world with the message of the Creator's reality and redemption.

B. Lesson Background

In the beginning God . . . . Today's lesson on creation deals with one of the grandest, most significant themes in all of Scripture. Without the Biblical doctrine of creation, man is left to see himself as the product of blind force and chance. He is virtually alone in a universe without meaning and purpose. We learn from Genesis 1 that a loving God created man as part of a wonderful plan, and as the "crowning glory" to everything He had made. He declared each phase of His creative process as "good" and concluded His activity by declaring all that He had made "very good" (Genesis 1:31).

The truths found in the early chapters of Genesis are foundational to Christian faith. Jesus referred to events found in the early chapters of Genesis (1-11) and treated them as historical events, not as fables or myths (Matthew 19:4, 5; 23:35; 24:37-39). Every New Testament writer refers to at least one event found in the early chapters of Genesis. Recall how Paul, in presenting the gospel to the philosophers on Mars' Hill in Athens, began by proclaiming "God that made the world and all things therein" (Acts 17:24).

While we often speak of the "Genesis account" of creation, the theme of creation is prominent throughout the Old Testament. The command to the Israelites to observe the Sabbath on the seventh day was grounded in the creation week (Exodus 20:8-11). Significant portions of the book of Job (38–41), the Psalms (8;

19:1-6; 33:6; 139:14-16; 148; and especially 104), and the prophets (Isaiah 40:26, 28; 42:5; 45:12, 18; Jeremiah 10:10-12; Amos 4:13; 5:8; 9:6; Malachi 2:10) call attention to the glory and majesty of all that God has created.

In today's lesson we examine the fundamental teachings of Genesis 1, with a view toward understanding some of the key issues that surround this portion of Scripture.

I. In the Beginning
(Genesis 1:1, 2)

A. Creation Introduced (v. 1)

1. In the beginning God created the heaven and the earth.

The fact of divine creation is affirmed in the opening statement of Scripture. Debate over the *how* or *when* should not overshadow the primary emphasis of this verse: the entire universe owes its existence to the will and power of Almighty *God*. The existence of God is not explained or analyzed; it is simply set forth as a foundational truth of Scripture. Ultimately it is a matter of faith (Hebrews 11:3); however, the evidence for believing in God as Creator is far more substantial than the evidence for not believing. [See question #1, page 352.]

B. Initial Chaos (v. 2)

2. And the earth was without form, and void; and darkness was upon the face of the deep. And the Spirit of God moved upon the face of the waters.

This verse describes the state of the *earth* before order was established. Later distinctions and specializations would be made: light and darkness; air and water; dry land and seas; plants and animals, and others. The work of *the Spirit of God* in creation is emphasized here. In the New Testament we find that Jesus was also involved in the creation (John 1:3; Colossians 1:16, 17; Hebrews 1:2).

This visual should be on display as you begin the class session. It is a beautiful reminder that God created our universe.

Visual for lesson 1

Some have suggested that there is an enormous time span between Genesis 1:1 and 1:2. This "gap theory" of creation holds that Satan and his followers were defeated during this time, and in the process the original created order was ruined. Such items as dinosaurs, the fossil records, and "cave men" are all relegated to the time of the "first creation." The events described after Genesis 1:2 refer to an alleged *second* creation. This approach, also called the re-creation view or the ruin-reconstruction view, seeks to harmonize modern scientific belief in an old earth with a literal approach to the events recorded in Genesis.

However, nowhere in Scripture is there any firm indication that Genesis speaks of two creations. In fact, certain Scriptures cause serious problems for the gap theory. For example, Exodus 20:11 says, "In six days the Lord made heaven and earth, the sea, and all that in them is." In other words, *everything* was created within the six days described in Genesis; there appears to be no room for any previous creative activity in the Biblical account.

Perhaps more damaging to the theory is Romans 5:12, which says, "As by one man sin entered into the world, and death by sin; and so death passed upon all men, for that all have sinned." Under the gap theory, death would have occurred *before* Adam's sin. But Paul's statement is clear that there was no death prior to Adam's sin. Thus the gap theory, while it may appear to provide another way of understanding the creation account, challenges other important Biblical teaching. It is far more preferable to view Genesis 1 as describing a single period of creation. [See question #2, page 352.]

II. Day Five
(Genesis 1:20-23)

Our printed text now brings us to the events of the fifth day of creation. The six days of creation can be divided into two groups of three. During the first three days, God created what we might call the territories where created objects or creatures should go; then during the last three days He created the objects and creatures to fill the space He had made. Note, according to the chart below, the correspondence between the first three days and the last three. One writer has called the first three days "days of forming," and the last three, "days of filling."

Day	Day
1—light	4—sun, moon, stars
2—heavens	5—fish, birds
3—earth, vegetation	6—land animals, man

A. God Creates (vv. 20, 21)

20, 21. And God said, Let the waters bring forth abundantly the moving creature that hath life, and fowl that may fly above the earth in the open firmament of heaven. And God created great whales, and every living creature that moveth, which the waters brought forth abundantly, after their kind, and every winged fowl after his kind: and God saw that it was good.

The phrase *let the waters bring forth abundantly* captures well the incredible quantity and variety of aquatic life. The same Hebrew term translated *living creature* also describes man in Genesis 2:7, where it is rendered "living soul." As we shall see, it is the fact that man is created in the image of God that distinguishes him from all other living creatures in God's creation.

The Hebrew word translated *whales* in the *King James Version* includes much more than just the large mammals that we associate with the term. "Sea creatures" is a better translation. Note also the important phrase *after his kind*, which appears elsewhere in Genesis 1 (vv. 11, 12, 24, 25). Whatever biological class is designated by a *kind* (whether a species or a broader group), the various "kinds" of creatures did not evolve from a common ancestor, as evolutionists claim. Each kind was made unique and distinct from every other. There was no need to evolve to some higher form of life, for *God saw* that what He had made *was good*. [See question #3, page 352.]

B. God Blesses (vv. 22, 23)

22, 23. And God blessed them, saying, Be fruitful and multiply, and fill the waters in the seas, and let fowl multiply in the earth. And the evening and the morning were the fifth day.

With this form of life, mating is in order, so God bids these creatures to *be fruitful and multiply*. This same imperative is given to man in verse 28. Of course, with regard to the birds and sea creatures, it was not a "command" to be obeyed; it simply indicates God's purpose and design for these living beings.

III. Day Six
(Genesis 1:24-31)

A. Land Animals Created (vv. 24, 25)

24, 25. And God said, Let the earth bring forth the living creature after his kind, cattle, and creeping thing, and beast of the earth after his kind: and it was so. And God made the beast of the earth after his kind, and cattle after their kind, and every thing that creepeth upon the earth after his kind: and God saw that it was good.

How to Say It

ADAM (Hebrew). uh-*dahm*.

The three terms used to describe the land animals are of a general nature. Involved are larger herd animals (*cattle*), some of which would become domesticated; every *creeping thing*, a term that could refer to anything that moves low to the ground (such as lizards and snakes); and every *beast of the earth*, an expression that is simply "living thing" in Hebrew, but likely designates wild, undomesticated animals.

B. Man Created (vv. 26, 27)

26. And God said, Let us make man in our image, after our likeness: and let them have dominion over the fish of the sea, and over the fowl of the air, and over the cattle, and over all the earth, and over every creeping thing that creepeth upon the earth.

The Hebrew word translated *man* (*adam*, which is also the name given to the first man) can also be translated "mankind." Being made in the *image* of God does not include physical characteristics. Involved instead are attributes such as intellect, self-consciousness, emotion, self-determination, and the capacity to love, communicate, and have fellowship with God. We might include the capacity to "create," or think independently and originally, as something we share with God.

Being made in God's image also involves a shared authority, by which man is granted *dominion* over the rest of the created order. Man was created to be a ruler; as David wrote, "Thou hast made him a little lower than the angels, and hast crowned him with glory and honor" (Psalm 8:5). But he is to rule out of compassion, not greed. Thus was Adam placed in the garden of Eden "to dress it and to keep it" (Genesis 2:15).

What does *let us make man* indicate? Most likely this is an early indication of the doctrine of the Trinity, a plurality of persons within the divine being. (As we have already noted, both Jesus and the Spirit of God were present at creation.) Others believe that the plural pronoun reflects what is called a "plural of majesty"—the use of the plural to express the grandeur of something or someone. Similar language appears in Genesis 11:7 ("Let *us* go down") and Isaiah 6:8 ("Who will go for *us*?").

Another question involves the significance of the terms *image* and *likeness*. Most likely these are simply interchangeable terms, as seen by a comparison of Genesis 1:27 with Genesis 5:1.

They indicate that man is set apart from the rest of creation and is given a position of honor above everything else God has made.

27. So God created man in his own image, in the image of God created he him; male and female created he them.

Here *man* is defined as comprising both *male and female*. Both share the blessings and responsibilities of being made *in the image of God*. Next week's lesson will focus on the more detailed description of man and woman's creation in Genesis 2. [See question #4, page 352.]

C. A Mandate Given (v. 28)

28. And God blessed them, and God said unto them, Be fruitful, and multiply, and replenish the earth, and subdue it: and have dominion over the fish of the sea, and over the fowl of the air, and over every living thing that moveth upon the earth.

The phrase *replenish the earth* simply means to fill it. The words *subdue* and *have dominion* describe the responsibility given man as a result of his being made in God's image. They encompass the realms of science and technology. Man is to seek to understand the created order and then utilize that knowledge, not selfishly or thoughtlessly, but to the glory of his Creator.

Psalm 8 refers to this "creation mandate," as David marvels at the glorious position bestowed on man at creation. However, man's fall has diminished his ability to fulfill such a mandate. Hebrews 2:5-9 teaches that only through Jesus Christ, whom the Father has "crowned with glory and honor," can man's dominion over creation be realized.

TOP OF THE LINE

Serious car enthusiasts know the names of the finest automobiles manufactured by the major manufacturers: Eldorado, Continental, Aurora, Imperial, Roadmaster, and others. These are called "top of the line," and they are roomier, safer, more luxurious, more powerful, and more comfortable than the other models. Only a certain affluent segment of society can afford these cars; the rest of us merely fantasize about driving one.

VISUALS FOR THESE LESSONS

The *Adult Visuals* packet contains classroom-size visuals designed for use with the lessons in the Summer Quarter. The packet is available from your supplier. Order No. 492.

When God created the world, He saved His best till last. He created humans in His image and gave them dominion over the rest of creation. Humans possess features surpassing the characteristics of all other species in the animal kingdom. Self-consciousness and superior intelligence endow us with capabilities that are unique and unsurpassed. We are God's "top of the line." As such we exercise dominion over the earth and its inhabitants, subduing even creatures much larger, stronger, and faster than we.

We are "fearfully and wonderfully made" (Psalm 139:14). God made us just "a little lower than the angels" and has "crowned [us] with glory and honor" (Psalm 8:5). How else can we respond except to say, "O Lord our Lord, how excellent is thy name in all the earth!" (Psalm 8:1, 9). —R. W. B.

D. God's Provision (vv. 29-31)

29, 30. And God said, Behold, I have given you every herb bearing seed, which is upon the face of all the earth, and every tree, in the which is the fruit of a tree yielding seed; to you it shall be for meat. And to every beast of the earth, and to every fowl of the air, and to every thing that creepeth upon the earth, wherein there is life, I have given every green herb for meat: and it was so.

These verses suggest that initially both man and animals fed only on plant life. (The word *meat* in the *King James Version* means "food.") Only after the flood is animal flesh specified for human consumption (Genesis 9: 2, 3). The significance of these instructions lies in God's gracious provision for what He has created.

31. And God saw every thing that he had made, and, behold, it was very good. And the evening and the morning were the sixth day.

At the culmination of His creative work—after man, the crown of His creation was fashioned—God pronounced it all as *very good*. A perfect world, unmarred by sin and its consequences, was in place. A being created in God's image was given dominion over this world.

An important element of man's being created in the image of God was his freedom of choice. Tragically, we know how man abused his freedom to disobey God—an abuse that continues to the present day. Apart from his Creator, man cannot become better; he can only grow worse. [See question #5, page 352.]

GOD THROUGH GLASS

I looked at the moon through a telescope recently, and I didn't see the "man in the moon." But I did see God—that is, I saw convincing evidence of God's design and creative excellence.

There were no shadows across the moon that night; the moon was "full." I could see one whole face of the entire sphere, brilliantly white. Craters were visible, too; the telescope's powerful magnification brought it all up close and beautiful.

To believe that our solar system, let alone the infinite universe beyond, came into existence as the result of some cosmic accident stretches my imagination too far. What I saw through the telescope confirmed my faith in a world created by an omniscient, benevolent, Supreme Being.

I've seen God through a microscope, too. Viewing the world that is invisible to the naked eye is another revelation of remarkable design and precision. Microscopic organisms deliver "sermons from science." The intricacies of form and function that one can see with the aid of powerful lenses speak of purposeful, intelligent creation.

Perhaps the most convincing argument for the truth of the Biblical account of creation is what one sees in the glass of a mirror. The only power that could possibly create such a remarkable specimen as man is Almighty God. He alone is responsible for the beauty of the earth. —R. W. B.

Conclusion

A. You and the Creation Debate

Today there is much controversy over whether both creation and evolution should be taught in public schools. Those who hold the evolutionary viewpoint often depict their view as scientific while portraying the Biblical account of creation as nothing more than religious folklore.

The simple fact is that both those who support the theory of evolution and those who believe in creation must come to their respective positions by faith. The Christian believes in divine creation because he considers the Bible to be the Word of God, and this is clearly an act of faith. However, one who believes in evolution must also come to his position by faith, since obviously there were no eyewitnesses to the beginning of living things.

Which, then, of these two faiths has more to commend it? One way to address this question is to ask which of them produces the most desirable results. If the physical universe and man came into existence by blind chance, then clearly there is no purpose in the universe. Without purpose, there can be no logical basis for morality. Man may propose rules for his own protection, but if there is no God behind the rules to give them authority, then man may break them whenever he "feels like it" or whenever he thinks he can get away with it.

On the other hand, if we believe that God created the universe with moral as well as physical laws to govern it, then our approach to life will be drastically different. When we have a sense of identity (Who am I?), origin (Where did I come from?), and destiny (Where am I going?), we will live lives that are filled with meaning and purpose, not despair and disillusionment.

How should we respond to the attacks that are often mustered against the creation viewpoint? First, we should seek to acquaint ourselves with the key issues and facts, recognizing (as noted earlier) that not everyone will be comfortable with the more technical aspects of the discussion. Second, we should seek God's wisdom as we try to discern that which is important for our faith and that which is not. Third, we should exhibit a gracious spirit in our discussions on the subject, whether verbal or written. We must contend for the revealed truth, not for man-made theories and opinions. God will bless our efforts as we commit our study of this subject to Him.

B. Prayer

God of Heaven and earth, we marvel as we consider the power and wisdom that You have displayed in the handiwork of Your creation. We are privileged to be created in Your image. May we use our lives to glorify You—our great Creator. Amen.

C. Thought to Remember

"Thou art worthy, O Lord, to receive glory and honor and power: for thou hast created all things, and for thy pleasure they are and were created" (Revelation 4:11).

Home Daily Bible Readings

Monday, May 31—Day One of Creation (Genesis 1:1-5)

Tuesday, June 1—Days Two and Three of Creation (Genesis 1:6-13)

Wednesday, June 2—Day Four of Creation (Genesis 1:14-19)

Thursday, June 3—Day Five of Creation (Genesis 1:20-23)

Friday, June 4—Day Six of Creation (Genesis 1:24-31)

Saturday, June 5—Day Seven; God Finishes Creation (Genesis 2:1-4a)

Sunday, June 6—O Lord, How Manifold Are Thy Works! (Psalm 104:24-35)

Learning by Doing

This page contains an alternate lesson plan emphasizing learning activities. Classes desiring such student involvement will find these suggestions helpful.

Learning Goals

As a result of participating in this session, the student will be able to:

1. Summarize the account of God's creative activity in Genesis 1.

2. Explain why the Biblical record of creation is superior to other explanations of man's origin.

3. Give thanks that he or she is not an "accident," but an individual created in the image of God.

Into the Lesson

As students arrive, give each one a copy of the following scrambled sentence.

"we appear made Through worlds so things that understand faith were the things which framed the word by God, are not of that which were seen of do."

Ask the students to try to unscramble the sentence, which is a verse of Scripture. After a few minutes, ask someone to read Hebrews 11:3, which is the solution. Ask how many had correctly unscrambled the verse. Award these a small prize, like a stick of gum or a bookmark.

Ask all the students, "What is the most confusing thing to you about the current evolution-creation debate?" Some may suggest the conflicting reports about what the fossil record indicates. Others may be confused about the "old earth" or "young earth" debate.

Point out that you will not resolve all the differences between the various views of creation in this class session. What we must all agree on is that the Bible certainly conflicts with any worldview that starts without a Creator. The most important thing to know about creation is not its exact process but its origin. The world is not a product of blind chance and probability; God created it!

Into the Word

Begin the exploration of Genesis 1 by asking your students to form small groups and complete the right-hand column of the chart shown below. (Note: the chart below has been filled in for you. A copy of the uncompleted chart can be found in the student book, or you can make your own worksheet leaving the "Creative Act" column blank.) This will help them to work through the basic outline of the Biblical account of creation.

Text	Day	Creative Act
Genesis 1:1-5	Day 1	Light & darkness/day & night
Genesis 1:6-8	Day 2	Earth's atmosphere (the firmament)
Genesis 1:9, 10	Day 3	Dry land and seas separated
Genesis 1:11-13	Day 3	Plants & trees
Genesis 1:14-19	Day 4	Sun, moon, & stars; seasons, days, years
Genesis 1:20-23	Day 5	Sea creatures & birds
Genesis 1:24, 25	Day 6	Land animals
Genesis 1:26-31	Day 6	Man

After a few minutes briefly summarize the creative acts so that you can be sure each group was able to complete the activity successfully.

Ask your students to return to their small groups and answer the following question: "What do we learn about God from the account of creation?" They will probably notice at least three things: (1) God is the Creator of all things, including man; (2) God is distinct from His creation; (3) God is eternal and is in control.

Into Life

Make the transition into application of the text by encouraging your students to answer the "so what?" question about each of the aspects of the character and nature of God mentioned above. What does it mean to them that God created the world? How do they live differently? How do they worship God differently? How do they view nature differently? How does it change the way they look to the future?

If you have time, a similar exercise can be done in the small groups with the question: "What do we learn about ourselves from the Biblical account of creation?" At least two responses may be (1) we are valuable to God since He chose to make us; and (2) we are more precious to Him than all of the rest of His creation.

Observe that after all their research is in, many scientists have found themselves in an undesirable position of staring in the face of the God whom they have desperately tried to avoid. Then lead your students in a prayer of praise that God has revealed Himself as the Creator and sustainer of our world. If time allows, ask each small group to spend some time offering sentence prayers of praise for the way in which God has created and cared for them.

Let's Talk It Over

The questions on this page are designed to encourage review of the lesson Scriptures and to promote discussion of the lesson by the class. The answers provided are only discussion starters. Let your class talk it over from there.

1. Suppose a member of your church said, "You don't believe all that stuff about God creating the world, do you? Science has proved the universe is the result of millions of years of chance process. Genesis is a record of ancient man's view of the origin of things. We can't take it literally today." How would you answer?

While it's true that a person can be wrong about some of his facts but still be right (that is, in a right relationship) with the Lord, there are some issues that leave no room for disagreement. This is an issue that divides believer from unbeliever. Either we believe God's Word is true or we don't. Jesus accepted the Genesis record as fact (Matthew 19:4, 5; 23:35; 24:37-39), and we must do likewise. If this person does not believe in the God of creation, then how can he believe in the God of salvation? He has too great a view of what science has done—or even can do—and too little appreciation for the God of the Bible.

2. Many theories are proposed that seek to reconcile contemporary scientific opinion and the Scriptures. The lesson writer has noted the "gap theory" and pointed out some shortcomings in that view. Besides, scientific opinion is constantly shifting, so that the "science" one harmonizes the Bible with today may be rejected by scientists tomorrow. How then should we view alleged discrepancies between science and the Bible? Can a person accept both "scientific truth" and "Biblical truth"? If so, how?

Truth is consistent with truth, so there is no discrepancy between "scientific truth" and "Biblical truth." Scientists, however, are not completely objective, so much of what is passed off as "science" is not truth at all, but theory. That is the reason science changes so much. Scientist Louis Pasteur proved that spontaneous generation of life is impossible; yet evolutionary scientists continue to believe in it. When trying to harmonize science with the Bible, it is the Bible that is the sure standard, not shifting scientific opinion.

3. One of the key questions in this debate is how life started. Even the simplest life form is unimaginably complex. No accident could have produced such a result. The evidence of careful design is everywhere. In spite of the evidence, many people refuse to accept the existence of God because they do not want to accept accountability to Him. How, then, would you attempt to share your faith with someone who refused to accept the existence of God, but chose to believe some other explanation for the existence of life?

One should not expect to convince such a person in a short time. This person will not likely listen to evidence, so a different approach is needed. Perhaps he or she can be shown that accepting any explanation is a matter of faith. Does he believe aliens colonized the earth? That's a matter of faith—he cannot prove it to be so. Does she believe in an "intelligent universe"? Again, that's a matter of faith. The question then might be posed, "Which faith produces the best results?" Faith in God has produced more hospitals, schools, and benevolence programs than any other kind of faith.

4. Our text declares that God made mankind, both male and female, in His image. What significance does that fact have to you? Why?

This is what gives meaning to life. We are made in God's image to have fellowship with Him, and not just in this life, but for eternity. It is no surprise that suicide has increased since schools started teaching children that they are nothing more than accidents of nature and have no purpose. Being made in God's image gives a person meaning, purpose, and hope.

5. Several events are listed for the sixth day. Some skeptics claim there would not have been enough time in a day, especially considering the twelve-hour daylight portion of the day, as the time span of activity. How would you respond to a skeptic with such a view?

We must remember that God requires very little time to accomplish His will. "Through faith we understand that the worlds were framed by the word of God . . ." (Hebrews 11:3). God spoke, and creation happened. God's causing the animals to pass by Adam in order for him to name them was the only time-consuming activity mentioned. God probably brought appropriate representatives of each group of animals to Adam, so it is reasonable that this could have been accomplished in a period of several hours.

God's Purpose for People

DEVOTIONAL READING: Ephesians 5:22-33.

LESSON SCRIPTURE: Genesis 2:4-25.

PRINTED TEXT: Genesis 2:7-9, 15-25.

Genesis 2:7-9, 15-25

7 And the LORD God formed man of the dust of the ground, and breathed into his nostrils the breath of life; and man became a living soul.

8 And the LORD God planted a garden eastward in Eden; and there he put the man whom he had formed.

9 And out of the ground made the LORD God to grow every tree that is pleasant to the sight, and good for food; the tree of life also in the midst of the garden, and the tree of knowledge of good and evil.

. . . .

15 And the LORD God took the man, and put him into the garden of Eden to dress it and to keep it.

16 And the LORD God commanded the man, saying, Of every tree of the garden thou mayest freely eat:

17 But of the tree of the knowledge of good and evil, thou shalt not eat of it: for in the day that thou eatest thereof thou shalt surely die.

18 And the LORD God said, It is not good that the man should be alone; I will make him a help meet for him.

19 And out of the ground the LORD God formed every beast of the field, and every fowl of the air; and brought them unto Adam to see what he would call them: and whatsoever Adam called every living creature, that was the name thereof.

20 And Adam gave names to all cattle, and to the fowl of the air, and to every beast of the field; but for Adam there was not found a help meet for him.

21 And the LORD God caused a deep sleep to fall upon Adam, and he slept; and he took one of his ribs, and closed up the flesh instead thereof.

22 And the rib, which the LORD God had taken from man, made he a woman, and brought her unto the man.

23 And Adam said, This is now bone of my bones, and flesh of my flesh: she shall be called Woman, because she was taken out of Man.

24 Therefore shall a man leave his father and his mother, and shall cleave unto his wife: and they shall be one flesh.

25 And they were both naked, the man and his wife, and were not ashamed.

GOLDEN TEXT: The LORD God formed man of the dust of the ground, and breathed into his nostrils the breath of life; and man became a living soul.—Genesis 2:7.

Lesson Aims

After completing this lesson, each student will:

1. Describe the creation of, and the relationship between, the first man and woman.

2. Explain how the belief that we are created in God's image gives purpose to living.

3. Choose an area of life in which he or she needs to reflect God's purpose better, and take steps to do so.

Lesson Outline

Introduction

A. What Is Man?

The year 1997 marked the spectacular appearance of an infrequent visitor in the skies above North America. The Hale-Bopp Comet, which is visible approximately every 2400 years, produced a dazzling display as the glow of its tail shone brightly in the heavens. For some, its appearance was a bit overwhelming. Our eleven-year-old daughter became rather unsettled by the sight and didn't even like to look at it. The comet's mystique was heightened by the bizarre mass suicide of thirty-nine members of a cult known as Heaven's Gate near San Diego, California. They believed that their deaths would somehow allow them to travel to Heaven by means of a spaceship in the tail of the comet.

In ancient times, the psalmist David understood the meaning of the heavens far better than many moderns do. In Psalm 8 he extols the majesty and splendor of God as revealed in the heavens. In verse 4 he asks an appropriate question, in view of the vast, impressive heavenly array above: "What is man, that thou art mindful of him? and the son of man, that thou visitest him?" To view man as the centerpiece of God's magnificent work of creation is truly mind-boggling. And yet that is what Genesis 1 states. Man alone was made "in the image of God" as the crown of His creation (Genesis 1:26, 27). In today's lesson from Genesis 2, we find further evidence of that wonderful truth.

B. Lesson Background

With grand and forceful style, the opening verses of the Bible provide a panoramic overview of God's act of creation. In six successive days, all that comprises our precious planet and the indescribable universe surrounding it was created by "the word of the Lord" (Psalm 33:6). God spoke, and it was so.

The sixth day begins with the creation of the land animals and culminates in the creation of man and woman. It is clear on several counts that woman's creation is a part of day six: (1) God created "male and female" on the sixth day (Genesis 1:27), then blessed "them" and commanded "them" to be fruitful and multiply (v. 28); (2) God pronounced the result of His work at the end of day six as "very good" (v. 31), implying that His creation of everything, including mankind, was finalized; and (3) God's seventh-day rest from His creative activity indicates that the female counterpart of Adam was already on the scene. This means that the events of Genesis 2:7-25 were all a part of day six and followed the creation of land animals earlier that day.

Not all Christians agree on the nature and length of the days in Genesis 1. It is best to view them as twenty-four-hour days in light of Exodus 20:8-11. There God tells Israel to observe the seventh day as a sabbath, "for in six days the Lord made heaven and earth." This command makes sense only if we are thinking in terms of literal twenty-four-hour days.

It has been pointed out that the events recorded in Genesis 2 make for a rather full day, since it includes the following events: land animals are brought forth; Adam is created and placed in the garden; he is prohibited from eating of the tree of the knowledge of good and evil; he is commissioned with the task of naming all the creatures brought before him; he is put into a deep sleep, awakens to find the woman God has fashioned from his rib, and names her. Still, it would not have been impossible for all of this to occur (we do not need to think of every subcategory of animal species as being involved in Adam's naming of the creatures). The sixth day thus included not only man's special creation, but also a series of events that reinforced his special place in God's creative purpose.

I. Man's Special Creation
(Genesis 2:7)
A. The Process (v. 7a)

7a. And the LORD God formed man of the dust of the ground, and breathed into his nostrils the breath of life.

The shift in focus from the first to the second chapter of Genesis is much like switching from a wide-angle lens to a close-up "zoom" lens. Several features in chapter 2 accentuate this transition. The phrase "the heaven(s) and the earth," found in Genesis 1:1; 2:1, 4 is replaced by "the earth and the heavens" (end of verse 4), as the emphasis now shifts to man's dwelling place. The name shift from *God* (the Hebrew word *Elohim*, used throughout chapter 1) to *Lord God* (*Yahweh Elohim*) throughout chapters 2 and 3 is also significant. While the name *God* designates God in His power (as reflected in His creative activity in chapter 1), the name *Lord* (*Yahweh*) is often used to emphasize God's covenant relationship with His people. From Genesis 4 to the end of the book *Lord* is frequently used, but the term *Lord God* does not appear at all. This suggests a special "linking" function of this compound name in chapters 2 and 3.

God *formed man of the dust of the ground*. The Hebrew word rendered *formed* signifies that God

Visual for
lesson 2

The visual for this lesson illustrates verse 7 of the text. Display it at the beginning of the class session.

fashioned or shaped man, much as the potter works a lump of clay. *Dust* is both the original source and ultimate state of man's physical existence (Genesis 3:19; Job 34:15). Man is made of the stuff of this world. Even today, the human body's survival depends on some sixty minerals derived from the ground. We are still closely tied to the earth from which we came. The similarity in the Hebrew words *adam* ("man") and *adamah* ("ground") serves to emphasize this association. [See question #1, page 360.]

B. The Result (v. 7b)

7b. And man became a living soul.

As noted in last week's lesson, the Hebrew phrase translated *living soul* is the same one rendered "living creature" in Genesis 1:21 (also in 1:24; 2:19; 9:10, 12, 16). Thus we should not use this phrase to defend man's superiority to the rest of creation or his immortality. Man's uniqueness is indicated by the special process through which God formed him (He did not breathe life into the nostrils of any other creature) and, especially, by the fact that he is created in the image of God (Genesis 1:26, 27).

II. Man's Special Environment
(Genesis 2:8, 9, 15-17)
A. A Special Territory (vv. 8, 9)

8. And the LORD God planted a garden eastward in Eden; and there he put the man whom he had formed.

The *garden* into which Adam was *put* was located in *Eden*. The paradise conditions described there apparently did not exist elsewhere outside the garden area. One suggestion for the location of *Eden* is the region at the northern tip of the Persian Gulf, in what is now the country of Iraq. The 1991 Gulf War was fought in this same area (although many speculate that modern-day Kuwait would have been under water in earliest times, with the shoreline being to the north of it).

From what we know concerning the terrain of that part of the world at present, it is hard to imagine a luxuriant, natural garden flourishing there. However, some climatologists now argue that this part of the world was much wetter in earlier times, with a major shift to a much drier climate occurring after 3000 B.C. or so.

9. And out of the ground made the LORD God to grow every tree that is pleasant to the sight, and good for food; the tree of life also in the midst of the garden, and the tree of knowledge of good and evil.

The *garden* is described as a beautiful and beneficial place. Two special trees are noted as being provided by God. It is unclear whether these were specially created or were simply ordinary trees endowed with extraordinary meaning. Not everything in the garden is simply laid out for man to enjoy, however. Many of the benefits will come only from the work of his hands, as the next verse of our printed text indicates.

B. A Special Task (v. 15)

15. And the LORD God took the man, and put him into the garden of Eden to dress it and to keep it.

Even in paradise, work was involved! Work was not part of the curse placed on man following the fall; it was part of the Creator's intention for him from the beginning. Adam was assigned the task of cultivating and caring for the *garden* in which God placed him. The Hebrew word translated *dress* means to "work." In this case, Adam was to work by tilling the soil: see verse 5, where it is noted that "there was not a man to till the ground." Adam's task filled this void. His responsibility in the garden was the beginning of the process of subduing the earth, in accordance with God's design (Genesis 1:28).

C. A Special Test (vv. 16, 17)

16, 17. And the LORD God commanded the man, saying, Of every tree of the garden thou mayest freely eat: but of the tree of the knowledge of good and evil, thou shalt not eat of it: for in the day that thou eatest thereof thou shalt surely die.

The garden was not only a place of pleasure, but also a place of probation. Man's continued enjoyment of the blessings there was conditioned on his adherence to God's rules. His love for his Creator was to be demonstrated by obedience to His will. Woman was not yet created at this point, so she would not have heard this initial prohibition. Either God repeated it for her, or it was communicated to her by her husband.

The tree of life is not mentioned in the prohibition given to man. Later we learn that once man disobeyed God and ate of the *tree of the knowledge of good and evil*, he no longer was permitted access to the tree of life. That access will be restored in the renewed paradise described in Revelation 22:1, 2. [See question #2, page 360.]

The phrase *in the day* may simply mean "when," as it does in 2:4. Spiritual death, that is, separation from God, occurred immediately upon Adam and Eve's transgression. This separation was symbolized by their expulsion from the garden. They did not die physically at the very instant of their rebellion, but the principle of death began to operate within their mortal bodies. This physical "death penalty" was then passed on to all future generations of Adam and Eve's descendants (for "all have sinned," according to Romans 5:12), but the curse is ultimately removed in Christ (Romans 5:12-21; 1 Corinthians 15:21, 22).

TALE OF TWO TREES

A Tale of Two Cities may not be the best known or most read work of Charles Dickens (*A Christmas Carol* probably is), but many can at least recognize that title as the name of a literary classic. In the same way, the names of two specific trees in the garden of Eden are recognized by many who are otherwise unfamiliar with much of what the Bible says. We could call those trees "The Tree of Life" and "The Tree of Temptation."

These two trees represent man's free moral agency—our choice and our dilemma. The conflict between good and evil began as soon as God planted that second tree, the one with a "No Trespassing" sign on it. He planted the tree to encourage man to exercise his freedom of choice wisely by obeying his Creator. Satan used the tree to plant the idea of disobeying the Creator.

Life-or-death choices are still a part of our daily experience. Without them we would be reduced to mere puppet-like clones with no personality and no opportunity for independent decisions and individual action.

When God planted His garden, He provided for all of our needs, including the freedom of choice. That is part of being made in His image. We exercise that freedom best when we choose to obey our Creator.   —R. W. B.

III. Man's Special Role (Genesis 2:18-20a)

A. A Helper Needed (v. 18)

18. And the LORD God said, It is not good that the man should be alone; I will make him a help meet for him.

Dominion over the rest of creation was given by God to both male and female (Genesis 1:27, 28). God knew that this task would require a team effort and purposed to provide the newly created *man* with a companion and helper.

How to Say It

ADAM (Hebrew). uh-*dahm*.

ADAMAH (Hebrew). ad-uh-*mah*.

ELOHIM (Hebrew). El-owe-*heem*.

ISHAH (Hebrew). ish-*ah*.

YAHWEH (Hebrew). *Yah*-weh.

While everything else in God's creation had been declared "good" thus far, here was a situation that was *not good*. [See question #3, page 360.]

The Hebrew phrase rendered *help meet for him* is better understood as "a helper corresponding to, or suitable for, him." It suggests the supportive role of woman and calls attention to her role as one who complements man and supplies what he lacks. Interestingly, the person in the Old Testament most frequently referred to as a helper is God (particularly in the Psalms).

B. An Authority Exercised (vv. 19, 20a)

19, 20a. And out of the ground the LORD God formed every beast of the field, and every fowl of the air; and brought them unto Adam to see what he would call them: and whatsoever Adam called every living creature, that was the name thereof. And Adam gave names to all cattle, and to the fowl of the air, and to every beast of the field.

Out of the ground . . . God formed the land animals and birds, just as He made man "of the dust of the ground" (v. 7). It thus appears that, according to Genesis 2, these creatures were created after Adam. However, since Genesis 1 describes man as the crown of God's creation and the last living being created, the animals mentioned in 2:19 must have been created before, not after, Adam. Verse nineteen should then be understood to say, "Out of the ground the Lord God *had formed* every beast of the field, and every fowl of the air; and [now] brought them unto Adam . . . ." As noted earlier, it is not necessary to think of every subcategory of animal species as being involved here. The term *cattle* likely designates larger domesticated animals, while the phrase *every beast of the field* describes wild animals.

The fact that the man was given the task of naming the animals emphasized his authority over the animal kingdom. Apparently Adam was created as an intelligent adult who looked like he had reached that stage through the normal process of being conceived, born, and nurtured to adulthood. We do not need to envision a lengthy learning process prior to Adam's being able to assign a multitude of names to the animals. He came into this world with a mind that possessed the capacity to think and reason on a high level.

It should be noted that this concept of "apparent age" has interesting ramifications if applied to other created objects besides man. For example, the stars could have been given an age of several thousand years at the time God created them. Thus the fact that they reflect that age does not indicate that they are actually that old.

IV. Man's Special Companion (Genesis 2:20b-25)

A. Suited for Man (v. 20b)

20b. But for Adam there was not found a help meet for him.

One may wonder why there was a delay in the creation of woman, since God knew that she was a necessary part of the picture. Several suggestions come to mind. One is that her separate creation emphasized her importance. Another is that she was created only after the man recognized his need for her. Nothing in the animal parade over which Adam officiated came close to filling the bill! The fact that God had said that it was not good for man to be alone (v. 18) signified how vital this final creative act really was.

As noted under the discussion of verse 18, the phrase *a help meet for him* designates a helper who will be suitable, fit, or appropriate for the man. In the English language the two words *help* and *meet* were eventually combined into one, *helpmeet*, which was then modified to create the term *helpmate;* but the result has not aided our understanding. The two words are better left separated, as one is a noun (*help*, i.e., helper) and the other is an adjective (*meet*, i.e., suitable) and belongs with the phrase *meet for him*. The woman was just the helper and companion the man needed—and still needs.

B. Fashioned From Man (vv. 21, 22)

21, 22. And the LORD God caused a deep sleep to fall upon Adam, and he slept; and he took one of his ribs, and closed up the flesh instead thereof. And the rib, which the LORD God had taken from man, made he a woman, and brought her unto the man.

God caused a deep sleep to fall upon Adam. The word for *deep sleep* indicates a state in which one is oblivious to any nearby sounds (a "dead to the world" kind of sleep). The Hebrew term is used in two other places where specific individuals are said to fall into a deep sleep (Abram in Genesis 15:12; Saul and his army in 1 Samuel 26:12).

The use of a *rib* suggests someone who is close to man's heart and who stands by his side to fulfill the role of helper. The Hebrew verb used in the phrase *made he a woman* means "to build." It carries the idea of a planned, precise construction of man's special companion.

C. United With Man (vv. 23-25)

23. And Adam said, This is now bone of my bones, and flesh of my flesh: she shall be called Woman, because she was taken out of Man.

Bone of my bones and flesh of my flesh. This expression has a ring of exclamation to it. The close physical similarity between man and woman as a result of God's creation is reinforced by the language in verse 24 describing the marriage bond. Another sound correspondence in Hebrew (similar to *adam* and *adamah* noted under the study of Genesis 2:7a) is found here in the words translated *Woman* (Hebrew, *ishah*) and *Man* (Hebrew, *ish*). (The similarity in the English words "woman" and "man" occurs because the term "woman" is derived from the phrase "wife [of] man.")

24. Therefore shall a man leave his father and his mother, and shall cleave unto his wife: and they shall be one flesh.

The teaching of Jesus in Matthew 19:5 indicates that the words of this verse are directly from God, and not a continuation of Adam's speech. In the context of Matthew 19:5 Jesus employs the designation *one flesh* as a prohibition against divorce. Indeed, in marriage it is God who joins man and woman together in a bond that is not to be broken. The words *cleave unto* further depict the closeness that marriage is to entail. For *a man to leave his father and his mother* marks the establishment of a new relationship of love and devotion that is to supersede all previous relationships. [See question #4, page 360.]

25. And they were both naked, the man and his wife, and were not ashamed.

Adam and Eve initially enjoyed a wonderful innocence and intimacy with one another as well as with God. The phrase *the man and his wife* signifies the special relationship of marriage that God designed to be a part of His creation order. At the beginning man and woman were truly "good," not only in design and origin, but

in actual thought and deed. [See question #5, page 360.]

Conclusion

A. "Crowned With Glory and Honor"

We learn much concerning God's plan and purpose for man in the opening chapters of Genesis. Made in the "image of God," men and women are to reflect the glory of God in their lives. Our lesson text for today singles out man as the capstone of God's creation. As the psalmist David proclaimed, we have been "crowned . . . with glory and honor" by our Creator (Psalm 8:5).

Although marriage is set forth as the divine model in our text, Christians who are unmarried, including those who do not plan to be married, should not see themselves as excluded from God's divine program for man as described in Genesis. The apostle Paul even notes that undistracted devotion to God may be best achieved in the unmarried state, since marriage carries with it other obligations and priorities (1 Corinthians 7:32-35).

Adam and Eve were created pure and sinless, yet there was no guarantee that they would remain so. Free will and self-determination were part of being made in God's image. Conditions were attached to Adam and Eve's continued enjoyment of God's blessings. Their control over the rest of creation would depend on their measure of self-control—their conscious decision to love and obey their Creator.

To look at today's text is to look into our own hearts. It seems that daily, as we recall God's provision and blessings toward us, we find ourselves standing beneath forbidden fruit in one form or another. We must ask ourselves whom we will serve. We can experience the glory and honor that we were created to possess only when we live to bring glory and honor to our Creator.

B. Prayer

Our Lord and Father, we marvel at how much we mean to You as the crown of Your creation. We thank You for Your provisions and blessings—for human love and companionship; for noble purposes and important tasks; for the freedom to serve You out of choice, not compulsion. Help us in our marriages and other relationships as we strive to fulfill Your plan for our lives. In the name of Jesus we pray. Amen.

C. Thought to Remember

We receive our greatest sense of fulfillment when we do what God wants, not what we want.

Home Daily Bible Readings

Monday, June 7—The Lord God Planted a Garden (Genesis 2:4b-14)

Tuesday, June 8—Therefore a Man Clings to His Wife (Genesis 2:15-25)

Wednesday, June 9—Husbands, Love Your Wives (Ephesians 5:18-33)

Thursday, June 10—Honor Your Father and Your Mother (Matthew 15:1-9)

Friday, June 11—Claiming to Keep the Commandments (Matthew 19:16-22)

Saturday, June 12—God Made Them Male and Female (Mark 10:1-9)

Sunday, June 13—Perishable to Imperishable (1 Corinthians 15:42-49)

Learning by Doing

This page contains an alternate lesson plan emphasizing learning activities.
Classes desiring such student involvement will find these suggestions helpful.

Learning Goals

As a result of participating in this session, the student will be able to:

1. Describe the creation of, and the relationship between, the first man and woman.

2. Explain how the belief that we are created in God's image gives purpose to living.

3. Choose an area of life in which he or she needs to reflect God's purpose better, and take steps to do so.

Into the Lesson

Ask the married couples in your class to form at least two small groups of no more than six—with husbands and wives in *separate* groups. Ask the members of each group to tell what they first found attractive about their mates and what they now appreciate most. If the two are not the same, explain why.

Have the singles form small groups, too. These should tell what they are looking for in a prospective mate. What physical, spiritual, intellectual, and emotional qualities do they hope to find? Which is most important? Why?

After a few minutes, tell the class that today's lesson looks at the origin of marriage. "Dating" in today's world can be confusing. The many people trying to give advice on marriage can make that relationship rather confusing as well. Things were much simpler in the garden of Eden. The one man met the one woman in the world, and God made them "one flesh." Let's see how that relationship can help us understand our own situations more clearly.

Into the Word

Lead into the Bible study portion of the lesson by asking a volunteer to read Genesis 2:7-9, 15-25 aloud. Then use the following questions to lead a discussion of the text.

1. What do you think Moses (the author of Genesis) is trying to convey to us about the creation of mankind when he uses the imagery "breathed into his nostrils the breath of life"? (God creates mankind in a very special, intimate way when compared with the way in which He created all that was created previously.)

2. The word "garden" literally means "a protected area" and "Eden" means "delight." In what way did the garden of Eden live up to its name? (Encourage your students to visualize the garden as it was before man sinned. Be sure to emphasize the fact that it was a place specially prepared by God for man, that it provided every physical thing necessary for life, and that man had the opportunity for intimate fellowship with God there.)

3. Why did God plant the tree of life in the garden? (He intended that man would not die but live forever.)

4. Why did God plant the tree of the knowledge of good and evil in the garden of Eden? (God desired man's obedience. In order to obey, Adam needed to have real choice. Without choice, Adam was a prisoner in the garden. True love and worship are not possible without choice.)

5. What was man's "job" in the garden? ("To dress it and to keep it." This was part of the mandate to subdue and have dominion over the earth. Work is not part of the curse; it was part of man's God-ordained role even before there was sin.)

6. What was the one thing that was "not good" in God's creation? (Man was alone. He needed companionship. He needed a mate with whom to reproduce and fill the earth with people.)

7. What is significant about the manner in which woman was created? (She was taken from man's side; so she was like him—made of the same stuff. She was to be at his side as a companion. The word for "made" in verse 22 suggests the idea of a planned, precise construction, much as the word "formed" suggests God made man in a special way. The man and the woman were both very special in design and in relationship to God.)

Into Life

Point out to your students that Adam and Eve lived in the garden of Eden as they were created to live—in a delightfully intimate relationship with each other and with their Creator. Ask, "How can we restore something of that purpose and relationship?" In your discussion, note that Adam and Eve had to choose to obey God. (Next week we'll see what happened when they did not.) We too can choose to obey God and act in a way that reflects the image of God.

Then lead in a time of prayer thanking God for creating us in His image. Seek His help in reflecting that image more clearly.

Let's Talk It Over

The questions on this page are designed to encourage review of the lesson
Scriptures and to promote discussion of the lesson by the class. The answers
provided are only discussion starters. Let your class talk it over from there.

1. We see a certain intimacy in God's creation of man. First He *formed* man out of dust, suggesting a more "hands-on" approach than merely speaking the words to create. Then He breathed the breath of life into man's nostrils. How might you use this description of man's creation to encourage a friend who suffers from low self-esteem?

Self-esteem is talked about and promoted in virtually every aspect of our society today, but low self-esteem remains a problem. Perhaps the reason for that is the acceptance of evolutionary theories about the origin of man. If we are but accidents of nature, we are no better than the beasts of the field. (Many animal rights activists would like us to believe just that!) But if we see ourselves made in God's image—and beyond that carefully and lovingly shaped and formed by our Creator, then we have cause to feel good about ourselves. This kind of self-esteem does not condone bad behavior, as secular theories of self-esteem do, but calls us ever higher to be like the God who formed us.

2. Man's free will required at least one ethical choice in order to function. This was the way man's obedience was to be tested. That was the purpose of the tree of knowledge of good and evil. What ethical choices do you find hardest to make today? Why? How can you consistently make right choices?

Each of us is challenged and tested in different ways. For some, sexual lust is a persistent problem; for others, the lust for power or wealth is more difficult to control. For most, maintaining integrity in the "little" issues of life—when "Who would know the difference?"—is a constant battle: obeying speed laws, not copying copyrighted material, being completely honest with family and friends. But faithfulness in the little issues will keep us faithful in the larger ones. We need more intimate time with our Creator to resist the tempter.

3. Suppose a Christian brother is thinking of asking an unbeliever to marry him. "I know the Bible says we are not to be 'unequally yoked,' he says, but the Bible also says, 'It is not good that the man should be alone.' What choice do I have?" What advice would you give?

God's statement in Genesis 2:18 should not be taken as an absolute command for every situation. Adam was not just single; he was *alone*. Some measure of intellectual and spiritual companionship is available to us today even without marriage, but Adam was alone. Eve was designed to be Adam's sexual and reproductive partner. Marriage provides that for us today, but it was especially important for Adam; he needed a wife to continue the human race. While it is more typical for people to marry, the apostle Paul notes that singleness can be an opportunity for undistracted devotion to God (1 Corinthians 7:32-35). At the very least, this person should be encouraged to wait until he can marry "in the Lord" (1 Corinthians 7:39).

4. Our text records that God instituted marriage when He presented Eve to Adam to be his mate. What do these verses teach us about the nature and intent of marriage?

This account shows us that God's will is for one man and one woman to be permanently united together as husband and wife. Once the two become one flesh in marriage, it is as unnatural to separate them as it would be for a man to pull off his own arm. Adam appears to have been overjoyed to receive his mate. Indeed, God designed the union of man and woman to be a source of joy, encouragement, celebration, cooperation, comfort, consolation, and pleasure for both partners. When each loves the other wholeheartedly and unselfishly, marriage is perhaps the strongest and sweetest of human bonds.

5. According to the Bible, all mankind has descended from Adam and Eve. What lesson does this teach us in regard to race relationships? How ought we to treat others who are different from ourselves?

Incredible as it may seem, God made the human genetic code so complex and yet so flexible that billions of humans could come from just two individuals; yet each of these people is unique. Apparently geographical isolation caused certain traits, such as color and other body features, to concentrate in different peoples, giving rise to the races. Yet all human beings are made in God's image, and all should be treated with respect, dignity, and compassion.

Consequences of Sin

DEVOTIONAL READING: 1 John 3:11-18.

LESSON SCRIPTURE: Genesis 4.

PRINTED TEXT: Genesis 4:1-16.

Genesis 4:1-16

1 And Adam knew Eve his wife; and she conceived, and bare Cain, and said, I have gotten a man from the LORD.

2 And she again bare his brother Abel. And Abel was a keeper of sheep, but Cain was a tiller of the ground.

3 And in process of time it came to pass, that Cain brought of the fruit of the ground an offering unto the LORD.

4 And Abel, he also brought of the firstlings of his flock and of the fat thereof. And the LORD had respect unto Abel and to his offering:

5 But unto Cain and to his offering he had not respect. And Cain was very wroth, and his countenance fell.

6 And the LORD said unto Cain, Why art thou wroth? and why is thy countenance fallen?

7 If thou doest well, shalt thou not be accepted? and if thou doest not well, sin lieth at the door: and unto thee shall be his desire, and thou shalt rule over him.

8 And Cain talked with Abel his brother: and it came to pass, when they were in the field, that Cain rose up against Abel his brother, and slew him.

9 And the LORD said unto Cain, Where is Abel thy brother? And he said, I know not: Am I my brother's keeper?

10 And he said, What hast thou done? the voice of thy brother's blood crieth unto me from the ground.

11 And now art thou cursed from the earth, which hath opened her mouth to receive thy brother's blood from thy hand.

12 When thou tillest the ground, it shall not henceforth yield unto thee her strength; a fugitive and a vagabond shalt thou be in the earth.

13 And Cain said unto the LORD, My punishment is greater than I can bear.

14 Behold, thou hast driven me out this day from the face of the earth; and from thy face shall I be hid; and I shall be a fugitive and a vagabond in the earth; and it shall come to pass, that every one that findeth me shall slay me.

15 And the LORD said unto him, Therefore whosoever slayeth Cain, vengeance shall be taken on him sevenfold. And the LORD set a mark upon Cain, lest any finding him should kill him.

16 And Cain went out from the presence of the LORD, and dwelt in the land of Nod, on the east of Eden.

GOLDEN TEXT: If thou doest well, shalt thou not be accepted? and if thou doest not well, sin lieth at the door: and unto thee shall be his desire, and thou shalt rule over him.
—Genesis 4:7.

Lesson Aims

After completing this lesson each student should:

1. Summarize the details surrounding Cain's murder of Abel.

2. Cite examples from modern society or personal experience that demonstrate the destructive consequences of sin.

3. Identify someone to whom he or she is (or will be) accountable in order to minimize the danger of falling prey to sin.

Lesson Outline

INTRODUCTION
    A. Paradise Lost
    B. Lesson Background
 I. CAIN AND ABEL (Genesis 4:1-5a)
    A. Two Sons (vv. 1, 2a)
    B. Two Occupations (v. 2b)
    C. Two Offerings (vv. 3, 4a)
    D. Two Responses (vv. 4b, 5a)
II. CAIN AND GOD (Genesis 4:5b-16)
    A. Cain's Anger (v. 5b)
    B. God's Response (vv. 6, 7)
    C. Cain's Violence (v. 8)
    D. God's Curse (vv. 9-12)
      Like Father, Like Son
    E. Cain's Protest (vv. 13, 14)
    F. God's Protection (vv. 15, 16)
      Murder Mysteries
CONCLUSION
    A. Learning From Cain
    B. Blood That Speaks
    C. Prayer
    D. Thought to Remember

Introduction

A. Paradise Lost

A tiny island dots the western Pacific Ocean just south of the equator between Australia and Hawaii. At one time abundant wildlife, lush foliage, and food-laden trees made the eight-square-mile island of Nauru (Nah-*oo*-roo) a delight for its seven thousand native inhabitants. But then "progress" replaced paradise. Nauru was discovered to be situated on one of the richest stores of phosphate rock on the globe. Millions of tons have been mined during this century, creating vast wealth—and untold misery. Greed and government intervention have combined to turn what was once a dreamland into a nightmare.

Although the island gained its independence in 1968, its new and improved status was quickly followed by the nationalization of the phosphate mines. Wasteful affluence soon manifested itself in many ways, and continues to do so today: thousands of cars, loads of high-tech gadgetry, multiple televisions per family, and the list goes on. The government subsidizes everything—health care, education, housing, and utilities, to name but a few items.

Major problems now exist on Nauru. Changes in diet have destroyed the health of the people. Nine out of ten are obese, and heart disease and diabetes are on the rampage. The average life expectancy is only fifty-five. Government handouts have created a lazy welfare state, and its misuse of earnings from the now nearly depleted mines has left a mortgage on the future that may bankrupt the island in a few years. Much of the once lush terrain now resembles a lunar landscape, and the excess heat from all the exposed rock has even severely lessened the rainfall on the island. For Nauru, paradise has indeed been lost—a victim of greed and folly.

B. Lesson Background

Last week's lesson focused on God's creation of Adam and Eve. Placed in a beautiful garden in Eden, they enjoyed the blessings of their Creator. However, Satan, in serpent form, succeeded in enticing them to eat from the tree of the knowledge of good and evil. He promised them that they would become like God with the knowledge gained from the tree's forbidden fruit. But loss, not gain, was the result of Adam and Eve's transgression. A spiritual separation from God occurred alongside the introduction of the process of physical death into their bodies. They were driven out of the garden (Genesis 3:23, 24). Their wonderful paradise was lost.

Amidst the punishment that God pronounced on the man and woman was a glimmer of hope. Through the promised seed of the woman, Satan would one day taste ultimate defeat. The curse upon man would be removed by a triumphant Redeemer, who would bruise Satan's head (Genesis 3:15).

For the present, however, Adam and Eve would continue to experience the devastation caused by sin. Today's lesson shows how much heartache sin brought to the first family. It will remind us that sin always yields bitter fruit, particularly when it affects a home.

I. Cain and Abel
(Genesis 4:1-5a)

A. Two Sons (vv. 1, 2a)

1, 2a. And Adam knew Eve his wife; and she conceived, and bare Cain, and said, I have gotten a man from the LORD. And she again bare his brother Abel.

The Hebrew word translated *knew* is regularly used in the Old Testament to describe intimate relations between a husband and wife. These relations were ordained prior to the Fall, for on the sixth day God had commanded, "Be fruitful, and multiply, and replenish the earth" (Genesis 1:28). Eve's name means "living" or "life," for she was to be "the mother of all living" (Genesis 3:20). She recognized that being able to conceive and give birth to *Cain* was a result of God's blessing. In contrast, very little information is given regarding Abel's birth.

B. Two Occupations (v. 2b)

2b. And Abel was a keeper of sheep, but Cain was a tiller of the ground.

Whether by necessity or by personal preference, Cain and Abel found themselves in different occupations. Both labors were valuable in providing for their family. Contrary to the picture painted by evolutionists (of man as a primitive being whose intelligence slowly "evolved"), the Bible portrays mankind as being involved from the beginning with advanced tasks such as soil cultivation and animal domestication.

C. Two Offerings (vv. 3, 4a)

3, 4a. And in process of time it came to pass, that Cain brought of the fruit of the ground an offering unto the LORD. And Abel, he also brought of the firstlings of his flock and of the fat thereof.

When and why did the first act of worship occur? Did God command the offerings mentioned here, or were they spontaneous? Had Adam made similar offerings? Were these the first offerings that *Cain* and *Abel* offered? And what was the exact purpose of such offerings: to atone for sins or to accomplish some other purpose? No definite answer can be given to any of these questions, so we must be cautious about whatever conclusions we draw based on our understanding of the offerings.

We should make two observations from our text. First, each man gave from the produce of his individual labors. Cain brought a grain or vegetable *offering*, while Abel brought an animal offering. Second, the phrase *firstlings of his flock* may have some significance. Abel brought from the "firstborn" of his animals—an offering

consistent with laws later given to Israel (Exodus 13:12; 34:19). Cain, however, *brought of the fruit of the ground*. The text does not say that he brought of the "firstfruits"—another practice later commanded of Israel (Exodus 23:16, 19; Nehemiah 10:35). Of course, only at certain times of the year could a farmer bring of the firstfruits, or first results, of his harvest.

D. Two Responses (vv. 4b, 5a)

4b. And the LORD had respect unto Abel and to his offering.

What caused the Lord to have *respect unto* Abel's *offering* but not to Cain's? Usually two answers are suggested. One is that Abel provided a blood sacrifice, presumably according to God's specific command. Cain's was only a grain offering. We later learn that apart from the shedding of blood, there is no remission of sins (Hebrews 9:22). However, we cannot be certain that a sin offering was involved here. The Hebrew word rendered "offering" here and in verse 5 is also used to describe the grain offering in Leviticus 2. [See question #1, page 368.]

A more common understanding is that the heart of the offerer was the key factor distinguishing the two offerings. An offering can be made according to exact specifications and yet be accompanied by an evil heart. The New Testament contrasts Cain and Abel with regard to their righteousness. We learn that Abel offered a "more excellent sacrifice than Cain" and obtained the testimony that he was righteous (Hebrews 11:4). First John 3:12 states that Cain's deeds were evil, while his brother's were righteous. Most likely Abel's act of worship arose from a right relationship with God, thus *the Lord had respect unto Abel and to his offering.*

5a. But unto Cain and to his offering he had not respect.

Cain's angry reaction to God's rejection of his *offering* (verse 5b) provides a clue to the real problem here. Rather than view Cain's offering as a well-intentioned but misguided attempt to approach God, we should see it as symptomatic of a deeper crisis in his spiritual life.

The problem of empty ritual in Israel was frequently addressed by the prophets. They endeavored to drive home the point that merely going

---

How to Say It

BATHSHEBA. Bath-*she*-buh.

ENOS. *Ee*-nuss.

LAMECH. *Lay*-mek.

SEPTUAGINT. Sep-*too*-ih-jent.

through the motions of worship, unaccompanied by genuine devotion to God, is an abomination to the Lord. "To obey is better than sacrifice," Samuel scolded a disobedient Saul (1 Samuel 15:22). "For I desired mercy, and not sacrifice," God chastened Israel through the prophet Hosea (Hosea 6:6). Following his sin with Bathsheba, David realized that multitudes of animal sacrifices would not suffice in restoring his relationship with God: "The sacrifices of God are a broken spirit: a broken and a contrite heart, O God, thou wilt not despise" (Psalm 51:17). See also Isaiah 1:11-20; Jeremiah 7:21-23; Amos 5:21-24; Micah 6:6-8; and Malachi 1:10-14.

Cain's corrupted offering casts a long, dark shadow. His failure is a foretaste of similar experiences in the history of Israel, and is even cited in the New Testament (Jude 11). It is sobering to think that the first acts of worship described in Scripture produced such tragic results. [See question #2, page 368.]

II. Cain and God
(Genesis 4:5b-16)

A. Cain's Anger (v. 5b)

5b. And Cain was very wroth, and his countenance fell.

Rebellion was followed by resentment. In what way God communicated that He was displeased with Cain is not clear, but in the next verse He spoke directly with Cain.

B. God's Response (vv. 6, 7)

6, 7. And the LORD said unto Cain, Why art thou wroth? and why is thy countenance fallen? If thou doest well, shalt thou not be accepted? and if thou doest not well, sin lieth at the door: and unto thee shall be his desire, and thou shalt rule over him.

God reasoned with Cain as He sought to restore him. Could Cain justify his anger? Had God been unclear or unfair in His dealings with

Visual for lesson 3

This visual dramatizes the danger Cain was in, and the danger each of us faces when temptation urges us to sin. Display it as you discuss verse 7.

him? We might categorize this confrontation as the Bible's first recorded counseling session. It is clear that the changes in attitude were Cain's to make. He had a problem; would he face it and deal with it? Sin is depicted as a savage beast, lurking *at the door* to devour Cain. The tense of the Hebrew verb used in the phrase *thou shalt rule over him* can also be rendered, "thou must rule over him." This is perhaps the sense of God's message to Cain: sin desired to overtake Cain, but he could still resist if he would make the effort. He had a choice in the matter. [See question #3, page 368.]

C. Cain's Violence (v. 8)

8. And Cain talked with Abel his brother: and it came to pass, when they were in the field, that Cain rose up against Abel his brother, and slew him.

The Hebrew text literally reads, "And Cain said unto Abel his brother." What is puzzling is that the Hebrew words, "said unto," are normally followed by what was said. Here we have no such statement. To compensate, the *King James Version* renders the statement, *And Cain talked with Abel his brother*, implying a give-and-take conversation. However, several ancient versions, including the Septuagint (the Greek text of the Old Testament), include the expected quotation of Cain's words. Following these, the *New International Version* reads, "Now Cain said to his brother Abel, 'Let's go out to the field.'"

Although a Jewish tradition states that Abel's death was the result of an argument that broke out between the brothers in the field, another view is that an angry, jealous Cain invited Abel to go with him to the field with the intent to kill him once they were there.

D. God's Curse (vv. 9-12)

9. And the LORD said unto Cain, Where is Abel thy brother? And he said, I know not: Am I my brother's keeper?

Having buried his slain brother's body to hide his evil deed, Cain was confronted by God. Cain's question, *Am I my brother's keeper?* is one of the most familiar (and quoted) questions from Scripture. It is also one of the most tragic. It conveys an attitude of contempt and neglect that sadly characterizes many in society today. [See question #4, page 368.]

LIKE FATHER, LIKE SON

Fathers hope their sons will imitate only their good and honorable characteristics and habits. Unfortunately, most sons don't exercise such discretion. They become just like Dad, "warts and all." A father's influence on his offspring exerts itself negatively as well as positively. From his father a son may learn dishonesty as well as integrity, profanity as well as purity, laziness as well as ambition.

Cain apparently developed shortcomings similar to Adam's. When confronted with his own transgression, Adam tried to shift the blame, refusing to accept responsibility for his own actions: "The woman whom thou gavest to be with me, she gave me of the tree, and I did eat" (Genesis 3:12).

When Cain killed Abel and was subsequently confronted with his sin, he tried the same gambit: "Am I my brother's keeper?" He had learned the "art" of dodging responsibility for his personal behavior and choices.

As members of the human race, we are all, in a sense, sons and daughters of Adam. We too have learned to shirk responsibility, to play the "blame game," and to resist repentance and confession of our sins. Christians, however, are "sons of God" (1 John 3:1). When we acknowledge our sin and seek forgiveness, we are promised that Christ will "cleanse us from all unrighteousness" (1 John 1:9).

Let us pursue the holiness of our heavenly Father so that others can readily identify us as His children.   —R. W. B.

10. And he said, What hast thou done? the voice of thy brother's blood crieth unto me from the ground.

God heard a *voice* that no human ear could detect. As David describes so vividly in Psalm 139 (especially vv. 1-12), no one can hide an act or even a thought of the heart from God. The testimony of Abel's *blood* before an all-knowing Judge called for justice and retribution.

11. And now art thou cursed from the earth, which hath opened her mouth to receive thy brother's blood from thy hand.

The Hebrew word rendered *earth* is best translated "ground." The ground, contaminated with Abel's *blood*, would be a source of cursing rather than blessing by not producing a harvest for Cain. This was a particularly painful punishment for Cain, since he was "a tiller of the ground" (v. 2). Cain would not be able to survive by doing what he had become most adept at doing.

12. When thou tillest the ground, it shall not henceforth yield unto thee her strength; a fugitive and a vagabond shalt thou be in the earth.

The word *earth* at the end of this verse is different from that rendered *ground*, and indicates a much larger region or area (or the entire planet). There was no place to which Cain could travel to escape the impact of this curse. He would be forced to wander as *a fugitive and a vagabond* and fend for himself as best he could.

E. Cain's Protest (vv. 13, 14)

13, 14. And Cain said unto the LORD, My punishment is greater than I can bear. Behold, thou hast driven me out this day from the face of the earth; and from thy face shall I be hid; and I shall be a fugitive and a vagabond in the earth; and it shall come to pass, that every one that findeth me shall slay me.

God's punishment did not set well with the volatile and violent disposition of Cain. (Adam, in contrast, offered no protest when God pronounced his punishment.) Cain complained about the severity of his sentence. He seemed to believe that he would be cut off (*hid*) from God's presence and care, but that was not true, as Cain would soon learn. Later God declared that death was the appropriate penalty for murder (Genesis 9:5, 6; Exodus 21:12); thus Cain's punishment was actually less severe than it could have been. [See question #5, page 368.]

Another concern expressed by Cain was the fear that he himself would be slain by an act of vengeance. We should keep in mind that all persons on the earth at this time were members of the same family, although the numbers of cousins, nephews, etc. already could have numbered into the hundreds or even thousands. We do not know how she learned of it, but Eve knew of Cain's deed (v. 25) and we assume that everyone else did as well. Cain's fears may have been well grounded (we know that feuds within families have often escalated, leaving numerous undeserving victims in their wake), but one

Home Daily Bible Readings

Monday, June 14—Sin Is Lurking at the Door (Genesis 4:1-7)

Tuesday, June 15—Cain Murders His Brother Abel (Genesis 4:8-16)

Wednesday, June 16—The Birth of Enoch and Seth (Genesis 4:17-26)

Thursday, June 17—Iniquities Are Barriers Between You and God (Isaiah 59:1-15)

Friday, June 18—Those Who Forsake Transgressions Will Obtain Mercy (Proverbs 28:9-14)

Saturday, June 19—"But I Say Unto You" (Matthew 5:21-26)

Sunday, June 20—Happy Are Those Whose Transgression Is Forgiven (Psalm 32:1-11)

wonders how much he read into other people's thinking the evils of his own heart. If others were like Cain, he was indeed in grave danger.

F. God's Protection (vv. 15, 16)

15. And the LORD said unto him, Therefore whosoever slayeth Cain, vengeance shall be taken on him sevenfold. And the LORD set a mark upon Cain, lest any finding him should kill him.

The term *sevenfold* is probably the use of the number *seven* to express completeness. Full *vengeance* will be *taken* on whoever kills Cain.

Commentators speculate about the meaning of the *mark upon Cain*. The Hebrew preposition translated as *upon* is best rendered as "for" or "for the sake of." The idea is probably not that a mark (literally, "sign") was placed on the body of Cain, but that a sign was given for Cain's sake either to indicate God's displeasure on anyone who would kill him or to warn Cain if someone seeking to take his life was approaching.

16. And Cain went out from the presence of the LORD, and dwelt in the land of Nod, on the east of Eden.

The name *Nod* means "wandering." It was a fitting location since Cain had been sentenced to live as a "wanderer." There Cain established a family line. Six generations, including the godless Lamech, are mentioned (vv. 17-24). However, it was not until Adam and Eve had Seth, and he in turn begat Enos, that men began to "call upon the name of the Lord" (v. 26).

MURDER MYSTERIES

Homicide cases unraveled by Sherlock Holmes, Colombo, Matlock, and others like them provide captivating drama by focusing on the psychological tension created by the presence of unknown details. Missing pieces of information make mysteries mysterious. The more question marks that punctuate the crime, the more convoluted the story line can be. Until the victim, the weapon, and the motive (as well as witnesses) are discovered, readers or viewers can only guess what the outcome will be. Usually, last-minute revelations provide surprise endings where the crime is solved and the perpetrators are brought to justice.

Genesis 4 tells of a murder mystery of sorts. Though we know who the victim and the murderer are, questions remain. Why was Cain's offering to God unacceptable? What weapon was used? What was the "mark upon Cain"? Exactly where was the "land of Nod"?

We can be certain of this: God tells us all we need to know about this tragic incident. He wants us to understand something about the origins and consequences of sin, His justice and punishment for disobedience, His grace and compassion for sinners, and our accountability to Him. We don't have to know any more details to be able to grasp these important concepts. About such truths as these there is no mystery.

—R. W. B.

Conclusion

A. Learning From Cain

Some important truths are evident from our lesson text today. First, God desires a personal relationship with us, not merely outward compliance to His laws. God accepted the sacrifice of Abel because it was offered by a man of faith (Hebrews 11:4). Second, we are reminded of the chaos that sin can produce in our lives. For Cain, God's rejection of his sacrifice drove him to anger, bitterness, and eventually even murder. God challenged Cain to master sin (Genesis 4:7). We also must heed that charge.

Cain's question, "Am I my brother's keeper?" speaks to the issue of accountability. The message of Genesis 4 is clear: we are accountable, both to our fellowman and to the One who created them and us in His image.

B. Blood That Speaks

The blood of Abel cried out from the ground calling for judgment on his murderer Cain. The one who had shed man's blood deserved for his own to be shed, since he had slain that which was made in the very image of God (Genesis 9:6). Abel's blood, therefore, cried out on behalf of justice and legal rights.

The book of Hebrews teaches that the blood of Jesus "speaketh better things than that of Abel" (Hebrews 12:24). The theme "better" is prominent in Hebrews, as the New Covenant through Jesus is shown to be superior to the Old in a variety of ways. Jesus' blood "speaketh better" because it calls, not for vindication and justice, but for mercy and grace.

C. Prayer

Father in Heaven, as Your children may we reflect the glory of Your image to a world blinded by sin's dark shadow. Help us to take sin seriously in our own lives, and to demonstrate Your love and Your grace to those around us who are trapped by sin. In Jesus' precious name we pray. Amen.

D. Thought to Remember

"The sacrifices of God are a broken spirit: a broken and a contrite heart, O God, thou wilt not despise" (Psalm 51:17).

Learning by Doing

This page contains an alternate lesson plan emphasizing learning activities.
Classes desiring such student involvement will find these suggestions helpful.

Learning Goals

As a result of participating in this session, the student will be able to:

1. Summarize the details surrounding Cain's murder of Abel.

2. Cite examples from modern society or personal experience that demonstrate the destructive consequences of sin.

3. Identify someone to whom he or she is (or will be) accountable in order to minimize the danger of falling prey to sin.

Into the Lesson

Ask your students to form small groups of no more than three or four to a group. Then ask each person to think of a time in his life when he had a clear choice between right and wrong and chose to do what he knew was wrong. Ask each person to describe that event to his group, tell why he chose to do wrong, and describe the result. Make this exercise less intimidating by telling the students that the choices they describe need not be examples from their adult lives but may be things they did as children. Break the ice by telling the results of some wrong choice of your own.

When every member of the class has had time to tell his or her story, ask, "Do you think you would have made a different choice if you had felt accountable to someone? Why or why not?" Allow some time for the groups to discuss this among themselves; then note that today's lesson introduces us to, perhaps, the most famous act of disobedience in the Scriptures: Cain's murder of Abel. His oft-quoted "Am I my brother's keeper?" shows he shirked accountability, and suggests the danger of our not being accountable today.

Into the Word

Ask a volunteer to read Genesis 4:1-16. Then distribute a worksheet with the names Cain and Abel at the top, heading two separate columns. Ask the class to use the worksheet to note points of comparison and contrast between Cain and Abel from the first five verses of the text. (Three specific contrasts should be noted in the two occupations, two offerings, and two results.)

Discuss why Abel's offering was accepted and Cain's was not. Use Hebrews 11:4 and the Scripture exposition on pages 363, 364 to help you.

Write the word *temptation* on your chalkboard. Ask, "What is temptation? Is temptation the same as sin? Why or why not?" (Temptation is an enticement to sin. It is not, generally, sin itself—except that sometimes our sin becomes temptation to further sin.)

Read verses 5b-7. Ask, "Is Cain guilty of wrong here, or is he merely being tempted? Explain." (Cain is clearly being tempted, as God's warning that "sin lieth at the door" reveals. His anger, and the reason his offering was rejected are also wrong, however. So he is guilty of sin, but he is being tempted to greater sin.)

Read verses 8-16 and discuss the following questions:

1. What were the results of Cain's sin? (Abel was dead, and Cain became an exile.)

2. Cite some other examples from modern society or personal experience that demonstrate the destructive consequences of sin. (Increasing violence in our society, declining moral standards, broken homes, and many other general consequences might be cited. Each class member may have a story of deception or jealousy or some other sin that caused painful personal consequences. Don't pressure anyone to share, but try to get everyone to reflect on what sin has done in his or her own life in order to see the repugnance of sin.)

Into Life

Point out that most of us find ourselves in the position of Cain at verse 7. Sin is "at the door," either because of our own mistakes or past unfaithfulness or in spite of our innocence. But sin is there, we are being tempted, and we must master it. Discuss some ways we can do that.

One way is by being accountable to another believer. Cain may not have believed himself to be his brother's keeper, but God did not accept that. Mutual accountability between two believers, or in a small close group, is a great help in avoiding sin.

Distribute index cards and ask each student to write the name of someone to whom he or she would be willing to be accountable in order to minimize the danger of falling prey to sin. Challenge the students to seek to initiate accountability relationships with the people whose names they have written. Then close your class session with prayer.

Let's Talk It Over

The questions on this page are designed to encourage review of the lesson Scriptures and to promote discussion of the lesson by the class. The answers provided are only discussion starters. Let your class talk it over from there.

1. Some have alleged God was unfair to Cain. Both he and Abel brought offerings from their own field of endeavor—Abel from his flock and Cain from his harvest—yet God accepted only the blood offering, which Cain was unable to give. How would you respond to such criticism?

We do not know what in particular God found wrong with Cain's offering—if anything. Perhaps God gave clear instructions about what to bring and Cain did not comply. On the other hand, it may have been Cain's attitude instead of the offering itself that was unsatisfactory. If the heart is wrong the offering can never be right. Perhaps Abel gave a spontaneous offering of a firstling lamb to the Lord, and Cain, not to be outdone, tried to imitate his brother's faith without really having any of his own.

We don't know enough details to be specific, so the allegation is unwarranted. The problem was not that Cain could not offer a sheep. The issue was faith. Abel's offering was offered in faith (Hebrews 11:4). Clearly, such faith was absent from Cain's heart.

2. Cain's reaction shows us much about his heart. Rather than accept responsibility and repent, he became angry. Some people still respond that way when their sins are exposed. How do you deal with such people? How can we lovingly lead them to repentance?

This attitude is not one that appears suddenly, and it is not likely to be erased suddenly. It develops over time, when a person has a need to be "right" all the time. He or she has an answer for every criticism. It is much better to *prevent* such an attitude from developing than try to *correct* it. When correction is needed, one will need great patience. Over time, perhaps a demonstration of unconditional love will demonstrate to the person that it's okay to admit to failings. Many, however, will go the way of Cain, who refused the loving urges of God Himself.

3. Cain's offering was rejected, but God's loving counsel with Cain shows that God still loved him. Christians are sometimes accused of hating those they believe guilty of sin (e.g., homosexuals, abortionists, etc.). How can we demonstrate that we truly do *hate the sin* but *love the sinner?*

This goes right to the heart of our mission. We need to imitate Jesus, who spent time with sinners to communicate His love to them in action. We need to avoid name-calling and other practices that make *personal* our protests against the *issues*. We need to remember that these people are not our enemy (Ephesians 6:12). We need to be open and honest and admit that we, too, are sinners, and that we only want to share the hope we have found in Jesus Christ.

4. Cain asked, "Am I my brother's keeper?" What do you think it means to be your brother's—or sister's—keeper? How do you perform such a role?

Cain's flippant question revealed that his heart contained no love for his brother. He does not appear to have been remorseful in the least for his terrible deed. One who is truly his brother's keeper starts with genuine love for his brother. Jesus' parable of the Good Samaritan teaches us that we must have genuine concern and compassion for every person and, as we have opportunity, give concrete expression to that concern by actually helping the needy person. Galatians 6:1 adds a spiritual dimension to being our brothers and sisters' keepers.

Perhaps some in your class can share specific acts done to help a brother or sister in need.

5. God's punishment was severe, but He stopped short of requiring Cain's life as He could justly have done. Nonetheless, Cain complained. Why is it that some people complain even when they are treated with grace? How do you deal with such people?

Cain's complaint clearly shows his unrepentant heart. His only concern was for the suffering he was going to experience, not for the suffering and death he had inflicted. It is always so in the unrepentant; they selfishly look out for themselves and complain at the least provocation. They will not be won by argument, and certainly not by our getting down to their level. We, like God, can only continue to show them grace, and perhaps that will turn them in time to see God's goodness. It takes maturity to respond in such a way, but God wants us to be mature. Perhaps we need to pray for an extra measure of grace to handle such situations.

Judgment and New Beginning

DEVOTIONAL READING: Isaiah 54:8-14.

LESSON SCRIPTURE: Genesis 6:5—9:17.

PRINTED TEXT: Genesis 6:5-8; 7:1-4; 9:12-17.

Genesis 6:5-8

5 And GOD saw that the wickedness of man was great in the earth, and that every imagination of the thoughts of his heart was only evil continually.

6 And it repented the LORD that he had made man on the earth, and it grieved him at his heart.

7 And the LORD said, I will destroy man whom I have created from the face of the earth; both man, and beast, and the creeping thing, and the fowls of the air; for it repenteth me that I have made them.

8 But Noah found grace in the eyes of the LORD.

Genesis 7:1-4

1 And the LORD said unto Noah, Come thou and all thy house into the ark; for thee have I seen righteous before me in this generation.

2 Of every clean beast thou shalt take to thee by sevens, the male and his female: and of beasts that are not clean by two, the male and his female.

3 Of fowls also of the air by sevens, the male and the female; to keep seed alive upon the face of all the earth.

4 For yet seven days, and I will cause it to rain upon the earth forty days and forty nights; and every living substance that I have made will I destroy from off the face of the earth.

Genesis 9:12-17

12 And God said, This is the token of the covenant which I make between me and you, and every living creature that is with you, for perpetual generations:

13 I do set my bow in the cloud, and it shall be for a token of a covenant between me and the earth.

14 And it shall come to pass, when I bring a cloud over the earth, that the bow shall be seen in the cloud:

15 And I will remember my covenant, which is between me and you and every living creature of all flesh; and the waters shall no more become a flood to destroy all flesh.

16 And the bow shall be in the cloud; and I will look upon it, that I may remember the everlasting covenant between God and every living creature of all flesh that is upon the earth.

17 And God said unto Noah, This is the token of the covenant, which I have established between me and all flesh that is upon the earth.

GOLDEN TEXT: I will remember my covenant, which is between me and you and every living creature of all flesh; and the waters shall no more become a flood to destroy all flesh.—Genesis 9:15.

Genesis: Beginnings
Unit 1: In the Beginning
(Lessons 1-4)

Lesson Aims

As a result of completing this lesson, the student will:

1. Explain the reason for the great flood, and how God dealt with faithful Noah.

2. Compare the need for a cleansing of the earth in Noah's day with the growing need for cleansing of the earth today.

3. Make a commitment to be ready for the Lord's return and to share in His deliverance from the final cleansing.

Lesson Outline

INTRODUCTION
    A. Sons of God?
    B. Lesson Background
 I. NEED FOR JUDGMENT (Genesis 6:5-8)
    A. Man's Wickedness (v. 5)
      What's on Your Mind?
    B. God's Grief (v. 6)
    C. God's Solution (v. 7)
    D. An Exception (v. 8)
 II. DELIVERANCE FROM JUDGMENT (Genesis 7:1-4)
    A. Provision of an Ark (v. 1)
    B. Provision for a Future (vv. 2, 3)
    C. Provision for Cleansing (v. 4)
III. AFTERMATH OF JUDGMENT (Genesis 9:12-17)
    A. A Sign Given (vv. 12-14)
      God's Bow in the Cloud
    B. A Sign Explained (vv. 15-17)
CONCLUSION
    A. Preacher of Righteousness
    B. Scoffers Be Warned
    C. Prayer
    D. Thought to Remember

Introduction

A. Sons of God?

The introductory verses of Genesis 6 demonstrate that bearing the "image of God" as a result of creation and bearing a resemblance to God in character and deed are two completely different matters. In these verses we are introduced to three groups, the identity of whom remains a matter of considerable discussion: the sons of God, the daughters of men, and the giants in the earth. These giants may be linked to a later group of giants, the sons of Anak, whom the spies who examined the land of Canaan saw (Numbers 13:33). There is also a possible connection to the family of Goliath of Gath (Joshua 11:22; 1 Samuel 17:4). The Hebrew name seems to mean "fallen/falling ones."

Three main proposals have been given for understanding who the "sons of God" and the "daughters of men" were: (1) fallen angels who intermarried with human women; (2) human rulers who began to multiply harems of wives for themselves; and (3) the godly line of Seth that began to commingle with the more wicked descendants of Cain. The least likely alternative would seem to be the first view mentioned, since Jesus taught that angels "neither marry, nor are given in marriage" (Matthew 22:30).

The third view, while it may possess its own difficulties, appears the most acceptable interpretation. That the line of Seth was a godly line seems to be indicated by the last verse in Luke's genealogy of Jesus, which traces Jesus' line back to the beginning: "the son of Enos, which was the son of Seth, which was the son of Adam, which was the son of God" (Luke 3:38).

What we must keep in mind is that bearing the image of God requires more than membership in the human race. In our lesson today, a righteous God faces the tragic task of having to pronounce judgment on a people made in His image, but who no longer reflected that image.

B. Lesson Background

How much time elapsed from the time of creation to the flood of Noah's day? The answer cannot be known for certain. If we assume that there are no gaps in the lengthy genealogy found in Genesis 5, then 1565 years passed.

Many Bible students, however, believe that such gaps probably do exist. Other genealogies in the Bible exhibit gaps, some of them rather significant. Perhaps the most obvious instance is the genealogy of Jesus in Matthew 1. That listing moves from King Jehoram to King Uzziah (v. 8), omitting Uzziah's father, grandfather, and great-grandfather. This does not mean that the Bible is in error or that the Biblical writers were careless in recording such matters. It was not always their purpose to give complete lists of names, but to call attention to prominent individuals within a genealogy.

If the genealogies of Genesis 5 and 11 are complete, several interesting situations emerge. For example, when Abraham turned fifty, Noah was still alive, while Noah's son Shem actually outlived Abraham! (To some, this appears unlikely.) In addition Methuselah, the man with the longest life recorded in Scripture (969 years), died in Noah's six hundredth year, the year of the flood (Genesis 7:11). This could be mere coincidence, but it does raise the question of whether or not Methuselah was one of those swept away by the flood. The spiritual status of Methuselah is not discussed in the Bible.

On the other hand, the spiritual status of Methuselah's grandson Noah is one of the key themes in the early chapters of Genesis. His righteous life shone brightly against the dark background of his wicked generation. Our lesson today examines the monumental events that transpired during his lifetime.

I. Need for Judgment (Genesis 6:5-8)

A. Man's Wickedness (v. 5)

5. And GOD saw that the wickedness of man was great in the earth, and that every imagination of the thoughts of his heart was only evil continually.

As the *wickedness* of Adam and Eve's descendants grew greater and greater, the patience of God reached its limits. *And God saw . . . .* The same God who had observed the first sin in the garden and then the murderous deed of Cain was also now keenly aware of the woeful conditions on the *earth* in Noah's day. Not only were the actions of wicked man known to Him, but also *every imagination of the thoughts of his heart.* [See question #1, page 376.]

WHAT'S ON YOUR MIND?

I recently revisited the Christian camp where I began my church camping experience at age nine. It was nostalgic to see the old buildings, the lake, the vespers site, and other familiar facilities. When I saw the boys' dorm, I remembered how much fun we had lying on our cots at night, thinking up pranks to torment the guys on the other side of the lockers. They, of course, were brainstorming how they would retaliate. Everything from pop-bottle caps to dirty socks to bars of soap were thrown over those lockers before the week was out.

Our imaginations were clearly active in those days, but generally not mean-spirited. In the days of Noah, however, most people were lying awake nights thinking of the evil that they had done, that they were doing, or that they planned to do. It certainly was no church camp! Those people were vile and wicked; they were unrepentant sinners, giving themselves totally to devising ever-new ways to transgress God's will. God was sorry He had created mankind—so sorry, in fact, that He decided to destroy His handiwork, including both man and beast.

What's been on your mind lately? Do your imaginations satisfy or sadden your Maker? "Whatsoever things are true, . . . honest, . . . just, . . . pure, . . . lovely, . . . of good report; if there be any virtue, and if there be any praise, think on these things" (Philippians 4:8).   —R. W. B.

B. God's Grief (v. 6)

6. And it repented the LORD that he had made man on the earth, and it grieved him at his heart.

The phrase *repented the Lord* seems to suggest that God did something wrong for which He needed to repent. The Hebrew verb translated *repented* simply means "to have sorrow, be sorry." God's regret was not for His own gracious actions, but for the way *man* had responded to those actions with rebellion and wickedness. God was *grieved* that the creature made in His image was acting so contrary to His purposes.

C. God's Solution (v. 7)

7. And the LORD said, I will destroy man whom I have created from the face of the earth; both man, and beast, and the creeping thing, and the fowls of the air; for it repenteth me that I have made them.

The Hebrew word translated *destroy* means "to wipe." It pictures someone taking a dish and wiping it clean with a rag. The same word is used in 2 Kings 21:13 to describe God's judgment on rebellious Jerusalem. Here in Genesis 6, the scope of God's judgment is stressed by listing all air-breathing forms of life created on days five and six (Genesis 1:20-31). Note that they are listed in the opposite order of that in which they were created—*man*, the land animal (*beast*), the *creeping thing*, and the *fowls of the air*. Most likely man is mentioned first because he is the creature primarily responsible for the earth's sorry condition.

Elsewhere in Scripture animals are described as suffering the consequences of man's sins (Joshua 7:24, 25). Apparently the animal world is considered to be creatures living under man's corrupted dominion; thus they share in his judgment. Note that in the book of Jonah, even the livestock of Nineveh participated in the fast of repentance and were donned with sackcloth (Jonah 3:5-8)! [See question #2, page 376.]

D. An Exception (v. 8)

8. But Noah found grace in the eyes of the LORD.

The name *Noah* means "rest, relief, comfort." His name was appropriate, given the relief he provided from a strife-torn world filled with men consumed by evil. Note how he fulfilled the words spoken at his birth, when his father declared, "This same shall comfort us concerning our work and toil of our hands, because of the ground which the Lord hath cursed" (Genesis 5:29). Noah is described as "a just man and perfect in his generations," and is said to have "walked with God" as did Enoch earlier (Genesis 6:9; 5:24). The word *grace* or "favor" is used frequently in the Old Testament to describe God's compassion and mercy toward man.

II. Deliverance From Judgment (Genesis 7:1-4)

A. Provision of an Ark (v. 1)

1. And the LORD said unto Noah, Come thou and all thy house into the ark; for thee have I seen righteous before me in this generation.

Interestingly, the only other portion of the Bible where the Hebrew word translated *ark* is found is in Exodus 2:3, 5, in reference to the "basket" that held the baby Moses as it floated among the bulrushes of the Nile River. The dimensions of Noah's boat made it an enormous vessel: 300 cubits long, 50 cubits across, and 30 cubits high (Genesis 6:15). A cubit generally measured a foot and a half, so we should envision a vessel some 450 feet long, 75 feet across, and 45 feet high.

The phrase *thou and all thy house* included Noah, his three sons (Shem, Ham, and Japheth), and their wives. These eight individuals entered the ark and therein found deliverance. Although only Noah's righteousness is mentioned, we may infer that this quality was present in the lives of his family as well. Perhaps they aided him in the massive undertaking of the construction of the ark. Others may have assisted as well, although apparently none heeded Noah's warnings (1 Peter 3:20; 2 Peter 2:5).

B. Provision for a Future (vv. 2, 3)

2. Of every clean beast thou shalt take to thee by sevens, the male and his female: and of beasts that are not clean by two, the male and his female.

A distinction was made regarding the animals that Noah was to gather into the ark. Although some commentators have interpreted the terminology *by sevens* to mean "seven each" (three pairs and an extra to be later sacrificed), it would seem best to understand that Noah was to set apart fourteen of each kind of *clean* animal—seven male-female pairs.

Leviticus 11 provides a lengthy explanation of clean and unclean animals as part of the regulations found in the law of Moses. No such analysis is given here, but a revelation of God's guidelines must have been made known to Noah. It is presumed that only the clean animals would be desirable for sacrifices (Genesis 8:20) and for food (9:3). This would explain why more of them were taken aboard the ark.

3. Of fowls also of the air by sevens, the male and the female; to keep seed alive upon the face of all the earth.

Noah was also to gather seven pairs of every kind of bird. The reason given was *to keep seed alive upon the face of all the earth*. The word *seed* can be translated "descendants" or "posterity."

C. Provision for Cleansing (v. 4)

4. For yet seven days, and I will cause it to rain upon the earth forty days and forty nights; and every living substance that I have made will I destroy from off the face of the earth.

Noah and his family boarded the ark *seven* full days before the *rain* came. We can imagine that such a circumstance itself would have been a test of faith. How many mockers came by and laughed? What were the feelings of the tiny crew as they fed huge numbers of livestock sitting in dry dock, waiting for the promised deluge? Some people believe the condition described in Genesis 2:5, in which the earth was watered by a mist going up from the earth, continued until the time of the flood. If so, then it had never rained at all on the earth when Noah's family entered the ark. That really would have stretched their faith! [See question #3, page 376.]

The time span of *forty days and forty nights* occurs elsewhere in Scripture in connection with certain occasions, which, like the flood, carried great spiritual significance. Examples are found in Exodus 24:18; 1 Kings 19:8; Jonah 3:4; Matthew 4:2; and Acts 1:3.

The word translated *earth* here is the word for "ground" or "soil." Those who argue against a worldwide flood and in favor of a localized one believe that this term is worth noting. However, the idea of a universal flood is suggested from other passages, such as Genesis 6:17: "I, even I, do bring a flood of waters upon the earth, to destroy all flesh, wherein is the breath of life, from under heaven; and every thing that is in the earth shall die." The word *earth* in this verse does indicate the entire planet. In addition, if the flood were localized, God's promise never to destroy the earth again by a flood (Genesis 9:11) would have been broken many times since Noah's day; for many destructive localized floods have occurred since then.

III. Aftermath of Judgment (Genesis 9:12-17)

At this point the flood has already taken place. God's righteous judgment has been administered. Following the departure of Noah and his family from the ark, God establishes His covenant with them.

A. A Sign Given (vv. 12-14)

12. And God said, This is the token of the covenant which I make between me and you, and every living creature that is with you, for perpetual generations.

God's *covenant* or promise included His assurance that He would never again destroy the earth as He had in Noah's day (8:21, 22; 9:11, 15; Isaiah 54:9). This promise was directed toward Noah and his sons (v. 8); the *you* in the verse before us is plural. The covenant was unlimited regarding subjects (*every living creature*) and duration (*for perpetual generations*).

13, 14. I do set my bow in the cloud, and it shall be for a token of a covenant between me and the earth. And it shall come to pass, when I bring a cloud over the earth, that the bow shall be seen in the cloud.

A rainbow was to serve as the pledge or symbol of God's covenant with Noah and his descendants. The Hebrew term translated *bow* generally refers to a weapon for hunting or warfare. Genesis 9 (vv. 13, 14, 16) and Ezekiel 1:28 are the only places in the Old Testament where the word describes a rainbow. The symbolism of God's act may lie in the fact that He was laying aside His weapon of destruction in keeping with the promise of the next verse.

Was this the first occurrence of a rainbow in the clouds? The importance attached to its appearance indicates that this was the case. If Noah's flood represented the first rain ever experienced, then this was indeed the first time such a visual effect in the sky was present. [See question #4, page 376.]

GOD'S BOW IN THE CLOUD

Is there any phenomenon in nature more beautiful than a rainbow? Especially fascinating are the so-called "double" rainbows. I've seen only two of those in my life. The first one was so breathtaking, I pulled my car off an interstate highway to the shoulder so we could safely look at the wonder with full attention.

The second double rainbow I saw appeared not long ago. There was no rain or mist in the air where I was, but apparently, moisture higher in the atmosphere diffracted light rays into two splendid spectra of color, ringing the sun. It was a truly spectacular sight.

That rainbows are singularly wonderful is no surprise. The Maker and His promises are wonderful, too. God's covenant with Noah and with all mankind was that the earth would never be destroyed by a flood again. There are many other promises in the Bible given to those who, like Noah, find "grace in the eyes of the Lord."

Imagine how thrilling it must have been for Noah and his family to have witnessed the splendor of the first rainbow. Rainbows are still the eye-pleasing reminder of God's "exceeding great and precious promises" (2 Peter 1:4). —R. W. B.

B. A Sign Explained (vv. 15-17)

15. And I will remember my covenant, which is between me and you and every living creature of all flesh; and the waters shall no more become a flood to destroy all flesh.

And I will remember my covenant. The promises of God are sure. As Moses reminded Israel, "Know therefore that the Lord thy God, he is God, the faithful God, which keepeth covenant and mercy with them that love him and keep his commandments to a thousand generations" (Deuteronomy 7:9).

I will remember my covenant between me and you and living creatures of every kind. Never again will the waters become a flood to destroy all life. Genesis 9:15, KJV

This cheery-looking visual is a reminder of God's promise, which He sealed with the rainbow.

Visual for lesson 4

As noted earlier, the wording of God's promise in this verse would be weakened by any view that the flood affected only a limited region. The expressions *every living creature of all flesh* and *a flood to destroy all flesh* point to a catastrophe of worldwide scope.

16, 17. And the bow shall be in the cloud; and I will look upon it, that I may remember the everlasting covenant between God and every living creature of all flesh that is upon the earth. And God said unto Noah, This is the token of the covenant, which I have established between me and all flesh that is upon the earth.

A new phase in God's dealings with mankind had begun, yet God knew that man's heart had not really changed. Hear His words from Genesis 8:21: "I will not again curse the ground any more for man's sake; for the imagination of man's heart is evil from his youth." Accompanying God's command for man to be fruitful and multiply (9:7) was the stern warning that "whoso sheddeth man's blood, by man shall his blood be shed" (9:6). God was still concerned with justice, but He would never again use a flood to administer justice. [See question #5, page 376.]

Conclusion

A. Preacher of Righteousness

Not only was Noah a portrayer of righteousness through his obedient conduct, but he was also, according to 2 Peter 2:5, a "preacher of righteousness." Thus Noah's testimony was communicated by both example and exhortation. No doubt the curiosity aroused by Noah's shipbuilding activities gave him numerous opportunities to proclaim God's message of coming judgment.

Not only was Noah the first "preacher" according to the Bible, but he was also the first to experience rejection by his audience. Of course,

in this he is not alone. He is joined by a host of "failures" in the Old Testament alone: Moses, Elijah, Isaiah, Jeremiah, Ezekiel, Amos—the list could go on of men who faithfully proclaimed the truth of God regardless of popular sentiment and opinion. Today's generation also has its host of faithful heralds of God's divine revelation. For them we should be thankful, because the needs of our time are as great as they were in Noah's. His generation was "corrupt in the sight of God" and "filled with violence" (Genesis 6:11, *New American Standard Bible*). So is ours. Noah had a message of deliverance to proclaim to the people of his day. So do we.

B. Scoffers Be Warned

As a precursor of the second coming of Christ, the flood offers a grim warning for those willing to heed it. Peter describes men in his day who sound a lot like a host of individuals in our present day. They are called "scoffers" (2 Peter 3:3), or mockers, who denied the supernatural, especially the fulfillment of the promise that God would bring this world to an end. "Where is the promise of His coming?" they jeered.

But Peter reminded the scoffers that there was once a great interruption to the regular course of things—a catastrophic event that destroyed the world of Noah's day (v. 6). Fire, not water, will be God's future instrument of devastation (v. 10). In the same way that God's patience delayed the sending of the flood waters in Noah's day, so today God's patience allows others the opportunity to "come to repentance" (v. 9). His schedule is controlled by an eternal perspective—"one day is with the Lord as a thousand years, and a thousand years as one day" (v. 8). And yet that day will at last arrive and judgment will be rendered. In light of this fact, Peter asks us, "What sort of people ought you to be in holy conduct and godliness?" (v. 11, *New American Standard Bible*).

C. Prayer

Father in Heaven, Judge of the living and the dead, we pray that we may lead lives that honor You in righteousness and obedience to Your will. Help us to be beacons of Your light in our own age of spiritual darkness. Amen.

D. Thought to Remember

"As the days of Noah were, so shall also the coming of the Son of man be. For as . . . they were eating and drinking, marrying and giving in marriage, until the day that Noah entered into the ark, and knew not until the flood came, and took them all away; so shall also the coming of the Son of man be" (Matthew 24:37-39).

How to Say It

ANAK. *Ay*-nak.

ELIJAH. Ee-*lye*-juh.

ENOCH. *Ee*-nock.

ENOS. *Ee*-nuss.

EZEKIEL. Ee-*zeek*-yul or Ee-*zeek*-ee-ul.

ISAIAH. Eye-*zay*-uh.

JAPHETH. *Jay*-feth.

JEHORAM. Jeh-*ho*-rum.

JEREMIAH. Jair-uh-*my*-uh.

METHUSELAH. Muh-*thoo*-suh-luh.

NINEVEH. *Nin*-uh-vuh.

UZZIAH. Uh-*zye*-uh.

Learning by Doing

This page contains an alternate lesson plan emphasizing learning activities.
Classes desiring such student involvement will find these suggestions helpful.

Learning Goals

As a result of participating in this session, the student will be able to:

1. Explain the reason for the great flood, and how God dealt with faithful Noah.

2. Compare the need for a cleansing of the earth in Noah's day with the growing need for cleansing of the earth today.

3. Make a commitment to be ready for the Lord's return and to share in His deliverance from the final cleansing.

Into the Lesson

As you prepare for today's lesson, watch for news items (from a magazine or newspaper) that would illustrate both the good and the bad in mankind. If your students generally sit at tables in small groups, place one news item in each group before class begins. As you begin the lesson, ask each group to summarize its article and give an opinion as to whether the activity reported in the story is more or less typical of human behavior.

Another possibility for getting into this lesson is to set up a debate among several class members as to whether our society demonstrates more good deeds than bad behavior. This activity should be arranged far enough in advance that those taking each side in the debate will have enough time to prepare.

Make the transition into the Bible study time by pointing out that regardless of how bad we think things may be now, there was a time in history when mankind was characterized by so much evil that God decided that he should wipe out creation and begin again with a small faithful remnant.

Into the Word

Divide the class into three groups. Ask one group to read Genesis 6:1-8, a second group to read Genesis 7:1-10, and the third to read Genesis 9:8-17. Ask each group to write ten questions that can be answered by its assigned text. Have each group select one member to be its "quizmaster." This person will ask the other groups the questions the group has written.

After about eight or ten minutes, ask the quizmaster for group 1 to stand and ask group 2 the first question from his or her list. If group 2 answers correctly, score one point for them and direct the quizmaster to ask group 3 the next question. If group 2 misses the question, group 3 gets a chance. The next question goes first to group 3 either way. Have quizmaster 1 continue alternating between groups 2 and 3 until all group 1's questions have been asked and answered. Have a volunteer read Genesis 6:1-8 aloud; then review the material to make sure everyone understands this section of Scripture before proceeding.

Next have quizmaster 2 stand and ask questions alternately of groups 1 and 3, scoring as before. Read and review the section as before, and then have quizmaster 3 stand and ask questions of groups 1 and 2. Read and review the section; then tally the scores and announce the winning group. If there is a tie, ask questions to the tying groups until you can crown a winner— or just declare a tie. If you want to award small prizes to the members of the winning group, be sure you have enough for everyone in case all the groups tie.

Into Life

Ask the class, "Which generation do you think was or is worse, Noah's or our own?" Discuss the similarities between the two. Does the fact that God sent the flood indicate that Noah's generation must have been worse, or does the fact that the next judgment is final suggest God is even more patient with our generation than with Noah's?

Point out that Noah and the flood are mentioned several times in the New Testament. Have a volunteer look up and read each of these Scriptures: Matthew 24:36-39; Hebrews 11:7; 1 Peter 3:17-22; 2 Peter 2:4, 5, 9. After each text is read, ask, "What do we learn from Noah's example in this text that helps us follow the Lord today?"

One of the most important lessons we can learn is that judgment is coming when the Lord returns, and we need to be ready for that great event. Close with a prayer circle, asking any who wish to participate to pray for your church, your community, your nation, and the world at large about the need to repent and to be right with God when the Lord returns. Also ask each one to pray, whether aloud or silently as others pray, and make a commitment to be personally ready for the Lord's return and to share in His deliverance from condemnation at the final judgment.

Let's Talk It Over

The questions on this page are designed to encourage review of the lesson Scriptures and to promote discussion of the lesson by the class. The answers provided are only discussion starters. Let your class talk it over from there.

1. Except for Noah and his family, the people of Noah's day were in open rebellion against God. They were so alienated from God that they thought only about doing evil. Compare the people of that day with people of today. What do you think God will do about the condition of the world of our day? What do you think the church should do about it?

We have ample cause to be concerned about the condition of our world. Homosexuality, violence, drunkenness and drug use, immorality, corruption, and abortion are just a few of the evils rampant in our society. Many Christians believe the judgment of God cannot tarry long under these conditions. Yet millions today still stand for God and righteousness, and perhaps it is their presence that holds off God's judgment. The church through the ages has stood for God's truth and God's will. We must continue to take that stand. Discuss specific actions the church or individual Christians might take to address the issues that are of greatest concern to your class.

2. From the great flood we learn that God has great, but not unlimited, mercy. We learn He is the righteous Judge of all. And we see beyond the shadow of a doubt that God has incredible power both to execute His judgment on sinners and to save the righteous. What warnings do you see in the flood that apply to people today? How might we communicate those warnings?

The flood is a warning to all mankind that God holds us accountable for our actions and that He can and will bring judgment on us. It warns us that none can withstand Him or escape from His judgment. The church must broadcast these warnings, and it must tell that God has planned a way of deliverance from His judgment through Jesus Christ. In an age of rapidly changing technology, our methods of communicating these warnings may be changing continually, and many good ideas may surface in your discussion. Follow up on as many of the better ones as you can.

3. Noah and his family entered the ark seven days before the rain started. With or without hecklers outside, the wait must have been a strong test of their faith. What tests your faith today? What helps you to persevere, even as Noah and his family held fast to their faith even when no rain fell for seven days?

Waiting is always hard. We like to see instant results, and not getting them can be disappointing. Noah had the word of God that the flood would begin in seven days after he entered the ark. Thus, even after six days of waiting, Noah could not say God had not done what He had promised—His word was still true. If we will focus on what God has actually said and not on what we want or expect, we will also find that God's word is true. That should bolster our faith.

4. God said the rainbow was the token of His covenant with the earth. How can we maintain this purpose of the rainbow today? Does knowing the scientific explanation for how the rainbow appears lessen this value in any way? Why or why not?

The psalmist said, "The heavens declare the glory of God; and the firmament showeth his handiwork" (Psalm 19:1). Everything the Lord has created affirms for the believer the awesome power of God. Knowing something of the processes He has used in creation does not diminish this. In fact, the study of science began as an attempt of believers to observe God's work in detail. It has been only in recent times that science and faith have been in conflict. Parents should teach their children at an early age to appreciate the lessons nature can teach us about God. When a rainbow appears, children—and adults, too—need to be reminded of God's promise in Genesis 9. Perhaps that can lead to a time of rehearsing other promises of God and thanking Him for them.

5. In the midst of such great destruction, God preserved the righteous Noah and his family. What encouragement does that give to you? Why?

Christians face trouble and difficulty, even persecution, so we should not get the idea that God will always protect us physically from danger. Many have died for their faith. But God's treatment of Noah should encourage us to know that God will ultimately deliver us. Peter used Noah as an example both of God's judgment on the wicked and of His deliverance of the righteous (2 Peter 2:4-10).

God's Call to Abram

DEVOTIONAL READING: Hebrews 11:8-12.

LESSON SCRIPTURE: Genesis 11:27—12:9.

PRINTED TEXT: Genesis 11:31—12:9.

Genesis 11:31, 32

31 And Terah took Abram his son, and Lot the son of Haran his son's son, and Sarai his daughter-in-law, his son Abram's wife; and they went forth with them from Ur of the Chaldees, to go into the land of Canaan; and they came unto Haran, and dwelt there.

32 And the days of Terah were two hundred and five years: and Terah died in Haran.

Genesis 12:1-9

1 Now the LORD had said unto Abram, Get thee out of thy country, and from thy kindred, and from thy father's house, unto a land that I will show thee:

2 And I will make of thee a great nation, and I will bless thee, and make thy name great; and thou shalt be a blessing:

3 And I will bless them that bless thee, and curse him that curseth thee: and in thee shall all families of the earth be blessed.

4 So Abram departed, as the LORD had spoken unto him; and Lot went with him: and Abram was seventy and five years old when he departed out of Haran.

5 And Abram took Sarai his wife, and Lot his brother's son, and all their substance that they had gathered, and the souls that they had gotten in Haran; and they went forth to go into the land of Canaan; and into the land of Canaan they came.

6 And Abram passed through the land unto the place of Sichem, unto the plain of Moreh. And the Canaanite was then in the land.

7 And the LORD appeared unto Abram, and said, Unto thy seed will I give this land: and there builded he an altar unto the LORD, who appeared unto him.

8 And he removed from thence unto a mountain on the east of Bethel, and pitched his tent, having Bethel on the west, and Hai on the east: and there he builded an altar unto the LORD, and called upon the name of the LORD.

9 And Abram journeyed, going on still toward the south.

GOLDEN TEXT: Now the LORD had said unto Abram, Get thee out of thy country, and from thy kindred, and from thy father's house, unto a land that I will show thee: and I will make of thee a great nation, and I will bless thee, and make thy name great; and thou shalt be a blessing.—Genesis 12:1, 2.

Lesson Aims

After this lesson students will be able to:

1. Recount the details of God's call to Abram and the promises God made to him.

2. Compare Abram's decision to leave his homeland in answer to God's call with the decisions that followers of Jesus are challenged to make today.

3. Embark on an adventure of faith by "breaking new ground" in one area of their Christian living.

Lesson Outline

INTRODUCTION
  A. Blind Faith
  B. Lesson Background
 I. FROM UR TO HARAN (Genesis 11:31, 32)
  A. Terah's Journey (v. 31)
  B. Terah's Death (v. 32)
 II. FROM HARAN TO CANAAN (Genesis 12:1-5)
  A. God's Call (v. 1)
   Destination Unknown
  B. God's Promises (vv. 2, 3)
   Leaving a Legacy
  C. Abram's Obedience (vv. 4, 5)
III. INTO THE PROMISED LAND (Genesis 12:6-9)
  A. Abram's Travels (v. 6)
  B. God's Promise (v. 7)
  C. Abram's Worship (vv. 8, 9)
CONCLUSION
  A. Mission Impossible
  B. Prayer
  C. Thought to Remember

Introduction

A. Blind Faith

An artist and a poet once examined a painting representing Jesus' healing of the two blind men of Jericho. The poet asked, "What seems to you the most remarkable thing in this painting?"

"Everything in the painting is excellently done," replied the artist. "The form of Christ, the grouping of the individuals, the expressions in the faces of the characters—all these are marvelously executed."

But the poet found the most significant touch elsewhere in the picture. Pointing to the steps of a house in the corner of the picture, he said to his friend, "Do you see that discarded cane lying there?"

"Yes, but what does that signify?"

"Why, my friend, on those steps one of the blind men sat with the cane in his hand, but when he heard that Jesus was coming, he was so sure that he would be healed that he left his cane there. He knew he would no longer need it, and hastened to the Lord as if he could already see."

Such was the faith of Abram. His faith in God was much more than just an acknowledgment that God exists. It was so powerful that he left comfort and safety behind as he journeyed from Ur to Haran to Canaan to answer God's call.

B. Lesson Background

The first four lessons in our study of Genesis this quarter were taken from the first eleven chapters of the book. These chapters, as we have seen, deal first with events surrounding the creation of the heavens and the earth and the creation and fall of man. They lay the groundwork for God's later dealings with mankind as He worked to offset the effects of the fall and the curse that resulted from man's disobedience in the garden.

The close of chapter 11 marks the introduction of the family of Abram, through whom God planned to send the Messiah as the one who would bruise the serpent's head (Genesis 3:15). It is difficult to date Abram (or Abraham, as he later came to be called) precisely. The most likely time of his birth was somewhere in the middle of the twenty-second century before Christ. (See the "Chronology of Genesis," p. 342.) The details of his life and times, according to the book of Genesis, reflect practices found among ancient Near Eastern peoples of that period.

The name Abram means "exalted father"; later God changed his name to Abraham, which means "father of a multitude," in reference to the great number of descendants that He promised to Abram (Genesis 17:5). Abram is introduced to us as the son of Terah, who lived in "Ur of the Chaldees" (Genesis 11:31). Scholars disagree about the location of Ur. Some place it in northern Mesopotamia near the city of Haran. However, the work of the British archaeologist Sir Leonard Woolley, between 1922 and 1934, provided strong evidence that ancient Ur was located in southern Mesopotamia. In its prime, Ur was a large, thriving city that provided a comfortable lifestyle for its inhabitants. It was also a city in which many gods were worshiped, with the worship of the moon god most prominent.

I. From Ur to Haran
(Genesis 11:31, 32)

A. Terah's Journey (v. 31)

31. And Terah took Abram his son, and Lot the son of Haran his son's son, and Sarai his daughter-in-law, his son Abram's wife; and they went forth with them from Ur of the Chaldees, to go into the land of Canaan; and they came unto Haran, and dwelt there.

Terah had three sons: *Abram*, Nahor, and Haran (Genesis 11:27). *Haran* died while the family was still in Ur (v. 28). Apparently Nahor chose to remain in Ur when Terah and other members of the family moved to *Haran*. (The Hebrew words for *Haran* the person and *Haran* the place have a slightly different spelling that does not come through in English.) Haran was located in northwestern Mesopotamia on a tributary of the Euphrates River and on a major trade route that led from Assyria to Syria and Palestine. Since Haran is more than six hundred miles from Ur, moving family and possessions as well as large flocks and herds from Ur to Haran must have been a slow and demanding trip. Later, members of Nahor's family also moved to that area. They were living there when Abraham sent his servant to find a wife for Isaac (Genesis 24:10, 15) and when Jacob fled there for refuge (28:2).

We are not told why Terah decided to move to Haran. However, we do know that God appeared to Abram while he was still in Ur, telling him to leave Ur and begin a quest for a land that God would eventually show him (Acts 7:2, 3). Perhaps Abram convinced his father to come with him on this move. Accompanying Abram and Terah were not only *Sarai*, Abram's wife, but also *Lot*, Terah's grandson and a nephew to Abram.

B. Terah's Death (v. 32)

32. And the days of Terah were two hundred and five years: and Terah died in Haran.

This verse raises a chronological question. Genesis 11:26 seems to say that Terah was seventy years old when Abram was born, which would have made Abram one hundred thirty-five years old when his father died. Yet Genesis 12:4 states that Abram was seventy-five when he left Haran (that he left Haran after his father's death is clear from Acts 7:4). The best solution to the problem is to say that Abram was not the son who was born when Terah was seventy. The order of "Abram, Nahor, and Haran" that appears in Genesis 11:26 does not reflect birth order, then, but Abram's prominence in the account that follows.

Visual for lesson 5

Today's visual is a map that traces Abram's trek from Ur to Haran to Canaan. Use the map throughout the quarter to locate important sites.

II. From Haran to Canaan
(Genesis 12:1-5)

A. God's Call (v. 1)

1. Now the LORD had said unto Abram, Get thee out of thy country, and from thy kindred, and from thy father's house, unto a land that I will show thee.

We do not know what method God used to reveal Himself to *Abram*. It may have been through an audible voice, in a dream, or in a vision. But regardless of the method, Abram had no doubt that it was God who spoke to him, nor did he have any problem understanding what God wanted him to do. The message was simple: Go!

Answering God's call demanded great faith on Abram's part. First, he had to leave his *father's house*. In addition he had no road map to guide him to his destination. All God told him was that he was to go to *a land that I will show thee*. Yet Abram was equal to the challenge. The New Testament tells us, "By faith Abraham, when he was called to go out into a place which he should after receive for an inheritance, obeyed; and he went out, not knowing whither he went" (Hebrews 11:8). [See question #1, page 384.]

Some students wonder whether this call came to Abram in Ur (his original home) or in Haran (where Terah's caravan had stopped). The context of this verse seems to indicate that it took place in Haran, since this is where the group had stopped (v. 31) and from which they continued their journey according to 12:4, 5. That a previous call in Ur had occurred is clear from Genesis 15:7 and from Stephen's statement in Acts 7:2-4. Most likely the call issued to Abram in Ur was repeated in Haran, which is why our text reads, *Now the Lord had said unto Abram*.

DESTINATION UNKNOWN

My youngest daughter's husband planned a surprise holiday for their first wedding anniversary. Charlotte knew that the two of them were going somewhere special, but Paul didn't reveal their destination until they boarded a plane (in Chicago) for Phoenix, Arizona! He had made all the arrangements for a fun weekend in the Southwest, including mountain hiking, sightseeing, elegant dinners, and room service breakfasts. The surprise aspect of the trip made the celebration especially exciting and memorable.

Most people are intrigued by mystery and enjoy being treated to surprises. Church youth groups like "Destination Unknown" parties, when they can only guess where sponsors are taking them.

Not knowing where we are going can be fun for a party or a holiday. Abram's experience, however, required more faith and courage. He was risking his future, and perhaps jeopardizing his family's welfare, when he heeded God's call to leave his homeland and travel to Canaan. "By faith Abraham, . . . obeyed and went, even though he did not know where he was going" (Hebrews 11:8, *New International Version*).

As Christians we know our final destiny: everlasting life in Heaven. Some of the details have not been revealed, but we can rest assured that there will be a great celebration. Not knowing *when* should enhance the journey!—R. W. B.

B. God's Promises (vv. 2, 3)

2. And I will make of thee a great nation, and I will bless thee, and make thy name great; and thou shalt be a blessing.

God made four distinct promises to Abram in this verse. First of all, He would make of him a *great nation*. From the world's point of view, this promise may have seemed impossible to fulfill, for at the time Abram was both childless and advanced in years. But God specializes in doing the impossible, as both Abram and Sarai learned. From this one man came the nation of Israel.

The second promise, *I will bless thee*, was fulfilled as Abram acquired great flocks, material wealth, and servants—even in a land where he "sojourned . . . as in a strange country" (Hebrews 11:9). There was also a spiritual dimension to Abram's blessings, for he was privileged to know God as his "shield" and his "exceeding great reward" (Genesis 15:1).

The third promise, that God would *make* Abram's *name great*, has been fulfilled beyond anything that he could ever have imagined. Today three great religions—Judaism, Christianity, and Islam, comprising a significant portion of the world's population—honor him in one way or another.

The final promise, *thou shalt be a blessing*, had even more far-reaching implications. From among Abram's descendants God would eventually call a special people, the Jews, and through them He would send His Son, Jesus Christ, as the Savior of the world. [See question #2, page 384.]

3. And I will bless them that bless thee, and curse him that curseth thee: and in thee shall all families of the earth be blessed.

Although God extended a tremendous challenge to Abram, He also gave him the assurance that He would watch over him during his travels. Those who treated Abram fairly could expect God's blessings. On the other hand, those who mistreated Abram would experience God's wrath. A good example of this is seen in Egypt when Pharaoh unwittingly prepared to make Sarai one of his wives. As a result, God brought great plagues on Pharaoh and his house. Realizing what he had done, Pharaoh quickly returned Sarai to Abram (Genesis 12:10-20). In this case God watched over Abram, even though he had tried to hide the real truth by claiming Sarai was his sister.

Here too it is important to note the broader implications of God's promise, according to the New Testament. God was calling just one man, yet with a view toward bringing *all families of the earth* back to Him. Paul goes so far as to say that God "preached . . . the gospel unto Abraham" when He promised him, "In thee shall all nations be blessed" (Galatians 3:8). Paul then adds, "So then they which be of faith are blessed with faithful Abraham" (v. 9), and, "If ye be Christ's, then are ye Abraham's seed, and heirs according to the promise" (v. 29).

LEAVING A LEGACY

You probably have seen the bumper sticker that reads: "I'm spending my kids' inheritance." Such a humorous thought is really true to life, because not many parents leave large legacies for their children these days. Most of us simply try to keep from becoming a burden in our final years; we try to provide for adequate retirement income, and for the possibilities of major illnesses and/or nursing home care. Leaving an inheritance of any size for the family is a luxury that average persons usually cannot afford.

Abram was by no means average. He was a wealthy patriarch with large herds and considerable possessions. However, when God promised that all his descendants (in fact, all people of the earth) would be blessed in him, He had in mind a spiritual rather than a material heritage. Among the descendants of Abram would finally come the Messiah—Jesus Christ, the Savior. No other inheritance can equal the faith, hope, and love bequeathed to those who are children of Abraham by faith in Christ (Galatians 3:29) and who belong to the church, the "Israel of God" (Galatians 6:16).

The legacy of faith, trust, and obedience must be passed on to each succeeding generation. Do you want to bless your children with an invaluable inheritance when you die? Leave an estate that includes Christian values and commitment. "May all who come behind us find us faithful!"

—R. W. B.

C. Abram's Obedience (vv. 4, 5)

4, 5. So Abram departed, as the LORD had spoken unto him; and Lot went with him: and Abram was seventy and five years old when he departed out of Haran. And Abram took Sarai his wife, and Lot his brother's son, and all their substance that they had gathered, and the souls that they had gotten in Haran; and they went forth to go into the land of Canaan; and into the land of Canaan they came.

Abram traveled the full length of the so-called Fertile Crescent that extended from lower Mesopotamia to upper Mesopotamia through Syria and into southern Palestine. The trade routes that connected ancient Egypt to the great kingdoms of Mesopotamia passed through this area. The shorter route connecting Egypt and Mesopotamia ran across a desert that was impassable for persons such as Abram, who was traveling with donkeys and large numbers of flocks.

How to Say It

ABRAM. *Ay*-brum.
AI. *Ay*-eye.
ASSYRIA. Uh-*sear*-ee-uh.
CANAANITE. *Kay*-nuh-nite.
CHALDEES. Kal-*deez*.
EBAL. *Ee*-bull.
EUPHRATES. You-*fray*-teez.
GERIZIM. *Gair*-ih-zim or Guh-*rye*-zim.
HAI. *Hay*-eye.
HARAN. *Hair*-un.
JERICHO. *Jair*-ih-ko.
LUZ. Luzz.
MESOPOTAMIA. *Mess*-uh-puh-*tay*-me-uh
    (strong accent on *tay*).
MOREH. *Moe*-reh.
NAHOR. *Nay*-hor.
NEGEB. *Neg*-eb.
SARAI. *Seh*-rye.
SHECHEM. *Sheck*-em or *Shee*-kem.
SICHEM. *Sye*-kem.
SYRIA. *Sear*-ee-uh.
TERAH. *Tair*-uh.

Abram started this trip to *Canaan* when he was *seventy and five years old*. Accompanying him were *Sarai his wife*, his nephew *Lot* and his family, and the *souls they had gotten in Haran*. Since Abram and Sarai were childless at this time, these additional *souls* must refer to servants and their families. We do not know how many people were with Abram at this time, but later, when he came to Lot's rescue, he was able to lead a force of over three hundred armed servants against Lot's captors (Genesis 14:14).

III. Into the Promised Land (Genesis 12:6-9)

A. Abram's Travels (v. 6)

6. And Abram passed through the land unto the place of Sichem, unto the plain of Moreh. And the Canaanite was then in the land.

Abram's travels took him from northern Canaan to the central highlands. *Sichem* is the same town referred to as "Shechem" elsewhere (Joshua 24:1; Judges 9:1). It was located about thirty miles north of Jerusalem in a valley between Mount Gerizim and Mount Ebal. The phrase *plain of Moreh* is translated "oak of Moreh" in the *New American Standard Bible* and "great tree of Moreh" in the *New International Version*.

The verse concludes by noting that Abram was not the only resident in the land of promise: *the Canaanite was then in the land*. If these Canaanites engaged in some of the wicked and idolatrous practices that later Canaanites did (Deuteronomy 7:1-4), then their presence may have constituted a serious test of Abram's faith in and commitment to the true God. [See question #3, page 384.]

B. God's Promise (v. 7)

7. And the LORD appeared unto Abram, and said, Unto thy seed will I give this land: and there builded he an altar unto the LORD, who appeared unto him.

This was it! After weeks, perhaps even months of travel, Abram had arrived at his destination. Once more God *appeared* to him and announced that this was the *land* that He had promised to Abram. Yet Abram would never really possess it himself, for the promise was to his *seed*. Joshua 21:43-45 records the fulfillment of this promise to Abram's descendants—the children of Israel.

Following God's revelation to him, Abram *builded . . . an altar unto the Lord*. On this altar he may have offered a sacrifice, perhaps an animal, as an expression of his faith and his gratitude toward God.

C. Abram's Worship (vv. 8, 9)

8, 9. And he removed from thence unto a mountain on the east of Bethel, and pitched his tent, having Bethel on the west, and Hai on the east: and there he builded an altar unto the LORD, and called upon the name of the LORD. And Abram journeyed, going on still toward the south.

Abram continued to travel southward, stopping this time near *Bethel*, about a dozen miles north of Jerusalem. The name Bethel means "house of God," a name given to the place by Jacob many years later after his dream of a ladder stretching to Heaven with angels ascending and descending on it (Genesis 28:12). (In Abram's day the town was called Luz, according to Genesis 28:19.) There he once more *pitched his tent* and again *builded an altar*. The town of *Hai*, or Ai as it is called elsewhere (Joshua 7:2), was located about two miles to the *east* of Bethel.

The altars that Abram built were probably nothing more than a few stones stacked on top of one another. Since he was constantly on the move, he had little time to build anything more elaborate. His practice should be an example for those of us who move or travel frequently. Have a place of worship wherever you are, even if your stay there is brief. [See question #4, page 384.]

And Abram journeyed, going on still toward the south. Literally, this reads something like, "he kept pulling up stakes," indicating frequent moves. These moves brought Abram into the Negeb, the arid region in southern Palestine, southwest of the Dead Sea, that provided very little pasture. Perhaps Abram was pressured by hostile Canaanites to move into this more desolate area, or God may have providentially moved

him there so that he would be in a better position to move on into Egypt when a famine befell the land (Genesis 12:10).

Conclusion

A. Mission Impossible

Several years ago *Mission Impossible* was a popular television program. At the beginning of the program, the main characters were given information about an extremely difficult task. Then they were given the opportunity either to accept the mission or to reject it. Of course, experts that they were, they always accepted. What followed was a series of ingenious and daring schemes that enabled them to accomplish their assigned mission.

In a way, the venture God challenged Abram to undertake was a "mission impossible." How could a man living in Ur of the Chaldees embark on a journey to an unknown destination hundreds of miles away? Yet Abram, like the characters in the television program, accepted the challenge.

Every one of us, like Abram, is challenged to embark upon a "mission impossible." We are called to journey through a society that subtly or often quite openly rejects the truths that Christianity embraces. More and more we feel like strangers having to make our way through spiritual and moral minefields that have been laid by Satan.

But we have some advantages that Abram did not. We have the fellowship of the church to give us support and companionship in our journey. In addition, God has given us the Scriptures as a road map for the journey, and He has promised the Holy Spirit as a Comforter.

We have one additional advantage. While Abram "looked for a city which hath foundations, whose builder and maker is God" (Hebrews 11:10), he did not know as much about that place as we do. We know that our ultimate destination is Heaven—an eternal "promised land" planned and built by God for us. Let's go! [See question #5, page 384.]

B. Prayer

Gracious God, help us to develop the faith that we need as we strive to serve You amidst the threats and challenges of our day. May the faith of Abram inspire us toward that goal. In Jesus' name we pray. Amen.

C. Thought to Remember

"By faith Abraham, when he was called to go out into a place which he should after receive for an inheritance, obeyed" (Hebrews 11:8).

Home Daily Bible Readings

Monday, June 28—Terah Leads His Family From Ur (Genesis 11:27-32)

Tuesday, June 29—God Calls Abram (Genesis 12:1-9)

Wednesday, June 30—Stephen Recounts Abram's History (Acts 7:1-8)

Thursday, July 1—God Calls Samuel (1 Samuel 3:1-10)

Friday, July 2—God Calls Amos (Amos 7:10-15)

Saturday, July 3—God Calls Saul (Acts 9:1-9)

Sunday, July 4—Jesus Calls Disciples (Mark 1:16-20)

Learning by Doing

This page contains an alternate lesson plan emphasizing learning activities.
Classes desiring such student involvement will find these suggestions helpful.

Learning Goals

Having participated in this session, students will be able to:

1. Recount the details of God's call to Abram and the promises God made to him.

2. Compare Abram's decision to leave his homeland in answer to God's call with the decisions that followers of Jesus are challenged to make today.

3. Embark on an adventure of faith by "breaking new ground" in one area of their Christian living.

Into the Lesson

As you begin the lesson, help your students focus their thoughts on one of the themes of today's text by asking, "What is the greatest promise anyone has ever made to you?"

If your students sit in small groups, encourage them to go around the group and take time for each one to share one promise that was made to him. This will allow everyone to get involved in the lesson right away. After everyone has had time to share, ask for a show of hands to indicate whether the promise was kept.

If time allows, you might also ask them to tell some of the promises that they have received from God. Make the transition into the lesson by pointing them to the promises of God to Abram in Genesis 12.

Into the Word

As a way of getting all of your students into the Biblical text, ask them to work in small groups on the chart shown below. You may want to make a chart like this (except for the answers, of course) for each group (or if you have student books available, they can use the chart provided there). If you have a small class, this exercise can be done with the whole class while you write their ideas on a chalkboard.

Ask your students to read Genesis 11:31—12:9 and Hebrews 11:8-10 and list the qualities they see in Abram and the ways in which he shows them.

Abram's Qualities	How He Shows Them
1. Courageous	He was willing to set out for an unknown land.
2. Obedient	Hebrews tells us that God called Abram when he was in Ur; apparently that was the reason for the move; he obeyed again when God repeated the call in Haran.
3. Persuasive	Abram convinced his father and nephew to make the trip from Ur with him.
4. Faithful	Abram trusted God, and that was the source of his obedience.
5. Reverent	He built altars to worship God; he "called upon the name of the Lord."

Now ask your students to read the passage again and list the promises made to Abram. Write these clearly on a large piece of poster board. (1. God would make of him a great nation; 2. God would bless him and make his name great; 3. He would be a blessing—those who blessed Abram would be blessed and those who cursed Abram would be cursed; 4. In him all families of the earth would be blessed; 5. The land would be given to Abram's seed.) Then ask the students to read Genesis 17:1-8 and indicate how many of these promises are repeated (confirmed).

Ask, "How are the promises related to the call?" To some, the promises may seem a reward for Abram's obedience to the call. But the Bible makes clear that "Abraham [i.e. Abram] believed God, and it was counted unto him for righteousness" (Romans 4:3). Abram obeyed the call because of his faith in God. Perhaps God had already made some of these promises in the original call to Abram in Ur. Abram believed them—he believed God—and so he obeyed.

Into Life

Ask your students to compare Abram's call with the call that comes to each of us to follow Christ. (Both require faith; both have promises attached; both are fulfilled ultimately in Christ.)

Ask the class, "How would relying more on God and His promises affect your current decisions and priorities?" After a brief discussion, say, "I'd like each of you to focus on one area of your Christian living in which greater faith would help you to 'break new ground' in your walk with the Lord. What specifically will you do about it?" Close with prayer that your students can exhibit greater faith in these areas.

Let's Talk It Over

The questions on this page are designed to encourage review of the lesson Scriptures and to promote discussion of the lesson by the class. The answers provided are only discussion starters. Let your class talk it over from there.

1. God's call to Abram required him to leave home and family, comfort, security, and the like in order to walk with God. When we become Christians, we pledge to follow the Lord however and wherever He leads. What has that call meant for *you*? Where has God led you since you answered His call? What have you left behind? What have you received?

Some of your students probably have parted with unbelieving family and friends. Some have left honorable, successful careers in order to train for the ministry. They have left their comfort zones in order to serve the hurting around them. If some have not left anything, perhaps they should consider things they never acquired simply because such acquisitions did not seem consistent with their faith or would distract them from their higher purpose.

Surely they have gained a precious extended family, riches untold even if not measured in the world's currency, and a hope that is more precious than all the gold in this temporal world.

2. God made several promises to Abram if he would follow Him. Similarly, the Lord makes many promises to those who follow Him today. He promises to provide food and clothing for those who seek first His kingdom and His righteousness (Matthew 6:25-33). Jesus promises He will return for His followers (John 14:3). He promises eternal life to those who believe in Him (John 3:16; 6:40, 47). He promises no more death, mourning, crying, or pain (Revelation 21:4). Which of these, or others of His promises, is most significant to you? Why?

This could be a good time for class members to tell how God has kept His promises with them. Perhaps one has come through financial stress, but the Lord was true to provide daily necessities. Perhaps another has lost a loved one, and the promises of no more death, mourning, crying, or pain are especially significant. Let them tell their stories, and praise God for His goodness.

3. The most remarkable thing about Abram, the thing that made him beloved of God, was his faith. Describe this kind of faith. How can we exhibit this faith in our Christian lives? How does this faith grow?

Abram was convinced in his heart that God could and would keep His promises. Thus he was able to obey God with no more assurances of a positive outcome than God's word. Though he sometimes stumbled, Abram lived a life of obedience to the Lord. He was not swayed by the practices of others, like the Canaanites, who lived around him.

We exhibit this same kind of faith when we obey God. We show it when we begin some new service to the Lord, such as teaching or serving in a leadership position. We have this kind of faith when we resist the attractions of the world in order to follow the Lord wherever He leads us.

4. Abram built altars at Shechem and near Bethel. What connection do you see between worship and obedience? How important do you think regular worship is in our walk with the Lord?

When we worship, we acknowledge who and what God is, we acknowledge our relationship to Him, and we reaffirm our allegiance and submission to Him. Regular worship helps us keep these things foremost in our minds and hearts. It reminds us to be true to Him because He is the only true God, to put our trust in Him because He is faithful. Regular, sincere worship tends to help us cast those things out of our lives that are offensive to God or that compete for God's place in our hearts.

5. The lesson writer notes that "we have some advantages that Abram did not." As examples, he cites the fellowship of the church, the Scriptures, the presence of the Holy Spirit, and our knowledge of Heaven. How are these helpful to you? How can we take full advantage of them to help us on our spiritual journey?

Tragically, many Christians fail to utilize these advantages to their full potential. Their attendance at church functions is sporadic, they seldom if ever read the Scriptures, they resist the urging of the Spirit to a walk of greater service or holiness, and thoughts of Heaven are reserved for funerals. We need to make a commitment to the Lord that says He gets first place, and thus we will utilize every gift the Lord has given to assist us in that relationship.

A Promise Fulfilled

DEVOTIONAL READING: Deuteronomy 7: 7-11.

LESSON SCRIPTURE: Genesis 15:1—18:15; 21:1-7.

PRINTED TEXT: Genesis 15:1-6; 17:17-21; 21:1-3.

Genesis 15:1-6

1 After these things the word of the LORD came unto Abram in a vision, saying, Fear not, Abram: I am thy shield, and thy exceeding great reward.

2 And Abram said, Lord GOD, what wilt thou give me, seeing I go childless, and the steward of my house is this Eliezer of Damascus?

3 And Abram said, Behold, to me thou hast given no seed: and, lo, one born in my house is mine heir.

4 And, behold, the word of the LORD came unto him, saying, This shall not be thine heir; but he that shall come forth out of thine own bowels shall be thine heir.

5 And he brought him forth abroad, and said, Look now toward heaven, and tell the stars, if thou be able to number them: and he said unto him, So shall thy seed be.

6 And he believed in the LORD; and he counted it to him for righteousness.

Genesis 17:17-21

17 Then Abraham fell upon his face, and laughed, and said in his heart, Shall a child be born unto him that is a hundred years old? and shall Sarah, that is ninety years old, bear?

18 And Abraham said unto God, O that Ishmael might live before thee!

19 And God said, Sarah thy wife shall bear thee a son indeed; and thou shalt call his name Isaac: and I will establish my covenant with him for an everlasting covenant, and with his seed after him.

20 And as for Ishmael, I have heard thee: Behold, I have blessed him, and will make him fruitful, and will multiply him exceedingly; twelve princes shall he beget, and I will make him a great nation.

21 But my covenant will I establish with Isaac, which Sarah shall bear unto thee at this set time in the next year.

Genesis 21:1-3

1 And the LORD visited Sarah as he had said, and the LORD did unto Sarah as he had spoken.

2 For Sarah conceived, and bare Abraham a son in his old age, at the set time of which God had spoken to him.

3 And Abraham called the name of his son that was born unto him, whom Sarah bare to him, Isaac.

GOLDEN TEXT: God said, Sarah thy wife shall bear thee a son indeed; and thou shalt call his name Isaac: and I will establish my covenant with him.—Genesis 17:19.

Lesson Aims

After completing this lesson students should be able to:

1. Summarize God's promise to Abraham and how He continually reaffirmed it even when Abraham doubted or misunderstood.

2. Tell why God's promises are no laughing matter—even when they seem incredible.

3. State a confident faith in one or more of the wonderful promises of God.

Lesson Outline

INTRODUCTION
    A. Stop the Bus
    B. Lesson Background
  I. GOD REAFFIRMS HIS COVENANT (Genesis 15:1-6)
    A. God's Reassurance (v. 1)
    B. Abram's Concern (vv. 2, 3)
    C. God's Answer (vv. 4-6)
      That's Incredible!
 II. GOD PROMISES A SON (Genesis 17:17-21)
    A. Abraham's Doubts (vv. 17, 18)
    B. God's Plans (vv. 19-21)
      Laughing at God
III. GOD KEEPS HIS WORD (Genesis 21:1-3)
    A. A Son Is Born (vv. 1, 2)
    B. A Son Is Named (v. 3)
CONCLUSION
    A. A Hero of Faith
    B. Prayer
    C. Thought to Remember

Introduction

A. Stop the Bus

A small boy riding a bus home from Sunday school was very proud of the card he had received, which had a picture and a caption that read: "Have Faith in God." Then to his dismay the card slipped from his hand and fluttered out the window. "Stop the bus," he cried, "I've lost my 'faith in God!'"

The driver pulled the bus to a stop, and as the lad climbed out and went to retrieve his card, one of the adult riders smiled and made a comment about the innocence of youth. A more perceptive adult observed, "All of us would be better off if we were that concerned about our faith. All too often we plunge ahead on our own when we have lost our faith in God."

Abraham provides an excellent example of this truth. God promised him that He would give him a son who would be the heir of all of His promises to Abraham. However, after many years passed and the promise had not been fulfilled, Abraham attempted to take care of the matter on his own. He plunged ahead, leaving his faith behind.

B. Lesson Background

Some years passed between the events covered in last week's lesson and the events narrated in today's lesson. During this time Abram had been forced by a famine to move into Egypt. There Sarai, who was quite attractive, caught the attention of Pharaoh, who desired to make her his wife. Fearing that Pharaoh would kill him in order to acquire her, Abram had told Pharaoh that Sarai was his sister, which was a half-truth (Genesis 20:12), and Pharaoh took Sarai into his house. But God plagued Pharaoh's house because of it, and Pharaoh sent Abram and Sarai away (Genesis 12:11-20). We are not told how Pharaoh knew the plagues were associated with Sarai. In a similar incident later God spoke in a dream to Abimelech, king of the Philistines (Genesis 20). We assume God made some specific revelation to Pharaoh in this case as well.

Abram and his company then left Egypt and returned to Canaan (Genesis 13:1). By this time, Abram and Lot both had become rather wealthy and their flocks quite large—so large that there was not adequate pasture for the flocks of both of them. To avoid strife between the herdsmen of the two men, they agreed to go their separate ways. While Abram remained in the highlands, Lot chose to move to the Jordan Valley, which was well watered and green.

Before long this area was attacked by a group of marauders, who defeated the rulers of Sodom and Gomorrah and their allies, carrying off Lot and his family as a part of their booty. When Abram learned what had happened, he led a rescue party that defeated the raiders and rescued the captives. As he returned from his victory, Abram was greeted by Melchizedek, "king of Salem, priest of the most high God" (Hebrews 7:1), who pronounced a blessing upon him. Abram then gave Melchizedek tithes of all he had obtained (Genesis 14:19, 20). It was "after these things" that the events found in the first part of today's printed text took place.

I. God Reaffirms His Covenant (Genesis 15:1-6)

A. God's Reassurance (v. 1)

1. After these things the word of the LORD came unto Abram in a vision, saying, Fear not, Abram: I am thy shield, and thy exceeding great reward.

Most likely the reassuring words *Fear not* were needed because the immediate response anyone has when brought into the presence of Almighty God is one of overwhelming fear. In the presence of His holiness, man feels himself "undone" (Isaiah 6:5). It is also possible that these words were meant to help prepare Abram for the developments that were to follow.

The Lord's description of Himself to Abram was appropriate in light of recent events. He was Abram's *shield*, promising to protect him if the marauders gathered reinforcements and tried to stir up trouble again. Although Abram had refused to take any kind of reward or booty following his victory (Genesis 14:22-24), he was promised a greater spiritual treasure: God Himself would be Abram's *exceeding great reward.* [See question #1, page 392.]

B. Abram's Concern (vv. 2, 3)

2, 3. And Abram said, Lord GOD, what wilt thou give me, seeing I go childless, and the steward of my house is this Eliezer of Damascus? And Abram said, Behold, to me thou hast given no seed: and, lo, one born in my house is mine heir.

When the Lord had spoken to Abram on previous occasions, He did the talking and Abram listened, then acted. On this occasion, Abram spoke up to voice his concern. What troubled him most was not that he was *childless*, having no *heir*. His question was how God could *give* him all He had promised without an heir to help fulfill those promises. How could God make of him a "great nation" (Genesis 12:2) when he didn't even have a son? We cannot tell for certain whether Abram's faith was wavering at this point, or whether he was simply asking how God planned to keep His promise. Note in the following verses that God responded to Abram, not by rebuking him for lack of faith, but by reassuring him of His promise. [See question #2, page 392.]

Archaeological discoveries of clay tablets dated only shortly after the time of Abram show that his description of *Eliezer* referred to a common practice of the day. A childless couple would adopt a servant, who would become their heir unless a child should be born later to them, at which time that child would become the heir.

Here Eliezer is described as the *steward* over Abram's household. Apparently he had been adopted by Abram at some point (perhaps his birthplace was *Damascus*, or he had been purchased from someone who lived there). The phrase *one born in my house* literally reads, "the son of my house." It indicates, not that Eliezer was born into Abram's household, but that he had attained a favorable status within it.

The Scriptures do not provide us any further information about Eliezer. He may be the servant in Genesis 24 whom Abraham sent to find a wife for Isaac.

C. God's Answer (vv. 4-6)

4, 5. And, behold, the word of the LORD came unto him, saying, This shall not be thine heir; but he that shall come forth out of thine own bowels shall be thine heir. And he brought him forth abroad, and said, Look now toward heaven, and tell the stars, if thou be able to number them: and he said unto him, So shall thy seed be.

Once more *the word of the Lord came unto him.* Abram's concern necessitated a further response from the Lord. First of all, God informed him that Eliezer would *not* be his *heir.* The heir would come from his *own bowels*, that is, his own body. The heir would be his own offspring.

Apparently it was night when this revelation occurred, and Abram was most likely inside a tent. So, to further assure him, God took Abram outside (the meaning of *abroad*) and told him to look up into the sky and *tell*, or count, the *stars.* The number of his descendants, God told him, would be equally vast. Such an impressive visual aid and the accompanying explanation would give Abram the assurance he needed and calm his anxieties.

Today astronomers tell us that there are millions upon millions of stars dotting the heavens. Such information would have really impressed Abram! God used this same illustration with him later (Genesis 22:17) and with Isaac (Genesis 26:4). Moses referred to this promise when interceding for the children of Israel (Exodus 32:13) and when addressing them as they prepared to enter the promised land (Deuteronomy 1:10; 10:22).

6. And he believed in the LORD; and he counted it to him for righteousness.

This is the first specific reference to Abram's faith in God, although he had already exercised faith when he left his homeland in answer to God's call (as Hebrews 11:8 notes). The use of this verse in the New Testament is significant in the writings of Paul (Romans 4:3; Galatians 3:6) and James (James 2:23). Both point out that

Christians are children of Abraham, for they must come to God by faith as he did. There is no other way to please God (Hebrews 11:6) or to be considered righteous before Him.

THAT'S INCREDIBLE!

Can you believe what some people believe these days? Thousands of "hot-line" subscribers swallow the prognostications of so-called "psychics" every day. And what about the untold numbers who fall prey to the con man? Promising something "too good to be true," he swindles otherwise sensible people out of millions every year. It's incredible that intelligent human beings could be so naive and gullible.

Abram seems to have wondered whether he had chosen to believe something that was "too good to be true." He was an elderly man and concerned that God's promise of an heir was quickly leaving the realm of possibility. Yet God insisted that Abram would have an heir "out of thine own bowels" (Genesis 15:4). And despite all the probabilities to the contrary, Abram "believed in the Lord" (v. 6). Now that is truly incredible—or is it?

We can believe that Abram believed because he trusted the same God whom we trust. We believe the record of Genesis because we regard the Bible as the inspired Word of God—totally true. And we believe in miracles, because we know that our God can do exceedingly more than we could ever ask or think (Ephesians 3:20).   —R. W. B.

II. God Promises a Son
(Genesis 17:17-21)

A. Abraham's Doubts (vv. 17, 18)

17, 18. Then Abraham fell upon his face, and laughed, and said in his heart, Shall a child be born unto him that is a hundred years old? and shall Sarah, that is ninety years old, bear? And Abraham said unto God, O that Ishmael might live before thee!

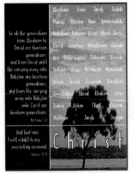

This visual shows how Jesus fulfills the promise to Abraham. The names in Jesus' family tree come from Matthew 1.

Visual for lesson 6

In the years that passed between the events studied in the previous verses and those recorded in these, several significant things had occurred. Even though God had promised that Abram would have a son, that seemed increasingly unlikely as the years passed. Finally, Sarai suggested that Abram take her handmaid, Hagar, as a surrogate wife so that she could bear children to him. (This too was an accepted custom of that time, although it was not what God intended Abram to do.) From this union a son, Ishmael, was born. [See question #3, page 392.]

Thirteen years later God once more appeared to Abram to reaffirm the covenant that He had previously established. In the process Abram's name was changed to Abraham, which means "father of many nations" (Genesis 17:5). At this point the circumcision of all males was introduced as a mark of the covenant. Sarai's name was changed to Sarah with the promise that she would bear a son and become the mother of nations (vv. 15, 16).

Such extraordinary promises as these seemed to raise doubts in the mind of Abraham. In the very presence of Almighty God, he *laughed* at such a thought. Of course, he was ninety-nine years old now (vv. 1, 24), so he would have to be *a hundred years old* by the time a child was born to him. Abraham's long experience told him that a hundred-year-old man did not father children with a wife who was *ninety years old*.

Some suggest that Abraham's laughter may have been the expression of joy or wonder at the thought that he and Sarah could be parents at their ages. That God repeated His promise in the next verse would indicate that Abraham entertained some doubts and needed reassuring. We ourselves who often struggle with taking God at His word can identify with Abraham at this point.

Abraham then asked God *that Ishmael might live before thee.* Earlier Abraham had proposed that Eliezer be his heir. Perhaps he was now proposing that Ishmael be that heir. Or Abraham's words may simply reflect his desire that God not ignore Ishmael while blessing the promised child.

B. God's Plans (vv. 19-21)

19. And God said, Sarah thy wife shall bear thee a son indeed; and thou shalt call his name Isaac: and I will establish my covenant with him for an everlasting covenant, and with his seed after him.

God was tolerant of Abraham's weakness and did not rebuke him. Instead, He reaffirmed His previous promise. In spite of Abraham's doubts, God would give him *a son*. In addition, God even named the son—*Isaac*, which means "he laughs" or "laughter." Was God displaying a subtle sense of humor by assigning this name just after Abraham had laughed at the idea that he would have a son?

20. And as for Ishmael, I have heard thee: Behold, I have blessed him, and will make him fruitful, and will multiply him exceedingly; twelve princes shall he beget, and I will make him a great nation.

I have heard thee. God had heard Abraham's petition on behalf of *Ishmael* and was granting it, but apparently not as Abraham had expected. God promised to do four things for Ishmael: bless him, *make him fruitful*, make him the father of *twelve princes* (see Genesis 25:12-16), and *make him a great nation*. However, God did not establish a covenant with Ishmael as He had with Abraham and would later do with Isaac. Regardless of the blessings that Ishmael would receive, he was not to be a part of God's plan to bless all the families of the earth through Abraham.

21. But my covenant will I establish with Isaac, which Sarah shall bear unto thee at this set time in the next year.

The *covenant* God established with Abraham did not include all of his physical descendants. It included only those who were descendants of *Isaac*. Of course, we today who are Christians are the spiritual children of Abraham, for we have come to God in faith as he did (Galatians 3:7-9, 29). Isaac is used to symbolize all Christians who live under the New Covenant (Galatians 4:21-31).

God added that the promised son of the covenant would be born *at this set time in the next year*. In His earlier promises of a son, God had not given a specific time for their fulfillment. Now He had set a date. [See question #4, page 392.]

LAUGHING AT GOD

Most everyone loves a good laugh. "Situation comedies" are featured on prime-time television every night. Sometimes our whole world seems locked into its own twenty-four-hour comedy channel.

No topic is sacred anymore; any subject is fair game for a laugh. Some people laugh at disabilities, misfortune, pain, religion, and sin (they may be laughing themselves right into Hell).

What was going through Abraham's mind when he laughed at God's promise of a son? Did he actually fall down laughing? Was it a laugh of amazement and wonder? Abraham had already expressed his faith in significant ways; God wanted to address the degree of unbelief that apparently he still possessed regarding this latest

Home Daily Bible Readings

Monday, July 5—Your Very Own Offspring Shall Be Your Heir (Genesis 15:1-6)

Tuesday, July 6—The Lord Makes a Covenant With Abram (Genesis 15:12-20)

Wednesday, July 7—Hagar Bears Abram a Son (Genesis 16:1-16)

Thursday, July 8—Your Name Shall Be Abraham (Genesis 17:1-14)

Friday, July 9—Sarah Shall Be Her Name (Genesis 17:15-27)

Saturday, July 10—Sarah Laughs to Herself (Genesis 18:1-15)

Sunday, July 11—Sarah Bears Abraham a Son (Genesis 21:1-7)

promise. He knew Abraham's heart was right; He knew this righteous servant *wanted* to believe. So, lovingly and patiently, God simply repeated His promise.

Do you suppose it seems to God that we laugh at Him and His promises sometimes? Some say that God has a sense of humor, but God never kids around with His promises. We may misunderstand God, and we may raise our eyebrows at some of His ways and methods; but we must always take Him seriously. He says what He means, and He means what He says. —R. W. B.

III. God Keeps His Word (Genesis 21:1-3)

Genesis 18 tells of the visit of three men to Abraham. While they ate the food that he had provided for them, one of them mentioned that Sarah would have a son. Sarah overheard the remark and, not believing it, laughed within herself. When confronted, she denied that she had laughed. The chapter also tells how God revealed to Abraham that the cities of Sodom and Gomorrah would be destroyed because of their wickedness. Upon learning this, Abraham made an impassioned plea on their behalf. While God was not willing to spare Sodom and Gomorrah (not even ten righteous people could be found there), He did spare Lot and his family when He destroyed these cities (Genesis 19).

Genesis 20 reveals yet another failure by Abraham to walk in faith. During his travels Abraham came into contact with Abimelech, king of Gerar. Fearing for his life, Abraham again claimed Sarah was his sister, just as he had in Egypt. In spite of Abraham's duplicity, Abimelech sent him away with additional livestock, servants, and silver.

A. A Son Is Born (vv. 1, 2)

1, 2. And the LORD visited Sarah as he had said, and the LORD did unto Sarah as he had spoken. For Sarah conceived, and bare Abraham a son in his old age, at the set time of which God had spoken to him.

When the Scripture says that *the Lord visited* someone, it does not necessarily mean that God actually appeared to that person or spoke to him in an audible voice. The phrase often describes God's action toward someone, and it can indicate either His favor and blessing, as it does here (see also Genesis 50:24, 25; Ruth 1:6; Jeremiah 29:10), or His displeasure (Exodus 20:5). Here the point is that God worked to fulfill the promise that He had made to Abraham earlier—the same promise that Sarah had ridiculed when she overheard it. Sarah's lack of faith did not prevent God from fulfilling His promise of *a son* in her old age.

The actual birth would not have come as a complete surprise to Sarah. *At the set time* would seem to indicate that the pregnancy covered a normal nine-month span. As the months passed, Sarah would have become increasingly aware of the new life developing within her womb. As the baby grew, so did her faith that God was able to do as He had promised.

B. A Son Is Named (v. 3)

3. And Abraham called the name of his son that was born unto him, whom Sarah bare to him, Isaac.

It was the normal practice for the father to name a child. In this case Abraham was carrying out the order that God had given him earlier (Genesis 17:19). As has already been noted, the name *Isaac* means "he laughs" or "laughter." What an appropriate name for a son born under such impossible conditions!

How to Say It

ABIMELECH. Uh-*bim*-eh-lek.
ABRAM. *Ay*-brum.
DAMASCUS. Duh-*mass*-kus.
ELIEZER. El-ih-*ee*-zer.
GERAR. *Gear*-ar.
GOMORRAH. Guh-*more*-uh.
HAGAR. *Hay*-gar.
ISHMAEL. *Ish*-may-el.
MELCHIZEDEK. Mel-*kizz*-ih-dek.
MESOPOTAMIA. *Mess*-uh-puh-*tay*-me-uh (strong accent on *tay*).
SARAI. *Seh*-rye.
SODOM. *Sod*-um.

Conclusion

A. A Hero of Faith

In the Scriptural "Hall of Faith" Abraham ranks high. His faith withstood numerous challenges during his long life. When his faith caused him to leave Ur, he had to give up a life of comfort. Archaeological findings from Ur indicate that citizens of that city, especially people of means as Abraham appears to have been, lived in comfortable, roomy houses and had numerous slaves to take the drudgery out of life. In addition, Abraham had to give up the security that people in Ur enjoyed. Evidence indicates that Ur in Abraham's day was not threatened by any outside forces and was able to provide adequate food supplies for its citizens. People of every age, ours included, desire these securities, and are usually very reluctant to give them up once they have them.

Once Abraham decided to leave Mesopotamia, he had to leave behind much of his family and all of his friends. Unless one has had the experience of "pulling up stakes" and leaving behind his loved ones, he has no way to understand the pain that such separation can bring. By faith Abraham made this move, taking along only Lot and his family (and they turned out to be more of a problem than a blessing).

Most important, Abraham believed God's promises even when there was no evidence of any kind that they would be fulfilled. As the years passed, Abraham was continually challenged to trust God to do what appeared impossible, and yet he kept his faith. Through it all "he believed in the Lord; and he counted it to him for righteousness" (Genesis 15:6).

Abraham's faith serves as a model for all of us today. Most of us have never had our faith tested as he did. Occasionally we may hit a little bump along life's highway, but these are usually not devastating. And often these challenges to our faith come because of our own carelessness or foolishness. When we do have severe tests, let us look to Abraham and take heart. [See question #5, page 392.]

B. Prayer

We thank You, Father, that You called Abraham and challenged him to live a life of faith. May we have the wisdom and the courage to follow You wherever You may lead us. May the world see in our lives the same kind of faith that Abraham demonstrated. In Jesus' name we pray. Amen.

C. Thought to Remember

The righteous shall live by faith.

Learning by Doing

This page contains an alternate lesson plan emphasizing learning activities.
Classes desiring such student involvement will find these suggestions helpful.

Learning Goals

As a result of participating in this session, the student will be able to:

1. Summarize God's promise to Abraham and how He continually reaffirmed it even when Abraham doubted or misunderstood.

2. Tell why God's promises are no laughing matter—even when they seem incredible.

3. State a confident faith in one or more of the wonderful promises of God.

Into the Lesson

Before the class arrives, write the words, *ABRAHAM BELIEVED IN THE LORD AND HE COUNTED IT TO HIM FOR RIGHTEOUSNESS,* on fifty-nine sheets of paper (half-sheets are adequate)—one letter per sheet. Post these on a wall where everyone will be able to see them, but hang them so the letters face the wall. (Be sure to leave spaces between the words.)

As you begin the class session, divide the class into two or three teams. Each team takes a turn suggesting a letter of the alphabet. If that letter appears in the sentence, turn the appropriate sheet(s) around to display the letter(s). That team gets a chance to guess what the complete sentence is. If the letter is not present, the next team gets a chance.

When the sentence has been solved, say, "We are going to see the origin of that statement in our lesson today. What some of us may be surprised to learn is that Abraham's faith was not without a few doubts and blunders along the way. Still, God's grace was with Abraham, and we can be certain it is with us today even if our faith seems a little shaky from time to time."

Into the Word

Recall last week's lesson on the promises made to Abraham (Abram) at his call. Ask a volunteer to read Genesis 12:1-3, 7. If you made the poster suggested last week (see "Into the Word" on page 383), display it and review the promises together.

Then assign each of three groups one of the following Scripture passages: Genesis 15:1-6; Genesis 17:17-21; Genesis 21:1-3. Ask each group to cite the promises from Genesis 12 that are mentioned, confirmed, or fulfilled in its assigned text. Note also signs of doubt on the part of Abraham and how God dealt with his doubt.

Allow about five minutes for the groups to work, and then ask for reports. Between reports, fill in details of what happened between the events recorded in the texts. (Use the exposition section of this book to help you.) Note how Abraham not only doubted, but at times took matters into his own hands to work things out (as with having a son by his wife's servant Hagar, Genesis 16:1-4, 15).

After the reports, ask, "When have you found yourself, like Abraham, taking matters into your own hands instead of waiting on the Lord? Have you ever acted in a way that cast doubt on your true belief in the promises of God?"

Point out that God changed Abram's name to Abraham (from "exalted father" to "father of a multitude") to constantly remind him of His promise.

Lead in to the next exercise by saying "God's promises are no laughing matter. There were others in the Bible (in addition to Sarah) who, by the direct intervention of God, conceived when it seemed impossible." Then have the class read the following passages and see who they were: Judges 13:2-24 *(Wife of Manoah)*; 1 Samuel 1:2-20 *(Hannah)*; Luke 1:7-25 *(Elisabeth)*; Luke 1:32-35 *(Mary)*.

Into Life

In Genesis 15:7 God spoke to Abram, calling Himself "the Lord that brought thee out of Ur ... to give thee this land." List the promises God makes to you in each of the following passages:

• Mark 9:23 (unlimited blessing)
• Mark 11:24 (answered prayer)
• Luke 17:6 (removal of obstacles)
• John 3:16 (eternal life)
• John 12:46 (spiritual light)
• John 14:12 (power for service)
• Romans 1:16 (salvation)

Give each student a three-by-five card and these instructions: "Write on this card one of these promises that you feel you especially need to be reminded of in the coming week. Follow this format:

"Write, 'I am the Lord who . . .' and finish the statement with one of the promises. Then write an encouragement based on the promise." For example, one who is timid in his witness might write, "I am the Lord who gives you power for service. Tell your neighbor of my love."

Let's Talk It Over

The questions on this page are designed to encourage review of the lesson Scriptures and to promote discussion of the lesson by the class. The answers provided are only discussion starters. Let your class talk it over from there.

1. The Lord appeared to Abram and described Himself as Abram's "shield" and his "exceeding great reward." Since Abram had just returned from battle, these terms were especially significant. If God appeared to you in such a way, what terms might He use to describe Himself? Why?

The shield suggests protection—especially significant if the battle were resumed—and the reward indicates that God's blessings are greater than temporal wealth. To the farmer God might be described as his "plow," more important than the tools the farmer uses to make his living, and his great "harvest." Encourage your students to think of the tools and rewards of their own professions for new metaphors. In all of these, the point is that God is greater than even the things we value so highly. If these were suddenly lost, we would still have God—and we would be rich.

2. Abram questioned God about His promise. It had been a long time since God first appeared to Abram, and still he was childless. Why is waiting on God such a test of faith? What do you do to keep your faith strong even when it seems nothing is happening to bring you closer to what you want or expect from God?

Abram may have felt confused, wondering if he really understood what God promised. He may have felt frustrated because it appeared that nothing was happening and time was slipping away. He may have felt doubt, or that his sins had separated him from God so that God would punish him instead of fulfilling His promise.

Abram took his concern to the Lord. We, too, can pray and study God's Word to be sure what we want or expect is in harmony with His revealed will.

3. Abraham's faith stumbled on some occasions. When he lied about his relationship with Sarah, and when he took Hagar to bear him a son, he was taking matters into his own hands instead of trusting God. The results were always trouble for Abraham and for others involved. What do you think is the difference between working to achieve our goals and dreams and taking matters into our own hands?

We can and should work toward our goals, but we must work within God's expressed will.

Abraham broke God's will when he lied. God obviously meant that Abraham and his wife Sarah would have a child, so Abraham was stepping outside of God's will to take Hagar, even if using a surrogate wife was an acceptable custom then. We must realize that we cannot help God along by violating His will and His laws. Such actions always produce trouble and do nothing to achieve the truly desired goals.

4. Abraham did have a very hard test of trust, but God appeared to him repeatedly through the years and reaffirmed His promises. We do not have the same benefit. How does God reaffirm His promises to us and encourage us to keep our faith strong?

Just like Abraham, the longer we walk with God the more reasons we have to trust Him. We may not see Him, but we see His hand in our lives. Many of us can look back and see how God guided us, even though we did not see it at the time. One of the real values of regular, fervent prayer, is that it gives God opportunity to answer us and thus to demonstrate His awareness and concern for us and His willingness and power to help. God may work through impossible coincidences, great blessings from unexpected and unlikely sources, or other means that show His direct intervention. Each time He does so, our faith is strengthened.

5. Though God delayed in fulfilling His promises to Abraham, His delay gave Him opportunity to display His greatness, power, and glory. For Isaac to be born when Abraham and Sarah were so advanced in age was truly miraculous. The result was that Abraham's faith, though sorely tried, was greatly strengthened. What positive results have come to you when you have had to wait to see God working in your life?

God sometimes may wait to work in our lives until our desired goals seem impossible. Then when what we want does come about, we know without doubt that the Lord has been working in our lives, and our faith is strengthened. Perhaps some of your students can tell of times they "tried everything" before finally submitting to God in faith, and His blessing was beyond their imagination!

A Test of Faith

DEVOTIONAL READING: Daniel 3:13-26.

LESSON SCRIPTURE: Genesis 22:1-19.

PRINTED TEXT: Genesis 22:1-14.

Genesis 22:1-14

1 And it came to pass after these things, that God did tempt Abraham, and said unto him, Abraham: and he said, Behold, here I am.

2 And he said, Take now thy son, thine only son Isaac, whom thou lovest, and get thee into the land of Moriah; and offer him there for a burnt offering upon one of the mountains which I will tell thee of.

3 And Abraham rose up early in the morning, and saddled his ass, and took two of his young men with him, and Isaac his son, and clave the wood for the burnt offering, and rose up, and went unto the place of which God had told him.

4 Then on the third day Abraham lifted up his eyes, and saw the place afar off.

5 And Abraham said unto his young men, Abide ye here with the ass; and I and the lad will go yonder and worship, and come again to you.

6 And Abraham took the wood of the burnt offering, and laid it upon Isaac his son; and he took the fire in his hand, and a knife; and they went both of them together.

7 And Isaac spake unto Abraham his father, and said, My father: and he said, Here am I, my son. And he said, Behold the fire and the wood: but where is the lamb for a burnt offering?

8 And Abraham said, My son, God will provide himself a lamb for a burnt offering: so they went both of them together.

9 And they came to the place which God had told him of; and Abraham built an altar there, and laid the wood in order, and bound Isaac his son, and laid him on the altar upon the wood.

10 And Abraham stretched forth his hand, and took the knife to slay his son.

11 And the angel of the LORD called unto him out of heaven, and said, Abraham, Abraham: and he said, Here am I.

12 And he said, Lay not thine hand upon the lad, neither do thou any thing unto him: for now I know that thou fearest God, seeing thou hast not withheld thy son, thine only son, from me.

13 And Abraham lifted up his eyes, and looked, and behold behind him a ram caught in a thicket by his horns: and Abraham went and took the ram, and offered him up for a burnt offering in the stead of his son.

14 And Abraham called the name of that place Jehovah-jireh: as it is said to this day, In the mount of the LORD it shall be seen.

Jul 18

GOLDEN TEXT: Lay not thine hand upon the lad, neither do thou any thing unto him: for now I know that thou fearest God, seeing thou hast not withheld thy son, thine only son, from me.—Genesis 22:12.

Lesson Aims

After this lesson students should be able to:

1. Summarize the account of how God tested Abraham's faith by commanding him to sacrifice Isaac.

2. Consider what their response would be if God commanded them to give up someone or something precious to them.

3. Explain how they have been, or are being, tested, and the lessons they have learned from the test.

Lesson Outline

INTRODUCTION
   A. Comparing Price Tags
   B. Lesson Background
 I. ABRAHAM IS TESTED (Genesis 22:1, 2)
   A. God Appears to Abraham (v. 1)
   B. God Commands Abraham (v. 2)
     Do You Have What It Takes?
 II. ABRAHAM OBEYS (Genesis 22:3-10)
   A. Abraham's Journey (vv. 3-5)
   B. Isaac's Question (vv. 6-8)
   C. Abraham's Preparation (vv. 9, 10)
III. GOD INTERVENES (Genesis 22:11-14)
   A. An Angel Speaks (v. 11)
   B. God Commends Abraham (v. 12)
     Tempted or Tried?
   C. The Substitute (vv. 13, 14)
CONCLUSION
   A. Testing Our Faith
   B. Prayer
   C. Thought to Remember

Introduction

A. Comparing Price Tags

A well-to-do merchant stood on the dock watching as final preparations were made for a ship to sail. As he stood there, he was joined by a stranger whose clothing revealed his poverty. Finally the stranger spoke up. "You seem mighty pleased about watching this ship sail," he said.

"Yes," replied the merchant. "I have seen many ships leave this harbor, but this one gives me more satisfaction than any other I can remember. You see, on this ship I am sending ten thousand dollars worth of equipment for a mis-

sion hospital in China. I just had to come down and see that it got off safely."

"Then we have something in common," said the stranger, "for I, too, have a gift on that ship."

"And what is that gift?" asked the merchant somewhat incredulously.

"My only daughter is on that ship. She's going to China as a missionary."

"Then my gift is nothing compared with yours," came the merchant's quiet reply.

Like this merchant, Abraham was a man of great wealth. His faith was so strong that he would readily have given any or all of his wealth to God. However, Abraham's material wealth was nothing compared with the gift God asked of him—his son Isaac. Yet Abraham passed even this test of faith in noble fashion.

B. Lesson Background

After the birth of Isaac (with which last week's printed text ended), the tensions between Sarah and Hagar continued to increase. They reached the breaking point when Isaac was weaned. Sarah demanded that Hagar and Ishmael be sent away, but Abraham was reluctant to give in to his wife's demands until God told him to do what Sarah asked. Isaac was to be the child of promise, God said, but Ishmael, too, would be made a great nation (Genesis 21:9-14). We find Sarah's behavior shocking, yet she was acting within her legal rights when she made her demand. (Some of the laws of ancient Mesopotamia allowed the primary wife almost complete control over a secondary wife.) Even though Hagar and Ishmael were sent out into the desert with only a little food and water to sustain them, God watched over them and cared for them. The young Ishmael grew to maturity in the wilderness of Paran, located in the Sinai Peninsula.

During this time, Abraham continued to travel about in southern Palestine, seeking pasture and water for his flocks. After a misunderstanding with Abimelech over a well that Abraham had dug, the two entered into an agreement that allowed them to live in peace with one another.

I. Abraham Is Tested
(Genesis 22:1, 2)

A. God Appears to Abraham (v. 1)

1. And it came to pass after these things, that God did tempt Abraham, and said unto him, Abraham: and he said, Behold, here I am.

God did tempt Abraham. Rather than *tempt* (a word that implies persuading someone to do something evil), the Hebrew word used is better rendered "test" or "prove." Satan often tempts us to sin, but James informs us that God will never do this (James 1:13). James also notes how "divers temptations" (in the sense of "testings") are a source of joy because they contribute to our Christian maturity (James 1:2-4).

This testing of Abraham's faith was for Abraham's benefit, not God's. God already knew Abraham's heart and knew that he was a man of faith. While Abraham had passed most of his earlier tests, his grade was not one hundred percent. Although his faith had grown through the years, the fact that his faith had wavered at times indicated that he still had room for growth. If he met the upcoming test successfully, it would mean that his faith had reached a new level of maturity and dedication. All of us are like Abraham: we never fully understand our strengths and weaknesses until we have been tested in the fires of pain, suffering, and defeat.

B. God Commands Abraham (v. 2)

2. And he said, Take now thy son, thine only son Isaac, whom thou lovest, and get thee into the land of Moriah; and offer him there for a burnt offering upon one of the mountains which I will tell thee of.

Of course, *Isaac* was not Abraham's *only son*. He had another son, Ishmael, but he had been sent away. So Isaac, the beloved son of Abraham's old age, was the *only son* with Abraham and the *only son* through whom God's covenant with Abraham would be fulfilled.

The very thought of sacrificing this son *for a burnt offering* must have struck Abraham's heart like a sledgehammer. To further complicate the matter, the idea of human sacrifice would have been abhorrent to Abraham. Some of the peoples around him practiced human sacrifice, but the God he worshiped was a life-giving God, not a life-taking God. To offer a human sacrifice would seem to contradict everything he had learned about God.

We know that God would never require us to kill one of our children to prove our faith in Him. Yet through the Great Commission of Jesus, He may call one of our children to serve in some distant and dangerous mission field. Should that occasion ever arrive, would we be as steadfast and unwavering in our faith as Abraham was?

The land of Moriah was located in central Canaan. Centuries later Solomon built the temple of Jerusalem on Mount Moriah (2 Chronicles 3:1). Many believe that Abraham journeyed to that mountain or, if not there, to *one of the mountains* in the vicinity of Jerusalem. [See question #1, page 400.]

Do You Have What It Takes?

Reports of widespread persecution of Christians around the world are deeply troubling. Believers in Communist China must worship "underground," fearing imprisonment or worse if they are discovered. Entire villages in the Sudan have been destroyed by militant Muslims, making corpses, slaves, or refugees of the Christians who live there. In Pakistan, the "Blasphemy Law" threatens anyone who is perceived as speaking or acting in disrespect of Mohammed. Christians are being tortured and sometimes killed in these and several other countries.

One has to wonder, "Could my faith withstand such pressure and abuse? Is my Christian commitment deep enough to risk or surrender my freedom and/or life if I were forced to make such a choice?" An even bigger question comes to mind when we consider Abraham's experience: "Would I be willing to sacrifice one of my children if God commanded me to do so?"

Spiritual giants are made, not born. Abraham probably never imagined he had such faith until he was actually confronted with the challenge. That day on the mountain in Moriah he grew a spiritual mile. We must remember that though few Christians have *what* it takes to be victorious in such situations, we all have *whom* it takes; and He has overcome the world (John 16:33).
—R. W. B.

II. Abraham Obeys
(Genesis 22:3-10)

A. Abraham's Journey (vv. 3-5)

3. And Abraham rose up early in the morning, and saddled his ass, and took two of his young men with him, and Isaac his son, and clave the wood for the burnt offering, and rose up, and went unto the place of which God had told him.

Early in the morning seems to indicate that God had spoken to Abraham during the night.

How to Say It

ABIMELECH. Uh-*bim*-eh-lek.
BEERSHEBA. Beer-*she*-buh.
HAGAR. *Hay*-gar.
ISHMAEL. *Ish*-may-el.
JEHOVAH-JIREH. Jeh-*ho*-vuh-*jye*-ruh.
MESOPOTAMIA. *Mess*-uh-puh-*tay*-me-uh (strong accent on *tay*).
MORIAH. Mo-*rye*-uh.
PARAN. *Pair*-un.
SINAI. *Sye*-nye or *Sye*-nay-eye.

Abraham's heart must have been heavy as he made the preparations that he believed would cost him his beloved son. The struggle he must have gone through was both emotional and intellectual. It was emotional because his own son was involved; it was intellectual because he could not see any way that God could fulfill the covenant promises if Isaac were sacrificed. Hebrews 11:19 suggests a solution to Abraham's intellectual problem. He believed "that God was able to raise him up, even from the dead." Thus, even if Isaac were sacrificed, Abraham believed that God would restore him to life and allow him to fulfill the covenant.

So Abraham left for Moriah, taking Isaac with him. He was also accompanied by *two of his young men* (probably servants). Perhaps with their help Abraham *clave*, or cut, the firewood that was to be used in the *burnt offering*. We wonder what the foursome talked about as they traveled. [See question #2, page 400.]

4, 5. Then on the third day Abraham lifted up his eyes, and saw the place afar off. And Abraham said unto his young men, Abide ye here with the ass; and I and the lad will go yonder and worship, and come again to you.

If Abraham started his trip at Beersheba (where he was when chapter 21 ended), then he had to journey about fifty miles to reach Moriah. Since Abraham had probably traveled over this area many times, he knew where he was going and would recognize *the place afar off.* Taking his leave of the two servants, he and Isaac started toward the mountain. The duty he was about to perform was too intensely personal to have anyone else present. Furthermore, had the servants been present and realized what was about to happen, they might have interfered.

Notice how strong Abraham's faith remained, even though the moment that he dreaded was drawing ever nearer. He told the servants that both he and Isaac (*I and the lad*) would return.

B. Isaac's Question (vv. 6-8)

6, 7. And Abraham took the wood of the burnt offering, and laid it upon Isaac his son; and he took the fire in his hand, and a knife; and they went both of them together. And Isaac spake unto Abraham his father, and said, My father: and he said, Here am I, my son. And he said, Behold the fire and the wood: but where is the lamb for a burnt offering?

As they trudged upward, Abraham carried the *knife* that he would need to slay the sacrificial victim. He also took *the fire in his hand*, probably a censer or pot containing live coals needed to start a fire and make the sacrifice a burnt offering. Isaac carried the *wood* for the fire.

Artists have often portrayed Isaac as a small boy at this time. Actually he was more likely an older teenager. A small child would not have been able to carry the wood, especially for as long as Isaac apparently had to. In addition, his question involved more rational thinking than one might expect from a child. At this point Isaac did not have an inkling about what Abraham was planning to do. *Where is the lamb for a burnt offering?* he asked. No doubt Isaac had witnessed other acts of worship involving a burnt offering, and so his question was reasonable enough. He may have wondered earlier about the absence of a lamb, but waited until he was alone with his father before he asked.

8. And Abraham said, My son, God will provide himself a lamb for a burnt offering: so they went both of them together.

Abraham may have answered calmly enough, but his heart must have experienced a turmoil of emotion. His response must have been confident enough to satisfy Isaac. (It may imply that he did not believe that God would allow him to sacrifice Isaac.) Christians recognize the prophetic significance in Abraham's statement, for God did *provide* His own Son as *a lamb* that would take away the sins of the world (John 1:29).

C. Abraham's Preparation (vv. 9, 10)

9. And they came to the place which God had told him of; and Abraham built an altar there, and laid the wood in order, and bound Isaac his son, and laid him on the altar upon the wood.

The Scriptures do not indicate that there was any further conversation between the distraught father and the unsuspecting son. Under the circumstances it is not likely that Abraham felt much like talking. Finally they arrived at the designated *place* of sacrifice. Abraham then gathered up some large stones and built an *altar*—something he had done many times in the past. Next he laid out the *wood* upon the altar. Finally he *bound Isaac his son* and *laid him* on top of the wood. During the process of being tied up, Isaac certainly must have realized what was about to happen. He was a young man in his physical prime and certainly could have resisted his father had he so desired, yet he humbly submitted to what was happening. This says a great deal about young Isaac's faith—both in his father and in God. [See question #3, page 400.]

10. And Abraham stretched forth his hand, and took the knife to slay his son.

The moment of truth had arrived. At every step along the way Abraham could have stopped and turned back, refusing to carry out God's order. But now "by faith . . . he that had received the promises offered up his only begotten son" (Hebrews 11:17).

III. God Intervenes (Genesis 22:11-14)

A. An Angel Speaks (v. 11)

11. And the angel of the LORD called unto him out of heaven, and said, Abraham, Abraham: and he said, Here am I.

Just as Abraham raised his knife to plunge it into the heart of his son, *the angel of the Lord* interrupted him. In that brief moment, the call of his name must have sent a storm of emotions surging through his heart. Were his orders being changed? Was he to receive new orders? What did it mean? God's revelations to him in the past had been frequent enough that he must have recognized the voice that was speaking, and so he quickly responded, *Here am I.*

B. God Commends Abraham (v. 12)

12. And he said, Lay not thine hand upon the lad, neither do thou any thing unto him: for now I know that thou fearest God, seeing thou hast not withheld thy son, thine only son, from me.

Abraham could not have heard words more wonderful than *Lay not thine hand upon the lad.* When Abraham began this solemn venture, he had no idea how it would turn out. As he journeyed along, he must have hoped that somehow his son would be spared, but he had no idea how this would happen. Now all his fondest hopes were realized. God assured him that he had passed the test. Although God knew from the beginning how the test would turn out, it was necessary that Abraham go through the entire process right up to the killing of Isaac. As noted earlier, the test was for the benefit of Abraham, not God. If he had *withheld* his *only son*, then his faith in God would have remained incomplete. Referring to this incident, James writes of Abraham, "His faith and his actions were working together, and his faith was made complete by what he did" (James 2:22, *New International Version*).

TEMPTED OR TRIED?

My wife recently took a Medical Assistant Certification test—four hours, three hundred questions. She had studied for some twenty weeks (about two hundred hours) in preparation. She won't know her score for three months, but she doesn't think she did very well. The questions did not reflect the study material or the sample quizzes that the candidates were

"Lay not thine hand upon the lad, neither do thou any thing unto him: for now I know that thou fearest God." *Genesis 22:12*

Visual for lesson 7

Today's visual pictures that dramatic moment when the angel of the Lord called to Abraham to prevent him from slaying his son Isaac.

given. One of my wife's friends said that she was confident of less than one-tenth of her answers!

This test apparently was designed to fail the testees. It was clearly unfair. By contrast, God's intent with Abraham's test was to prove his faith, not cause his failure. Certain events in life are allowed to try the quality of our trust and the courage of our convictions. We say such trials are tests of our faith. That's different from temptation.

James teaches us that God tempts no one (James 1:13). Temptation is designed by the devil to cause our failure. God allows us to be tested to strengthen our Christian character (James 1:2-4). Satan wants to destroy us; God wants to reward us with the "crown of life" (James 1:12). His purpose in our trials is positive—to temper our commitment and to harden our resolve. God wanted Abraham to be a spiritual giant, and He wants that for you and me, too.   —R. W. B.

C. The Substitute (vv. 13, 14)

13, 14. And Abraham lifted up his eyes, and looked, and behold behind him a ram caught in a thicket by his horns: and Abraham went and took the ram, and offered him up for a burnt offering in the stead of his son. And Abraham called the name of that place Jehovah-jireh: as it is said to this day, In the mount of the LORD it shall be seen.

Earlier Abraham had told Isaac that God would provide an offering, but of course, he had no idea how this would be accomplished. Now, in God's perfect timing, a *ram* was made available as a substitute for *his son.* Again note the prophetic element in this act: God's provision suggests a sacrifice that was to occur centuries later when He substituted His Son for us at the cross. [See question #4, page 400.]

Abraham, who only a few moments before had been filled with anguish, now experienced a joy that knew no bounds. This is the normal response when faith triumphs over doubt. We can know that same joy when we overcome a particularly severe temptation or a personal disaster, such as a serious illness, that tries our faith.

The name *Jehovah-jireh* means "Jehovah sees." Here the sense of the word seems to include not merely seeing but "seeing to," or providing for, a certain need, as God had done for Abraham. Abraham was able to keep his earlier promise (v. 5): "I and the lad will go yonder and worship, and come again to you."

Conclusion

A. Testing Our Faith

We live in an age of testing. Millions upon millions of dollars are spent every year on testing. Such items as the food we eat, the water we drink, and the clothes we wear are all subjected to countless tests before they are sold to us. Although these tests are expensive and often time-consuming, we accept them as a part of our complicated lifestyle. When we visit a physician's office, we are likely to be tested so that he can make a better diagnosis of our ailments. Our automobiles are safer than ever because they have been tested both in the designing and the manufacturing process. We must pass a test to receive a driver's license, and if we should be caught driving erratically, we may be tested by an officer for our sobriety. And the word *school* is one that for many students becomes synonymous with tests.

Our faith in God involves testing. Just as our everyday life involves testing, so does our relationship to God. On rare occasions that test may come in one defining moment, as did Abraham's when he was told to sacrifice Isaac. But most of us will never have an experience like that with

all of its intensity and drama. Our tests usually come frequently, even daily. They arise in the seemingly small, insignificant events of life. They come when we are exasperated by another person and cut him down with a sarcastic remark. They arise when we "forget" about the posted speed limits on the highway. They occur when, in a group that may be critical of Christ or the church, we remain silent rather than speak up for our Lord. When we fail to live up to our faith in these and a thousand similar situations, we will rarely be criticized. Often our consciences won't even bother us. And in addition, when we pass these tests of faith, we will not receive an instant commendation from the Lord as did Abraham. Yet these tests are still important.

We need to prepare for tests of our faith. As a teacher I spend a great deal of time preparing, giving, and grading tests. Normally I give students advance notice of tests and tell them how to prepare for them. Some students listen, prepare, and usually make good grades. Others don't listen, or they prepare inadequately, and they suffer the consequences. Occasionally I give a "pop quiz" just to make sure that the students stay alert.

Life is much like this. We often know when and where major tests of faith will come in our lives, and we can prepare for those times. When we move or take a new job or make new friends, we should be aware that such situations often put our faith to the test. At other times, tests come like the dreaded pop quizzes—unannounced and unexpected. These are usually the most difficult tests because our guard is not up. [See question #5, page 400.]

Tests can make our faith stronger. Most of us don't enjoy tests when we have to take them. But James reminds us to "count it all joy when ye fall into divers temptations" (James 1:2). Abraham was able to rejoice when he successfully passed his test, and so can we. God gives us this assurance: "Blessed is the man that endureth temptation: for when he is tried, he shall receive the crown of life, which the Lord hath promised to them that love him" (James 1:12).

B. Prayer

We thank You, dear Lord, for Abraham, whose life of faith serves as a model for us. Give us the wisdom to learn from his life and the strength to follow his example. In our Master's name we pray. Amen.

C. Thought to Remember

"Faith is to believe, on the word of God, what we do not see, and its reward is to see and enjoy what we believe."   —Augustine

---

Home Daily Bible Readings

Monday, July 12—Take Your Son, Your Only Son Isaac (Genesis 22:1-8)

Tuesday, July 13—Abraham . . . Took the Knife to Slay His Son (Genesis 22:9-14)

Wednesday, July 14—I Will Indeed Bless You (Genesis 22:15-19)

Thursday, July 15—We Will Not Serve Your Gods (Daniel 3:16-26)

Friday, July 16—Remove This Cup From Me (Mark 14:32-42)

Saturday, July 17—One Who in Every Respect Has Been Tested (Hebrews 4:14—5:4)

Sunday, July 18—The Greatest of These Is Love (1 Corinthians 13:1-13)

Learning by Doing

This page contains an alternate lesson plan emphasizing learning activities. Classes desiring such student involvement will find these suggestions helpful.

Learning Goals

After this lesson students should be able to:

1. Summarize the account of how God tested Abraham's faith by commanding him to sacrifice Isaac.

2. Consider what their response would be if God commanded them to give up someone or something precious to them.

3. Explain how they have been, or are being, tested, and the lessons they have learned from the test.

Into the Lesson

As you begin the lesson, ask your students, "What is the most difficult test you have faced in your life?" Ask several students to share their stories if they are willing.

It might be best to do this exercise in small groups. In this way each student will have the opportunity to get involved in a less threatening environment. After allowing enough time for several to share, ask anyone in the class who is willing to tell what they learned from being tested. In what ways are they different?

Lead into the Bible study by pointing out that one of the great patriarchs of the Old Testament was greatly tested—and passed with flying colors! It is his story that we will consider today.

Into the Word

Ask a volunteer to read Genesis 22:1-14 aloud. Then divide the class into groups of three to five students each and give each group one of the following three assignments:

1. Imagine that Abraham kept a journal or diary. What might he have written in it upon returning home with Isaac after this event?

2. Imagine that Isaac kept a journal or diary. What might he have written in it upon returning home with Abraham after this event?

3. Write what Abraham and Isaac might have said to each other as they walked home. What fatherly advice might Abraham have given his son based on this experience?

Encourage each group to include a review of the details of the event, something of the emotional drama that must have been present as Abraham and Isaac looked back at the experience, and any lessons they might have learned. Allow ten minutes; then have several groups share their results. You need not have every group read its work unless each one is eager to do so. A sampling will provide a good review.

Discuss the areas in the writings where the groups were speculating. Do their conclusions seem reasonable? What lessons are there for us in these events? Use information from the Scripture exposition section to explain any details that are unclear to the students or to answer their questions.

Into Life

After the students have completed this exercise, read Hebrews 11:17-19. Ask the students what they think God was asking Abraham to give up by sacrificing Isaac. (He may have been asking Abraham to give up control and let God lead. At least three times before, Abraham had taken matters into his own hands—twice calling Sarah his sister to protect himself, and once by fathering a child with Hagar.) Why was this test necessary? (It demonstrated that God had Abraham's full trust and confidence—not just when Abraham could see a good purpose.) What was God really after? (Abraham's heart.) How might God make a similar demand on us? (How about when He calls our children to serve Him as missionaries in far-off lands, or in ministerial professions that won't earn the kind of money they have the potential to make in secular employment?)

Say, "God has not asked any of us to sacrifice our children on an altar, but probably there are some of us who are being tested. What tests are you facing right now or have you faced? What lessons have these trials taught you?"

It appears from verse 19 that Abraham believed that even if he obeyed the Lord and killed his son, God could bring Isaac back again. Ask your students how this reflects on Abraham's faith in God to keep His promises. Then ask your students to think about what God has asked them to sacrifice (to give up). Do they believe that God can provide what was given up?

Close by reminding your class that Abraham called the place of the sacrifice *Jehovah-jireh*—"God sees" or "God provides." Tradition says that this is the same mount where the temple was later built and near the place called *Golgotha,* where a sacrifice was made that "provides" for us in a very special way.

Lead your class in singing the chorus "Jehovah-jireh, My Provider" before you pray.

Let's Talk It Over

The questions on this page are designed to encourage review of the lesson Scriptures and to promote discussion of the lesson by the class. The answers provided are only discussion starters. Let your class talk it over from there.

1. Isaac was the most precious thing in Abraham's life. No test could have been more severe! What are some of the things that are most precious to you? How might God demand you to give them up to serve Him?

For us parents, of course, our own children would be most precious. Other special items might include a talent or skill, wealth, or a position of status. Your students can probably name several others.

God does not ask for burnt offerings today, but for a living sacrifice (Romans 12:1). Thus, rather than ask us to kill one of our children on an altar, God might ask us to send a child into a ministry where we will seldom if ever see him or her again. Another might be asked to leave a very well-paying job to avoid corruption in the company or simply to have more time for serving the Lord. Again, your students will have many good ideas on this.

2. Sometimes when we face a tough challenge, we don't refuse; we just procrastinate. Abraham, however, "rose up early in the morning" to initiate his obedience. What benefits do you see in taking immediate action in order to obey? What dangers do you see in putting it off?

The real danger in procrastination is that it can become indefinite. Thus, with our mouths we say yes to God, but in deed we say no. Taking immediate action is a sign of faith; we are trusting God to help us, and we are eager to see that help displayed. Probably some of your students can tell of opportunities that were wasted because they procrastinated to the point that doors began to close before they could take action.

3. Through all of this, Abraham taught Isaac a powerful lesson in trusting God. Isaac's behavior shows that he already had a high degree of trust in God and in Abraham; otherwise he could and would have resisted. The lesson was not a new one, then, but a vivid demonstration of an old one, and proof that what Abraham had taught Isaac about his faith was completely genuine. How may we use crises to teach our children or others who look to us for guidance to trust in God?

We must teach them to trust in God before times of testing come. Then, when a crisis does come, we teach them by example, by keeping our own faith strong. Lessons learned while watching a parent keep faith in the face of pain, danger, sacrifice, or apparent impossibility are lessons not soon forgotten. But we cannot lead where we have not gone. We must be sure our faith is sound in order to teach valid faith lessons to others.

4. Though Abraham had no way of knowing it, his actions were a dramatic and powerful portrayal of God's actions some two thousand years later. Abraham was called to give his only son of promise, his beloved son; God gave His only begotten and beloved Son. Abraham took Isaac to a mountaintop in the land of Moriah, a mountain close to, or maybe even the same as, the temple mount, or perhaps Calvary. Isaac was innocent of anything that called for his death; Jesus was absolutely pure and innocent. Isaac willingly obeyed his father by accepting that he would be sacrificed; Jesus made His sacrifice of His own will, in obedience to the will of His heavenly Father. How do these things strengthen your faith?

Abraham's actions prophesied the work of his divine seed, thus showing us that our heavenly Father planned far in advance to give His Son as a sacrifice for our sins. Jesus' death was no afterthought or, as some skeptics have claimed, a failure of God's plan. It was God's plan. It shows that God is in control, even in times that look the most grim. Whatever trial we are facing, God is in it with us.

5. The lesson writer says we need to prepare for tests of our faith. How do you think one does that? What do you do to prepare for such tests?

Simply knowing they will come is one way. Some people mistakenly believe that becoming a Christian eliminates testing from one's life. Such people are ill-prepared for testing! Rather than develop patience by it (James 1:3), they may become exasperated and give up. Regular Bible study and prayer, fellowshiping with other believers, and fasting are all good disciplines that can help us. Perhaps some of your students can tell of trials they faced successfully because they were prepared, and can tell what prepared them for those trials.

Deceit and Blessing

DEVOTIONAL READING: Luke 16:1-14.

LESSON SCRIPTURE: Genesis 25:19-34; 27:1-40.

PRINTED TEXT: Genesis 25:29-34; 27:30-37.

Genesis 25:29-34

29 And Jacob sod pottage: and Esau came from the field, and he was faint:

30 And Esau said to Jacob, Feed me, I pray thee, with that same red pottage; for I am faint: therefore was his name called Edom.

31 And Jacob said, Sell me this day thy birthright.

32 And Esau said, Behold, I am at the point to die: and what profit shall this birthright do to me?

33 And Jacob said, Swear to me this day; and he sware unto him: and he sold his birthright unto Jacob.

34 Then Jacob gave Esau bread and pottage of lentils; and he did eat and drink, and rose up, and went his way. Thus Esau despised his birthright.

Genesis 27:30-37

30 And it came to pass, as soon as Isaac had made an end of blessing Jacob, and Jacob was yet scarce gone out from the presence of Isaac his father, that Esau his brother came in from his hunting.

31 And he also had made savory meat, and brought it unto his father, and said unto his father, Let my father arise, and eat of his son's venison, that thy soul may bless me.

32 And Isaac his father said unto him, Who art thou? And he said, I am thy son, thy firstborn, Esau.

33 And Isaac trembled very exceedingly, and said, Who? where is he that hath taken venison, and brought it me, and I have eaten of all before thou camest, and have blessed him? yea, and he shall be blessed.

34 And when Esau heard the words of his father, he cried with a great and exceeding bitter cry, and said unto his father, Bless me, even me also, O my father.

35 And he said, Thy brother came with subtilty, and hath taken away thy blessing.

36 And he said, Is not he rightly named Jacob? for he hath supplanted me these two times: he took away my birthright; and, behold, now he hath taken away my blessing. And he said, Hast thou not reserved a blessing for me?

37 And Isaac answered and said unto Esau, Behold, I have made him thy lord, and all his brethren have I given to him for servants; and with corn and wine have I sustained him: and what shall I do now unto thee, my son?

GOLDEN TEXT: [Isaac] said, Thy brother came with subtilty, and hath taken away thy blessing. And he said, Is not he rightly named Jacob? for he hath supplanted me these two times: he took away my birthright; and, behold, now he hath taken away my blessing.—Genesis 27:35, 36.

Lesson Aims

After this lesson the student will be able to:

1. Tell how Jacob tricked his brother and father to secure rights and blessings for himself.

2. Cite instances (from Scripture or from personal experience) of the alienation caused by deceitful words and actions.

3. Determine to live by the truth in every relationship, especially those within his or her own family.

Lesson Outline

INTRODUCTION

  A. Sisters Who Didn't Speak

  B. Lesson Background

I. JACOB SECURES A BIRTHRIGHT (Genesis 25:29-34)

  A. A Hungry Brother (vv. 29, 30)

  B. A Scheming Brother (vv. 31, 32)

  C. A Clever Deal (vv. 33, 34)

    Living Beneath One's Privilege

II. JACOB STEALS A BLESSING (Genesis 27:30-37)

  A. Jacob's Departure (v. 30)

  B. Isaac's Discovery (vv. 31-33)

  C. Esau's Disappointment (v. 34)

  D. Isaac's Declaration (vv. 35-37)

    Favorite Sons

CONCLUSION

  A. The People God Uses

  B. Sibling Rivalries

  C. Prayer

  D. Thought to Remember

Introduction

A. Sisters Who Didn't Speak

In many churches people have a favorite pew. Week after week they will be found occupying the same pew for the worship services. That was true in the small-town church in which I grew up. I remember two couples who were always in the same separate pews, one couple on the left side of the sanctuary and the other on the right.

I was grown and had left home before I learned that the two women in these couples were sisters. Years before, the two had become involved in a bitter dispute about an inheritance from their parents. One felt that the other had received an unfair share. In the years that followed they never spoke to one another though they continued to attend the same church. They always sat on opposite sides of the sanctuary and always entered and left by different doors, insuring that they would never have to speak to one another. As far as I know, they died without ever being reconciled to each other.

As we study the household of Isaac, we may be tempted to dismiss the conflict within it as just another ancient story that has little relevance in our day. However, on every hand we can see the same kind of family scheming and plotting. And in many of today's conflicts, the results are far more deadly.

B. Lesson Background

The previous lesson (which was taken from Genesis 22) ended with Abraham passing the test of faith when he was commanded to offer up Isaac as a sacrifice. Chapter 23 records the death and burial of Sarah. Chapter 24 then tells how Abraham sent his servant back to northern Mesopotamia (to the area near Haran, where Abraham had formerly lived) to secure a wife for Isaac from among his own kinsmen. Rebekah returned with the servant and became Isaac's wife.

Some time after Isaac and Rebekah were married, Abraham died and was buried in the cave of Machpelah, where Sarah had been buried. Eventually Rebekah gave birth to twin sons—Jacob and Esau. Even before they were born, they struggled within her womb—a precursor to the events described in today's text. It should be pointed out that Isaac and Rebekah contributed to much of the tension that developed between their sons by "playing favorites." Genesis 25:28 tells us, "And Isaac loved Esau, . . . but Rebekah loved Jacob."

I. Jacob Secures a Birthright (Genesis 25:29-34)

A. A Hungry Brother (vv. 29, 30)

29, 30. And Jacob sod pottage: and Esau came from the field, and he was faint: and Esau said to Jacob, Feed me, I pray thee, with that same red pottage; for I am faint: therefore was his name called Edom.

While *Jacob* and *Esau* were twins, their personalities and interests were quite different, as verse 27 indicates. Esau was "a cunning hunter, a man of the field." We might label him an "outdoorsman." For this reason he was his father's favorite. Contributing to Isaac's preference for Esau was his fondness of the food that Esau supplied him. Verse 28 refers to this as "venison," though the Hebrew word is a more general term, perhaps best rendered as "wild game."

Jacob, in contrast, was a "plain man, dwelling in tents." The word translated "plain" can mean "upright" or "blameless"; however, Jacob's behavior shows that such a definition is not accurate. Both the *American Standard Version* and the *New International Version* read "quiet man," suggesting that Jacob was meek and not as aggressive as his brother. Apparently he had also developed some cooking skills and was quite handy around the tent. It is not surprising, then, that he was Rebekah's favorite son.

In the rearing of children there is always a temptation for those of us who are parents to play favorites. And even when we diligently try to avoid this, our actions may be perceived as favoring one child over another. Even when we try our best to treat our children alike, we end up treating them differently simply because each child is different. However, though we cannot treat our children alike, we must try to treat them fairly. From the account of Jacob and Esau, it seems obvious that Isaac and Rebekah had failed in this critical area.

Jacob sod pottage. This is good *King James* English, but it may sound a bit quaint to our modern ears. It means that Jacob was cooking (literally, "boiling") a stew. When Esau came in *from the field* where he had been hunting or perhaps caring for the flocks, he was *faint*, or exhausted, and hungry. The aroma from the stew no doubt whetted his appetite even more, and he had to have some of it now—right now!

These two verses tell us a great deal about the two brothers. Esau was clearly a captive of his own appetites. No doubt he was hungry after being out in the field for a time, but he was in no danger of starving to death as he would later claim (v. 32). He just thought he was! Like many today, he lived for the moment. Jacob, on the other hand, looked to the future and cleverly took advantage of his brother's weakness to provide for his own future. Had Jacob been a true brother, he would have generously offered Esau

some of the stew he was preparing, not expecting any kind of personal gain from the favor.

Verse 25 of this chapter tells us that Esau received the name that he did because he was "hairy" at his birth. Now he was given another name (perhaps a nickname) based on his desire for the *red pottage* that Jacob was preparing (probably red because of the meat in the stew). The name *Edom*, meaning *red*, became the name by which Esau's descendants were known—Edomites (Genesis 36:9).

B. A Scheming Brother (vv. 31, 32)

31, 32. And Jacob said, Sell me this day thy birthright. And Esau said, Behold, I am at the point to die: and what profit shall this birthright do to me?

Sell me this day thy birthright. It was a common practice in the ancient Near East that when a man died, his oldest son received a double portion of the inheritance along with his father's family responsibilities. This was what Jacob wanted. He wanted Esau to give it to him at that very moment, while Esau was tired and hungry. Once Esau had eaten and rested, Jacob knew that he wouldn't be such an easy mark.

Esau's response must have seemed quite logical to him. After all, if he was going to *die* very shortly, why worry about a birthright that might be years in coming? The only problem with his logic was that he was not even close to starving to death. But Esau was such a slave to his physical appetites that he exaggerated his need and easily convinced himself that he was on the verge of starvation. We wonder why he didn't appeal to Jacob's mercy, but he had probably had enough experience with Jacob to know that this would never work. [See question #1, page 408.]

C. A Clever Deal (vv. 33, 34)

33, 34. And Jacob said, Swear to me this day; and he sware unto him: and he sold his birthright unto Jacob. Then Jacob gave Esau bread and pottage of lentils; and he did eat and drink, and rose up, and went his way. Thus Esau despised his birthright.

According to verse 23 of this chapter, Rebekah was told that Esau, her older son, would serve Jacob, her younger son. Since Rebekah was closer to Jacob, she may have shared this revelation with him. Jacob, schemer that he was, may have seen in Esau's hunger the opportunity to fulfill what God had prophesied. In his own mind he may have justified his actions on this basis. "After all," he may have said to himself, "I'm going to come out ahead in the future. Why not cooperate with God and hurry the process along?" [See question #2, page 408.]

How to Say It

ABIMELECH. Uh-*bim*-eh-lek.
EDOM. *Ee*-dum.
EDOMITES. *Ee*-dum-ites.
GIDEON. *Gid*-ee-un.
HARAN. *Hair*-un.
MACHPELAH. Mack-*pea*-luh.
MESOPOTAMIA. *Mess*-uh-puh-*tay*-me-uh (strong accent on *tay*).

This verse provides some information as to the ingredients of Jacob's stew: it was a *pottage of lentils*. The lentil is a member of the legume family and was widely grown in the ancient Near East. The lens-shaped seed is less than a quarter of an inch in diameter. It is nutritious, and when mixed in a stew containing meat and other vegetables it is quite delicious.

Had someone challenged Jacob's actions in this matter, he might have responded that it was a good deal for everyone involved. Esau got what he wanted—a meal—and went away satisfied; Jacob got what he wanted—the *birthright*. The concluding statement of verse 34 provides us with the correct understanding: *Esau despised his birthright*. There was no way that a bowl of stew was worth the birthright. But guided by his carnal mind, Esau was unable to keep the two items in proper perspective. The conniving Jacob understood quite well how Esau thought and cleverly took advantage of his brother's weakness. [See question #3, page 408.]

LIVING BENEATH ONE'S PRIVILEGE

What's the value of a name? Ask "John-John" Kennedy, or Lucy Arnaz, or Franklin Graham, or any of the Rockefeller clan.

What is a family legacy worth? Ask the Walt Disney heirs, or the Hearst family, or the children of people like Jimmy Stewart, Henry Fonda, and Judy Garland.

Most people value their "birthright." Most consider it a privilege to inherit a family legacy of wealth or of character, good reputation, and positive values. Not Esau. He "despised his birthright"—his family name and his promised inheritance. He surrendered it all for nothing more than the instant gratification of his carnal appetites.

Home Daily Bible Readings

Monday, July 19—Jacob and Esau Are Born (Genesis 25:19-26)
Tuesday, July 20—Esau Sells His Birthright (Genesis 25:27-34)
Wednesday, July 21—Rebekah Schemes to Deceive Isaac (Genesis 27:1-17)
Thursday, July 22—Jacob Deceives Isaac (Genesis 27:18-29)
Friday, July 23—Esau Pleads for a Blessing (Genesis 27:30-40)
Saturday, July 24—Because He Had Acted Shrewdly (Luke 16:1-9)
Sunday, July 25—Clean Hands and Pure Hearts (Psalm 24:1-6)

Esau's descendants are legion. Think of the millions who sacrifice or risk integrity, purity, virginity, trust, and reputation for just a few moments of pleasure, indulgence, or adulation. The family of man is "desperately wicked" (Jeremiah 17:9), but the family of God is also often guilty of trading Christian privileges for temporal and sensual rewards.

We are privileged to be called the sons of God, and that is what we are (1 John 3:1). But so often we live beneath our privilege, selling our heavenly birthright for little more than a mess of earth's stew.   —R. W. B.

II. Jacob Steals a Blessing (Genesis 27:30-37)

A. Jacob's Departure (v. 30)

The preceding verses of chapter 27 tell how Rebekah plotted with Jacob to gain a blessing from Isaac that properly belonged to Esau. It is hard to imagine a mother and son who would plot to deceive an aged and blind husband and father as Rebekah and Jacob did. Or is it? Not really, for again, we see similar acts happening about us all the time. The plot was cleverly planned—the goatskins on Jacob's hands and neck to make him feel like his hairy brother, and Esau's clothes to make Jacob smell like a man of the field. But even with these preparations, the scheme almost failed. "The voice is Jacob's voice," old Isaac said, "but the hands are the hands of Esau" (v. 22). Nevertheless, Isaac proceeded to bless Jacob.

30. And it came to pass, as soon as Isaac had made an end of blessing Jacob, and Jacob was yet scarce gone out from the presence of Isaac his father, that Esau his brother came in from his hunting.

Apparently Esau returned sooner than Jacob had expected, but Jacob was able to get away just in time. Otherwise, a bloody confrontation might have occurred right in the presence of Isaac. The *blessing* that Isaac pronounced on Jacob included an abundance of physical blessings. Isaac asked God to give Jacob "the dew of heaven, and the fatness of the earth, and plenty of corn and wine" (v. 28). But there were other blessings beyond the physical. Jacob was also given mastery over other nations and over his brethren (v. 29).

B. Isaac's Discovery (vv. 31-33)

31, 32. And he also had made savory meat, and brought it unto his father, and said unto his father, Let my father arise, and eat of his son's venison, that thy soul may bless me. And Isaac his father said unto him, Who art thou? And he said, I am thy son, thy firstborn, Esau.

Although Esau was a hunter and a man of the field, apparently he had also gained some cooking skills; for after returning from a successful hunt, he prepared the *savory meat* that his father loved. He may have come into his father's presence with an air of triumph. He had fulfilled Isaac's request and now he expected to receive his due reward—the coveted blessing.

What a shock Isaac must have received when he heard Esau's voice! He thought he had already blessed Esau, but now came the devastating realization: he had been deceived. To confirm his suspicions, he asked, *Who art thou?* Perhaps he thought that it might be Jacob who had just arrived. But Esau's answer was emphatic: *I am thy son, thy firstborn, Esau.* The emphasis in his reply on being *thy firstborn* suggests that he had already begun to suspect that something was amiss.

33. And Isaac trembled very exceedingly, and said, Who? where is he that hath taken venison, and brought it me, and I have eaten of all before thou camest, and have blessed him? yea, and he shall be blessed.

When Esau responded to Isaac's question, *Isaac trembled very exceedingly*, realizing that he had been deceived. The statement indicates his intense emotions. Not only was he distraught because he had been deceived by his own son, but his distress was intensified because he could not undo what had been done. He had pronounced the blessing upon Jacob: *yea, and he shall be blessed.* In our culture a contract that has been agreed to under duress or fraud can be challenged in the courts. But in that day there was no legal remedy for what happened in this case. Furthermore, when Isaac blessed Jacob, he had called upon God to honor Jacob's blessing. Isaac knew there was no way that God would rescind the blessing even if he tried to.

C. Esau's Disappointment (v. 34)

34. And when Esau heard the words of his father, he cried with a great and exceeding bitter cry, and said unto his father, Bless me, even me also, O my father.

Now it was Esau's turn to express his anguish. His *cry* is described as *great and exceeding bitter.* It was a soul-wrenching cry of bitter disappointment—a spontaneous outburst at the realization of what had been taken from him. The bitterness that he felt would soon begin to fester and would burst forth in anger against his brother, calling for revenge.

Hoping that there was still some blessing left for him, Esau pleaded, *Bless me, even me also, O my father.* Even though Jacob had cheated him out of his birthright and now had stolen the

blessing that rightfully belonged to him, surely, thought Esau, there ought to be something left for him. [See question #4, page 408.]

D. Isaac's Declaration (vv. 35-37)

35, 36. And he said, Thy brother came with subtilty, and hath taken away thy blessing. And he said, Is not he rightly named Jacob? for he hath supplanted me these two times: he took away my birthright; and, behold, now he hath taken away my blessing. And he said, Hast thou not reserved a blessing for me?

Isaac now realized the full impact of what had happened. He may have begun to realize something else. Even while Rebekah carried the twin brothers, God told her that "the elder shall serve the younger" (Genesis 25:23). She certainly must have shared this information with Isaac. Yet knowing this, Isaac had worked to secure God's blessing for Esau, who was his favorite son. His efforts to thwart the will of God had failed, even though Jacob had accomplished it by devious and unacceptable means. [See question #5, page 408.]

There is a note of bitter sarcasm in Esau's reply: *Is not he rightly named Jacob?* The name Jacob means "heel grabber" (Genesis 25:26), or one who tries to trip up (deceive) another. Esau realized that he had been cheated *two times* by his brother. He had lost his standing as the favored son. In desperation Esau asked, *Hast thou not reserved a blessing for me?*

FAVORITE SONS

I was visiting an elderly widow recently. As she spoke of her several children, she told me without apology that one of her sons was her "favorite." Such admissions make me nervous, for I know that they can lead, or have led, to serious problems in the family. When parents choose favorites among their children, they almost certainly will indulge their favoritism in some way or another. Equal treatment and fairness are hardly possible in such circumstances.

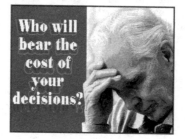

Visual for lesson 8

Has this man been hurt by another's actions (as Esau was by Jacob's)? Or is he a repentant "Jacob"? Either way, the caption is quite challenging!

Rebekah preferred Jacob, and she led him to become manipulating and dishonest. Isaac loved Esau better and influenced him (perhaps inadvertently) to develop self-centered instincts and a carnal outlook on life. Values became unbalanced, relationships became jealous and competitive, and the family became, in today's jargon, "dysfunctional."

Not every case of parental favoritism results in such obvious failure. That such situations are potentially harmful, however, is clear. Every child is a gift from God (Psalm 127:3) and needs to be instructed carefully in His ways (Proverbs 22:6). Though we may feel more comfortable with the temperament and personality of some children than with others, our preferences should never be detected by any of our offspring. Nonpartisan parenting should be the aim of every mom and dad. We have the perfect model, for our heavenly Father is "no respecter of persons" in His grand family.   —R. W. B.

37. And Isaac answered and said unto Esau, Behold, I have made him thy lord, and all his brethren have I given to him for servants; and with corn and wine have I sustained him: and what shall I do now unto thee, my son?

Isaac's answer was not very reassuring, for it seemed to suggest that there was nothing left for Esau. In the verses that follow, Esau continued to plead for a blessing. Finally Isaac agreed to bless him, but it was not nearly what Esau had hoped.

The New Testament summarizes the tragedy of Esau in this way: "For ye know how that afterward, when he would have inherited the blessing, he was rejected: for he found no place of repentance, though he sought it carefully with tears" (Hebrews 12:17).

Conclusion

A. The People God Uses

God in His infinite wisdom chose Abraham to begin the family line through which He would send His Son to bless the earth. Abraham was not perfect by any means. On two occasions he lied about Sarah's being his sister in order to save his life. Yet God was able to use him.

Isaac, Abraham's son, was a good man but did not seem to have the same high level of faith that his father did. However, he did imitate his father in one respect: he used the same ruse that Abraham had used and lied to Abimelech about Rebekah (Genesis 26:6-11). Yet God was able to use him.

The situation got worse with the third generation. As we have seen, neither Esau nor Jacob demonstrated exemplary character. Esau was a slave of his physical passions. He was impatient and lived for the moment. Because the satisfaction of his hunger meant more to him than the birthright to which he as the eldest son had claim, the Scriptures say he "despised his birthright." Jacob, on the other hand, wanted the birthright and was willing to plan ahead to secure it. To acquire it he took advantage of his brother's weaknesses. Today's texts from Genesis show Jacob to be a conniving schemer. Yet God was able to use him.

We could add others to our list of unlikely instruments of God, including Moses, Gideon, David, Peter, and Paul. Regardless of whom we choose, the lesson is the same: God uses imperfect people. There is no other kind for Him to use! He still meets us where we are and challenges us to let Him use us for His glory. As someone has pointed out, it isn't *ability* that God wants as much as *availability*.

B. Sibling Rivalries

Esau and Jacob give us a vivid example of a sibling rivalry that was made worse because the parents, Isaac and Rebekah, took opposite sides in the conflict. Although the Bible relates only two incidents that highlight this tension, we can be certain that the conflict was an ongoing one over many years.

Such rivalries are common in families where there is more than one child. How can we deal with these in our own families? First of all, we need to treat all of our children equally and try not to play favorites. Our children will not always understand that we are being fair, but we should not allow them to manipulate us. (Also, we ought not to let them manipulate their grandparents.)

We have to do the best we can, bathe our efforts in prayer, and, above all, never give up. We can find consolation in the fact that in many cases children who were bitter rivals while they were growing up become the closest of friends when they become adults. Keep in mind that Esau and Jacob, though separated for many years, later reunited and were reconciled (Genesis 33:1-16).

C. Prayer

O God of Abraham, Isaac, and Jacob, it is to You that we lift up our prayer. We thank You that in Your infinite wisdom and bountiful grace You were able to use these men in such a way that we today enjoy Your blessings of salvation. In the name of Your Son and our Savior. Amen.

D. Thought to Remember

Let spiritual priorities guide your daily living.

Learning by Doing

This page contains an alternate lesson plan emphasizing learning activities.
Classes desiring such student involvement will find these suggestions helpful.

Learning Goals

As a result of participating in this session, the student will be able to:

1. Tell how Jacob tricked his brother and father to secure rights and blessings for himself.

2. Cite instances (from Scripture or from personal experience) of the alienation caused by deceitful words and actions.

3. Determine to live by the truth in every relationship, especially those within his or her own family.

Into the Lesson

Write the words *sibling rivalry* on the chalkboard. Ask your students to list as many examples of sibling rivalry as they can. (This activity may be more effective if students work together in small groups. If at all possible, divide your students into four equal-size groups.)

Students will, no doubt, suggest many examples either from their own families or from the families of friends and neighbors they have known. After the students have shared a few stories, encourage them to suggest examples from the Bible. They may list Cain and Abel, Jacob and Esau, Joseph and his brothers, and perhaps others.

Lead into the Bible study by saying that today's story of Jacob and Esau will show that God is able to use even sibling rivalry to accomplish His purpose.

Into the Word

Ask your students to read Genesis 25:27-34 aloud in their small groups and then make a list of the personality characteristics that distinguish Esau and Jacob. In what ways do these traits come from their parents? *Students should be able to identify Esau's character as a manly outdoorsman (like his country-boy father), outgoing, living for the moment, a captive of his own appetites. They should also be able to identify Jacob as quiet (like his city-girl mother), logical, patient, cunning, taking tactical advantage of others' weaknesses, and one who takes the longer view of events.*

After each group has had the opportunity to share their ideas with the rest of the class, ask your students to think of modern examples of these two personality types. They should be able to think of any number of modern personalities

like Esau who live for the moment and are captives of their own appetites. They should also easily be able to identity modern examples of Jacob's cunning—those who are more than happy to take advantage of the weaknesses of others to gain what they want in life.

Next, assign each of four small groups one of the main characters in the story (Isaac, Rebekah, Esau, and Jacob). Ask them to use the following passages to determine what each of them did wrong.

* Isaac (Genesis 25:23, 28; 27:1-4)
* Rebekah (Genesis 25:28; 27:5-17, 42-46)
* Esau (Genesis 25:29-34; 27:34, 38, 41)
* Jacob (Genesis 25:29-34; 27:11-27)

As they share their answers with the rest of the class, help them to see that even though Rebekah had been told God's plan for her sons (and she had probably shared this information with the family), none of them gracefully accepted God's desires without trying to work things out themselves.

Into Life

Ask each of the four groups to write a summary of the events of chapter 27 told from the viewpoint of the character they were assigned earlier. Encourage each group to tell the story in such a way as to try to justify their character's actions. After they have each had an opportunity to tell their version, ask them, "Did God need all of this help to accomplish His purpose?"

The Bible says that Esau "despised his birthright." We could list examples of the same attitude from modern life—exchanging integrity for a pittance, trading honor for a good test grade, or a good reputation for popularity. Ask the class to take time in their small groups to share some ways in which they have "despised their birthright"—times in which they found themselves so enslaved to their immediate desires that they were able to convince themselves to do something as illogical as trading a birthright for stew.

Allow several in each group to share their thoughts; then close by reminding your students that in spite of the dishonorable way in which each of these family members acted, God still blessed them and honored His covenant. Even though Jacob did not deserve God's favor, he received it—and so do we.

Let's Talk It Over

The questions on this page are designed to encourage review of the lesson Scriptures and to promote discussion of the lesson by the class. The answers provided are only discussion starters. Let your class talk it over from there.

1. Esau and Jacob were not the first siblings to squabble over family matters, and they certainly haven't been the last. What kinds of things do brothers and sisters fight about today? What, if anything, is worth fighting to keep?

Like Isaac's twins, siblings today fight over inheritances, be it riches or sentimental mementos. In fact, some fight over what they can get from their parents while the parents are still living. They become jealous of each other and fight for their parents' affections and praise. In all such fights and struggles, they forget that no family possession is worth the destruction of the family itself. A whole family, serving God together, is worth whatever effort is needed to preserve!

2. Jacob, and later Rebekah, might have justified their actions by appealing to the prophecy that the older would serve the younger. They were taking matters into their own hands, however, as surely as Abraham did when he fathered a child by Hagar. How do people today use "God's will" to justify wrong? How can we prevent such errors?

Some Christians have divorced their mates because they were "unhappy" and rationalized, "I know it's not God's will for me to be unhappy." Misguided abortion foes have resorted to terrorism and violence to stop abortion. Short-sighted church members have been divisive and caused church splits over petty issues, all the while claiming they were following "God's will." We must remember, there is never a right reason to do wrong, no matter how appealing it may seem to us. If our view of "God's will" violates His revealed will, we have the wrong view.

3. Esau seems to have had no use for and no interest in the most important things in life. He let his birthright go without hesitation. What are the most important things in your life? What would you do to protect or preserve them?

Some of your students might quickly say "family," but Jesus taught that even family must come second to Him (Luke 14:26). Of course, providing for one's family is important, and providing the best and essential things for one's family is certainly among the most important things one can do. But what are those best and essential "most important" things?

The most important things are spiritual, for only the spiritual is eternal. So one might say the most important thing any of us possesses is his own eternal soul. Yet millions of people sell their souls into eternal agony for momentary pleasures or bits of gold. Put another way, the most important thing any of us can acquire is a relationship with Jesus Christ, or redemption, or eternal life. These are synonymous, but most people today do not value these things at all. Those who do must guard them carefully, "redeeming the time," as Paul says, for "the days are evil" (Ephesians 5:16).

4. Deceit hurts. Genesis 27:34 shows Esau's anguish over Jacob's deceit, but that was just the beginning. Everyone was hurt by Jacob's deed. Isaac's heart was broken; Esau wanted to kill Jacob; Rebekah never saw Jacob again after he fled from Esau. Isaac and Rebekah may have died without the hurt's ever having been healed.

Many people today have deceived or been deceived. How can relationships be healed after such a hurt?

Years later, when Jacob returned to Canaan, he and Esau were reconciled. This was possible only because both men chose to value their relationship over their rights. When we admit our faults and ask for forgiveness or we forget our anger and give up our "right" to revenge, we can also find healing for broken relationships.

5. Isaac and Rebekah bear part of the blame for this sad story. They definitely had favorites, which contributed to the resentment that grew between the brothers. The fact that Isaac's blessing, mistakenly given to Jacob, left no way in which he could bless the other son demonstrates the extent of his favoritism. What lessons can modern parents—or anyone who works with youth—learn from their poor example?

Parents and youth workers should learn from this sad story that they must love each child— not necessarily in the same ways, but to the same extent. Each child is different and will have a unique relationship with his or her parents or other authority figures in the child's life. Still, every child must rest assured in the fact that he or she is loved in a way that is not diminished by the presence of other children or any other factor.

Jacob's Flight and Vision

DEVOTIONAL READING: Psalm 121.

LESSON SCRIPTURE: Genesis 27:41—28:22.

PRINTED TEXT: Genesis 27:41; 28:10-16, 18-22.

Genesis 27:41

41 And Esau hated Jacob because of the blessing wherewith his father blessed him: and Esau said in his heart, The days of mourning for my father are at hand; then will I slay my brother Jacob.

Genesis 28:10-16, 18-22

10 And Jacob went out from Beersheba, and went toward Haran.

11 And he lighted upon a certain place, and tarried there all night, because the sun was set; and he took of the stones of that place, and put them for his pillows, and lay down in that place to sleep.

12 And he dreamed, and behold a ladder set up on the earth, and the top of it reached to heaven: and behold the angels of God ascending and descending on it.

13 And, behold, the LORD stood above it, and said, I am the LORD God of Abraham thy father, and the God of Isaac: the land whereon thou liest, to thee will I give it, and to thy seed;

14 And thy seed shall be as the dust of the earth; and thou shalt spread abroad to the west, and to the east, and to the north, and to the south: and in thee and in thy seed shall all the families of the earth be blessed.

15 And, behold, I am with thee, and will keep thee in all places whither thou goest, and will bring thee again into this land; for I will not leave thee, until I have done that which I have spoken to thee of.

16 And Jacob awaked out of his sleep, and he said, Surely the LORD is in this place; and I knew it not.

. . . .

18 And Jacob rose up early in the morning, and took the stone that he had put for his pillows, and set it up for a pillar, and poured oil upon the top of it.

19 And he called the name of that place Bethel: but the name of that city was called Luz at the first.

20 And Jacob vowed a vow, saying, If God will be with me, and will keep me in this way that I go, and will give me bread to eat, and raiment to put on,

21 So that I come again to my father's house in peace; then shall the LORD be my God:

22 And this stone, which I have set for a pillar, shall be God's house: and of all that thou shalt give me I will surely give the tenth unto thee.

Aug 1

GOLDEN TEXT: Behold, I am with thee, and will keep thee in all places whither thou goest, and will bring thee again into this land; for I will not leave thee, until I have done that which I have spoken to thee of.—Genesis 28:15.

Genesis: Beginnings
Unit 3: A People Tested
(Lessons 9-13)

Lesson Aims

After participating in this lesson, each student should:

1. Summarize the details surrounding God's appearance to Jacob at Bethel.

2. Relate a personal experience in which God was at work even though he or she was initially unaware of God's presence.

3. Praise God for granting His presence and blessings even though we are undeserving.

Lesson Outline

INTRODUCTION
    A. The Lord Is in This Place
    B. Lesson Background
  I. ESAU'S HATRED (Genesis 27:41)
 II. JACOB'S FLIGHT (Genesis 28:10-16)
    A. Jacob's Rest (vv. 10, 11)
    B. Jacob's Dream (v. 12)
    C. God's Revelation (vv. 13-15)
       Better Than a Dream
    D. Jacob's Response (v. 16)
III. JACOB'S MEMORIAL (Genesis 28:18-22)
    A. The Anointed Pillar (v. 18)
    B. A New Name (v. 19)
    C. Jacob's Vow (vv. 20-22)
CONCLUSION
    A. God Is Now Here
    B. Prayer
    C. Thought to Remember

Introduction

A. The Lord Is in This Place

When the first Russian cosmonaut returned to earth, he triumphantly announced to the world that now he had proof that there was no God. He had circled the earth in his spacecraft, and in all of outer space he had seen nothing of God or nothing to indicate God's presence. We stand amazed at the naivete of this man, who in many other respects must have been quite intelligent.

Yet consider Jacob. He was fleeing for his life from the wrath of his brother. But it also seems obvious that he was fleeing from the presence of God. Perhaps he was deliberately fleeing God and the responsibility that the presence of God involved, like Jonah many centuries after him.

Or perhaps he simply believed the God of his fathers was limited to the place where his father was—that fleeing his father's house necessitated fleeing his God. For whatever reason, it is clear he believed he had left God behind from his cry of amazement when he awoke from his dream: "Surely the Lord is in this place; and I knew it not."

Now let us consider ourselves, for we are all like Jacob. Our actions occasionally betray the fact that we think we have wandered too far from God for Him to reach us, or that we can deliberately run far enough to get beyond the presence of God. We ought to pray that when this happens, God will jar us back to our senses and cause us to cry out, "Surely the Lord is in this place; and I knew it not."

B. Lesson Background

The events described in today's lesson follow immediately after those covered in last week's lesson. That lesson ended with Esau pleading with his father for some kind of a blessing to replace the one out of which Jacob had cunningly cheated him. But the blessing that Isaac gave was more like a curse than a blessing. It included the promise that Esau would live by the sword and serve his brother (Genesis 27:40). While Esau himself did not experience the fulfillment of these words, his descendants (the Edomites) would later be in frequent submission to the descendants of Jacob (the Israelites). It is not surprising, in view of the blessing that Esau missed and the blessing that he received, that he reacted with hatred toward his brother and began to plot against him.

I. Esau's Hatred
(Genesis 27:41)

41. And Esau hated Jacob because of the blessing wherewith his father blessed him: and Esau said in his heart, The days of mourning for my father are at hand; then will I slay my brother Jacob.

When Esau first learned that his brother had cheated him out of his father's blessing, he "cried with a great and exceeding bitter cry" (v. 34). With the passing of time, his disappointment grew into a seething hatred.

Driven by this hatred, Esau began to plot how he would even the score against his brother. One who acts out of passion on the spur of the moment can be a dangerous and violent person. But once the moment of rage has passed, such a person usually regains control of his emotions and begins to behave more rationally. Far more dangerous is the man who is able to control his emotions for the moment, but allows them to simmer slowly until they become intensely bitter. This type of person is able to plot his revenge calmly, often carrying it out in violence. [See question #1, page 416.]

At this point Isaac was advanced in years, and it seemed evident that his death was not far away. Esau, who loved and respected his *father*, did not want to cause him grief by an act of violence within the family. Instead he determined to restrain his revenge until Isaac's death and *the days of mourning* had passed.

We do not know how long the *the days of mourning* typically lasted. In Genesis 50:3 Jacob was mourned seventy days by the Egyptians. Then, when his body was taken back to Canaan for burial, the caravan mourned him an additional seven days just before entering Canaan (Genesis 50:10). The seven days more likely reflects the more common mourning period in the family of Abraham.

Esau's plan was to wait until his father had died and been "properly mourned"; *then* he would *slay* his *brother Jacob*. However, Isaac lived for many years after this, and at his death was buried by both Jacob and Esau (Genesis 35:29). By then, Esau had put aside his anger and no longer wished to kill Jacob.

II. Jacob's Flight
(Genesis 28:10-16)

Esau felt so strongly about getting revenge that he was not able to keep his intentions to himself. He may have confided his desire to kill his brother to some of his friends, or he may inadvertently have let slip what he had in mind. In any event Rebekah learned about it and told Jacob about Esau's plan. Her advice, which made good sense under the circumstances, was for Jacob to flee to her brother Laban in Haran. Perhaps she had maintained some degree of contact with Laban and knew that Jacob could find a refuge there. Or perhaps she simply believed the family ties would be strong enough for Jacob to be welcome even though he was a stranger to Laban. After all, Abraham's servant had showed up there several years earlier and had been welcomed. That was how Rebekah had come to be Isaac's wife (Genesis 24).

However, Rebekah did not want to reveal to Isaac the real purpose for Jacob's departure. Instead, she told him that she wanted Jacob to find a wife among her own people rather than from among the pagan peoples around them in Canaan. Esau had married two Canaanite wives, and Rebekah complained that they were a source of frustration to her (Genesis 27:42-46).

This seemed plausible enough to Isaac, so he called Jacob in, blessed him, and sent him on his way. When Esau learned the stated reason for Jacob's departure, he realized that his father did not approve of his taking Canaanite wives. It appears that Esau tried to get back in his father's good graces by marrying a daughter of Ishmael. He apparently believed that since Ishmael was related to Abraham, this would be acceptable to Isaac. However, God had already made very clear His intention to establish His covenant with Isaac, not Ishmael (Genesis 17:19-21). Thus Esau's marriage may only have added to the tension between him and his father.

A. Jacob's Rest (vv. 10, 11)

10. And Jacob went out from Beersheba, and went toward Haran.

Jacob's journey from *Beersheba*, located in the southern part of Canaan, to *Haran*, located in northern Mesopotamia east of the Euphrates River, would cover several hundred miles through rugged, semi-desert terrain. Furthermore, there was a good chance that Jacob would encounter some hostile tribes or individuals along the way. We are not told what provisions Jacob took along with him for the trip, which may have taken several weeks. Since he left in haste (Genesis 27:43), he probably did not have much. [See question #2, page 416.]

11. And he lighted upon a certain place, and tarried there all night, because the sun was set; and he took of the stones of that place, and put them for his pillows, and lay down in that place to sleep.

Beersheba, where Jacob started, was about forty-five miles southwest of Jerusalem. Luz (later named Bethel), where Jacob stopped, was about a dozen miles north of Jerusalem; thus Jacob had traveled close to sixty miles since he left home. He had been on the road probably three or four days, then, at this point. Exhausted as he must have been by a long day's journey, all he wanted was a place where he could stop and rest. At sunset, *he lighted upon a certain place.* The Hebrew has the definite article ("*the* place"), suggesting that Jacob's arrival at this particular location was no accident. It was not by Jacob's plan that he arrived at this place, however. Jacob was soon to discover that Another was guiding his steps on this journey.

As Jacob prepared for a night's rest, *he took of the stones of that place, and put them for his pillows.* The Hebrew text reads, "He took from the stones of the place and set up his pillow." That one stone was used by Jacob for a pillow is clear from verse 18. His heavy outer garment likely served as bedding.

Today's visual illustrates Jacob's dream at Bethel and highlights God's promise to protect him and bring him back to the land of promise (v. 15).

Visual for lesson 9

B. Jacob's Dream (v. 12)

12. And he dreamed, and behold a ladder set up on the earth, and the top of it reached to heaven: and behold the angels of God ascending and descending on it.

At some point during the night Jacob *dreamed*, but this was no ordinary dream! This is one of several accounts recorded in the Old Testament of divine revelation coming to someone through a dream. Later, Jacob's son Joseph had a number of dreams and was also given the ability to interpret dreams.

In his dream Jacob saw *a ladder set up on the earth*. Some versions use the word "stairway" instead of "ladder" (*New International Version, Today's English Version*). This stairway or ladder *reached to heaven*. Years before men had attempted to build their own stairway to Heaven (the tower of Babel), and God had thwarted their efforts (Genesis 11:4-9). Now God Himself opened the way. Communication between Heaven and earth must take place on God's terms, never on man's.

Apparently the vision conveyed to Jacob that no matter how far he had run, he had not moved beyond God's care and control. We are not told the significance of the angels both *ascending and descending*, but it may have symbolized the communication that was to take place between God and Jacob, as well as that which He desires with all mankind. Was Jesus thinking of this incident when He was speaking to Nathanael and referred to Himself as the one upon whom the angels of God would be "ascending and descending" (John 1:51)? Jesus is the "stairway" by which God has reached down to communicate with mankind (John 1:1, 14).

C. God's Revelation (vv. 13-15)

13. And, behold, the LORD stood above it, and said, I am the LORD God of Abraham thy father, and the God of Isaac: the land whereon thou liest, to thee will I give it, and to thy seed.

Above this stairway *the Lord stood.* We are not given a description of what the Lord looked like, and appropriately so, for "no man hath seen God at any time" (John 1:18). Jacob knew from the words spoken to him that this was no ordinary dream; it was clearly of the Lord. Probably the last thing in the world that he expected at this time was a revelation from God. And although he did not deserve such a revelation, Jacob—a cheat and a swindler—certainly needed one. In spite of his sins and failures, God intended to use him in His plan for the salvation of the human race.

When the Lord began to speak to Jacob, He identified Himself as *the Lord God of Abraham thy father, and the God of Isaac.* God had made a covenant with both Abraham and Isaac, promising them a large posterity and the land of Canaan as their own. How much information about this covenant Isaac had shared with Jacob we do not know, but certainly Jacob knew something about it. Now God indicated that He was renewing this covenant with Jacob. The very *land* on which Jacob was sleeping was a part of the land that God had promised to his father and grandfather. The idea that this promise could ever be fulfilled in him must have struck Jacob as highly improbable. How could Jacob—a fugitive from his brother and a stranger in the land where he traveled—ever hope to inherit anything but more trouble?

Note, too, the irony. Jacob had schemed and deceived to achieve for himself greater rights and blessings, and he had only made himself a fugitive. Now, helpless and virtually hopeless, he achieves a greater blessing than he could have imagined—simply by God's grace!

14. And thy seed shall be as the dust of the earth; and thou shalt spread abroad to the west, and to the east, and to the north, and to the south: and in thee and in thy seed shall all the families of the earth be blessed.

Now the dream became even more amazing. *Thy seed shall be as the dust of the earth.* How could this promise ever be fulfilled in a man who not only had no children, but was not even married? Yet the situation was not entirely hopeless. After all, Jacob's own grandfather and grandmother had been blessed with a son after all hope of having a child had passed.

Thou shalt spread abroad. In every direction from where he lay, Jacob's descendants would scatter. Furthermore, through his seed *all the families of the earth* would be *blessed.* How ironic that one who was then a curse to his own family should someday become a source of blessing to the nations! We know that blessing to be Jesus Christ, who many generations later would be born to descendants of Jacob and would draw in many "from the east, and from the west, and from the north, and from the south" to be part of His kingdom (Luke 13:29).

15. And, behold, I am with thee, and will keep thee in all places whither thou goest, and will bring thee again into this land; for I will not leave thee, until I have done that which I have spoken to thee of.

Jacob was just beginning a journey that would take him far from home for a long time (twenty years, according to Genesis 31:38). He certainly must have been apprehensive about what the future held for him. Now came God's reassuring words. God promised to be *with* Jacob—to watch over him, protect him every step of the way, and eventually return him to this land. He would never *leave* Jacob until He had accomplished what He had promised. [See question #3, page 416.]

BETTER THAN A DREAM

Not long ago a popular retort to someone's plans or ideas was, "In your dreams!" It meant that someone's ambitions or fantasies were far less than likely to be fulfilled. Dreams that actually do come true seem to be disproportionately outnumbered by those that don't. Occasionally, however, one's dreams are realized: a girl actually marries a "knight in shining armor," a college graduate lands the perfect job, and nice guys finish first rather than last.

In some cases dreams challenge individuals to do some serious self-examination and make some long overdue changes. Consider the account of Jacob's dream in today's lesson text. We, like him, would react with awe and reverence if God spoke to us in a dream. Indeed, perhaps we wish that He *would* communicate His purposes and promises in such a direct manner or tell us personally, "I will not leave you . . . ." Jacob was truly blessed to be reassured of God's covenant through the miracle of a dream.

But think about this: we have our own miracle of God's revelation. The Bible is God's book; it is "God-breathed" (2 Timothy 3:16, *New International Version*). In it God *has* communicated His purposes and promises to us. He *has* said that He will never leave us (Hebrews 13:5). We should treat this sacred record with awe and reverence—for through it God speaks. —R. W. B.

D. Jacob's Response (v. 16)

16. And Jacob awaked out of his sleep, and he said, Surely the LORD is in this place; and I knew it not.

When Jacob awoke, he was a different man. Perhaps he had believed that God could operate only in a small area, specifically the area where his family lived. Now he realized that God knows no geographical limitations. Not only was God back home with his family, but God was also in the very spot where he lay!

Many today share Jacob's limited faith. Because God permits evil in the world, they believe that He has limited power. Or because He fails to extricate them from the mess they have made of their lives, they reject Him as powerless. Or because they deem their sins so terrible, they refuse to believe that He can forgive them.

III. Jacob's Memorial (Genesis 28:18-22)
A. The Anointed Pillar (v. 18)

18. And Jacob rose up early in the morning, and took the stone that he had put for his pillows, and set it up for a pillar, and poured oil upon the top of it.

Verse 17 tells us that Jacob was filled with fear as a result of his experience during the night. When he *rose up early in the morning*, he *took the stone* that had been his pillow during the night and used it to construct a *pillar*. Then he *poured oil* upon it as an act of consecration. Actually, Jacob was not consecrating the stone; he was consecrating the spot where God had revealed Himself to him. [See question #4, page 416.]

B. A New Name (v. 19)

19. And he called the name of that place Bethel: but the name of that city was called Luz at the first.

The Hebrew word rendered *Bethel* means "house of God." Jacob's encounter with God had

---

How to Say It

BEERSHEBA. Beer-*she*-buh.
BETHEL. *Beth*-ul.
CANAANITE. *Kay*-nuh-nite.
EDOMITES. *Ee*-dum-ites.
ESAU. *Ee*-saw.
EUPHRATES. You-*fray*-teez.
HARAN. *Hair*-un.
ISHMAEL. *Ish*-may-el.
JEROBOAM. Jair-uh-*boe*-um.
LABAN. *Lay*-bun.
LUZ. Luzz.
MELCHIZEDEK. Mel-*kizz*-eh-dek.
MESOPOTAMIA. *Mess*-uh-puh-*tay*-me-uh (strong accent on *tay*).
NATHANAEL. Nuh-*than*-yull (*th* as in *thin*).

so overwhelmed him that he had no doubt that God was present there. Jacob was not proclaiming this spot to be the only place where God lived; like the erection of the pillar, the new name marked this location as one of great meaning for Jacob. We are told that the earlier name for this place was *Luz*, which means "nut tree" or "almond tree." Bethel played a significant part in later Hebrew history. It was one of the places where Samuel held court and "judged Israel" (1 Samuel 7:16); and it was there that Jeroboam, who ruled the northern kingdom following the division of Israel, erected a golden calf to keep the people in the north from going to Jerusalem to worship (1 Kings 12:28-33). [See question #5, page 416.]

C. Jacob's Vow (vv. 20-22)

20, 21. And Jacob vowed a vow, saying, If God will be with me, and will keep me in this way that I go, and will give me bread to eat, and raiment to put on, so that I come again to my father's house in peace; then shall the LORD be my God.

If God will be with me . . . then shall the Lord be my God. Some believe that these words show that Jacob was driving a bargain with God. His reputation would certainly leave him open to such a charge. However, at this point in Jacob's spiritual pilgrimage, we might better see this as claiming God's promise and responding to it: "If God will be with me [and I believe He will], then. . . ." Jacob obviously had some growing to do, but the next verse indicates that he was not thinking simply of getting things from God; he also wanted to give a portion of God's provisions back to Him.

22. And this stone, which I have set for a pillar, shall be God's house: and of all that thou shalt give me I will surely give the tenth unto thee.

This stone . . . shall be God's house. Jacob was not affirming that he believed that God actually lived in the stone that he had set up. Such a crude form of paganism may have been accepted by some of the Canaanites in the land around Jacob, but this was not his religion. This statement may be taken as Jacob's pledge that someday he would build here a more fitting altar, monument, or structure to the glory of God. And indeed, Jacob did eventually return to Bethel, and built there an altar to mark the time when God appeared to him (Genesis 35:6, 7).

I will surely give the tenth unto thee. Jacob made a second commitment. Recognizing that all of his material blessings would come from God, he pledged to return to Him a tenth, or a tithe, of all those blessings. Abraham earlier had given tithes to Melchizedek (Genesis 14:18-20). These two examples indicate that tithing was an accepted practice many years before the instructions in the law of Moses were given.

Conclusion

A. God Is Now Here

An atheist wanted to proclaim his denial of the existence of God. So he hired a skywriter to write the following message across the sky: GOD IS NOWHERE. But just as the pilot finished writing the words, a shift in the wind changed the message to read: GOD IS NOW HERE.

Jacob was not an atheist, but his idea of God was a rather limited one. The way he lived his life indicated that God did not have an important place in his decision-making. When he left his home and fled for his life, he apparently left his convictions about God at home. Then God confronted Jacob in the way that God often confronts us—when we are tired, lonely, and hurting. Jacob's dream convinced him that God was not confined to one small locality but was everywhere! We too need to come to that same conclusion—and do so before we are confronted with dire circumstances.

B. Prayer

Dear God, help us learn from the experiences of Jacob. Keep us from seeking to take advantage of our family and our friends through questionable practices or misleading words. Help us to grow in faith as Jacob finally did. In Christ's name we pray. Amen.

C. Thought to Remember

"Whither shall I flee from thy presence?" (Psalm 139:7).

Home Daily Bible Readings

Monday, July 26—Esau Hates Jacob (Genesis 27:41-46)
Tuesday, July 27—Isaac Sends Jacob Away (Genesis 28:1-5)
Wednesday, July 28—Jacob's Dream at Bethel (Genesis 28:6-17)
Thursday, July 29—If God Will Be With Me (Genesis 28:18-22)
Friday, July 30—Jacob Meets Rachel (Genesis 29:1-14a)
Saturday, July 31—Jacob Is Tricked by Laban (Genesis 29:14b-30)
Sunday, Aug. 1—The Faithfulness of God (Deuteronomy 30:1-5)

Learning by Doing

This page contains an alternate lesson plan emphasizing learning activities.
Classes desiring such student involvement will find these suggestions helpful.

Learning Goals

As a result of this lesson, your students should be able to:

1. Summarize the details surrounding God's appearance to Jacob at Bethel.

2. Relate a personal experience in which God was at work even though he or she was initially unaware of God's presence.

3. Praise God for granting His presence and blessings even though we are undeserving.

Into the Lesson

Introduce this lesson by asking your students to suggest various ways that God makes Himself known. Write their answers on a sheet of newsprint. Some answers are through the Bible, through a personal tragedy (death, disease, financial reverse), through answered prayer, through another person's witness, through a sermon, through music, or through a special blessing (such as the birth of a child).

In today's lesson we will learn how God encountered Jacob and made Himself known in a dream. The promises God made to Jacob in that dream still have relevance for us today, as we shall see in our lesson.

Into the Word

Review the events that happened in last week's lesson. Jacob's flight to Haran in this lesson was necessitated by his acts of deception in last week's lesson, which angered Esau to the point of murderous hatred (Genesis 27:41).

In this lesson we see that God is faithful to reveal Himself even when we are not looking for Him. God's self-disclosure to Jacob was actually a reaffirmation of the covenant He had made with Abraham and renewed with Isaac. As such, it contained multiple promises. Ask your students to read Genesis 28:12-16 and identify and explain each promise:

• Land (v. 13). Jacob was heir to the same land God had promised to Abraham—Canaan, the land of promise.

• Descendants (v. 14a). As Israel, Jacob would give his name to the descendants of Abraham—the Israelites (Jews).

• A Descendant (v. 14b). This promise was fulfilled in Jesus Christ.

• Presence (v. 15). God promised to go with Jacob even to faraway Haran. This contradicted the popular belief that gods were assigned specific areas and functions.

Ask the class, "If God appeared to you in a spectacular vision and spoke in an audible voice, what would your response be?" Obviously, life for a person who had such an experience would be changed forever. Such was the case with Jacob. Have a volunteer read Genesis 28:18-22. Then distribute a sheet of paper with the title "Jacob's Response" at the top and verse numbers 18-22 down the left side. Working individually or in small groups, students should fill in the chart by noting what is said of Jacob's response in each verse.

18: He worshiped God by building an altar.

19: He named the place "Bethel," which means "house of God."

20, 21: He acknowledged God's promises and vowed to serve God.

22: He promised to build a proper altar or sanctuary for the worship of God at Bethel and to give God a tithe of everything he received.

Into Life

In Genesis 28:20-22 Jacob made what appears to be a bargain with God. Have any of your students ever tried to negotiate a deal with God? How do your students feel about making deals with God? What are the hazards?

There is a better way to look at Jacob's "bargain" with God. He may have been making a promise to God as a result of this life-changing encounter. In that case it was not so much a bargain as an expression of praise to God and an affirmation of faith in God.

Tell the class, "Jacob apparently thought he was leaving everything—including God. But in his vision he learned that God was still with him." Then ask, "What experiences have you had when you were not specifically aware of God's presence for a time but then came to realize He was with you?" Be prepared to relate a personal example to initiate the discussion. Perhaps it was when a loved one died and you found a strength not your own to hold up under your grief. Or perhaps you took on a job you feared you could not handle but found God gave you the strength to do it.

In closing, challenge your students to praise God during the coming week for all the blessings and promises that flow from His hand.

Let's Talk It Over

The questions on this page are designed to encourage review of the lesson Scriptures and to promote discussion of the lesson by the class. The answers provided are only discussion starters. Let your class talk it over from there.

1. Esau had a legitimate complaint—he had been cheated! The more he thought about it the madder he became until he hated his brother. The only thing that kept him from killing Jacob was respect for their father. That still happens today. People are wronged, hurt, or offended in some way, and they nurse their anger until it grows into hatred. They begin to look for ways to exact revenge. What advice would you give someone who had been wronged by another? What would you do to help the two restore their broken relationship?

It is easy to say one ought to forgive but much harder to practice it. Of course, that is what's needed, but maybe a cooling-off period would help first. Jacob and Esau were parted for twenty years and, while that was a symptom of some real trouble, it did allow time for cooler heads to prevail. At other times, a third party might be able to arbitrate between divided brothers. In the end, the wronged party must yield his right to revenge—even if the offending party does not apologize or repent.

2. Jacob was in a mess of his own making, and it seemed that the best thing to do was to leave for a while. Sometimes we find ourselves in bad situations of our own making, too. When is it wise to try to escape such situations, and when should we stay and confront the issues? How can we tell which is better?

There are times when it is wise to put some distance between ourselves and a bad situation for a time. If another is angry or, especially, abusive, then some time and distance may be prudent. We should not use flight as a mere "easy way out," however. If we are guilty of creating the situation, usually the only way to fix it is to admit our guilt, repent of it, and seek forgiveness—even making restitution if that is possible.

3. Some people read verse 15 of our text and claim it guarantees a sort of immortality until we accomplish what God wants us to do. How would you caution a person who took unnecessary risks because he was sure God had not done with him all He planned to do, and thus he believed himself immortal?

This was a special promise to Jacob, not a blanket assurance for people of all time. Some

people never submit to God's will. If this idea were true, such people would never die! This concept also leaves unanswered the cause for so many infant deaths (especially including all the unborn who die either by natural causes or by violence). God does promise to be with us (Matthew 28:20), but He does not promise us immortality in *this* life—only in eternity.

4. Jacob erected a simple monument to mark the place where he had met God. What kind of monuments do you have to help you recall special events or truths?

The Lord's Supper is a type of monument or memorial, which reminds us of Jesus' sacrificial death every time we partake of it. Christian symbols, such as a cross, a dove, or a fish are types of simple memorials, testifying to the faith. Important events in the life of the church that are seen as extraordinary examples of God's blessing may be memorialized by anniversary observances or physical reminders. Let each class member share what he or she uses as a memorial to something especially significant in his or her walk with the Lord.

5. Jacob probably worshiped God before he had his dream, and genuinely so. But when God appeared to him, Jacob's worship took on a whole new dimension. He submitted to God, trusted in Him, and attempted to walk with Him. It went from ritual to real. It became important to Jacob that he know God and please Him. How can we move our own worship from the ritual to the real? What impact does real worship have on your life?

We cannot duplicate Jacob's experience to deepen our worship, but we can focus on the God who initiated it. Worship that is mere habit will make little impact on our lives. But when we submit to the Lord and make it our utmost desire to know and please Him, our worship naturally goes to a deeper level. Putting aside the interests of the world, we devote our hearts to the Lord. The prophets repeatedly chastised Israel for maintaining a form of worship while their day-to-day lives were out of sync with God's will. When we desire fellowship with God every day of the week, our fellowship on the first day of the week is even sweeter.

Jacob's Struggle at Peniel

DEVOTIONAL READING: **Psalm 25:1-7.**

LESSON SCRIPTURE: **Genesis 32:3—33:17.**

PRINTED TEXT: **Genesis 32:9-11, 24-30; 33:1-4.**

Genesis 32:9-11, 24-30

9 And Jacob said, O God of my father Abraham, and God of my father Isaac, the LORD which saidst unto me, Return unto thy country, and to thy kindred, and I will deal well with thee:

10 I am not worthy of the least of all the mercies, and of all the truth, which thou hast showed unto thy servant; for with my staff I passed over this Jordan; and now I am become two bands.

11 Deliver me, I pray thee, from the hand of my brother, from the hand of Esau: for I fear him, lest he will come and smite me, and the mother with the children.

· · · · · · · · · · · ·

24 And Jacob was left alone; and there wrestled a man with him until the breaking of the day.

25 And when he saw that he prevailed not against him, he touched the hollow of his thigh; and the hollow of Jacob's thigh was out of joint, as he wrestled with him.

26 And he said, Let me go, for the day breaketh. And he said, I will not let thee go, except thou bless me.

27 And he said unto him, What is thy name? And he said, Jacob.

28 And he said, Thy name shall be called no more Jacob, but Israel: for as a prince hast thou power with God and with men, and hast prevailed.

29 And Jacob asked him, and said, Tell me, I pray thee, thy name. And he said, Wherefore is it that thou dost ask after my name? And he blessed him there.

30 And Jacob called the name of the place Peniel: for I have seen God face to face, and my life is preserved.

Genesis 33:1-4

1 And Jacob lifted up his eyes, and looked, and, behold, Esau came, and with him four hundred men. And he divided the children unto Leah, and unto Rachel, and unto the two handmaids.

2 And he put the handmaids and their children foremost, and Leah and her children after, and Rachel and Joseph hindermost.

3 And he passed over before them, and bowed himself to the ground seven times, until he came near to his brother.

4 And Esau ran to meet him, and embraced him, and fell on his neck, and kissed him: and they wept.

GOLDEN TEXT: I am not worthy of the least of all the mercies, and of all the truth, which thou hast showed unto thy servant.—Genesis 32:10.

Genesis: Beginnings

Unit 3: A People Tested

(Lessons 9-13)

Lesson Aims

After this lesson each student will be able to:

1. Tell how Jacob was reconciled with Esau and of the prayer and divine struggle that preceded the event.

2. Explain the significance of Jacob's actions as he prepared to meet Esau, and describe the change in his character these actions represent.

3. Examine his or her life for an occasion of struggling with God, and seek God's blessing in it.

Lesson Outline

INTRODUCTION

  A. Fixing the Works

  B. Lesson Background

I. JACOB PRAYS (Genesis 32:9-11)

  A. A Prayer of Humility (vv. 9, 10)

  B. A Prayer for Deliverance (v. 11)

II. JACOB WRESTLES WITH AN ANGEL (Genesis 32:24-30)

  A. The Struggle (vv. 24, 25)

  B. Jacob's Demand (v. 26)

  C. The Angel's Response (vv. 27, 28)

    A New Name

  D. Jacob's Realization (vv. 29, 30)

III. JACOB MEETS ESAU (Genesis 33:1-4)

  A. Jacob's Preparation (vv. 1, 2)

  B. Jacob's Greeting (v. 3)

  C. Esau's Response (v. 4)

    A Parable of Grace

CONCLUSION

  A. Wrestling Through the Night

  B. Bethel and Peniel

  C. Prayer

  D. Thought to Remember

Introduction

A. Fixing the Works

An old mountaineer came one day into a watchmaker's shop, bringing with him the hands from a large old-fashioned clock. "I want you to fix these," he said to the watchmaker. "They jist don't keep the right time anymore."

"But there's nothing wrong with these hands," replied the watchmaker. "Apparently the trouble is in the works. Bring the clock in and let me look at it. That's the only way I can fix it."

"But it's the hands that don't work," argued the old man. Nothing that the watchmaker said could convince him that the real trouble was in the works and not in the hands. Finally in anger the mountaineer cried, "I knowed it! I knowed it all along. You jist want to git that clock in here so's you kin work on it and charge me a fancy price. Well, I'm not dumb enough to let you git away with it!"

Foolish as this man was, his caution was very much like that of Jacob, who tried to control and manage his life without addressing the real problems on the inside. His promise at Bethel was a good start (recall last week's lesson), but for the next twenty years Jacob still had difficulty putting himself under God's authority. Perhaps he feared that the price would be too high. But at Peniel he finally realized that true victory would never be his unless he was willing to surrender the "works" of his life to God.

B. Lesson Background

Rebekah had sent Jacob to her brother Laban to escape the revenge of Esau and to find a wife from among her own people. Jacob's mission was successful on both counts. He spent seven years working for Laban, after which he married his two daughters, Leah and Rachel. To complete the agreement for Rachel, Jacob had to work seven more years, and then six additional years in order to have his own livestock. Thus the "few days" that Rebekah had urged him to tarry with Laban (Genesis 27:43, 44) turned into twenty years!

During this twenty-year period, Jacob prospered. His wives and their handmaidens bore him eleven sons and a daughter. In addition God blessed him materially and, especially in the last six years, his flocks increased. Laban's flocks, which Jacob tended, had grown large during the first fourteen years Jacob worked for Laban. But in the last six, while Jacob's flocks were growing stronger, Laban's grew weaker. This led to growing tensions between Laban and Jacob.

Eventually God told Jacob to leave Haran and return to Canaan—"the land of thy fathers" (Genesis 31:3). Jacob realized that Laban would not be happy with his leaving, and so he slipped away secretly.

Learning of Jacob's departure, Laban pursued him; but before he caught up with him, God spoke to Laban in a dream, telling him not to deal violently with Jacob (Genesis 31:24). The meeting of the two men was not exactly congenial, but they agreed to go their separate ways. They raised a heap of stones, which they agreed would mark the boundary beyond which neither would pass. Laban's words to Jacob formed a benediction that many Christians still use: "The Lord watch between me and thee, when we are absent one from another" (Genesis 31:49). After this meeting, Jacob and his family and flocks continued to move southward toward the territory where Esau lived.

I. Jacob Prays
(Genesis 32:9-11)

A. A Prayer of Humility (vv. 9, 10)

As Jacob and his company drew closer, he sent messengers to meet Esau, who was living in "the land of Seir, the country of Edom" (Genesis 32:3), located south and east of the Dead Sea. The messengers were instructed to convey to Esau the word that Jacob came in peace, seeking reconciliation with him. But when the messengers returned, they brought word that Esau was coming to meet Jacob with four hundred men. Jacob assumed the worst and became "greatly afraid and distressed" (v. 7). He figured that Esau had organized a group of men in order to gain the revenge against Jacob that he had never been able to obtain.

9. And Jacob said, O God of my father Abraham, and God of my father Isaac, the LORD which saidst unto me, Return unto thy country, and to thy kindred, and I will deal well with thee.

Jacob had good reason to go to God in prayer. He knew that the sizable group approaching him, led by Esau, could easily overpower him. And with the numbers of family and flocks accompanying him, there was really no way he could escape if Esau chose to pursue him.

Jacob began his prayer by addressing Jehovah as the God of his *father Isaac* and his grandfather *Abraham*. Then he mentioned the promise that God had made to him earlier during his flight from Laban. Jacob was in this precarious situation because God had told him to return to the *country* of his fathers. He claimed that God had promised to *deal well* with him. But that is not exactly what God had said. God had promised Jacob, "I will be with thee" (Genesis 31:3). God's abiding presence with us is no guarantee that everything will "go well" or that our circumstances will always come out the way we want them to. [See question #1, page 424.]

10. I am not worthy of the least of all the mercies, and of all the truth, which thou hast showed unto thy servant; for with my staff I passed over this Jordan; and now I am become two bands.

During his twenty-year "exile," Jacob had grown in his faith. He approached God with a humility that was not evident earlier in his life.

Formerly he had depended on his cleverness and cunning to get what he wanted. Now he acknowledged that God had showered His *mercies* on him and had opened his heart to new *truth*. Jacob was showing signs of real spiritual growth.

Jacob indicated how God had blessed him by noting that when he had first crossed the Jordan River during his flight from Esau, he had nothing but his *staff*. Now his possessions were so many that he could divide them into *two bands*, or groups (vv. 7, 8). Jacob's sentiments can be echoed by every Christian: we realize that we have been brought out of spiritual poverty into immeasurable wealth and that we are *not worthy* of such treatment. [See question #2, page 424.]

B. A Prayer for Deliverance (v. 11)

11. Deliver me, I pray thee, from the hand of my brother, from the hand of Esau: for I fear him, lest he will come and smite me, and the mother with the children.

Jacob remembered *Esau* as he had been twenty years earlier. As far as we know, there had been no communication between the two during that time. Jacob remembered Esau as impulsive and ill-tempered, and that caused him to *fear* for his own safety and for the safety of his wives and *children*. Apparently it never occurred to Jacob that Esau might have changed, even as he himself had changed during that time. Still, even if Jacob had tried to give Esau credit, we can understand why he felt as he did. After all, why else but for battle did Esau need a four-hundred-man escort?

II. Jacob Wrestles With an Angel
(Genesis 32:24-30)

A. The Struggle (vv. 24, 25)

As the moment drew near for the two brothers to meet, Jacob selected a sizable number of sheep, goats, camels, cattle, and donkeys to be sent by his servants as a gift to Esau. He also sent his family across the Jabbok River, a tributary of the Jordan that flows east, about halfway between the Dead Sea and the Sea of Galilee. Only Jacob remained behind.

24, 25. And Jacob was left alone; and there wrestled a man with him until the breaking of the day. And when he saw that he prevailed not against him, he touched the hollow of his thigh; and the hollow of Jacob's thigh was out of joint, as he wrestled with him.

Jacob was left alone with his thoughts and fears. Suddenly, or so it appears, he was attacked without warning. Here we have no description of the assailant except that he was a *man*. Hosea 12:4 tells us that he was an angel.

Jacob, in spite of the fact that he was advanced in years (according to the information provided in Genesis, he would have been close to one hundred years old), struggled valiantly and held his own until the dawning of the new day. The angel then demonstrated his supernatural ability when he *touched . . . the hollow of Jacob's thigh* and wrenched it *out of joint.*

B. Jacob's Demand (v. 26)

26. And he said, Let me go, for the day breaketh. And he said, I will not let thee go, except thou bless me.

When the stranger touched his thigh joint and left him crippled, Jacob must have realized that he was not just an ordinary desert marauder, but was in some sense divine, or a divine messenger. (He had already encountered angels of God, according to Genesis 32:1, 2.) Thus, when the stranger asked to be released, Jacob refused to let him go unless he received a blessing.

Hosea 12:4 provides an interesting commentary on this contest. Speaking of Jacob, the prophet said, "He had power over the angel, and prevailed: he wept, and made supplication unto him." From wrestling, Jacob turned to supplication—a most significant change in attitude. Thus the most important wrestling that took place during this incident was spiritual, not physical. God's angel could have overpowered Jacob at any point. But when a man is struggling for God's blessing, God does not want to prevail against him and make him abandon the struggle. God may delay the giving of His blessing because the man needs the time of waiting and struggling to help him realize his need for God and appreciate His blessing when it comes. Apparently Jacob continued to suffer the effects of his injury (v. 31), but the greater spiritual battle had been won.

Home Daily Bible Readings

Monday, Aug. 2—Jacob Undertakes Reconciliation With Esau (Genesis 32:3-8)
Tuesday, Aug. 3—Jacob Prepares Gifts for Esau (Genesis 32:9-21)
Wednesday, Aug. 4—Jacob Wrestles With a "Man" at Jabbok (Genesis 32:22-32)
Thursday, Aug. 5—Esau and Jacob Are Reunited (Genesis 33:1-11)
Friday, Aug. 6—Esau and Jacob Go Separate Ways (Genesis 33:12-17)
Saturday, Aug. 7—Jesus' Teaching on Anger (Matthew 5:21-26)
Sunday, Aug. 8—Forgive Seventy Times Seven (Matthew 18:21-35)

C. The Angel's Response (vv. 27, 28)

27, 28. And he said unto him, What is thy name? And he said, Jacob. And he said, Thy name shall be called no more Jacob, but Israel: for as a prince hast thou power with God and with men, and hast prevailed.

Of course, the angel knew Jacob's *name;* he asked for it only to emphasize the change that he was about to make. Jacob confessed that his name was *Jacob,* the "heel grabber," the "supplanter." The name described his earlier life quite accurately—a cheat, a clever trickster, one who had taken advantage of his blind father and his hungry brother.

Then came the dramatic announcement: *Thy name shall be called . . . Israel.* This name is interpreted by some as meaning "prince of God"; however, the Hebrew term can be translated as "one who strives, or struggles, with God" and seems to be the preferred meaning among Bible students. The word is thus rendered in the *New International Version* ("you have struggled with God and with men") and the *New American Standard Bible* ("you have striven with God and with men"). This is not to be understood in the bad sense (as though Jacob opposed God), but in the good sense (that he worked vigorously to obtain God's blessing). Jacob had learned to prevail through *power with God,* not through his own craftiness. [See question #3, page 424.]

A NEW NAME

Names make a big difference to some people. Think of the Hollywood celebrities whose whole public persona has been shaped around their screen names. Some brides choose not to take the family name of their husbands; keeping their own name is an issue of personal independence for them. Others prefer to be called by a nickname rather than by their given name—in fact, sometimes their legal name becomes a closely guarded secret.

Names had great significance in early Hebrew culture. Names often called attention to appearance and achievements, as well as character and personality. *Jacob* meant "supplanter." The name was actually a kind of prophecy, which came to pass when the younger twin born to Rebekah and Isaac stole the birthright and blessing of his older brother. Jacob's new name, *Israel,* identified him as one who had "struggled" or "striven" with God and secured divine favor.

Most Westerners don't pay that much attention to names and their meanings. Christians, however, wear the name and title of Jesus, and "there's just something about that name!" Blessed be the name of the Lord!   —R. W. B.

O Lord, ...
I am unworthy
of all the
kindness and
faithfulness
you have shown.

Genesis 32:9, 10 NIV

Visual for
lesson 10

Today's visual cites Genesis 32:10 and reminds us that none of us is worthy of the grace of God. Praise God that He gives it to us anyway!

D. Jacob's Realization (vv. 29, 30)

29, 30. And Jacob asked him, and said, Tell me, I pray thee, thy name. And he said, Wherefore is it that thou dost ask after my name? And he blessed him there. And Jacob called the name of the place Peniel: for I have seen God face to face, and my life is preserved.

Tell me . . . thy name. Jacob was interested in much more than his opponent's name; he wanted to know his identity, who he really was. Jacob must have already strongly suspected that his opponent was more than human. Through his question, he wanted to confirm his suspicions. The angel did not answer Jacob's question directly, but by blessing him, he confirmed that he was indeed supernatural. The blessing apparently included God's assurance that His presence would sustain Jacob through the upcoming meeting with Esau.

Jacob called the name of the place Peniel, which means "the face of God." By now Jacob had begun to understand the fuller implications of his experience, and the impact left him filled with awe. *I have seen God face to face.* Of course, no man has actually seen God with his physical eyes (John 1:18), for God is a Spirit. But Jacob's experience was just as vivid as if God had been visible, and he was overwhelmed by the fact that he had survived such an intimate encounter with God.

III. Jacob Meets Esau (Genesis 33:1-4)

A. Jacob's Preparation (vv. 1, 2)

1, 2. And Jacob lifted up his eyes, and looked, and, behold, Esau came, and with him four hundred men. And he divided the children unto Leah, and unto Rachel, and unto the two handmaids. And he put the handmaids and their children foremost, and Leah and her children after, and Rachel and Joseph hindermost.

As the new day dawned, the moment of truth for Jacob and his family arrived. Since Esau was accompanied by *four hundred men,* Jacob believed he had good reason to expect the worst. And yet he did not turn back because he had faith that God would protect him. Having prevailed with God the night before, he had every reason to believe that God would help him prevail against his brother.

Apparently, however, Jacob had no guarantee that he would prevail without a struggle or that the struggle would be without casualties. He began to take precautions to save some of his party from the anticipated conflict. He placed the *handmaids* and their children first, followed by *Leah and her children,* and finally *Rachel and Joseph hindermost* (or farthest to the rear). In this arrangement Jacob showed the order of his preference for the family members involved. Perhaps he thought that if Esau was bent on revenge, then at least his favorite wife (Rachel) and son (Joseph) could escape. We wonder what those placed in the front of the group may have thought about this strategy! [See question #4, page 424.]

B. Jacob's Greeting (v. 3)

3. And he passed over before them, and bowed himself to the ground seven times, until he came near to his brother.

Whatever the different groups of his family thought about the precautions Jacob had taken, they could not accuse him of being a coward. He himself boldly stepped forward and placed himself at the front of his family. If violence ensued, he would be the first to suffer. Note the contrast: twenty years earlier he had fled in fear to escape his brother. Now, as he approached Esau, Jacob *bowed himself . . . seven times* as a gesture of respect and submission. Probably he bowed once, took a few steps toward Esau, then bowed again, repeating this action until he stood before *his brother.*

C. Esau's Response (v. 4)

4. And Esau ran to meet him, and embraced him, and fell on his neck, and kissed him: and they wept.

Like the father who ran to meet his prodigal son, Esau laid aside any proper protocol and *ran to meet* his long-lost brother, embracing him and kissing him in a display of his affection. In spite of his earlier treatment by Jacob, Esau obviously accepted his brother's gesture as sincere. Gone was the bitterness and hostility of the past. At first Jacob was likely taken aback by Esau's response, but he soon shared with his brother in tears of joy. In words that reflected his experience of the previous night, Jacob told Esau, "I have seen thy face, as though I had seen the face of God, and thou wast pleased with me" (v. 10).

A PARABLE OF GRACE

Parables—"earthly stories with heavenly meaning"—are a frequent teaching device in the Bible. Jesus often used them (Matthew 13:34), employing both fictional and historical parables. Old Testament parables are fewer and farther between, but they do exist.

Jacob's reconciliation with Esau may be considered an historical parable of the doctrine of grace. Jacob sins against Esau; Esau sentences the sinner to death; Jacob, acknowledging his sin, first runs in fear of retribution but then returns to Esau in humble repentance; Esau forgives Jacob, receiving him with open arms of reconciliation.

This touching story is somewhat reminiscent of Jesus' well-known parable of the prodigal son. The rebellious and wasteful son finally comes to his senses; and when he returns home in penitent humility, the forgiving father welcomes him with love and acceptance.

In the Old and New Testaments, we find the drama of redemption prophesied, illustrated, and fulfilled according to God's will. Today we are the leading characters in the drama—as sinners saved by grace.   —R. W. B.

Conclusion

A. Wrestling Through the Night

Engaging in a wrestling match with an angel was a unique experience that none of us is likely to have. But most of us have at one time or another wrestled with God emotionally and spiritually. When we were younger, those prolonged wrestling matches may have come as we struggled to make a choice about our life vocations. Perhaps we struggled in choosing between an honorable profession and one that was not so honorable. Or we had to choose between two vocations, both of which were honorable. Such a match is not usually settled in one night but may go on for weeks or even months.

What about the wrestling that one addicted to alcohol must endure to free himself from its shackles? Many caught in this kind of struggle are never able to succeed on their own. They need the help of God and the faithful encouragement of others to make it.

Or perhaps a Christian is married to one who is not a Christian. This struggle may go on for months and years. Sometimes it is resolved when the Christian compromises his or her faith. But it can also come to a happy conclusion with the conversion of the non-Christian mate.

From these and similar wrestling matches we can learn at least two lessons. One of them comes from Jacob's experience. Even though he prevailed against his opponent, he was wounded in the conflict. Sometimes this happens to us. In the process of prevailing in our efforts to serve God, we may lose a friend, a job, or even a mate. But if our wounds serve the cause of Christ, then we should rejoice.

The second lesson we need to learn is that as we struggle to resist temptation or to serve the Lord more faithfully, we gain strength in victory. Each triumph makes us better equipped to win the next contest.

B. Bethel and Peniel

During his first great encounter with God, Jacob was so impressed with the experience that he called the place *Bethel*, meaning "house of God." His second great encounter with God, related in today's lesson, led him to name the place *Peniel* or "face of God," because the confrontation had been so direct and so personal. It is doubtful that Jacob could have ever become a faithful, effective servant of God without this second experience.

Christians regularly visit Bethel—the house of God—where they worship and fellowship with other Christians. But Christians must also go to Peniel; they must have a personal relationship with God that goes beyond assembling each Lord's Day. This relationship must be a growing one that develops within them a mature Christian faith. [See question #5, page 424.]

C. Prayer

O God of Abraham, Isaac, and Jacob, help us learn the lessons You have for us in the lives of these patriarchs. Let us never forget that we, like they, are pilgrims in this world, seeking our promised land. In Jesus' name we pray. Amen.

D. Thought to Remember

Jacob's struggles with God taught him that the path to victory lies in surrender.

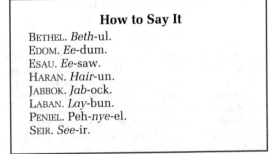

How to Say It

BETHEL. *Beth*-ul.
EDOM. *Ee*-dum.
ESAU. *Ee*-saw.
HARAN. *Hair*-un.
JABBOK. *Jab*-ock.
LABAN. *Lay*-bun.
PENIEL. Peh-*nye*-el.
SEIR. *See*-ir.

Learning by Doing

This page contains an alternate lesson plan emphasizing learning activities.
Classes desiring such student involvement will find these suggestions helpful.

Learning Goals

As a result of this lesson, each student should be able to:

1. Tell how Jacob was reconciled with Esau and of the prayer and divine struggle that preceded the event.

2. Explain the significance of Jacob's actions as he prepared to meet Esau, and describe the change in his character these actions represent.

3. Examine his or her own life for an occasion of struggling with God, and seek God's blessing in it.

Into the Lesson

To introduce the lesson, distribute copies of a worksheet as follows: On the left side of the page is a vertical column of words (see below). To the right of that column and at the top of the page are the words *Positive* and *Negative*. Students are to look at each word on the left and determine whether it has a positive or negative connotation and then make a mark (✔) under the appropriate heading. (Words considered "neutral" can be marked "positive.") The words for the column on the left are as follows: *cross, desire, forward, liberal, radical, sophisticated.*

Allow a couple of minutes for the students to mark their sheets; then poll the class on each word. Probably there will not be unanimity on any of these, for each word can be taken in different ways. For example, the *cross* is a reminder of our salvation, but someone who is *cross* is hard to get along with. A conservative theologian opposes *liberal* theology, but *liberal* giving is praiseworthy. *Sophisticated* suggests education and refinement, but it also has to do with not being naive or innocent. Sometimes *sophisticated* suggests the loss of innocence that pornography represents.

Suggest the word *struggle*—is it positive or negative? In past lessons we have seen Jacob struggle in the sense of resisting God and trying to get by on cunning. Today we'll see him struggle for God's favor.

Into the Word

Set the scene for this lesson by listing in scrambled order several events from Jacob's life (from Genesis 29:1 through 32:8). List these on newsprint or on a handout and ask the students to put them in the correct chronological order.

(Begin with Jacob's journey to Haran and end with Jacob's learning that Esau is coming with four hundred men.)

Ask a volunteer to read Genesis 32:9-11. Observe that we see Jacob here dealing with a potentially threatening situation with prayer instead of cunning. Ask, "Is that how the 'old Jacob' would have handled things? What made the difference?"

Tell the students that the answer is in the text just read. Ask them to identify Jacob's character qualities that can be seen in that passage. For example: devout (v. 9), aware of his religious heritage (v. 9), humble (v. 10), thankful to God for His blessings (v. 10), dependent on God (v. 11), concerned for others (v. 11).

Ask another volunteer to read Genesis 32:24-30. Discuss what Jacob's struggle with the angel represented. Use the Scripture exposition section, as well as discussion question #3 (page 424), to help you.

Now have another volunteer read Genesis 33:1-4. Discuss the relationship between trusting God in a difficult or dangerous situation and taking sensible precautions. At what point do our precautions suggest we are lacking in faith? Discuss also how this picture of reconciliation is similar to God's grace. (See "A Parable of Grace" on page 422.)

Into Life

Observe that God wants to give us grace. Ask, "Why, then, do we sometimes have to struggle for it? Why did Jacob have to struggle with the angel in order to find God's blessing?"

Be sure to point out that we cannot struggle for grace in the sense that if we work hard enough we can earn God's favor. But God allows tests in our lives to refine and purify us (James 1:2-4; 1 Peter 1:6, 7). Jacob could have bolted and looked to some other source for security against his brother. But he realized he needed God's blessing, and he stayed with the fight to get it. When difficulties come to us, we can bolt and look for the best the world has to offer, or we can stay in the fight and seek God's blessing. It's a matter of submission to His will.

Challenge the students to think about their relationship with God. What obstacles are making it a struggle? Pray for endurance to continue to seek God's blessing through their struggles.

Let's Talk It Over

The questions on this page are designed to encourage review of the lesson Scriptures and to promote discussion of the lesson by the class. The answers provided are only discussion starters. Let your class talk it over from there.

1. Jacob assumed that the Lord had promised more than He actually had. Jacob claimed the Lord had promised to "deal well" with him. What the Lord had actually promised was to be with Jacob. Why is it so easy to assume the Lord has promised us more than He has? What alleged promises do people put stock in that are without foundation? How can we help them see what God has actually promised?

Humans have an amazing capability of believing what they want to believe. Thus people quote Scriptures that don't exist or otherwise misrepresent God's promises. "The Lord helps those who help themselves" is widely believed, but it's not in the Bible. "A God of love couldn't send anyone to Hell" is another popular but wrong belief. The "health and wealth" gospel has many adherents, but it is a distortion of what God has actually promised.

2. After reading Genesis 32:10—"I am not worthy of the least of all the mercies, and of all the truth, which thou hast showed unto thy servant"—a friend says, "I thought we were supposed to feel good about ourselves—you know, have 'good self-esteem.' This sounds like we should feel worthless!" How would you answer?

Jacob truly was unworthy, but he was not worthless. As he moved closer to God and placed himself more fully in subjection to God's will, he learned more and more what God could do with him. Christians are no more worthy of God's blessings than Jacob. We are sinners; we have earned punishment for our sin. But God's love and grace are greater than our sin. This gives us great self-esteem. The Almighty God values us in spite of our sin and extends His grace to us!

3. Though Jacob and the angel had wrestled through the night, it is obvious that the angel could have disabled Jacob at any time. It was not the physical struggle that was important here, except that it illustrated the spiritual struggle that Jacob had experienced. Jacob's struggle was not one of resisting or opposing God. Jacob had done that all his life! Here he was struggling to find God's favor, God's blessing. Jacob "prevailed" in that his prayer for deliverance from Esau was answered. How have you struggled with God? What was the result?

We struggle the same way when we grieve over past sin in honest repentance (like Peter in Matthew 26:75). We struggle this way when we submit to prayer and fasting before making a major decision. This kind of struggle always has positive results. Jacob had become the man that God wanted him to be. We, too, can be who God wants us to be.

4. Jacob had finally put wholehearted faith in God. He had struggled with God and had prevailed. Still, as Esau approached, he took some practical precautions. How do you mix faith and practicality? At what point is planning for a contingency simply a lack of faith, and when is it just good sense?

Some people say Jacob's precautions show he still didn't quite trust God one hundred percent. Others find no fault in Jacob's "plan B." Perhaps we need to be careful to observe exactly what God has promised and what He has not. God promised to make Jacob a great nation, but He did not specifically say there would be no casualties among his family. That left some room for Jacob to take precautions. God has promised to meet our needs (Matthew 6:31-33), but He never promised to make us rich. Some today believe having an insurance policy shows a lack of faith. But God has not promised us a life of ease or of protection from every natural calamity. Experience has shown that insurance policies can be good stewardship.

5. The lesson writer uses Jacob's experiences at Bethel and Peniel to illustrate our need for corporate worship (Bethel, "house of God") and private worship (Peniel, "face of God"). Suggest some ways to enhance either our public worship times or our private worship.

Your students probably have some good ideas about how they would like to see the worship service improved. Guide the discussion to focus more on the condition of our hearts in public worship than on the style, format, and other externals. As for our private worship times, ask volunteers to share how they do this at home, either in individual or family worship. Some class members may be wanting to initiate family worship but don't know how. This could be a good time to learn!

Favored Son to Slave

DEVOTIONAL READING: 1 Samuel 18:1-9.

LESSON SCRIPTURE: Genesis 37.

PRINTED TEXT: Genesis 37:3, 4, 17b-28.

Genesis 37:3, 4, 17b-28

3 Now Israel loved Joseph more than all his children, because he was the son of his old age: and he made him a coat of many colors.

4 And when his brethren saw that their father loved him more than all his brethren, they hated him, and could not speak peaceably unto him.

. . . .

17b And Joseph went after his brethren, and found them in Dothan.

18 And when they saw him afar off, even before he came near unto them, they conspired against him to slay him.

19 And they said one to another, Behold, this dreamer cometh.

20 Come now therefore, and let us slay him, and cast him into some pit, and we will say, Some evil beast hath devoured him; and we shall see what will become of his dreams.

21 And Reuben heard it, and he delivered him out of their hands; and said, Let us not kill him.

22 And Reuben said unto them, Shed no blood, but cast him into this pit that is in the wilderness, and lay no hand upon him; that he might rid him out of their hands, to deliver him to his father again.

23 And it came to pass, when Joseph was come unto his brethren, that they stripped Joseph out of his coat, his coat of many colors that was on him;

24 And they took him, and cast him into a pit: and the pit was empty, there was no water in it.

25 And they sat down to eat bread: and they lifted up their eyes and looked, and, behold, a company of Ishmaelites came from Gilead, with their camels bearing spicery and balm and myrrh, going to carry it down to Egypt.

26 And Judah said unto his brethren, What profit is it if we slay our brother, and conceal his blood?

27 Come, and let us sell him to the Ishmaelites, and let not our hand be upon him; for he is our brother and our flesh: and his brethren were content.

28 Then there passed by Midianites merchantmen; and they drew and lifted up Joseph out of the pit, and sold Joseph to the Ishmaelites for twenty pieces of silver: and they brought Joseph into Egypt.

Aug 15

GOLDEN TEXT: Now Israel loved Joseph more than all his children, because he was the son of his old age: and he made him a coat of many colors.
—Genesis 37:3.

Genesis: Beginnings
Unit 3: A People Tested
(Lessons 9-13)

Lesson Aims

After this lesson students should be able to:

1. Tell why Joseph's brothers were jealous of him and what they did to him because of their jealousy.

2. Suggest some ways the sibling rivalry in Joseph's family could have been prevented by Jacob.

3. State some principles that fathers and grandfathers today can follow to promote greater peace in their families.

Lesson Outline

INTRODUCTION
  A. A Deadly Acid
  B. Lesson Background
 I. JOSEPH, A FAVORED SON (Genesis 37:3, 4)
  A. Jacob's Gift (v. 3)
  B. Reaction of Joseph's Brothers (v. 4)
    Joseph's Sin
 II. THE PLOT AGAINST JOSEPH (Genesis 37:17b-22)
  A. The Brothers' Plan (vv. 17b-20)
  B. Reuben's Suggestion (vv. 21, 22)
III. JOSEPH TAKEN TO EGYPT (Genesis 37:23-28)
  A. Joseph Seized (vv. 23, 24)
  B. Ishmaelites Pass By (vv. 25-27)
  C. Joseph Sold Into Slavery (v. 28)
    Three Wrongs Make One Right?
CONCLUSION
  A. The Big Picture
  B. Prayer
  C. Thought to Remember

Introduction

A. A Deadly Acid

A military leader in an ancient Grecian city had rendered an outstanding service to his fellow citizens, and they in turn had honored him by erecting a statue of him in the public plaza. A brother of this hero became terribly jealous and looked for a way to destroy him. Since a personal attack on the hero was out of the question, the brother decided to deface the statue honoring him. Late at night, when everyone was asleep, he secretly went to the plaza and tried to push the statue over. But try as he might, he couldn't budge it. In desperation he started digging away

at the foundation supporting the statue. His efforts proved all too successful, for the next morning he was found crushed to death beneath the statue that had toppled over when its foundation was removed.

In similar fashion Joseph's brothers learned that jealousy is a destructive passion. While their jealousy did not result in their deaths, their jealous actions against Joseph wreaked havoc and heartache within their family. Like a powerful acid, jealousy, once spilled out, burns and corrodes all that it touches.

B. Lesson Background

After the peaceful reunion between Esau and Jacob (which we studied in last week's lesson), the two brothers went their separate ways. Esau returned to Seir and Jacob moved on to Succoth, where he built a house and a shelter for his livestock (Genesis 33:16, 17). Succoth, located east of the Jordan River in the Jordan Valley, was not far from Peniel, where Jacob wrestled with an angel. Jacob then moved across the Jordan River and settled at Shalem, a village near Shechem. There occurred the shameful incident, recorded in Genesis 34, involving Dinah, the daughter of Leah. After this happened, God told Jacob to move to Bethel (35:1). Then he moved on to Ephrath (later called Bethlehem), where Rachel died while giving birth to Benjamin (35:16-19). Also during this period, Isaac died at the age of one hundred eighty and was buried by Esau and Jacob (35:28, 29).

I. Joseph, a Favored Son (Genesis 37:3, 4)

A. Jacob's Gift (v. 3)

3. Now Israel loved Joseph more than all his children, because he was the son of his old age: and he made him a coat of many colors.

As we learned last week, *Israel* was the new name given to Jacob at Peniel. In the narratives that follow, the two names are used interchangeably (Genesis 42:4, 5; 45:21, 25-28; 46:1-8).

That Jacob *loved Joseph* was admirable; the problem was that he loved him *more than all his children, because he was the son of his old age.* Within many families the youngest child often receives special privileges. However, Benjamin was younger than Joseph, and yet at this point was apparently not as favored as Joseph. This leads us to believe that Joseph may have had other qualities that endeared him to his father.

Jacob showed his preference for Joseph by giving him *a coat of many colors.* The *New International Version* translates this as "a richly ornamented robe." Some commentators suggest that this was a tunic with long sleeves, designed more for leisure than for work. Others have suggested that such a coat designated its owner as the son whom the father desired to become the future leader of the family—a privilege normally given to the firstborn. From his own experience (Genesis 25:28), Jacob should have known that this obvious partiality to Joseph would kindle resentment among the other sons. [See question #1, page 432.]

B. Reaction of Joseph's Brothers (v. 4)

4. And when his brethren saw that their father loved him more than all his brethren, they hated him, and could not speak peaceably unto him.

Strong feelings and impulsive actions came easily to Joseph's brothers. Their behavior in the case involving their sister Dinah (Genesis 34) showed how violent they could become. Concerning Joseph, they *could not speak peaceably unto him*. How, then, did they speak to him? Did they tease and taunt him? Were they openly hostile? Did they just not speak to him at all? The second option seems least likely since Jacob and Joseph both seemed unaware of the danger Joseph would be in by being in their presence far from home (v. 18). That the Scripture says they "could not *speak peaceably*" to Joseph suggests they did speak, but it was not nice. Probably their speech was filled with innuendo and sarcasm, and they must have delighted to point out any mistake he might have made, no matter how trivial.

Joseph did not help matters by some of his own actions. Genesis 37:2 tells us he brought an "evil report" to his father about four of his brothers. We do not know whether this was a case of "tattling" some misdemeanor or whether it was a serious case of wrongdoing that needed to be reported. Either way, his brothers would not have appreciated it. What really angered his brothers, however, was his relating of his dreams (v. 5). In them his brothers and even his parents were subservient to Joseph (vv. 6-11). Did Joseph realize even at the young age of seventeen that these were messages from God? If so, perhaps he felt an obligation to report them. Or was he trying to get even with his brothers for their hatred toward him? Or was Joseph simply naive about the way his brothers would take these reports? These are questions we cannot answer with certainty, but it appears that Joseph might have used better judgment even if he was not particularly vindictive. His father rebuked him, but even so he seems to have felt there might be something worth noting in the dreams (vv. 10, 11). [See question #2, page 432.]

JOSEPH'S SIN

I once heard a powerful sermon about Joseph in which the preacher proclaimed, "If Joseph ever sinned, the Bible doesn't tell us about it!" That statement and that sermon made an impact on me and on hundreds of youth at a huge rally. Joseph remained faithful to the Lord despite many trials and temptations. That makes him a fitting role model for modern teens who struggle with all sorts of seductions in today's world.

Upon reflection and further study, however, I see at least one potential flaw in Joseph's character. This seventeen-year-old told his older brothers about dreams that unmistakably predicted that Joseph would one day rule over his own family. Such news would hardly be welcomed, especially since the brothers already were jealous and resentful. We don't know whether Joseph was vindictive or simply naive, but it seems he could have used better judgment.

Whatever the case, Joseph was not perfect. In that, he is like all of us, for "all have sinned" (Romans 3:23). This truth is not meant to serve as an excuse for the sins we commit. What it should do is drive us to the recognition of how much we need God's mercy and forgiveness.

—R. W. B.

II. The Plot Against Joseph (Genesis 37:17b-22)

A. The Brothers' Plan (vv. 17b-20)

17b. And Joseph went after his brethren, and found them in Dothan.

Jacob's family was dwelling at Hebron at this time (Genesis 35:27; 37:14), but apparently the pastures there became barren. So the older brothers took their father's flock to Shechem, more than fifty miles north of Hebron. After some time had elapsed, Jacob decided to check up on the brothers, and he sent Joseph to find them and then report back to him. It seems strange that Jacob would send his teenage son

This visual, for use with this week's lesson and next week's, depicts Joseph's fall from "favored son" to "slave," and then his elevation to second to Pharaoh over all of Egypt.

Visual for lessons 11, 12

(Joseph was seventeen, according to Genesis 37:2) all alone on such a mission. Apparently Jacob was unaware of how the older brothers felt about Joseph—or, at least, he underestimated how bitterly they hated him.

When Joseph reached Shechem, however, his brothers were not there. A stranger told him that they had moved to *Dothan*, about a dozen miles to the north and located on a major caravan route connecting northern Palestine and Egypt. Later it was the scene of a great miracle by Elisha (2 Kings 6:11-18). There Joseph *found them*.

18, 19. And when they saw him afar off, even before he came near unto them, they conspired against him to slay him. And they said one to another, Behold, this dreamer cometh.

Although the brothers were not expecting Joseph, they were able to recognize him at a distance, probably because of his coat. Even before he arrived *they conspired against him to slay him.* Their jealousy and bitterness had been growing and festering and now had an opportunity to come to the surface.

Contemptuously the brothers referred to Joseph as *this dreamer.* They resented the special treatment that Joseph had received from their father, but it was Joseph's dreams that really "stuck in their craw." Had their attitudes been different, they might have been able to laugh off their teenage brother's dreams. But now those dreams had become the basis of all their hatred. Most of us have been guilty of similar attitudes when we have allowed one incident or one act by another person to become the catalyst of a continuing resentment.

How to Say It

BETHEL. *Beth*-ul.
BILHAH. *Bill*-ha.
DOTHAN. *Doe*-thun (*th* as in *thin*).
ELISHA. Ee-*lye*-shuh.
EPHRATH. *Ef*-rath.
ESAU. *Ee*-saw.
GILEAD. *Gil*-ee-ud.
HAGAR. *Hay*-gar.
HEBRON. *Hee*-brun or *Heb*-run.
ISHMAELITES. *Ish*-may-el-ites.
KETURAH. Keh-*too*-ruh.
MIDIANITES. *Mid*-ee-un-ites.
PENIEL. Peh-*nye*-el.
REUBEN. *Roo*-ben.
SEIR. *See*-ir.
SHALEM. *Shay*-lem.
SHECHEM. *Shek*-em or *Shee*-kem.
SUCCOTH. *Soo*-kawth.

Even though the brothers seem to have made their feelings about Joseph obvious to him, he appears to have felt no apprehension as he approached them. Joseph was basically a decent person and, harboring no ill will toward his brothers, was not suspicious of their motives.

20. Come now therefore, and let us slay him, and cast him into some pit, and we will say, Some evil beast hath devoured him; and we shall see what will become of his dreams.

The temptation to kill Joseph, which may have begun as a momentary impulse, quickly grew into a full-blown scheme. Perhaps none of the brothers acting alone would have carried out such a violent act; but in a group of men with similar feelings, the wicked thoughts of each one stimulated the wicked thoughts of the others. "Evil companionships corrupt good morals" (1 Corinthians 15:33, *American Standard Version*). For this reason, all of us ought to be concerned about the company we keep. We need to be especially concerned about the company our children or our grandchildren keep.

As their plot began to develop, the brothers even came up with a plausible cover-up: *some evil beast hath devoured him.* At that time lions and bears still roamed the land, and either one could pose a deadly threat to a person traveling alone or sleeping outdoors.

B. Reuben's Suggestion (vv. 21, 22)

21. And Reuben heard it, and he delivered him out of their hands; and said, Let us not kill him.

Reuben was certainly not a model of high moral character. On one occasion he had slept with Bilhah, his father's concubine—an act that Jacob never forgot (Genesis 35:22; 49:3, 4). But now, in the face of his brothers' sinister plot, Reuben demonstrated a commendable degree of responsibility. As the oldest son he would normally be looked to for leadership, and his opinion would be given some respect by his brothers. He certainly realized the grief that Joseph's death would cause Jacob. Perhaps his conscience grieved him because of his own sin against his father, and thus he was more sensitive to his father's feelings than were the others.

22. And Reuben said unto them, Shed no blood, but cast him into this pit that is in the wilderness, and lay no hand upon him; that he might rid him out of their hands, to deliver him to his father again.

Perhaps the mention of shedding *blood* would focus the brothers' attention on the heinous nature of the crime they were about to commit. How horrible it would be to have the blood of their own brother on their heads! Instead,

Reuben suggested that they *cast him into this pit.* Most likely this was a cistern hewn out of the ground. It was used to collect water during the rainy season. Cisterns were usually shaped like a bottle with a wide basin at the bottom and a narrow opening at the top that could be covered by a stone. It would have been very difficult for a person to escape from one without help from someone else.

Had Joseph been left in the cistern, he almost certainly would have died; but at least the brothers would not have felt the guilt of actually shedding his blood. They agreed with Reuben's suggestion, and so Joseph was thrown in the cistern. Reuben planned to return later and rescue Joseph and *to deliver him to his father again.* [See question #3, page 432.]

III. Joseph Taken to Egypt (Genesis 37:23-28)

A. Joseph Seized (vv. 23, 24)

23, 24. And it came to pass, when Joseph was come unto his brethren, that they stripped Joseph out of his coat, his coat of many colors that was on him; and they took him, and cast him into a pit: and the pit was empty, there was no water in it.

Even before Joseph reached his brothers, they had discussed their two plans and had decided to follow Reuben's suggestion. Joseph had no forewarning of their intentions, and as soon as he arrived they seized him. The first thing they did was to strip him of his beautiful *coat,* which perhaps symbolized all their jealousy toward him. Joseph must have pleaded with his brothers not to do this to him, but his protests fell on deaf ears. Even Reuben, who seemed not to favor their actions, did not speak up in his defense at this point. Perhaps he felt that his brothers' willingness to go along with his plan was about the only concession he could hope to get from them.

Without hesitation, the brothers carried out their plan and *cast* Joseph *into a pit.* Fortunately for him *there was no water in it;* otherwise he probably would have drowned within just a few minutes. [See question #4, page 432.]

B. Ishmaelites Pass By (vv. 25-27)

25. And they sat down to eat bread: and they lifted up their eyes and looked, and, behold, a company of Ishmaelites came from Gilead, with their camels bearing spicery and balm and myrrh, going to carry it down to Egypt.

The reader is shocked by the callousness of Joseph's brothers. In a matter of minutes they plotted to kill their brother, took action that seemed certain to ensure his death, and then calmly *sat down to eat.* As they ate, they saw a caravan of *Ishmaelites* approaching. The Ishmaelites were descendants of Abraham through Hagar (Genesis 16:15). However, the term was sometimes applied more broadly to all the nomads who roamed the desert areas east of the Jordan River and south of the Dead Sea. Some were engaged in the lucrative business of carrying various *spicery* to Egypt. *Gilead,* a fertile territory southeast of the Sea of Galilee, was famous for its *balm* that reputedly possessed outstanding medicinal properties (Jeremiah 8:22; 46:11). *Myrrh* was used not only as a spice, but also in pain-relieving medicines (Mark 15:23). It was brought to Jesus as a gift following His birth (Matthew 2:11) and was applied to His body after His death (John 19:39, 40).

Since Dothan was on a major trade route that went to Egypt, it was not surprising that a caravan should be passing by. The timing of its arrival, however, was surely by divine providence, to send Joseph to Egypt (Genesis 45:5).

26, 27. And Judah said unto his brethren, What profit is it if we slay our brother, and conceal his blood? Come, and let us sell him to the Ishmaelites, and let not our hand be upon him; for he is our brother and our flesh: and his brethren were content.

Once these men had a little time to think about how cruelly they were treating their *brother,* they may have had some second thoughts. But they had a problem. If they took Joseph out of the pit and allowed him to return to their father, he would certainly report to him what they had done. That could only make the family situation worse.

The sight of the passing caravan of *Ishmaelites* gave the brothers a way out of their dilemma. *Judah* suggested that they *sell* Joseph to the Ishmaelites. That way they could get rid of "the dreamer" and make a little *profit* for themselves. Note the brothers' twisted reasoning: they did not want to kill Joseph, *for he is our brother and our flesh;* but that fact did not prevent them from selling him into slavery!

C. Joseph Sold Into Slavery (v. 28)

28. Then there passed by Midianites merchantmen; and they drew and lifted up Joseph out of the pit, and sold Joseph to the Ishmaelites for twenty pieces of silver: and they brought Joseph into Egypt.

The *Midianites* were descendants of Abraham by Keturah (Genesis 25:1, 2). They lived in the same general area as the Ishmaelites and apparently were considered as part of the larger Ishmaelite group. (That *Midianites* and *Ishmaelites* could be used interchangeably is clear from a comparison of Genesis 37:36 and 39:1.) When the brothers began to negotiate with the Midianites, Joseph realized what the future held in store for him. He pleaded with his brothers not to carry out their plan. Years later in Egypt the brothers admitted this: "We saw the anguish of his soul, when he besought us, and we would not hear" (Genesis 42:21).

The brothers received *twenty pieces of silver* for Joseph, which was later recognized in the law of Moses as the price of a male slave five to twenty years old (Leviticus 27:5). We wonder how long the brothers kept these grim reminders of their terrible crime! [See question #5, page 432.]

THREE WRONGS MAKE ONE RIGHT?

When youngsters justify some act of meanness with "He hit me first!" conscientious parents are likely to respond with a maxim so familiar it has become a cliché: "Two wrongs don't make a right." Children later see the wisdom of such instruction when they acknowledge the sinfulness of vengeance and retaliation.

The scenario in today's text presents at least three wrongs. Jacob was wrong when he showed favoritism to one son over the others. Joseph was wrong when he provoked greater animosity among his already jealous brothers by relating his dreams of his superiority and their submission to him. The angry brothers were wrong when they retaliated hatefully and violently against Joseph.

None of these wrongs can be excused, regardless of the circumstances. But God ultimately brought right out of all these wrongs. In Egypt, Joseph providentially was promoted to a posi-

tion that allowed him to save Israel (Jacob and his growing family) from the effects of famine, thereby furthering God's plan for His chosen people.

None of our wrongs ever makes a right, but our Father's will prevails even when His children sin.   —R. W. B.

Conclusion

A. The Big Picture

Today's lesson ends on a tragic note. Even those of us who have become hardened by the frequency of violent crime all about us cannot avoid being shocked by what Joseph's brothers did to him. However, before we spend too much time bemoaning this act of violence, we need to step back and take a look at the big picture.

God did not force the brothers to mistreat Joseph, and He did not condone their actions. Yet in spite of their crimes, God was able to use their actions to achieve a greater purpose. Years later in Egypt, the brother who had been sold into slavery became the instrument whom God used to save the family of Jacob from a severe famine. Joseph recognized that God, not his brothers, was responsible for his coming to Egypt when he did: "You intended to harm me," Joseph later told his brothers, "but God intended it for good to accomplish what is now being done, the saving of many lives" (Genesis 50:20, *New International Version*). Furthermore, God used Joseph as a model for us of remaining morally upright and determining to trust in Him through all kinds of adversity.

Central to the Christian faith is the truth that our God allows us individual freedom of choice, yet, at the same time, He is also able to control the flow of history. When bad things happen to us, we need to step back a bit and try to see the big picture. Situations may seem out of control, but God is always in control.

B. Prayer

Gracious God, we are appalled at the tragedy we have seen unfolding in the family of Jacob. Help us to learn ways to avoid such situations in our own families. Give us the knowledge and the wisdom that it takes to rear God-fearing families, united in their desire to please Him. May we seek, in every circumstance of life, to live so that You are honored by our words and actions. In Jesus' name we pray. Amen.

C. Thought to Remember

Anger long smoldered can burst into a consuming flame at the slightest provocation and scorch everyone in its path.

Home Daily Bible Readings

Monday, Aug. 9—Joseph, the Tattletale and Dreamer (Genesis 37:1-11)

Tuesday, Aug. 10—Joseph's Brothers Become Jealous of Him (Genesis 37:12-24)

Wednesday, Aug. 11—Joseph Is Sold to Ishmaelites (Genesis 37:25-28)

Thursday, Aug. 12—Jacob Mourns Joseph's Imagined Death (Genesis 37:29-36)

Friday, Aug. 13—Saul Is Jealous of David (1 Samuel 18:1-9)

Saturday, Aug. 14—The First Workers Are Jealous of the Last (Matthew 20:1-16)

Sunday, Aug. 15—The Disciples Wonder Who Is the Greatest (Luke 14:7-11)

Learning by Doing

This page contains an alternate lesson plan emphasizing learning activities.
Classes desiring such student involvement will find these suggestions helpful.

Learning Goals

As a result of this lesson, your students should be able to:

Tell why Joseph's brothers were jealous of him and what they did to him because of their jealousy.

2. Suggest some ways the sibling rivalry in Joseph's family could have been prevented by Jacob.

3. State some principles that fathers and grandfathers today can follow to promote greater peace in their families.

Into the Lesson

Some of your students may be old enough to remember Tom Smothers' lament to his brother that "Mom always liked you best." In reality, however, parental favoritism is no laughing matter. Ask your students to suggest some of the harmful results and consequences of parental favoritism. For example: jealousy, resentment, pride, arrogance, negative self-image, broken relationships, shattered family, even violence.

In today's lesson we see what happened when Jacob lavished special attention on his favorite son, Joseph, the first child born to Rachel, his beloved wife.

Into the Word

Fill in the Biblical background for this lesson by asking one of your students (in advance, early in the week) to summarize the events that happened in Jacob's life since last week's lesson. This information is contained in Genesis 33:5—37:2. See also "Lesson Background" on page 426.

Dysfunctional is a word that psychologists and family counselors use when describing a family in which the relationships are not healthy and do not work. Jacob had been raised in a dysfunctional family, and now largely as a result of his own errors in judgment his own family was dysfunctional.

Ask your students to read Genesis 37:3-28 in search of indicators that this family was dysfunctional. Write their responses on the chalkboard or newsprint. Here are some suggestions:

• parental favoritism—by Jacob (v. 3).
• sibling jealousy and hatred—by Joseph's brothers (v. 4).
• pride or insensitivity—by Joseph (vv. 5-10).
• envy—by Joseph's brothers (v. 11).

• hatred to the point of deciding to murder their brother—by Joseph's brothers (vv. 18-20).
• violence—by Joseph's brothers (vv. 23, 24).
• callous insensitivity—by Joseph's brothers (v. 25).
• willingness to sell a brother into slavery—by Joseph's brothers (v. 28).

Divide your class into three groups.

• Assign one group to think about what Jacob could have done differently to have prevented the horrible tragedy that struck his family when Joseph was sold into slavery.

• Assign the second group to think about what Joseph could have done differently. Was he so naive that he didn't realize that relating the content of his dreams would incense his brothers? Or didn't he care?

• The third group can think about what Joseph's ten older brothers could have done differently. Were they so out of touch with godly values that they didn't realize that their jealousy and murderous hatred would inevitably lead to violence? Or didn't they care?

After about five minutes, call for reports from each group. If there were things that Jacob, Joseph, and the brothers could have done to avert disaster, why didn't they? What do your students think?

Into Life

Use the following "case study" to help your students talk about what parents (and/or grandparents) can do to promote peace and positive, healthy relationships in their families.

Alan has two sons. Steve is a natural athlete, and is on the high school football team. Jeff is more interested in computers and music than in sports. Since Alan was a high school football star himself, he naturally has more in common with Steve.

• How can Alan prevent his natural preference from becoming a problem?

• What can he do to demonstrate that he is not showing favoritism?

• What might happen if Alan shows more interest in Steve than in Jeff?

In closing, challenge the parents in your class to be aware of the temptation to play favorites. What will they do during this coming week to assure all their children that they are loved and valued?

Let's Talk It Over

The questions on this page are designed to encourage review of the lesson Scriptures and to promote discussion of the lesson by the class. The answers provided are only discussion starters. Let your class talk it over from there.

1. We might have expected that Jacob, knowing firsthand what it felt like to have his father favor his brother, would have been careful not to repeat this mistake. But he did just as his father did. Adults often repeat the mistakes of their parents. Why is this? How can adults break with the patterns of the past?

So much of what we learn comes through observation and imitation. The son of a man who beats his wife all too often beats his own wife. Paradoxically, this can happen even when the son hates his father for what he did to his mother. But it is possible to break the cycle. The most important way in which this happens is through a person's submitting to Christ as Lord and experiencing the renewing power of the Holy Spirit working in his life.

2. What kinds of things make people jealous of others today? How can parents and grandparents help prevent this within the family?

Jealousy is a form of coveting: we want what the other person has. It might be a talent, our father's favor, a more winsome personality, or any number of things. To prevent it we need to appreciate the uniqueness and the value of each individual—including ourselves.

Parents and grandparents can help by teaching this truth to children and by encouraging the unique gifts and qualities in each child. Siblings are prone to be jealous of those things that bring others attention or praise while disparaging their own gifts. Children need constant reminders that God entrusts different gifts to each person, but each is needed and important. Parents must value what every child has and is and help all to develop their potentials.

3. Reuben's intention to rescue his brother is commendable even if his method is not. After all, he failed. What do you think would have happened if Reuben had simply said, "No! We must not do anything to harm Joseph, for to do so would be sin"? Have you ever had to stand up to a crowd and say no? What does it take to do so?

Reuben was a coward. It's not likely the brothers would have harmed him along with Joseph. He simply did not want to risk their disapproval. But one voice acting as the conscience of the group could very well have averted this travesty of justice. It is not easy to stand up to a crowd. It takes faith and courage, and a confidence that doing the right thing is its own reward no matter what the consequences.

4. It is one thing to be jealous and have hard feelings toward someone, but Joseph's brothers acted violently and, when they were done, he was as good as dead. And they didn't even lose their appetites! How could they be so cold? What precautions do we need to take to be sure we don't get to that point?

The stage was set for this when Joseph was born. His ten older brothers, born of three mothers, understood that Joseph's mother was Jacob's true love. As Joseph's status as favorite son became apparent, their resentment grew. The brothers were enraged when Joseph reported to their father that they were not doing their jobs. They refused to acknowledge that Joseph's dreams were a prophecy sent by God, and so they hated him on account of them. Cherished and nourished for seventeen years, with brother encouraging brother, their hatred grew into a raging fire that roared for Joseph's destruction. The same thing will happen to us if we allow jealousy and hatred to find a home in our hearts. We must cast them out and ask God's forgiveness, lest we commit greater sins.

5. Joseph was sold into slavery by his brothers. Many people are unfairly put in difficult situations by the evil deeds of others. Thieves and swindlers can rob people of most everything that they have, placing them in very hard economic situations. Spouses walk out and cause great emotional and economic hardship for the one who is left behind. When the sin of another leaves us in difficulty, what is a proper response?

Perhaps some of your students have firsthand experience with such situations. Can they tell how they handled it? Did they handle it well? If we find ourselves in such circumstances, we must not be resentful, for then we put ourselves in danger of becoming like Joseph's resentful brothers. We can only put our hope and trust in the God who has promised never to forsake us. Such hope is never misplaced.

Opportunity to Serve

DEVOTIONAL READING: Acts 21:7-14.

LESSON SCRIPTURE: Genesis 39—41.

PRINTED TEXT: Genesis 41:14-16, 25-40.

Genesis 41:14-16, 25-40

14 Then Pharaoh sent and called Joseph, and they brought him hastily out of the dungeon: and he shaved himself, and changed his raiment, and came in unto Pharaoh.

15 And Pharaoh said unto Joseph, I have dreamed a dream, and there is none that can interpret it: and I have heard say of thee, that thou canst understand a dream to interpret it.

16 And Joseph answered Pharaoh, saying, It is not in me: God shall give Pharaoh an answer of peace.

.   .   .   .

25 And Joseph said unto Pharaoh, The dream of Pharaoh is one: God hath showed Pharaoh what he is about to do.

26 The seven good kine are seven years; and the seven good ears are seven years: the dream is one.

27 And the seven thin and ill-favored kine that came up after them are seven years; and the seven empty ears blasted with the east wind shall be seven years of famine.

28 This is the thing which I have spoken unto Pharaoh: What God is about to do he showeth unto Pharaoh.

29 Behold, there come seven years of great plenty throughout all the land of Egypt:

30 And there shall arise after them seven years of famine; and all the plenty shall be forgotten in the land of Egypt; and the famine shall consume the land;

31 And the plenty shall not be known in the land by reason of that famine following; for it shall be very grievous.

32 And for that the dream was doubled unto Pharaoh twice; it is because the thing is established by God, and God will shortly bring it to pass.

33 Now therefore let Pharaoh look out a man discreet and wise, and set him over the land of Egypt.

34 Let Pharaoh do this, and let him appoint officers over the land, and take up the fifth part of the land of Egypt in the seven plenteous years.

35 And let them gather all the food of those good years that come, and lay up corn under the hand of Pharaoh, and let them keep food in the cities.

36 And that food shall be for store to the land against the seven years of famine, which shall be in the land of Egypt; that the land perish not through the famine.

37 And the thing was good in the eyes of Pharaoh, and in the eyes of all his servants.

38 And Pharaoh said unto his servants, Can we find such a one as this is, a man in whom the Spirit of God is?

39 And Pharaoh said unto Joseph, Forasmuch as God hath showed thee all this, there is none so discreet and wise as thou art:

40 Thou shalt be over my house, and according unto thy word shall all my people be ruled: only in the throne will I be greater than thou.

GOLDEN TEXT: Pharaoh said unto Joseph, Forasmuch as God hath showed thee all this, there is none so discreet and wise as thou art: thou shalt be over my house, and according unto thy word shall all my people be ruled: only in the throne will I be greater than thou.—Genesis 41:39, 40.

**Aug
22**

Lesson Aims

After completing this lesson each student should:

1. Recount Joseph's interpretation of Pharaoh's dream and the favorable treatment he then received.

2. Compare Joseph's situation and his faith in God's providence with the situation many Christians face at the workplace.

3. Make a commitment to live with integrity and to serve with honor wherever God places him or her.

Lesson Outline

INTRODUCTION
    A. I'll Be Honest
    B. Lesson Background
I. PHARAOH SUMMONS JOSEPH (Genesis 41:14-16)
    A. Joseph's Preparation (v. 14)
    B. Pharaoh's Problem (v. 15)
    C. Joseph's Reply (v. 16)
II. JOSEPH INTERPRETS THE DREAM (Genesis 41:25-36)
    A. Feast, Then Famine (vv. 25-32)
    B. Joseph's Advice (vv. 33-36)
      Saving Up for a Dry Day
III. PHARAOH'S RESPONSE (Genesis 41:37-40)
    A. Joseph Commended (vv. 37, 38)
    B. Joseph Given Authority (vv. 39, 40)
      All Things for Good
CONCLUSION
    A. God Has a Plan
    B. Prayer
    C. Thought to Remember

Introduction

A. I'll Be Honest

Years ago in a Southern slave market, a young man was to be sold at an auction. Before the bidding began, he was examined by several prospective buyers. Most of them were concerned about his health and his strength. One man, after examining him, told him, "I will be a kinder master to you than some of the other slave owners. But I want to know one thing. If I buy you and you become my slave, will you be honest?"

The young man drew himself up to his full height, looked the man in the eye, and said, "Sir, I'll be honest whether you buy me or not!"

Joseph would have echoed this young man's sentiment. Sold into slavery by his brothers, Joseph experienced difficult, faith-trying times. He suffered imprisonment because he refused to compromise his integrity. Eventually, however, his honesty was rewarded.

B. Lesson Background

The Ishmaelites who purchased Joseph from his brothers took him to Egypt where he was sold to Potiphar, an official in Pharaoh's government. Joseph prospered for a time; but when he resisted the seductive advances of Potiphar's wife, he was falsely accused and thrown into prison. There Joseph was able to gain the respect of the jail keeper. Later Pharaoh's baker and butler were imprisoned, and during their imprisonment each had a dream. Joseph was able to interpret their dreams, each of which came true in the way Joseph had said it would.

Some time after this, Pharaoh had a dream that none of his wise men could interpret. The butler, by now restored to Pharaoh's favor, remembered Joseph and mentioned to Pharaoh his ability to interpret dreams. Upon learning this, Pharaoh sent for Joseph to have him interpret his dream. [See question #1, page 440.]

I. Pharaoh Summons Joseph (Genesis 41:14-16)

A. Joseph's Preparation (v. 14)

14. Then Pharaoh sent and called Joseph, and they brought him hastily out of the dungeon: and he shaved himself, and changed his raiment, and came in unto Pharaoh.

When *Pharaoh sent* for *Joseph*, the servants acted *hastily* to bring him *out of the dungeon*. However, there were special preparations that Joseph had to make before he could present himself to Pharaoh. First of all he *shaved himself*. Hebrew men ordinarily wore beards. The Egyptian men, on the other hand, shaved their beards (they are thus depicted in ancient statues, monuments, and paintings); and so it is likely that Joseph followed the Egyptian custom in deference to Pharaoh. Joseph also changed from his prison *raiment* (clothing) to more appropriate garments.

B. Pharaoh's Problem (v. 15)

15. And Pharaoh said unto Joseph, I have dreamed a dream, and there is none that can interpret it: and I have heard say of thee, that thou canst understand a dream to interpret it.

Pharaoh immediately told Joseph of his predicament. He was disturbed by the fact that none of the Egyptian wise men could *interpret* his *dream*. Then he had learned from the butler who had been in prison with Joseph that Joseph could interpret dreams.

When Joseph had interpreted the butler's dream, he had asked that the butler remember him when he was restored to Pharaoh's favor. The butler, however, promptly forgot about Joseph when he returned to his post. Two years passed before the butler mentioned Joseph (Genesis 40:23—41:1), and that was only after none of the Egyptians could interpret Pharaoh's dream—an incident that apparently jogged the butler's memory.

C. Joseph's Reply (v. 16)

16. And Joseph answered Pharaoh, saying, It is not in me: God shall give Pharaoh an answer of peace.

Joseph's immediate response was to deny that he himself possessed any special powers that allowed him to interpret Pharaoh's dream. He then acknowledged that the *answer* would come from *God*. His affirmation that there was but one God was a significant statement of faith in Egypt, where the people worshiped many gods. In fact, even Pharaoh himself was considered to be a god. Joseph also assured Pharaoh that the answer he would receive would be *an answer of peace*. Even though Pharaoh had not yet revealed the contents of his dream to Joseph, God had given Joseph enough knowledge about it to know that it conveyed good news to Pharaoh. [See question #2, page 440.]

II. Joseph Interprets the Dream (Genesis 41:25-36)

A. Feast, Then Famine (vv. 25-32)

Verses 17-24 give the details of Pharaoh's dream, which was in two parts. In the first part, Pharaoh was standing on the bank of a river (most likely the Nile) when he saw seven kine, or cattle, "fat-fleshed and well-favored" come up out of the river. They were followed by seven lean and sickly cows—the ugliest cows he had ever seen. Then an amazing thing happened—the lean cows devoured the fat cows, yet even after such a bountiful feast they still looked lean and ugly. Obviously in the real world cows are not cannibalistic, eating other cattle. But dreams know no such limitations.

In the second dream, Pharaoh saw seven heads of grain (probably wheat), "full and good." Then seven more heads of grain sprang up, but they were "withered, thin, and blasted with the

east wind." This most likely described the east wind that came in from the Arabian Desert and was hot and dry, withering much of the vegetation in its path. The withered heads of grain then attacked and devoured the good heads of grain. Cannibalistic grain is even stranger than cannibalistic cattle. But then again, even stranger things than these sometimes happen in dreams.

25. And Joseph said unto Pharaoh, The dream of Pharaoh is one: God hath showed Pharaoh what he is about to do.

Although Pharaoh had two dreams, the message they brought was *one* and the same. He would soon see a demonstration of the power of the *God* whom Joseph served. God in His providential mercy was using Joseph to inform Pharaoh of what He was *about to do*.

26, 27. The seven good kine are seven years; and the seven good ears are seven years: the dream is one. And the seven thin and ill-favored kine that came up after them are seven years; and the seven empty ears blasted with the east wind shall be seven years of famine.

Again Joseph emphasized that Pharaoh's *dream* conveyed *one* message. Both the good cattle and grain and the inferior cattle and grain represented *seven years*. Pharaoh was about to learn how these years would affect his country and the people whom he governed.

28. This is the thing which I have spoken unto Pharaoh: What God is about to do he showeth unto Pharaoh.

Joseph also stressed once more that even though he was speaking to Pharaoh in answer to his inquiry, his words described what *God* was *about to do*. Joseph was only God's spokesman.

29-31. Behold, there come seven years of great plenty throughout all the land of Egypt: and there shall arise after them seven years of famine; and all the plenty shall be forgotten in the land of Egypt; and the famine shall consume the land; and the plenty shall not be

Visual for lessons 11, 12

Display again the visual used with last week's lesson, which depicts Joseph's fall from "favored son" to "slave," and then his elevation to second to Pharaoh over all of Egypt.

known in the land by reason of that famine following; for it shall be very grievous.

The seven fat cattle and the seven good heads of grain represented seven years of *great plenty* in *Egypt*. Egypt was richly blessed by the Nile River, which stretched the full length of the country. At almost exactly the same time each year, the Nile rose and flooded the land, not only providing water for the crops but also renewing the fertility of the soil by the silt it carried from upstream. Egyptians could normally count on a good crop, and rarely did they experience a famine. As a result, for centuries their country served as the breadbasket of the ancient world. Earlier Abram had traveled to Egypt because of a famine in Canaan (Genesis 12:10); eventually the brothers of Joseph would be forced to do the same.

However, in this case the coming famine would hold Egypt in its grip as well. The seven years of plenty would be followed by *seven years of famine* so severe that *all the plenty shall be forgotten in the land of Egypt*. The famine would not be just a local or regional one; it would *consume the land*. Joseph also described it as *very grievous*. Likely no one in Egypt would be able to recall a famine of this magnitude.

Quite often in the Old Testament, when disasters were predicted or came to pass, they were acts of God against sinful people. There is nothing in the Scriptures to indicate that any kind of divine judgment was being administered through this famine. However, as later chapters in Genesis reveal, this famine was providentially used of God to bring Joseph's family to Egypt.

32. And for that the dream was doubled unto Pharaoh twice; it is because the thing is established by God, and God will shortly bring it to pass.

For a dream to be *doubled* or "given to Pharaoh in two forms" (*New International Version*) emphasized its importance. Joseph's dream concerning his brothers was thus repeated (Genesis 37:5-11). (See another example of this in Amos 7:1—8:3.) Here the repetition of Pharaoh's

dream signaled its certainty (*the thing is established by God*) and its imminence (*God will shortly bring it to pass*). Clearly there was nothing *Pharaoh* could do that would change God's decree. The best he could do was to prepare for the coming famine.

It may seem surprising that the Egyptian magicians and wise men, who had earlier failed to interpret Pharaoh's dream, raised no objections to Joseph's interpretation. They had every reason to be suspicious and jealous of him; not only was he a foreigner, but he also did not belong to their group of "experts." Apparently the logic and clarity of Joseph's interpretation (and of his subsequent suggestion for dealing with the famine) were such that they had no basis for objection.

B. Joseph's Advice (vv. 33-36)

33. Now therefore let Pharaoh look out a man discreet and wise, and set him over the land of Egypt.

In this situation Joseph functioned both as a *fore*teller, predicting future events, and as a *forth*teller, giving advice about how to deal with the situation. Many of the prophets in Israel's later history functioned in this same double capacity. Joseph advised Pharaoh to select a man *discreet and wise* who would have the responsibility of directing Egypt's efforts to meet the coming crisis. There is nothing to indicate that Joseph was seeking the job for himself. [See question #3, page 440.]

34. Let Pharaoh do this, and let him appoint officers over the land, and take up the fifth part of the land of Egypt in the seven plenteous years.

Joseph's suggestion included not only a leader, but also a plan that this leader could begin to implement. *Officers* would be in charge of collecting and storing the grain produced during the *seven plenteous years*. The *fifth part* may be considered as a kind of tax, or "double tithe," levied against the people. Or perhaps the government could *take up* that portion of the grain by offering to pay for it. In a plentiful year the price of grain would be low, allowing the government to buy it up cheaply. In either case, the grain would be collected and stored for future use rather than allowed to go to waste as it might have otherwise.

35, 36. And let them gather all the food of those good years that come, and lay up corn under the hand of Pharaoh, and let them keep food in the cities. And that food shall be for store to the land against the seven years of famine, which shall be in the land of Egypt; that the land perish not through the famine.

How to Say It

DARIUS. Duh-*rye*-us.
EGYPTIANS. Ee-*jip*-shuns.
ELOHIM (Hebrew). El-o-*heem*.
ISHMAELITES. *Ish*-may-el-ites.
NEBUCHADNEZZAR. *Neb*-uh-kad-*nezz*-er
 (strong accent on *nezz*).
PHARAOH. *Fair*-o or *Fay*-ro.
POTIPHAR. *Pot*-ih-far.

The word *corn* is often used in the *King James Version* to describe grain of any kind (as in John 12:24). Here it describes wheat or some other grain, rather than what we today know as corn. The grain was to be stored in the *cities* where it would be most needed and where it could be better protected. While Joseph did not mention the subject at this point, his plan probably necessitated building many new storage facilities. However, these tasks could be undertaken and completed within the seven prosperous years that would come first.

SAVING UP FOR A DRY DAY

Thoughtful people have always considered it prudent and thrifty to "save up for a rainy day." Laying back money and other resources to provide for leaner times is sensible. Insurance policies, annuities, IRAs, savings accounts, mutual funds, and investments of every kind are generated by a cautious, plan-ahead spirit.

Joseph's resourceful strategy to supply Egypt with food during the coming famine years could be called, "Saving Up for a Dry Day." The seven-year drought was inevitable. The Egyptians, however, had a seven-year period of plenty to prepare for the "dry day" that was sure to come.

We do not possess the supernatural foresight to know when our rainy or dry days will come, but we do know that they will come at some point. Jesus predicted, "In the world ye shall have tribulation" (John 16:33). Since we know that tests, trials, and hardships are certain, "saving up" spiritually in preparation for them makes good sense. During all of our good days, when "heaven comes down and glory fills our souls," we should store up as many spiritual resources as possible to sustain us in bad times.

Then, like Joseph, we can remain faithful—rain or shine. —R. W. B.

III. Pharaoh's Response (Genesis 41:37-40)

A. Joseph Commended (vv. 37, 38)

37, 38. And the thing was good in the eyes of Pharaoh, and in the eyes of all his servants. And Pharaoh said unto his servants, Can we find such a one as this is, a man in whom the Spirit of God is?

Apparently Pharaoh had made no comment about Joseph's interpretation of his dream. Perhaps he was so overwhelmed by the interpretation that he was left speechless. But when Joseph began to suggest some practical ways to address the famine that Egypt would one day face, Pharaoh immediately began to show an interest. Both he and his *servants*, or advisors, were impressed with the suggestions that Joseph made.

Joseph had gained administrative experience in the household of Potiphar when he was made the overseer in charge of all Potiphar's affairs (Genesis 39:1-6). He gained similar experience in prison where he was put in charge of all the other prisoners (vv. 21-23). This was all part of how "the Lord was with Joseph" (vv. 2, 21), preparing him for a task that would require such leadership. Pharaoh realized that Egypt needed someone uniquely qualified to head up the program that Joseph had just suggested.

Among all the other qualifications, such a person had to be *a man in whom the Spirit of God is.* The Hebrew word for *God* is *Elohim*, which can be translated "gods" as well as "God." Thus it is difficult to know exactly what Pharaoh meant by this statement. Although the Egyptians were polytheists, worshiping many gods, perhaps Pharaoh had heard and seen enough of Joseph to realize that he worshiped a God who was different from the Egyptian gods. His admission may be similar to that of King Nebuchadnezzar in Daniel 3:28-30 and King Darius in Daniel 6:25-27. [See question #4, page 440.]

B. Joseph Given Authority (vv. 39, 40)

39. And Pharaoh said unto Joseph, Forasmuch as God hath showed thee all this, there is none so discreet and wise as thou art.

After conferring with his advisors, *Pharaoh* immediately selected *Joseph* as the man for this new and important position. From the advisors, he may have learned that Joseph was a man of integrity—a man who could command the respect of those who served under him, and (probably most important) a man who had no personal ambitions. Autocratic rulers are usually fearful of having ambitious people around them who might try to take their jobs.

40. Thou shalt be over my house, and according unto thy word shall all my people be ruled: only in the throne will I be greater than thou.

What a dramatic change had occurred in Joseph's status in only a few hours! When the day began, he was a despised prisoner. Now he was second only to the Pharaoh of Egypt. If there were any objections to his rapid elevation to such a high position, no one voiced them in the presence of Pharaoh. Apparently Joseph was one of those persons who impressed everyone he met as a man of integrity and ability. Of course, behind all of this was the hand of God, who had blessed Joseph in the house of Potiphar and in prison. [See question #5, page 440.]

ALL THINGS FOR GOOD

Was the apostle Paul simply stating a theory when he wrote Romans 8:28? Do all things really work together for good to those who love God? Paul had earned the right to write such a powerful truth. He could testify from experience to its authority. Despite almost constant trials and persecutions, God worked through all Paul's circumstances to bless his life and ministry in ways the apostle had never asked nor imagined.

Joseph suffered much, too. Hated and ridiculed by his own brothers, he was threatened, abused, and finally sold into slavery. Though faithful to God and to Potiphar in Egypt, he was wrongfully accused by Potiphar's wife and imprisoned for something he didn't do. He could have complained bitterly and wondered, "Why me, Lord?" But there is no record of self-pity or doubt on Joseph's part.

In the end, Joseph's integrity was vindicated, and all things did work out for his good. His example should encourage all of us. If we continue to trust God's promises and determine to fulfill His purposes, we can depend upon His faithfulness in making all things work out for our good and His glory.   —R. W. B.

Conclusion

A. God Has a Plan

Some persons come to power by virtue of birth into a ruling family. Some do so by violence and intrigue, others just by accident, and some because of their ability, along with a helping hand from some other person or persons. Joseph belonged to the latter class. He was a person of great leadership ability; and he had the best kind of helping hand, for it was the hand of God.

As a young man, Joseph's prospects of reaching the top certainly seemed dim or even nonexistent. Sold into slavery as a teenager and then unjustly thrown into prison and forgotten, what chance did he have? Yet through all of his experiences Joseph never forgot that he belonged to God. At times he certainly must have wondered why his faithfulness always seemed to be "rewarded" by suffering, but he never wavered in his commitment to God. Deep in his heart he must have nurtured the belief that somewhere, sometime, God would use him for a significant purpose. He had to have great patience to survive many years of disappointment. Great leaders must learn such patience, for God never seems to be in a big hurry to accomplish His purposes in history. But the years that Joseph spent as a slave and as a prisoner were not wasted years. God was training him and disciplining him for a crucial task. When the time came, Joseph was ready and willing.

God has a plan for every one of us. That fact presents us with some sobering responsibilities. First of all, we must be willing to surrender our lives to God and seek and accept His plan for us. If we are not willing to make that effort, then we can never be effectively used by Him. Second, we must have the patience to prepare for carrying out that plan, whatever it may be. Moses spent forty years in Egypt and another forty years in the wilderness of Sinai before God could use him.

Perhaps the most difficult part of all of this is discovering the exact place where God wants us to serve. Sometimes we have to choose among several places or avenues of service, all of which seem equally good. At other times we are forced to choose from a set of options, none of which seems to be good. Joseph's options seemed quite limited until the very moment he was thrust into the place where God wanted him. When that time came, Joseph was ready because he never lost faith that God was still there, caring for him and planning his destiny.

B. Prayer

Father God, You know the struggles that we sometimes face. When trials come, may we not despair. Instead, like Joseph, may we have the strength to trust You even in our defeats. Keep us strong in the faith and prepared to accept any task You have for us. Through Christ, amen.

C. Thought to Remember

May each of us strive to become a person "in whom the Spirit of God is."

Home Daily Bible Readings

Monday, Aug. 16—Joseph Resists Potiphar's Wife (Genesis 39:1-18)

Tuesday, Aug. 17—Joseph Is Imprisoned (Genesis 39:19—40:8)

Wednesday, Aug. 18—Joseph Interprets Dreams of Fellow Prisoners (Genesis 40:9-23)

Thursday, Aug. 19—The King's Butler Remembers Joseph (Genesis 41:1-13)

Friday, Aug. 20—Pharaoh Relates His Dream (Genesis 41:14-24)

Saturday, Aug. 21—Joseph Interprets Pharaoh's Dream (Genesis 41:25-45)

Sunday, Aug. 22—Joseph Stores Grain for Egypt (Genesis 41:46-57)

Learning by Doing

This page contains an alternate lesson plan emphasizing learning activities.
Classes desiring such student involvement will find these suggestions helpful.

Learning Goals

As a result of this lesson, each of your students should be able to:

1. Recount Joseph's interpretation of Pharaoh's dream and the favorable treatment he then received.

2. Compare Joseph's situation and his faith in God's providence with the situation many Christians face at the workplace.

3. Make a commitment to live with integrity and to serve with honor wherever God places him or her.

Into the Lesson

Much of the success—or failure—of one's life has to do with time and place. The person who is in the right place at the right time gets the opportunity. The person who appears on the scene too soon or too late misses the opportunity.

Your students no doubt can give examples of this from their own lives. For example, some people have been annoyed when they missed a plane—later they learned that the plane crashed. Or two people bump into each other in the grocery store, and before long a romance develops. Ask your students to tell their stories.

Ask, "Do you see God's hand in such things? Do you think God controls events to put the right person in the right place at just the right time? Why or why not?"

In today's lesson we see that Joseph was always in the right place at the right time. At the beginning of the lesson he was in an Egyptian prison, but that was just where God wanted him.

Into the Word

To begin the Bible-study portion of the lesson, draw the following "wave" on newsprint:

Point out that Joseph's life was a series of ups and downs. When things were going well for him, something bad happened to reverse his situation. When things looked hopeless, something good happened to turn things around again.

With the students' help, chart Joseph's ups and downs on the "wave" you have drawn. Have them read each of the following Bible passages to discover the up or down event in Joseph's life.

(A similar exercise appears in the student book, *Adult Bible Class.*)

1. UP: Genesis 37:3 *(receives coat);* 2. DOWN: Genesis 37:23-28 *(sold to slave traders);* 3. UP: Genesis 39:1-6 *(became Potiphar's steward);* 4. DOWN: Genesis 39:7-20 *(falsely accused and imprisoned);* 5. UP: Genesis 39:21-23 *(put in charge of prisoners);* 6. DOWN: Genesis 40:12-15, 20-23 *(forgotten);* 7. UP: Genesis 41:39-44 *(made second to Pharaoh).*

Ask: "What do these ups and downs tell you about God's involvement in Joseph's life?" (God was continually with Joseph. Even the "down" events were necessary to put Joseph in position for the "ups.")

Next, ask the students to read Genesis 41:14-16, 25-40 and call out Joseph's positive character traits that they see demonstrated. Write these traits on the chalkboard as they are called out. Here are some ideas: humility (vv. 16, 25, 28), Joseph knew God was the one who interpreted the dreams; courage (vv. 25, 28), Joseph was a Hebrew and a prisoner, but he had the courage to stand before Pharaoh and declare God's message; insightful (vv. 33-36), Joseph had a plan, which he was bold enough to share with Pharaoh; discrete (v. 33), Joseph could have pushed himself forward and said, "I'm your man," but he didn't.

Into Life

Begin the life-application section of the lesson by writing this open-ended sentence on newsprint: "I could be a dynamic, powerful, and successful Christian if only . . ."

Ask the students to write a completion of that sentence on a card or piece of paper. No doubt every person in your class will have a different idea. Without asking anyone to reveal what he or she wrote, complete the sentence this way: "I trusted God the way Joseph did."

Observe that many of us sit around waiting for our situation to be ideal. When everything is just right and working perfectly, then we will be able to serve Christ effectively. But if Joseph had waited for everything to be perfect, he never would have served the Lord. Instead, he had the courage and the determination to serve the Lord wherever he was and no matter how dark his situation. Challenge your students to serve Christ in this less-than-ideal world.

Let's Talk It Over

The questions on this page are designed to encourage review of the lesson Scriptures and to promote discussion of the lesson by the class. The answers provided are only discussion starters. Let your class talk it over from there.

1. The Bible points out two critical things that Joseph did. First, he maintained his faith in God even when it appeared that God had forsaken him. Second, he maintained his integrity. What situations challenge your faith and integrity? How can you imitate Joseph's example in these situations?

Each person will have different areas that are most challenging, but there will be much in common as well. One may have a co-worker making sexual advances. Resisting may be especially difficult if the forward one is in a supervisory position. A student may have a professor who takes delight in ridiculing his or her faith. Let the ones in your class who have weathered some of these storms encourage the others.

2. Joseph said, "God shall give Pharaoh an answer." Pharaoh did not accept the God of the Hebrews. He could have refused to hear Joseph. People who reject God today often refuse to hear Christians when they appeal to God or the Bible. How can we take a stand for God and His Word in such a way as to be heard and to have influence for Him?

Joseph did not know how Pharaoh would receive his remark about God's having the answer, but he gave credit to God nonetheless. Sometimes we will take a stand for the Lord, and we will be rejected. Still we stand. Sometimes we are able to demonstrate good sense and integrity and then give God the credit. Our faith in action helps our faith in word to go farther. If we can further our witness by good timing, we should do so. But we should never refuse to stand for the Lord just because others do not believe.

3. Pharaoh did not ask for advice but for information. When someone asks for information about the Bible or about our faith, is it okay to give advice as well, or should we wait until the person asks for it? Explain why you think it is proper or improper to give unsolicited spiritual advice.

Some people believe we should never give unsolicited advice—spiritual or otherwise. Such people will seldom offend anyone. Others believe we should look for opportunities and take them, even when we are not invited. Such a one will offend people occasionally, but he or she will share the gospel more often. We need to use discretion. Pharaoh, impressed by Joseph's knowledge, was ready to hear his advice. If we know a person, often we can tell when he is ready to hear more than he specifically asked for. Then we need to tell him.

4. Probably the last thing that Joseph expected that fateful day was to be elevated from the dungeon to the palace. Unexpected challenges may happen in our lives, too. How should we react to them? How can we prepare for them?

Unexpected challenges and unsought responsibilities may come upon us at work when we are tapped for an important assignment. They may come upon us in the family, perhaps through a birth or someone's death or illness. They may come upon us in the church when something important needs to be done, and no one else is able to do it. In one way or another, most of us shoulder more responsibility as we get older. Joseph was ready for this challenge because he was "a man in whom the Spirit of God is." If we continually "walk in the Spirit," as Paul says (Galatians 5:16, 25), and continue to grow in our faith, God will enable us to handle each new challenge that comes our way.

5. Who would have expected Joseph, a teenager sold into slavery, to end up as the second in command of all Egypt? God did! God did not force Joseph's brothers to sell him. He could have accomplished His purposes in other ways. But once it was done, God preserved Joseph until it was time to face Pharaoh. No matter what man does, God is able to work His plans and accomplish His goals. What assurance does that give you today? How does that assurance apply to some situation about which you have been especially concerned?

It often seems as if the world is going against God and His will at every turn. But we can be assured that this will not stop God from accomplishing His will or fulfilling His promises. Perhaps some of your students have been concerned about their own effectiveness in the kingdom, or about "saying the right thing" when they try to share their faith. This lesson assures us that when we put our lives in God's hands, He will use them as He wills!

Forgiveness and Reunion

August 29
Lesson 13

DEVOTIONAL READING: Psalm 105:7-22.

LESSON SCRIPTURE: Genesis 42—45.

PRINTED TEXT: Genesis 44:16-20, 33, 34; 45:1-7.

Genesis 44:16-20, 33, 34

16 And Judah said, What shall we say unto my lord? what shall we speak? or how shall we clear ourselves? God hath found out the iniquity of thy servants: behold, we are my lord's servants, both we, and he also with whom the cup is found.

17 And he said, God forbid that I should do so: but the man in whose hand the cup is found, he shall be my servant; and as for you, get you up in peace unto your father.

18 Then Judah came near unto him, and said, O my lord, let thy servant, I pray thee, speak a word in my lord's ears, and let not thine anger burn against thy servant: for thou art even as Pharaoh.

19 My lord asked his servants, saying, Have ye a father, or a brother?

20 And we said unto my lord, We have a father, an old man, and a child of his old age, a little one; and his brother is dead, and he alone is left of his mother, and his father loveth him.

·   ·   ·   ·   ·   ·   ·   ·   ·   ·   ·   ·

33 Now therefore, I pray thee, let thy servant abide instead of the lad a bondman to my lord; and let the lad go up with his brethren.

34 For how shall I go up to my father, and the lad be not with me? lest peradventure I see the evil that shall come on my father.

Genesis 45:1-7

1 Then Joseph could not refrain himself before all them that stood by him; and he cried, Cause every man to go out from me. And there stood no man with him, while Joseph made himself known unto his brethren.

2 And he wept aloud: and the Egyptians and the house of Pharaoh heard.

3 And Joseph said unto his brethren, I am Joseph; doth my father yet live? And his brethren could not answer him; for they were troubled at his presence.

4 And Joseph said unto his brethren, Come near to me, I pray you. And they came near. And he said, I am Joseph your brother, whom ye sold into Egypt.

5 Now therefore be not grieved, nor angry with yourselves, that ye sold me hither: for God did send me before you to preserve life.

6 For these two years hath the famine been in the land: and yet there are five years, in the which there shall neither be earing nor harvest.

7 And God sent me before you to preserve you a posterity in the earth, and to save your lives by a great deliverance.

GOLDEN TEXT: Be not grieved, nor angry with yourselves, that ye sold me hither: for God did send me before you to preserve life.—Genesis 45:5.

Aug 29

Genesis: Beginnings
Unit 3: A People Tested
(Lessons 9-13)

Lesson Aims

After this lesson, each student should:

1. Summarize the process by which Joseph made himself known to his brothers and the words of reconciliation that he spoke to them.

2. Explain how God's providence was accomplished through Joseph's forgiving spirit.

3. Make a commitment to forgive someone who has wronged him or her, being confident that God's providence is at work in this effort.

Lesson Outline

INTRODUCTION
    A. From Manliness to Godliness
    B. Lesson Background
 I. JUDAH'S DEFENSE (Genesis 44:16-20)
    A. Judah's Admission (v. 16)
    B. Joseph's Response (v. 17)
    C. Judah's Urgent Plea (vv. 18-20)
 II. JUDAH'S PROPOSAL (Genesis 44:33, 34)
    A. Judah's Offer (v. 33)
    B. Judah's Concern for Jacob (v. 34)
III. JOSEPH'S DISCLOSURE (Genesis 45:1-7)
    A. Weeping (vv. 1, 2)
    B. Revealing His Identity (vv. 3, 4)
       Family Reunions
    C. Explaining God's Purpose (vv. 5-7)
       Forgiveness Begins With Grace
CONCLUSION
    A. But God
    B. To Forgive Is Divine
    C. Prayer
    D. Thought to Remember

Introduction

A. From Manliness to Godliness

A man once approached his minister, terribly upset over something that a fellow church member had done to him. After the man had explained the nature of the incident, the minister readily agreed that he had good reason to be upset. Then the man began to tell the minister his plans for gaining revenge. When it became obvious from the minister's expression that he did not approve of the plans for revenge, the man blurted out, "Well, don't you consider it manly to seek revenge for such an insult?"

"Certainly," replied the minister, "it is quite manly to seek revenge. But it is *godly* to forgive such an offense."

Joseph surely had good reason to seek revenge for the insults and injuries he had suffered at the hands of his jealous brothers. In his day it would have been perfectly acceptable for him to have exacted vengeance on his brothers once he had them under his authority. Yet Joseph was able to rise above the "manliness" of revenge to the "godliness" of forgiveness.

B. Lesson Background

Famine had struck Egypt and many of the surrounding lands, including Canaan. Because of Joseph's wise stewardship of Egypt's crops during its seven good years of harvests, Egypt had food enough not only for its own people but even for some of its neighbors. In Canaan Jacob learned that grain was available in Egypt, so he sent his ten oldest sons to Egypt to purchase some.

When Joseph saw them, he recognized them, but they did not recognize him. Joseph accused them of being spies and said they would have to bring their youngest brother, Benjamin, to prove that they were not. Simeon was held as a hostage until they returned. Joseph then provided them the grain that they needed but secretly returned their money in their grain sacks.

The nine brothers returned home and told their father what had happened, but he refused to allow Benjamin to accompany them back to Egypt. But the supply of grain ran out, and the famine remained severe. Faced with starvation, Jacob finally gave permission for the brothers, including Benjamin, to go to Egypt.

In Egypt the brothers were reunited with Simeon and were able once again to purchase grain. Once again Joseph secretly had their money returned to them; but this time he also had his silver cup placed in Benjamin's sack. After the men had left, Joseph sent his steward to overtake them and search for the cup. When it was found in Benjamin's sack, the brothers were forced to return to Joseph and try to explain what had happened.

I. Judah's Defense
(Genesis 44:16-20)

A. Judah's Admission (v. 16)

16. And Judah said, What shall we say unto my lord? what shall we speak? or how shall we clear ourselves? God hath found out the iniquity of thy servants: behold, we are my lord's servants, both we, and he also with whom the cup is found.

At this point, the brothers must have been beside themselves, fearing not so much what might happen to them, but what would happen to Benjamin. All of them fell on the ground before Joseph (v. 14), dreading the judgment that seemed certain to fall on them.

The evidence against Benjamin seemed so obvious that there was no way that they could *clear* themselves. Judah, who became their spokesman, did not even try to deny the evidence. He volunteered the whole family to become Joseph's *servants*. They were not willing to leave Benjamin to suffer the consequences alone.

Note Judah's confession of *the iniquity of thy servants*, apparently referring to the brothers' cruel treatment of Joseph. Judah's admission marked a significant change from the man who had so callously suggested that they ought to make a profit from Joseph's misery (Genesis 37:26, 27). [See question #1, page 448.]

B. Joseph's Response (v. 17)

17. And he said, God forbid that I should do so: but the man in whose hand the cup is found, he shall be my servant; and as for you, get you up in peace unto your father.

Joseph further tested his brothers by asserting that only the one in whose sack the *cup* had been *found*—Benjamin—would be punished. Apparently Joseph was trying to find out if they were the same selfish, jealous men that they had been years before when they mistreated him. They could return to their *father* in *peace* if they left Benjamin behind to suffer for the alleged theft. If they were willing to go along with Joseph's offer, that would indicate that they had not changed.

What would Joseph have done if the brothers had accepted his offer? Perhaps he had already heard enough to convince him that they had changed. If so, he knew that they would refuse. Or perhaps he felt, if they had not changed, that Benjamin was in the same kind of peril he had been in. In that case, this plan would have rescued Benjamin from them. [See question #2, page 448.]

C. Judah's Urgent Plea (vv. 18-20)

18. Then Judah came near unto him, and said, O my lord, let thy servant, I pray thee, speak a word in my lord's ears, and let not thine anger burn against thy servant: for thou art even as Pharaoh.

The brothers must have been shaken by Joseph's rejection of their offer to remain as his slaves. Judah was not willing to accept Joseph's decision; he *came near* so that he could make his appeal even more personal. He recognized

that Joseph was *even as Pharaoh*, with the power of life and death over them. To approach such a powerful official could mean signing his own death warrant, but Judah was willing to take the chance.

19, 20. My lord asked his servants, saying, Have ye a father, or a brother? And we said unto my lord, We have a father, an old man, and a child of his old age, a little one; and his brother is dead, and he alone is left of his mother, and his father loveth him.

When it became apparent that Joseph was going to allow Judah to speak, he recounted the events of their first visit to Egypt. On that occasion Joseph had asked them about their *father*. Naturally he had an interest in learning about Jacob, for since the day that he had been sold into slavery he had not seen his father nor heard any word about him. For all Joseph knew at that time, his father was dead; and so he must have rejoiced when he first learned that Jacob was still alive.

Judah went on to remind Joseph how he and his brothers had told him about their youngest *brother*, Benjamin, whom they described as *a child* of Jacob's *old age*. Judah also mentioned Benjamin's *brother*, who was *dead*. At this point in the conversation, Joseph must have had to restrain himself to avoid giving away his secret.

In the verses that follow this portion of the printed text, Judah went on to recount how Joseph had demanded that the brothers bring Benjamin with them if they returned for more grain. When the famine forced them to do so, their father permitted Benjamin to accompany them with great reluctance and only after much persuasion. Judah pointed out Jacob's great love for Benjamin and that Jacob was certain to die if

Home Daily Bible Readings

Monday, Aug. 23—Jacob Sends His Sons to Buy Grain (Genesis 42:1-17)
Tuesday, Aug. 24—Joseph Arranges to See Benjamin (Genesis 42:18-38)
Wednesday, Aug. 25—Jacob Agrees for Benjamin to Go to Egypt (Genesis 43:1-15)
Thursday, Aug. 26—Joseph Arranges a Meal for His Brothers (Genesis 43:16-34)
Friday, Aug. 27—Benjamin Is Threatened With Slavery in Egypt (Genesis 44:1-17)
Saturday, Aug. 28—Judah Offers to Take Benjamin's Place (Genesis 44:18-34)
Sunday, Aug. 29—Joseph Reveals His Identity (Genesis 45:1-28)

Benjamin were not returned safely. Judah sought to appeal to Joseph's sense of compassion for an old man who would be devastated at the loss of the son with whom his life was "bound up" (v. 30). This argument was much more forceful than Judah realized at the time, because he did not know that he was talking to Joseph. Joseph was the last person in the world who would have wanted anything bad to happen to his father.

II. Judah's Proposal (Genesis 44:33, 34)

A. Judah's Offer (v. 33)

33. Now therefore, I pray thee, let thy servant abide instead of the lad a bondman to my lord; and let the lad go up with his brethren.

Judah had a stronger reason for returning Benjamin to his father than his brothers did. Verse 32 tells us that he had made a personal pledge to his father that he would be responsible for Benjamin's safe return. Perhaps Judah originally made this promise because of the pressure of having to buy grain a second time in Egypt. However, his willingness to keep his word shows that he had not taken his pledge lightly.

The irony of this situation would not have escaped Joseph. Judah had suggested that the brothers sell Joseph into slavery (Genesis 37:26, 27). Now this same man was willing to become a slave that his younger brother might go free. [See question #3, page 448.]

B. Judah's Concern for Jacob (v. 34)

34. For how shall I go up to my father, and the lad be not with me? lest peradventure I see the evil that shall come on my father.

When Judah had been a party to selling Joseph into slavery, he had shown no concern for how his action would affect his *father*. He and his brothers possessed such an intense hatred for Joseph that they completely disregarded any consideration for Jacob. Now that had changed. Judah was unwilling to do any thing that would bring down Jacob's "gray hairs with sorrow to the grave" (Genesis 44:29).

III. Joseph's Disclosure (Genesis 45:1-7)

A. Weeping (vv. 1, 2)

1, 2. Then Joseph could not refrain himself before all them that stood by him; and he cried, Cause every man to go out from me. And there stood no man with him, while Joseph made himself known unto his brethren. And he wept aloud: and the Egyptians and the house of Pharaoh heard.

This is certainly one of the most moving scenes in the entire Bible. Joseph's test of his brothers had been completed. Judah's speech clearly demonstrated that they were no longer the heartless villains who sold him into slavery. When it became obvious to Joseph that his brothers had truly changed, he could no longer hold back his emotions. Earlier during his brothers' first visit and later when he had first seen Benjamin, he had been able to recover his composure (Genesis 42:24; 43:29-31), but not this time. His test of his brothers had turned out the way that he had hoped, and when it did, he could no longer *refrain* (or restrain) *himself*.

As Joseph prepared to reveal his identity to his brothers, he sent all the *Egyptians* from the room. This was to be a private family moment that he was not ready to share with anyone else. That would come later at a more appropriate time.

When Joseph was alone with his brothers, *he wept aloud*. His pent-up emotions burst forth with such force that those who had just left the room could hear him, along with *the house of Pharaoh*. From the nature of his crying, those outside the room knew that he was in no physical danger from the "strangers" who were with him. Otherwise they might have burst into the room to rescue him.

B. Revealing His Identity (vv. 3, 4)

3. And Joseph said unto his brethren, I am Joseph; doth my father yet live? And his brethren could not answer him; for they were troubled at his presence.

Now came the climactic moment—the moment that Joseph had postponed until the time was just right. A bolt of lightning striking in the brothers' midst could not have produced a greater shock than the words they heard: *I am Joseph!* Joseph followed this introduction with a question about Jacob. Judah's previous speech had already indicated that their *father* was still living. Thus Joseph's question was not so much for information as it was to confirm what he had hoped all along was true.

The brothers were still so shocked at what they had just heard that they could not talk. They may also have been *troubled*, or apprehensive, about what would follow, and for good reason. They realized that Joseph had the authority to do anything he wanted to with them. Had they been in his situation, they might very well have thought about exacting revenge. [See question #4, page 448.]

4. And Joseph said unto his brethren, Come near to me, I pray you. And they came near. And he said, I am Joseph your brother, whom ye sold into Egypt.

More than twenty years had passed since the brothers had last seen Joseph, so no doubt they had difficulty believing what they were hearing. To reassure them that they had heard him correctly, Joseph repeated, *I am Joseph your brother.* Then he added *whom ye sold into Egypt*, indicating the knowledge of a detail that validated his claim. These words may have frightened the brothers, but no doubt Joseph's tone was gentle, even forgiving, rather than harsh.

FAMILY REUNIONS

In a few days our family reunion will convene in Atlanta, Georgia. This will be our sixth annual get-together—a tradition begun when miles and marriages precluded all of us getting together for holidays, as we had done for many years. We decided, for the sake of relationships, unity, and family identity, that we needed a yearly planned gathering where we can reminisce, reaffirm our love, and renew our commitment to family ties. So we annually come together (sometimes at considerable expense and inconvenience) in order to "catch up," laugh, pray, eat together, sympathize, and encourage—the kind of fellowship only a family can enjoy.

We can imagine Joseph's joy in arranging his family's first reunion. Don't you suppose that the tears and laughter in Egypt were an unforgettable experience for Jacob's large family? Our family is small by comparison, but our reunions are always memorable—as well as they should be.

Christ's church is the family of God. Each congregation becomes someone's extended family, and the weekly reunions are truly special. Let us not forsake "the assembling of ourselves together" (Hebrews 10:25).   —R. W. B.

C. Explaining God's Purpose (vv. 5-7)

5. Now therefore be not grieved, nor angry with yourselves, that ye sold me hither: for God did send me before you to preserve life.

Joseph did not mention anything about forgiving his brothers for the way they had treated him. But he did not have to. From the tone of his voice and his explanation of what had happened, it was obvious that he had already forgiven them. There was no need for them to feel burdened by a sense of guilt.

Here we see a marvelous statement of the faith that sustained Joseph during his ordeal in a foreign land. Joseph's faith in God permitted him to see beyond his brothers' wicked deeds to God's larger purposes. *God did send me before you to preserve life.* What a profound theological statement! How did Joseph come to this conclusion? It is not likely that he had held such a view as a seventeen-year-old who had just been

Now therefore be not grieved, nor angry with yourselves, that ye sold me hither: for God did send me before you to preserve life.

The visual for today's lesson portrays Joseph's brothers kneeling before him, just as his dreams had predicted they would do.

Visual for lesson 13

sold into slavery. There is nothing to indicate that Joseph had received a special revelation from God about this matter. The fundamentals of the faith that he had learned in his father's household followed by many years of experience, some of them very painful, had brought Joseph to this conclusion.

Joseph likely knew of the covenant that God had made with Abraham, Isaac, and Jacob. Through the eyes of faith he understood that what had happened to him had not occurred by chance. Only by God's providence had he been brought to Egypt so that when the time of famine came he was able *to preserve life* and thus keep alive God's covenant family. [See question #5, page 448.]

6. For these two years hath the famine been in the land: and yet there are five years, in the which there shall neither be earing nor harvest.

Joseph then informed his brothers that the present period of famine had only begun. It had lasted *two years* thus far, but there were still *five years* (a total of seven, in accordance with Pharaoh's dream) during which there would be neither plowing *nor harvest.* (*Earing* is an old English word meaning "plowing.")

7. And God sent me before you to preserve you a posterity in the earth, and to save your lives by a great deliverance.

God sent me. Joseph's brothers sent him to Egypt as a slave, but in time he was able to see the bigger picture. It was God who actually sent him to Egypt by using their evil intentions to accomplish His purposes. *Posterity* is translated "remnant" in some other versions. The idea that God works through a remnant persists throughout the entire Bible (Isaiah 1:9; Jeremiah 23:3; Joel 2:32; Romans 9:27; 11:5; Revelation 12:17).

The verses that immediately follow our printed text tell how Joseph sent his brothers back to Canaan in order to bring their father Jacob to Egypt. There they, along with their children and their flocks, would live in the land of

Goshen during the five years of famine that remained. However, that five years stretched into four hundred years before the children of Israel were again able to leave Egypt under the leadership of Moses.

FORGIVENESS BEGINS WITH GRACE

A lady counselee says that she feels no obligation to notify two of her siblings when her mother dies. She reasons that since this brother and sister have shown absolutely no interest in their aging and ill mother for several years, they have forfeited their right to know. "Besides," she adds, "they probably won't care anyway."

This counselee's attitude is understandable, but not justifiable. All children have a right to know of a parent's death. No good can come from adding another wrong to the wrongful neglect and indifference of these guilty children.

Everyone would have understood if Joseph had sentenced his brothers to imprisonment or even execution. They did not deserve anything better. But Joseph graciously forgave them of their hateful deeds and sinful offenses. Nothing would have been gained by seeking vengeance.

The bitter sister in the situation described earlier finally agreed to telegram *all* the children when her mother dies. It's the right thing to do; it's the forgiving thing to do. The unloving brother and sister don't deserve to be forgiven, but grace is *always* undeserved. None of us merits God's love and redemption, yet "He looks beyond our fault and sees our need." That truly is amazing grace.   —R. W. B.

Conclusion

A. But God

Genesis 47:28 tells us that Jacob "lived in the land of Egypt seventeen years." After his death, Joseph's brothers became fearful that Joseph would seek revenge for the evil they had done against him. But when they came before Joseph, he quickly dismissed their fears with words similar to those found in today's text: "Ye thought evil against me; *but God* meant it unto good" (Genesis 50:20). What a very important lesson this is for all of us today! The world often views events through the narrow lens of time. Christians have a different viewpoint because they look at life through the lens of eternity. What a difference it makes to see events the way God sees them!

Paul tells us that "all things work together for good to them that love God" (Romans 8:28). Such a view should not lead us to a Pollyannaish attitude that never sees any evil anywhere. The truth is that we are surrounded by an evil world, full of pain and suffering. As Christians we must confront evil wherever we see it and try to alleviate as much of the suffering as we can.

Many of us have suffered because of the wicked deeds of others. During the time that we are going through such a trial, we may not see or understand how any good could come out of the situation. However, the passing of time can give us a broader view, as it did Joseph. Let us never forget that the world may declare a certain situation hopeless or useless, *but God* always has the last word.

B. To Forgive Is Divine

Joseph stands out as one of the noblest characters in the Bible. Mistreated by his brothers, he refused to allow his life to be consumed by a burning hatred or a desire for revenge. He had every opportunity to get even with his brothers for what they had done to him. Instead, he returned good for evil.

How often we bear grudges about petty issues that don't really matter a whit! We may try to get even for these perceived offenses, and in the process cause the other person to retaliate. Over the years this little game can escalate until it becomes a festering sore that poisons the souls of those involved.

Joseph refused to allow his life to become scarred by what others had done to him. As a result he looked on his reunion with his brothers as an opportunity for restoration, not revenge. Revenge may seem sweet for a time, but that sweetness soon turns bitter. Long before Jesus stated it in the Sermon on the Mount, Joseph had learned to love his enemies, bless them that cursed him, and do good to them that hated him.

C. Prayer

Loving and forgiving Father, we thank You for revealing to us the life of Joseph, a man who knew how to forgive and forget. Show us how to follow his example and the even greater, nobler example of Your Son. In His name, amen.

D. Thought to Remember

"Even as Christ forgave you, so also do ye" (Colossians 3:13).

How to Say It

CANAAN. *Kay*-nun.
EGYPTIANS. Ee-*jip*-shuns.
GOSHEN. *Go*-shun.
PHARAOH. *Fair*-o or *Fay*-ro.
SIMEON. *Sim*-ee-un.

Learning by Doing

This page contains an alternate lesson plan emphasizing learning activities.
Classes desiring such student involvement will find these suggestions helpful.

Learning Goals

After this lesson, each student will be able to:

1. Summarize the process by which Joseph made himself known to his brothers and the words of reconciliation that he spoke to them.

2. Explain how God's providence was accomplished through Joseph's forgiving spirit.

3. Make a commitment to forgive someone who has wronged him or her, being confident that God's providence is at work in this effort.

Into the Lesson

Write this statement on a sheet of newsprint to introduce this lesson:

Some deeds are so awful that forgiveness is neither expected nor required.

How do your students feel about that statement? Do they agree? Do they think it needs some editing or revision?

Would anyone in your class be willing to talk about a personal situation in which forgiveness was all but impossible? If no one wants to share, suggest these situations:

• A woman cheats on her husband with his best friend. Can he forgive her?

• A sexual predator kidnaps, assaults, and then murders a young girl. Can the parents of that girl be expected to forgive that man?

• A man and a woman are in line for the same promotion. The man spreads lies suggesting the other worker is stealing from the company. As a result, the woman is fired. Can she forgive a person who acted so viciously?

Today's lesson shows the ultimate level of forgiveness in Joseph's forgiveness of his brothers. His act is a human model of divine forgiveness.

Into the Word

Summarize the events that happened in Joseph's life since last week's lesson. This information can be found in Genesis 41:41—44:15. See also the "Lesson Background" on page 442.

Point out that Joseph was putting his brothers to the test to see if they had changed in the more than twenty years since they had sold him into slavery. By framing Benjamin for stealing his cup, Joseph gave the brothers a perfect opportunity to look out for their own skins and feel quite justified about it. Would they take the opportunity, or could they think of Benjamin and their father ahead of themselves?

Ask a volunteer to read Genesis 44:16-20, 33, 34; 45:1-7. Assign half the class to consider Genesis 44:16-20 and to compare Judah's attitude here with his attitude in 37:23-27. What has changed? What might account for this change? *(Judah's confession in v. 16 cannot be a confession of theft; he must be referring to what the brothers did to Joseph. While they appeared callously indifferent, their consciences must have been working on them. Witnessing their father's profound grief must also have affected them.)*

The other half of the class is to study 45:1-7. List as many positive actions or attitudes Joseph displays in this scene. *(Obviously, forgiveness is the most apparent; note also Joseph is eager to be reconciled with his family—not all forgiveness includes reconciliation; he is concerned about his father; he expresses faith in God and in His providence; he demands no penalty; he does not mention his earlier dreams and say, "I told you so!")*

Discuss, "What if the brothers had failed Joseph's test? What if they had proved by their actions that they were no different? Or what if Joseph had not been willing to forgive his brothers? How would this story have been different? How is God's providence seen in this event as it did actually happen?"

Into Life

When we are wronged, it is up to us to decide what to do and how to act and react. Ask the students to suggest possible responses to being wronged. To give flesh and blood to this activity, remind the students of the situations discussed at the beginning of the lesson. Note that there are times we can forgive without reconciliation. Reconciliation requires a change on the part of the other party; we can control only our own behavior.

Forgiveness opens the door to healing. But emphasize that forgiveness is not easy or automatic—even for mature Christians. It may take a long time to work toward the point of forgiveness. And it's not something we can do on our own. Forgiveness is possible only through the grace and the strength that come from Christ.

In closing, ask the students to review their past, looking for grudges and open wounds. Encourage them to be willing to forgive old wrongs, and then to make a commitment to express their forgiveness during the coming week.

Let's Talk It Over

The questions on this page are designed to encourage review of the lesson Scriptures and to promote discussion of the lesson by the class. The answers provided are only discussion starters. Let your class talk it over from there.

1. Even though he and his brothers were innocent of stealing from Joseph, Judah did not pursue that. Instead he said that God had found out their iniquity, referring to their treatment of Joseph so many years earlier. His guilty conscience had condemned him. He knew they were reaping exactly what they had sown. Judah and the others were facing up to their terrible sin, perhaps for the first time. No forgiveness and no healing can occur, whether from man or from God, until a person faces and admits his sin. How does that happen today? Can we help people face their sin, or must people come to that point on their own? If so, how?

The Holy Spirit convicts of sin (John 16:8), so ultimately it is He who brings people to this point. We can assist in this process by teaching Biblical standards of righteousness and sin, informing the consciences of those whom we teach. We can also help by confessing our own sin and demonstrating the power of God's forgiveness.

2. Joseph offered his ten brothers an easy way out in verse 17. They could return to Jacob, tell him Benjamin had stolen the cup—they themselves had seen it in his sack—and put the whole mess behind them. What situations tempt us to take the easy way out today? How can we have the character to stand up under pressure, even at risk of personal loss?

So often today silence is the easy way out. We hear people around us mock Christian ideals and standards—even the God who saved us—but do we respond? It's easier to let it pass than to risk a confrontation. Sometimes the easy way out is to avoid a situation. We might be at odds with a neighbor, fellow church member, relative, etc., and, instead of talking things out, we avoid the person. Read Romans 8:28-39.

3. Judah's plea to be taken as Joseph's slave in the place of his brother Benjamin is a very powerful example of self-sacrifice. Under what conditions would you sacrifice your own life or freedom in behalf of another? To what extent have you sacrificed self in behalf of Christ?

Judah's offer was the most he could give. Only love motivates a person to do this. His love for his brother and his father made it intolerable to him that Benjamin be lost. Judah's noble and selfless deed looks forward to the self-sacrifice of his greatest descendant, Jesus Christ. Responding to His love, millions of Christians give up time, comfort, finances, and even their lives for the sake of serving the Lord by helping others and testifying to them about God's love.

4. Joseph had been separated from his father for over twenty years, but his affection was still strong. In modern society frequent moves are a fact of life. The result is that many of our families are separated by hundreds of miles. How can we keep this separation from causing our families to disintegrate or become alienated?

Joseph's separation from his family was very unusual, but today families frequently become separated for a variety of reasons. Children leave out of anger or a desire to be free of the restraints of home. Others may go to college and then settle far from home. Some move seeking a better job. The reasons are many, but the separation is the same. Whether the family lives near or far, the key to keeping close is communication. We are blessed today in that long-range communication is simple and inexpensive. However, we must put forth the effort. Too often we let our busy lives or an old offense keep us from making time to communicate with distant family. Who is waiting for your call today?

5. Joseph told his brothers not to be grieved with themselves for selling him, but the brothers had difficulty finding peace because of their heinous deed. Guilt has a way of eating at our hearts and destroying our peace. How do you deal with guilt and overcome it?

Our sins don't seem so terrible when we commit them, but later their true ugliness becomes undeniable. Our consciences condemn us even when no man knows or accuses us. Guilt becomes a beast that stalks at every turn.

We must learn to trust God's power of forgiveness. Through the blood of Christ, God is able to forgive any sin. Of course, we can know that in our heads, but our guilt sometimes continues to cry from our hearts. We can forget the past by focusing more on the future—and eternity. We can forget ourselves by focusing more on others. Of course, spending more time in God's Word and in prayer is also helpful.